Irish Political Studies Reader

D1427814

Since its inception in 1986, *Irish Political Studies* (IPS) has published some of the most stimulating research in the field. This book reprints 17 IPS articles, covering a wide range of issues including: the electoral system, the development of the Irish party system, political culture, the Good Friday Agreement, the rise of Sinn Féin and the DUP, national identity, the economic foundations of the independent Irish state, and conflict resolution in Northern Ireland. Each article, chosen for both their academic rigour and the accessibility of their writing for a non-specialist reader, is followed by a specially commissioned new commentary which analyses recent developments in the area. Its coverage is broad, yet each area is dealt with in conspicuous detail.

The combination of the best original scholarship and contemporary commentaries on the core political issues makes *Irish Political Studies Reader* an invaluable resource for all students and scholars of Irish politics.

Conor McGrath is an Independent Scholar, and was Lecturer in Political Lobbying and Public Affairs at the University of Ulster from 1999 to 2006. He is author of *Lobbying in Washington, London and Brussels: The Persuasive Communication of Political Issues* (2005), and co-editor of *Challenge and Response: Essays on Public Affairs and Transparency* (2006). He has been President of the Political Studies Association of Ireland since 2005.

Eoin O'Malley is a Lecturer in Political Science at the School of Law and Government in Dublin City University. He has published articles in *Government and Opposition*, *International Political Science Review* and *British Journal of Politics and International Relations* on prime ministers and executive power. He is also continuing research on cabinet government in Ireland, some of which has been published in *Irish Political Studies*.

Contributors: Maura Adshead; Paul Arthur; Arthur Aughey; John Coakley; Michael Cunningham; David M. Farrell; Christopher Farrington; Michael Gallagher; John Garry; Tom Garvin; Brian Girvin; Bernadette C. Hayes; William A. Hazleton; Thomas Hennessey; Adrian Kavanagh; Bill Kissane; Michael Laver; Adrian Little; Michael Marsh; Ian McAllister; James W. McAuley; Anthony McIntyre; Iain McMenamin; Claire Mitchell; Gary Murphy; J.P. O'Carroll; Niall Ó Dochartaigh; Kirsten E. Schulze; Richard Sinnott; Clifford Smyth; Jennifer Todd; Jonathan Tonge; Timothy J. White; Stefan Wolff.

Irish Political Studies Reader

Key contributions

**Edited by
Conor McGrath and
Eoin O'Malley**

Routledge
Taylor & Francis Group

LONDON AND NEW YORK

First published 2008
by Routledge
2 Park Square, Milton Park, Abingdon, Oxon OX14 4RN

Simultaneously published in the USA and Canada
by Routledge
270 Madison Ave, New York, NY 10016

*Routledge is an imprint of the Taylor & Francis Group,
an informa business*

© 2008 Conor McGrath and Eoin O'Malley for selection and
introductory matter; the Political Studies Association of Ireland for
original articles from *Irish Political Studies*; the contributors for
their individual commentaries

Typeset in Times New Roman by
Newgen Imaging Systems (P) Ltd, Chennai, India
Printed and bound in Great Britain by
Antony Rowe Ltd, Chippenham, Wiltshire

British Library Cataloguing in Publication Data
A catalogue record for this book is available from the British Library

Library of Congress Cataloging in Publication Data
A catalog record for this book has been requested

ISBN10: 0–415–44647–3 (hbk)
ISBN10: 0–415–44648–1 (pbk)
ISBN10: 0–203–93567–5 (ebk)

ISBN13: 978–0–415–44647–1 (hbk)
ISBN13: 978–0–415–44648–8 (pbk)
ISBN13: 978–0–203–93567–5 (ebk)

Dedicated with admiration and appreciation
to all those colleagues who founded the
Political Studies Association of Ireland
at its constitutive meeting on 19–20 March 1982

Contents

Notes on contributors

Maura Adshead is Senior Lecturer in Politics and Public Administration in the Department of Politics and Public Administration at the University of Limerick. She is author of *Developing European Regions?* (Ashgate, 2002) and co-editor (with Michelle Millar) of *Public Administration and Public Policy in Ireland: Theory and Methods* (Routledge, 2003) and (with Peadar Kirby and Michelle Millar) *Contesting the State: Lessons from the Irish Case* (Manchester University Press, forthcoming). She has published articles on Irish politics and policy in *Economic and Social Review*, *Electoral Studies*, *Policy and Politics*, *Public Administration*, *Public Policy and Administration* and *West European Politics*. She is a former President and current Treasurer of the Political Studies Association of Ireland.

Paul Arthur is a Professor of Politics at the Magee campus of the University of Ulster. He is Course Director of the MA in Peace and Conflict Studies. His last book was *Special Relationships: Britain, Ireland and the Northern Ireland Problem* (2001). He has acted as consultant on the Carnegie Commission on Preventing Deadly Violence; and on the United Nations Research Institute for Social Development's (UNRISD) project on political violence. In 1997–98 he was a Senior Fellow at the United States Institute of Peace in Washington DC. Currently he is on a Fulbright fellowship at Stanford University.

Arthur Aughey is Professor of Politics at the University of Ulster. He has published widely on Northern Ireland politics, British Conservatism and constitutional change in the United Kingdom. His recent publications include *Nationalism, Devolution and the Challenge to the United Kingdom State* (Pluto Press, 2001) and *Northern Ireland Politics: After the Belfast Agreement* (Routledge, 2005). Recently he has examined the diverse elements of the contemporary English Question in R. Hazell (ed.) *The English Question* (MUP, 2006) and his own book *The Politics of Englishness* was published by MUP in 2007. He is also writing jointly with John Oakland a major text for international students on *Irish Civilisation* for Routledge which will be published in 2008.

John Coakley is an Associate Professor in the School of Politics and International Relations at University College Dublin. He specialises in the study of Irish politics, comparative politics and ethnic conflict. He is vice-president of the International Social Science Council, and was formerly director of the Institute of British-Irish Studies at UCD and secretary-general of the International Political Science Association. He has edited or co-edited *Politics in the Republic of Ireland* (4th ed., 2005), *The Territorial Management of Ethnic Conflict* (2nd ed., 2003), and *The Social Origins of Nationalist Movements* (1992).

Michael Cunningham is Senior Lecturer in Politics at the University of Wolverhampton. He is author of *British Government Policy in Northern Ireland 1969–2000* (Manchester University Press, 2001) and has published a number of chapters and articles on aspects of Northern Ireland politics, including contributions to *Irish Political Studies*. His other principal research interest and area of publication is the politics of apology.

David M. Farrell holds a Jean Monnet chair in European politics and is Head of the School of Social Sciences at the University of Manchester. An expert on electoral systems and party politics, Professor Farrell edits two key journals in these areas (*Representation*; *Party Politics*). His most recent books include: (with Ian McAllister) *The Australian Electoral System* (University of New South Wales Press, 2006), and (with Roger Scully) *Representing Europe's Citizens?* (Oxford University Press, 2007). He is currently working on a new edition of his textbook, *Electoral Systems* (Palgrave Macmillan).

Christopher Farrington is a Lecturer in Politics in University College Dublin. He is the author of *Ulster Unionism and the Peace Process in Northern Ireland* (Basingstoke: Palgrave Macmillan, 2006) as well as articles in *Political Studies*, *British Journal of Politics and International Relations*, *Contemporary European History* and *Irish Political Studies*.

Michael Gallagher is Professor of Comparative Politics in the Department of Political Science, Trinity College, University of Dublin, and has been Visiting Professor at New York University and at the City University of Hong Kong. His research interests include electoral systems and political parties. He is co-author of *Representative Government in Modern Europe* (4th ed., 2005) and *Days of Blue Loyalty* (2002), and co-editor of *The Politics of Electoral Systems* (2005), *Politics in the Republic of Ireland* (4th ed., 2005), *How Ireland Voted 2002* (2003), *The Referendum Experience in Europe* (1996) and *Candidate Selection in Comparative Perspective* (1988).

John Garry is a Lecturer in the School of Politics, International Studies and Philosophy in Queen's University Belfast. His research interests are in the areas of elections, public opinion and political parties. He is one of the authors of a forthcoming book on electoral behaviour in the Republic of Ireland, *The Irish Voter: Parties, Issues and Candidates*, to be published by Manchester University Press.

Tom Garvin is Professor of Politics at the School of Politics and International Relations at University College Dublin. He is an alumnus of the Woodrow

Wilson International Center for Scholars, Washington D.C., has been Burns Scholar at Boston College, and is a Member of the Royal Irish Academy. He is the author of many books and articles in both Irish and international journals on Irish and comparative politics, including *The Evolution of Irish Nationalist Politics* (1981, 2005), *Nationalist Revolutionaries in Ireland* (1987, 2005), *1922: the Birth of Irish Democracy* (1996, 2005), *Mythical Thinking in Political Life* (2000) and *Preventing the Future* (2004, 2005). He is at present engaged in a study of Irish democratic politics in the 1950s.

Brian Girvin is Professor of Comparative Politics in the Department of Politics at the University of Glasgow. His publications include *The Right in the Twentieth Century* (1994), *Union to Union: Nationalism, Democracy and Religion in Ireland* (2002) and *The Emergency: Neutral Ireland 1939–45* (2006). He is currently working on 'Crisis and Continuity in Liberal Democratic States, 1966–1989' and 'Small States in Europe: A Comparative Perspective'.

Bernadette C. Hayes is Professor of Sociology at the University of Aberdeen. She has published extensively in the areas of gender, religion and politics. Her most recent work – *Conflict and Consensus: A Study of Values and Attitudes in the Republic of Ireland and Northern Ireland* (Brill, 2006) – co-authored with Tony Fahey and Richard Sinnott, provides a detailed and comparative account of the complex value patterns on the island of Ireland, North and South.

William A. Hazleton is a member of the political science department at Miami University in Oxford, Ohio. He received his PhD from the University of Virginia in Foreign Affairs and held visiting appointments at the University of East Anglia, Queen's University of Belfast, and the University of Adelaide. His publications have focused on foreign policy-making, human rights, and more recently on voting behaviour and electoral outcomes in Northern Ireland.

Thomas Hennessey is Reader in History at Canterbury Christ Church University. Among his publications are: *The Evolution of the Troubles 1970–72* (2007); *Northern Ireland: the Origins of the Troubles* (2005); *The Northern Ireland Peace Process. Ending the Troubles?* (2000); *Dividing Ireland: World War One and Partition* (1998); and *A History of Northern Ireland, 1920–1996* (1997). He is a Fellow of the Royal History Society.

Adrian Kavanagh hails from Co. Laois. He is a contract lecturer and researcher in the Department of Geography in NUI Maynooth and is a research associate of the National Institute for Regional and Spatial Analysis and the National Centre for Geocomputation. His main research interests lie within the field of electoral geography (in particular, the geography of voter turnout and election boundaries), but interests also include other political geographical topics, such as the geographical background to conflicts. He is currently a committee member of the Geographical Society of Ireland, with responsibility for the editing of the *GeoNews* newsletter.

Bill Kissane was born in Wexford and educated at Trinity College Dublin and the London School of Economics. He has degrees in English literature, Sociology, and Political Science. He is presently a Senior Lecturer in Political Science at the London School of Economics, specialising in Irish and Comparative Politics. His first book *Explaining Irish Democracy* (UCD Press, 2002) was based on his PhD, while his second book, *The Politics of the Irish Civil War* (Oxford University Press, 2005), is the first comprehensive political study of the conflict. He also published articles in many journals including *Comparative Political Studies*, *The Journal of Commonwealth and Comparative Politics*, *The Journal of Political Ideologies*, and the *Journal of Contemporary History*. He is currently working on the study of the relationship between constitutionalism and democracy in the Irish Republic.

Michael Laver is Professor of Politics at New York University, having previously been Professor of Political Science at Trinity College Dublin. His main research interests are in the theory and practice of party competition, especially competition between elections within parties and governments and most especially the dynamic modelling of these, and on methods for estimating the policy positions of political actors, in particular the use of expert surveys and computerised text analysis. He has been co-editor of the *European Journal of Political Research* and is author or co-author of over 100 articles and 15 books on various aspects of political science, examples of which include *Multiparty Government*, *Making and Breaking Governments*, and *Representative Government in Modern Europe*.

Adrian Little is Senior Lecturer in Political Theory at the University of Melbourne. He is the author of several books including *The Politics of Community: Theory and Practice* (2002) and *Democracy and Northern Ireland: Beyond the Liberal Paradigm?* (2004). His latest work, *Democratic Piety: Complexity, Conflict and Violence,* will be published by Edinburgh University Press in 2008.

Ian McAllister is Professor of Political Science at The Australian National University. He is the co-author of *How Russia Votes* (Chatham House, 1998) and *The Australian Electoral System* (UNSW Press, 2006), and co-editor of *The Cambridge Handbook of the Social Sciences in Australia* (Cambridge University Press, 2003). He has been director of the Australian Election Study since 1987 and chair of the 50-nation Comparative Study of Electoral Systems project since 2003. He is currently working on comparative electoral behaviour, the Northern Ireland conflict, and democratisation in postcommunist societies.

James W. McAuley is Professor of Political Sociology and Irish Studies at the University of Huddersfield. He has written widely on the sociology and politics of the situation in Northern Ireland. Currently he is engaged in ESRC-funded research on the political and social attitudes of members of the Orange Order (with Jon Tonge) and former paramilitary prisoners (with Jon Tonge and

Peter Shirlow), funded by the Leverhulme Trust. His latest book, *Ulster's Last Stand?*, is due to be published by Pluto Press in 2007.

Conor McGrath is an Independent Scholar, but was Lecturer in Political Lobbying and Public Affairs at the University of Ulster from 1999 to 2006. He is author of *Lobbying in Washington, London and Brussels: The Persuasive Communication of Political Issues* (2005), and co-editor of *Challenge and Response: Essays on Public Affairs and Transparency* (2006). His articles have appeared in *Journal of Public Affairs*, *Irish Political Studies*, and *Journal of Communication Management*. He has been President of the Political Studies Association of Ireland since 2005.

Anthony McIntyre is a former Provisional IRA prisoner who completed a doctoral thesis on the formative years of the Provisional Movement upon his release from prison. The chapter that appears in this book led to him being carpeted by the Sinn Féin leadership and informed that academic contributions must not contradict the party line. McIntyre has worked as an academic researcher for a US university and is currently a member of the National Union of Journalists. He is a regular public broadcast commentator, and is a weekly columnist for the online journal *The Blanket*.

Iain McMenamin is a Lecturer in the School of Law and Government, Dublin City University. He is interested in most aspects of comparative politics. His articles have appeared in the *European Journal of Research*, *British Journal of Political Science*, *Political Studies* and other journals.

Michael Marsh is Head of the School of Social Sciences and Philosophy in Trinity College Dublin. He has published extensively on parties and elections and has been a principal investigator for the 2002 and 2007 Irish Election Studies and is a co-author of *The Irish Voter*, the report on the 2002 study that will be published later this year.

Claire Mitchell is a Lecturer in the School of Sociology, Social Policy and Social Work at Queen's University Belfast. Her research focuses on religion and politics and her first book, *Religion, Identity and Politics in Northern Ireland: Boundaries of Belonging and Belief*, was published by Ashgate in 2005. She has published numerous articles on religion, identity, ethnicity, politics and research methodology in *Sociology*, *Ethnic and Racial Studies*, *Political Studies*, *Sociology of Religion*, *Nations and Nationalism*, *Contemporary Politics* and *Irish Political Studies*.

Gary Murphy is Senior Lecturer in Government in the School of Law and Government at Dublin City University. He has published extensively on Irish politics in a number of journals and texts. He is currently engaged in research on political lobbying and was co-editor of *Irish Political Studies* from 2002 to 2005.

J.P. O'Carroll taught Sociology at UCC from 1971 to 2003 mainly in the areas of the sociology of community and of politics. His main focus has been in the area of cultural politics and from this perspective he has published on the politics of the divorce referenda, of commemoration, of de Valera, of blood, of social work and of the effects of the ideology of community, nation and partnership on the processes of policy formation.

Niall Ó Dochartaigh is lecturer in the Department of Political Science and Sociology, National University of Ireland, Galway. He is the author of *From Civil Rights to Armalites: Derry and the Birth of the Irish Troubles* (Cork University Press, 1997; Palgrave, 2005).

Eoin O'Malley is a Lecturer in Political Science at the School of Law and Government in Dublin City University, where he teaches courses on Irish politics. His main research area is executive politics. He has published articles in *Government and Opposition, International Political Science Review* and *British Journal of Politics and International Relations* on prime ministers and executive power. He is also continuing research on cabinet government in Ireland, some of which has been published in *Irish Political Studies*.

Kirsten E. Schulze is senior lecturer in International History at the London School of Economics. She works on conflict and conflict resolution, in particular the Northern Ireland Conflict, the Arab-Israeli Conflict, the Lebanese Civil War, and the Aceh Conflict. Her publications include *The Free Aceh Movement (GAM): Anatomy of a Separatist Organisation* (East-West-Center, 2004); *The Jews of Lebanon: Between Coexistence and Conflict* (Sussex Academic Press, 2001); and *The Arab-Israeli Conflict* (Longman, 1999) as well as *Insurgency and Counter-insurgency: Strategy in the Aceh Conflict* (Singapore University Press, 2006); 'Decommissioning and Paramilitary Strategy in Northern Ireland: A Problem Compared' (*The Journal of Strategic Studies*, 2000), and *Taking the Gun out of Politics: Conflict Transformation in Lebanon and Northern Ireland* (Oxford University Press, 2001).

Richard Sinnott is Professor of Political Science in the School of Politics and International Relations at University College Dublin (UCD) and Director of the Public Opinion and Political Behaviour Research Programme at the UCD-Geary Institute. He is author of *Irish Voters Decide: Voting Behaviour in Elections and Referendums since 1918* (MUP, 1995) and co-author of *People and Parliament in the European Union: Democracy, Participation and Legitimacy* and of *Conflict and Consensus: A Study of Values and Attitudes in the Republic of Ireland and Northern Ireland* (Leiden: Brill Academic Publishers, 2006). A graduate of Georgetown University (PhD 1983), he has held senior visiting fellowships at the European University Institute, Harvard University, Waseda University and Nuffield College, Oxford.

Clifford Smyth is a historian and former politician. His doctoral thesis, undertaken at Queen's University Belfast in 1984, was on religious and political convergence in the DUP and he wrote a biography of Ian Paisley three years later. In the 1970s he was an elected DUP member of the Northern Ireland Assembly and the Northern Ireland Constitutional Convention, but later stood as an Ulster Unionist candidate in the 1979 general election.

An active member of the Ulster-Scots community, Dr Smyth was recently awarded an Arts Council of Northern Ireland grant to research the cultural significance of the kilt and Ulster tartan.

Jennifer Todd publishes on ethnicity and identity change (including in *Archives Européennes de Sociologie*, 2004; *Theory and Society*, 2005; and an edited special double issue of *Nationalism and Ethnic Politics*, 2006). She was Director of the Institute for British Irish Studies, UCD, 2005–6; IRCHSS Government of Ireland Senior Research Fellow, 2006–7; Member of the Royal Irish Academy, 2007; and is based in the School of Politics and International Relations, University College Dublin. Since 1987, Jennifer Todd has written (individually and jointly) on the Northern Ireland conflict, including *Dynamics of Conflict in Northern Ireland* (Cambridge UP, 1996) and articles in *Irish Political Studies* (1990, 1991, 1995) and *Political Studies* (2001, 2007). Between 2003–6 she led research projects on identity formation and change (funded by the Irish Higher Education Authority and the EU Programme for Peace and Reconciliation).

Jonathan Tonge is Professor of Politics at the University of Liverpool. He has been involved in four ESRC projects and one Leverhulme Trust project on the politics of Northern Ireland since the Good Friday Agreement. Recent books include *Northern Ireland* (Polity, 2006), *The New Northern Irish Politics* (Palgrave, 2005), *Sinn Féin and the SDLP* (Hurst/O'Brien, 2005), and *Northern Ireland: Conflict and Change* (Pearson, 2002). Recent articles include pieces in *Electoral Studies*, *Party Politics*, *Political Psychology* and *Political Studies*. He was co-editor of *Irish Political Studies* from 2003 to 2006 and is currently Chair of the Political Studies Association of the United Kingdom.

Timothy J. White is Professor of Political Science at Xavier University and past Visiting Professor at NUI-Galway. His recent publications include: 'Why So Few Women in Dáil Éireann? The Effects of the Single Transferable Vote Election System', *New Hibernian Review*, 2006, pp. 71–83; 'Decoupling Catholic and National Identity: Secularisation Theories in the Irish Context' in *Irish and Catholic? Towards an Understanding of Identity*, ed. L. Fuller, J. Littleton, & E. Maher, Columba, Dublin, 2006; and 'Elite Construction of Identity: Comparing Nehru and de Valera as National Founders' in *India and Ireland: Colonies, Culture, and Empire*, ed. T. Foley & M. O'Connor, Irish Academic Press, Dublin, 2006.

Stefan Wolff is Professor of Political Science at the University of Nottingham and Senior Non-resident Research Associate at the European Centre for Minority Issues in Flensburg, Germany. He has extensively published on ethnic conflict and conflict resolution, including *Ethnic Conflict: A Global Perspective* (Oxford University Press, 2006). Wolff is editor of the journal *Ethnopolitics* (Routledge) and co-chair of the Specialist Group on Ethnopolitics of the Political Studies Association of the UK.

Acknowledgements

First and foremost, we wish to thank the authors and commentators whose work is presented here for their willingness to be included in this volume.

A very particular and significant contribution has been made to the development of the Political Studies Association of Ireland by all those who have published in, and refereed for, *Irish Political Studies* over the years. While it is impossible to single each of them out for personal commendation, we would especially like to take this opportunity to note our appreciation of the journal's editors: Paul Arthur, John Coakley, Richard English, Michael Gallagher, John Garry, Tom Garvin, Vincent Geoghegan, Brian Girvin, Alan Greer, Richard Jay, Michael Laver, Michael Marsh, Paul Mitchell, Gary Murphy, Nicholas Rees, Jon Tonge, and Ben Tonra.

The PSAI's current committee members have all been most supportive of this project: Maura Adshead, Andrew Cottey, Aaron Edwards, Christopher Farrington, John Garry, Cillian McGrattan, Niall Ó Dochartaigh, Theresa Reidy, Jane Suiter, and Liam Weeks. Very practical assistance in the manuscript's preparation was provided by Marian Hughes and Maria Laura Sudulich. At Routledge, Craig Fowlie and Natalja Mortensen have been very helpful indeed.

On a personal note, the editors would like to record their deep gratitude to Paula and Alicia, and Catherine and Martha, for their enduring support and constant tolerance of the encroachments of work into family life.

1 Introduction

Politics in Ireland, 1982–2007

Eoin O'Malley and Conor McGrath

Twenty-five years ago, when the Political Studies Association of Ireland (PSAI) was established, a book was published which sought to reflect the changes Ireland had undergone in the previous 25 years. Despite having just suffered a depression, the (very) late 1950s had been a time of hope in the Republic of Ireland – not least because of the Whitaker Report which promised to open up Ireland to external economic forces. However by 1982 the introduction of that book, intriguingly titled *Unequal Achievement*, painted a bleak picture:

> The Irish economy is in recession. Unemployment is rising and the social problems which follow from economic stagnation are growing. Despondency seems to be on the increase, as though the intractability of our problems had at last sapped our will to solve them.
>
> (Litton, 1982, p. ix)

As well as the stagnation of the Republic's economy, the other great intractable problem on the island – the inter-communal dispute in Northern Ireland – was going through one of its severest tests. It had just witnessed the hunger strikes and the upsurge in violence and social unrest associated with them. A solution to the Northern Ireland problem seemed further away than ever; indeed it was common to cite Richard Rose's (1976, p. 139) devastating conclusion that, 'The problem is that there is no solution'. In the last 25 years, since 1982, hopelessness, depression, stagnation and violence have largely given way to self-confidence, economic boom, vibrancy and political progress. In 2007 the island of Ireland is a different place – one worthy of Hartley's phrase 'the past is another country, they do things differently there'. In some respects the Ireland of 2007 is infinitely better than the Ireland of 1982, in others perhaps worse; it is, however, unarguably different.

Economy

By the end of the twentieth century the Republic of Ireland had transformed itself from the 'poor man of Europe' to one of its leading lights. The extent to which this wealth is real or illusory is debatable – much of the growth is based on Foreign Direct Investment (FDI) from multinational companies and an unsustainable property and construction boom – but that Ireland has been transformed following years of economic growth is clear. Ireland's unemployment rate hovered at about four per cent for much of the 2000s (down from 18 per cent in 1987), a position of effective full employment. Ireland's per capita Gross Domestic Product was among the highest in the European Union (EU).

How this happened is the subject of debate but a number of contributing factors can be identified. Ireland opened itself up to foreign investment, offering low corporation tax rates and comparatively liberal labour markets. This relieved it of its dependence on trade with Britain and on agricultural produce. Ireland 'bet' on developing a specialisation in information technology, which happened to be the major growth industry in the 1990s. It can be argued that demographic and social factors helped. Ireland had a much younger population than many places in Western Europe and because of a series of decisions in the 1960s to invest in education, these people were now reasonably well educated for the labour market. That these people were English-speaking and culturally close to the U.S. – the major source of FDI – may have helped. Ireland also benefited from pump-priming from the EU which invested heavily in Ireland's infrastructure. Ireland's system of 'social partnership' may also have given stability to previously fractious industrial relations, enabling further investment. A series of public expenditure cuts from the late 1980s designed to get the public finances under control probably gave more confidence to business to invest, as did a series of measures which both liberalised the economy and offered stability to investors (for instance, membership of the European Monetary Union). Another factor which is difficult to measure but clear anecdotally is the development of an entrepreneurial culture to an extent not previously seen in Ireland. None of these factors alone could account for the unprecedented economic growth. For instance, Ireland's demographic make-up could have led to greater emigration as it had in the past. But what is certain is that Ireland's depressions and boom were related to public policy and ultimately political choices (see Garvin, 2004; and Girvin in this volume). Less certain is whether the Republic of Ireland will be able to hold on to these gains over the next 25 years in the face of rising house prices and wages, competition from developing economies in Asia and Eastern Europe, a continued reluctance by the state to divest itself of direct ownership in a host of industries, and an infrastructure system which is clearly much improved but still with substantial room for further development. Explaining these developments adequately will thus be an important research question for social scientists.

The Northern Ireland economy, once one of the most vibrant industrial centres in the world, suffered from stagnant unionist rule, its being tied to the relatively declining British economy and then the violence of the Troubles, which meant that little inward investment could take place. The economy became, and remains, dependent on transfers from Britain, which account for 20 per cent of economic product, and the public sector as a whole accounts for about 60 per cent of activity in the Northern Irish economy, much higher than either Britain or the Republic. Still there has been a 'peace dividend' and a dividend from its proximity to the

Republic. By 2007 Northern Ireland's growth rates were higher than Britain's or the Republic's, and house prices there were rising faster than in most of the United Kingdom, leading many to hope that it could eventually emulate its southern neighbour.

As a result of these developments the physical differences between north and south narrowed significantly. In the 1980s the Republic of Ireland's roads were the subject of ridicule. A cartoon by Martyn Turner in the *Irish Times* contrasted 'Dear, old Ireland' with 'Cheap, new Northern Ireland'. The physical difference on crossing the then heavily fortified border was marked. Northern Ireland had a well-built road network and well maintained public spaces. The Republic's road network has improved since then and the physical changes in the countryside reflect the country's economic growth if not taste. However, the countryside in the Republic is blighted by ribbon development along the roads of Ireland with incongruous mansions in many places. The cities have seen poorly built apartment blocks already in decay and at risk of becoming ghettoes of the poor. Out-of-town shopping centres, already common in Northern Ireland, have thrived at a cost to city centres which have been neglected up until recently. These decisions resulted in increasing traffic problems and are not helped by poor public transport networks. Many of the planning decisions which allowed this type of development we now know (thanks to the work of various tribunals of inquiry set up to investigate certain payments to politicians and planning decisions) to have been taken as a result of political corruption. Again we see the primacy of politics.

Political or 'peace' process

At the time the Political Studies Association of Ireland was being formed in 1982, the Troubles were (with the benefit of hindsight) just about at their mid-point. It is difficult to exaggerate the toll they exerted – in lives taken and lives ruined, in economic terms, in inter-group relations. One account provides a reckoning of the murder rate as around one in every 400 people in Northern Ireland, and conflates this as being equivalent to 150,000 and 600,000 killings in Britain and the United States respectively, while further noting that by comparison 52,000 U.S. soldiers died in Vietnam and total US military casualties in World War II were 274,000 (Smith, 2002, p. 21; also see the remarkable book by McKittrick *et al*, 2004). On whatever measurement and by any standard, the violence in Northern Ireland was enormously destructive.

The course of the violence and of the rather intermittent and sporadic efforts at political progress have been well charted by now (Bell, 1993; Bew and Gillespie, 1999; Bloomfield, 1998; Cunningham, 2001; Elliott and Flackes, 1999; Prior, 1986; Rees, 1985; Taylor, 1997, 1999 and 2001; Thatcher, 1993). So too has the more substantial political momentum which has been achieved in the second half of the Troubles and since, much of the material coming from the first-hand perspective of insiders (Adams, 2003; Cox *et al*, 2000; de Bréadún, 2001; Finlay, 1998; Godson, 2004; Major, 1999; Mallie and McKittrick, 2001; Mitchell, 1999; Mowlam, 2002; Needham, 1999; Rafter, 2002; Tonge, 2005; Wilford, 2001).

The economies of both Northern Ireland and the Republic have both benefited from the stable peace achieved in Northern Ireland. Ireland no longer instinctively evokes images of car bombs. In the 1980s a solution to the conflict seemed a long way off; the hunger strikes had radicalised a new group of nationalists, and unionists balked at the possibility of interference from Dublin through institutions set up by the Anglo-Irish Agreement. The ongoing process towards a normalised political framework for the rule of Northern Ireland started in the late 1980s with secret meetings between the Social Democratic and Labour Party (SDLP) and Sinn Féin leaders, John Hume and Gerry Adams. It was helped by the increased contact and subsequently improved relations between the two governments. By the early 1990s the Provisional movement – both the Irish Republican Army (IRA) and Sinn Féin – made conciliatory gestures in the form of ceasefires and the British and Irish governments engaged fully and, more importantly, publicly with Sinn Féin. The major Agreement signed in Belfast in 1998 between the then largest unionist party, the Ulster Unionist Party (UUP), and the two nationalist parties as well as a host of smaller parties took the form of a sectarian Executive and Assembly which would through a series of mechanisms govern many aspects of Northern Ireland. It included other institutions such as the North–South Ministerial Conference which would attempt to make policy in a small number of areas on an all-island basis, a British–Irish Inter-governmental Conference and a British–Irish Council. By 2007 the Executive and Assembly had been in suspension rather than operation for most of the period, and while functioning had exhibited little success in governing. However, the two most (British and Irish) nationalist parties, the Democratic Unionist Party (DUP) and Sinn Féin, also became the largest parties and their electoral success made each secure enough to make significant concessions. The IRA decommissioned its weapons and Sinn Féin agreed to support the police force, while the DUP – once opposed to the Agreement – signalled its willingness to go into government with Sinn Féin.

While progress has been and is being made, it remains to be seen whether Northern Irish politics can be fundamentally transformed. The two moderate partners at the centre of the Good Friday Agreement – the Ulster Unionist Party and the SDLP – have both lost ground since the Agreement was signed. Even they were unable to work entirely harmoniously together while in office. How the DUP and Sinn Féin will meet this challenge is as yet unknown, but it is undoubtedly a problematic relationship. While power-sharing has long been regarded, for under-standable historical reasons, as a 'good thing', it may be difficult for politics in Northern Ireland to make the transition from a sectarian, constitutional, focus to a discourse and electoral competition based primarily on socio-economic or ideological priorities until such time as the system – and the people – can come to terms with a more traditional form of government. The existence of a single-party government, or of a multi-party voluntary coalition, exercising power through collective responsibility, with a clearly-defined and significant grouping of opposition parties offering both legislative oversight and electoral choices, are all still some way off for Northern Ireland. It is, though, clear in 2007 that while the process to a long-term political settlement is ongoing, the comparative peace and stability being experienced in Northern Ireland makes it a radically different place.

Attitudes in the Republic apparently also changed. Many in the Republic had been actively hostile to Britain, and it could be plausibly argued that opinions on the approach towards Britain and the 'Northern Problem' formed the basis of the major political division in the Republic. The importance of nationalism is still evident but survey evidence shows that by 2003 young people in the Republic felt much closer to people in Britain than to those in Northern Ireland (British Council Ireland, 2003). This, coupled with Northern Ireland's addiction to London's tax revenue, perhaps makes the likelihood of a united Ireland much less. Indeed, it is at least arguable that the population of the Republic of Ireland would never have voted in favour of a united Ireland had that been a realistic possibility over the last 30 years, given the common ignorance and fear which many felt towards Northern Ireland then, and moreover that they would not now be prepared to vote for unification on the basis that its economic costs could imperil the Republic's relative prosperity. There is a real sense in which the Troubles were fuelled by a feeling on all sides of being unwanted – unionists often perceiving the United Kingdom as being only too willing to be rid of Northern Ireland if it could, and nationalists/republicans perceiving that the Republic was willing to abandon them if support came with a tangible price-tag.

Social and demographic changes

In 1982 Ireland was a country of emigration. Later, the continuing high emigration throughout the 1980s was excused by one minister, Brian Lenihan, who exclaimed in a U.S. magazine that 'after all we can't all live on a small island' (*Newsweek*, 19 October 1987). By 2007 ten per cent of the Irish population was foreign born, up from negligible levels in the 1980s. Immigration rates are among the highest in Europe. This has led to a physical change in Irish society. Most towns and villages have significant non-Irish populations, and most school children are in schools with children of many other nationalities. These changes will undoubtedly have an impact on social attitudes in the coming decades – and indeed signs of a degree of racism are becoming evident for the first time in Ireland, both north and south. Predicting and explaining changing social attitudes should mean that there are exciting times ahead for Irish social scientists.

Parts of the west of Ireland in 1982 still conformed to what many would describe as pre-modern society – one in which traditionalism, religiosity and conservatism abound. Superstition and myth gripped much of the country in 1985 when alleged sightings of statues of the Virgin Mary moving, first in Ballinspittle, Co. Cork and then in much of the rest of the country, resulted in mass religious fervour. Of course none of these sightings was confirmed but in the 1980s the Republic of Ireland was still a conservative and religious place. Ireland was in the throes of a debate on abortion, with parties fighting over who could please the Church more. The referendum was not about legalising abortion, but the extent to which its illegalisation should be cemented in law. A few years later the so-called 'crusade' of Garret FitzGerald to liberalise the country lost any of its credibility when the Irish voted strongly in favour of the ban on divorce. However, the next decade would see a major change in the power of and attitudes to the Catholic Church. The Church went through a crisis following revelations that it had protected from prosecution priests who were serial sex offenders. The hypocrisy of the Church was further exposed when it was revealed that a number of prominent clergy were in relationships with women or had fathered children. The economic boom, which allowed greater social and geographic mobility, can probably also in part explain changing mores in Irish society – although see Garry, Hardiman and Payne (2006) for evidence of some stability in social attitudes. So the moving statues could be seen as the death throes of this pre-modern society and certainly now people would view with disbelief an Ireland in which such visions could have been taken seriously; indeed, the moving statues phenomenon has become the subject of satire rather than sociology (Binchy, 1991). Ireland arguably has moved from a pre-modern to modern society where secularism, liberalism and urban values are the norm, and moved from a pre- to a post-industrial society, in the space of only three or four decades.

Social attitudes in Northern Ireland are of much less interest to social scientists than have been the attitudes there towards the other community. Traditionally Protestants were seen as more liberal than Catholics, who received their attitudes from Rome. However, there has been an increase in evangelism in Northern Ireland (see Mitchell in this volume) and the largest unionist party, the DUP, is religious whereas Sinn Féin, the largest party representing Catholics, is much more secular so this assumed division may not stand up to empirical examination. It is notable however that one of the few issues on which Sinn Féin and the DUP voted together was against the extension of the UK's 1967 Abortion Act to Northern Ireland (NI Assembly, 20 June 2000).

Political culture

1982 was a vintage year for Irish political scandals (Kerrigan and Brennan, 1999). On 18 February that year, Pat O'Connor was alleged to have voted in the general election at Malahide and then again later in the day at Kinsealy; Mr O'Connor also happened to be Charles Haughey's election agent. He was charged but the case was eventually dismissed by the High Court on a technicality. We know now that the Minister for Justice, Seán Doherty, had been tapping the phone conversations of two journalists during 1982; Doherty's claim a decade later that he had given Charles Haughey transcripts of those phone calls was the immediate cause of Haughey's retirement from public life (at least until tribunals forced him back to centre-stage). Nor was this the only political bugging in 1982: Minister for Finance, Ray MacSharry, secretly recorded a conversation he had with Martin O'Donoghue, another Fianna Fáil TD, in which O'Donoghue was asking MacSharry to lead a putsch against Haughey. Brian Lenihan's 1990 presidential campaign was derailed when a researcher produced a tape-recording of an interview Lenihan had given him in which he admitted that in January 1982 he had phoned the then president, Paddy Hillery, asking him not to dissolve the Dáil for a general election but to instead ask Haughey to attempt to form a government; Lenihan had denied making any such phone calls.

Also in August 1982, the Attorney General, Patrick Connolly, was forced to resign after police arrested Malcolm Macarthur, a friend who was staying in Connolly's apartment. Macarthur was subsequently found guilty of the murder of a nurse in the Phoenix Park. When Macarthur was arrested, Connolly left Ireland for a planned holiday the next day but by the time he arrived in New York there was public astonishment over the incident and he flew back to resign. Haughey described the events as 'grotesque, unprecedented, bizarre and unbelievable' which Conor Cruise O'Brien turned into 'GUBU'; GUBU then became a common shorthand for the various controversies which Haughey both courted and was dogged by.

Whether Ireland's political culture – 'attitudes towards the political system and its various parts and attitudes towards the role of the self in the system' (Almond and Verba, 1963, p. 13) – has changed much since 1982 is moot. Some of the articles in this volume point to a culture of individualism and 'cute hoorism' – where people try to get the political system to work for their own individual desires rather than for broad policy changes. As recently as the 1990s, Chubb (1992, chapter 1) wrote about a peasant culture, loyalty, anti-intellectualism and authoritarian values in Ireland. Earlier Raven and Whelan (1976) found 'distrust of authority on which personalism can thrive' (Whyte, 1976, p. 5). The election campaign in 2007 equally produced many examples of politicians acting in what has (incorrectly) become known as a clientelistic manner. For instance, a story confirmed to one of the authors shows that Taoiseach Bertie Ahern's constituency office arranged for a lamp-post to be moved in advance of the election because it hindered a constituent's ability to get in and out of her driveway.

Political culture in Northern Ireland continues to be dominated by group identity, although there are still elements of this which are relatively under-explored. For instance, we know little about the beliefs and values of those middle-class Catholics who are largely indifferent, or even opposed, to the idea of a united Ireland. It has been suggested that their professional status is responsible for their political views (i.e. that in well-paid and respected jobs such as the law, medicine, academia, and business, they enjoy a relatively high standard of living and are thus essentially content with the status of Northern Ireland), but no comprehensive or systematic study of Catholic unionists has yet been attempted. Equally, to what precisely are loyalists loyal, when they attack or criticise the British government, its police or soldiers, its people and even on occasions its Queen? The various groupings within Northern Ireland are by no means as one-dimensional as a simple headcount of Catholics and Protestants might suggest, but it can by no means yet be said that the political system is structured such as to allow the full expression of each grouping's range of socio-politico-economic interests.

Party system

The Irish party system was in the midst of substantial realignment at the time of the PSAI's foundation – 1977 was the last general election at which the electorate in the south produced a single-party majority government, and there has been permanent government by coalition there since 1989; indeed, it is difficult now to imagine a future single-party government. In 1981–82 there were three elections in the Republic of Ireland. Fianna Fáil under the controversial leadership of Charles J. Haughey lost power, before regaining it temporarily and then lost it again. Fine Gael under a new leader, Garret FitzGerald, underwent an organisational and ideological renovation to pose a real challenge to Fianna Fáil's electoral dominance for the first time in decades. Fine Gael repositioned itself as a liberal, social democratic party under FitzGerald's leadership, even as he retained many conservatives still in senior positions in the party. The coalition with the Labour Party, which was led by a then inexperienced Dick Spring, may have brought the possibility of repositioning the Irish party system between a centre-left and liberal block of Fine Gael and Labour, and a centre-right, conservative Fianna Fáil. In 1982 the two biggest parties accounted for nearly 85 per cent of the vote, and almost 94 per cent of voters supported the three established parties. However, this two-block system failed to cement itself. Distrust between the coalition parties and economic differences led to that government's eventual break up. A division in Fianna Fáil led to the founding of the Progressive Democrats (PDs) and these two parties eventually went into coalition leading to a complete change in the Irish party system (Mair, 1993).

This decision has had a major impact on the party system as Fine Gael is no longer necessary for changes in government, and Fianna Fáil could pick new coalition partners as it saw necessary (O'Malley and Kerby, 2004). Unsurprisingly the number and electoral support of smaller parties increased. Sinn Féin, the Greens and the PDs all increased their representation in 2002, whereas Fianna Fáil and Fine Gael together only accounted for 64 per cent of the vote – Fine Gael falling to just 22 per cent. By 2007 the election campaign was dominated more by who would coalesce with whom than any substantial policy disagreement. The answer seemed to be – anybody with anybody. All political parties, including Sinn Féin and the Greens, were keen not to threaten the economic model which was credited with Ireland's economic growth. These parties would only tinker at the edges. The lack of salient political divisions between the parties perhaps can account for the declining turnout in Ireland.

Over the years of the PSAI's existence, we have seen a remarkable transformation in the Irish presidency. Generally regarded as something like a retirement home for aging statesmen for its first three decades, the presidency is no longer the sole preserve of elderly men with a long background in Fianna Fáil party politics (with the exception of the first president, Douglas Hyde, who received an all-party nomination, as the Labour Party candidate in 1990 Mary Robinson is the only president not from Fianna Fáil). Indeed, 1997 was the first time that one woman succeeded another as elected head of state anywhere in the world. Moreover, both Mary Robinson and Mary McAleese consciously expanded the office – they held 13 meetings of the Council of State between them (to date), compared to 13 meetings in total prior to 1990; they addressed the Houses of the Oireachtas on three occasions, something which had only happened once before; and they have both been active in terms of promoting social issues of national importance.

Northern Ireland was possibly unique in Europe in having a dominant party for much of the twentieth century. The Official or Ulster Unionist Party continuously formed the devolved government. However the outbreak of violence, and the imposition of Direct Rule, led to challenges to its hegemony. The DUP, formed by a religious firebrand, Ian Paisley, grew slowly but eventually overtook the UUP as the largest party in Northern Ireland. On the nationalist side, the Nationalist Party gave way to the SDLP which dominated through the 1980s, but the hunger strikes gave Sinn Féin a way into electoral politics, which after a series of failures bore the party fruit, eventually dominating the SDLP. By 2007 the raison d'être of the two establishment parties could be questioned and their futures are uncertain.

Overview

This book has been produced to mark the 25th anniversary of the establishment of the Political Studies Association of Ireland. The PSAI exists to promote the study of politics both in and of Ireland. The Association is concerned with politics, not simply Irish politics, and to this end it now operates a number of specialist groups which deal with a broad range of sub-disciplinary areas. In addition, since 1986 the PSAI has published its academic journal, *Irish Political Studies*, which does focus on Irish politics and which has evolved from an annual into a quarterly publication and from an essentially self-produced journal into one now in the hands of an internationally respected academic publisher – reflecting the extent and vibrancy of academic study of politics in Ireland.

The present volume does not aim to track or explain all the changes Ireland has undergone in the last 25 years, though many will be the themes of some of the contributions. Rather we have brought together some of the best, most controversial and/or most thought-provoking articles from *Irish Political Studies* over its life-time. These are broken into two broad themes – Political Culture and Traditions; and Electoral Politics and Political Institutions. The first group of articles covers a range of topics such as analyses of the different political traditions in Northern Ireland – nationalism, unionism, republicanism and loyalism. This section also contains discussions of the political culture of Ireland and the nature of its democracy. The second section looks at topics including the basis for voting on both sides of the Irish border, political attitudes and political institutions.

After each article another academic offers a commentary on the topic which considers how (and how well) the original article has stood the test of time. These specially-commissioned commentaries do not summarise the article; rather they may take the original author to task on some issue, offer an updated assessment of the topic, and provide some pointers for future research and reading. The original articles and new commentaries taken together offer a firm basis for the study of each topic. What is notable is the quality and prescience of many of the articles, which stand up to scrutiny even after many years. This is a credit to the authors, to the editors of *Irish Political Studies*, and to the wider body of scholarship that exists in the political science community in Ireland today. It is our hope and expectation that the community of scholars studying politics in Ireland will continue to use and benefit from the PSAI and *Irish Political Studies* well into the future. While highlighting and celebrating the research which has already been published in *Irish Political Studies*, at the same time we look forward with renewed interest and anticipation to see how this distinctive field develops over the next 25 years and beyond.

References

Adams, Gerry (2003) *Hope and History: Making Peace in Ireland*. Dingle: Brandon.

Almond, Gabriel A. and Sydney Verba (1963) *The Civic Culture: Political Attitudes and Democracy in Five Nations*. Boston, MA: Little, Brown.

Bell, J. Bowyer (1993) *The Irish Troubles: A Generation of Violence, 1967–1992*. Dublin: Gill and Macmillan.

Bew, Paul and Gordon Gillespie (1999) *Northern Ireland: A Chronology of the Troubles, 1968–1999*. Dublin: Gill and Macmillan.

Binchy, Dan (1991) *The Neon Madonna*. London: Century.

Bloomfield, David (1998) *Political Dialogue in Northern Ireland: The Brooke Initiative, 1989–92*. New York: St. Martin's Press.

British Council Ireland (2003) *Through Irish Eyes: Irish Attitudes Towards the UK*. Dublin: British Council.

Chubb, Basil (1992) *The Government and Politics of Ireland*. Third Edition. Harlow: Longman.

Cox, Michael, Adrian Guelke and Fiona Stephen (eds.) (2000) *A Farewell to Arms?: From 'Long War' to Long Peace in Northern Ireland*. Manchester: Manchester University Press.

Cunningham, Michael (2001) *British Government Policy in Northern Ireland, 1969–2000*. Manchester: Manchester University Press.

de Bréadún, Deaglán (2001) *The Far Side of Revenge: Making Peace in Northern Ireland*. Wilton: Collins Press.

Elliott, Sydney and W.D. Flackes (1999) *Northern Ireland: A Political Directory 1968–1999*. Fifth Edition. Belfast: Blackstaff.

Finlay, Fergus (1998) *Snakes and Ladders*. Dublin: New Island.

Garry, John, Niamh Hardiman and Diane Payne (2006) *Irish Social and Political Attitudes*. Liverpool: Liverpool University Press.

Garvin, Tom (2004) *Preventing the Future: Why Was Ireland So Poor for So Long?* Dublin: Gill and Macmillan.

Godson, Dean (2004) *Himself Alone: David Trimble and the Ordeal of Unionism*. London: HarperCollins.

Kerrigan, Gene and Pat Brennan (1999) *The Great Little Nation: The A–Z of Irish Scandals and Controversies*. Dublin: Gill and Macmillan.

Litton, Frank (1982) 'Preface', pp. ix–x in Frank Litton (ed.) *Unequal Achievement: The Irish Experience 1957–1982*. Dublin: Institute of Public Administration.

Mair, Peter (1993) 'Fianna Fáil, Labour and the Irish Party System', pp. 162–73 in Michael Gallagher and Michael Laver (eds) *How Ireland Voted 1992*. Dublin: Folens.

Major, John (1999) *John Major: The Autobiography*. London: HarperCollins.

Mallie, Eamonn and David McKittrick (2001) *Endgame in Ireland*. London: Hodder and Stoughton.

McKittrick, David, Seamus Kelters, Brian Feeney and Chris Thornton (2004) *Lost Lives: The Stories of the Men, Women and Children Who Died as a Result of the Troubles*. Second Revised Edition. Edinburgh: Mainstream.

Mitchell, George (1999) *Making Peace*. London: William Heinemann.

Mowlam, Marjorie (2002) *Momentum: The Struggle for Peace, Politics and the People*. London: Hodder and Stoughton.

Needham, Richard (1999) *Battling for Peace: Northern Ireland's Longest Serving British Minister*. Belfast: Blackstaff.

O'Malley, Eoin and Matthew Kerby (2004) 'Chronicle of a Death Foretold? Understanding the Decline of Fine Gael', *Irish Political Studies*, 19 (1), pp. 39–58.

Prior, James (1986) *A Balance of Power*. London: Hamish Hamilton.

Rafter, Kevin (2002) *Martin Mansergh: A Biography*. Dublin: New Island.

Raven, John and C.T. Whelan (1976) 'Irish Adults' Perceptions of Their Civic Institutions and Their Own Role in Relation to Them', pp. 7–84 in John Raven, C.T. Whelan, Paul A. Pfretzschner and Donald M. Borock (eds.) *Political Culture in Ireland: The Views of Two Generations*. Dublin: Institute of Public Administration.

Rees, Merlyn (1985) *Northern Ireland: A Personal Perspective*. London: Methuen.

Rose, Richard (1976) *Northern Ireland: Time for a Change*. London: Macmillan.

Smith, Jeremy (2002) *Making the Peace in Northern Ireland*. Harlow: Pearson Education.

Taylor, Peter (1997) *Provos: The IRA and Sinn Féin*. London: Bloomsbury.

Taylor, Peter (1999) *Loyalists: Ulster's Protestant Paramilitaries*. London: Bloomsbury.

Taylor, Peter (2001) *Brits: The War Against the IRA*. London: Bloomsbury.

Thatcher, Margaret (1993) *The Downing Street Years*. London: HarperCollins.

Tonge, Jonathan (2005) *The New Northern Ireland Politics?* Basingstoke: Palgrave Macmillan.

Whyte, John H. (1976) 'Introduction', pp. 1–6 in John Raven, C.T. Whelan, Paul A. Pfretzschner and Donald M. Borock (eds.) *Political Culture in Ireland: The Views of Two Generations*. Dublin: Institute of Public Administration.

Wilford, Rick (ed.) (2001) *Aspects of the Belfast Agreement*. Oxford: Oxford University Press.

Part One

Political culture and traditions

2 The not-so-amazing case of Irish democracy[1]

Bill Kissane

Originally published in *Irish Political Studies*, 10, 1995, pp. 43–68.

When in 1923, over a year after independence, and just four months after the end of a bitter Civil War, the Irish Free State held its first proper, free and fair, competitive election, *The Times* commented 'that a people untrained, by the accidents of history, in self-government, and congenitally disposed towards political instability, should complete a critical election without bloodshed or even social disturbance is indeed proof that its present governors are men of understanding' (quoted in Lee, 1989, p. 173). Given the political disposition of the Irish, that the state should retain a democratic form of government was, in short, a surprise. In so far as Irish democracy has subsequently been studied by democratic theorists it has been analysed in a post-colonial framework in which the failure of democracy is the norm. As 'a poor new nation' that remained democratic it provides a useful limiting case for generalisations about the experience of new nations in the Third World (Munger, 1976, p. 34).

The resilience of democracy in social conditions allegedly unpropitious for the survival of democracy has been explained in two ways; as a product of the diffusion of a British political culture into Irish life (Farrell, 1971; Chubb, 1982), or as the product of the ability of British institutions to accommodate the cultural expectations of a backward society (Carty, 1983; Garvin, 1981; Prager, 1986; Schmitt, 1973). Both theories assume some incongruity between aspects of Irish society and an advanced democratic system. I question that assumption and suggest that the Irish inherited a social structure typically favourable to democracy. The Irish case is not relevant to democratic theory because it developed and survived in unmodern conditions but is a case that can be explained by comparative macro-sociological theories of democratisation.

Post-colonial theories of political culture

Of states classified by Lipset in 1959 as stable democracies the number with a previous experience of British rule amounted to almost half of the overall total (Lipset, 1959). All ex-colonies with a population of one million or more that have remained democratic since independence have been British colonies (Weiner, 1987). In contrast the Dutch, Portuguese, and French colonial empires together have left behind no stable democracy. On a worldwide scale experience of British rule 'overwhelms other variables' as a predictor of democratic stability.[2]

The British tutelary model

Weiner identifies three features of British rule which may account for the persistence of democracy after independence. One was the creation of bureaucratic structures that 'stressed the legitimate role of state authority in the preservation of order in societies that left to themselves, would have descended into anarchic violence' (Weiner, 1987, pp. 4–5). A second was the opportunity given to native politicians to compete in elections, form political parties, and gain experience of office. This enabled rival elites to internalise the norms that regulate the peaceful competition for power. This is related to the third feature, peaceful regime-change. When independence came power was transferred to elected officials not armed revolutionaries.

The emphasis on the diffusion of a British political culture is the most common approach to the study of democratic stabilisation in the Irish Free State (Chubb, 1982; Farrell, 1972, pp. 13–26 and 208–23). Irish MPs had been attending Westminster since 1801. Elections had been popular events in Irish life since the 1820s. Democratisation in Ireland was gradual and the British system became 'internalised'.

> As is the case of the white communities of the British Commonwealth, many of the currently held political traditions and values were inculcated and absorbed during a most critical and formative period: the period of the advent of mass democracy ... Extensions of the franchise in Britain were followed by extensions, with modifications, in Ireland; and Irish people acquired democratic habits and values.
>
> (Chubb, 1982, p. 6)

Farrell also argues that the achievement of political stability 'was primarily part of Ireland's British inheritance from the nineteenth century parliamentary tradition' (1972, p. 212). He emphasises the significance of Dáil Éireann during the nationalist struggle from 1919 to 1922. It was 'a Westminster import'; a consistent effort was made to maintain Westminster procedures, the Speaker's rulings were accepted by the members, priority was given to parliamentary questions, the authority of the Dáil over the military campaign was stressed, and the creation of the Dáil courts showed 'a concern to preserve as far as possible the existing and accepted system' (Farrell, 1972, p. 211).

The implicit suggestion that the outcome was inevitable underestimates the problems faced by the Free State. Kevin O'Higgins described the Provisional Government which took over from the British as

> simply eight young men in the City Hall [the adjoining Dublin Castle's centuries-old association with British oppression made it unsuitable as a seat of government for Irish ministers] standing amidst the ruins of one adminis-tration, with the foundations of another not yet laid, and with wild men screaming through the keyhole. No police force was functioning through the

country, no system of justice was operating, the wheels of administration hung idle, battered out of recognition by rival jurisdictions.

(cited in Fanning, 1983, p. 10)

Britain left the Free State with a lot of problems: partition, a discredited parliamentary tradition, and a monarchical constitution repugnant to its sense of nationality. The Anglo-Irish Treaty of 1921 had solved the Irish question by stabilising 'Ireland' but temporarily destabilising the two states. After 1916 'the wild men' seized the initiative and turned their guns on the Pro-Treatyites. This forced the Free State's elites into a tutelary attitude themselves. They were concerned with order, legality, and the irresponsible and irrational nature of Irish political culture.[3]

> Ten years ago the Provisional Government assumed control of a country reduced by war and misgovernment to a state bordering on chaos. During the preceding struggle, the entire machinery of government had been disorganised, and respect for law had disappeared, in the absence of law which could command respect. An urgent and difficult task confronted the new Executive. The restoration of order and the rule of law, were the first necessity.
>
> (Hobson, 1932, pp. 15–16)

For some Pro-Treatyites the Civil War was the product of fantasy and lawlessness. 'Leavened in with some small amount of idealism and fanaticism, there is a good deal of greed, envy, and lust, and drunkenness and irresponsibility' (quoted in Lee, 1989, p. 98). Garvin suggests that two distinct political traditions within the nationalist movement were expressed in the war:

> 1921–22 is the founding date of democratic Ireland's political life, not just because of the coming of the truce in July 1921 or the signing of the treaty in December 1921, but because of the emergence, for the first time in Irish history, of popular expression of two poles of Irish Catholic political culture: the vision of the Republic as a moral community, as a community of equals submerging individual identity and self interest for the common good on the one hand, and a non-magical, lawyers' pragmatic nationalism on the other, which saw Irish independence as a means to the construction of a commercialised, mechanically representative democracy.
>
> (*Irish Times*, 28 December 1991)

The republican sub-culture had more in common with the secret society mentality of Southern Europe. Fenianism, the Irish Republican Brotherhood, the Irish Republican Army (IRA), were all part of a 'public band' tradition. It saw society as a 'moral community' and republicans saw themselves as guardians of that community's highest values and aspirations. The nature of their commitment was expressed by the role of the secret oath; they were answerable only to themselves; as de Valera put it, the majority had no right to do wrong. The Treaty split can be seen as a conflict between 'the public band' tradition personified by the anti-Treatyite IRA, and the world of 'civil society': the Church, the business community, the ex-unionists, and the electorate who supported the Treaty in 1922. Democracy was not inevitable but the product of the defeat of one way of thinking by the other in 1923. After this the 'unenthusiastic democrats' of Fianna Fáil rejoined civil society in 1927 (Garvin, 1993a and 1993b).

This suggests that in those areas where an experience of good government would be most obvious, respect for the law, faith in the political process, and an acceptance of the ultimate writ of the state, the inheritance was an ambiguous one (see Garvin, 1991, pp. 21–5). This was especially the case with regard to the republican assault on the Free State. 'The primary misfortune of the Irish state was that from the very beginning its existence constituted a violation of the principles of its founders' (O'Brien, 1968, p. 229). It is common to see signs of a healthy civic spirit in public participation in state holidays, which celebrate independence days and re-enact foundation myths in the U.S. vein. There is no such thing in Ireland. For decades the commemoration of the 1916 Rising was the only such ritual. On the walls of Irish primary schools are hung copies of the 1916 Proclamation of the Irish Republic, not the constitutions of 1922 or 1937. There are also photos of the martyred heroes of 1916, not of the real founding fathers of the Irish state, Cosgrave, Mulcahy, Collins, and O'Higgins. The terms 'the Free State' or 'Free Stater' were used either to denigrate the state's status or to question someone's nationalist credentials.

To Cardinal Logue, in 1922 de Valera unleashed a 'wild and destructive hurricane... from a thin insubstantial vapour' (quoted in Foster, *The Independent on Sunday*, 17 October 1994), yet for republicans the oath of allegiance, the amending of the 1922 constitution, and the Boundary Commission fiasco were all signs of Ireland's subordination. When de Valera tried to challenge the oath by using the constitutional right to initiate a referendum on it in 1927, the provision for referenda was removed from the constitution. The Free State government was strong, but not legitimate. How did it became so, and how in turn did Irish republicanism, at least in the south, become a purely constitutional form of politics? The constitutional republican thesis is that the role of Fianna Fáil was crucial in creating a more legitimate state. Along with the Blueshirts, Fianna Fáil was under threat from the IRA, which had around 30,000 members in 1932. When the government was debating the renewal of Article 2A which allowed the establishment of military tribunals in 1935 they complained that they were people, 'who had given one would have thought sufficient proof of their attachment to the Republican ideal and who were now held up to obloquy as the instruments of British oppression' (Department of An Taoiseach, *Constitutional Documents*, S2 454). A Garda document suggested that repression was not enough; it should look to 'legislative acts directed towards the political and economic emancipation of our country'. In particular a republican constitution 'will, I feel certain, succeed in demilitarising the IRA, and remove the organisation of a serious menace to democratic government' (Department of An Taoiseach, *Constitutional Documents*, S2 454).

This view suggests that the bulk of the population, including those who correctly saw the Treaty as a stepping-stone towards greater freedom, were in favour of undoing the Treaty. The 1937 constitution made republicanism constitutional for the first time. The leadership of de Valera was the *sine qua non* of this process.

> Indeed, if we take together de Valera's move away from 1916 militarism to the constitutionalism of elections in 1916 and 1918, his break with abstentionist and extra-parliamentary Sinn Féin in 1926 and the stern, if professedly anguished, steps against the IRA in the 1940s, we can say that not only did he epitomise at the outset of his career the ambivalence of constitutionalist and violent traditions of Irish nationalism but that he also bridged and transcended them, and finally and firmly asserted the supremacy of the civil over the military tradition, the constitutionalist principle over that of physical force, and majority rule over the people have no right to do wrong assertion.
>
> (Murphy, 1983, p. 2)

The route to stability was not smooth. The victory of the Free State army in 1923, the entry of Fianna Fáil into the Dáil in 1927, the changeover in 1932, and the 1937 constitution were all important stages in the consolidation of the system. 'From our present acquaintance with political processes in new nations we know how strange these events are' (Munger, 1976, p. 6), but it is not clear how the emphasis on a British political culture helps to explain these events; 'the principal evidence that such a culture existed lies in the fact that it purports to explain' (Munger, 1976, p. 23).

Irish political culture and political integration

Chubb argued that British influence ensured that 'the values of an industrial, urbanised liberal democratic society would prevail' (1982, p. 14), but when he asks why the 26 counties did not remain tied to Britain he turns to a broader conception of culture. Ireland's social structure was different and Irish social values – Catholicism, authoritarianism, loyalty and anti-intellectualism – reinforced this difference. Yet Chubb did not discuss how these values affected the process of democratic stabilisation. Garvin suggests that the legitimacy of the new state depended to an important extent 'on the degree to which it could be seen as being loyal to traditional values' (1981, p. 6). The relationship between culture and legitimacy has been analysed by three authors who reject the tutelary model 'which fails to account for the successful persistence of democratic institutions in post-independence Ireland' (Carty, 1983, p. 3). Prager states that the Irish success 'can hardly be viewed as an example of pre-modern, traditional convictions giving way to modern, universalistic ones; rather, the Irish example of stability demonstrates the accommodations made by political institutions to already existing social understandings' (Prager, 1986, p. 11).

These writers argue that the state overcame three problems typical of post-colonial experience: a tendency to see political roles in particularistic and ascriptive terms; a disjuncture between the type of authority exercised throughout the society, based on tradition and personal ties, and that exercised by a modern state; and finally, a deep cultural division, expressed by the Civil War. These problems are typical of backward societies. All three writers share an incongruity thesis, that the new state inherited a culture usually incompatible with the requirements of a democratic system. Table 2.1 compares the three variants of the incongruity thesis. All assume Irish society is essentially backward; two out of three adopt a model of peasant culture. The shared emphasis on the post-1922 period is because the analysis is of how the new political system accommodated itself to a traditional culture. For Prager the problem was how to overcome deep cultural divisions, or more specifically how to absorb a pre-modern Gaelic Romantic tradition, a sub-culture, into the institutions and forms of the Irish Enlightenment tradition. For Schmitt the problem was to have the decisions of the state accepted as authoritative, or to reconcile modern with pre-modern forms

Table 2.1 Three variants of the incongruity thesis compared

	Carty	Schmitt	Prager
Social base	Relatively underdeveloped	Traditionalist peasant society	Rural, pre-industrial society
Comparative context	Southern Europe	Third world new states	Third world new states
Description of Irish culture	Traditional, clientelistic, personalistic, peasant culture alongside autonomous elite culture	Traditional peasant culture characterised by personalistic and authoritarian social values	Deeply divided by two historic cultural divisions; and Anglo-Irish enlightenment and a Gaelic romantic tradition
Political symptom of cultural backwardness	Long history of clientelistic politics	Deference towards authority, preference for strong charismatic leadership and general conformism	Poor 'civic spirit', Treaty tension between parliamentary non-sectarian principles and Catholic middle classes
Obstacle to democracy	Lack of elite-mass linkages	Rejection of legal rational authority of the State	Deep cultural division blocks growth of collective solidarity and state legitimacy
Mechanism of cultural integration	Clientelism	Fusion of traditional and modern sources of authority	Fianna Fáil reconciled worlds of politics and culture
Decisive phase	1917–23	1922–23	1927–32
Decisive party	Sinn Féin	Cumann na nGaedheal	Both civil war parties

Sources: Carty (1983), Schmitt (1973) and Prager (1986).

of authority. For Carty the problem was how to build effective durable party structures on pre-modern clientelist traditions of political representation.

Prager sees the society as divided by profound cultural antinomies which were expressed by the Civil War:

> There was the Irish-Enlightenment tradition, deriving its original insights from the Anglo-Irish ascendancy and articulating modern secular aspirations for the Irish nation. Here the objective was to construct a social order characterised by autonomous individuals and independent spheres of social life in which the Irish citizen could rationally influence the course of Irish affairs. On the other side, there was a competing Gaelic-Romantic set of thoughts and beliefs. Its aim was to promote a solidary nation without conflict and disharmony, imbued with a vivid sense of the past in the functioning of the present. Neither secular nor individualistic, this orientation expressed a yearning for a social order protective of the values and patterns of interaction putatively characteristic of the ancient Gaelic Ireland.
>
> (1986, p. 16)[4]

He believes that the Irish public 'was hardly a healthy one' (Prager, 1986, p. 16), but nevertheless sees the entry of Fianna Fáil into the political arena as a decisive moment. As evidence of an unhealthy public he notes that the IRA and Sinn Féin remained active after 1922, opposed to 'the politics of reform'. Turnout in 1922 and 1923 was quite low. One reason allegedly was that the public could not vote for candidates that reflected their local concerns or their cultural orientations.[5] In his view, neither Labour nor Cumann na nGaedheal 'shared the same cultural universe as most Irish men and women' (Prager, 1986, p. 192). Until the entry of Fianna Fáil into the Dáil, those who held Gaelic-Romantic sentiments still felt excluded, culture was estranged from politics, and since Gaelic-Romantic impulses were not expressed politically this 'ensured the continued insecurity of the democratic order'. They were reconciled by Fianna Fáil who 'accomplished a cultural integration whereby Gaelic-Romantic and Irish-Enlightenment beliefs both appeared compatible with Free State politics' (Prager, 1986, p. 197).

These writers share three basic assumptions. Firstly, they deny the modernity of Irish society. Carty sees Ireland as an exception to the rule that democracy blossoms only in modern, developed societies (Carty, 1983, p. 3). Schmitt argues that Ireland displayed many of the features of post-World War II developing nations (1973, p. 88). Prager puts Ireland firmly within a Third World perspective:

> as a twentieth century nation faced with the problems of decolonization, it is more comparable in character and conviction, in many respects, to the new nations of the Third World than to Denmark, Switzerland, or other small Western democracies to which it is more frequently compared. Its economy and social structure bear the strong imprint of its colonially dependent status. It still remains a largely rural, agriculturally oriented nation, unlike most of its Western counterparts.
>
> (1986, p. 29)[6]

Secondly, all assume that Ireland's pre-modern culture posed problems for democratic politics. Prager's book is sub-titled *Political Order and Cultural Integration in a Newly Independent Nation*.[7] Schmitt is also concerned with the relationship between political culture, which in Ireland was characterised by 'authoritarian norms' and a 'personalistic style', and political development. He titled his work *The Irony of Irish Democracy*. Carty set out to 'discover how it managed successfully to organise democratic politics in a relatively unmodern society' (1983, p. 30). Finally, they argue that the central values of this culture proved to be congruent with a modern political system. Prager refers to the 'remarkable ability of the political institutions to accommodate to the cultural beliefs of the citizens' (1986, p. 223). Schmitt's hypothesis is that 'traditional norms can contribute significantly to the early stages of political development in new nations' (1973, p. 77). Carty suggests that the system became stable because 'the organisational forms of Irish politics are highly congruent with the norms of the political culture which, in their turn, epitomise the dominant social authority patterns of the society' (1983, p. 24). Although the success of the Fianna Fáil party was 'a function of a particular "irrational" commitment to an authoritarian politics that provided personal payoffs to its supporters', it was vital to incorporate these cultural traditions into the system (Carty, 1983, p. 213).

The Irish state remained democratic, not because it imposed its rules on Irish society but because it compromised them. So rather than saying the outcome was undemocratic, they say it was amazing. Can they consistently maintain the second and third arguments; that on the one hand the culture was pre-modern, and that on the other the reason for the durability of Irish institutions was due to their incorporation of that culture's norms?[8] This is the really 'amazing' thesis: that Irish democracy survived, because the public in 1922–23 accepted the law of the Church as more authoritative than that of the state, that the party system was stable because it was clientelistic, and that the Civil War split was healed because of the emergence of an irrational authoritarian party in the depression of the late 1920s. It would be more plausible to maintain that the public in 1922–23, after six years of chaos, said yes to peace and no to militarism, that in the late 1920s Fianna Fáil won over new voters because the politics of Cumman na nGaedheal, which Prager calls 'the politics of reform', had produced no legislation aimed at combating the depression, and that 'culture' (meaning republicanism) and politics were reconciled, because de Valera succeeded in revising the Treaty.

Their analysis is not only illogical; it is misleading. After 1922 constitutional provisions for referenda were ignored, executive decision-making was centralised and secretive, the army was denied a political role, and the civil service became more meritocratic than it had ever been. This is not evidence of a legal-rational state making concessions to the expectations of a backward society! Consider the case of local government. In 1922 a Ministry of Local Government was established. All appointments were made centrally and a county manager, a civil servant, directed local government policy. The government argued that the growth of local government functions made it plain that 'the appointment of local officials could no longer be exposed to the evils of patronage, of family, local and political influences' (Mansergh, 1934, p. 233). The local authorities had no right to reject these appointments. One challenge came in 1930 when Mayo County Council rejected a recommendation for the post of county librarian, a Protestant. The Council was dissolved by the minister. In 1932 Fianna Fáil ordered the commissioners to send down two names to choose from but this choice was removed in 1933 amidst allegations of bribery and canvassing (Mansergh, 1934, pp. 225–51).

The post-colonial legacy reconsidered

The post-colonial perspective has been misapplied to the Irish case although a comparison with other ex-colonies might yield insights. First, I suggest that it was not a backward peasant society. Then I show that the state had a social structure typically favourable to the emergence and stabilisation of democracy. Lastly I suggest that a modernisation approach combined with a post-colonial approach yields better insights into the British legacy.

Democracy and modernity

Small states are usually compared to their closest neighbour, for Ireland the most industrialised country in the world. The condescending description of the society as 'a peasant society' hides fundamental similarities between it and many other contemporaneous democracies. The Irish state is rarely compared to Europe's other small north-western democracies despite the fact that 'the rulers of the Free State entered on the task of state building with many advantages. Ireland was already a relatively modernised society' (Farrell, 1971, pp. xv–xvi; Lee, 1989, p. 69).

In 1959 Lipset (p. 53) put forward the argument that a stable democratic system is the probable result of a given level of socio-economic development. At first glance the Irish state seems to refute the thesis. His cross-national sources for that year showed that the Irish case was really an anomalous case. By then the Irish state had fallen well behind the other democracies. Table 2.2 shows how widely the Free State diverged from these levels in terms of industrialisation. The stability of the Irish state could not be explained in terms of its economic success after 1921.

Table 2.2 Level of industrialisation in the Republic of Ireland in 1956 compared to mean figures for democracies and non-democracies

Indices of industrialisation	Percent males in agriculture	Annual per capita energy consumption
Democracies	21	3.6
Non-democracies	41	1.4
Ireland	46	1.4

Sources: Mean figures taken from Lipset (1959). Individual figures: Agriculture, *United Nations Demographic Yearbook*, 1956, Table 12, pp. 350–370. Energy, *United Nations Statistical Yearbook, 1956*, op. cit., table 127, pp. 308–310. Refers to commercially produced energy in 1955, in equivalent numbers of metric tons of coal.

However, even if in 1959 the Free State was 'a Third World democracy' the starting point for the new state had compared favourably with its contemporaries (Lee, 1989, pp. 69–94). In fact Ireland was a semi-industrial state rather than a peripheral agricultural state, a category which then included states like France, Sweden, Norway and Denmark.[9]

A Finnish political scientist argues that quantitative data should be used to explore the extent to which power resources are distributed throughout society (Vanhanen, 1984). Vanhanen argues that the wider the distribution of power resources in society the less likely one group would impose itself on the society. He constructed an 'index of power resources' (IPR) which measured the dispersal of power resources and found that by independence the Irish IPR 'was so high (6.2) that democracy was on a firm footing right from the start' (Vanhanen, 1984, p. 79). Vanhanen's findings suggest democracy may be unconvincing in the Irish case, social pluralism may have been greater than is generally thought.

A third approach is that of Barrington Moore who sees modern political systems as the outcome of class conflicts in agrarian society, with a strong landed elite and a landless peasantry as major obstacles to democratisation (Moore, 1966). Discussing the roles of lord and peasant in the emergence of modern political systems Moore suggests that on the basis of the French, British and American experience the 'bourgeois-democratic' route to modernity involved the emergence of five structural preconditions.

The first of these preconditions was the development of a balance to avoid too strong a Crown or too independent a landed aristocracy. Up to the Act of Union the Irish political system was dominated by a landed aristocracy. In the course of the nineteenth century the British state, responding both to popular demands and to international pressure, took the institutions of government in Ireland out of the hands of the landed aristocracy. The decisive step was the Act of Union itself which placed the whole of Ireland under the jurisdiction of Westminster. The separation happened on a number of levels. Firstly, the means of coercion were centralised. Local militias, recruited and led by the gentry, were disbanded. After 1801 the constabulary was directed and organised at Dublin Castle. Secondly, the ways in which a landed elite could legitimate its position were undermined. The introduction of Catholic Emancipation in 1829, and the disestablishment of the Anglican Church in Ireland, marked a symbolic separation of church and state. Extensions of the franchise in 1850, 1868, 1884, and 1918, the introduction of secret ballots, the abolition of rotten boroughs, and the establishment of a system of local government in 1898 meant that the gentry lost the ability to represent local constituencies and to control voters. Thirdly, as Catholic education developed and meritocratic reforms were introduced more and more Catholics were recruited into the state itself. This happened slowly but was an unmistakable trend in the last decades before independence (McBride, 1992).

Moore's argument is that a balance of power must emerge between the Crown and the landed aristocracy. While Land Reform Acts and the achievement of religious equality might suggest that the Anglo-Irish were powerless to resist the government it has to be stressed that the British aristocracy as a whole which had close links with the Anglo-Irish retained its power. The House of Lords succeeded in blocking Home Rule Bills until 1911. Likewise senior positions were still disproportionately held by Protestants in the professions and in the Irish civil service at the turn of the century (see O'Leary and McGarry, 1993, Figure 2.4, p. 82). Anglo-Irish institutions such as the Bank of Ireland, Trinity College, and the Church of Ireland retained their importance. Nevertheless the landed aristocracy in Ireland was relatively powerless to resist the slow growth of political equality in Ireland after 1801.

The second precondition was the turn towards an appropriate form of commercial agriculture. By this Moore means the production of agricultural produce for the market which allows for capital accumulation and industrial growth. Moore is equivocal on what form this must take. His analysis of the English enclosure movements leads him to suggest that 'getting rid of agriculture as a major social activity is one prerequisite for successful democracy' (Moore, 1966, p. 429). Alternatively he suggests that if the peasant is turned into a farmer producing for the market rather than for his own consumption or that of the landlord, small-scale proprietorship is not incompatible with capitalist development. If the opportunities for market production, the existence of market towns, appropriate financial institutions, and an adequate transport system, are present, the peasants can become part of the democratic capitalist system, as happened in Scandinavia (Moore, 1966, p. 422). In Ireland the growth of domestic and external markets combined with a series of land reforms led to a decline of labour-repressive agricultural production based on landlords absorbing the surplus produced by their tenants. Ireland benefited from one of the most extensive land reforms in western history. Over a period of 70 years or so, 15 million acres out of a total of 19 million acres were transferred from landlord to peasant (Dovring, 1965, p. 241). The two classes Moore considers least likely to support democratic modernisation, landlords and their peasants, hugely declined in importance and were superseded by independent farmers more inclined to produce for the market. The extent to which small-scale proprietorship was compatible with capitalist development has been questioned but there is no doubt that late-nineteenth-century Ireland experienced a turn towards a more appropriate form of agriculture (for a discussion see Lee, 1973). Table 2.3 gives an indication of the dimensions of the changes.

The third and fourth preconditions were the weakening of the landed aristocracy and the prevention of an aristocratic-bourgeois coalition against the peasants

Table 2.3 Percent of Irish farmers as owner-occupiers, 1870–1929

Year	% owner-occupiers	% others
1870	3.0	97.0
1906	29.2	70.8
1916	63.9	36.1
1929	97.4	2.6

Source: Hooker, cited in Rumpf and Hepburn (1977, p. 227).

and workers. Both have to be related to the ethnic makeup of Irish society. The ability of Catholic elites to mobilise and unite the Catholic peasants and the inchoate middle class against the Ascendancy and the Union with Britain was based on the prior existence of deep ethnic cleavages within Ireland. The emerging Catholic politicians opted to oppose the *status quo* because the British state was only relatively autonomous from the Protestant landed interest. Catholic Emancipation came a quarter of a century after the Union and religious equality was not formally attained until Disestablishment in 1869. Indeed the Catholic Association, the first mass organisation to represent Catholic interests, emerged half a century before any significant suffrage extension or land reform had taken place and almost a full century before they had been completed. The masses were mobilised into political movements well before enfranchisement which structured the pattern of political mobilisation for the next century (Garvin, 1981). Both Catholic elites and masses faced a type of double-domination whereby the subordination of Ireland within the UK at the macro-level was reproduced at the micro-level in terms of the subordination of one religion to another, of the peasantry to their landlords, and in terms of finance, status, and opportunities, of the Catholic elite to the Protestant elite.

Only in Northern Ireland did a reactionary alliance against peasants and workers develop between the Protestant bourgeoisie and the landed elites. This was reinforced by a pre-existing ethno-religious cleavage which determined that the Protestant working class would support this alliance in the form of Ulster unionism (see Wright, 1987, pp. 86–112). Under certain circumstances the solidity of the nationalist movement weakened, as in 1922 when the Sinn Féin movement split. Garvin argued that the Treaty split reflected a profound divide in Irish society between those who for cultural, geographical, or class reasons 'assume a natural affinity between Ireland and Britain and those who do not, or would rather such an affinity did not exist' (Garvin, 1981, p. 133). Others have suggested that the division did reflect social divisions within the Free State itself (Rumpf and Hepburn, 1977). Yet since the conflict was largely confined to the 26 county area a realignment of class forces in the shape of a Pro-Treaty alignment between moderate nationalists and Ulster unionists was impossible. A 32 county offer of Home Rule that was acceptable to moderate nationalists and unionists may well have produced the type of reactionary alliance within Ireland that Moore discusses.

The fifth precondition Moore discusses, a revolutionary break with the past, was not present in the Irish case. The modernisation of the Irish social structure in class terms had occurred before the War of Independence. Irish farmers did not achieve the right to own the land they farmed through revolution but through legal reform. Violence in Ireland was more a precondition of democratic breakdown than anything else. This almost happened in the Free State in 1922 and did happen in Northern Ireland half a century later. Moore's work nonetheless provides a powerful framework for the analysis of the structural transformation of Irish society at the turn of the century. The limitation derives from its neglect of demographic variables which were just as important in effecting the modernisation of the Irish social structure. The crucial precondition of nineteenth-century democratisation nevertheless was the emergence of a balance to avoid too strong a Crown or too weak an aristocracy. Moore's analysis also suggests that by 1921 the Irish social question was essentially solved (see the essays in Boyce, 1988), in so far as both landlord and peasant had largely been removed from the country-side, the former through emigration and the latter through expropriation often by consent. Furthermore, partition removed the possibility of a reactionary alliance in the twentieth century between moderate nationalist and unionist elites who would have preferred modernisation from above within the British Free Trade area.

The agrarian roots of Western democracy

Dahl suggests that many societies have became polyarchies before being substantially industrialised and urbanised (1989, p. 251).

> Even more telling, however, are countries in which the institutions of polyarchy became strongly rooted well before they developed Modern Dynamic and Plural societies, while they were still preponderantly agrarian. For example, when the institutions of white male polyarchy took form in the United States in the early nineteenth century, the population was over-whelmingly rural and agricultural ... Yet as Tocqueville observed (among many others), the agrarian society of the United States possessed the two crucial features that make an MDP society favourable to polyarchy; it produced a wide dispersion of power and it strongly fostered democratic beliefs. In fact, ideologues of agrarian republicanism like Thomas Jefferson and John Taylor were so firmly convinced that an agrarian society of independent farmers was absolutely essential to the existence of a democratic republic that they were unable to foresee the possibility that a republic might continue to exist in the United States even after farmers became a minuscule minority. As in the United States, polyarchy also developed in other countries in which independent farmers were numerically preponderant: among newly settled countries – Canada, Australia, and New Zealand – and among old European countries – Norway, Sweden, Denmark, and Switzerland.
>
> (Dahl, 1989, p. 254)

Iceland, Finland, France, and Ireland could be added to the list of agrarian democracies. The general correlation between a large free farming, agricultural sector and the emergence of Western democracy is clear. This suggests that Ireland presents no paradox for democratic theory.

There is also considerable comparative evidence to suggest that the relationship between a modernised but egalitarian agrarian class structure and democratic stability is systematic. Table 2.4 classifies inter-war European regimes along two dimensions; whether the political elite is landed to any significant extent,[10] and whether the peasantry is a modern one (meaning essentially independent farmers) or backward (meaning farmers that do not own the land they farm whether as crofters or tenant farmers).

Table 2.4 Agrarian base and political outcomes in inter-war Europe

	Landed elite	Urban elite
Free farming, commercialised peasantry	Austria Germany UK	Sweden Denmark Norway Finland Netherlands France *Irish Free State* Belgium Switzerland
Backward or landless peasantry	Romania Greece Poland Yugoslavia Spain Italy Hungary Portugal	Bulgaria Latvia Estonia Lithuania

Sources: adapted from Rueschemeyer, Stephens and Stephens (1992). Eastern European countries classified according to Seton-Watson (1982), Polanski (1975) and Lieven (1993).

It suggests that when a large agrarian sector dominated by independent farmers is combined with a politically dominant urban elite, democracy is the likely outcome. Where a politically dominant landed elite is combined with tenant or semi-feudal farming, authoritarian government is the likely outcome. The absence of a strong landed elite and the presence of a prosperous landowning peasantry are necessary prerequisites for the stabilisation of a democratic system. Where the elite was landed, regardless of the nature of the peasantry, a democratic breakdown followed. Britain is the one exception. In countries with a backward peasantry, an urban elite was not sufficient to effect a transition to democracy, whereas where a backward peasantry and a landed elite existed together democratic breakdown followed. In those countries with a modern independent peasantry and an urban elite democracy survived the inter-war era.

The conclusion that neither peasants nor a surviving aristocratic tradition are conducive to democracy has also been reached by other analysts of inter-war European politics (Seton-Watson, 1982, pp. 75–123; Polanski, 1975, pp. 3–14). In stark contrast with countries like Bulgaria where the agricultural population increased between 1924 and 1937 leading to congestion and sub-division, Irish land reform was ultimately linked to the long-run demographic decline of the agricultural proletariat and the embourgeoisement of previously radical farming communities. Ireland ceased to be a mass peasant society before the turn of the century. Intimations of agrarian radicalism in the early years, and of fascism later on, were largely histrionic echoes of other times and other places. The former lacked a political organisation while the latter lacked a mob. Ireland was not a 'peasant society' but a society of free farmers. Free farming communities provide an appropriate social base for democracy for one simple reason: 'the greater the concentration of property, the less likely it is that democratic rule will be consolidated' (Hall, 1993, p. 278).

The British state and civil society in the colonial world

A modernisation approach can also be consistent with a post-colonial approach. British rule has resulted in stable democracy in two regions, the White Settler colonies and the English-speaking Caribbean. Australia, New Zealand and Canada differ from Ireland in that they enjoyed self-rule at a much earlier stage of political development whereas the Caribbean countries gained statehood much later. Rueschemeyer *et al* (1992) combine a historical-sociological account of the transformation of class relations with an emphasis on the conditions which facilitated the emergence of a strong and resilient civil society.

They argue that the White Colonial route to democracy was shaped by four factors (Rueschemeyer *et al*, 1992, pp. 121–40). Firstly, the 'transplantation' of British state structures meant that representative government took hold relatively early on and that political struggles tended to centre on these institutions. They analyse the 'Tocquevillian' effect of state structures whereby British political institutions had a much more democratic effect than they had in Britain (Rueschemeyer *et al*, 1992, p. 280). Secondly, due to the availability of cheap land for settlement and the prior demise of the aboriginal populations all of these colonies developed systems of agricultural production based on free family farmers. Except in the American South attempts to introduce systems based on labour-repressive agriculture failed and in the absence of feudal traditions landed elites failed to establish an ideological hegemony over the lower classes. Thirdly, for a variety of reasons ties between the state and the landed elite were weak. Lastly, democratisation in these countries was crucially affected by changes in Britain's role in the world.

In the cases of the English-speaking Caribbean (Rueschemeyer *et al*, 1992, pp. 226–68), British rule was direct and fully representative institutions were not established until independence. Only a small white minority acquired experience in government. Secondly, in several of these countries labour-repressive agriculture on plantations was the dominant mode of production. The authors compare this combination of a racially exclusive conception of citizenship with plantation agriculture with that of the American Deep South. Thirdly, while colonial officialdom was relatively independent they were supportive of the planters and there were few government-instigated reforms until pressure from London after 1945 forced a rethink in policy. Nevertheless the authors argue that a comparison with Central America shows that in the British Caribbean the relative autonomy of the colonial state and the influence of London prevented the landed upper class from using the state to repress the political mobilisation of subordinate classes, in contrast to the repression exercised by the large landlords in central America

(Rueschemeyer *et al*, 1992, p. 281). In contrast to ex-British and ex-French colonies in Africa parties and trade union movements were relatively strong. This allowed for the emergence of alliances between the middle and working classes. The subsequent consolidation of democracies in the Caribbean was dependent on the emergence of a vigorous civil society. The crucial condition allowing for the emergence of these civil societies was the relative autonomy of the state from the landed class. This relates of course to the fourth factor, that changes in Britain's geo-political role crucially affected the prospects of democratisation.

Ireland gained self-rule relatively late and the aboriginal population survived colonisation. Like the Caribbean countries it experienced self-rule and independence relatively late and its land structure was labour-repressive. Up to 1829 the majority of the population were excluded from citizenship on religious grounds and there were initially close ties between the landed elite and the bureaucracy. On the other hand full-scale political mobilisation and social reform preceded independence so the Irish experience differs from the Caribbean cases too. Nevertheless the analysis provided by these authors can profitably be applied to Ireland. Firstly, British rule did have 'Tocquevillian effects'. By allowing organised opposition a mass party emerged in Ireland earlier than in Britain. The landed aristocracy which played a large role in British politics into the next century had lost its political power in Ireland well before 1900. The British state in Ireland engaged in social reforms that were never introduced in Britain. Church and state in Ireland were separated whereas England still has an established Church. Secondly, by 1921 Irish agricultural reforms gave rise to a class of independent family farmers that would play a large role in Irish political life well after 1921. Thirdly, the state was slowly divorced from the landed interest. The ideological hegemony of landlordism was weakened not only by the rise of Catholic nationalism but also by developments within Britain. Lastly, Irish democratisation has to be understood in the context of geo-political developments beginning with the end of the Napoleonic Wars and ending with the changes in Dominion Status and the era of appeasement in the second half of the 1930s.

As in the Caribbean the opportunities for political mobilisation meant that a strong civil society would emerge. Etzioni-Halevy argues that the relative autonomy of elites from the elites of the state, and, within the state itself (1990, p. 322), is the product of elite struggles that have been couched as struggles for the principles of democracy: the right to free speech, to freedom of association, to free elections, and so on.[11] As a result these principles come to protect and justify the elite's autonomy 'which in turn comes to be a core mechanism that protects democracy' (Etzioni-Halevy, 1990, p. 322). Elite autonomy in Ireland came partially as a result of a successful struggle for rights within Ireland and such struggle reinforced the commitment of Irish elites to maintain their autonomy but it was also a by-product of British democratisation in general.

Firstly, the opposition parliamentary parties that dominated nationalist politics in the nineteenth century drew on their own membership funds, recruited their own leaders and were able to survive intermittent attempts at repression. Free from the onus of forming governments they were relatively free from government patronage and control. As more people became enfranchised the autonomy of political parties increased especially as British governments came to rely on Irish votes in the House of Commons. Secondly, the autonomy of the bureaucratic elite in nineteenth-century Ireland emerged in the late nineteenth and early twentieth century as a result of a series of modernising reforms instigated by the British civil service itself. What concerns us here however is the autonomy of the bureaucratic elite *vis-à-vis* the nationalist parties. This was absolute up to the War of Independence but while some senior figures in the service after 1921 were government-appointed the bulk had been recruited before independence and as part of the Treaty settlement their position was constitutionally guaranteed (Munger, 1976, p. 26). Furthermore over the first decades the bureaucrats served essentially inexperienced governments which were reliant on their expertise (Fanning, 1983, pp. 60–79). Thirdly, the religious elite found itself in a position of increased autonomy both from the government and the established political parties. This applied in different ways to both the Catholic Church and the Church of Ireland. Like the parties the Catholic Church provided a potential source of social control for the state; its ultimate resource was its ability to shape and articulate public opinion. This made it a potential ally of the state. However, attempts to establish the Catholic Church and give the state some say in ecclesiastic appointments were defeated. The Catholic Church developed its own educational institutions, financed its own activities, and trained its own clergy. Conversely, as the Church became part of a prototypic welfare state the Church maintained its relative autonomy from the nationalist parties. Although the Church did play a direct role in nationalist mobilisation the relative autonomy of the Church was due to a split between its functional and its symbolic role. Functionally the Catholic Church was part of the state but as the Church of an ostensibly nationalist population it was also an institution of opposition. This enabled it to accumulate more institutional power while maintaining its political, financial, and intellectual autonomy. The Anglican Church in Ireland in contrast began the century as a state-endowed Church. The state had a say in ecclesiastic appointments, clerical salaries were paid for by the state, and religious taxes were also collected by the state. This changed with the coming of Emancipation and Catholic political power. A rival educational sector was set up, tithes were slowly suspended and the Church was disestablished in 1869. Autonomy was not fought for but it came about none the less.

The same type of analysis would hold for the economic, intellectual, and media elites all of which were relatively free from government interference. Ireland by 1918 had a relatively developed press, a free market economy, and a nascent university system relatively free from government control. Not surprisingly in the 1922 election the Labour Party and the Farmer's Party, both of whom developed out of economic interest groups, showed that nationalist parties had no monopoly over political resources. The very existence of elite autonomy in a society with a long tradition of political monopoly by nationalist parties was a considerable advantage. The nature of this autonomy was two-fold. On the one hand elected elites possessing the same claim to authority as nationalist politicians had done since the early nineteenth century had an autonomy from the state. On the other hand the army, the civil service, and the police were autonomous from the party elite. This meant that the state could not be taken over by either side in the Civil War split and that genuine opposition was possible. Whatever the objectives of the party elite, the army, the police, and the bureaucracy allowed the 1932 changeover to happen; the autonomy of the state from the parties was the basic precondition of democratic consolidation (see Munger, 1976). Likewise the Catholic Church which distanced itself from the government in the late 1920s (Fanning, 1983, p. 103) maintained its autonomy. In reinforcing this autonomy from and within the state the Civil War was vital since it split the Sinn Féin elite and made both sides dependent not only on the bureaucracy but the smaller parties too if they wanted to govern. The Irish experience after 1921 confirms the hypothesis that in countries where democracy stabilised, 'there would be clear historical evidence of the previous development of the relative autonomy of elites' (Etzioni-Halevy, 1990, p. 344).

Conclusion: an unsurprising outcome

This analysis lends credence to the view that Ireland was already a modern society by 1921. If Vanhanen's work can be taken to be an accurate measure of pluralism, then this supports the view that Irish civil society was resistant to the public band tradition. This can be related to three consequences of British rule. Firstly, the elimination of landlords and peasants from the Irish countryside prevented the Civil War becoming a class war (Farrell, 1971, p. xv). Partition was also crucial here. Secondly, by 1921 Ireland had developed a tradition of relative state autonomy which was a consequence of the slow divorce between the British Crown and the Anglo-Irish in the nineteenth century. The decline of the landed aristocracy was tempered by their over-representation in the bureaucracy and the professions. The Anglo-Irish became an urban and professional elite:

> in 1926, when they were 8.4 per cent of the population they still accounted for 28 per cent of farmers with over 200 acres, and 18 per cent of the entire professional class. By 1936 the Protestant proportion of Irish employers and business executives was 20–25 per cent; bank officials, 53 per cent; commercial representatives, 39 per cent; lawyers, 38 per cent.
>
> (Foster, 1988, p. 534; see also Munger, 1976, pp. 26–8)

This structural transformation ensured that the bureaucracy would remain autonomous from Civil War politics. Thirdly, the development of a strong civil society meant that the Sinn Féin split did not polarise the whole society. It has been argued that a democratic regime change requires that those committed to partial, negotiable and flexible objectives in politics must outnumber those who hold 'all or nothing' views.[12] The simple fact that less than half of the eligible electors voted in the 1922 Pact Election and that non-Sinn Féin candidates got 34.6 per cent of the vote in the 1923 general election suggests that not all of the public were in thrall to Civil War politics. The anti-Treatyite tactic in the Civil War was to rally the public behind them; it didn't happen.

The course of Civil War politics after 1923 suggests that even for the anti-Treatyites ambition had its limits, especially with respect to partition. The significance of the Civil War may well have been to provide a salutary warning to both sides, that unity and the legitimacy of the new state was more important than anything else. Did mass culture matter in the stabilisation of the system? The legitimacy of the state was not challenged by any major social institution or by the majority of the public. The requirement that the way a country is governed must conform to the preferences of the politically conscious public (Coakley, 1993, p. 25) need only extend to the active elites. Majority rule was accepted by both the Civil War sides. By refusing to be bound by any law other than Dáil majorities Cosgrave was merely preparing the ground for de Valera's assault on the Treaty. The mechanism of 'integration' was majority rule. Democracy involves building a high degree of trust between political elites. This was slow coming but was aided by a number of inherited factors: the common background of the elite, the neutral role of the Church, the existence of a stable administration, and the elite's relative success in undoing the Treaty. The Treaty split was not an argument over nothing, but it was soluble in a way acceptable to most people. For this reason 1937 signifies the end of Civil War politics. After that, as in many small states dominated by a powerful neighbour, consensus on foreign policy after 1939 provided another powerful incentive for unity.

Tactically Irish democracy was a product of compromise. Spain and Greece are also supposed to have political cultures marked by personalism, authoritarianism, and clientelism. In each of them the transition to democracy involved a number of factors – the role of centre-right parties in initiating and establishing the bound- aries of change early on, the policy of compromise and conciliation between parties and between old and new elites, the co-option of the old military-bureaucratic elites, the demise of radical socialist parties and the eventual emergence of reformed socialist governments – which echo the Irish case. It had a 'civilised right', and a radical politics faded after independence; the changeover in 1932 was also a '*ruptura pactada*' where Fianna Fáil gave guarantees of security to the old administration and thereby co-opted them. The Fianna Fáil government may initially have been radical but the party became moderate very quickly. The Irish case does not appear as an exception so much as a precursor of a general European process. Like in Southern Europe a generation was faced with a clear and immediate choice between a gradualist unadventurist system and something much worse, and collectively chose the former. As in the other cases it may have concluded that the challenge of creating a stable democracy was the limit of one generation's capacity (Ami, 1991, pp. 23–40).

COMMENTARY BY TIMOTHY J. WHITE

Bill Kissane's article answers a question that has long simmered among students of Irish politics. How unique was Irish political development? While some compare the arrival of Irish democracy to other post-colonial states, Kissane believes that Irish political development was closer to that of other European states. Nevertheless, Kissane seeks to demonstrate that a post-colonial understanding of Ireland's development does not hinder but helps us understand how Ireland became democratic when it is seen as supplementing modernisation theory. Before Kissane's article, many agreed with John Whyte's (1974) analysis that Ireland was unique compared to other European states in that it lacked a social basis to its politics. Others have contested this claim (Laver, 1986a, 1986b and 1987; Mair, 1986; McAllister and O'Connell, 1984), but none of these efforts did so based on an examination of the modernisation literature that is at the heart of Kissane's analysis. Previous work had attempted to see Irish political development and the rise of stable democracy as an anomaly due to the unique characteristics of Irish political culture (Farrell, 1971). What separates Kissane's article from earlier scholarship is its use of modernisation literature to explain how Ireland's political development conformed to other states' transition to democracy.

Kissane's article begins by identifying earlier scholarship that stressed how Ireland's historic status as a colony and its traditional political culture made democratic political stability unlikely. In a famous work on democratisation and modernisation, Lipset (1959, p. 80) hypothesised that 'the more well-to-do a nation, the greater the chances that it will sustain democracy'. Thus, previous authors saw the arrival of Irish democracy as exceptional (Carty, 1983; Prager, 1986; Schmitt, 1973). Kissane wonders if these authors were correct in assuming the necessary socio-economic prerequisites for democracy were not in place when Ireland gained its independence. Rather, Kissane contends it is wrong to characterise Ireland as a backward state at the time of independence. He presents Ireland as a state with a 'social structure typically favourable to the emergence and stabilisation of democracy'. Kissane argues that Ireland's economic and social development prepared it well for the arrival of democracy early in the twentieth century.

Kissane's analysis rests on his utilisation of modernisation theorists. For example, even though Ireland was an outlier in the data presented by Lipset (1959), Kissane attempts to make the argument that Ireland 'was a semi-industrial state rather than a peripheral agricultural state'. Lipset's theory specified that states needed to experience the kind of economic growth associated with an industrial take-off in order to develop the social basis for democracy. No matter how Kissane tries to interpret the data, Ireland was not a state whose social and economic measures of development suggested conditions conducive to democracy according to Lipset's theory. Even the Ireland of the 1950s was plagued by economic stress, emigration, and a collective view of failure (Garvin, 2004).

Another development theorist that Kissane uses to attempt to explain Ireland's typical pattern of political development was Barrington Moore Jr. When reviewing Moore's (1966) conditions of democracy, Kissane contends that Ireland experienced the kind of agricultural transition in the nineteenth century that meets Moore's criterion of a move towards an appropriate form of commercial agriculture. The problem with this argument is that even if Ireland experienced an agrarian transformation in the nineteenth century, the critical factor for Moore was that this agricultural transition led to an industrial revolution. This never happened in Ireland. Moore's (1966, p. 418) most famous quote is 'No bourgeois, no democracy'. The Ireland of the first half of the twentieth century remained a state that had yet to experience an industrial revolution, and no serious student of Moore would argue that Ireland's transition was the equivalent of the Enclosure Movement that is critical to the development of English democracy.

Kissane attempts to link Irish political development, especially in the era before independence, with an appreciation of the legacy of British rule. He believes that the British colonial presence made democracy possible in White Settler colonies and the English-speaking Caribbean. Relying on Rueschemeyer *et al* (1992), Kissane contends that the British successfully transplanted state structures of representative government to their settler colonies like Ireland. The reforms of the nineteenth century in terms of land redistribution and the end of the penal laws allowed the Catholic majority to be ready to take their roles as citizens when independence came. By the early part of the twentieth century elites intent on holding onto power or repressing social or religious groups no longer existed in Ireland. An indigenous administrative elite emerged which was more than capable of operating the administrative apparatus of the state. Political elites operated in a competitive political framework that sought to mobilise mass support through democratic means. Thus, for Kissane, the legacy of British colonial rule and practice prepared Ireland well for its transition to democratic self-governance.

The most compelling evidence Kissane employs is that which compares Ireland to other agrarian democracies in the European context. Relying primarily on Dahl's (1989, p. 251) argument that democracies can emerge before a society is industrialised and urbanised, Kissane finds that – as a result of late-nineteenth-century land reform – Ireland (like Iceland, Finland, France, and some other European states) had a large free farming commercialised peasantry with a smaller urban elite. This allowed a sense of egalitarianism to emerge in society associated with modern democracy. If a rural elite had continued to dominate Irish society, Kissane believes the arrival and stability of democracy would have been in greater question in the Irish case.

Kissane concludes his article emphasising that by 1921 Ireland had a mass public built on agrarian egalitarianism ready and accustomed to operating in a democratic political framework based on their experience in the British imperial system. Ireland also had a bureaucracy professionalised enough to stay aloof from civil war politics and keep the state operating in its infancy. Kissane also believes that Ireland possessed a strong sense of civil society that lent democratic legitimacy to the new Free State government and quickly marginalised those who sought to use violence against the new state in the Civil War. One factor that remains under-explored in Kissane's analysis is his stress on the role of level of trust among elites that was critical to the success of Irish democracy, something that has been highlighted in the work of Di Palma (1990) and Inglehart (1999), among others.

While Kissane's article sought to challenge the inherited assumption that Irish democracy was exceptional, not all have been fully convinced by his argument. Perhaps the most important competing interpretation of Ireland's political development has come from Tom Garvin. Garvin emphasises the unenthusiastic and exceptional nature of Irish democratic development (1981, 1988 and 1993b). Garvin's later work (1996, p. 191), published after Kissane's article, identifies the political skills achieved by the Irish mass public and elites based on their long struggle for independence as the critical factor that explains the arrival of Irish democracy. Garvin (1996, p. 194) also highlights the tremendous skills of those who led the initial Free State government as successful agents solidifying Ireland's young democracy. While Garvin concedes Kissane's point that Ireland may not have been as poor as is commonly depicted, he emphasises the role of political factors in explaining Ireland's democratic development. He does admit that 'Irish exceptionalism has been much exaggerated' (Garvin, 1996, p. 206), thus conceding a central point of Kissane's argument but not for the socio-economic reasons given by Kissane.

Kissane expanded the argument he developed in this article in a book published seven years later (Kissane, 2002). In this book Kissane incorporates theories of democracy that became popular in the 1990s that emphasise the role of elites and their commitment to the democratic transition process. He builds upon the work of Linz (1978) to employ a 're-equilibrium model' to explain how Fianna Fáil emerges as a party initially of those who threatened the nascent democracy and then come to participate and finally lead it, thereby ensuring the consolidation of Irish democracy (Kissane, 2002, pp. 165–94). Overall, this book demonstrates the refinement and advancement of Kissane's interpretation of the not-so-amazing case of Irish democracy.

Kissane's article represents a major contribution. It attempts to explain more of the social and political context of the development of Irish political institutions than previous scholars such as Chubb (1982) and Ward (1994) who focused on the legal and constitutional framework of Irish government. This article also places Ireland's development in a comparative framework so that one can appreciate the similarities of Irish politics to others in Europe and perhaps to those who emerged later in a colonial context. While not everyone will agree with Kissane's interpretation of Irish political development, he clearly has made those who emphasise Ireland's exceptional development as a democracy recognise that it is difficult to contend that Ireland lacked the socio-economic basis for democracy and then argue Ireland became democratic nonetheless.

Notes

1   I would like to thank Dr Brendan O'Leary for encouraging me to write this article and commenting helpfully on earlier drafts. I would also like to thank the two anonymous reviewers and Dr Terry Mulhall for their helpful comments. The views expressed are of course mine alone.

2   Seymour Martin Lipset, 'The Social Basis of Democracy in Eastern Europe', speech given at the London School of Economics, 17 January 1995. The British-influenced

countries in his 1959 sample of 13 stable democracies were Ireland, the U.S., Canada, Australia, and New Zealand. India, a curious omission, would make the proportion exactly half.

3 Kevin O'Higgins for example did not think his fellow citizens were quite fit for democracy: 'What are the social convictions behind our Irish democracy? They are not Catholic in the measure to be expected but an unquestionable admixture of feudalism and brigandage in one quarter, and a deplorable amount of grabber and gombeen morality generally' (cited in de Vere White, 1948, p. 181).

4 One problem with this attempt to find differing traditions behind the Civil War is that it ignores the extent to which the Sinn Féin elite were united on fundamentals. With respect to cultural, educational and religious policy, the Fianna Fáil governments merely reinforced legislation passed by the Cosgrave governments. 'Holy Ireland', the view of society as a moral community, transcended the Treaty. While the proposition that political stability cannot be achieved at the expense of a state's cultural roots is an important one, the application of this *problematique* to independent Ireland, a highly homogeneous society, is puzzling.

5 Garvin notes that non-voters were generally more prevalent in peripheral areas where Fianna Fáil's early vote would be strongest (1981, pp. 162–7). Prager doesn't explore the possibility that these areas were mobilised by Fianna Fáil, not because that party was more Gaelic-Romantic than Cumann na nGaedheal, but because that party was the first party to address their material interests. Furthermore there is no evidence to suggest that the leaders of both sides differed greatly in social origin or outlook. Prager has merely superimposed on the Civil War split the alleged conflict between the cultural values of the Anglo-Irish and the Irish-Ireland values which Prager identifies with the anti-Treatyites. In fact there is evidence to suggest that the Anglo-Irish political elite (not to mention the Pro-Treatyites) were favourably disposed towards Irish cultural nationalism (see O'Callaghan, 1984).

6 For a critique of this perspective see Liam Kennedy (1992–93). Kennedy notes that on every significant socio-economic indicator Ireland, north and south, is placed among the richest countries of the world.

7 The inference is that the Irish experience holds lessons for Third World states which are deeply divided on ethnic/linguistic lines. Yet the most striking thing about the new state was its near total homogeneity – religious, ethnic, and social. Compare it to India which is, unlike the Irish case, a genuine paradox for democratic theory: Indian culture is hierarchical and traditional unlike Ireland's which is egalitarian and has only tenuous roots in the Gaelic past; India suffered from a degree of poverty and ignorance/illiteracy which in the Ireland of 1900 was only a folk memory; India's social cleavages are deep, diverse, and apparently permanent; its land structure had not been modernised before independence and the rural poor still live in a semi-feudal world of social relations (see Weiner, 1991). Notably post-colonial theorists shy away from comparisons with the Third World preferring only to show how the Irish experience deviated from the Western European experience. For a more useful comparison with the successor states of Eastern Europe see the articles by Coakley (1986 and 1987).

8 At this stage it is necessary to clarify the argument which is not with the post-colonial framework *per se* or with the argument that Irish political culture exhibits a combination of democratic and authoritarian norms (see Coakley, 1994), but to criticise the causal argument derived from that conception of Irish political culture. Once you accept the thesis that Irish political culture contains strong pre-modern elements there are two possibilities. (1) You may assume that such a culture could not possibly be supportive of democratic values. (2) You explain the system's resilience in terms of how the post-colonial state came to incorporate the norms of a peasant society into its institutional practices, through clientelism, veneration of Irish cultural nationalism, or institution-alised co-operation with the Catholic Church. My central objection to this explanation is that an explanation of why the Free State remained democratic should explore the

factors which prevented the state becoming completely theocratic, pervasively corrupt, and radically nationalistic. These authors do precisely the opposite. Schmitt's thesis for example is that personalistic and authoritarian norms *facilitated* democratic political development which, logically speaking, is absurd.

9 In a test of Lipset's theories for the inter-war period, Berg-Schlosser and De Meur chose a threshold level for four of Lipset's indicators of the 'economic development complex': per capita GNP below $200, population in towns with more than 20,000 inhabitants below 50 per cent, literacy below 75 per cent, and industrial labour force below 30 per cent of the economically active population. Although omitted from the review, like Sweden the Irish state in 1930 would have been 'a democratic state with high levels of wealth and education and low levels of industrialisation and urbanisation' (Berg-Schlosser and De Meur, 1994, p. 257). Noting that the level of industrialisation does not really separate stable democracies from democratic breakdowns the authors conclude that Sweden does not contradict Lipset's hypothesis, as would be the case for Ireland.

10 Landed elites were never numerically preponderant in the age of mass democracy, but where the elite included a landed element in a conservative alliance, where it was dependent on a landed elite for military or economic support, where bourgeois elite values were shaped by the values of an established aristocratic tradition, or where landed elites developed alliances with other groups, the outcome was likely to weaken democracy.

11 Etzioni-Halevy argues that the relative autonomy of elites exists when two conditions are met: a) elites control resources (material, coercive, organisational, political, or symbolic) which enable them to influence social and political processes; b) these elites are not repressed by the state.

12 Naomi Chazan, speech to the Association for the Study of Ethnicity and Nationalism at LSE, Spring, 1994.

References

Ami, Shlomo Ben (1991) 'The Concept of Southern Europe and the New Mediterranean Democracies', pp. 23–40 in S.N. Eisenstadt (ed.) *Democracy and Modernity*. Leiden: E.J. Brill.

Berg-Schlosser, Dirk and Giesele De Meur (1994) 'Conditions of Democracy in Interwar Europe: A Boolean Test of Major Hypotheses', *Comparative Politics*, 24 (3), pp. 253–81.

Boyce, David G. (ed.) (1988) *The Revolution in Ireland, 1879–1923*. London: Macmillan.

Carty, R. Kenneth (1983) *Party and Parish Pump: Electoral Politics in Ireland*. Dingle: Brandon Press.

Chubb, Basil (1982) *The Government and Politics of Ireland*. Second Edition. London: Longman.

Coakley, John (1986) 'Political Succession and Regime Change in New States in Interwar Europe: Ireland, Finland, Czechoslovakia and the Baltic Republics', *European Journal of Political Research*, 14 (1/2), pp. 187–207.

Coakley, John (1987) 'Political Succession During the Transition to Independence: Evidence from Europe', pp. 161–70 in Peter Calvert (ed.) *The Process of Political Succession*. London: Macmillan.

Coakley, John (1993) 'Society and Political Culture', pp. 25–49 in John Coakley and Michael Gallagher (eds.) *Politics in the Republic of Ireland*. Second Edition. Limerick: PSAI Press/Folens.

Dahl, Robert (1989) *Democracy and Its Critics*. New Haven, CT: Yale University Press.

de Vere White, Terence (1948) *Kevin O'Higgins*. Dublin: Mercier Press.

Di Palma, Giuseppe (1990) *To Craft Democracies: An Essay on Democratic Transitions*. Berkeley, CA: University of California Press.

Dovring, Folke (1965) *Land and Labour in Europe in the Twentieth Century: A Comparative Survey of Recent Agrarian History*. Third Edition. The Hague: M. Nijhoff.

Etzioni-Halevy, Eva (1990) 'Democratic-Elite Theory: Stabilisation Versus Breakdown of Democracy', *European Journal of Sociology*, 31, pp. 317–50.

Fanning, Ronan (1983) *Independent Ireland*. Dublin: Helicon.

Farrell, Brian (1971) *The Founding of Dáil Éireann: Parliament and Nation Building*. Dublin: Gill and Macmillan.

Farrell, Brian (1972) *The Irish Parliamentary Tradition*. Dublin: Gill and Macmillan.

Foster, Roy (1988) *Modern Ireland, 1600–1972*. London: Allen Lane.

Garvin, Tom (1981) *The Evolution of Irish Nationalist Politics*. Dublin: Gill and Macmillan.

Garvin, Tom (1991) 'The Rising and Irish Democracy', pp. 21–9 in Mairin Ni Dhonnchadha and Theo Dorgan (eds.) *Revising the Rising*. Derry: Field Day.

Garvin, Tom (1993a) 'Democratic Politics in Independent Ireland', pp. 250–61 in John Coakley and Michael Gallagher (eds.) *Politics in the Republic of Ireland*. Second Edition. Limerick: PSAI Press/Folens.

Garvin, Tom (1993b) 'Unenthusiastic Democrats: The Emergence of Irish Democracy', pp. 9–23 in Ronald J. Hill and Michael Marsh (eds.) *Modern Irish Democracy*. Dublin: Irish Academic Press.

Garvin, Tom (1996) *1922: The Birth of Irish Democracy*. New York: St Martin's.

Garvin, Tom (2004) *Preventing the Future: Why Was Ireland So Poor for So Long?* Dublin: Gill and Macmillan.

Hall, John A. (1993) 'Democratic Consolidations', pp. 271–91 in David Held (ed.) *Prospects for Democracy: North, South, East, West*. Cambridge: Polity Press.

Hobson, Bulmer (1932) 'Introduction', pp. 15–17 in *Irish Free State Official Handbook*. London: Ernest Benn.

Inglehart, Ronald (1999) 'Trust, Well-Being and Democracy', pp. 88–120 in M.E. Warren (ed.) *Democracy and Trust*. Cambridge: Cambridge University Press.

Kennedy, Liam (1992–93) 'Modern Ireland: Post–Colonial Society or Post-Colonial Pretensions?', *Irish Review*, 13, pp. 104–21.

Kissane, Bill (2002) *Explaining Irish Democracy*. Dublin: UCD Press.

Laver, Michael (1986a) 'Ireland: Politics with Some Social Bases: An Interpretation Based on Aggregate Data', *Economic and Social Review*, 17, pp. 107–31.

Laver, Michael (1986b) 'Ireland: Politics with Some Social Bases: An Interpretation Based on Survey Data', *Economic and Social Review*, 17, pp. 193–213.

Laver, Michael (1987) 'Measuring Patterns of Party Support', *Economic and Social Review*, 18, pp. 95–100.

Lee, J.J. (1973) *The Modernisation of Irish Society 1848–1918*. Dublin: Gill and Macmillan.

Lee, J.J. (1989) *Ireland 1912–1985: Politics and Society*. Cambridge: Cambridge University Press.

Lieven, Anatol (1993) *The Baltic Revolutions: Estonia, Latvia, Lithuania and the Path to Independence*. New Haven, CT: Yale University Press.

Linz, Juan J. (1978) *The Breakdown of Democratic Regimes: Crisis, Breakdown, and Reequilibrium*. Baltimore, MD: Johns Hopkins University Press.

Lipset, Seymour M. (1959) 'Some Social Requisites of Democracy: Economic Development and Political Legitimacy', *American Political Science Review*, 53 (1), pp. 69–104.

Mair, Peter (1986) 'Locating Irish Political Parties on a Left–Right Dimension: An Empirical Enquiry', *Political Studies*, 34 (3), pp. 456–65.

Mansergh, Nicholas (1934) *The Irish Free State: Its Government and Politics*. London: George Allen and Unwin.

McAllister, Ian and Declan O'Connell (1984) 'The Political Sociology of Party Support in Ireland: A Reassessment', *Comparative Politics*, 16 (2), pp. 191–204.

McBride, Lawrence W. (1992) *The Greening of Dublin Castle: The Transformation of Bureaucratic and Judicial Personnel in Ireland 1892–1992*. Washington, DC: Catholic University of America Press.

Moore, Barrington (1966) *Social Origins of Dictatorship and Democracy: Lord and Peasant in the Making of the Modern World*. Boston, MA: Beacon.

Munger, Frank (1976) *The Legitimacy of Opposition: The Change of Government in Ireland in 1932*. Beverly Hills, CA: Sage.

Murphy, John A. (1983) 'The Achievement of Eamon de Valera', pp. 1–7 in J.P. O'Carroll and John A. Murphy (eds.) *De Valera and His Times*. Cork: Cork University Press.

O'Brien, Conor Cruise (1968) 'The Embers of Easter, 1916–1966', pp. 225–40 in Owen Dudley Edwards and Fergus Pyle (eds.) *The Easter Rising*. London: MacGibbon and Kee.

O'Callaghan, Margaret (1984) 'Language, Nationality and Cultural Identity in the Irish Free State, 1922–7: The Irish Statesman and the Catholic Bulletin Reappraised', *Irish Historical Studies*, 24 (94), pp. 226–45.

O'Leary, Brendan and John McGarry (1993) *The Politics of Antagonism: Understanding Northern Ireland*. London: Athlone Press.

Polanski, Anthony (1975) *The Little Dictators: The History of Eastern Europe Since 1918*. London: Routledge and Kegan Paul.

Prager, Jeffrey (1986) *Building Democracy in Ireland: Political Order and Cultural Integration in a Newly Independent Nation*. Cambridge: Cambridge University Press.

Rueschemeyer, Dietrich, Evelyne Huber Stephens and John D. Stephens (1992) *Capitalist Development and Democracy*. Cambridge: Polity Press.

Rumpf, Erhard and A.C. Hepburn (1977) *Nationalism and Socialism in Twentieth Century Ireland*. Liverpool: Liverpool University Press.

Schmitt, David E. (1973) *The Irony of Irish Democracy: The Impact of Political Culture on Administration and Democratic Political Development in Ireland*. Lexington, MA: Lexington Books.

Seton-Watson, Hugh (1982) *East Central Europe Between the Two World Wars: 1918–1941*. Boulder, CO: Westview Press.

Vanhanen, Tatu (1984) *The Emergence of Democracy*. Helsinki: Societas Scientiarum Fennica.

Ward, Alan J. (1994) *The Irish Constitutional Tradition: Responsible Government and Modern Ireland, 1782–1992*. Dublin: Irish Academic Press.

Weiner, Myron (1987) 'Empirical Democratic Theory', pp. 3–37 in Myron Weiner and Ergun Ozbudun (eds.) *Competitive Elections in Developing Countries*. Durham, NC: Duke University Press.

Weiner, Myron (1991) 'The Indian Paradox: Violent Social Conflict and Democratic Politics', pp. 69–85 in S.N. Eisenstadt (ed.) *Democracy and Modernity*. Leiden: E.J. Brill.

Whyte, John H. (1974) 'Ireland: Politics Without Social Bases', pp. 619–52 in Richard Rose (ed.) *Electoral Behavior: A Comparative Handbook*. New York: Free Press.

Wright, Frank (1987) *Northern Ireland: A Comparative Analysis*. Dublin: Gill and Macmillan.

3 Strokes, cute hoors and sneaking regarders

The influence of local culture on Irish political style

J.P. O'Carroll

Originally published in *Irish Political Studies*, 2, 1987, pp. 77–92.

The importance of the local community in Irish politics has long been recognised. Garvin (1981) traces many aspects of current politics back to their communal roots in the late eighteenth century. In particular, present-day styles of mobilisation and the organisation of party politics can be traced to this source. A number of writers have explored the features of this 'parish pump' politics (Carty, 1983; Sacks, 1976; Bax, 1976). On the ideological front community looms even larger. Peillon (1984) places the concept at the heart of Irish culture and ideology. The aim of this article is to explore a number of aspects of communal culture and to demonstrate their implications for Irish political development.

The conceptualisation of community as an orally-constructed portrait, the idea that talk convenes a community by the sharing of experiences and that such talk represents a 'public trial of truths', seems to constitute a fruitful starting point for the examination of the popular bases of political culture (Berger and Luckmann, 1967; Berger, 1985; García Márquez, 1978). Community as a cultural phenomenon can be most usefully conceptualised as a 'bounded symbolic whole' (Cohen, 1985) – i.e. it is most fruitfully viewed 'from inside'. This not only solves problems of definition but also avoids methodological debates which arise when it is treated primarily as social structure. An essential part of communal life can be seen by viewing community as the result of a continuous portrayal of itself by its members, a portrayal comprised of 'words, spoken and remembered: opinions, stories, eyewitness reports, legends, comments and hearsay' (Berger, 1985). Since this never-finished portrait was, until recently, the only reflection of the meaning of their existence – apart from the physical achievement of the work of local people – it is the obvious locus in which to search for the subjective elements of both community culture and popular political culture.

Four key aspects of community culture are explored: the image of place; the role of talk itself; the idea of unity; and the conceptualisation of time. First, a shared sense of place is still an important aspect of community for most people (Tovey, 1985). The name of the place which people regard as their community is a symbol of the unique, sovereign possession which forms the basis of their identity. In the communal portrait which is constructed by talk, place and the image of place symbolise the boundary which differentiates them from the anonymous mass of humanity.

Second, the implication of the process of constructing community through talk is that the nature of community itself and the politics of community are shaped by the formal characteristics of that talk. Form, as well as content, is of importance. Third, the main attraction of community for its members may be that the sense of belonging to a large social group of like-minded people imparts a needed feeling of security. The idea of unity is thus a compelling feature of such thought.

Finally, because the communal portrait is constructed of words, spoken and remembered, it has an important in-built time element. Local elites must constantly control perceptions of time in order to protect their authority. Images of time thus become an important element in the politics of local life. The aim of this study is to explore these aspects of communal culture. In the final section of the paper the effect of the predomination of communal culture on Irish political development is considered.

A number of caveats must be entered at this point. First, community is not considered to be more rural than urban. The difficulties which social scientists, both foreign and Irish, have had in this regard tells more about themselves than about the nature of community. Second, it is not helpful to classify community as either traditional or modern. The main attraction of the traditional view of community is that it is often a neoconservative flight from the conflictual realities of the present to a mythical conflict-free utopia. Third, the social function of community and its importance for politics is to be found in the realm of the conative or emotional rather than in the instrumental (Cohen, 1969). Politicians interested in the mobilisation of bias find community a very useful resource. Fourth, community is not conceived as passive in relation to its societal environment. Though it may at times appear passive, it is continually talking and judging. Its anti-structure and syncretist capabilities are considerable (Turkle, 1975). Finally, because community and our conceptualisation of it are based on belief, the criteria of validity to be applied are those appropriate to a sociology of belief (Dixon, 1980).

Communal images of place and the influence of property

Locality is an essential part of the popular conceptualisation of community. It plays an important role in the formation and maintenance of individual and communal identity. It is also intrinsically associated with the notion of possession and hence with property, both collective and individual. These two aspects of community are explored here and their implications for Irish politics are examined.

The frequency with which conversations between strangers in Ireland open with the question, 'Where do you come from?', indicates the importance of place in the identity of a large proportion of the population. Images of place are highly selective (Hourihan, 1978). This topic has been well explored in recent years (Smyth, 1985; Tovey, 1985). Place and images of place are a fundamental part of all portraits of community. Indeed, its paramount importance lies in the fact that, because of its concreteness, it is very often the only symbol of the existence of the community which outsiders recognise. This recognition by outsiders plays a vital role in the formation of identity because it acknowledges the insiders' view of themselves. The concrete and indestructible aspect of place makes it a reassuring focus for identity, particularly for a community fearful of change. Finally, because locality is so much associated with community, political leaders lack credibility if they are not local. By definition, a leader should be an intrinsic part of the community and therefore of the locality. These cultural traits have ensured that, historically and currently, Irish politics at all levels is heavily influenced by interaction of place and identity. Because of the extent of the correspondence of the geographic and the social, much Irish politics might be properly classed 'topological'. Bax (1976), Bowman (1982), Carty (1983), Rumpf and Hepburn (1977) and Sacks (1976) have all documented the importance of locality, territory or geography for Irish politics, both local and national. Electoral boundaries, bailiwicks, vote transfers, nomination of candidates as well as the appointment of ministers are still rigidly determined by social-geographical factors. Paradoxically, public administration reflects social structures such as parish, county and region much less than it does in other European countries.

The influence of images of place on national and international relations in Ireland has been well explored by MacDonagh (1983) in his chapter on place. 'In one sense the Irish problem has persisted because of the power of geographical images over men's minds. In particular, the image of the island, with its surrounding water carving out a territorial identity, has been compelling' (MacDonagh, 1983, p. 15). The island as a 'symbol of separateness, mystery and peculiarity' (MacDonagh, 1983, p. 15) is common to both the indigenous occupiers and their arriviste conquerors. Ascendancy and Dissenter both conceived the national community in terms of the entire island.

Protestant nationalism's image of Ireland reflected the communal notion of unity in its two leading articles of faith: 'Ireland's geographic integrity and Ireland's irrefragable unity as a society...From all this sprang the respective neuroses concerning place which afflicted the different Irish sections in the nineteenth and twentieth centuries' (MacDonagh, 1983, p. 18). These concepts of territoriality have thus shaped the forces of history since and their influence persists, for example, in the recent Anglo-Irish Agreement. The second key element associated with the communal sense of place is the notion of possession. Collective possession of a territory by members implies communal sovereignty. The high proportion of citizens owning private property such as businesses, farms and private homes makes property ownership a key feature of many communities. Many communities, particularly in rural areas, are locality descent groups where the same families have shared the area for generations. There is little mobility of property in rural areas (Sheehy and O'Connor, 1985). Overall more than 70 per cent of family homes are owner-occupied. Possession is, therefore, a key feature of both the image and the reality of most communities. The outlook of such communities is moulded by this experience.

The most important characteristic of these communities is the high proportion of people who were born there and who continue to live their whole lives in them.

This can lead to considerable mental immobility (Becker and Barnes, 1961). Possession thus becomes a basic value and achievement is considerably undervalued. This trait is deeply ingrained at all levels of culture including business and commerce (O'Carroll, 1987). This emphasis on possession and the concomitant undervaluing of achievement may have their roots in the land struggles of the past: 'the myth or model of a "territory" belonging to a group, worked as a means of living and supporting homes *rather than for profit* and subject to a customary code of rights and duties always underlay the peasant attitude' (MacDonagh, 1983, p. 39, my emphasis). Despite the modern move to a very absolutist idea of individual ownership, the above argument is being used today by the Irish Farmers' Association against bank foreclosures. The communal notion of property has been used in the attempt to prevent both upward and downward mobility. The political implications of a culture which emphasises ascription to such an extent are manifold. It would appear that the consequences of ascription for belief, cognition, notions of validity and legitimation, and standards of discourse all have considerable impact at the political level, particularly in the domains of decision-making, choice of policy, debate, discussion and problem definition. For example, lack of options greatly limits choice, and therefore it limits the possibility of acquiring the skills needed for choice-making. It should also be noted that pursuit of a family business particularly limits choice and thus weakens the ability to identify problems, and to develop criteria of validity in argument and debate. The results are poor standards of problem identification, poor awareness of options, a considerable tendency toward fundamentalism (Daly, 1983) and poor skills in decision-making. At the individual level, lack of options prevents the development of responsibility and the sense of the moral and political adulthood which can only be achieved when opportunity for the exercise of choice is offered. Publics which have not developed a sense of political efficacy are easy prey to politicians who wish to create a dependent following.

At a deeper level the possession of property is seen to validate knowledge and authority, particularly among the self-employed in family businesses and farming. In these cases both inheritance and knowledge generally depend on age. Property, age and experience validate authority and knowledge. The implications of this syndrome for the strongly anti-intellectual tone of Irish politics (Chubb, 1970) might well be profitably explored. In these areas familism and authoritarianism still hold considerable sway. The view that 'authority is God' (Keane, 1972) still receives much support.

In sum, notions of place and property structure the content of the communal portrait. Images of place have become a vital part of local and national politics and of our relations with Britain and Northern Ireland. The implications of property are to be seen in popular styles of validation of authority, truth and logic, and in poor sense of individual efficacy. Perhaps the most damaging legacy of the preponderance of property-ownership in the community is the limitation and weakening of the ability to choose between options. Ascription inhibits decision-making in many areas of life. It may foster irresponsibility, passivity and an inability to handle complex political issues.

Local culture and the language of competitive politics

> Every town has its quota of Bright Boys – the characters who either make the news or interpret the news in the way they like best.
>
> (Power, 1984)

Membership of a community means that each person contributes to the collective portrait both as a portrayer and as an element portrayed. The portrait is created by a process of communication in which each day's events are recounted. Each recounting invites comment which is the speaker's 'personal response – in the light of that story – to the riddle of existence' (Berger, 1985, p. 8). The commentator, in that way, builds his own identity. He also confirms the identity of the speaker. The sum total of communication constitutes a large part of the identity of the community as a whole. This process of definition is an organic part of communal life. Should it cease, Berger notes, the community would disintegrate. The implications of this aspect of social life are profound (Marshall, 1961). They need, however, to be examined in much greater detail. In this section we will illustrate some ties between local culture and the language used in the discussion of politics.

As a first step we examine the characteristics of the talk which constitutes and recreates the communal portrait. To the outsider who happens to become involved in communal life such talk often seems mundane, trivial, boring, irrelevant, idle, sometimes scandalous or vicious, sometimes moralistic or righteous. To the more careful listener, however, it will become clear that, on the whole, very few stories are narrated either to idealise or condemn. As Berger (1985, p. 8) notes, a key feature of such stories is that they 'testify to the always slightly surprising range of the possible. They are mystery stories.' This fundamental characteristic of community life – a preoccupation with the extraordinary in everyday events, a predilection for talking about the surprising – has not received anything like the attention it deserves. It may well underlie many aspects of communal culture. The savouring of 'news', the love of watching a contest of skill, strength and wits, the appreciation of the skills of the 'fixer', of cleverness in the market and the popularity of the 'playboy', are all grist to the mill of the portrayers who create the communal portrait. They also contribute to the evolution of the idioms of politics in a number of ways.

First, they deal with elements of the 'mysterious' and the 'extraordinary', a necessary ingredient for the evolution of any political relationship in which uncertainty, arising from crises of various sorts, is to be replaced by 'hope and confidence' (Wallis, 1982; O'Carroll, 1983). This, of course, is the key element in the growth of a charismatic relationship, whether directed toward hero, priest, king, politician or poet (Ó hÓgáin, 1985). In order to be successful in politics aspirants to office have to be able to show they have power. Those who can deliver material favours are said to have 'pull' (Bax, 1976). In the continuous, intense competition necessitated by the electoral system, 'pull' indicates an ability to 'deliver' more than other competitors for political office. The fact that most of that which is delivered is imaginary in no way lessens the degree of confidence in the person who is seen to have 'pull'.

In local parlance the actions which most strikingly demonstrate power, however, are termed 'strokes'. The perpetrator of a stroke is called a 'cute hoor', a term which denotes a certain admiration for the way in which he outmanoeuvres his competitors. The 'stroke' justifies the aspirant's claim to the loyalty and support of the local constituents. Their use of the term acknowledges the validity of that claim. It should also be noted that, at the cultural level, politics is also expected to provide the thrills of a spectator sport. Humour, style and imagination are all convertible into power. Flamboyance is the result. How you present yourself (form) is as important as what you have to present (content). This makes for great adaptability (Eisenstadt, 1973) because form, not content, is the essence of culture (Cohen, 1985).

Second, though neither idealised nor condemned, the behaviour involved was well recognised as being on the margins of social acceptability. The cuteness of the 'cute hoor' may imply sharp practice. This is generally not politically acceptable to the authorities. If all or part of the community supports those ('the lads') who cock a snook at the establishment, they may be dubbed 'sneaking regarders' by the authorities. However, when the establishment seek to augment formal power by tapping informal channels, they signal their intention in language which is instantly recognised by those that might otherwise be called 'sneaking regarders' (Luhmann, 1979). Lemass' characterisation of the Fianna Fáil government as 'slightly constitutional' is a classic example of such communication. The implications of this idiom for the communication of power and its contribution to the strengths and weaknesses of Irish political development will be examined later.

Third, the communal culture described above gives low priority to the ordinary and the mundane and the complexity of the economy relegates it, by and large, to this category. As a result, when the economy must be discussed, the idiom of the extraordinary is used wherever possible. A coup in the market – just once in a lifetime – is preferable to years of routine production. The economy is mundane, complex and threatening and no amount of politically flamboyant documentation of economic plans will hide the fact. National pride is also infinitely 'warmer' than national produce. Public discourse on matters economic is considerably contaminated by this inappropriate idiom. Few, even among those who support development, are aware of the incongruity of the use of the idiom in their discourse. For example, although many commentators including historians and journalists have welcomed the replacement of an obsession with romantic nationalist politics by concern for the economy, the idiom still remains unchanged. The nationalist hero is now replaced by the 'economic' hero or saint. Lemass was canonised soon after his death and Whitaker is beatified in his own lifetime. The content may change but the political forms remain.

All of this points to an imbalance in the tone of public discourse. We favour the language of the extraordinary, of the hope-giving vision, to such an extent that we leave little room for the mundane in public discourse. As a result there are large areas of silence in public life.

Community is thus ideological in three senses of the word. First, it expresses an ethos – a necessary constituent of all social life. Second, this ethos can be manipulated so as to control others. Very often the emotions unleashed by this ideology directly negate the possibility of action or seriously limit action in the public interest. As a result, the problem which occasioned the activation of the ideology remains ignored. The ideology may evoke vast areas of silence. In its silence about the 'mundane' there is an element of conspiracy to hide important truths.

Community, wholeness, belonging

There is only one communal portrait. No matter what internal divisions there may be, the community generally strives to present a single face to the public. The communal portrait is thus unique. It is a coherent whole. These and associated formal characteristics of community powerfully influence the construction of political reality. In Ireland this influence is much greater than in other European countries because of its intense magnification by three other elements of the culture. First, at the societal level, community is a major ideological theme. It is seen to be desirable and is always juxtaposed to the idea of society which is seen to be undesirable (Peillon, 1984). Second, many of the themes of community find a perfect resonance in the major tenets of nationalism. Third, the meaning has been further strengthened by its consonance with Catholicism (Hurst, 1969), and by the ties between church and state (Clarke, 1984).

In this section we will examine in some detail some general aspects of community, of identification with community, and some characteristics of thought and belief which arise in the communal experience. These are then all related to relevant aspects of the polity, the party system and the pattern of government.

First, uniqueness, unity and wholeness characterise the communal portrait. There is also the strong notion of centre (Barden, 1977). These ideas all raise the issue of boundary which in turn intensifies their meaning (Weber, 1978). Conflict based on community identity is by definition zero-sum conflict (McAllister, 1982). Superiority, indivisibility and unity of belief, authority and leadership are the result. These are the characteristics which in a subliminal way render community a potent symbol.

The most powerful political notion to emerge from this is, of course, that of unity. Territory, nation, polity, party and the belief system are all judged by this absolute standard. Re-unification of the 'national territory', self-sufficiency and neutrality have a powerful attraction. The nation is 'one and indivisible'. The party has one leader and one voice. The obverse of this is the fears generated by the notion of pluralism. Recognition of minority rights, it is felt, would constitute an 'injustice to the majority' or 'would bring about the collapse of society'. Even the ubiquitous 'split' could be judged as symptomatic of the purist's notion that unity cannot be based on agreement to differ. This is the essence of corporatism and also the basis of much anti-individualism.

The notion of unity has likewise structured the party system and the possibilities for coalition formation. Fianna Fáil traced its pedigree back to the united pre-Treaty Sinn Féin party. After the Civil War it soon successfully convinced a majority of the public of its claim to be the bearer of the authentic nationalist tradition. With its emphasis on Gaelic culture it created a strong 'moral' sense of community. Its claim to be 'not so much a party, more a national movement' reflected not only doubts even about the correctness of oppositional politics, but also their claim to the support of the nation as a whole. Coalition was seen to be anathema, reflecting the dilemma of all who would claim the absolute. In the world of true believers, whether of Fianna Fáil or of traditional Catholicism, the untrue and the bad cannot be joined with the true and the good. Accordingly the only alignment, for the foreseeable future, can be Fianna Fáil versus the rest. The only coalition possibilities are among 'the rest'.

The second outcome of the communal experience is its creation of a powerful sense of identification. The sense of belonging, in both its active (Ryan, 1984) and passive senses, and of exclusivity imparted by community give rise to a strong sense of attachment and loyalty. Because many members tend to see community as indiscriminately good, it has a magnetic effect on those who seek a large group in which to invest their identity.

Irish politics also reflects this second major communal characteristic, i.e. the powerful attachments and loyalties it evokes. Party support overwhelmingly arises from a powerful sense of loyalty and partisanship which forms part of individual identity (Bax, 1976; Garvin and Parker, 1972; Gallagher, 1978; Carty, 1983). The appeal of this identification for a majority of supporters is so great that it amounts almost to what has been called political religion (Apter, 1963). John Healy has even suggested that it also substituted for sex in the case of many of its celibate supporters. In fact, he has highlighted the exceptionally strong pull of Fianna Fáil for its members by coining the term 'Moral Community' (Carty, 1983). So strong and religious in fervour is this feeling that confession of political agnosticism brings reactions only of incomprehension or frank disbelief. Recent defections from Fianna Fáil have been termed 'apostasy' and they have given rise to the statement that 'outside Fianna Fáil there is no salvation'.

Community time and political time

> All villages tell stories. Stories of the past, even the distant past ... And equally, stories of the very same day ... this combination of the sharpest observation, of the daily recounting of the day's events and encounters, and of lifelong mutual familiarities is what constitutes the so called village gossip.
>
> (Berger, 1985, p. 8)

Community is symbolically constituted, as has been noted above, of words both remembered and spoken. What has been generally missed is that talk mixes themes from both present and past. The past is therefore embedded in the present. Each community has its own unique map of time. It is an intrinsic part of community. No outsiders share or even acknowledge this version of time. It has its characteristic lacunae, elisions and foreshortenings. To the extent that a locality descent group is a community, every interaction bears to some extent the imprint of the shared past, a past selectively defined in terms of persons, circumstances, events and occasions. This aspect of reality is recognised even by the courts which are prepared, in assault cases, to accept as a mitigating plea the information that 'it started in their grandfathers' time'.

As a result it is exceptionally difficult to alter the nature of such relationships. The community's knowledge of an individual is not much less than God's. There is, therefore, almost no latitude for role playing (Berger, 1985; Giddens, 1984; Tenbruck, 1961). Because of this, it is almost impossible to break the mould of communal history – unless you can bring the whole community with you. However, the pull of primordial loyalties (Alavi, 1973; Inhetveen, 1982) and the tendency to deny such changes as do occur (Horton, 1967a and 1967b) considerably reduce the possibility of such a conversion.

In the communal portrait perception of time is closely associated with authority, identity, meanings, values and, above all, change. 'Moving with the times' implies acknowledgement of changes in meanings and values. Such a step is fraught with hazard for the authorities because it could be interpreted to imply that they were wrong. To prevent any possibility of a crisis of legitimacy change tends to be avoided. The future is a *terra incognita* full of terrors. If change does occur, it is often ignored or denied by authorities. If the authorities decide on change, the implementation of the decision is heavily underwritten by reference to the past. All this is reflected in the ebb and flow of discourse which creates the communal portrait.

It is remarkable that the analogue of many of these communal 'peculiarities' in regard to time can be found in the political field. As a result, Chubb (1970, p. vi) has found it necessary to issue an important warning: 'In no other country more than Ireland is a knowledge of the past, even the distant past, essential to an understanding of the present'. Ireland's dead are continually called on to validate and justify the policies of its politicians. On the 200th anniversary of his death, Berkeley, the philosopher bishop of Cloyne, found himself being called on by de Valera to justify the policies of Fianna Fáil (Moynihan, 1980; O'Carroll, 1983). The proposal to issue a stamp in 1969 to commemorate the Norman invasion and the celebration of the anniversary of the granting of a charter to Cork evoked controversy, though both events had occurred 800 years before.

Irish historiography, too, has not been unaffected by the malaise. Communication between communities, whether between Britain and Ireland or between Protestant and Catholic, was confounded by differences in notions of time which were often produced by historians. MacDonagh (1983, p. 1) noted apropos of the first meeting between Lloyd George and de Valera in the Treaty negotiations of 1922: 'To Lloyd George, the seventeenth century was dead, irrelevant to current difficulties, except perhaps in helping to explain how they might, remotely, have come into being. To de Valera, the seventeenth century lived on in that it had generated still unexpiated and irredeemed injustices; the mere intervention of years, however many, could do nothing whatever to change the ethical reality. When and how did this Irish habit of historical thought arise?'

Historians of each community painted their own portrait of time. Protestants saw Irish history as movement towards civilisation. Catholics viewed it as a retreat from a golden age, at first pre-Christian and heroic but, as sectarianism increased, the image of our 'island of saints and scholars' was born (MacDonagh, 1983). In Ireland the continual frustration of aspirations led to a circular idea of time – 'an endless repetition of repelled assaults without hope of absolute finality or of fundamental change in their relationship to their surroundings and surrounded neighbours' (MacDonagh, 1983, p. 14). By 1830 the two fundamental myths of Irish nationalism, those of repetitive heroic violence and of an early Christian Elysium of saints and scholars, had been established.

This timeless view of history is typical of a community which lacks its own clear view of the future and which is content to massage its identity by wallowing in its miseries. 'It renders the past an arsenal of weapons with which to defend both inveterate prejudice and that ignorance which wishes only to remain invincible' (MacDonagh, 1983, p. 7). Furthermore, it allows no statute of limitations to soften the judgement to be made on past events, however distant. 'In such a view, no prescriptive rights can be established by the passage of time' (MacDonagh, 1983, p. 17).

Community time and the economy

The failure to recognise differing conceptualisations of time is associated with the failure also to perceive the considerable amount of syncretism which occurs in Ireland. The implication of syncretism is that the community identity is so powerful that changes urged on it by the world outside are ransacked of their essential and intended meaning. The goals of the centre are thus totally deflected. For example, the capital grants supplied to agriculture by many agencies over the past 150 years, agencies such as the Congested Districts Board, the Department of Agriculture and the EEC, have in many cases been treated by farmers merely as a form of dole, for current consumption, rather than as a basis for expansion of future production. These are two entirely different time scales.

The inability to take a realistic long-term view is also the origin of wild swings between over-confidence and gloom. Community is more about being than about doing. It emphasises solidarity based on a shared past and is less interested in change and development. The over-confidence of the boom years toward the end of the 1970s was the analogue of the doom which has descended since the onset of depression in 1980.

Our orientation to time has also influenced our approach to planning at the national level. Whitaker (1978) has noted a degree of 'political flamboyance' in later national plans. Recent plans have, for example, been criticised because of lack of adequate details (NESC, 1985). They have often depended for their successful execution primarily on the intervention of a *deus ex machina*, such as changes in exchange rates, to create favourable conditions. In popular thought the possible discovery of oil played a similar role (Neary, 1984). Planning documents, therefore, seem to share some ideas found in the cargo cults of the south Pacific (Worsley, 1967).

It is important to recognise that the primary and key function of such plans lies in the domain of ideology. As a statement of good intentions they bear witness to their authors' commitment to the common good. This is an example of 'verbal politics' (Healy) and of the preference for saying rather than doing (Lee, 1984). The origin of this proclivity arises in the talk which creates community. National plans should, therefore, be recognised also as moral statements which affirm the identity of the community. Their impact is instant and automatic because they speak a language first made familiar in the local community – the language of identity and solidarity. They also convey the image of a state which is benevolent and subsidy-oriented, and in many ways like familiar local communities, both real and imagined.

National plans appear, therefore, to have two conflicting aims: first, the creation of a following, and, second, the much more tenuous programming of action (Edelman, 1971). Publication of a national plan creates the impression that the authorities have the situation in hand and are about to 'get the nation going again'.

However, because the primary aim of this activity is to mobilise emotions in favour of the government, it is not conducive to rational thought. Because recent economic plans have been so politicised, they have lacked the coherence to be expected of them. They have been found wanting in regard to their goals, their priorities, their scope and their strategy (NESC, 1985). The elements which are lacking are those which might conflict with the need for legitimation. There is nothing new about all this, however. Hurst (1969, p. 18) notes that in Maria Edgeworth's time 'popular leaders ... did not have a proper social programme, yet their emotional contact with the masses was automatic and immediate, engendered by countless unspoken elements of history and kept alive through the great agency of their religious faith'. As a result they had no trouble in outbidding reformist opponents.

Community is primarily concerned with identity, solidarity and unity. Identity is based on a shared version of past events. Communal discourse continually mixes the present and the past. Authorities orchestrate the discourse and thus control the reaction to changes which are pressed on community by society. Whether they react negatively or positively to change, or choose inertia, they invoke the past. The main attraction of the past may lie in the fact that a communal past is presented as a single seamless web. For authorities seeking to avoid conflict at all costs such a version of the past is a vital resource. It also explains why Irish society chooses to go 'backwards into the future'. The broader implications of the use of communal ideology as a resource in political development are discussed below.

Community and political development

The importance of community for Irish political development must now be considered. In this section it will be argued that Irish politics suffers from a surfeit of the communal in its culture, its style, and in their influence on the organisation and the processes of politics. As a result of this imbalance, politics is archaic and out of tune with many of the needs of a modern society. Because of an over-emphasis on issues of national identity and on the maintenance of political tranquillity – often to the exclusion of many other aspects of politics – political discourse on major issues is minimal and decision-making, particularly in regard to the economy, is rendered ineffective.

Community itself is a powerful cultural asset. Its power lies in its contribution to identity, solidarity and to partisanship. At a deeper level it conveys images of unity and wholeness which help to shape our view of the world. It is constituted largely of talk and the form as well as the content of the discourse shape its potentialities. However, though it is an important resource, overuse can lead to a narrowing of the limits of political culture.

The origins of this imbalance, ironically, can be found in the important place that the notion of community won for itself through its crucial contribution to the building of Irish identity. Most newly-independent states must solve their problems of institution-formation and of identity-building so that they can proceed successfully with the third aspect of development, the pursuit of social and economic well-being. A strong sense of local community is the ideal tool for the creation of national identity and for political mobilisation (Gellner, 1983). De Valera recognised this and, as a result, he almost always used this idiom. By 1948 he was successful in having his version of Irish identity clearly established and accepted by a majority.

De Valera's genius lay in the proper recognition of what was needed by the body politic at that time, identity-building, and in the use of the most appropriate tool, the rhetoric of community, to achieve it. De Valera's rhetoric not only created a national political community by using an image of Ireland as a parish writ large, he also built a most effective machine for the creation and expansion of political power – a prime requisite in the conditions of the early years of independence. De Valera's populist approach was designed to broaden the appeal of his party, particularly to sectors of the polity which would have been ambivalent in regard to constitutional politics. This antinomian dimension has long been recognised as characteristic of both populist (Laclau, 1977) and corporatist (Winkler, 1975) politics. Luhmann (1979), however, has best explored its characteristics and their implications for the expansion of informal power. It is remarkable how closely his delineation of the phenomenon corresponds to the Irish case and to the traits of parish-pump politics.

Luhmann (1979, p. 134) notes three characteristics of such informal power codes. First, they have 'greater concreteness and dependence on the circumstances'. Second, they have 'a lesser capacity for social legitimation and so also less "presentability" '. Finally, they depend for their functioning on access to beliefs 'which cannot be shared by the outside world'. The existence of this symbolic boundary was clearly recognised by one former Irish politician, himself outside the belief system, when he admitted to finding the people of Bandon 'as inscrutable as orientals'. Another even more prominent politician placed himself firmly outside the boundary by his failure to recognise the significance of the red and white scarf presented to him in Cork. What is important for our argument is that those capable of tapping the informal, communal, culture have a powerful advantage because of the broadening of the base of their power. No modern politician can afford to neglect such a bonus. Hence the predominance of the communal style in politics today.

However, although this form of communication is excellent for the purpose of political mobilisation and identity-building, it is a poor tool for motivating economic and social growth. It may even hinder such growth. This political style is archaic. It imparts a powerful sense of belonging, of distinctiveness, of security, of identity, of loyalty and of partisanship. As such, it can impart a strong sense of place but not a sense of direction. It is primarily conservative and focussed ultimately on survival, a key angst of the petite-bourgeoisie. Paradoxically its highest achievement, apart from the building of identity, was a contribution to the intense degree of centralisation within the new state. The new state's political colonisation of the cultural space of the community was so total that local politics became merely a proxy for national party politics (Barrington, undated; Lee, 1985; Muintir na Tire, 1985). Today, there is almost no sign of the move toward local government so prevalent in Europe (Machin and Wright, 1985).

Communal-style politics, though an excellent harvester of the marginal influence that counts in elections, is unable to handle the problems of a modern society. Industrial society necessitates wide acceptance of forms of organisation which transcend the community. The division of labour which characterises the new way of living implies interdependence and co-operation which is based, not on communication involving concreteness and on immediate circumstance, but on the ability to handle ideas, abstract relationships and, above all, options implied by ephemeral encounters and non-repetitive situations (Bernstein, 1971; Douglas, 1966; Martin, 1981; Turner, 1974). Gellner (1964, p. 155) has pointed out that the burden of comprehension then 'is shifted from the context to communication itself... the message must itself become intelligible – it is no longer understood as was the case in traditional society, before it was even articulated'. The latter, according to Ó Crualaoich (1983), aptly described de Valera's style of communication. In fact, de Valera himself became the key symbol of the party. This study has attempted to demonstrate, however, that such politics establishes an unduly rigid and fixed political system by limiting the number of parties and their possible combinations, by creating a most rigid type of partisanship and a narrow parochial outlook which is incapable of responding to the challenges offered to it by the modern world.

In conclusion, Irish politics, as a result of its communal underpinnings, is best interpreted as an exercise in expressiveness, in the assertion of inherited loyalties and partisanship – rather than as an exercise of individual choice. By its tendency to limit choice, the culture contravenes the first two characteristics of modern democracy, the possibility of open discussion and the exercise of individual will and consent. Finally, its idealisation of the concept of unity contravenes the third and last key notion of modern democracy, that of pluralism. For these reasons Irish political culture has failed to adjust to the problems of social and economic mobilisation. No amount of striving for such mobilisation will be effective as long as the belief continues to exist which portrays community as a key cultural value which is indiscriminately good, and society as a value which is indiscriminately bad.

COMMENTARY BY GARY MURPHY

J.P. O'Carroll's 1987 article posits the view that the notion of community in Ireland is best seen as a set of locally shared attitudes to place, territory, property, time and language. It goes on to argue that local culture in Ireland portrays community as good and society as bad and finishes with the startling conclusion that Irish politics is more an exercise in expressiveness than an expression of choice and that such expressiveness is manifested in the assertion of inherited loyalties and partisanship where Ireland is full of politicians, or 'cute hoors', able to pull 'strokes' on behalf of a grateful public full of 'sneaking regarders'. In this context O'Carroll's thesis is as much about democracy as it is political. O'Carroll notes that by its tendency to limit choice, political culture Irish style contravenes the first two characteristics of modern democracy, the possibility of open discussion and the exercise of individual will and consent. Furthermore Irish political culture's idealisation of the concept of national unity contravenes the third and key notion of modern democracy, that of pluralism and in this context he ultimately rationalises that Irish political culture has failed to adjust to the problems of social and economic mobilisation.

J.P. O'Carroll (or Paddy as he was known to generations of undergraduate sociology students in UCC, of which I was one) published this piece in 1987 just at the time that the Irish body politic was about to embark on an economic journey which had the tool of social partnership as its navigational sextant. During the February 1987 general election campaign Fianna Fáil had stressed its traditional commitment to economic growth via social partnership. Facing a grave fiscal crisis, the new Fianna Fáil government, acting in conjunction with the social partners, agreed a strategy to overcome Ireland's economic difficulties based on the premise of partnership whereby interested actors such as farmers' organisations, trade unions and business interests would negotiate with the government in what might be called the process of economic governance that continues to the current day (Hardiman, 2002). The 1987 general election resulted in a single-party Fianna Fáil minority government under Charles J. Haughey, the last single-party government to govern in Ireland. In 1989 Haughey called a snap general election in the hope of gaining an overall majority, which had eluded him and Fianna Fáil since Jack Lynch's crushing victory in 1977. The upshot of the 1989 election was Fianna Fáil's breaking of one of its 'core values' with its entry into coalition government, where it has resided remarkably comfortably pretty much ever since. More startling still was Fianna Fáil's decision to enter coalition with the Progressive Democrats (PDs), formed just four years earlier in a break-away from Fianna Fáil, mainly over the leadership of Charles Haughey (Laver and Arkins, 1990).

Single-party government is an important point in the context of O'Carroll's thesis. For O'Carroll, the genius of Eamon de Valera lay in his recognition of what was needed by the body politic at the time of Independence – identity-building – and in the use of the most appropriate tool – the rhetoric of community – to achieve it. By 1948, and the end of Fianna Fáil's first 16-year period of rule, de Valera was (in O'Carroll's words) 'successful in having his version of Irish identity, clearly established and accepted by a majority'. De Valera's rhetoric not only created, according to O'Carroll, a national political community by using an image of Ireland as a parish writ large, but he also built a most effective political machine for the creation and expansion of political power. This political machine, among the most successful in Western Europe, has dipped below 40 per cent of the first preference vote on only two occasions, both since the party embraced coalition. Once Fianna Fáil accepted the politics of coalition, party competition became more volatile and unstable. The 1992 general election saw a Fianna Fáil-led coalition government with the Labour Party, who would see themselves on the opposite side of the political fence to the PDs. Fianna Fáil found itself back in power after the 1997 general election by coalescing once again with the PDs.

By going into coalition government with the PDs after previously having coalesced with both the PDs and Labour, it appeared that coalition politics would become the norm (Mair and Weeks, 2005). The very crux of O'Carroll's article, however, is based on the politics of single-party government. This allows him to comment that the notion of unity has structured the party system and the possibilities for coalition formation. In that context Fianna Fáil saw itself as more of a national movement than a political party and through this movement had created a strong moral sense of community for itself whereby doubts about the correctness of oppositional politics are perfectly normal. According to O'Carroll:

> Coalition was seen to be anathema, reflecting the dilemma of all who would claim the absolute. In the world of true believers, whether of Fianna Fáil or of traditional Catholicism, the untrue and the bad cannot be joined with the true and the good. Accordingly the only alignment, for the foreseeable future, can be Fianna Fáil versus the rest. The only coalition possibilities are among 'the rest'.

O'Carroll quotes John Healy's coining of the term 'Moral Community' (Carty, 1983), to highlight the exceptionally strong pull of Fianna Fáil for its members and echoes Healy's suggestion that it substituted for sex in the case of many of its celibate supporters. Overall O'Carroll suggests that so strong and religious in fervour is this feeling that any confession of political agnosticism brings reaction of incomprehension and frank disbelief and tells us that the recent defections from Fianna Fáil are viewed as 'apostasy' and have given rise to the statement that 'outside Fianna Fáil there is no salvation'. The trouble here for us as students of politics is that the chief of this tribe, Charles J. Haughey, did not seem to view the national movement in much the same way as the members of his tribe. Single-party government was jettisoned on the altar of maintaining Fianna Fáil government.

That Fianna Fáil's first experiment with coalition government should be in partnership with the apostates from the PDs suggests that for the elected members of the national movement, political survival meant much more than membership of a moral, pure community; a community that was now infected from outside by those who had once been part of the said same community.

In macro-economic terms, social partnership has, since 1987, and this article's publication, become the vehicle through which the modern Irish economic phenomenon has flourished. O'Carroll devotes part of his analysis to what he terms as 'Community Time and the Economy' wherein he asserts that it is important to recognise that the primary and key function of a variety of national plans in Ireland – which he suggests share some of their ideas with those found in the cargo cults of the south Pacific – lies in the domain of ideology. This ideology seems to have as its defining characteristic a form of goodness as these plans bear witness to their authors' commitment to the common good. In O'Carroll's words national plans should thus be recognised as 'moral statements which affirm the identity of the community. Their impact is instant and automatic because they speak a language first made familiar in the local community – the language of identity and solidarity.' In this context the Irish devotion to plans, in which O'Carroll detects a trend back to the early nineteenth century, is an exercise in verbal politics and of the preference for saying rather than doing. This gives such plans two conflicting aims; first the creation of a following, second the much more tenuous programme of action.

Examining O'Carroll's analysis in 2007, after 20 years of social partnership, what is striking is just how much true national planning, involving all the social partners, as distinct from just sections of the civil service like previous plans, has achieved the twin aims of following and action. For instance, Bertie Ahern has long been of the view that there is no alternative to social partnership. While social partnership has come under strain from all sides, farmers, trade unionists, business interests and the voluntary sector at different times in its 20 year history, it has proved enormously durable – even elastic – and has not lost its initial following, created in times of crisis. This following also inhabits the political sphere. While Fine Gael has occasionally voiced reservations about social partnership having superseded politics, there are no major political voices calling for an end to the construct of social partnership. It is also important to note that when Fine Gael was in power from late 1994 to mid-1997 it actively embraced social partnership. While the original 1987 Programme for National Recovery was very much a response to the grave fiscal crisis of the mid-1980s, subsequent agreements developed into a strategy for facilitating steady growth and the inward investment that fuelled such growth, over a much longer time period than was originally expected, and this strategy, the action, was central to the successes of the Irish economy from the mid-1990s. O'Carroll's view that national plans are not conducive to rational thought as their primary aim is to mobilise emotions in favour of the government would seem not to fit the social partnership model. His argument that recent (pre-1987) economic plans lacked coherence because they were so politicised, while unquestionably valid – one need only think of Fianna

Fáil's 1977 election manifesto with its promise to abolish rates amongst other things – would also not seem to hold if we test it in the era of social partnership. However, as Fianna Fáil has been in office for 18 of the 20 years, this could well confirm Garvin's view that

> the penetration of Fianna Fáil into the bureaucracy appears to be very great, and is due mainly to the fact that the party has had a near monopoly on public office for almost fifty years and has, by its own success, generated social categories created in its own image.
>
> (1981, p. 224)

We could also possibly see social partnership as an element of this bureaucracy and perhaps see O'Carroll's own view of the communal experience, in this case social partnership, as a sense of identification.

Fianna Fáil's decision to enter coalition in 1989 fundamentally changed the nature of Irish electoral politics. Its almost religious attachment to social partnership as the means by which the macro-economy is run has been equally as important in understanding the changing nature of Irish domestic politics since J.P. O'Carroll's article in the second volume of *Irish Political Studies*. O'Carroll's seminal placing of community, expressed in his immortal phrase of 'strokes, cute hoors and sneaking regarders', in Irish local culture as being 'good', with 'society' being 'bad' was then the latest in a number of important studies which examined the importance of the local community in Irish politics (Bax, 1976; Carty, 1983; Garvin, 1981; Sacks, 1976). Such community found its political expression in voting either for or against Fianna Fáil with the result that Irish politics became in O'Carroll's view more an exercise in expressiveness than an exercise of choice. In the two decades since its publication, however, Irish politics has undergone profound change due to the twin developments of coalition government and social partnership. For O'Carroll the politics of community was the product of an unduly rigid system, which limited the number of parties and their possible combinations by 'creating a most rigid type of partnership and a narrow parochial outlook which is incapable of responding to the challenges offered to it by the modern world'. Yet today Ireland ranks amongst the most globalised states in the world (Murphy, 2006, pp. 301–2) and in the run up to the 2007 general election, Fianna Fáil, Fine Gael, Labour, the Progressive Democrats, the Green Party, and Sinn Féin all had legitimate hopes of being in government. In that context it would seem that the influence of local culture on Irish political style had its heyday with J.P. O'Carroll's 'Strokes, Cute Hoors and Sneaking Regarders'.

References

Alavi, Hamza (1973) 'Peasant Classes and Primordial Loyalties', *Journal of Peasant Studies*, 1 (1), pp. 23–62.

Apter, David (1963) 'Political Religion in the New Nations', pp. 57–104 in Clifford Geertz (ed.) *Old Societies and New States: The Quest for Modernity in Asia and Africa.* New York: The Free Press.

Barden, Garrett (1977) 'Centre', *The Crane Bag*, 1 (2), pp. 45–6.

Barrington, T.J. (undated) *From Big Government to Local Government: The Road to Decentralisation.* Dublin: Institute of Public Administration.

Bax, Mart (1976) *Harpstrings and Confessions: Machine-Style Politics in the Irish Republic.* Assen: Van Gorcum.

Becker, Howard P. and Harry Elmer Barnes (1961) *Social Thought from Lore to Science: Volume 1.* New York: Dover Publications.

Berger, John (1985) *Pig Earth.* London: Chatto and Windus.

Berger, Peter L. and Thomas Luckmann (1967) *The Social Construction of Reality: A Treatise in the Sociology of Knowledge.* New York: Doubleday.

Bernstein, Basil B. (1971) *Class, Codes and Control: Volume 1.* London: Routledge and Kegan Paul.

Bowman, John (1982) *De Valera and the Ulster Question 1917–1973.* Oxford: Clarendon Press.

Carty, R. Kenneth (1983) *Party and Parish Pump: Electoral Politics in Ireland.* Dingle: Brandon Press.

Chubb, Basil (1970) *Government and Politics of Ireland.* London: Oxford University Press.

Clarke, Desmond M. (1984) *Church and State: Essays in Political Philosophy.* Cork: Cork University Press.

Cohen, Abner (1969) 'Political Anthropology: The Analysis of the Symbolism of Power Relations', *Man*, 4 (2) (New Series), pp. 215–35.

Cohen, Anthony P. (1985) *The Symbolic Construction of Community.* London: Tavistock Publications.

Daly, G. (1983) 'On Formulating National Goals', pp. 29–35 in An Foras Forbartha [colloquy proceedings] *Ireland in the Year 2000: Towards a National Strategy – Issues and Perspectives.* Dublin: An Foras Forbartha.

Dixon, Keith (1980) *The Sociology of Belief: Fallacy and Foundation.* London: Routledge and Kegan Paul.

Douglas, Mary (1966) *Purity and Danger: An Analysis of Concepts of Pollution and Taboo.* London: Routledge and Kegan Paul.

Edelman, Murray J. (1971) *Politics as Symbolic Action: Mass Arousal and Quiescence.* New York: Academic Press.

Eisenstadt, S.N. (1973) 'Post-Traditional Societies and the Continuity and Reconstruction of Tradition', *Daedalus*, 102 (l), pp. 1–27.

Gallagher, M. (1978) 'Party Solidarity, Exclusivity and Inter-Party Relationships in Ireland, 1922–1977: The Evidence of Transfers', *Economic and Social Review*, 10 (1), pp. 1–22.

García Márquez, Gabriel (1978) *The Autumn of the Patriarch.* London: Picador.

Garvin, Tom (1981) *The Evolution of Irish Nationalist Politics.* Dublin: Gill and Macmillan.

Garvin, Tom and Anthony Parker (1972) 'Party Loyalty and Irish Voters: The EEC Referendum as a Test Case', *Economic and Social Review*, 4 (1), pp. 35–9.

Gellner, Ernest (1964) *Thought and Change.* London: Weidenfeld and Nicolson.

Gellner, Ernest (1983) *Nations and Nationalism.* Oxford: Basil Blackwell.

Giddens, Anthony (1984) *The Constitution of Society: Outline of the Theory of Structuration.* Cambridge: Polity Press.

Hardiman, Niamh (2002) 'From Conflict to Co-ordination: Economic Governance and Political Innovation in Ireland', *West European Politics*, 25 (4), pp. 1–24.

Horton, Robin (1967a) 'African Traditional Thought and Western Science: Part One', *Africa*, XXXVII (1), pp. 50–71.

Horton, Robin (1967b) 'African Traditional Thought and Western Science: Part Two', *Africa*, XXXVII (2), pp. 155–87.

Hourihan, Kevin (1978) 'Social Areas in Dublin', *Economic and Social Review*, 9 (4), pp. 301–28.

Hurst, Michael (1969) *Maria Edgeworth and the Public Scene: Intellect, Fine Feeling and Landlordism in the Age of Reform*. London: Macmillan.

Inhetveen, H. (1982) ' "Nie Fertig mit Anschaffen und Anpassen": Kleinbäuerinnen zwischen Tradition und Fortschritt', *Sociologia Ruralis*, 22 (3/4), pp. 240–63.

Keane, John B. (1972) *Letters of an Irish Parish Priest*. Cork: Mercier Press.

Laclau, Ernesto (1977) *Politics and Ideology in Marxist Theory: Capitalism, Fascism, Populism*. London: New Left Books.

Laver, Michael and Audrey Arkins (1990) 'Coalition and Fianna Fáil', pp. 192–207 in Michael Gallagher and Richard Sinnott (eds.) *How Ireland Voted 1989*. Galway: PSAI Press.

Lee, Joseph (1984) 'Reflections on the Study of Irish Values and Attitudes', pp. 107–24 in Michael Patrick Fogarty, Liam Ryan and Joseph Lee (eds.) *Irish Values and Attitudes: The Irish Report of the European Value Systems Study*. Dublin: Dominican Publications.

Lee, Joseph (ed.) (1985) *Ireland: Toward a Sense of Place*. Cork: Cork University Press.

Luhmann, Niklas (1979) *Trust and Power: Two Works*. London: John Wiley.

MacDonagh, Oliver (1983) *States of Mind – A Study of Anglo-Irish Conflict 1780–1980*. London: George Allen and Unwin.

Machin, Howard and Vincent Wright (eds.) (1985) *Economic Policy and Policy Making Under the Mitterrand Presidency 1981–1984*. London: Frances Pinter.

Mair, Peter and Liam Weeks (2005) 'The Party System', pp. 135–59 in John Coakley and Michael Gallagher (eds.) *Politics in the Republic of Ireland*. Fourth Edition. Abingdon: Routledge and PSAI Press.

Marshall, Lorna (1961) 'Sharing, Talking and Giving: Relief of Social Tensions Among Kung Bushmen', *Africa*, 31 (3), pp. 231–49.

Martin, Bernice (1981) *A Sociology of Contemporary Cultural Change*. Oxford: Basil Blackwell.

McAllister, Ian (1982) 'The Devil, Miracles and the Afterlife: The Political Sociology of Religion in Northern Ireland', *British Journal of Sociology*, 33 (3), pp. 330–47.

Moynihan, Maurice (ed.) (1980) *Speeches and Statements by Eamon de Valera*. Dublin: Gill and Macmillan.

Muintir na Tire (1985) *Towards a New Democracy?: Implications of Local Government Reform*. Dublin: Institute of Public Administration.

Murphy, Gary (2006) 'Assessing the Relationship Between Neoliberalism and Political Corruption: The Fianna Fáil–Progressive Democrat Coalition, 1997–2006', *Irish Political Studies*, 21 (3), pp. 297–317.

National Economic and Social Council (1985) *Economic and Social Policy Assessment Report No. 79*. Dublin: Stationery Office.

Neary, P. (1984) 'The Failure of Economic Nationalism', *The Crane Bag*, 8 (1), pp. 68–77.

O'Carroll, J.P. (1983) 'Eamon de Valera, Charisma and Political Development', pp. 17–34 in J.P. O'Carroll and John A. Murphy (eds.) *De Valera and His Times*. Cork: Cork University Press.

O'Carroll, J.P. (1987) 'Ireland: Political Domination of Business', pp. 84–113 in Rinus van Schendelen (ed.) *The Politicisation of Business in Western Democracies*. London: Croom Helm.

Ó Crualaoich, Gearóid (1983) 'The Primacy of Form: A "Folk Ideology" in de Valera's Politics', pp. 47–61 in J.P. O'Carroll and John A. Murphy (eds.) *De Valera and His Times*. Cork: Cork University Press.

Ó hÓgáin, Dáithí (1985) *The Hero in Irish Folk History*. Dublin: Gill and Macmillan.

Peillon, Michael (1984) 'The Structure of Irish Ideology Revisited', pp. 46–58 in Chris Curtin, Mary Kelly and Liam O'Dowd (eds.) *Culture and Ideology in Ireland*. Galway: Galway University Press.

Power, Larry (1984) *The Bright Boys: Revenge for Tipperary Tim and Other Stories*. Dublin: Glendale Press.

Rumpf, Erhard and A.C. Hepburn (1977) *Nationalism and Socialism in Twentieth Century Ireland*. Liverpool: Liverpool University Press.

Ryan, Liam (1984) 'The Changing Face of Irish Values', pp. 95–106 in Michael Patrick Fogarty, Liam Ryan and Joseph Lee (eds.) *Irish Values and Attitudes: The Irish Report of the European Value Systems Study*. Dublin: Dominican Publications.

Sacks, Paul M. (1976) *The Donegal Mafia: An Irish Political Machine*. New Haven, CT: Yale University Press.

Sheehy, Seamus J. and Robert O'Connor (1985) *Economics of Irish Agriculture*. Dublin: Institute of Public Administration.

Smyth, William J. (1985) 'Explorations of Place', pp. 1–20 in Joseph Lee (ed.) *Ireland: Toward a Sense of Place*. Cork: Cork University Press.

Tenbruck, Friedrich H. (1961) 'Zur deutschen Rezeption der Rollentheorie', *Kölner Zeitschrift für Soziologie und Sozialpsychologie*, 13, pp. 1–40.

Tovey, H. (1985) 'Local Community: In Defence of a Much Criticised Concept', *Social Studies*, 8 (3/4), pp. 149–63.

Turkle, Sherry Roxanne (1975) 'Symbol and Festival in the French Student Uprising (May and June 1968)', pp. 68–100 in Sally Falk Moore and Barbara G. Myerhoff (eds.) *Symbol and Politics in Communal Ideology: Cases and Questions*. London: Cornell University Press.

Turner, Victor Witter (1974) *Dramas, Fields and Metaphors: Symbolic Action in Human Society*. London: Cornell University Press.

Wallis, Roy (1982) 'The Social Construction of Charisma', *Social Compass*, XXIX (1), pp. 25–39.

Weber, Max (1978) *Economy and Society* [Guenther Roth and Claus Witich (eds.)]. Berkeley: University of California Press.

Whitaker, T.K. (1978) *Economic Development: Twenty Years On – Lessons and Prospects*. Cork: Commerce and Economics Society.

Winkler, J.T. (1975) 'Law, State and the Economy: The Industry Act 1975 in Context', *British Journal of Law and Society*, 2 (2), pp. 103–28.

Worsley, Peter (1967) *The Trumpet Shall Sound: A Study of "Cargo" Cults in Melanesia*. Second Edition. London: Paladin.

4 Political culture, political independence and economic success in Ireland[1]

Brian Girvin

Originally published in *Irish Political Studies*, 12, 1997, pp. 48–77.

One of the key arguments promoted by nationalists in favour of independence has been the economic benefits which could be derived from national control of economic management (O'Brien, 1921). The Republic of Ireland has been independent for 75 years, yet as late as 1989 Lee (1989) concluded his study on an extremely pessimistic note in respect of the economy. More recently, economic performance has been much better, yet there has not been a comprehensive assessment of why these outcomes should differ to this degree (OECD, 1995). Ireland needs to be placed alongside other small states in Europe if its experience of independence and its economic performance are to be realistically evaluated (Kennedy, 1996). It is also important to disaggregate various sub-periods since independence to adjudicate on economic success. Four sub-periods have been identified for the purposes of this discussion. These are: first, 1922 to 1932 when the Irish Free State continued to be integrated economically into the United Kingdom; second, 1932 to c.1966 when Ireland adopted a policy of isolationism and protectionism; the third lasts from the early 1960s to 1982 and can be characterised as a transitional phase during which Ireland becomes fully reintegrated into the international economy and the European Community (EC); the fourth is currently underway and the main features of this period are successful economic management and self-sustained growth which is maximising benefits for the society.

Performance differs across all four sub-periods, but the most important features are the relative decline of the Irish economy and income in respect of most other European states between 1932 and 1966, the gradual but difficult reversal of this trend during the 1970s and the closing of the relativity gap within the European Union in the 1990s. The argument here is that economic explanations are not sufficient when assessing why Ireland declined when it did and why it recovered. The use of political culture provides a more comprehensive and nuanced means of appreciating the long-term (and non-economic) factors which led to the specific outcomes described. On this reading political independence is of considerable importance in reinforcing features within the political culture which obstructed change, especially after the introduction of protection in the 1930s. The slow response to external change can also be explained in terms of the dominance of certain features of the political culture into the 1970s, though by this stage the features are becoming increasingly residual. Consequently changes in the political culture since the 1970s may have altered the balance of the political culture in favour of a more dynamic and modernising framework. This it is suggested is a necessary condition of the economic success of the recent past (Girvin, 1996).

The use of political culture

The use of political culture as a concept for explaining human action has often been criticised for either being too general or too specific in its claims. The model may be so general that its applications to specific cases is impossible, or so specific that it can only be applied to one case (Lane and Ersson, 1994, pp. 113–17; Dogan and Kazancigil, 1994). Almond and Verba (1963) most famously operationalised the model of civic culture for general use, an attempt which has been defended and criticised ever since (Almond and Verba, 1980; Girvin, 1989a; Diamond, 1993). More recently, Welch (1993) has attempted to ground the model within a phenomenological context, while Woshinsky (1995) has adapted and expanded earlier approaches in the light of new studies. From a somewhat different standpoint, Inglehart (1990, pp. 3–65) insists that there is a need to reconceptualise the relationship between culture, economics and politics. This revival in the use of political culture is a clear challenge to other models of explanation within politics, such as rational choice, Marxism or post-modernism.

One of the strengths of a political culture model is that it is well placed to explain persistence and stability, though it is not always as successful in explaining change, certainly radical and disruptive change. The model outlined in Table 4.1 attempts to address this tension by identifying three levels at which political culture operates and suggests that there are different elements which operate at different levels.

This is a general model, suggesting that when applied it is necessary to be clear as to the level of analysis (Girvin, 1989a and 1997; Welch, 1993). It presupposes mass political involvement, though not the specific form of political authority

Table 4.1 Three levels of political culture

Level	*Macro*	*Meso*	*Micro*
Constitutive elements in each level	Hegemonic Values Norms Stable Organic Permanent (?) Rules of the game Absolute presuppositions	Institutional Consensual Evolutionary Strains Longstanding constitution, political system, legislative etc.	Routine Conflictual Dynamic Unstable (?) Immediate Party political Political action Individual behaviour

Source: adapted from Girvin (1989a), pp. 34–36.

(a political culture can exist within an authoritarian, totalitarian, militaristic or democratic system). The macro-level includes those elements which are long standing and which provide 'permanent' features of the political and social architecture. Within this level there are different points of emphasis. The static, organic and permanent elements within Table 4.1 reflect the long-established patterns within a culture and are usually normative in character. Those features characterised as hegemonic, values or as rules of the game reflect the need to specify what the attributes might be, but also to give the culture at this level some substance. Its hegemonic character emphasises the dominance of one set of values over another as worked out through the rules of the game. A value which is hegemonic in one culture may not have any influence in another. Permanent is used in a qualified fashion and does not imply that nothing ever changes. It is used in the sense that for practical purposes and short of radical upheaval, these features occupy the lives of successive generations in a political community and are independent of each generation as part of this membership. This level of analysis is essentially a form of collective system maintenance and it allows the political authority to be legitimised without regular recourse to repression.

Societies cannot function without these higher-order features and they are internalised by each generation. The most powerful value in contemporary societies is national identity. This gives collective meaning to the individual and to the society in general. National identity and nationalism have replaced or subordinated other forms of identity such as class, religion and language as the primary source of meaning within political cultures. National identity has the merit of being long standing, normally unquestioned, but is quickly defended if challenged. If, as Pye (1985, p. 20) argues, culture is persistent, the strongest political form it takes in the contemporary era is through nationalism. Woshinsky (1995, p. 93) notes that

> Nations generally remain true to their historical traditions. Once set in place, the cultural norms of a given society take hold and exert enormous impact on thought and behavior. Change can occur, or course, but short-term change will almost always occur within the confines of the traditional pattern. Thus, leaders do change frequently in places like Bolivia and Liberia. What doesn't change is the long-term pattern of violence and anarchy.

Nor does this analysis need to be restricted to Asia, Africa or Latin America; the same features identified here can be found in the developed liberal democratic states of Europe and North America.

Despite this the macro political level is not unchanging, but to secure stability within the culture it is necessary for the macro level to be long standing and system maintaining. The nature of change at this level is complex, but not absent. Two types of changes are possible. A dramatic break with the past may lead to a society reformulating its political culture fairly quickly. This is what seems to have happened to Germany after the defeat in the Second World War. At first a new set of institutions and political practices (meso and micro) were imposed on Germans, but in time these were internalised and integrated into the macro political culture. If as Goldhagen (1996) has argued anti-Semitism was one of the dominant features of the pre-war political culture, it is one which has subsequently been eradicated (Conradt, 1980). A less dramatic process can be identified in stable systems where change takes place at the lower levels over a long period of time, but which leads to significant changes in the self-image of the society. If these changes at the meso and micro level are gradual and consensual it is possible for the macro level to be altered to assimilate those changes. This is what has happened in Ireland over the past 20 years (Girvin, 1996 and 1997; Dowding and Kimber, 1983).

The system maintaining and ordering features of a political culture may be taken for granted by its members, and when this is so it is at its most cohesive and consensual. Critics of this approach (Pateman, 1980) reject this consensual aspect of political culture by highlighting arenas of conflict, dissent and indeed violence or repression. If, however, these latter engagements are located at the intermediate and routine levels of the political culture, it is possible to integrate these unstable aspects of political behaviour with the stable and long-standing features associated with the macro level. Thus a rational choice model for political behaviour may be quite appropriate for action at the micro level, an institutional model for the meso level, yet neither might apply to the influence of the macro level on the society as a whole. This model provides a means for integrating the long-term influence on politics with the short and medium term (Bartolini and Mair, 1990; Elster, 1989, pp. 13–51; Hibbs and Fassbender, 1981).

It is the macro level which emphasises uniqueness because cultural attributes are difficult to compare even among similar states. Within comparative research there is a growing recognition (Dogan and Kazancigil, 1994) that there are elements unique to individual states and that these can often account for the different behavioural patterns observed in research. The role of history may be far more important than realised. Dogan and Kazancigil (1994, p. 11) note that 'Two or several countries may have many features in common, but they are never identical, because the attributes are combined differently for each country'. These differences can be best explained by paying attention to the macro-political culture of a society, and to the features which make it unique. Harrison (1992) argues that the success or failure of individual economies in generating economic growth since 1945 can in large part be explained by recourse to cultural factors. For him the historic traditions of a society can reinforce, neutralise or weaken the conditions which bring about economic success.

Is there a cultural reason for success or failure?

One reason why writers are reluctant to use culture as a tool for analysis is that there is a danger that blame will be transferred to those who fail. If it is 'their fault', or it is 'in their genes', then nothing can be done (Kohn, 1995; Herrnstein and Murray, 1994; Goldhagen, 1996). This view has been advanced most seriously in the United States, but is at the heart of much nationalist thought (for example, Catholic and Protestant stereotyping in Northern Ireland). This is not the intention of this contribution, but to assess whether the constituent elements of a political culture have an effect on the economic outcome of specific societies. The observation that different states perform differently, while operating under similar conditions, requires an explanation. Regime type does not appear to play the main role in this: authoritarian, military and democratic states may have similar outcomes or no similarity at all (Rueschemeyer *et al*, 1992; World Bank, 1993). Even when states with similar regime types are compared, the outcome can be quite different as comparisons between Japan, the United States and India demonstrate (Yoshino, 1992; Harrison, 1992; Franklin, 1978). This is not simply a question of economic management, but of the cultural environment within which decisions about management are taken.

There is a growing recognition that culture affects the environment within which policy making takes place. This study takes for granted two assumptions central to the twentieth century: the demand for self-determination and the desire for economic development (Hobsbawm, 1994). However, it also recognises that political independence in itself does not necessarily promote economic development, and that the policy package endorsed or imposed in individual societies will have an important impact on the outcome (Tivey, 1981; Girvin, 1992). Political independence may have a positive, negative or neutral impact on economic development, but in itself this tells us relatively little about how the economy would have performed in the absence of political independence. As is evident from the new democracies in central and eastern Europe (and indeed in Africa) political independence or democracy do not guarantee success. A case might be made that while independence provides a basis for choice, the choices taken are dependent on the nature of the political culture. Within a society there will be features which will obstruct or facilitate economic development and the outcome will depend on the balance between them. Traditional features in a society will not necessarily impede development; it will depend on how traditions affect the policy-making process (Haselitz, 1961; Yoshino, 1992, pp. 9–38; Keating and Desmond, 1993). There is a causal relationship to be considered in this case. A specific political culture can adapt its traditions in such a way as to facilitate economic success, while another will adapt in such a way as to obstruct such an outcome.

Nor are the historical conditions which underwrite political culture static: a society is not condemned to permanent underdevelopment or decline simply because its ability to develop has been historically weak. Notwithstanding this, it would be mistaken to ignore the influence of the macro-political culture on the choices made by human agents, because these choices will determine the actual outcome. The relationship between choice and political culture is central to the political process and to the methods by which policy is formulated and executed. For example, all the following have been cited as reasons why one state or another experiences success, failure or decline: class relations, religion, nationalism, race or colonialism. It is only through the careful construction of the political culture and how it affects the society's choices that it is possible to evaluate the causal relationship between political culture in its general sense and its applicability in any individual case.

The Irish case: long-term failure, or intermittent decline?

The Irish Republic provides a useful case study for the relationship between political culture and the economy. It has been independent since 1922, it has achieved long-term democratic stability and it has experimented with a number of different economic policies over time. Additionally, it has been a member of the European Community (now the European Union) since 1973 and shares with other members a commitment to European values (Coakley, 1993; Ashford and Timms, 1992). In these circumstances, Ireland might provide a model for the newly emergent democracies in Europe, or for secessionist nationalists in Scotland, Quebec or the Basque region in Spain. Its recent success has attracted some attention, but its long-term patterns have not been such as to offer a model for other small states. It is one of the puzzles about Ireland that it has had at best an indifferent economic experience since independence, despite many positive political and economic attributes. This has led Lee (1989, p. 521) to conclude that

> It is difficult to avoid the conclusion that Irish economic performance has been the least impressive in western Europe, perhaps in all Europe, in the twentieth century.

The nationalist elite which came to power when the Irish Free State was established in 1922, had been committed to economic nationalism as a means of achieving development (Garvin, 1987). However, there was no necessary connection between this view and the assertion that independence would bring significant changes to the independent economy. If Ireland had not realised its economic potential within the United Kingdom, would it be able to do so as an independent state? The relative economic success or failure of independent Ireland may have wider relevance. With the end of empire and colonialism, the normal unit of political organisation has become the independent state and many of these new, and often small, states believe that political independence can enhance the prospects for growth and development (Mjøset, 1992, pp. 35–42).

Was Ireland, in fact, a poor and underdeveloped economy prior to political independence? Irish nationalists certainly believed this to be the case (O'Brien, 1921; O'Riordan, 1906). However, Cullen (1968) and Meenan (1970) challenged this historical relationship between Britain and Ireland and the causal connection between independence and economic development. The figures tell a complex story. Irish Gross Domestic Product (GDP) per capita in 1913, depending on the assumptions, was between 55 and 62 per cent of the United Kingdom figure. On this measure Ireland was a relatively poor region of the United Kingdom (Kennedy *et al*, 1988, p. 14). However, if the comparison is with other European economies, the outcome is more positive. Bairoch (1981, p. 10) places Ireland close to the European average in 1913, as do Kennedy *et al* (1988). Ó Gráda (1994, p. 380) adopts a more cautious approach, but his data confirm the view that Ireland was not an especially poor country before the First World War.[2]

Ireland may have been a relatively poor region of the richest state in the world, but in a European context its performance and income compare favourably.

These data highlight the limitations of drawing comparisons between Ireland, the United Kingdom and, perhaps also, with Northern Ireland. Ireland was an agrarian region of the United Kingdom and, though part of the British state, its economic development was in many respects quite different to that of the industrialising areas of Britain. As a consequence Ireland, before and after independence, can be more adequately compared to those states in Europe which, though not poor, had not developed a strong industrial dynamic (Mjøset, 1992).[3] Though Ireland compares favourably with many European states in 1913, the performance of the economy since then can be characterised as, at best, poor. Independent Ireland does quite badly when compared with levels of income, growth rates or labour force participation in other parts of Europe. From a position which can be considered average in 1914, Ireland falls almost to the bottom of the European league table by 1988, whether measured in respect of the United Kingdom or the European Community (Bairoch, 1981, p. 10; Kennedy *et al*, 1988, pp. 12–21; Kennedy, 1992, pp. 7–12). The agricultural nature of Ireland in itself does not account for poor performance: after all in 1913 four out of the eight richest states were agricultural (Bairoch, 1981, p. 10), and Denmark was to maintain its high income status throughout the inter-war period while remaining an agricultural economy (Sørensen, 1993, pp. 88–92). Complementing Lee's approach, Mjøset (1992, pp. 29–42 and 237–53) sought to identify forces within Ireland which contributed to this outcome. The historical and comparative framework is enriched by his suggestion that in a number of small European states 'a functioning system of innovation' was in place at the end of the nineteenth century, but not in Ireland.

The assumption contained in Lee's study is that independence *should* have led to better economic performance. This was a long-standing view in nationalist politics, and continues to influence the thinking of policy makers, politicians, economists as well as the general public in most states. Central to this is the view that the state can make a difference to outcome and that economic policy is best formulated on the assumption that the economy is independent (O'Brien, 1921; O'Malley, 1981, pp. 38–40). However, the question of sovereignty and economic performance is not without ambiguity. The possibility for independent action by small states can be quite limited, especially if they are in close proximity to a large and powerful state with different interests (Seers, 1983, pp. 55–90). A state can acquire and sustain its sovereignty if this is taken to mean 'the ability of a nation to act on its own rather than under the coercion of other nations'. Ireland acquired this status in 1922, and has maintained it ever since. However, sovereignty should not be confused with 'autonomy', which is the belief that a nation can take 'unilateral action' to achieve its objectives. A distinction has to be drawn between non-interference by one state in the affairs of another and the insistence by a state that it is autonomous and can do what it wants (Bradley, 1990, p. 128). The connection between achieving sovereignty, having it recognised by other nations and economic success is not a given, but a political objective which may or may not be reached in the specific historic circumstances. Additionally, weak economic performance is not necessarily connected to a failure of sovereignty. In the Irish case loyalty to the state and to its institutions has remained high since independence, and shows levels of approval similar to those found in states with more successful economies (Ashford and Timms, 1992, pp. 86–107; Martinotti and Stefanizzi, 1995). To adapt Hirschman (1970), 'loyalty' has been the primary attribute of Irish behaviour, though 'exit' has been quite a strong pattern, while there has been relatively little 'voice'.

The fact remains, however, that since independence Ireland has experienced high levels of unemployment, continuing under-employment and persistent emigration. It seems that political independence had little or no impact on economic performance. Despite the introduction of quite different policy packages at different times, the effect of such seems quite limited. In 1944 the Taoiseach's economic adviser noted in a comment on agriculture, that

> Evidently, there are some fundamental forces at work which render agriculture so inelastic to both price, legislative and educational influences.[4]

Given the contribution of the agricultural sector to the Irish economy this conclusion had serious implications, but it might have been applied to the economy generally at the time. Despite the political revolution which Ireland experienced between 1916 and 1922, the Civil War and subsequent changes in government, the economy on this reading remained largely impervious to governmental influence (Girvin, 1989, pp. 131–68). This raises the possibility that the quality of economic management itself might not be the crucial factor in economic success. If existing structures inhibit new policies, the cost of implementing them could be so high as to be impractical. To blame civil servants (Girvin, 1989) in these circumstances may therefore be quite wide of the mark.

Lee's pessimistic view of performance can be endorsed with some qualifications. It is one which is now shared by many analysts, though there are different points of emphasis. One challenge to Lee focuses on the adequacy of the data used to establish the pre-war ratios and the subsequent comparative decline. If the 1913 figure is too high, then performance can be shown to be better than hitherto thought. Lee's data are derived from Cullen and Smout's (1977) figures, and these have been questioned by Johnson (1991) and Ó Gráda (1994) among others. However, Cullen (1994) has more recently reiterated his original estimate, while Bielenberg and O'Mahony (1994), providing the most recent and comprehensive analysis of data, suggest that a figure higher than Cullen's original is in order. Bielenberg and O'Mahony provide an estimate for Irish Gross National Product (GNP) in 1907 which places Irish per capita GNP at approximately 65 per cent of the British figure. Their figure, arrived at by taking a cautious and conservative approach to the data, place Ireland even higher on the European league table than Ó Gráda's recent data suggest. In comparative context, the Bielenberg and O'Mahony data place Ireland on a par with Germany and France, well ahead of Norway, Italy, and Sweden and closer than hitherto thought to Denmark and the Netherlands. The most recent refinement of these data by Bielenberg and O'Mahony (1995) confirms the relatively affluent nature of pre-independence Ireland, including that region which became independent.[5]

The secular trend between 1913 and 1988 is poor, and over the same time comparative performance is weak. However, this may not be the case for every period, but might be restricted to certain sub-periods. Ireland was neither a late starter in 1913, nor was it a peripheral economy. Furthermore, Mjøset (1992, pp. 35 and 140–3) suggests that even as late as 1945 Ireland did not lag that far behind the states he compares Ireland with. This seems to contradict his earlier view that the creation of a national system of innovation was already underway by the end of the nineteenth century in the states analysed, giving them their subsequent advantage over Ireland. If this is the case then the first half of the twentieth century should provide evidence for Ireland lagging behind the rest of Europe. For the most part the evidence is inconclusive. Ireland certainly grew somewhat slower than the west European average of 1.0 per cent. Ireland's 0.7 per cent was lower than this, only slightly behind the United Kingdom at 0.8 per cent, but grew a lot faster than Austria. The comparison with Austria is a useful one, because it shows that an economy which did not seem to have a national system of innovation during the inter-war period could develop one subsequently and achieve considerable success during the 1950s.

The first decade after independence was quite a successful one for the Irish Free State. Although a dismal picture is sometimes painted of the decade, this is no longer justifiable. It is assumed that the state could have been more active than it actually was: promoting industrialisation, pursuing an expansionary fiscal policy and (perhaps) an independent monetary policy. Most policy options were carefully evaluated by the new government after the receipt of the reports of independent committees and found wanting. Critics assumed that radical policies could have been introduced without significant costs, yet were usually unable to demonstrate this. For most of the 1920s there was no significant body of public opinion in favour of these changes. It is questionable if the society actually wanted industrialisation or if it was prepared to pay for it (Fiscal Inquiry Committeee, 1923; Girvin, 1989, pp. 11–46; Daly, 1992, pp. 13–36). In this context the criticism of the Department of Finance may be misguided (Fanning, 1978; Lee, 1989). That Department was not imposing a policy on government, but reflecting the predominant current within government and society. It made economic sense to concentrate on agricultural exports during the 1920s; cattle exports rose in value by 12 per cent between 1925 and 1930, and national income may have increased by around 11 per cent between 1926 and 1931 (Kiernan, 1933; Duncan, 1939–40; Ó Gráda, 1994, pp. 389–90). The comparison with the Netherlands and Denmark is instructive here for they were also heavily dependent on agricultural exports to the United Kingdom, yet responded quite well to changing circumstances. Furthermore, if the period up to 1930 can be characterised as successful in economic terms, this has implications for the nature and quality of economic management before as well as after 1932.

Economic continuity reinforced the patterns of economic behaviour which had been established by 1914. It is questionable whether an alternative in the 1920s could have achieved a more optimal outcome. Critics then and now compared what existed with what might exist in an ideal world, and often with the benefit of Keynesian hindsight. Free Trade with the United Kingdom during the 1920s probably enhanced Irish economic performance and almost certainly did not affect it in a detrimental fashion. Exports increased, incomes improved and the government intervened selectively in the economy, but within the constraints established by a cautious fiscal policy and the monetary union with the United Kingdom. In this, Irish governments did not depart radically from the policies adopted by most other states in Europe or North America (Girvin, 1994, pp. 59–74). This is not to conclude that economic policy and performance was optimal at every level. Efficiency in agriculture did not significantly improve, nor did strong agro-industrial linkages emerge. The evidence we have suggests that the entre-preneurial spirit in industry was weak. Furthermore, Ireland concentrated more of its resources on agriculture and less on industry than most other states in Europe. Moreover, the gap in real GNP per capita between Ireland and other European states is beginning to widen by 1929, but despite this the Irish Free State remained confident about its overall performance by this date (Ó Gráda, 1994, pp. 391 and 435–6; Clark, 1940, p. 41). The political culture reinforced these trends by contributing to the stability of the new state. The most important expression of this was the failure of the republican opposition to maintain its anti-system position in respect of the state and its institutions (Prager, 1986; Kissane, 1995). The maintenance of pre-independence economic structures and trends reinforced this stability.

If it is possible to offer a positive, if qualified, approval for the 1920s, the period after 1932 is less conclusive. The world depression, a change in government and an economic war with the United Kingdom provided the environment for a radical change in policy. The Fianna Fáil Government introduced a comprehensive policy of industrial protection, intervened actively to change the direction of agricultural production and sustained a relatively expansionary fiscal policy. One consequence of this policy was to weaken the most efficient sector of the agrarian economy by depriving it of the British market between 1933 and 1937. One estimate suggests that national income could have been 25 per cent higher in 1939 if the economic war had not taken place. This may be exaggerated, but the slump in farmers' income and the relative stagnancy in national income is certainly true (Meenan, 1967), while income in the Irish Free State rose by around two per cent between 1931 and 1938 (Johnson, 1985, pp. 39–40). A more positive evaluation is also possible in the context of a world depression. Irish unemployment was low by international standards, a significant number of new jobs were generated by industrial expansion and the evidence suggests that the welfare provisions introduced by Fianna Fáil involved a degree of redistribution (Dunphy, 1995). However, it should be noted that the 'economic war' was only economic in form. The substance of this conflict was political and reflected de Valera's belief that this was part of the process of de-anglicising Ireland and republicanising the society (Coogan, 1993, pp. 486–520).

Some reservations have been noted concerning the real number of jobs generated as a consequence of protection and import substitution (FitzGerald, 1959; Johnson, 1985, pp. 27–30). The balance of judgement now rests on the higher figures for job creation, notwithstanding some doubts concerning the data from which the conclusions have been drawn (Daly, 1992, pp. 75–81; Ó Gráda, 1994, pp. 397–407). Despite this, protection did not develop a system of national innovation, although Seán Lemass certainly hoped to do so. The main reason for introducing the policy was not to promote national innovation, but reflected the ideological disposition of the ruling party. Economic nationalism, the 1937 constitution, the emphasis on agrarian self sufficiency all reinforced the isolation of Ireland by the end of the 1930s. This decade disrupted patterns which had been in place for nearly a century; linkages with the United Kingdom were damaged which were not to be repaired until the 1960s. The state and the society now emphasised the most traditional and conservative elements of the political culture and institutionalised most of them within the constitution, the education system and the civil service (Girvin, 1996). It is questionable if the change in economic policy during the 1930s was in fact based on a developmental strategy, but even if it was the method of doing so actually weakened the economy by the 1940s.

By 1939, outside the Department of Industry and Commerce, there was no force in Irish society prepared to deepen industrialisation beyond import substitution. Nor did war-time experience provide one, as was the case with a number of other states. The main problem with protection may not have been its introduction in the 1930s, but its continuation after 1945 (Ó Gráda, 1994, pp. 411 and 433). Ó Gráda further suggests that protection involved an intergenerational trade off between those who acquired employment during its expansionary phase and those who lost it three decades later (Girvin, 1989, pp. 88–130; Mjøset, 1992, pp. 262–7). This outcome was due to the suspicion concerning change which had become widespread by the end of the 1930s, and to the way in which political and social institutions frustrated change during the 1940s (Girvin, 1989, pp. 131–68).

The real challenge to the independent Irish economy occurs after the first phase of import substitution ends in 1938. The Second World War and post-war recovery disguised this challenge, but by the 1950s some of the difficulties had become apparent. Ireland continued to maintain one of the largest agricultural labour forces and the smallest industrial labour force in Europe. It is between 1940 and 1960 that Ireland becomes peripheral within Europe. During that time most other economies increased the relative distance between themselves and Ireland. By 1960 Ireland had more in common with peripheral Europe than with northern and northwest Europe, with whom it would previously have been appropriate to compare it with (Mjøset, 1992, pp. 113–14; Kennedy, 1992, pp. 5–15; Peillon, 1994). The most obvious contrast between Ireland and the smaller industrialising states of Europe was the rapid expansion of the latter, their involvement in the global economy and the enhancement of their employment prospects and income. Throughout the late 1940s and the 1950s, Irish policy makers and public opinion generally resisted these trends (Girvin, 1995).

The constraints on change

In particular, between 1950 and 1960, Ireland experienced what was probably its worst decade since the Famine; characterised by declining income, rising unemployment and accelerating emigration. A number of explanations can be given for this. The first is the continuing commitment to autarchy, though this was now an essentially passive process rather than active as in the 1930s. Continuing dependence on the British market for exports contributed to slow growth, given the relatively low levels of growth in the United Kingdom. More important was the continuing importance placed on agriculture as the main instrument of economic growth (Girvin, 1989, pp. 190–201). Moreover, until 1960 successive Irish governments resisted free trade and the economic liberalisation being promoted by the General Agreement on Tariffs and Trade (GATT) and the Organisation for European Economic Co-operation (OEEC). In contrast, Denmark and the Netherlands, also heavily dependent on agriculture, began to shift their policy priorities from agriculture to industry in order to share in the benefits of an expanding world economy (Griffiths, 1990; Sørensen, 1993, pp. 94–116; Griffiths and Girvin, 1995; Olesen, 1995). In comparison with most other 'small' states in western Europe Irish economic management between 1945 and the early 1960s did not maximise the state's economic opportunities.

Ireland remained dependent on agriculture for employment and exports much longer and to a greater degree than was to be the case with these other states. Consequently, when Irish agriculture collapsed during the 1950s and the flight from the land accelerated to crisis proportions, the Irish experience proved to be closer to that of the Italian Mezzogiorno than to the experience of the now industrialising states in northern Europe (Del Monte and Giannola, 1979; Camagni, 1991). It is, however, only of limited value to compare Ireland to Mezzogiorno, as the latter is one region within an existing state. Although Ireland was closely linked to the United Kingdom, it was not simply a region in political terms. It was fully independent and had the freedom to make whatever policy decisions it considered appropriate, that it did not do so is the crucial factor. Yet this is only a partial explanation. Policy making throughout the 1940s and 1950s was constrained by a set of assumptions which valued a society which was traditional in structure, morally repressive in character, conformist in intention and protectionist in economic matters. A high premium continued to be placed on continuity and stability, one reinforced by both public opinion and the political culture (Biever, 1976; Girvin, 1997). Irish policy makers chose, for the most part, to reinforce traditional policies rather than undertake new or innovative approaches. Other independent states chose to behave differently and frequently benefited from the risks taken (Olesen, 1995; Griffiths, 1990).

If the crisis of the 1950s prompted a change in policy and a renewed commitment to free trade and economic integration, this in itself did not secure economic success for Ireland (O'Malley, 1989, pp. 89–91). In secular terms the Irish economy grew at its fastest rate since independence between 1960 and 1973, but even at this it lagged behind growth rates elsewhere in Europe, and especially those in peripheral Europe (Mjøset, 1992, p. 35; Ó Gráda and Ó Rourke, 1994, p. 6). The tendency for Ireland to diverge from European norms accelerated between 1940 and 1960, yet subsequent policy changes and considerable growth did not assure convergence with Europe. In particular membership of the European Community did not guarantee convergence. Indeed, as Boltho (1985) noted, the regional variation within the European Community is greater than that within the United States. This can be attributed to the existence of a federal state in the United States and competing jurisdictions within the EC. It also highlights the different outcomes across cultures in Europe, but it illustrates that political independence, even with integration, does not bring about convergence. Irish GDP per capita as a percentage of the European Community has grown from 59 per cent to 69 per cent between 1973 and 1990. However, when measured in terms of Gross National Disposable Income the increase was much smaller; from 61 to 66 per cent. The most dramatic shift occurs when the measurement is in terms of GDP per worker which shows an increase from 69 per cent to 89 per cent over the same time span (NESC, 1989, p. 117). One conclusion to be drawn from these data is that the Irish economy suffered an appreciable relative decline between 1940 and 1960 and after a period of subsequent growth has returned to its relative position in respect of Europe by the end of the 1980s (Kennedy, 1995, pp. 23–30; Ó Gráda and Ó Rourke, 1994, pp. 26–7). Could these patterns have been achieved earlier and the crisis of the 1950s avoided? It was probably possible in economic terms to do so, but if the constraints in the political culture are taken into consideration the practical obstacles were probably too high.

Between 1960 and the early 1990s the Irish economy has changed significantly, ceasing to be an agricultural economy and becoming 'a somewhat industrial society' (Kennedy, 1989, pp. 55–6). The non-agricultural labour force expanded rapidly, urbanisation increased and industrialisation became the main dynamic for growth (Breen *et al*, 1990; Goldthorpe and Whelan, 1992). Despite these changes, the Irish economy continued to confront serious difficulties. Economic performance during the 1980s was especially poor when contrasted with the previous 20 years. Unemployment soared to one of the highest levels within the European Community, while emigration, legal and illegal, returned to very high levels (NESC, 1991, pp. 156–60; Jacobsen, 1994, pp. 141–58).

Since 1987, Irish manufacturing output and exports, fiscal policy and its international credit rating suggest that economic policy has achieved some level of success when compared to the more recent past. Ireland's current account deficit between 1979 and 1981 as a percentage of GDP stood at 10 per cent, a figure considered unsustainable; by 1994 the provisional estimates suggest a current account surplus of 7.9 per cent placing Ireland at the top of the Organisation for Economic Co-operation and Development (OECD) for this measurement. Figures for the period 1970–1989 show that Irish manufacturing output had been second only to Japan and that, over time, the Irish position relative to Japan has improved. While employment creation has not been as successful, Ireland has done better on this measure than most other European states (NESC, 1992, pp. 31–44 and 109–13). Although the reliability of some of these data may be questioned (especially with reference to transfer pricing) the relative strength of the Irish economy should not be underestimated, even if it is recognised that a number of underlying difficulties remain. This positive performance has continued throughout the 1990s. The poor performance between 1977 and 1987 can be attributed to the second oil crisis and bad judgement in terms of policy making. If the reason for weakness was not structural, then the pessimistic view promoted by Lee may have been based on short-term factors. The OECD (1995, pp. 100–7) concluded that Ireland's macro-economic policy was proving successful in narrowing the gap between it and the other OECD states.

Assessing political culture and economic development

It is one thing to argue, as I have just done, that poor policy making and cyclical trends account for the specific outcome for a particular sub-period, it is another to claim that all difficulties can be explained in these terms. The history of the Irish economy in the twentieth century is not one of unmitigated disaster, as Lee claims, but of qualified success during the first half of the century, followed by decline, collapse and real failure during the 1950s. This, in turn, led to a crisis of confidence in the state and the transformation of policy which generated the growth patterns of the 1960s. The difficulties encountered during the 1980s were of a qualitatively different kind to those of the 1950s. This latter decade marked the end of the pre-industrial and traditional character of the society and economy. The crisis reflected the difficulties Ireland experienced in making the transition from one type of economic system to another. In comparative terms, Denmark also experienced some difficulties with its transition, but it was better prepared for that shift in policy and the outcome was less traumatic and more beneficial. The downturn of the 1980s was cyclical and reflected the problems associated with transition and integration. These difficulties are not insurmountable, though as Mjøset points out, a solution may not be easily secured. The heavy dependence on Foreign Direct Investment for employment and exports, the nature of transfer pricing and the weakness of backward and forward linkages has come in for considerable criticism since the 1980s. This has led to a re-evaluation of industrial policy and a renewed interest and emphasis on domestic industry, as well as a search for 'indigenous' factors to generate further growth in the economy (NESC, 1982; O'Malley, 1992, pp. 43–52).

If there is a renewed emphasis on the domestic, this does not entail that Ireland is pursuing a more 'nationalistic' economic policy. There is, however, a recognition that decisions taken in Ireland, in the context of the European Union, GATT and free trade, can make a difference to the outcome. While this limits the extent of unilateral action, it still provides an area for domestic policy making (Bradley, 1990, pp. 138–43). If this makes a difference, is it possible to make an overall assessment of the impact of independence on the Irish economy and its performance? Mjøset believes that the existence of 'autocentric' development and a 'national system of innovation' are the features which distinguish the successful states he surveys from Ireland. The unstated assumption here, and in Lee, is that political independence is an important contributory variable in explaining success. It implies, at least, that if Irish governments and entrepreneurs had made different decisions during the 1940s and 1950s, then Ireland too could have generated a 'national system of innovation'. That this was not the case reinforces the claim that the causal relationship between political independence and economic development is consequently fairly weak. What it implies is that while political independence provides the opportunity for improving economic performance, it does not guarantee it.

An alternative way of approaching this question is to ask whether independence made any difference to the Irish economy. On a number of grounds the economy might well have performed more successfully if it had remained in the United Kingdom. Independence can be justified without hesitation on political grounds, but the economic rationale for independence is weaker. Successive Irish governments sought to prove that Ireland performed better than Northern Ireland, yet for the most part the southern economy came out of the comparison quite badly (Johnson, 1985, pp. 36–43; Kennedy, 1989, pp. 6–13). Economic arguments to justify independence are nearly always subordinate to arguments based on identity, culture or emotion. Poor economic performance in itself will not lead to demands for independence, in the same way that appalling economic performance under an independent government does not lead to demands for reintegration into the former state (Girvin, 1992).

Among the arguments for Ireland remaining within the United Kingdom the following might be considered. The United Kingdom economy grew faster than that of independent Ireland between 1913 and 1960, and it is possible that if Ireland had remained an economic region of the United Kingdom it would have benefited from this. More directly, Ireland would have benefited from open access to the British market for cattle and agricultural products, whereas independent Ireland, especially between 1932 and 1966, used considerable resources to protect its position. Trading as part of a larger economic unit might have generated pressures for agriculture to diversify further and after the Second World War to develop more substantial agro-business. In addition, Irish agriculture would have benefited from the protection available in the United Kingdom after 1931 and from the 1947 Agricultural Act. The evidence from Northern Ireland suggests that agriculture was stimulated by this new environment. As a relatively poor region of the United Kingdom, southern Ireland would have benefited from the extension of the welfare state after 1945. Whether the absence of partition would have contributed to economic growth is debatable, as it is clear that the two parts of the island had very little in common economically. Large open markets provide opportunities for innovation and a discipline for producers, whereas closed and protected markets reduce competition, innovation and strengthen distributional coalitions (Olson, 1982).

Any possible benefits have to be balanced against other factors. It is likely that sectarian politics would have remained important throughout the island. Emigration would have continued, but emigration was lower during the 1920s, when the Irish economy was fully integrated into the United Kingdom, than during the nationalist phase of development between 1932 and 1966. In purely economic terms, it is likely that Ireland would have done just as well by remaining within the United Kingdom, and certainly no worse, as it was to do as an independent state.[6] This does not mean that Ireland *should* have remained in the United Kingdom, but it does draw attention to the essentially weak link between political independence and economic development in this case. The Irish experience, though similar in some respects, is not the same as the sub-state regions of Europe. The existence of the Irish state offers policy makers more flexibility and choice in the context of policy formation. Although in some respects (until c.1966) Ireland did remain an agricultural region of the United Kingdom, it was not condemned to be so indefinitely. The experience of protection, the decision to join the European Community and the policy of industrialisation demonstrated a capacity for autonomous decision making by a region with political independence. Political independence does not assure successful policy making. Irish economic performance was at its worst when policy was most nationalistic, whereas under free trade the economy has consistently performed better. It is impossible to predict outcomes, but within the restrictions imposed by size and location independence offers more policy choices than would be available to a region within a state.

Political culture and economic change

The other factor which requires consideration is whether the political culture prevented the changes which might have advanced a more dynamic development after 1945. The evidence cited here suggests that the nature of the political culture inhibited change in the Irish case. Complacency after the Second World War and the failure of more innovative approaches prolonged the commitment to protection. Moreover, the strength of agrarian pressure groups and political fragmentation also contributed to policy paralysis. Thompson (1995, pp. 6–7) argues that the economic success of some states in Pacific Asia is closely related to the length of time economic nationalist policies were in place. In Ireland protection lasted 30 years and this weakened the propensity to export and to participate in the global economy. The political culture contributed to this outcome to the extent that an institutional framework was in place between 1937 and 1957 which inhibited changes in a more open direction. Neutrality during and after the Second World War may also have enhanced the extent of Irish isolation from Europe, as did the moral uniformism which prevailed during the 1940s and 1950s (Inglis, 1987). But there was also a strong cultural element to this. The political culture of Irish nationalism affected not only the economy, but foreign policy and relations with Northern Ireland. The Catholic 'moral monopoly' (Inglis, 1987) had an important impact on social life, on education and on health policy. Moreover, as Ireland became more isolationist these features were enhanced rather than diminished.

To explain success is quite another matter. These features are frequently intangible and more difficult to evaluate. In particular, the use of culture to explain differences between societies is not always treated seriously by economists. Ó Gráda and Ó Rourke (1994, p. 45), though not adopting a cultural model, suggest that powerful factors existed within Irish society which help to explain its poor performance after 1945. These include the dominance of agriculture, rent seeking in industrial relations, firm size and the quality of investment decisions. It is here that Lee's analysis is important, for he asserts (1989, p. 528) that, 'it is at the human level that the solution to the mystery of the mediocrity of Irish socio-economic performance seems to lie'. Furthermore (pp. 390–6) the dominance of a 'possessor' mentality contributed to this outcome, while recommending the careful analysis of Irish character, identity, institutions and intellect to explain performance. The main implication is that if one or all of these features functioned differently, or if they were modified in some way, then the balance would be redrawn in favour of those promoting growth and entrepreneurship; what Lee characterises as the performer ethos. In a tantalisingly brief comment, Lee asks (pp. 522–3) whether the Irish actually wanted economic growth, but does not make the connection between this behavioural dimension and the concepts he selects for analysis.

This suggests an explanation based on political culture; that some behavioural patterns in the society prevented it from maximising the opportunities available. However, Lee does not pursue this line of analysis and indeed offers the view that the Irish are as materialist as any one else, as if this demonstrated an Irish commitment to economic growth. Acquisitiveness, or placing a high value on material possession, is not synonymous with the dynamic of capitalist accumulation and expansion central to the industrial system; nor does it reinforce the acceptance of technological change which again appears to be a central characteristic of the market economy. What Lee describes as materialism is closer to the behaviour exhibited by many peasant, pre-modern or traditional societies. Materialist behaviour according to Lee includes clientelism, population control to enhance income, strong social and patriarchal control within marriage and the family (see also, Hannan, 1979; Hannan and Commins, 1992; Inglis, 1987, pp. 63–94 and 187–214). These behavioural patterns are normally associated with pre-industrial societies whose values are often in conflict with the market and industrialism (Shanin, 1971). Such characteristics are likely to obstruct industrial development rather than promote it. If it is assumed that the characteristics required for a successful agricultural economy are different to those which promote industrialisation, then if the former are dominant it is likely that the latter will be obstructed (Gellner, 1988). This means that the relative weakness of the Irish economy can be explained for the most part in the unwillingness of sections of the community and society to pay the price associated with industrial change until a crisis hit the economy during the late 1950s, even then the changes were cautious and limited in impact. If this is contrasted with Denmark, where change was also painful, another factor can be highlighted. In Denmark (Sørensen, 1993; Mjøset, 1992) the role of the Social Democratic Party was crucial during the 1950s in promoting the case for rapid expansion of industry in the light of agricultural decline; similarly in the case of the Netherlands (Gladdish, 1991, pp. 33–49) the

Labour Party and the Catholic Party agreed on the need for industrialisation. In contrast, there was no policy or political commitment in Ireland to industrialise and integrate until after the crisis of the late 1950s. This reluctance separates Ireland from most other small states in Europe at the time (Mjøset, 1992; Katzenstein, 1984).

If Lee had developed an explicit cultural argument, he might have explained some of the structural factors which obstructed Irish growth during the 1950s. Harrison (1992, pp. 1–23) has suggested that certain forms of behaviour, values and mentalities can contribute to economic success, whereas others impede it. One study of the Irish economy (Keating and Desmond, 1993, pp. 110–32) has suggested that its poor performance can be attributed to the influence of the Catholic Church, the importance of rural social values and a reluctance to accept the consequences of the modern industrial economy and its values. The persistence of pre-industrial (and often anti-industrial) cultural attributes during the period of industrialisation often has a negative impact on economic success (Hannan and Commins, 1992; Inglis, 1987). Lee, however, is reluctant to discuss this possibility, largely because he believes that the major existing cultural forms, the Catholic Church, the Irish language, nationalism and the agrarian economy, are either neutral in their effect or have a positive contribution to make. In his unwillingness to confront the possibility that the political culture itself is an impediment to achieving the growth levels he desires, he falls back on a lack of intellectual quality without recognising that intellectuals are often hostile to the market and capitalism as well. In reality Lee describes some of the superficial problems facing the Irish economy, but he fails ultimately to identify those features which, if cultivated, would actually have contributed to a smoother transition between 1940 and 1960. An alternative view, and the one suggested by this analysis, is that political culture is crucial to the success or failure of an economy, especially when facing change and the need to innovate. Some factors will have a positive impact, while others may be neutral or negative, what is required is an analysis which distinguishes between the various elements to explain why certain behavioural traits are dominant at this time. At its most general it means that some states will be more open to change than others. The lack of intellectual quality in Ireland cannot be separated from the failure of the political culture to reinforce the innovative elements in Irish society in the four decades after independence. The political culture rewarded certain traits with status and income, but the cost of this was conformity, an acceptance of rural traditionalism and intellectual uniformity. Nor did these characteristics disappear during the 1960s, they remained in a dominant position until the 1980s, though by this date they were contested by a significant section of the society (Girvin, 1996 and 1997).

Conclusion

There is consequently a strong case to be made that aspects of the culture were responsible for weak economic performance. Political and economic isolation in the 1940s and 1950s meant that Irish industry and agriculture were ill equipped to meet the challenge of free trade in the 1960s (Committee on Industrial Progress, 1973; Girvin, 1989, pp. 202–11). The weakness of Irish industry was such that the government turned to Foreign Direct Investment to secure the investment and technology for the expansion of the economy. The success of the Foreign sector further weakened both the effectiveness and influence of Irish business because of that failure (Hirschman, 1968). Nor should the role of the Church be ignored. Intellectually it remains one of the main critics of capitalism and the inequities of the market. In a society with high religious participation rates and piety, its influence should not be underestimated. Furthermore, the high status traditionally associated with the ministry prompted many to join the Church who might have used their talents elsewhere. Joining the Church can also be seen as a form of rent-seeking in a society with a limited amount of land and opportunity; this feature can also be seen in the civil service, many skilled occupations and in the professions (Olson, 1982). The attempt to secure a rent on educational investment is a factor which continues to influence decisions especially in rural areas.

Furthermore agriculture remains heavily dependent on subsidies from the European Union for survival and this inhibits more adventurous investment strategies. In addition the percentage of land holders, as distinct from farmers, remains quite high in comparative terms and this may prove an obstacle to the modernisation of opinion on questions related to industrialisation and expansion (Keating and Desmond, 1993, pp. 198–230; Mjøset, 1992, pp. 282–91; O'Toole, 1995). It is also no accident that the Beef Tribunal found that major companies in the agricultural sector were not, as claimed, innovative entrepreneurs in export markets. The picture which emerges is of collusion between companies and government under the pretence of national interest to maintain the dominance in certain, unstable, markets of these companies. These companies are risk averse and owe their position to their relationship to political parties, especially Fianna Fáil (O'Toole, 1995). This might be applied more generally. There is some evidence to suggest that Irish public opinion endorses a strong interventionist role for the state in economic matters; a positive view is taken to the proposition that the government has a responsibility to provide employment, control prices and to aid industrial growth (Jowell *et al*, 1993, p. 83). The continuance of traditional beliefs into the modernising process should not be discounted, though the impact of them has to be carefully assessed and documented (Whelan, 1994).

It is not the purpose of this argument to suggest that the behaviour of Irish farmers or the business community was inappropriate in terms of their own self-interest or self-image. However, if one of the objectives of a society is to generate levels of economic growth which would maintain Irish income at levels comparable to those of other similar European states, then not only did economic management fail to maintain this between 1930 and the 1970s but the self-interest of these economic groups ran counter to the national interest. Short-term defence of existing priorities and arrangements, especially in rural Ireland, was legitimised by the political culture and reflected in government policy until the 1970s. Consideration should therefore be given to the view that certain behavioural features of modern Irish society impeded economic development. However, as suggested above, most of these constraints may now be residual, in that they are products of a pre-industrial society and associated with more marginal sectors of the economy; sectors now in decay. Olson's view (1982, pp. 36–71) that long-term stability will enhance the influence of distributional coalitions and affect the pace of change and the introduction of new technologies may have some merit in Irish circumstances. The state and economy remain very stable, and interest groups are very powerful, especially those organised in agriculture. Such stability could prevent change when it is required, as it did until the 1970s. In contrast, the corporatist arrangements which have been in place since 1987, and which reinforce a policy of low inflation, low to medium wage increases, a strong currency, high investment and employment increase, have enhanced stability to which can be attributed the strong growth in the economy and living standards (OECD, 1995). The patterns established at the time of independence have been broken and new forms of behaviour have been established; this is most apparent in the relationship between the government, the trade unions and the industrial sector but has wider application.

Olson's argument 'fits' the experience of the protectionist phase of development in the 1940s and 1950s rather than the period after 1970. One conclusion which can be drawn from these considerations is that the performance of an economy is dependent on a set of complex variables at any one time. Some of these will be objective, while others will be subjective or cultural. The balance necessary in any one case is a delicate one, but success is dependent on getting that balance right (Harrison, 1992). In the Irish case the balance was about right in the 1920s, and perhaps during the 1930s, but woefully wrong during the 1940s and 1950s. A new balance was put in place during the 1960s; while this was undermined between 1977 and 1987 this in turn has been replaced by a new balance and one which has secured significant growth since then. To continue development, the balance between the different factors will have to be continuously redrawn. Economic development will probably always be problematic for small economies, though the history of independent Ireland shows that a small economy is not helpless, if it is prepared to make the difficult decisions. However, these decisions are not only economic, but require that attention be paid to the cultural prerequisites for change.

COMMENTARY BY IAIN McMENAMIN

Brian Girvin's article is an Irish application of one of the most famous ideas in social science: that cultural differences explain differences in economic development. In 1905, Max Weber, widely seen as the founder of modern sociology, published two articles on the 'Protestant Ethic and the Spirit of Capitalism'. Weber wrote that under capitalism, 'Man is dominated by the making of money, by acquisition as the ultimate purpose of his life. Economic acquisition is no longer subordinated to man as the means for the satisfaction of his material needs' (1976, p. 53). Many Protestant sects thought that individuals would be predestined for salvation. These 'select' individuals would be marked by a sober industrious career. Wealth in itself was not condemned. It was only sinful if it supported a life of idle luxury. Thus, a new religious culture gave birth to a new economic system.

Girvin's work was a pioneering attempt to systematically demonstrate a relationship between Irish political culture and economic development. Political culture had been a central concern of students of Irish politics since Chubb's pioneering textbook (1970). While culture was often briefly mentioned in reviews of Irish economic policy and development, it had not been treated as a serious explanation. One partial exception, and seemingly a particular inspiration for Girvin's article, was the work of historian Joseph Lee (1989). Lee argued that the major cultural characteristics of Ireland (religion, language, nationalism, agrarian economy) were compatible with economic development. Instead, he blamed the economic failure of independent Ireland on a lack of intellectual quality. Girvin's essay was an important riposte to Lee in two respects. First, it emphasised how Ireland's relative economic performance has varied over the decades of independence. This meant that the 1950s could be identified as the era of greatest failure and as a turning point. Second, Girvin argued that the failure to make similar successful policy choices to other Western European countries cannot be understood as merely a failure of intellectual analysis, but a wider elite and popular cultural refusal to commit to the pursuit of economic development and acknowledge the social and political changes such a commitment would entail.

Girvin's article also exists in the context of a much wider literature on politics, culture and economic development. While some authors continue to emphasise the importance of culture (Landes, 1999, p. 516), the concept of culture is nowadays completely avoided by most scholars concerned with economic development. This is not to say that cultural explanations are wrong *per se*, just that they are difficult to prove. There seem to be three reasons for this. First, culture is difficult to define and measure. Second, even if cultures can be reliably identified, it is questionable whether they have any independent effect. In particular, it is difficult to disentangle political institutions and political culture. Do democratic institutions cause a democratic political culture or does a democratic political culture cause the adoption of democratic institutions (Lijphart, 1980, pp. 47–9)? Third, cultural explanations frequently have insulting and pessimistic implications. Africa is poor because of its culture; Africa's poverty is its people's fault; there is little that can be done about African poverty. Whatever about the third of these defects, the first two clearly apply to Girvin's article.

Girvin's conception of political culture is extremely wide and seems to encompass virtually all political values, institutions and behaviours. However, at least within his introduction, Girvin divides this all-encompassing concept into three different levels. It is more usual to adopt a narrow definition of political culture that restricts it to the 'pattern of cognitive, evaluative and affective orientations towards political objects' (Lijphart, 1980, p. 38; see also Brown and Gray, 1979). This narrow definition focuses on what is so difficult to measure about political culture. Basic information about political institutions is easy to find. At least some rules and procedures, frequently the most important ones, are written down. Similarly, a lot of basic information about political behaviour is relatively easy to access. Elections provide a huge amount of important and reliable information. Strikes and demonstrations can be tracked relatively easily. It is much more difficult to accurately see into the heads of individuals to understand the way they think about politics and then to generalise reliably from some individuals to a whole culture. Girvin, like others, is able to make detailed arguments about elite political culture from documentary evidence. Nonetheless, it is not clear that the same conclusions would have been drawn from a different selection of documents or a different interpretation of documents. Mass political culture is even more difficult to study, given that, politics students aside, most non-elites never write about politics. A common way to study mass political culture is by survey but surveys are crude and horribly expensive. Girvin does not refer to any surveys in his article.

A narrower definition of culture makes it easier to disentangle culture, institutions and behaviour. Even so, the challenges are formidable. Take culture and institutions. It is difficult to decide which causes which because, in most political systems, there is a fit between the culture and the institutions. Authoritarian cultures are found together with authoritarian institutions. Entrepreneurial institutions are found together with entrepreneurial cultures. The best opportunities for disentangling cultures and institutions are when there is a sudden and comprehensive political change such as happened in Germany after the Second World War. A change of similar suddenness and magnitude is not available to Girvin and other students of economic development and political culture in independent Ireland.

These criticisms of the cultural approach are implicit in the currently dominant approach to the explanation of economic development in both political science and economics. It focuses on institutions and policies and essentially argues that people will react to the incentives created by institutions and policies in essentially identical ways (Alt and Shepsle, 1990; Hall and Soskice, 2001). What matters is not cultural variation but variations in institutions and policies. Some policies are more conducive to economic growth than others. For example, low stable interest rates encourage investment. Some institutions make it easier to achieve a given policy objective. For example, if interest rates are set by politicians rates are likely to be more volatile and, on average, higher. Politicians will be tempted to cut rates going into elections to stimulate the economy, but will then have to raise them to combat inflation. However, if an independent central bank controls interest rates and is legislatively obliged to focus on low inflation, the policy objective of low inflation is much more likely to be achieved. Figure 4.1 summarises this approach to politics and economic development.

Figure 4.1 The institutional approach.

Girvin's argument accepts the importance of policy: 'Irish economic management between 1945 and the 1960s did not maximise the state's economic opportunities'. In his earlier book, Girvin more clearly separates out institutional and cultural explanations (Girvin, 1989, p. 170). Although Girvin does not do so explicitly, he is presenting a synthesis of the institutional and cultural approaches. A brief, but systematic attempt, to see how this might be done suggests that the cultural approach is important; that it consists of a number of arguments about how institutions and policy relate to economic development; and that accumulating the evidence to make this synthesis a convincing explanation for Ireland's economic development is a daunting challenge. Figure 4.2 shows a summary of this synthesis.

Figure 4.2 Synthesis of cultural and institutional approaches.

Culture, of both the elites and the masses, clearly has an important influence on the choice of institutions in many political systems. For example, it is often argued that the conservative culture of the Irish 'revolutionary' elite and the wider population led to the adoption of a very conservative set of institutions for the new state. Institutions interact with culture. They will produce different policies depending on the interests and culture of the political elites that make political decisions. Girvin argues that it was against the particular interests of many powerful political actors in the Irish political system to adopt policies which might lead to general economic development. A classic example would be businesses, which in a protected economy are able to take a large share of a small national wealth but who would not be able to compete in a freer economy, even if that freer economy raised the overall national wealth. Girvin also argues that there was a cultural brake on the choice of developmental policies, not just because of the difficulty of making such choices in the existing institutional structure but also because of the absence of a 'growth consciousness' amongst the elite. The incentives presented by policies also interact with the culture of the mass of economic actors. For example, a state can provide incentives for further education and technical education with the provision of free or paid courses. However, a conservative culture may resist such education, even if it promises higher returns, because it can disrupt well-established routines and hierarchies.

Girvin's work has now effectively been superseded by Tom Garvin's *Preventing the Future: Why Was Ireland So Poor for So Long?* (2004). Garvin acknowledges his debt to Girvin at several points (Garvin, 2004, pp. 54 and 196). His book addresses the implicit and explicit research problem posed by Girvin's article.

In terms of the explicit agenda, firstly, it concentrates at length on the 1950s, identified by Girvin as comparatively the most exceptional decade of Ireland's economic development. (He was writing before the Celtic Tiger period of the 1990s.) Secondly, Garvin follows Girvin in stressing how Irish political culture prevented the choice of similar successful policies to other European states. Garvin goes further than Girvin in addressing the problems of integrating cultural and institutional explanations. His introduction separates culture, institutions and interests while proposing a synthesis aimed at explaining varying levels of economic development. The main body of Garvin's book is replete with detailed examples, many of them convincing, of how culture, in combination with other factors, influenced important policy decisions and non-decisions. Garvin's book is so bubbling with hypotheses that it cannot but fail to prove most of them. In spite of the current unfashionable status of cultural explanations, these unproven hypotheses will provide an irresistible temptation for students of Irish politics to pursue Girvin's research agenda in years to come.

Notes

1 Earlier versions of this paper were read by Geoff Roberts and Rona Fitzgerald. I would also like to thank Andy Bielenberg and Steve McCarthy for discussing specific aspects of it with me. I alone am responsible for content and interpretation.
2 For a detailed assessment of the pre-war state of the Irish economy and in particular the nature of its industrial sector see Bielenberg (1994).
3 Mjøset's study compares Ireland with Austria, Denmark, Finland, Sweden and Switzerland, but it is possible to add Norway and the Netherlands to this list.
4 National Archives: Department of the Taoiseach. S11563, 'National Income', Smiddy to de Valera, 4 December 1944; Crotty (1966, p. 159) offers some support for this view.
5 I am indebted to Andy Bielenberg for providing me with unpublished data and for discussing many aspects of this question with me.
6 This view has greater strength for the period before 1960 than after.

References

Almond, Gabriel A. and Sidney Verba (1963) *The Civic Culture: Political Attitudes and Democracy in Five Nations*. Princeton, NJ: Princeton University Press.
Almond, Gabriel A. and Sidney Verba (eds.) (1980) *The Civic Culture Revisited*. Boston, MA: Little, Brown.
Alt, James and Kenneth Shepsle (eds.) (1990) *Perspectives on Positive Political Economy*. Cambridge: Cambridge University Press.
Ashford, Sheena and N. Timms (1992) *What Europe Thinks*. Aldershot: Avebury.
Bairoch, Paul (1981) 'The Main Trends in National Economic Disparities Since the Industrial Revolution', pp. 3–17 in Paul Bairoch and M. Lévy-Leboyer (eds.) *Disparities in Economic Development Since the Industrial Revolution*. London: Macmillan.
Bartolini, Stefano and Peter Mair (1990) *Identity, Competition, and Electoral Availability*. Cambridge: Cambridge University Press.
Bielenberg, Andy (1994) *Industrial Growth in Ireland, c.1790–1910*. Unpublished PhD thesis. London: London School of Economics.

Bielenberg, Andy and Patrick O'Mahony (1994) 'An Expenditure Estimate of Irish GNP (at Market Prices) in 1907'. Cork: Unpublished paper.

Bielenberg, Andy and Patrick O'Mahony (1995) 'An Expenditure Estimate of Irish GNP (at Market Prices) in 1907'. Cork: Revised paper.

Biever, Bruce Francis (1976) *Religion, Culture and Values: A Cross Cultural Analysis of Motivational Factors in Native Irish and American Irish Catholicism*. New York: Arno Press.

Boltho, Andrea (1985) 'European and United States Regional Differentials: A Note', *Oxford Review in Economic Policy*, 5, pp. 105–15.

Bradley, John (1990) 'The Legacy of Economic Development: The Irish Economy, 1960–1987', pp. 128–50 in J.F. McCarthy (ed.) *Planning Ireland's Future: The Legacy of T.K. Whitaker*. Dublin: Glendale.

Breen, Richard, Damien F. Hannan, David W. Rottman and Christopher T. Whelan (1990) *Understanding Contemporary Ireland: State, Class and Development in the Republic of Ireland*. Dublin: Gill and Macmillan.

Brown, Archie and Jack Gray (eds.) (1979) *Political Culture and Political Change in Communist States*. London: Palgrave Macmillan.

Camagni, R.P. (1991) 'Regional Deindustrialization and Revitalization Processes in Italy', pp. 137–67 in L. Rodwin and H. Sazanami (eds) *Industrial Change and Regional Economic Transformation*. London: HarperCollins.

Chubb, Basil (1970) *The Government and Politics of Ireland*. London: Oxford University Press.

Clark, Colin (1940) *The Conditions of Economic Progress*. London: Macmillan.

Coakley, John (1993) 'Society and Political Culture', pp. 25–49 in John Coakley and Michael Gallagher (eds.) *Politics in the Republic of Ireland*. Second Edition. Limerick: PSAI Press/Folens.

Committee on Industrial Progress (1973) *General Report*. Dublin: State Paper Office.

Conradt, David P. (1980) 'Changing German Political Culture', pp. 212–72 in Gabriel A. Almond and Sidney Verba (eds.) *The Civic Culture Revisited*. Boston, MA: Little, Brown.

Coogan, Tim Pat (1993) *De Valera: Long Fellow, Long Shadow*. London: Hutchinson.

Crotty, Raymond (1966) *Irish Agricultural Production*. Cork: Cork University Press.

Cullen, Louis M. (ed.) (1968) *The Formation of the Irish Economy*. Cork: Mercier.

Cullen, Louis M. (1994) 'Irish National Income in 1911 and its Context'. Unpublished Working Paper. Dublin: Economic and Social Research Institute.

Cullen, Louis M. and T. Christopher Smout (1977) 'Economic Growth in Scotland and Ireland', pp. 3–18 in Louis M. Cullen and T. Christopher Smout (eds.) *Comparative Aspects of Scottish and Irish Economic and Social History 1600–1900*. Edinburgh: Edinburgh University Press.

Daly, Mary (1992) *Industrial Development and Irish National Identity, 1922–1939*. Dublin: Gill and Macmillan.

Del Monte, A. and A. Giannola (1979) *Il Mezzogiorno Nell'Economia Italiana*. Bologna: Il Mulino.

Diamond, Larry (ed.) (1993) *Political Culture and Democracy in Developing Countries*. Boulder, CO: Lynne Rienner.

Dogan, Mattei and Ali Kazancigil (eds.) (1994) *Comparing Nations*. Oxford: Basil Blackwell.

Dowding, Keith and Richard Kimber (1983) 'The Meaning and Use of Political Stability', *European Journal of Political Research*, 11 (3), pp. 229–43.

Duncan, George A. (1939–40) 'The Social Income of the Irish Free State, 1926–38', *Journal of the Statistical and Social Inquiry Society of Ireland*, 16, pp. 1–16.

Dunphy, Richard (1995) *The Making of Fianna Fáil Power in Ireland 1923–1948*. Oxford: Clarendon Press.

Elster, Jon (1989) *Nuts and Bolts for the Social Sciences*. Cambridge: Cambridge University Press.

Fanning, Ronan (1978) *The Irish Department of Finance, 1922–58*. Dublin: Institute for Public Administration.

Fiscal Inquiry Committee (1923) *Reports*. Dublin: State Paper Office.

FitzGerald, Garret (1959) 'Mr Whitaker and Industry', *Studies*, XLVIII, pp. 138–50.

Franklin, Francine R. (1978) *India's Political Economy, 1947–1977*. Princeton, NJ: Princeton University Press.

Garvin, Tom (1987) *Nationalist Revolutionaries in Ireland, 1858–1928*. Oxford: Oxford University Press.

Garvin, Tom (2004) *Preventing the Future: Why Was Ireland So Poor for So Long?* Dublin: Gill and Macmillan.

Gellner, Ernest (1988) *Plough, Sword and Book: The Structure of Human History*. London: Paladin.

Girvin, Brian (1989) *Between Two Worlds: Politics and Economy in Independent Ireland*. Dublin: Gill and Macmillan.

Girvin, Brian (1989a) 'Change and Continuity in Liberal Democratic Political Culture', pp. 31–51 in J.R. Gibbins (ed.) *Contemporary Political Culture*. London: Sage.

Girvin, Brian (1992) 'Nationalism, Economic Growth and Political Sovereignty', *History of European Ideas*, 15, pp. 177–84.

Girvin, Brian (1994) *The Right in the Twentieth Century: Conservatism and Democracy*. London: Pinter.

Girvin, Brian (1995) 'Irish Agricultural Policy, Economic Nationalism and the Possibility of Market Integration in Europe', pp. 203–22 in Richard T. Griffiths and Brian Girvin (eds.) *The Green Pool and the Origins of the Common Agricultural Policy*. London: Lothian Press.

Girvin, Brian (1996) 'Church, State and the Irish Constitution: The Secularisation of Irish Politics?', *Parliamentary Affairs*, 49 (4), pp. 599–615.

Girvin, Brian (1997) 'Ireland', pp. 122–38 in Roger Eatwell (ed.) *European Political Cultures: Conflict or Convergence?* London: Routledge.

Gladdish, Ken (1991) *Governing From the Centre*. London: Hurst.

Goldhagen, Daniel (1996) *Hitler's Willing Executioners: Ordinary Germans and the Holocaust*. New York: Knopf.

Goldthorpe, John H. and Christopher T. Whelan (eds.) (1992) *The Development of Industrial Society in Ireland*. Oxford: Oxford University Press.

Griffiths, Richard T. (ed.) (1990) *The Netherlands and the Integration of Europe 1945–1957*. Amsterdam: NEHA.

Griffiths, Richard T. and Brian Girvin (eds.) (1995) *The Green Pool and the Origins of the Common Agricultural Policy*. London: Lothian Press.

Hall, Peter A. and David Soskice (eds.) (2001) *Varieties of Capitalism: The Institutional Foundations of Comparative Advantage*. Oxford: Oxford University Press.

Hannan, Damien F. (1979) *Displacement and Development: Class, Kinship and Social Change in Irish Rural Communities*. Dublin: Economic and Social Research Institute.

Hannan, Damien F. and P. Commins (1992) 'The Significance of Small-Scale Landholders in Ireland's Socio-Economic Transformation', pp. 79–104 in John H. Goldthorpe and

Christopher T. Whelan (eds.) *The Development of Industrial Society in Ireland*. Oxford: Oxford University Press.

Harrison, Lawrence E. (1992) *Who Prospers?: How Cultural Values Shape Economic and Political Success*. New York: Basic Books.

Haselitz, Bert F. (1961) 'Tradition and Economic Growth', pp. 83–113 in R. Brashanti and J.J. Spengler (eds.) *Tradition, Values and Socio-Economic Development*. Durham, NC: Duke University Press.

Herrnstein, Richard J. and Charles Murray (1994) *The Bell Curve: Intelligence and Class Structure in American Life*. New York: Free Press.

Hibbs, D.A. and H. Fassbender (eds.) (1981) *Contemporary Political Economy*. Amsterdam: North Holland.

Hirschman, Albert O. (1968) 'The Political Economy of Import-Substituting Industrialisation in Latin America', *Quarterly Journal of Economics*, LXXXII (1), pp. 1–32.

Hirschman, Albert O. (1970) *Exit, Voice and Loyalty*. Cambridge, MA: Harvard.

Hobsbawm, Eric (1994) *Age of Extremes*. London: Michael Joseph.

Inglehart, Ronald (1990) *Culture Shift*. Princeton, NJ: Princeton University Press.

Inglis, Tom (1987) *Moral Monopoly: The Catholic Church in Modern Irish Society*. Dublin: Gill and Macmillan.

Jacobsen, John K. (1994) *Chasing Progress in the Irish Republic: Ideology, Democracy and Dependent Development*. Cambridge: Cambridge University Press.

Johnson, David (1985) *The Interwar Economy in Ireland*. Dundalk: Economic and Social History Society of Ireland.

Johnson, David (1991) 'The Economic Performance of the Independent Irish State', *Irish Economic and Social History*, XVIII, pp. 48–53.

Jowell, Roger, Lindsay Brook and Lizanne Dowds (1993) *International Social Attitudes*. Aldershot: Dartmouth.

Katzenstein, Peter (1984) *Small States in World Markets*. Ithaca, NY: Cornell University Press.

Keating, Paul and Derry Desmond (1993) *Culture and Capitalism in Contemporary Ireland*. Aldershot: Avebury.

Kennedy, Kieran A. (1992) 'The Context of Economic Development', pp. 5–30 in John H. Goldthorpe and Christopher T. Whelan (eds.) *The Development of Industrial Society in Ireland*. Oxford: Oxford University Press.

Kennedy, Kieran A. (1995) 'The National Accounts of Ireland in the Nineteenth and Twentieth Centuries'. Unpublished Working Paper. Dublin: Economic and Social Research Institute.

Kennedy, Kieran A., Thomas Giblin and Deirdre McHugh (1988) *The Economic Development of Ireland in the Twentieth Century*. London: Routledge.

Kennedy, Liam (1989) *The Modern Industrialisation of Ireland, 1940–1988*. Dundalk: The Economic and Social History Society of Ireland.

Kennedy, Liam (1996) 'Modern Ireland: Post-Colonial Society or Post-Colonial Pretensions?', pp. 167–81 in Liam Kennedy, *Colonialism, Religion and Nationalism in Ireland*. Belfast: Institute for Irish Studies.

Kiernan, T.J. (1933) 'The National Income of the Irish Free State in 1926', *Economic Journal*, 43, pp. 74–87.

Kissane, Bill (1995) 'The Not-So Amazing Case of Irish Democracy', *Irish Political Studies*, 10, pp. 43–68.

Kohn, Marek (1995) *The Race Gallery: The Return of Racial Science*. London: Jonathan Cape.

Landes, David S. (1999) *The Wealth and Poverty of Nations*. London: Abacus.

Lane, Jan-Erik and Svante Ersson (1994) *Comparative Politics*. Cambridge: Polity Press.

Lee, J.J. (1989) *Ireland 1912–1985: Politics and Society*. Cambridge: Cambridge University Press.

Lijphart, Arend (1980) 'The Structure of Inference', pp. 37–56 in Gabriel A. Almond and Sidney Verba (eds.) *The Civic Culture Revisited*. Boston, MA: Little, Brown.

Martinotti, Guido and Sonia Stefanizzi (1995) 'Europeans and the Nation State', pp. 163–89 in Oskar Niedermayer and Richard Sinnott (eds.) *Public Opinion and Internationalized Governance*. Oxford: Oxford University Press.

Meenan, James (1967) 'From Free Trade to Self Sufficiency', pp. 69–79 in Frank Macmanus (ed.) *The Years of the Great Test*. Cork: Mercier.

Meenan, James (1970) *The Irish Economy Since 1922*. Liverpool: Liverpool University Press.

Mjøset, Lars (1992) *The Irish Economy in a Comparative Institutional Perspective*. Dublin: National Economic and Social Council.

National Economic and Social Council (1982) *A Review of Industrial Policy*. Dublin: National Economic and Social Council.

National Economic and Social Council (1989) *Ireland in the European Community: Performance, Prospects and Strategy*. Dublin: National Economic and Social Council.

National Economic and Social Council (1991) *The Economic and Social Implications of Emigration*. Dublin: National Economic and Social Council.

National Economic and Social Council (1992) *The Association Between Economic Growth and Employment Growth in Ireland*. Dublin: National Economic and Social Council.

O'Brien, George (1921) *The Economic History of Ireland from the Union to the Famine*. London: Longmans, Green.

Ó Gráda, Cormac (1994) *Ireland: A New Economic History, 1780–1939*. Oxford: Oxford University Press.

Ó Gráda, Cormac and Kevin Ó Rourke (1994) *Irish Economic Growth, 1945–88*. London: Centre for Economic Policy Research.

Olesen, Thorsten B. (ed.) (1995) *Independence Versus Integration: Denmark, Scandinavia and Western Europe 1945–1960*. Odense: Odense University Press.

Olson, Mancur (1982) *The Rise and Decline of Nations*. New Haven, CT: Yale University Press.

O'Malley, Eoin (1981) 'The Decline of Irish Industry in the Nineteenth Century', *Economic and Social Review*, 13, pp 21–42.

O'Malley, Eoin (1989) *Industry and Economic Development: The Challenge for the Latecomer*. Dublin: Gill and Macmillan.

O'Malley, Eoin (1992) 'Problems of Industrialisation in Ireland', pp. 31–52 in John H. Goldthorpe and Christopher T. Whelan (eds.) *The Development of Industrial Society in Ireland*. Oxford: Oxford University Press.

Organisation for Economic Co-operation and Development (1995) *Ireland 1994–1995*. Paris: OECD.

O'Riordan, M. (1906) *Catholicity and Progress in Ireland*. London: Kegan Paul, Trench, Trübner.

O'Toole, Fintan (1995) *Meanwhile Back at the Ranch: The Politics of Irish Beef*. London: Vintage.

Pateman, Carole (1980) 'The Civic Culture: A Philosophic Critique', pp. 57–102 in Gabriel A. Almond and Sidney Verba (eds.) *The Civic Culture Revisited*. Boston, MA: Little, Brown.

Peillon, Michel (1994) 'Placing Ireland in a Comparative Perspective', *Economic and Social Review*, 25, pp. 179–95.

Prager, Jeffrey (1986) *Building Democracy in Ireland*. Cambridge: Cambridge University Press.

Pye, Lucian W. (1985) *Asian Power and Politics: The Cultural Dimensions of Authority*. Cambridge, MA: Harvard University Press.

Rueschemeyer, Dietrich, Evelyne Huber Stephens and John D. Stephens (1992) *Capitalist Development and Democracy*. Cambridge: Polity.

Seers, Dudley (1983) *The Political Economy of Nationalism*. Oxford: Oxford University Press.

Shanin, Teodor (ed.) (1971) *Peasants and Peasant Societies*. Harmondsworth: Penguin.

Sørensen, Vibeke (1993) 'Between Interdependence and Integration: Denmark's Shifting Strategies', pp. 88–116 in A.S. Milward, F.M.B. Lynch, F. Romero, R. Ranieri and V. Sørensen, *The Frontiers of National Sovereignty*. London: Routledge.

Thompson, Mark R. (1995) *Late Industrializers, Late Democratizers: Developmental States in Pacific Asia*. Dresden: Institut für Soziologie.

Tivey, Leonard (1981) 'States, Nations and Economics', pp. 59–81 in Leonard Tivey (ed.) *The Nation State*. Oxford: Basil Blackwell.

Weber, Max (1976) *The Protestant Ethic and the Spirit of Capitalism*. London: Allen and Unwin.

Welch, Stephen (1993) *The Concept of Political Culture*. London: Macmillan.

Whelan, Christopher T. (ed.) (1994) *Values and Social Change in Ireland*. Dublin: Gill and Macmillan.

World Bank (1993) *The East Asian Miracle: Economic Growth and Public Policy*. Oxford: Oxford University Press.

Woshinsky, Oliver H. (1995) *Culture and Politics*. Englewood Cliffs, NJ: Prentice-Hall.

Yoshino, Kosaku (1992) *Cultural Nationalism in Contemporary Japan*. London: Routledge.

5   A state of exception

The concept of the political in Northern Ireland[1]

Arthur Aughey

Originally published in *Irish Political Studies*, 12, 1997, pp. 1–12.

In the preface to his invaluable and award winning study, *Interpreting Northern Ireland*, John Whyte (1990) noted that since the beginning of the troubles in 1968 there had been an explosion of work in the area. His estimate in 1990 was that there were 7,000 published items. It is possible that the figure today might well be in excess of 10,000. The enormous and patient labour of John Whyte was to transform that dubious inheritance into a set of propositions about Northern Ireland which have been not only accessible to students but also persuasive to academics. John Whyte was a scholar not a political commentator or political analyst. He was prepared to accept the burden of Montesquieu's view that until one has read all the old books one has no reason to prefer new ones instead (Montesquieu, 1993, p. 198). Nature, according to Montesquieu, had so arranged it that men's stupidities would be ephemeral and their books would make them immortal. The passion for publication in his own day was, he believed, the most absurd of vanities. An incautious author would inform posterity of his existence and it would be forever known that he was a fool (Montesquieu, 1993, p. 134).

In his commentary on such incautious modern-day authors, John Whyte was too much of a gentleman to linger long on the foolishness of others. His magisterial criticism, more in sorrow than in anger, was always prepared to give credit for effort. There is no doubt that the immortality of John Whyte has been secured by his own books. For the rest of us, one would have to admit that there is nothing so embarrassing as conducting your education in public – which embarrassment is the inevitable consequence of the illusion that one has – at any one point – something meaningful to say. However, as John Whyte's tolerant approach implied, those who err have also a contribution to make even if it is only to sharpen the scholar's critical faculties.

Pride and solace, argued Norman Jacobson, are the dubious wares purveyed by political philosophers. It was his view that a student of politics will turn to particular theorists because of different moods and different circumstances. 'Perhaps the time to read Hobbes to maximum effect', argued Jacobson, 'is when we ourselves are in a fearful state' (1986, p. xiii). Some solace may be had in the act of interpreting one's own predicament through works of political theory, where such works can have both the dramatising effect of a Greek tragedy and the reconciling effect of a Biblical text. In other words, finding some representation of one's own experience in political thought can help one confront its reality and help one adjust to its intractability.

Intractability was the theme of a recent speech to the British-Irish Association in September 1996 by the Secretary of State, Sir Patrick Mayhew. He made the following comment on the events of that year in Northern Ireland.

> It was thought that a reassuring crust had formed over the volcano's crater. On the surface of that crust we had been executing many an elegant design and had been proposing many an exciting structure. But the volcano was not extinct, and when it erupted it did so with horrifying ferocity.

Sir Patrick's interpretation of events would be shared by many. The question remains: how do we make sense of the politically volcanic character of Northern Ireland? In the mood and the circumstances of that summer, turning to the work of the German theorist Carl Schmitt provided me with one way of trying to make some sense of what had happened and was happening in Northern Ireland. One can often take perverse comfort in a 'shatterer of illusions'.[2]

Schmitt is not particularly well-known in the English-speaking world mainly because his collaboration with the Nazi regime after 1933 has been read back into his theoretical works of the Weimar period. Traditionally, he has been judged as one of those who paved the way, intellectually, for the enormities of Hitler. Recently, however, Schmitt has experienced rehabilitation on both the right *and* the left. This is not the place to examine this interesting return to Schmitt which ranges from the pages of *Telos* to the pages of *Nouvelle Ecole*, from radicals like Chantal Mouffe to Oakeshottians like Noel O'Sullivan. It may be that just as Schmitt was forced to think through the disintegration of a way of life at the beginning of this century, so too are contemporary intellectuals forced to think through changing expectations at the end of the century – changes including the decay of the social democratic project, the evaporation of communism and the trials of the parliamentary system.[3]

In so doing, they may find some of his views compelling. Others they may find repellent. On R.G. Collingwood's principle, one might conclude that critics are seeking answers to questions they once thought had been settled and are finding interesting suggestions or horrible reminders in the work of Schmitt. What follows is *not* an exercise for or against Schmitt. It is not an exercise in recommendation or dismissal. It is an exercise which shamelessly plunders some of his concepts in order to get some hooks upon which to hang certain reflections about the current crisis in Northern Ireland.

A state of exception

For Schmitt, what is taken to be the norm is not the best guide to understanding the political. Stable political communities, experiencing an orderly and settled administration of public affairs under the rule of law, represent not only an achievement of civilisation but also a decisive outcome of previous conflicts and struggles. For instance, Schmitt was fond of quoting Arthur Balfour's introduction to Bagehot's *The English Constitution* to the effect that the 'whole political machinery presupposes a people so fundamentally at one that they can safely afford to bicker; and so sure of their own moderation that they are not dangerously disturbed by the never-ending din of political conflict'.[4] That is a satisfactory condition, one experienced by Great Britain and the Republic of Ireland.

Under such stable legality it is often forgotten, though Schmitt will not let us forget, that: 'Sovereign is he who decides on the exception', and this sovereign authority stands ultimately beyond legal norms and decides when, in a crisis, those norms can be set aside or re-instated. Politics, Schmitt believes, is ultimately about decisions and not about discussion and it is the exceptional decisions which are, as one might expect, those which Schmitt believes reveal most about the nature of the political. Even though the extreme case of political conflict may appear to be an exception – as Northern Ireland does to citizens in the Republic and in Great Britain – that 'does not negate its decisive character but confirms it all the more' (1976, p. 35). For Schmitt:

> The exception is more interesting than the rule. The rule proves nothing: the exception proves everything. It confirms not only the rule but also its existence, which derives only from the exception... one only needs to look around for a true exception. It reveals everything more clearly than does the general.
>
> (1985b, p. 15)

Like Kierkegaard – the Protestant existentialist for whom the Catholic authoritarian Schmitt had the highest regard – this assumes that the exception thinks the general with an intense passion. I suppose no better justification could be made for all those books which have been written about Northern Ireland, the very point, indeed, which John Whyte made in his inaugural professorial lecture. It may appear to be stretching things a little bit too far, nevertheless, to appropriate Schmitt for the purposes of elucidating matters in Northern Ireland. After all, he was mainly concerned about international relations and conduct between sovereign states.

However, one is reminded of the comment by David Miller in his influential study *Queen's Rebels* that, from the early 1970s, the 'absence of a state became the essence of the Northern Ireland problem, subsuming all other candidates for the distinction of being *the* problem' (1978, p. 150). If one substitutes the 'stability of the state' for the 'absence of a state' then Schmitt's idea of the exception does indeed have some relevance. Political debate has focused almost exclusively upon the question of sovereignty. And sovereignty has been understood to mean more than formal constitutional doctrine. A constitution can only survive if it is upheld by some political power (Hirst, 1987, p. 19). Paramilitary violence in Northern Ireland has been about influencing, by direct action or the threat of direct action, the disposition of that power.

Schmitt owes to Hobbes the insight that there exists a 'mutual relation between Protection and Obedience', that it is authority alone and not what is true which determines whose writ will run in any political community. 'The one who has authority can demand obedience – and that it is not always the legitimate sovereign who possesses this authority' (1985b, p. xiii). Despite moments of apparent anarchy, no Hobbesian state of nature has existed, mainly because the resources of the British government have been sufficient to ensure that legal and administrative order has prevailed.

However, those who have researched the phenomenon of punishment beatings understand the localised political impact of the relationship between authority and obedience. Indeed, one suspects that some of the recent flirtation with the idea of cantonisation is a sign of the sort of liberal fatigue and failure of nerve which affected Weimar. If, as Schmitt suggests, the cutting edge of the liberal enlightenment has been its rejection of 'the exception in every form' it is a very different cutting edge that would benefit from *accepting* the exception in every form. Accepting the exception seems to be the logic of cantonisation (1985b, p. 37). The consequence would be separation of a stronger form than that explored in Boyle and Hadden's recent book (1994).

Friend and enemy

The most famous of Schmitt's works is his *The Concept of the Political* which was published in 1932. His object was to capture the ultimate distinction to which all action with a specifically political meaning can be traced. If the appropriate distinctions in morality are good and evil, in aesthetics beautiful and ugly, in economics profitable and unprofitable, then for Schmitt the specific 'distinction to which political actions and motives can be reduced is that between friend and enemy'. The 'friend/enemy' distinction is a criterion denoting 'the utmost degree of intensity of a union or separation, of an association or dissociation' (Schmitt, 1976, p. 27). It is irrelevant, according to Schmitt, whether one rejects this criterion, finds it barbaric or atavistic, hopes that it will some day disappear or imagine that enemies no longer exist.

He is concerned only with 'inherent reality and the real possibility of such a distinction' and not 'with abstractions or with normative ideals'. As an ultimate criterion of the political, this does not necessarily mean that communities are actually engaged in war or civil war. The distinction remains, irrespective of reason or idealism, as 'an ever present possibility for every people existing in the political sphere' (Schmitt, 1976, p. 20). The enemy in the political sense is collective and not personal and need not be hated individually. Reflecting on the Christian injunction to love one's enemies, Schmitt argues that never in a 1,000 year struggle did it occur to Christians to surrender out of love for the Turks rather than defend Europe. In the private sphere only does it make sense to love one's enemy. 'It certainly does not mean that one should love and support the enemies of one's own people' (1976, p. 29). In Schmitt's uncompromising and startling view, there is little room for equivocation: 'If a part of the population declares that it no longer recognizes enemies, then, depending on the circumstance, it joins their side and aids them. Such a declaration does not abolish the reality of the friend-and-enemy distinction' (1976, p. 51). Those who have been close to political life in Northern Ireland will be familiar with the meaning of that. However, the picture is not so simple or indeed so bleak. Dualism often expresses a truth but not the whole truth.

In her excellent essay – 'Beyond the Community Conflict: Historic Compromise or Emancipatory Process?' – Jennifer Todd (1995) identified not only two apparently contradictory realities of life in Northern Ireland – the polarisation of traditional politics and the plurality of contemporary attitudes – but also revealed what is the truth of the matter, namely that both of these experiences intermingle. To put that another way, it is possible to understand people in Northern Ireland who express, when asked, *liberal sympathies* about, for instance, the need for equality, fairness, compromise and so on. Personal relationships between Catholic and Protestant are often good (for instance, in the Greater Belfast area it is estimated that 20 per cent of marriages are mixed marriages) and civility is generally the norm between individuals (Trew, 1996, p. 143).

It is also possible to understand those same people who have *illiberal instincts* when it comes to matters to do with identity, statehood and belonging. There is enough *sympathy* to acknowledge that experience is more complex and varied than stereotypical views of the other side would represent it. There is a strong *instinct*, however, which tells people that, irrespective of such complexity within and between communities, collective unity strengthens your position. The value of Jennifer Todd's work is to show that this is not an irrational condition but perfectly logical in the circumstances. Logical, but not necessarily frozen and immutable. That insight is the basis of political realism.

Political realism

Political realism should be based on reliable knowledge, on the acceptance of certain boundaries set by necessity and on a sense of practical possibilities. In the words of the late Bob Berki, it is not anyone's subjective dreams or fancies, not a realm of infinite experimentation, but it is open to the lights of limited possibilities (1981, p. 29). In other words, political realism is not about optimism or pessimism. Neither optimism nor pessimism is an inappropriate disposition on the part of those trying to identify possibilities in Northern Ireland. The problem with the optimistic view, as Michael Oakeshott observed, is that it mistakes the world we live in as something merely to be set to right. The problem with the pessimistic view is that it fails to catch sight of valuable possibilities in the confusion of the present (Minogue, 1996, p. 6). If the former is subject to imaginative illusions the latter is subject to a fixed perspective which is equally illusory.

Thus it is possible to go some way towards interpreting the Northern Ireland problem in Schmittian terms: that is, as one in which the *political* relationship between unionist and nationalist communities is that of friend and enemy. Some way but not the whole way. Again, this relationship does not necessarily entail widespread inter-communal conflict. There is a definitive identity, however, which is based on the assumption that there does exist the real possibility of such conflict. More broadly, there is some justification for arguing that every political utterance here is judged according to source – friend or enemy? – and according to purpose – friendly or hostile? Those who refuse to define themselves as either unionist or nationalist, a surprisingly large group comprising now one third of the population, would also acknowledge that reality. Indeed, the political intensity of the friend/enemy relationship explains why those who fall into this category are often spoken of with contempt or treated with suspicion, an experience traditionally felt by members of the Alliance Party. More to the point, it helps to explain why disagreements *within* communities about the nature of the struggle *between* the communities tend to be so bitter.

The powerful instinct which tells people that communal solidarity is ultimately essential (mobilising friends to challenge the enemy) has been more than a countervailing force to rationalist models of institutional accommodation or exhortations to respect the diversity of cultural traditions. The business of definitive compromise has been interpreted consistently by political leaders as a threat to friends and to their own positions without satisfying the ambitions of the enemy. And in this political leaders generally reflect the concerns of their respective electorates. Much of what happens in the political life of Northern Ireland may be gauged by that practical rule of thumb.

Problem with talks

Such is the incapacity in practice to engage in *definitive* compromise that the political investment in talks between the parties has so far brought little reward. Again, this is a feature of political conflict recognised by Schmitt who argued that it was an article of liberal faith that what Locke called 'the way of the beasts' – naked power and force – 'could be overcome through openness and discussion alone, and the victory of right over might achieved. There is an utterly typical expression for this way of thinking: "discussion in place of force"' (1985a, p. 49). This might indeed be an achievement of a settled polity. It had less meaning in a state of exception. The real suspicions which are focused on negotiations about Northern Ireland's future illustrate the point. For instance, one can identify at least three (rather optimistic) understandings of what is meant by political talks.

First, there exists an expectation that talks should be about persuading one's opponent by debate and discussion of the justice of one's case. It is thought that, in a free and open debate across the table, parties will be persuaded by the logic or coherence of arguments and agree to move to a plane of understanding where old antagonisms and bitterness will be resolved (or transcended). Despite all the evidence that such an expectation is unrealistic and fabulous, it is a faith which has been held to tenaciously by people who are far from naive though who are, ironically, also generally dismissive of the world of politics.

Second, there exists also a view that talking is an end in itself. There may be scepticism about ever arriving at complete agreement. Nevertheless, it is believed that exploring differences between the parties is of itself a valuable activity. Talking in this sense is not about coming to any concrete decision. It is about avoiding physical confrontation. Indeed, it is about putting off any decision until all the elements of the problem have been aired sufficiently, considered and reconsidered. This understanding of talking as political therapy has a distinguished pedigree, especially in the world of community relations.

Third, there is the view that talks are about reckoning the impossibility of winning and should be about building alliances to attain one's interests, conceding on some points to gain advantage on others. It is hoped that through such hard bargaining, mutual respect – if not affection – will be built up between the parties and that a balance of compromises can be arrived at to the mutual satisfaction of all sides. This is taken to be hard-headed realism.

However, even *harder-headed* realists work on a fourth (and pessimistic) understanding and this understanding corresponds closely to what has actually been taking place over the last months. Talks, in this view, are *indeed* about winning and losing, about victory and surrender, about mastery and humiliation. That, it is believed, is the true nature of the political. Real enemies have nothing to discuss. They can only manoeuvre. This, it is assumed, is politics as Machiavelli described it. Schmitt has some interesting things to say about Machiavelli, the most pointed being that had Machiavelli been Machiavellian as this term is commonly understood then he 'would sooner have written an edifying book than his ill-reputed *Prince*' (1976, p. 66). (Beneath the unremitting, unsentimental realism, the German does seem to have a sense of humour.)

Ultimately on this point, the final word should go to Kenneth Minogue (another Oakeshottian). For Minogue, such cynical realism is a good servant but a bad master.

> The cartoon character Mr Magoo is a caricature of a Machiavellian whose conviction that he has seen through every deception always lands him in the soup. In other words, human affairs are marked by an element of contingency which sets limits to the range of any general doctrine, including any system of total cynicism.
>
> (*Times Literary Supplement*, 20 September 1996, p. 8)

The lesson for Northern Ireland would seem to be that conspiracy theories and manipulative stratagems often lose touch with reality, to such an extent that the possibilities for compromise or constructive opportunities are lost through politicians and officials being either too clever by half or too paranoid for their own good.

Communal expectations and misreadings

For instance, the generality of unionist opinion attributed the peace process from which the 1996 talks derived to the design of a 'pan-nationalist front' dedicated to the undoing of Northern Ireland's constitutional status. The evidence for this accusation lay in the purpose informing the strategy of northern nationalism which was judged to be an attempt to maximise the network of nationalist friends against the unionist enemy; and a calculation that unionist isolation and demoralisation could be increased to such an extent that its 'veto' on moves towards Irish unity could be surmounted. The British government had no bottom line and the Irish government was simply negotiating at one remove for the Irish Republican Army (IRA). The events at Drumcree may be read in the light of Schmitt's stark proposition that only a weak people will perish. Those who took to the streets were determined to make the point that if the British government was weak, unionists were not. While few Protestants actually engaged in the disruption and many would have been appalled at the images of confrontation, the concern which that disruption represented does permeate widely.

But this reading ignores, however, the modulated approach brought to Irish policy by John Bruton and Proinsias de Rossa. It cannot explain why, if the British government had indeed no bottom line, it had held the line for 18 months against Sinn Féin demands. It does not acknowledge sufficiently the report of the Forum for Peace and Reconciliation and cannot properly explain why the IRA went back to war in February 1996.

Equally, there is evidence to suggest that the peace process helped to polarise northern Catholic opinion in favour of Irish unity because that option now seemed more attainable – despite all the public statements by nationalist Ireland that an agreed Ireland did *not* mean a united Ireland. A change in the means *ought* to have meant a change in the end to be attained. Yet the social attitudes surveys from 1989 to 1993 showed that an average of 34 per cent of Catholics favoured remaining within the UK, with an average of only 53 per cent favouring Irish unity. In 1994 these figures were 24 per cent and 60 per cent respectively. In 1993 the overall figures for Northern Ireland showed that 70 per cent favoured staying within the UK and 20 per cent favoured Irish unity. In 1994 the figures were 63 per cent and 27 per cent respectively (Breen, 1996). The comment by Fergus Finlay that without Sinn Féin, talks were not worth a penny candle, damaged the Irish government's *bona fides* amongst unionists, for it suggested that unionist concerns were not taken seriously and, moreover, could be discounted. That is possibly one of the reasons why Drumcree was such a shock to nationalism on the island.

In some ways, then, the problem for talks in Northern Ireland is rather like the conundrum faced by social contract theory. If there were sufficient agreement (or 'consensus') between unionist and nationalist to formulate an elaborate political contract then such a contract – especially of the byzantine sort outlined in the Framework Documents – would be unnecessary. If there were not such sufficient agreement (or 'consensus') then a contract of that sort would be impossible anyway. Indeed, as Robin Wilson commented recently, the Framework Documents read 'as if a couple were to draw up a contract for their relationship, so replete with checks and balances that they could only be left wondering why they wanted to live together at all' (*Irish Times*, 13 September 1996). It might be suggested, therefore, that talks are only of value if the parties already desire to reach an accommodation, the shape of which they were already broadly agreed upon. The mutually suspicious approach to such an accommodation tends to reflect La Rochefoucauld's maxim that: 'We have not the courage to declare as a general principle that we have no shortcomings and our enemies no good qualities; but when it comes to details that is what we are none too far from believing' (1959, p. 397). Except that in Northern Ireland there is a self-righteous habit for politicians to act as if this were true not only on the details but also on the general principle.

Parity of esteem

What we witnessed in 1996 was a peculiarly malignant working out of this self-righteousness under the cover of the liberal concept of parity of esteem. Rather, we witnessed the meaning of parity of esteem as it works itself out in a society politically conscious of friends and enemies. Parity of esteem is here understood as parity of communal assertion. Activists have frequently chosen to interpret as communal humiliations the practical compromises necessary in any civilised society. Such an activist style of identity politics has only encouraged alienation and discontent. Why might this be so?

Since one's identity is something that only one can define for oneself it is a short step to arguing that in the public sphere what a group defines as necessary for its own self-esteem must be met. When or if it proves impossible to meet these essential demands – for all demands tend to take on an essential quality – then the disappointed community will feel that it has been humiliated. That approach attenuates the idea of a common public sphere. As Bertie Ahern, leader of Fianna Fáil, put it at the Forum for Peace and Reconciliation, parity of esteem should be 'practised in a commonsense way and any principle, if carried to illogical extremes, would be rendered virtually unusable' (1995, p. 55). He is absolutely right.

The lack of a sense of proportion and the lack of a sense of a common public sphere in Northern Ireland has meant that parity of esteem has been about denial rather than acceptance. Against the grain of that tendency which Schmitt believed to characterise Western liberalism, namely the tendency towards neutralising and depoliticising social antagonisms, the policy confusion surrounding parity of esteem has only served to activate and politicise the tensions between the communities in Northern Ireland. And the inevitable confrontations have increased since 1994, from the stopping of marches to the picketing of churches, from the boycotting of shops to the blocking of football supporters, from arson attacks on Orange Halls to arson attacks on Catholic churches. This incivility in society drains the lifeblood of intelligent politics.

Conclusion

The position we are in at the moment may be best described in the words of Richard Rorty. We are probably 'between an entrenched vocabulary which has become a nuisance and a half-formed new vocabulary which vaguely promises great things' (1990, p. 9). Much of the language of traditional nationalism and traditional unionism has become a nuisance. The political challenge is to transform the vaguely promising new vocabulary of, for instance, the Downing Street Declaration into a viable political grammar. The difficulty remains one which Schmitt would have recognised. It is fear of the 'tyranny of values'. For Schmitt 'all political concepts, images, and terms have a polemical meaning...A word or expression can simultaneously be reflex, signal, password, and weapon in a hostile confrontation' (1976, p. 31). The 'peace process' is a good example. Put very simply, in terms appropriate to the Northern Ireland case, it is the fear which unionists have of being redefined and redescribed in terms conducive to nationalism; and it is the fear which nationalists have of being confined in terms conducive to unionism. Those fears remain unresolved.

One of the sharpest critics of Schmitt's concept of the political, Hermann Heller, wrote that the value of liberal democracy lay in the 'belief in the existence of a common ground for discussion and in fair play for the opponent, with whom one wants to reach agreement under conditions that exclude naked force'.[5] The tragedy of Northern Ireland lies in the fact that we are still not certain whether such common ground exists, whether we are agreed on the meaning of fair play or, indeed, whether we want to reach agreement under any conditions.

COMMENTARY BY ADRIAN LITTLE

The publication of Arthur Aughey's article marked a significant turning point in the study of politics in Northern Ireland. Where previously theorising about Northern Ireland had played a minimal role in the conceptualisation of the 'problem' there, Aughey provided a more foundational analysis which returned to the most basic of theoretical questions: what is the nature of the *political*? In asking this question he understands that the relative absence of theoretical analysis of the political in Northern Ireland is inherently problematic because it is only through

> careful examination of political vocabulary, by scrutinizing the semantics of politics, that the theorist can gain access to that manner in which the political, all political phenomena and the political modality and quality of these phenomena, are perceived within a given culture.
>
> (Vollrath, 1987, p. 19)

Thus, where the 'real' events and politics of the conflict have dominated the study of Northern Ireland, Aughey reintroduced a more fundamental issue: how is the political formed in which these events and politics take place? The political is not just concerned with boundaries, borders, jurisdictions, political parties or indeed the ethical issues and social problems which are the major concern of politics. Instead, the political is the foundational moment in which these different procedural institutions and spaces are established and maintained. Thus, from this perspective, the decision taken over the nature of 'the political' is a point that has a significant bearing not only on the form of institutions and procedures but also on the kinds of issues that emerge in the space of politics.

The primary contention put forward by Aughey is that Northern Ireland is a prime example of what the German political and legal thinker, Carl Schmitt, had termed a state of exception (Schmitt, 1976 and 1985b). This reflects the rediscovery of Schmitt's work in political theory in the 1990s and a variety of attempts to apply his insights and critique of the liberal democratic state to modern political events. It leads Aughey to reflect darkly on the nature of the political in Northern Ireland and provide a prognosis for progress in Northern Irish politics which seemed overly gloomy in the light of the political developments in the years immediately after 1997 (when the article was published). However, this analysis appears somewhat prescient in the light of the stuttering political progress since then and, in particular, the continuation of the notion of a state of exception despite changes to the nature of the Northern Irish state since 1998. With hindsight, and the increase in debate about the state of exception since the attacks on the World Trade Center and Pentagon in 2001 (Agamben, 2005; Žižek, 2004), Aughey's article appears as a seminal paper in the study of contemporary political ideas. It stands out as a beacon of theoretical clarity amongst the paucity of analysis of the nature of the political in Northern Ireland (Little, 2004).

The notion of the state of exception suggests that there is nothing 'natural' about the given form of a political order. Instead, all polities are forged in moments of decision and this imbues those with the role of making decisions the kind of power that rarely appears explicitly once the decision over the nature of the political has been taken. In other words, as Schmitt and Aughey see it, the *sovereign* (be it a state, a government or an elite) ultimately decides on the operation of the rule of law and, once this decision is made, the established procedures may come to seem the natural order of things. For Schmitt, in his critique of parliamentary democracy, there is nothing inherently natural about the institutions which are established except that they suit the purposes of the sovereign power. More significantly still, not only does the sovereign decide the jurisdiction of the political, but it also decides where and when the law and established procedures can be superseded. Thus, it is only the sovereign that is empowered to decide when it is necessary to move towards a state of exception when the 'normal' procedures can be suspended or abandoned. According to this view, these decisions about the nature and institutions of engagement are the pivotal moments of 'the political'. Politics, on the other hand, is that which takes place within those institutions and ways of life once the political decision has taken place. Of course, from time to time there may be events which unsettle and disrupt the political, but these are infrequent. Such is the power invested in the sovereign, that any substantial threat to its authority may lead to the declaration of a state of exception.

Aughey's original article generated a fascinating debate with Alan Finlayson on the nature of the political in Northern Ireland (Aughey, 1998; Finlayson, 1998). Finlayson criticises Aughey's acceptance of Schmitt's rather stable interpretation of the political order. Thus, there is an assumption at work in the notion of the state of exception that the power of the sovereign is stable and accepted to some extent. This then is a power that enables the sovereign power to reproduce itself. However, Finlayson contends that no such stability ever exists. Instead, for the sovereign power, the political is comprised of the ongoing struggle to establish and maintain a hegemonic order to prevent moments of political upheaval re-emerging. The key aspect of this process is the definition of boundaries as to the nature of political engagement and the actors that can take part in this engagement. This perspective suggests that it is in the interests of the sovereign to police politics to ensure that no substantial threat emerges from within the established order.

This is why Schmitt's idea of the friend/enemy distinction is so pivotal to his political theory. As Aughey correctly argues (and as Finlayson agrees), much political discourse in Northern Ireland has been conducted in terms of friends and enemies in the absence of a genuinely consensual initiative. However, this is bemoaned by Aughey who would prefer to see the emergence of a space where 'normalised' political interaction can take place within the confines of a liberal democratic polity broadly construed. For Finlayson, on the other hand, Aughey has constructed a false dualism between a hypothetical 'normal' politics bereft of such communal tensions and the prevalence of the antagonistic model based on the friend/enemy distinction. For this reason Finlayson (1998, p. 118) argues, persuasively, that 'Aughey denies the full salience of the friend/enemy distinction in order to preserve a space for "non-political", liberal sympathies but this space is secured by antagonisms that are themselves variations on the antagonism of friend and enemy'. Instead of a hypothetical liberal democratic model, Finlayson sees the perpetual working out of the friend/enemy distinction as the foundational feature in 'the political' in Northern Ireland. This process is one that we can see within as well as between the 'two communities' if we are wont to refer to them as such. (Incidentally, we should note that both Aughey and Finlayson are renowned as critics of the notion of parity of esteem in the pieces referred to here and elsewhere. The attention paid to parity of esteem in their debate in *Irish Political Studies* is evidence of the prominence of the concept in Northern Irish political debates in the late 1990s.)

One further point to note here is the disagreement between Aughey and Finlayson on whether Northern Ireland is or was a good example of the state of exception. Despite both of them noting the issues that arise from the contested nature of the Northern Irish polity, Aughey notes that a semblance of order has been maintained under the auspices of the British state. Thus, for Aughey, despite 'moments of apparent anarchy, no Hobbesian state of nature has existed, mainly because the resources of the British government have been sufficient to ensure that legal and administrative order has prevailed'. This is important because it alludes to the real sovereign power at work in Northern Ireland during 'the Troubles'. This was a time when, despite the existence of an elected government in Stormont or the assumed control of the Westminster government, exceptional measures were deemed necessary to maintain order in Northern Ireland. Diplock courts, internment, the Special Powers Act and so forth were indeed the creations of a sovereign power (or its proxy). Ultimately, this sovereign power may have been contested but everyone knew where authority ultimately lay and that was with the British state.

Aughey quite rightly notes that it was the authority of the British state (deeply opposed as it was by some) that enabled the exercise of the exception and the unusual provisions which such a situation enabled. Thus, whilst Finlayson is correct to note that 'no class or set of institutions is currently able successfully to hegemonise itself and bring about the stability and legitimacy that is taken as a norm in liberal democratic states' (1998, p. 116), he fails to point out that this was part of the state of exception in operation. The failure to establish hegemony (either unionist or British) is what required the British state (the sovereign power) to enact the state of exception. To put it another way, in Northern Ireland at least, the state of exception did not require hegemony – it was the absence of the latter which led to the institutionalisation of the former. There was a decisive sovereign body in Northern Ireland – the British state – although it failed to make that position concrete. This contributed to a process whereby the British state increasingly came to see the transferral of considerable power to Northern Irish political parties and the establishment of a bipartisan approach with the Republic of Ireland as the best means of putting an end to 'the Troubles'. To make the point even more explicit, the peace process of the 1990s would never have emerged in the way it did without British governments that wanted to move towards the kinds of arrangements that have emerged. Northern Ireland in the 1990s was a form of the state of exception then and it was the British state that exercised sovereign power.

In the last ten years the renewal of interest in the state of exception has been applied in many different political settings (Mouffe, 2005). It is increasingly commonplace to use the insight of theorists such as Schmitt and Walter Benjamin (1996) to highlight the fundamental links between liberal democracy (with its policing of political conduct and consensual impetus) and the idea of the state of exception. In these circumstances Aughey's conclusion that the 'tragedy of Northern Ireland lies in the fact that we are still not certain whether... common ground exists, whether we are agreed on the meaning of fair play or, indeed, whether we want to reach agreement under any conditions', looks a little anachronistic. Aughey regards as a tragedy that which is sometimes viewed today as the ontological condition of the political. In other words, the state of exception is viewed by contemporary critics of liberal democracy as an inherent part of the condition of the political rather than as an anomaly. In investing the state of exception with particular significance, Aughey contributes to perceptions of the uniqueness of Northern Ireland as a place apart.

However, other political philosophers contend that the 'state of exception is not a special kind of law (like the law of war); rather, insofar as it is a suspension of the juridical order itself, it defines law's threshold or limit concept' (Agamben, 2005, p. 4). This normalisation of the state of exception is evident in the new discourses of the war on terror: rendition, Camp X Ray, torture, the lesser evil, and so forth. The really harrowing fact is not that Northern Ireland is a place apart in adhering to the idea of the state of exception – it is actually the opposite. Instead, as Agamben makes clear, one of the 'essential characteristics of the state of exception – the provisional abolition of the distinction among legislative, executive, and judicial powers – here shows its tendency to become a lasting practice of government' (Agamben, 2005, p. 7).

Arthur Aughey's essay is a turning point in the theoretical analysis of Northern Irish politics. Not only did it signify a point at which the study of political theory was to make a new contribution to understanding Northern Irish politics, but it also highlighted the resurgence of interest in Schmitt and the idea of the state of exception. That these ideas have become more commonplace in theoretical debates since 1997 is a sign of Aughey's prescience, although the concept of the state of exception in contemporary political theory leads to potentially more radical conclusions than Aughey imagined in his diagnosis of the state of exception in Northern Ireland.

Notes

1 This paper was originally given as the John Whyte Memorial Lecture at Queen's University, Belfast in 1996.
2 The phrase is Bernard Tucker's.
3 For a critical review of the literature see Neocleous (1996, pp. 12–23).
4 Schmitt, *Legalitat und Legitimitat*, Berlin, 1980, pp. 41–2, cited in George Schwab's introduction to Schmitt (1985a, p. xxiii).
5 Cited in introduction to Schmitt (1985a, p. xxxviii).

References

Agamben, Giorgio (2005) *State of Exception*. Chicago, IL: University of Chicago Press.
Aughey, Arthur (1998) 'Reconceptualising the Political in Northern Ireland: Reply to Finlayson', *Irish Political Studies*, 13, pp. 123–6.
Benjamin, Walter (1996) *Selected Writings: Volume One, 1913–1926*. Cambridge, MA: Harvard University Press.
Berki, Robert (1981) *On Political Realism*. London: Dent.
Boyle, Kevin and Tom Hadden (1994) *Northern Ireland: The Choice*. Harmondsworth: Penguin.
Breen, Richard (1996) 'Who Wants a United Ireland?', pp. 33–48 in Richard Breen, Paula Devine and Lizanne Dowds (eds.) *Social Attitudes in Northern Ireland: The Fifth Report 1995–96*. Belfast: Appletree Press.
Finalyson, Alan (1998) 'Reconceptualising the Political in Northern Ireland: A Response to Arthur Aughey', *Irish Political Studies*, 13, pp. 115–22.
Forum for Peace and Reconciliation (1995) *Report of Proceedings*. Vol. 5, 10 February.
Hirst, Paul (1987) 'Carl Schmitt's Decisionism', *Telos*, 72, pp. 18–24.
Jacobson, Norman (1986) *Pride and Solace*. London: Methuen.
La Rochefoucauld (1959) *Maxims*. Harmondsworth: Penguin.
Little, Adrian (2004) *Democracy and Northern Ireland: Beyond the Liberal Paradigm?* London: Palgrave.
Miller, David (1978) *Queen's Rebels*. Dublin: Gill and Macmillan.
Minogue, Kenneth (ed.) (1996) *Conservative Realism*. London: HarperCollins.
Montesquieu (1993) *Persian Letters*. Harmondsworth: Penguin.
Mouffe, Chantal (2005) *On the Political*. London: Routledge.
Neocleous, Mark (1996) 'Friend or Enemy? Reading Schmitt Politically', *Radical Philosophy*, 79, pp 13–23.
Rorty, Richard (1990) *Contingency, Irony and Solidarity*. Cambridge: Cambridge University Press.
Schmitt, Carl (1976) *The Concept of the Political*. New Brunswick, NJ: Rutgers University Press.

Schmitt, Carl (1985a) *The Crisis of Parliamentary Democracy*. Cambridge, MA: MIT.

Schmitt, Carl (1985b) *Political Theology*. Cambridge, MA: MIT.

Todd, Jennifer (1995) 'Beyond the Community Conflict: Historic Compromise or Emancipatory Process?', *Irish Political Studies*, 10, pp. 161–79.

Trew, Karen (1996) 'National Identity', pp. 140–52 in Richard Breen, Paula Devine and Lizanne Dowds (eds.) *Social Attitudes in Northern Ireland: The Fifth Report 1995–96*. Belfast: Appletree Press.

Vollrath, Ernst (1987) 'The "Rational" and the "Political": An Essay in the Semantics of Politics', *Philosophy and Social Criticism*, 13(1), pp. 17–29.

Whyte, John H. (1990) *Interpreting Northern Ireland*. Oxford: Clarendon Press.

Žižek, Slavoj (2004) *Iraq: The Borrowed Kettle*. London: Verso.

6 Two traditions in unionist political culture[1]

Jennifer Todd

Originally published in *Irish Political Studies*, 2, 1987, pp. 1–26.

In this article I distinguish two traditions within unionism in terms of their different ideological structures – the Ulster loyalist and the Ulster British traditions. Ulster loyalism, defined in terms of its imagined community of northern Protestants, has been the subject of much recent research.[2] The Ulster British tradition has not received sustained academic attention. Together, the Ulster loyalist and Ulster British traditions constitute the two main strands in unionism, but not the only traditions open to northern unionists or northern Protestants. They are distinct from socialism, in which class identification is primary; from Dissent, whose imagined community is Ireland and whose ideology is rooted in northern non-conformist religion; from bridge-building ideologies which take Northern Irish Protestants and Catholics as their imagined community; and from Irish nationalism and republicanism which have always had some northern Protestant adherents.

My primary aim in this article is descriptive – to present the Ulster loyalist and Ulster British ideologies as coherent and intelligible. I do not wish to defend them. Rather, I believe that all the ideological positions within Northern Ireland should be understood, however much one may disagree with them. An understanding of the ideologies at work in the Northern Ireland conflict is a precondition of meaningful dialogue and while such dialogue may not presently be possible it must be held open as a future option. Further, ideologies have some causal efficacy in conditioning political responses and in limiting the directions of future ideological change. It is therefore of some political importance accurately to assess their structure. In the final section of this paper I draw some conclusions from my analysis as to the possibilities of change in Ulster loyalist and Ulster British ideologies.

My analysis is geared at the level of ideological structure – the interrelated and often unspoken cultural assumptions and beliefs which are reproduced not primarily by state action or elite manipulation but by typical modes of experience and practice in the society, which are themselves conditioned by wider socio-economic structures. This is not the level of observable political behaviour and explicit political preference. The relation between underlying cultural-ideological assumptions and political behaviour is much mediated, in this case particularly by the Unionist Party whose origins and rationale lie in the political alliance of Ulster loyalist and Ulster British traditions. To give behavioural evidence of the ideological distinction

I draw would be the topic of another article. But the empirical distinction between Ulster loyalist and Ulster British is clear to participants and observers: it is the distinction between Ian Paisley and Robert McCartney; between Alan Wright of the Ulster Clubs and Sam McAughtry; between Martin Smyth and the civil servant and author, John Oliver; between Sammy Wilson and the one-time Northern Ireland Labour Party (NILP) politician, Charles Brett. As this list suggests, each ideology crosses class lines and endemic to each is class tension and class conflict.

Many northern Protestants cannot so easily be categorised for they have a foot in each camp and share aspects of each ideology. Unionist politicians, in particular, play to both audiences. Individuals' beliefs are often over-determined products of several ideological traditions, lacking in coherence and constantly changing. I think, however, that my categories are more than theoretically motivated ideal types. They represent the real ideological poles on which the views of individuals and groups settle over time. Those real individuals whose ideas are in flux and lack coherence live, after all, in Northern Ireland where their views are constantly subject to explicit or implicit questioning and criticism, where their practices reproduce these ideologies, and where the ideologies are articulated in relatively coherent fashion within the culture. In such a context, the tendency is to gravitate to one or other relatively coherent pole.

Many typologies of unionism have been suggested by participants and academics. Among academics, Frank Wright (1973, pp. 220–3) distinguishes between extreme and liberal unionists, the former opposing and the latter favouring the attempt to bring Catholics into unionism. Wallis *et al* (1986, pp. 1–2) distinguish the majority sectarian unionist position – a Protestant state for a Protestant people – from the minority of liberal unionists or Alliance supporters who conceptualise politics pragmatically in terms of compromise, tolerance and balance. Richard Rose (1971, p. 33) distinguishes the Ultra who gives only conditional loyalty to the British state from the fully allegiant person. My distinction of Ulster loyalism and Ulster British ideology does not fully coincide with these typologies although I would suggest that it shows them to be signs or symptoms of an underlying distinction which is recognised but not theorised by participants.

The interests of Wright, Rose and Wallis *et al* lie in the extreme, Ultra form of unionism – in my terminology, Ulster loyalism. They scarcely begin to specify the ideological structure of the other liberal form of unionism. They define their categories in terms of one issue or principle without arguing that this is the most central distinguishing feature, for example, in terms of its interrelation with the other features which divide northern unionists or in terms of its identification of long-lasting social groups. While the issues chosen, attitudes to sectarianism and political obligation, are closely interrelated with the other distinguishing features of Ulster loyalism, they do not similarly define features central to the ideological structure of the more liberal tradition of unionism. For example, there are conditions when the most liberal unionist would refuse compliance with British laws while supporting the British connection and constitution. Equally, it was perfectly possible for a liberal unionist in the 1950s to oppose the suggestion that Catholics be admitted to the Unionist Party on the grounds that this would be divisive with no chance of success and thus a 'phony' issue.[3] The identification of liberal unionists by Wallis *et al*, is accurate of many O'Neillite unionists and Alliance supporters but it misses the long-lasting Ulster British liberal tradition of which this is but one strand.

I distinguish Ulster British ideology from Ulster loyalism and the other ideologies open to northern Protestants in terms of its imagined community and the way it nests its senses of community in a distinctive order of priority. The imagined community is defined in contrast to other communities and thus this approach requires a multi-dimensional identification of each ideology. The focus on imagined community reveals ideological affinities and family resemblances over time, despite changes in explicit principles or policies. Within restricted timespans, my typology coincides quite neatly with the other proposed typologies of unionism.

The concept of imagined community was originally theorised by Benedict Anderson (1983). It is of especial importance in analysing ideologies in situations of boundary dispute, as in Northern Ireland. It allows analysis of a group's self-ascribed identity without the theorist imposing alien categorisations on the group. As such, one test of the accuracy of my analysis is whether or not participants recognise themselves in my categories.

The structure of Ulster loyalist ideology

Ulster loyalism is probably the most numerous and certainly the most vociferous ideological grouping of northern Protestants. I will use the existing literature on Ulster loyalist ideology, suggesting that the Orange Order, the Democratic Unionist Party (DUP) and secular working-class loyalism share central aspects of the Ulster loyalist structure of meanings.

To anticipate, the essential characteristics of Ulster loyalist ideology are that its primary imagined community is northern Protestants while its secondary identification with Britain involves only a conditional loyalty. It views political life as a recurrent struggle between good and evil with its own existence continually threatened by evil forces. It maintains its boundaries and imaginatively overcomes its internal tensions by potentially dominatory rituals, most notably marches. Ulster loyalism approximates a closed system resisting refutation by experience or argument. In its deep structure it derives its intelligibility and power from the evangelical fundamentalist religious tradition. Its core assumption is that the only alternative to Ulster loyalist dominance is Ulster loyalist defeat and humiliation.

Level of Ulster loyalist experience

A.T.Q. Stewart (1977, especially parts 2 and 4) has described the Ulster loyalist patterns which have been sedimented in the Northern Irish political landscape and political culture since the seventeenth century. The geography of settlement has created the Protestant town or city encircled by Catholic districts, as well as the inter-penetrating settlement patterns which raise fears of 'traitors in our midst'.

Stories and stereotypes highlight these patterns which have kept their emotional relevance because of continuing Protestant privilege and political division. Such patterned feelings of isolation and insecurity are not the only cultural patterns in country and town. There are also the well-documented patterns of neighbourliness, mutual aid and local loyalties which integrate Protestant and Catholic (Donnan and MacFarlane, 1986a) and the class-conditioned experiences and practices which divide Protestants and lead to class conflict within and between loyalist organisations (Patterson, 1980; Harris, 1972, pp. 194ff). Equally, there are the patterns derived from the democracy, independence and strict discipline character-istic of Presbyterian Church organisation. Yet for those in whom settler insecurity remains strong, nationalist assertion serves to reactivate the associated patterns while relegating the other cultural patterns to a recessive role. For these people, there is an underlying tendency to see the political world in terms of nationalist threats and encroachments.

At a second level, as D.W. Miller (1978) has shown, Ulster loyalism is dependent on the public banding tradition, itself a response to settler insecurity. Orange and other loyalist marches strengthen the cultural patterns outlined above; by responding to perceived threats with domination, any challenge to domination becomes itself a threat.

The rituals and political education associated with Orangeism lead into the third level of Ulster loyalism, the explicitly formulated ideology which typically takes a religio-political form. This ideology, as expressed by Orange Order, DUP or Ulster Clubs leaders, is more coherent, more theologically informed and more closed to refutation than the beliefs held by many ordinary loyalists. Nonetheless, in its structural affinity with and justification of the patterns of culture and practice it can be seen as an intellectualised expression of ordinary loyalist experience, an expression to which ordinary individuals are driven when forced to justify their beliefs and practices.

Politics and religion

Consider the self-definition of Ulster loyalists. In a statement of basic principle for all Lodge members, the Grand Orange Lodge of Ireland's primary definition of its imagined community is of a society of reformed Protestants. This Protestantism is of the fundamentalist-evangelical kind, the political implications of which Frank Wright (1973, pp. 223–32) has analysed – Bible Truth, Gospel Liberty or Protestant Liberty are the religio-political values for which Orangemen stand. These values do not require tolerance for error, evil or tyranny for 'when ungodliness abounds our heritage is imperilled' (LOLI, undated, p. 6). Here the religious concept of sin parallels and reinforces the political concept of the nationalist threat. Sin is thought of as a blot or a stain, passed on as if by contagion and requiring purification and removal of the source of the stain. Sin is not thought of as a mere wandering from a path to which one can later return or be led back. Thus there is a need to secure a Protestant ethos in all social, political and educational institutions (Dewer *et al*, 1969, pp. 174ff). The concept of sin as stain is paralleled in the political realm so that, for example, the very presence of the Irish Tricolour or Garret FitzGerald speaking Irish at Hillsborough, is seen as an insult to the purity of the Protestant state. These views of liberty and sin are not, it must be emphasised, typical of the entire Protestant or Presbyterian tradition. New Light Presbyterians, intellectual Calvinists, twentieth-century theologians and contemporary churchmen would variously reject the fundamentalist dogma, the immediate equation of religious and political values, the literal physical view of sin as concentrated in particular bodies, institutions or objects and for some the view of sin solely as stain, not also as wandering.[4] Yet this evangelical fundamentalist Protestantism is typical of the faith of Ulster loyalist leaders. Paisley's acceptance of these views is well documented (Wright, 1973, p. 224). Alan Wright of the Ulster Clubs declares himself 'a reformed Protestant man' who is ever conscious of the 'encroachment' of nationalists (Wright, 1986 and interview, *Today Tonight*, RTE 1, 8 April 1986). The oft-repeated desire of loyalist extremists to 'wipe out', 'eradicate' or 'exterminate' the Irish Republican Army (IRA) shows how pervasive this concept of political sin is even among secular loyalists.

Loyalty

Secondly, Ulster loyalists are loyal citizens, but the loyalty is of the conditional type which D.W. Miller has analysed (1978, pp. 1–6 and 61ff). As a leading Orangeman said on the Belfast platform this Twelfth, 'we cannot be expected to give *carte blanche* loyalty to a Conservative government who have never been loyal to Northern Ireland' (John McCrea, *Irish Times*, 13 July 1986). The constitution securing Protestant liberties is understood as having been secured once and for all by the 'Glorious Revolution' of the seventeenth century. With clear echoes of sixteenth-century theology, popular resistance to government is said to be justified only to preserve those liberties and only by properly constituted bodies (e.g. covenanting bands), for: 'All evil conspiracy and rebellion are forbidden by our faith. Tyranny may indeed be resisted as our history attests. But no private individual may treat with contumely the laws of our land' (LOLI, undated, p. 8). Miller (1978, pp. 71–2) points out that historically loyalists have seen themselves as defending or restoring the lawful order, even when this takes the form of a riot. So, too, contemporary loyalist politicians justify Protestant disorder and condemn Catholic disorder, defend unionist rights as against nationalist rights, on the grounds that the actions of nationalists are always geared to undermine the proper order ('the will of the ballot box') while the actions of unionists are always geared to uphold it (for example, interview with D. Calvert, DUP Portadown, *Today Tonight*, RTE 1, 8 April 1986).

Ulster loyalists are British citizens. Their loyalty is to 'the Queen and Constitution' (LOLI, undated, p. 8). The Union Jack is a centrally important symbol to them. Sarah Nelson (1984, pp. 12, 63 and 96ff) reports a deeply felt patriotism among some Belfast loyalists, a sense that they had built and fought for the British Empire and paid the ultimate sacrifice; the Somme is deep in Belfast folk-memory. Yet I think that Miller is correct to insist that loyalist

Britishness is neither a nationalist sentiment nor a sense of community with the peoples of Great Britain. At centre it is a loyalty to a Queen and constitution that guard the rights of the 'loyal Ulster people'. The Protestant people of Northern Ireland are emphasised in Ulster loyalist writings and speeches over and above the British connection, and the flag and the Queen symbolise the guarantee of Ulster loyalist liberties.

The Ulster loyalist people

That the Ulster loyalist people are the primary imagined community is borne out by an analysis of the symbolism of loyalism. Anthony Buckley (1985–6, pp. 20ff) has shown in his detailed analysis of the symbolism of the Royal Black Institution that the imagined community is a people, defined in terms of its religious and moral principles. The loyal Godfearing Ulster Protestant people are seen as akin to the Children of Israel, beset by enemies and strangers. Much the same can be said of Orangeism. Martin Smyth (1974, pp. 22–3 and 31ff) has preached that the Ulster Protestant today can learn much from Daniel's courage and refusal to compromise even while in the lion's den, and has seen an analogy between the politico-religious statement of Christ's entry to Jerusalem on Palm Sunday and the Twelfth marches. While Orange intellectuals emphasise the international heritage of Orangeism, the subject of narrative and sermons seems preponderantly to be the Ulster Protestant people from the Convenanters to the Somme to the present Troubles.[5] Similarly, Paisley sees the loyalist people constantly fighting the enemies of God and Ulster (Taylor, 1984, p. 64).

The loyalty is primarily to people rather than to place (see Bell, 1986, p. 37, for interesting evidence to this effect). Although loyalty to and love of the place of Ulster is strong, it is seldom spoken of. The 'homeland', 'province', or 'this beloved place' are mentioned but not emphasised in speeches and interviews (McMichael, 1986; Wright, 1986; *Irish Times*, 11 September 1986). More obvious is loyalist territoriality which defines place in terms of its inhabitants and asserts Protestant power over as wide a territory as possible. I think this reticence about place shows an underlying insecurity about the place they occupy. Some evidence of this insecurity lies in the references to land in the symbolism of the Royal Black Institution. Buckley's explication of the symbols (1985–6, pp. 15–20) contains almost as many references to a land as to a people, but the land is always a foreign land, a promised land or a land appropriated from the Canaanites. Even God's promise of the land does not seem to allow loyalists fully to appropriate it in their imaginations. It is as if the imaginative justification of loyalists as God's chosen people in their recurrent battles is gained only at the cost of continued uncertainty about the place of that people.

Ulster loyalists see their political future as in large part pre-determined. A constant theme of Orange speeches and writings is the view that Protestants must constantly repeat the defence of their faith and liberty against Catholic attack. Protestants of the twentieth century fight the same battles of the righteous against the ungodly as did those of the seventeenth and sixteenth centuries, or as did the

Jews of the Old Testament. 'The price of liberty is eternal vigilance' because the battle between the principles of light and darkness is itself eternal. The demand to stand for the faith of one's fathers is based on the view that neither the faith nor its enemies have changed. 'The errors and superstitions of Romanism are not less dangerous now than when our Order was founded' (Kerr in Dewer, 1959, p. 3; also pp. 7, 9, 18 and 20; and Dewer *et al*, 1969, p. 17). Paisley identifies the contemporary battles of loyal Ulster Protestants with battles of the Biblical and historical past (Taylor, 1984, p. 74; Wallis *et al*, 1986, pp. 19ff). The very rituals of secular loyalists, as of religious, identify contemporary loyalist battles with those of their Protestant forefathers.

Democracy, meaning majority rule in Northern Ireland, is defended in political speeches but I do not think that this concept is central to the structure of Ulster loyalist ideology. It is more consistent with the other aspects of the ideology to claim that the Ulster Protestant people have their rights (to a Protestant state) whatever about majorities.

The Other

The Other of the God-fearing loyal Protestant is the Roman Catholic Church, seen as an international source of political treason and tyranny as well as a barrier to the true faith: 'Papal powers and political tyranny are children of one womb' (LOLI, undated, p. 2). The perceived religious evil of the Roman Catholic Church's doctrines and practices (which systematically separate one from and deny Christ, on this view) is imaginatively identified with the 'murdering traitors' of the IRA. Some make a literal identification. Alan Wright of the Ulster Clubs sees the Church of Rome's ultimate target as the throne of England, and a United Ireland the first step on the way (interview, *Today Tonight*, RTE 1, 8 April 1986). Rhonda Paisley believes that 'the Roman Catholic Church is behind the Irish Republican Army ... Certainly there is complete alignment between the IRA and the Catholic Church today' (interview, *Irish Times*, 21 February 1986). Any Catholic or nationalist self-assertion is seen as a strain on the Protestant ethos of the society and as an opening for bloody republican rebellion (Dewer *et al*, 1969, p. 118). The Republic of Ireland is seen as Ulster's enemy in religion, culture and politics; it is a 'sick country' (Smyth, 1974, p. 32), 'not a civilized or Christian nation among the nations of Europe' (Paisley, speech at DUP conference, *Irish Times*, 21 April 1986).

Symbolically, the Catholic threat is seen as a corruption or besmirching of the true faith. This imagery is integrated with the historical image of the siege of Derry where the defenders protected the purity of the maiden city. Sometimes one finds a rich interrelation of gender, religious and historico-political themes in the writings: 'the Border is secure as a bulwark to his religious faith and his political freedom, under the ample folds of the Union Jack, as were the grey old walls of Derry beneath her Crimson Banner nearly three centuries ago' (Dewer, 1959, p. 22). This is a clear, although paradoxical, identification of the Orangeman with the virgin threatened with violation. The Orangeman is both defender and defended, assertively male but behind the defences possessing a powerless female core. The defences are at once physical (walls, security forces) and symbolic (flags), both manned by the vigilant loyalist who spans the divide between 'rough'/male and 'religious'/female.[6]

Ecumenism is a second and more insidious enemy which attempts to persuade Protestants to compromise on their true principles. Smyth (1974, pp. 31ff) and others preach the need to 'stand fast' against ecumenist pressure to conform to their definitions of the religious and political divide. Ecumenism is identified with liberalism, compromise with Republicans, and treachery, whether from within the Protestant population or from England.

Middle-class liberal unionists, for example, the O'Neillite 'fur coat brigade', are seen as unsteady allies, snobbish, patronising, ungrateful for loyalist defence of their liberties and often exploiting loyalist sacrifices.[7] The loyalists simply see the English as well-known betrayers of principle (for example, see Paisley in the *Irish Times*, 9 January 1986).

The logic of loyalism

In Orange writings first principles – defence of Protestant faith and liberties – are clearly and constantly stated. Arguments against Catholicism and ecumenism are deduced from these principles in what appears to be a clear logical fashion. Once the principles of Ulster loyalism are accepted, the closure of the system ensures that the right political and religious views are held on every topic. However, the writing style is not purely deductive but is rich in narrative and symbolism, often allegories where Bible stories are taken as illustrations of contemporary problems. The colourful language often disguises the closure of the system. The literal identifications, for example, of the Catholic Church and the IRA, seem to be the height of irrationality. I will take one such seemingly absurd argument and show its rationale in terms of its concealed religio-political premises.

After the killing of an Ulster Defence Regiment (UDR) man in Fermanagh, Ian Paisley claimed that his blood 'drips from the hands of Garret FitzGerald' who is 'only one remove from the actual man who pulled the trigger' (*Irish Times*, 5 February 1986). Paisley's evidence was FitzGerald's criticism of the UDR and supposed aspiration to have it disbanded. The general claim, often assumed in Ulster loyalists' arguments, is that criticising the security forces is equivalent to murdering them. This argument is valid if we insert two religio-political premises central to fundamentalist evangelical thinking.

The first premise is that unjust forces should be resisted, to the death if necessary. It follows that criticism of the security forces as unjust amounts to a justification of physical resistance to them, even of killing them. The second premise is that he who sins in his heart is as bad as he who commits the deed, i.e. the view that there is no gradation of sin. It follows that justifying murder is morally equivalent to murdering. Criticising the security forces is murdering them.

This conclusion and others similar are often repeated by secular loyalists. My argument is that the view becomes intelligible only in terms of a religio-political theory to which many of these loyalists do not explicitly adhere but which parallels and rationalises their views.

Ulster loyalists themselves have come into conflict with the security forces since the Anglo-Irish Agreement and have criticised them harshly. This provides a contradiction in the ideology from which there are two ways out. On the one hand, the premises can be followed through, as when William McCrea warns that 'Ulster people may even yet have to fight the British to remain true British' (*Irish Times*, 13 February 1986). On the other hand, the premises may be abandoned and nationalist criticisms of the security forces reassessed (Nelson, 1984, p. 135). In either case it signals a change in the loyalist position.

Ritual marches

Marching is central to the ideology of loyalism. It is at once an affirmation of Protestant values and cultural traditions and a constitution of communal identity as Ulster Protestants by creating real networks and by magical symbols and rituals which are emotionally and imaginatively effective. It is a practical assertion of territorial dominance and at the same time an imaginative overcoming of the real tensions, insecurities and contradictions experienced by loyalists. It is a mode of maintaining the existing boundaries between Protestants and Catholics in Northern Ireland. Since the *status quo* involves Protestant dominance, boundary maintenance is a mode of social dominance, as is seen most clearly in Protestant marches through Catholic areas. As Dewer points out in a discussion of early Orangeism, 'where you could walk you were dominant' (Dewer *et al*, 1969, pp. 118 and 125ff).

The Twelfth marches ritually commemorate the eternal battle faced by Protestants and their winning of that battle in 1690. They provide a motivation and rationale for the continuing battle and they imaginatively resolve the exciting contradictions faced by northern Protestants by having them win the battle. They destroy all ambiguities which might disrupt the binary opposition of good and evil in Orange ideology by clarifying and completing the proper social boundaries. Further, the celebratory aspects of the day – preparations, paraphernalia, noise, picnics with the women and children – reaffirm for Orangemen the benefits of their Protestant identity by having their rigid creed culminate in festival (Larsen, 1982a). These are typical functions of ritual in many and varied societies studied by anthropologists (Cohen, 1985, pp. 50–7).

In normal Northern Irish conditions of Protestant dominance, marching simply maintains boundaries. In circumstances where the British state, or nationalist assertion, has temporarily overturned Protestant dominance in any sphere, marching takes on a different function. It becomes a ritual restoration of the proper order, a restoration which often takes the form of a reversal of the dominant Orange values. The orderly and disciplined Protestants become riotous; they take on the characteristics of their Other. Thus they highlight the values and conventions constitutive of their group as if by saying 'see how disorderly and rebellious we could be if we wanted'. Such riotous protests are more than shows of force and signs of frustration. They also reconstitute the Ulster loyalist community by magically overcoming the contradictions which they manifest (loyalty/disloyalty, order/disorder) by repeating the actions of ancestors who overcame these contradictions in their legitimate resistance to tyranny.

The ideological structure

The elements of Ulster loyalist ideology derive from the sixteenth-century reformation, the public banding and convenanting traditions of the seventeenth century, eighteenth-century faction fighting and early Orangeism, and nineteenth-century evangelical preaching and sectarian patterns of housing and industrialisation in Belfast. Its more recent history has involved endemic class tensions and the emergence of breakaway working-class loyalist associations (Miller, 1978; Senior, 1966; Gibbon, 1975; Patterson, 1980). This package represents within itself definite historical changes even in religious principles. It is presented as embodying eternal and unchanging truth.

Despite the very real differences among Ulster loyalist organisations, I have suggested that they share a common ideological structure. I think it is of political importance to emphasise this for it shows an ideological factor which is important in limiting the splintering tendency of loyalist organisations, ensuring closure of the ideological system and preventing any gradualist move from within loyalism towards the class-based ideology of socialism. Two aspects of Ulster loyalist ideology are of especial importance in this regard – the concept of history and the existential assumptions.

History is seen as repeating an eternal pattern and battle of good against evil, light against darkness, loyalty against treachery, truth against error. Protestantism and Unionism are on the side of right. Thus, politics, for Ulster loyalists, is a zero-sum game. Refusal to compromise is treated as a sign of honesty (Nelson, 1984, p. 37; Miller, 1978, p. 89). Political enemies are treated mythically; Catholicism and ecumenism are personified as evil monoliths, like demons, ultimately equatable with republicans and betrayers. Ulster loyalist rituals reproduce and partially constitute this structure of meanings.

Existentially, political life is seen as a constant battle to defend the good and the pure from its surrounding assailants. Constant vigilance and assertion of Ulster loyalist principle is necessary to maintain the 'walls' defending the good and pure. Betrayal is always possible by those whom one defends – e.g. by the British state or by Protestant leaders and clergy. This vulnerability is expressed in the image of the maiden city. Betrayal leads to a seething anger, defeat to an intense sense of humiliation.[8] When the power of their male-assertive marches and speeches is taken from them they are in fantasy thrown defenceless to those who mock and stain their purity simply by their Being. The absolutist binary structure of Ulster loyalist thought can be maintained only insofar as Protestant dominance is maintained, for compromise is defeat and defeat is destruction and despoliation of the identity of group and individual.

The meaning of dominance

Basic to my argument is that Ulster loyalism is more than mere dominance. The ideological structure of Ulster loyalism is such that loyalists see dominance as the only means of preserving their identity. It is not simply Protestants' desire to hold onto material or even status advantages that explains Ulster loyalist practices although this is an important factor. Whatever advantage lower-class loyalists may have are surely outweighed by the costs to them of continued violence and turmoil. Not domination *per se* but the meaning of domination to loyalists explains their practices. It is because the dominatory practices are perceived as the only alternative to humiliation that they are fought for to the last. And to the extent that they continue, they reproduce the binary structure of Ulster loyalist thought. Ulster loyalism is dominance, but it is dominance legitimated and garbed in imaginatively rich and coherent ideas. These essentially religious ideas help explain the long-lasting appeal of loyalist movements and their role in cultural cohesion as well as boundary maintenance, for they imaginatively resolve the sense of insecurity at the heart of loyalism. Further, loyalist religious ideology has such structural affinity with loyalist experiences and practices that it retains some appeal even for more secular loyalists who cannot accept the whole religious system but who will accept some pieces of it and use them to justify their actions.

The structure of Ulster British ideology

Ulster British ideology, although unionist, has a radically different structure from Ulster loyalist ideology. Its imagined community is Greater Britain, although within this there is a secondary regional identification with Northern Ireland. Religious values are not primary in the structure of Ulster British thought although moral principles are important in defining their community. This ideology may be either integrationist or devoluntionist at the level of political programmes; I have attempted to define its structure of meaning at a more general level than that of explicit political policy. Ulster British ideology shares many characteristics with liberal ideology but within a social and political context where it is constantly challenged by the realities of loyalist sectarianism, the policies of the British state and nationalist grievances and achievements.

Levels of Ulster experience

The underlying pattern of landscape, thought and political culture upon which Ulster British ideology is based, expresses nothing of the loyalist sense of threat and insecurity. The Ulster British are sympathetic observers of the Northern Ireland political landscape seeing symbols of the British connection in marks of progress like new roads, hospitals, schools and industry, in the effects of the welfare state on individual health, education and welfare, in the ubiquitous war memorials and in the English literature and English media which still predominate in Northern Ireland.

Ulster British ideology is reproduced in their life-paths which take them to Great Britain and beyond to further their education, business and careers and in times of war. It is institutionalised in the evident linkages between Great Britain and Northern Ireland in industry and trade union organisation, and in British state economic and welfare policies which focus interests, action and thought within the British context.

Ulster British ideology has been articulated by unionist organic intellectuals, usually professional middle-class men, sometimes landed gentry, less frequently working-class writers.[9] Despite a pronounced middle-class and male bias in its written form, the structure of Ulster British ideology is as available to working-class experience as to middle-class and is open to a wide range of expressions, from the Ulster Anglo-Irish to the Anglophobic, from conservative to left-liberal, from Thatcherite to trade-unionist, from Unionist Party to NILP and Alliance, from integrationist to devolutionist, from the Ulster centred to the Irish oriented. All are unionist; most are Unionist Party supporters or voters. At the extremes, for example of Irish patriotism or Ulster loyalty, there may be a gradual transition from an Ulster British ideological structure to a different ideological structure. Within the ideology endemic class conflict exists which was clearly manifested in the NILP challenge to unionism in the late 1950s and early 1960s.

The historical context

The origins of Ulster British ideology lie with the late-nineteenth-century British Empire when Belfast industrialists in particular expressed a modernising unionist ideology in imperial terms (Gibbon, 1975, pp. 127–38). The aspects of imperial ideology drawn on in Ulster British ideology were primarily the sense that progress and civilisation were spread by Empire and the notion, emphasised by Lord Milner in Britain, that bonds of citizenship and loyalty unite every British person across all the states of the Empire (Bennett, 1953, pp. 352 and 359). There was a turn-of-the-century Belfast labour variant of this Empire unionism which argued that the Empire brought progress through the internationalisation of capital which in turn promoted working-class international solidarity (Patterson, 1980, p. 48).

The opposition to Home Rule united Ulster British and Ulster loyalist tendencies within the Unionist Party with the Ulster British gentry and bourgeoisie as leaders and intellectuals of the movement. The unification of these political traditions was ridden with class, urban–rural and ideological tensions and accomplished in large part symbolically (Gibbon, 1975, pp. 132–6). Intellectuals like Ronald McNeill produced effective symbolic unifications of the imperial and loyalist symbols. Those who opposed the first Home Rule Bill were like the heroes of Empire:

> men who felt as if living in a beleaguered citadel, whose flag they were bound in honour to keep flying to the last . . . a populace that came more and more to regard themselves as a bulwark of Empire, on whom destiny while

conferring on them the honour of upholding the flag, had imposed the duty of putting into actual practice the familiar motto of the Orange Lodges – No Surrender.

(McNeill, 1922, p. 13)

Here seventeenth-century sieges only gain a meaning through their analogy with nineteenth-century sieges; the imperialist discourse incorporates and limits the role of the loyalist discourse.

Many aspects of the imperial Ulster British ideology were taken up by the explicitly liberal, post-imperialist generation who served in the Second World War and whose most prominent spokesmen were in the professional middle class. This Ulster British generation tended to distance itself from involvement in Unionist Party politics until O'Neill's premiership although some were involved in Labour Party politics. O'Neill's failure and the subsequent IRA campaign provoked a range of responses, most typically: a retrenchment within the unionist alliance; the liberal unionist move to the Alliance Party; or an opting out of political life and debate.

The distinctiveness of the Ulster British has often been ignored and they see themselves as misunderstood (Oliver, 1978b, p. 68). Consistently they emphasise that their unionism is not a product of prejudice but a cherishing of British ideals (1918 Unionist letter to President Wilson, in McNeill, 1922, p. 297; Ervine, 1949, p. 104; Oliver, 1978b, p. 68). In part, the distinctiveness of this tradition has been ignored because its intellectuals have tended to assume that their moral-political principles needed little elucidation. In part it is because the professed liberal and progressive ideology of the Ulster British has been allied with crude sectarianism within the Unionist Party. While some unionists have been hypocritical in their professions of these liberal values, I intend to take the ideology as the authentic expression of the thought of many northern Protestants.

Ideological themes

Consider the self-image of the Ulster British. They see themselves as primarily British, where being British means having a particular ethos, holding particular ideals and moral principles. W. Brian Maginnis (1956), the liberal unionist Minister of Finance, emphasised that 'Partition is based not upon geographical, racial or language differences but on differences of ideas'. The ethos involves being progressive, liberal and democratic, at the forefront of modern ideas. St John Ervine emphasises the liberal and progressive tradition in Northern Ireland which, by the paradox of Irish politics, must retain these values by alliance with the British conservatives (Ervine, 1949, pp. vii, 6 and 103–4; see also O'Neill, 1972, p. 20). When pressed hard they will admit that these ideals are aspirations rather than realities, but they will point out that aspirations can define a society. R.L. McCartney argues that 'the true and essential Union is not an exclusive union of loyalists or protestants, but a union between peoples who believe in liberal democracy and civil and religious liberty for all in the fullest sense of a pluralist society' (McCartney, 1985, pp. 25–6; 1983, p. 147; Dunlop, 1986, p. 16).

The Ulster British see themselves as valuing progress and a future orientation for 'to Ulster, as to America, the past is past; it is the present and future that count' (Maginnis, 1956; see also Ervine, 1949, p. 70; Nelson, 1984, p. 50). They see themselves as rational, efficient and scientific with no time for superstitions and archaisms.[10] They take pride in technological advances in Northern Irish industry (Dunlop, 1986, p. 17).

The Ulster British see themselves as valuing liberty, understood in the traditional liberal sense of the negative freedom of individuals to choose their life plan and reach their own conclusions free from outside authorities, by their conscience alone: 'the fundamental rights... to think, to debate, to express our opinions, to differ from our neighbours... to exercise our minds without trammel or restriction, to develop our outlook as we each individually desire, to pursue knowledge no matter from which source it comes' (Maginnis, 1956). Liberty in this sense depends not on who governs, Protestant or Catholic, but on the justice of the constitution and the laws (McCartney, 1985, pp. 6–8).

The Ulster British understand democracy in the sense of majority rule. This is taken to be the normal understanding in the civilised world. The majority in Northern Ireland is therefore taken to have a right to decide on its basic form of government. While there are divisions among the Ulster British between integrationists and devolutionists, those who defend devolved majority rule within Northern Ireland do so not on grounds of retaining Protestant power but because any other arrangement would be incompatible with liberal democratic principles (Oliver, 1978b, p. 27).

The Ulster British consider themselves to have international, not merely parochial concerns and interests. They see themselves as part of a great tradition, recognising the need for world leadership and statesmanship to attain human excellence rather than accepting a 'small is beautiful' philosophy. As St John Ervine (1949, p. 247) puts it with his usual clarity: 'The Ulster people were not, and are not, willing to turn away from a prominent partnership in a galaxy of nations to an introspective obscurantist, Gaelic-speaking agricultural republic'. From a different political perspective, Charles Brett (1978, p. 62) contrasts nationalism to his own European and internationalist concerns. Ulster British internationalism, however, is routed through London.

The Ulster British are patriotic in their love for British ideals and institutions and in a willingness to fight for British interests. The patriotism is deeply felt. Britain here is conceived not as a nation but as a sphere of influence which encompasses diversity within it. The Crown is 'the symbol of the headship of a great family of nations of which we are a unit' (Maginnis, 1956). The Ulster people 'is devoted to a far greater thing than England, to the Commonwealth of the British people' (Ervine, 1949, p. 526). To safeguard British values the Ulster British middle class tends to be concerned with world strategic issues, state stability and to be anti-Communist. The Ulster British working class is less high-flown in its praise of British ideals but no less patriotic.[11]

The British values are clearly expressed in often repeated narratives. In the earlier twentieth century, writers like Ronald McNeill and St. John Ervine emphasised the part Ulstermen played in building the British Empire. Post World War Two, Ulster British like W. Brian Maginnis emphasise the part Ulstermen played in saving the free world during the world wars and their wholehearted acceptance of the progressive values and ideals of the post-war free world. The question is still 'What is Ulster's place in contemporary history?' and the answer is that Ulster stands 'on the side of freedom', a 'bridgehead between a free Europe and a free America' (Maginnis, 1956). Here the 'free world' and NATO take the same place in Ulster British ideology as the British Empire did previously, and the Northern Irish conflict is seen as the microcosm of the wider world conflict between freedom and modernity, on the one hand, and totalitarianism, on the other.

The reproduction of Ulster British ideology

The limited ritual of Ulster British ideology is all official British state ritual: Poppy days, the national anthem, the flag, the Queen's speeches, royal visits and walkabouts, OBEs, MBEs and other honours. While some of these rituals are shared with Ulster loyalists, I think that they have a different meaning to the Ulster British. They symbolise to them a sense of belonging to a wider community rather than conditional loyalty to a constitution.

Ulster British ideology is in large part a product of the British state presence in Northern Ireland and has varied from imperialist to welfare-state-liberal in tone as the form of the British state has changed. It is not, however, that Ulster British individuals merely passively accept ideas originating in London. Rather British state and economic structures exist within the socio-political structures of Northern Ireland and create typical opportunities and life-paths for individuals whose concrete life-experiences reproduce their Ulster British ideology. Bew *et al* (1979, chapter 3) have shown how the structure of relations between Stormont and London produced an 'anti-populist', anti-sectarian tendency within the pre-war Stormont government and administration. This allowed the retention within the predominantly sectarian regime of some liberal political norms and practices which themselves reinforced the liberal tendencies of the Ulster British population. The changing role of the British state in Northern Ireland conditions the changing weights of Ulster loyalist and Ulster British ideology within Unionist Party politics and the Northern Ireland administrative structure. This, however, is not my present concern. For the impact of the British state presence goes beyond direct political structures to condition the life-paths of many northern Protestants and thus provides a basis in socio-economic practices for Ulster British ideology.

Northern Protestants (and not only Protestants) served in the British army and the colonial service during the Empire; they volunteered for the two World Wars. Many families have relatives who emigrated to Canada, Australia or New Zealand. The present adult generation is still coloured by their parents' experience of

World War. In working-class Belfast it was common to join the British forces or merchant navy. Many trade-unions are British-based and working-class interests crucially depend on British state economic strategy, and protective and welfare legislation. In the professional middle class, further education in Great Britain is common, a period of work there not uncommon, and conferences there regular events, while businessmen have even more regular contacts. The very organisation of work for the middle and higher levels of industry, research, health, education, and administration has been integrally tied to British policies and practices. Robin Boyd, the Presbyterian clergyman and ecumenist, accurately describes the effects of these real linkages when he describes the feeling 'as I drive ashore at Holyhead or step off a plane at Heathrow: This too belongs to me and no one can take it from me' (Boyd, 1986). It is a feeling specific to those who frequently travel to Great Britain and is rooted in the fabric of their lives. Survey evidence supports this view for Protestants who travel to Britain are significantly more likely to share the Ulster British disapproval of loyalist influence on Northern Irish politics than are those who do not travel.[12]

A multi-levelled identity

The Ulster British stance involves an Ulster identity as well as a British identity. It involves a strongly felt patriotism towards the region, evidenced in a love of place, of the distinctive landscape, and a pride in regional distinctiveness whether of landscape, sport, education, food, or patterns of social interaction (Oliver, 1978a, pp. 132ff; McAughtry, 1985). For example, the Ulster British recognise and prize the informal mode of social interaction common to Ulster British, loyalists and nationalists and distinct from the more distant English pattern of interaction.

There is also, to a lesser extent, an Irish identity, expressed in support for the Irish rugby team or for Irish athletes at the Olympics and manifested in holidays in Donegal or trips to Dublin for the horse show, golf, rugby, the theatre, or just for a long weekend. The island is not alien to them. Many clergy and professionals were educated at Trinity College, Dublin and there are other limited professional and more extensive ecumenical linkages. As a place, the island of Ireland brings forth affection of a milder kind than the regional patriotism for Northern Ireland (Oliver, 1978b, pp. 14–15; Boyd, 1986; letter by G.B.G. McConnell, *Irish Times*, 1 August 1986).

Ulster British patriotism is multi-levelled. Charles Brett illustrates these multiple loyalties when he addresses his book to 'first, my fellow Ulstermen . . . also to my fellow countrymen throughout Ireland, and my fellow citizens throughout Britain' (1978, p. x). However, in terms of ideals and principles the Ulster British see themselves as British and in any conflict between ideals and sense of place the ideals clearly win out. Only when the perceived connection between their ideals and their concrete sense of Britishness is loosened can they begin to gain a critical detachment about their own unionist culture; this, however, is to move to the limits of Ulster British ideology.[13]

There are also distinctively Northern Irish characteristics of Ulster British ideology which the Ulster British do not themselves recognise and which distinguish Ulster British ideology from ideologies in Great Britain. For example, in England a major aspect of conservative ideology is the emphasis on tradition, continuity, the institutionalisation of values, and the possibility of only gradual, organic change for the better (Scruton, 1986, pp. 107ff; Schwarz, 1986, p. 155). In contrast, the Ulster British seldom argue from precedent and often from first principles. They value their principled approach to politics and tend to argue deductively from principles of liberty and progress which, it is assumed, no decent person would disagree with. British state ideology also diverges from Ulster British ideology in its English nationalism, in its pragmatism with respect to its own ideological principles, in its preference for informal influence over its peripheries rather than formalised control, in its tendency to make centrally important decisions in 'high politics' by executive decree not parliamentary debate and to leave parliamentary politics for issues of bargaining and compromise (Bulpitt, 1978 and 1986).

Part of the cultural specificity of Ulster British ideology lies in its assumption that politics and morality are closely intertwined. Religion is not directly important to the Ulster British concept of politics but the Presbyterian religious tradition has affected the Ulster British view of morality. Morality is thought to be a matter of principles and of conscience, not merely a product of civility, custom or social interaction. Individual liberty of conscience and the individual's duty to guard his own conscience and find his own relation with God are central to the non-conformist tradition in its non-evangelical-fundamentalist form. The New Light strand of Presbyterianism with its emphasis on rationality, rational assent to moral principles and the improvability of mankind has a faint echo in the moral optimism of the Ulster British.

The Ulster British and sectarian realities

The Ulster British tend to be personally 'tolerant'. For example in middle-class circles friendships with middle-class Catholics are common and there would be no qualms about friendships with British or Southern Irish middle-class Catholics (Larsen, 1982b; McAughtry, 1985, pp. 108–13; also participant observation). However, there are relatively few occasions where northern Protestants can meet northern Catholics unselfconsciously; Brett (1978, p. 65) lists the arts and trade union activity and one might also mention some sports. The etiquette of friendships between northern Protestants and Catholics, however, is that contentious political or religious issues cannot easily be raised.[14] While political discussions between Protestants and Catholics do occur, they tend to be limited in scope and duration except where the explicit intent is to institute dialogue. This tendency to avoid political discussions allows the continuation of stereotypes and also limits the depth of the relationships.

The positive self-image of the Ulster British is of an honourable people, equal to any, without chips on the shoulders or bad consciences. It is noticeable that the two central political forces in Northern Ireland – Catholics and loyalists – are all but absent from this self-image, at least in its middle-class variant. It is as if Catholics did not exist on this world horizon, except as a few individuals who are known socially, and as if loyalists were merely peripheral to unionist politics.

The middle-class professional Ulster British, in particular, have been shielded from the ugliness of communal violence and the sordid sectarianism of Unionist Party politics. Oliver, although close to party politicians in his work, saw himself as a professional administrator and giver of technical or factual advice although he also criticises the tendency of middle-class Protestants to stay aloof from party politics (Oliver, 1978a, pp. 71–9; 1978b, p. 67). The distance of his social group from the Catholic experience in Northern Ireland is illustrated by his account of the voluntary clubs he helped run in the 1930s:

> Our attitude – if we thought about it at all – would have been to welcome Roman Catholic boys and men insofar as they took part in our activities; insofar as they did not, then we would have regretted the fact but not been put out or surprised in the least. We all knew that Roman Catholics had their own point of view on such matters and we respected it. It would not have occurred to us to attempt to press or cajole them into the clubrooms, much less to construct any system of bridge-building or integration. In a very small way I suppose our philosophy reflected that of the service as a whole at the time.
>
> (Oliver, 1978a, p. 47)

Many of the middle class were unaware of the systematic discrimination against Catholics under Stormont. Robin Boyd, from such a background, states the position:

> the failure to share our rights and freedoms with our Roman Catholic fellow citizens; our failure even to *know* anything much about their problems, their alienation, their sense of exclusion in their own country which was also ours. We simply did not know. We were not encouraged to know. I had left Ireland before I made my first real Catholic friend. My parents would never let us speak a word against Roman Catholics but we never met any. Young people growing up in a middle class Belfast suburb simply did not know what was happening.
>
> (Boyd, 1986)

The sense of having been unaware of the injustices of the system and how Catholics felt about it has been expressed to me by people both older and younger than Boyd, not all in the Belfast suburbs. It must be added, however, that the evidence was there for the asking, and that some Labour activists tried to publicise it and oppose it.[15]

The high moral and optimistic tone of the Ulster British is in part a function of their distance from sectarian politics. Yet the conflict in Northern Ireland inevitably impinges on them and presents the Other of the Ulster British which questions their own integrity and thus is deeply disturbing to them. The Ulster British categorical structure, however, provides the framework in which they interpret Northern Irish politics. They retain their positive self-image through their negative stereotypes of their Other.

The Other

The obverse of the Ulster British self-image is a negative image of those who oppose their self-defined liberal, progressive and international orientation. Such groups are by definition intolerant, backward looking and parochial. Just as the Ulster British define their own British political allegiance in terms of moral principles so they divide their political world into those who share and those who reject their moral principles. The Others of the Ulster British reject Britishness, that is in Ulster British eyes they do not value individual freedom, social progress or democracy or share the moral virtues of patriotism and political principledness which the Ulster British see as essential to civilised society. The opposite of civilised society is backwardness and barbarism, and Seamus Deane has reminded us that the binary opposition of civilians and barbarians is typical of the colonial mentality (1983). Within the Northern Irish political context, the Ulster British find it all too easy to categorise unionists on the side of civilisation and nationalists on the side of barbarism.

The Others of the Ulster British do not share the moral principles which define their identity. At worst, the Other consciously rejects these principles and attempts to destroy them, as does the IRA. The IRA and the republican movement in general is, on this view, absolutely evil. It is felt that any attempt to understand the motives of such people underestimates their evilness and thus many Ulster British tend to focus on military rather than political 'solutions' to the Northern Ireland problem.

Nationalists are categorised and judged according to the strength of their opposition to the British state. Even St. John Ervine distinguished good nationalists, 'men of honour' like the Redmonds, W.T. Cosgrave and Joseph Devlin ('a friendly, generous hearted man, an Ulsterman in the marrow of his bones'), from bad (de Valera) (Ervine, 1949, pp. 328, 338, 378 and 528). However all nationalists are thought of as potential traitors. Their refusal to recognise the legitimacy of the British state in Northern Ireland or to participate in its rituals is felt to be insulting at least and traitorous at worst (Oliver, 1978b, pp. 25–6; Dunlop, 1986, p. 19). It is compared unfavourably with the attitude of southern unionists who quickly recognised the legitimacy of the Irish Free State. It is taken to show an intransigence, a disrespect for democracy and therefore a lack of moral character.

The Ulster British have, with a few individual exceptions, been slow to recognise nationalist complaints about discrimination and repression. Their complaints have been taken as merely ritualised and often dismissed as when the historian of the B Specials clearly agrees with the Protestants' 'firm conviction that you could believe very little of what the native Irish told you' (Hazlet, 1972, p. 9). I think Sarah Nelson is correct in explaining this blindness to nationalist grievances in terms of the challenge to their personal integrity which the accusations posed (Nelson, 1975, p. 163; see also Dunlop, 1986, p. 18). If true, their positive self-image would be badly shaken.

The Ulster British clearly defined the southern Irish as traitors in World War Two; southern neutrality rankles deeply especially with the older generation. The political intentions of the Republic are distrusted; southern politicians are considered 'devious', merely masking their irredentist nationalism, and their interference in Northern Irish politics is deeply resented (Oliver, 1978a, p. 68; 1978b, p. 21). It is thought, with some accuracy, that a Catholic ethos predominates in the Republic which restricts the negative liberty that the Ulster British value. McNeill (1922, p. 12) wrote of the 'mental and moral atmosphere' of southern Catholicism as tainting any legislature there and a similar point is made over 60 years later by McCartney (1985, pp. 15f). The Republic is also thought of as a backward country, industrially and socially (Maginnis, 1956; Ervine, 1949, p. 225; Oliver, 1978b, p. 21). There is no understanding of the value of preserving the Irish language and little interest in historical traditions or Gaelic games. Often an attitude of superiority, based on ignorance, is taken by middle-class, educated Ulster British Protestants. However, I have observed that many Ulster British people like southern Irish people although there is a very clear sense that their culture and assumptions are very different from their own.

Catholicism is clearly distinguished from nationalism. The Roman Catholic religion, especially in its Irish form, is thought to promote superstition and subservience to priests. Terence O'Neill's condescension to Catholics who can learn to live like Protestants when they are treated decently has been much quoted, and illustrates the attitudes of some Ulster British towards the Catholic population (Hepburn, 1980, p. 182; McNeill, 1922, pp. 9ff; Ervine, 1949, pp. 416, 463 and 518; O'Donnell, 1977).

Among the Protestant population, sectarians, religious fanatics and aggressive loyalists are thought of by the Ulster British as their Other. There is sometimes a rather condescending amusement at Orange processions but in my experience the Ulster British person is never an Orangeman and there is genuine shock if they are mistaken for sectarian loyalists (Oliver, 1978b, p. 66). Unionist politicians, of course, have combined Ulster British ideology and Ulster loyalist practices but they are a special category. However, many Ulster British have been willing to ally with Ulster loyalists as the lesser evil against the nationalist threat (McCartney, 1985, pp. 24–5). They tend to treat loyalist sectarianism as an unfortunate but inevitable fact of life and therefore advise that the national question not be raised as it will inevitably provoke trouble from loyalist and prevent progress in Northern Ireland (Garrett, 1986; McAughtry, 1986).

The Others of the Ulster British also typically include the southern English, perceived as snobbish and patronising, whose demonstration that Ulster Britishness is not their sort of Britishness is resented, and left-intellectuals and other 'misfits' who challenge the claim that the British-made world was well made. St John Ervine as usual gives vicious stereotypes and even combines the two in his disdain for 'English softies of the Left' (1949, p. 72).

Morality and politics

The elements of Ulster British ideology derive from official British state ideology: the progressive future-oriented sense of time; the view that the British Empire was a progressive, civilising and moralising force; the sense of Britain as a wider and more diverse entity than either England or the UK; the liberal tradition of British thought from Locke to Mill; the ideology of the free world. Yet the Ulster British have not simply taken over British state ideology but have chosen those elements and aspects that best fit their life experiences and have added to them a regional patriotism and a particular concept of politics in which politics and morality are intertwined. Their moral and political principles and their freedom to arrive at their own principles are central to the Ulster British concept of their own integrity as individuals.

Changes in unionist political culture

Change in unionist ideology is partially determined by the pre-existing structure of ideology. Consider the limits and possibilities of change in the Ulster loyalist and Ulster British traditions.

Change in Ulster loyalist ideology

Ulster loyalist ideology approximates a self-contained, closed system. The binary structure of thought – purity vs. corruption, domination vs. humiliation – does not allow for any gradual move towards compromise with or understanding of political opponents. No new evidence or argument can prove that humiliation won't follow from loyalists letting down their guard. It follows that there can be no gradual change in loyalism towards a more moderate or tolerant stance. There will be no slow 'modernisation' of Ulster loyalist ideology. Change in Ulster loyalist ideology can only be radical change in the basic structuring binaries of thought. But there is little within Ulster loyalist ideology that could internally generate such a change. It appears that radical change can only be externally produced, when Ulster loyalists face what they have perceived as defeat and humiliation and if they find the experience different from what they had anticipated.

Political developments within Ulster loyalism illustrate this analysis. Despite the abolition of Stormont, the destruction of Unionist Party hegemony, the proliferation of loyalist groupings and the increased class consciousness among working-class loyalists (Nelson, 1984, chapter 11), no loyalist grouping has radically redefined its imagined community in class rather than sectarian terms. Direct Rule and loyalist conflicts with the British state have weakened the sense of British loyalty among some loyalists but the primary imagined community of northern Protestants remains. A non-sectarian Ulster nationalism appears to have little appeal to the loyalist public (Aughey and Hume, 1986, p. 324). It has, however, been the repeated experience of defeats by the British state that has interested some loyalist groups in socialism or Ulster nationalism and it is often the (humiliating) experience of prison that turns some loyalists into socialists or ecumenical Christians. And the few occasions when individual loyalists have become Irish nationalists have been in part the product of defeats by the British state and the capitalist class.[16] The direction of change in loyalist ideology depends on the alternative ways of understanding their experience that are available to loyalists. They are acquainted with socialist and ecumenical Christian ideologies to which they may turn if events provoke radical change in their ideology. But not since the early years of the twentieth century when Lindsay Crawford had contact with advanced nationalists in Dublin have Irish nationalists succeeded in presenting their ideology in a way potentially available to loyalists.

Change in Ulster ideology

Ulster British ideology, in contrast, is not a closed ideological system. Its liberal ideals are in principle distinct from Unionist Party allegiance. Although these ideals are associated with the British connection by the Ulster British, in certain circumstances the ideals can be used to criticise the effects of the union. Change in Ulster British ideology can occur either by the Ulster British following the implications of their liberal ideals, or by structural changes in the British state and its relation with Northern Ireland disrupting the sense of a Greater British community.

While there is a possibility of internally generated change in Ulster British ideology, this possibility is limited by the structure of the ideology. The liberal ideals are understood in a relatively narrow and technocratic fashion which makes it difficult for the Ulster British to understand nationalist grievances or Irish culture. The group is constantly tempted to veer between an overly positive self-image and an overly negative image of their Other. The impact of republican violence has been to strengthen the negative image of nationalists. Thus many Ulster British justify to themselves the overturning of many of their liberal ideals in order to destroy what they perceive as the evil of terrorism. This more conservative wing of the Ulster British would fully support the Unionist Party and underestimate the validity of nationalist grievances. While internally generated self-criticism and change is highly unlikely in this group (Gallagher and Worrall, 1982, pp. 80 and 210–11), the only possibility of dialogue with them rests on an acknowledgement of their principles and a liberal critique of them. To treat them simply as bigots is, paradoxically, to reinforce their overly positive self-image and their overly negative image of their Other, for, in their eyes, only the unprincipled would fail to appreciate their liberal principles.

Some Ulster British, having been made aware of the sectarian realities of Northern Irish society, have become critical of Unionist Party politics and moved towards Alliance, Labour and other forms of bridge-building politics. This move has typically been on principled liberal grounds. It is clear that these Ulster British take their principles seriously enough to withstand strong loyalist and unionist pressure and are unlikely to accept any new orthodoxy.

Internally generated change is possible for this group. Their very contact with nationalists may lead to an understanding of the rationale of the nationalist viewpoint, a broadening of their liberal principles and a weakening of their association of their ideals with the British connection. They may move from a primary imagined community of Greater Britain to placing as much importance on an Irish imagined community as on a British imagined community – from Ulster British to British Irish.[17] This is a clear example of one possibility of the 'reconciliation' of traditions on this island. For it to be generalised among the Ulster British, however, depends on increased linkages in terms of work and interaction between Northern Ireland and the Republic which would begin to balance the established linkages with Great Britain which reproduce the Ulster British imagined community.

Finally, change in Ulster British ideology may be provoked by changes in British state policy. The very integration of the Ulster British into the British politico-economic system promotes tension between Ulster British ideology and contemporary British ideologies, few of which leave a clear place for the Ulster British. The very fact of British involvement in the European Economic Community (EEC) has institutionalised close contact with the Republic of Ireland and changed the arena of British influence and interests in a manner not easily assimilable in Ulster British ideology. Direct Rule, and especially the Anglo-Irish Agreement, show increasing acceptance in the higher reaches of the British state of the nationalist definition of the Northern Ireland problem. To the Ulster British this has threatened the end of the British community in which they had believed and in terms of which they had defined themselves. Their basic sense of Britishness has been shaken. The direction of change is not yet clear. It will depend on whether or not the possibilities of internally generated change discussed above can be encouraged.

Conclusion: The current situation

The analysis given above allows a preliminary understanding of the effects of the Anglo-Irish Agreement on unionist ideology. The initial reaction of unionists was predictable. For loyalists it was a betrayal, a breach of contract and an overturning of the proper order by giving power to the corrupt forces of the Republic. For the Ulster British it was a breach of a relationship between peoples, a casting of the northern unionists out from the British community, and a clear statement that the British government had turned its back on the Ulster British.

The Agreement has, however, had very different effects on the two unionist groups. It has tightened the circle of domination/humiliation through which loyalists perceive the political world and thus has provoked extreme ritual protests and dominatory violence, while it may be a catalyst for slow but self-generating change in Ulster British ideology. Political actors in Ireland and Britain should take account of the very different possibilities of change for these two groups.

COMMENTARY BY JAMES W. McAULEY

The number of academic and journalistic works on the politics of Ulster unionism and loyalism has grown rapidly in recent years. Any that claim to represent serious work should refer to the conceptualisations of Ulster unionism first presented by Jennifer Todd in her 1987 article. Todd crucially distinguished between the categories of 'British unionists' and 'Ulster loyalists', the former identifying primarily with Britain, rather than Northern Ireland, while the latter look to the six counties of Northern Ireland (most often referred to as Ulster) as their primary imagined community.

Revisiting the article I was reminded how limited the analysis of unionism was in the mid-1980s. Todd's understanding clearly moved beyond the dismissive interpretations of unionist politics that still abounded at the time, or Marxist interpretations such as those by Bell (1976, 1984), McCann (1974) and Farrell (1976, 1983) that largely portrayed unionists as pawns, moved at will around an imperialist game board. Hence, one of the strengths of Todd's article was the acknowledgement of an internal dynamic in the construction of unionist political identity, allowing commentators to move beyond an understanding of unionism simply as 'irrational, backward and deviant' (McBride, 1996, p. 1). Todd further considered loyalist culture as profoundly religious and covenantal, indeed she sees religion and politics as inextricably intertwined. In so doing, however, her argument – unlike that of Bruce (1986 and 1994) – never collapsed into the overstated premise that unionism represents a distinct ethnic group dependent on Protestant evangelicalism as the glue that holds it together.

Identification with Ulster Britishness remains central to unionism. In the 2001 census, 46 per cent of Northern Ireland's population defined themselves as Protestant. Of these around three out of four categorised themselves as unionists, while less than one per cent saw themselves as Irish nationalists. One aspect that therefore continues to unite unionists of all hues is a belief in the obviousness of two distinct 'peoples' in Ireland; underpinning their core claim that those in the north-east of Ireland form a community which differs in decisive ways – culturally, politically, and socially – from the people of the rest of the island. Further, as Brewer (2004) suggests there is little evidence to suggest that the strong sense of identity amongst Protestants is likely to change in the foreseeable future.

Given the consistent strength of this identification, other writers have given prominence to defining the political aspects of unionism. For Arthur Aughey (1989, p. 1) the Union is defensible in rational terms, and unionism is based on a straightforward political preference which has 'little to do with the idea of the nation and everything to do with the idea of the state' (1989, p. 18). Such an understanding has been highly contested. Both Coulter (1994, p. 16) and Cochrane (1997, p. 77) correctly point out that a concentration on British citizenship fails to recognise the obvious – that people, including unionists, are fluid and that at different times unionists give emphasis to different cultural or social aspects that make up their political identity.

Indeed, Coulter's (1994) strongest contribution remains his evidence of the continued salience of class to an understanding of unionism (something missing in Todd's article). Unionism has always been fragmented along class lines and as Buckland (2001, p. 218) reminds us, the 'unity of Ulster Unionism had constantly to be managed'. Within this framework the factions and tensions within it must be outlined with precision, a process that Todd added to in her article. Further, because of such factionalisms unionism (or the imagined community of unionism) must be constantly reconstructed and reproduced, framed and presented in ways that make sense of the world to its core adherents.

So how useful is Todd's model in understanding contemporary unionist politics? Even as her article was drying on the page, the face of unionist politics was changing dramatically. Early 1985 saw the development of the negotiations between the UK and Irish governments, which manifested in the Anglo-Irish Agreement. Unionists fundamentally objected, their overall reactions neatly encapsulated in the *News Letter* editorial (16 November 1985), which suggested that now 'the ghosts of Cromwell and Lundy walked hand in hand'. The feelings of betrayal, anger, humiliation and shock that were widespread have remained a core construct within large sections of unionism, resurfacing strongly in recent years.

Such views appeared to have been put on the back-boiler, however, as in the late 1990s the main protagonists in the conflict began to re-evaluate their main approaches to achieving long-term political goals. The search had begun for a settlement revolving around the notion of integrating political representatives from the constitutional parties and both loyalist and republican paramilitaries into a new political process. The 'peace process' was conceived and became a reality. Unionist reactions were complex. Most of the recent altercations within unionism can be seen in the context of its response to the subsequent political accord of the Belfast Agreement. Indeed, as Mitchell (2003) points out, while there may be only one Agreement, interpretations of it, within just the Protestant community, differ dramatically.

What shape did these new forms of political expression take within unionism? Cash (1996) is correct in distinguishing the broad response between exclusivist and inclusivist constructs of unionism. Inclusivism was at the forefront of unionism's initial response, witnessed by widespread support for the Ulster Unionist Party (UUP) under the leadership of David Trimble. Building on ideas of civic unionism, Trimble projected a vision of politics that sought to build institutions with which both nationalists and unionists could identify.

The idea of a new inclusive unionism was a core feature of those supportive of the Belfast Agreement. The UUP's vision as a party projected a sense of Britishness defined as inclusive of all sections of Northern Ireland's community and their 'willingness to take part in the affairs of the British nation' (UUP Westminster election manifesto, May 2001). This was in part matched by the political direction taken by key factions of loyalist paramilitarism. They too were promoting their own form of civic values, which was to gain increasing importance and prominence as they projected a coherent political position, most notably through the new loyalism of the Progressive Unionist Party.

Such views have been marginalised within unionism. The parties representing loyalist paramilitaries have all but disappeared from the political radar, while the UUP, once regarded as the 'natural' party of government, has been humbled at the polls by the Democratic Unionist Party (DUP). Unionist hegemony has reconstructed around the leadership of Ian Paisley. There are several reasons for this switch in support, including the sincere belief increasingly held by many unionists that the peace process has brought about political and social decline and that the nationalist community has made huge political gains.

Further, there is an embedded broad fear that the Union is under direct threat. Recent election results demonstrate that the DUP is capable of mobilising large sections of unionist opinion against any perceived 'sell-out to the enemies of Ulster'. Crucially any perceived concessions within the political process are presented as a weakening of unionism's core identity and a lessening of what it is to be British, Protestant and a unionist. The entire DUP political project is driven by the construction of discourses that re-emphasise and reinforce the central anxieties of many unionists. This discourse of fear and betrayal so straightforwardly projected by the DUP is non-party specific in its appeal to unionists. It is capable of arousing and mobilising across several of the factions of the unionist political bloc, and from within other sections of non-aligned unionists.

Contemporary unionist and loyalist political cultures need to be understood as the product of specific constructed identities and histories that draw on identifiable political memories. Indeed, as Todd reminds us in a later work (with Ruane, 1996) conflict in Northern Ireland rests on an intricate set of social relationships resulting in two communities with radically different, and often conflicting, aspirations and identities. Unionist identity is comprised of a complex set of interrelated ideological strands, but two elements are particularly important. First, those attributes that refer to the strength of the internal bonds of unionism as a collectivity; and second, those attributes that are seen to differentiate unionism from other collectives, most centrally Irish nationalists.

Unionism thus seeks to construct an inclusive sense of identity by excluding identifiable others. Some of the major discourses and symbolism that legitimise unionism as a defence of identity and as security against external and internal threat are understood and broadly accepted by many unionists, across all social and economic groupings and broadly identified as 'Britishness'. While unionists and loyalists often draw on the same understandings, icons and slogans, they do in sometimes differing ways, albeit under the broad banner of a British identity.

Moreover, the very notion of Britishness has become much more problematic and contested since Todd wrote her piece. Devolved working government is a reality in Scotland and Wales. Issues surrounding social diversity and cohesion are now much higher on the contemporary political agenda, especially following the recognition of institutional racism after the publication of the *MacPherson Report* (1999) into the death of Stephen Lawrence. Debates about refugees and asylum seekers, the *Runnymede Trust Report* (2000) on multiculturalism, the increase in 'Islamaphobia' following the attack on the World Trade Centre and the war in Iraq, have all brought the politics of ethnic differences to centre ground. The comfortable consensus that 'Britishness' reflects a society characterised by tolerance and respect for social diversity has been challenged. This has been brought into even sharper focus by the outbreak in 2001 of street violence in several northern English towns and the London bombings of July 2005.

In Northern Ireland, unionist concerns that their strength of identity is being diluted have raised core issues surrounding meanings of Britishness and their place in a multi-ethnic and multicultural UK state. From within traditional perspectives, Britishness was seen almost as the 'natural' entity. If, however, we approach the nation and Britishness as social and political constructions, subject to constant invention and reinvention, the notion is radically reconstructed. As Parekh (2000) indicates, multiculturalism has too often has been set in a context of an unproblematic understanding of British national homogeneity.

Rather, Britishness remains a highly contested signifier of personal, political and social identity. This is as true of Belfast as it is of Bradford. Further, Hall (2000) argues that in order to develop a common feeling of belonging in the new millennium, the British need to redefine national identity in a way that is more encompassing and acceptable to all of its citizens. At one level this will no doubt involve continuing the divorce of Britishness from Englishness. At another it must involve a more acute awareness of the differences between all those groupings who claim Britishness as their prime identity, including Ulster unionists.

So given the nature of contemporary unionist politics and current debates around Britishness, has Todd's article borne the burden of time? Certainly within Northern Ireland's Protestant community, Britishness remains the dominant expression of identity. Amongst that faction, attachment to symbolism – such as the Union Flag – remains much stronger than those who identify as British in other parts of the UK (Heath *et al*, 2005). Further, as they also point out there remains a sizeable minority who demonstrate hyper-loyalty to British symbolism, this faction located predominantly in lower socio-economic groupings – most commonly seen as Ulster loyalists.

However, while there is still validity in Todd's analysis, the strength of the ideological dichotomy she identifies within unionism has been weakened greatly. Today political unionism displays growing indications of political disengagement and a lack of confidence with the ability of the broader political process, and a strong perception that the British state cannot assure a future for unionism. Large sections across both British unionism and Ulster loyalism are now equally suspicious and distrustful of the relationship with the British state and the political direction of the UK government. What remains robust in Todd's model is her notion that loyalist and unionist identities are fluid and that the dominant social constructs within unionism do not go unchallenged from within. It is an article to which many will rightfully continue to turn when seeking to understand the political culture of unionism.

Notes

1 I thank all those who have commented on other drafts of this paper and who have helped in various ways, in particular, Joe Ruane, and John Whyte and also Paul Arthur, Richard Sinnott and anonymous reviewers.

2 The most important studies are Miller, 1978; Nelson, 1984; Wright, 1973. See also Bell, 1985 and 1986; Buckley, 1985–6; Hickey, 1984; Roberts, 1971; Smith, 1984; Taylor, 1984; Wallis *et al*, 1986.

3 Brian Faulkner (1978, p. 44) claims that this was his rationale.

4 Bonhoeffer, 1981. See also the statement by 24 Presbyterian ministers in opposition to the government committee of the Presbyterian church in its reaction to the Anglo-Irish Agreement (*Irish Times*, 29 November 1985) and the Belfast Declaration of Christians (*Irish Times*, 25 June 1986).

5 For example, S.E. Long's defence of the Union (1972) is aptly entitled *Rather Be An Ulsterman*.

6 See Buckley (1984, pp. 29ff) for a discussion of the loyalist binary oppositions rough/religious and male/female.

7 Nelson (1984, pp. 51ff). This is parallel to the liberal unionist view of the English as unsteady allies, snobbish, patronising and exploitative.

8 For example, Dewer *et al*, 1969, p. 137. Also the sense of humiliation felt by unionists after the signing of the Anglo-Irish Agreement as expressed, for example, by A.T.Q. Stewart in his talk of 'the anniversary of the Humiliation', *Irish Times*, 6 September 1986.

9 For examples of Ulster British writers, see McNeill, 1922; Ervine, 1949 (although Ervine is too outspoken to be typical of the Ulster British, there are strong elements of Ulster British ideology in his writing); Brett, 1978; Dunlop, 1986; Hazlet, 1972; McAughtry, 1985; McCartney, 1985; Oliver, 1978a and 1978b; O'Neill, 1972.

10 Oliver's autobiography (1978a) shows such a rational, efficient, modernising administrator.

11 For example, McAughtry's patriotism comes out when others suggest that it is questionable (1985, p. 22).

12 In Rose's loyalty survey. Protestants who had taken trips to Britain were more likely to disapprove of or hold mixed views on the Orange Order (42.1 per cent) than those who had not taken such trips (24.6 per cent) (significance: $p < .001$). Similarly they were less likely to think that the government should attend more to the views of strong loyalists (trips: 57.1 per cent; no trips: 67.4 per cent; significance: $p < .05$). I thank Richard Sinnott for analysing the data for me.

13 Brett (1978, pp. 152–3) appears to have moved to the margins of Ulster-British ideology; Boyd (1986) may or may not have passed over the limits.

14 Larsen, 1982b, pp. 154–5; Harris, 1972, pp. 146ff; Donnan and MacFarlane, 1986b, p. 387. The anthropological literature may underestimate the amount of political discussion that does take place, judging from my experience and the information others have given me.

15 For example, Sam Thompson in his play 'Over the Bridge'.

16 Nelson (1984, pp. 135 and 178). See a former Ulster Volunteer Force man's account of his conversion to ecumenical Christianity while in prison, *Irish Times*, 5 May 1986. For an account of Lindsay Crawford's career see Gray (1985).

17 Examples of individuals who appear from their writings above to have moved some part of the way along this path are Charles Brett, Sam McAughtry and Robin Boyd.

References

Anderson, Benedict (1983) *Imagined Communities: Reflections on the Origin and Spread of Nationalism*. London: Verso.

Aughey, Arthur (1989) *Under Siege: Ulster Unionism and the Anglo-Irish Agreement*. Belfast: Blackstaff Press.

Aughey, Arthur and David Hume (1986) 'Developments Within the UDA: A New Paramilitary Emphasis?', *Teaching Politics*, 15 (2), pp. 315–87.

Bell, Desmond (1985) 'Contemporary Cultural Studies in Ireland and the "Problem" of Protestant Ideology', *The Crane Bag*, 9 (2), pp. 91–5.

Bell, Desmond (1986) 'Acts of Union: Youth Sub-Culture and Ethnic Identity Amongst Protestants in Northern Ireland', paper presented at the annual meeting of the Sociological Association of Ireland, Dublin.

Bell, Geoffrey (1976) *The Protestants of Ulster*. London: Pluto Press.

Bell, Geoffrey (1984) *The British in Ireland: A Suitable Case for Withdrawal*. London: Pluto Press.

Bennett, George (ed.) (1953) *The Concept of Empire: Burke to Attlee 1774–1947*. London: Adam and Charles Black.

Bew, Paul, Peter Gibbon and Henry Patterson (1979) *The State in Northern Ireland, 1921–72*. Manchester: Manchester University Press.

Bonhoefer, Dietrich (1981) *Letters and Papers from Prison: An Abridged Edition*. London: SCM Press.

Boyd, Robin (1986) 'Northern Protestants – By Themselves', *Irish Times*, 20 March.

Brett, Charles (1978) *Long Shadows Cast Before: Nine Lives in Ulster, 1625–1977*. Edinburgh: Bartholomew.

Brewer, John D. (2004) 'Continuity and Change in Contemporary Ulster Protestantism', *The Sociological Review*, 52 (2), pp. 265–83.

Bruce, Steve (1986) *God Save Ulster: The Religion and Politics of Paisleyism*. Oxford: Oxford University Press.

Bruce, Steve (1994) *The Edge of the Union: The Ulster Loyalist Political Vision*. Oxford: Oxford University Press.

Buckland, Patrick (2001) 'A Protestant State: Unionists in Government, 1921–39', pp. 211–26 in D. George Boyce and Alan O'Day (eds.) *Defenders of the Union: A Survey of British and Irish Unionism Since 1801*. London: Routledge.

Buckley, Anthony D. (1984) 'Walls Within Walls: Religion and Rough Behaviour in an Ulster Community', *Sociology*, 18 (1), pp. 19–32.

Buckley, Anthony D. (1985–6) 'Chosen Few: Biblical Texts in the Regalia of an Ulster Secret Society', *Folk Life*, 24, pp. 5–24.

Bulpitt, Jim (1978) 'The Making of the United Kingdom: Aspects of English Imperialism', *Parliamentary Affairs*, 31 (2), pp. 174–89.

Bulpitt, Jim (1986) 'The Discipline of the New Democracy: Mrs Thatcher's Domestic Statecraft', *Political Studies*, 34 (1), pp. 19–39.

Cash, John Daniel (1996) *Identity, Ideology and Conflict: The Structuration of Politics in Northern Ireland*. Cambridge: Cambridge University Press.

Cochrane, Feargal (1997) *Unionist Politics and the Politics of Unionism since the Anglo-Irish Agreement*. Cork: Cork University Press.

Cohen, Anthony P. (1985) *The Symbolic Construction of Community*. London: Tavistock.

Coulter, Colin (1994) 'The Character of Unionism', *Irish Political Studies*, 9, pp. 1–24.

Deane, Seamus (1983) *Civilians and Barbarians: Field Day Pamphlet No. 3*. Derry: Field Day.

Dewer, Michael Willoughby (1959) *Why Orangeism?* [Foreword by Bishop W.S. Kerr]. Belfast: Jordan.

Dewer, Michael Willoughby, John Brown and Samuel Ernest Long (1969) *Orangeism: A New Historical Appreciation*. Belfast: Grand Orange Lodge of Ireland.

Donnan, Hastings and Graham MacFarlane (1986a) 'Social Anthropology and the Sectarian Divide in Northern Ireland', pp. 23–37 in Richard Jenkins, Hastings Donnan and Graham MacFarlane, *The Sectarian Divide in Northern Ireland Today*. Occasional Paper No. 41. London: Royal Anthropological Institute of Great Britain and Ireland.

Donnan, Hastings and Graham MacFarlane (1986b) 'You Get on Better with Your Own: Social Continuity and Change in Rural Northern Ireland', pp. 380–99 in Patrick Clancy, Sheelagh Drudy, Kathleen Lynch and Liam O'Dowd (eds.) *Ireland: A Sociological Profile*. Dublin: Institute of Public Administration.

Dunlop, John (1986) 'The Self Understanding of Protestants in Northern Ireland', pp. 5–20 in Enda MacDonagh (ed.) *Irish Challenges to Theology*. Dublin: Dominican.

Ervine, St John (1949) *Craigavon, Ulsterman*. London: George Allen and Unwin.

Farrell, Michael (1976) *Northern Ireland: The Orange State*. London: Pluto Press.

Farrell, Michael (1983) *Arming the Protestants: The Formation of the Ulster Special Constabulary and the Royal Ulster Constabulary, 1920–27*. London: Pluto Press.

Faulkner, Brian (1978) *Memoirs of a Statesman* [ed. J. Houston]. London: Weidenfeld and Nicolson.

Gallagher, Eric and Stanley Worrall (1982) *Christians in Ulster 1968–1980*. Oxford: Oxford University Press.

Garrett, Brian (1986) ' "Processing" Not Softening Unionism', *Irish Times*, 12 November.

Gibbon, Peter (1975) *The Origins of Ulster Unionism: The Formation of Popular Protestant Politics and Ideology in Nineteenth Century Ireland*. Manchester: Manchester University Press.

Gray, John (1985) *City in Revolt: James Larkin and the Belfast Dock Strike of 1907*. Belfast: Blackstaff.

Hall, Stuart (2000) 'A Question of Identity: What is Britain?', *The Observer*, 15 October.

Harris, Rosemary (1972) *Prejudice and Tolerance in Ulster: A Study of Neighbours and Strangers in a Border Community*. Manchester: Manchester University Press.

Hazlet, Sir Arthur (1972) *The 'B' Specials: A History of the Ulster Special Constabulary*. London: Tom Stacey Ltd.

Heath, Anthony, Catherine Rothon and Robert Andersen (2005) 'Who Feels British', Working Paper 2005/5. Oxford: Department of Sociology, University of Oxford.

Hepburn, Ronald (ed.) (1980) *The Conflict of Nationality in Modern Ireland*. London: Edward Arnold.

Hickey, John (1984) *Religion and the Northern Ireland Problem*. Dublin: Gill and Macmillan.

Larsen, S. Saugestad (1982a) 'The Glorious Twelfth: The Politics of Legitimation in Kilbroney', pp. 278–91 in Anthony P. Cohen (ed.) *Belonging, Identity and Social Organisation in British Rural Cultures*. Manchester: Manchester University Press.

Larsen, S. Saugestad (1982b) 'The Two Sides of the House: Identity and Social Organisation in Kilbroney, Northern Ireland', pp. 132–56 in Anthony P. Cohen (ed.) *Belonging, Identity and Social Organisation in British Rural Cultures*. Manchester: Manchester University Press.

Long, S.E. (1972) *Rather Be An Ulsterman*. Dromara: Slieve Croob Press.

Loyal Orange Lodge of Ireland (LOLI) (undated) *Here We Stand: A Brief Outline of Orange Principle*. Belfast: Loyal Orange Lodge of Ireland.

Maginnis, W. Brian (1956) 'The Right to Dissent – Making Democracy Work', in Lord Brookeborough, W. Brian Maginnis and George B. Hanna, *Why the Border Must Be: The Northern Ireland Case in Brief*. Belfast: Government of Northern Ireland.

McAughtry, Sam (1985) *McAughtry's War*. Belfast: Blackstaff.

McAughtry, Sam (1986) 'The Hay and the Troubles', *Irish Times*, 28 August.

McBride, Ian (1996) 'Ulster and the British Problem', pp. 1–18 in Richard English and Graham Walker (eds) *Unionism in Modern Ireland: New Prespectives on Politics and Culture*. London: Macmillan.

McCann, Eamonn (1974) *War and an Irish Town*. Harmondsworth: Penguin.

McCartney, Robert L. (1983) Interview in Padraig O'Malley, *The Uncivil Wars: Ireland Today*. Belfast: Blackstaff.

McCartney, Robert L. (1985) *Liberty and Authority in Ireland: Field Day Pamphlet No. 9*. Derry: Field Day.

McMichael, John (1986) Interview, *Fortnight*, 24 March.

McNeill, Ronald (1922) *Ulster's Stand for Union*. London: John Murray.

Miller, David W. (1978) *Queen's Rebels: Ulster Loyalism in Historical Perspective*. Dublin: Gill and Macmillan.

Mitchell, Claire (2003) 'Protestant identification and political change in Northern Ireland', *Ethnic and Racial Studies*, 26 (4), pp. 612–31.

Nelson, Sarah (1975) 'Protestant "Ideology" Reconsidered: The Case of "Discrimination" ', pp. 155–87 in Ivor Crewe (ed.) *The Politics of Race*. London: Croom Helm.

Nelson, Sarah (1984) *Ulster's Uncertain Defenders: Loyalists in the Northern Ireland Conflict*. Belfast: Appletree.

O'Donnell, Edward Eugene (1977) *Northern Irish Stereotypes*. Dublin: College of Industrial Relations.

Oliver, John A. (1978a) *Working at Stormont*. Dublin: Institute of Public Administration.

Oliver, John A. (1978b) *Ulster Today and Tomorrow*. London: PEP Broadsheet No. 574.

O'Neill, Terence (1972) *The Autobiography of Terence O'Neill*. London: Rupert Hart Davies.

Parekh, Bikkhu (2000) 'Changing What it Means to be British', *The Daily Telegraph*, 18 October.

Patterson, Henry (1980) *Class Conflict and Sectarianism: The Protestant Working Class and the Belfast Labour Movement 1868–1920*. Belfast: Blackstaff.

Roberts, David A. (1971) 'The Orange Order in Ireland: A Religious Institution?', *British Journal of Sociology*, 22 (3), pp. 269–83.

Rose, Richard (1971) *Governing Without Consensus: An Irish Perspective*. London: Faber.

Ruane, Joseph and Jennifer Todd (1996) *The Dynamics of Conflict in Northern Ireland: Power, Conflict and Emancipation*. Cambridge: Cambridge University Press.

Schwarz, Bill (1986) 'Conservatism, Nationalism and Imperialism', pp. 154–86 in James Donald and Stuart Hall (eds.) *Politics and Ideology*. Milton Keynes: Open University Press.

Scruton, Roger (1986) 'Authority and Allegiance', pp. 105–9 in James Donald and Stuart Hall (eds.) *Politics and Ideology*. Milton Keynes: Open University Press.

Senior, Herrward (1966) *Orangeism in Ireland and Britain 1795–1835*. London: Routledge and Kegan Paul.

Smith, A. Clifford (1984) *The Ulster DUP: A Case Study in Political and Religious Convergence*. Unpublished PhD thesis. Belfast: Queen's University Belfast.

Smyth, W. Martin (1974) *Stand Fast*. Belfast: Orange Publications.

Stewart, A.T.Q. (1977) *The Narrow Ground: Aspects of Ulster 1609–1969*. London: Faber and Faber.

Taylor, David (1984) 'Ian Paisley and the Ideology of Ulster Protestantism', pp. 59–78 in Chris Curtin, Mary Kelly and Liam O'Dowd (eds.) *Culture and Ideology in Ireland*. Galway: Galway University Press.

Wallis, Roy, Steve Bruce and David Taylor (1986) ' "No Surrender": Paisleyism and the Politics of Ethnic Identity in Ireland'. Belfast: Unpublished paper.

Wright, Alan (1986) Interview, *Fortnight*, 10 February.

Wright, Frank (1973) 'Protestant Ideology and Politics in Ulster', *European Journal of Sociology*, 14, pp. 213–80.

7 The political language of John Hume

Michael Cunningham

Originally published in *Irish Political Studies*, 12, 1997, pp. 13–22.

> Protestants are really puzzled by what they feel is the ambiguous attitude of Catholics and their failure to define ordinary concepts in a clean, straightforward way. There is much more of what I would call sophistry, casuistry, in the Roman Catholic approach to honesty.... Protestants sometimes find it very difficult to understand the sophistry, the playing with words which we (sometimes) get from Catholics.
>
> (Griffin, 1993, p. 37)

The above statement neatly encapsulates criticisms that have been levelled at John Hume, leader of the Social Democratic and Labour Party (SDLP) and arguably the most significant political figure in Northern Ireland (NI) in the last 25 years. The principal aim of this article is to examine Hume's recent use of key concepts to be found in his political statements; their evolution and influence will be briefly considered in the conclusion.[1] Three of the most significant, and inter-related, phrases (or variations upon them) are those of self-determination, post-nationalism and the European dimension.

Self-determination

Before turning to Hume's ideas some preliminary comments will be offered on the first concept; that of self-determination. It is a commonplace to record that the concept is problematic in that the theoretical basis of a people's claim to self-determination is contested; for example whether it can be based upon individual or collective rights, or indeed whether one accepts the concept of rights at all and its application in any specific case is difficult. The most obvious problem is how to decide who are the people who constitute the nation. Another concrete concern of many writers in the field of international relations is that an absolute right to self-determination promotes the likelihood of secessionary movements which can undermine the structure of international order. If one applies this to the Irish case it does not self-evidently support a unionist or nationalist case; nationalists may argue that unionist secession in 1921 was illegitimate while unionists may claim that Ireland was only one political unit under the Union and therefore nationalism was 'guilty' of secession. Gallagher (1990) argues convincingly both that the concept is imprecise and that neither unionists nor nationalists have an absolute right to self-determination and, in a later article, he highlights the complexities by identifying six different interpretations of how many 'nations' are to be found on the island of Ireland (Gallagher, 1995; see also McGarry and O'Leary, 1995, pp. 35–44).

It is not clear that recent theoretical attempts to refine the concept can help to resolve the Irish case. To give two examples; first, one strand of communitarian thinking argues that the right of a group to self-determination is weakened if its culture is 'pernicious' and denigrates or persecutes those of another culture (Freeman, 1996, p. 755). Both unionists and nationalists have claimed that the other group has acted perniciously which the accused would generally deny; this raises the question of who is to judge these claims or accusations? Secondly, Beran's liberal-democratic reformulation of the concept lays down conditions for secession which, it could be argued, were breached by unionist refusal to join with the rest of Ireland (Freeman, 1996, p. 757).

With these problems in mind, the following quotations provide a flavour of recent statements on this question.

> We accept that an internal settlement is not a solution because it obviously does not deal with all the relationships at the heart of the problem. We accept that the Irish people *as a whole* have a right to national self-determination . . . the exercise of self-determination is a matter for agreement between the people of Ireland.
>
> (Hume, 1993. Emphasis added)

> We are accepting the Sinn Féin statement that it is the Irish people *as a whole* who have the right (to self-determination) and the Irish people should be defined as those people domiciled on the island of Ireland.
>
> (SDLP, 1988. Emphasis added)

> Unfortunately the Irish people are divided on how to exercise the right to self-determination. The Irish people are divided on how to exercise the right to sovereignty. It is the search for agreement among the Irish people on how to exercise these rights that is the real search for peace and stability in Ireland.
>
> (Hume, 1988)

Many other statements could be included here but would largely replicate the points made. There are three inferences to be drawn from these formulations which appear to sit uneasily with Hume's invocation of post-nationalism (see below). Firstly, the phrase 'as a whole' echoes a 'traditionalist' 32 county approach to self-determination; this may be in part influenced by protracted and difficult discussions with Sinn Féin but is unlikely to reassure unionists or be compatible with the espousal of the validity of, and respect for, the two traditions.

Secondly, the suspicion of casuistry may be reinforced by the claim that the Irish people are divided over how to exercise the right to self-determination.

Rather than being divided the fundamental and perhaps irreconcilable problem is that, as indicated above, there is no agreement on the legitimate unit within which this right is exercised – a notion obscured in Hume's formulation. In a critique of the Sinn Féin position, Hume argues that Ireland is first and foremost a people, and not to be defined territorially. However this seems insufficient to distinguish his position from that of Sinn Féin since it makes no material difference in that it does not permit self-determination for Northern Ireland (or its unionist constituency) if that exercise of self-determination entails a rejection of identities or structures beyond what could be termed a 'traditional unionist' one.

Thirdly, Hume's conception of self-determination is self-consciously located in the Republican tradition of unifying Catholic, Protestant and Dissenter with the invocation of Parnell and, more frequently, Tone. This appears to have a twofold purpose; it distinguishes Hume's vision of a future Ireland from a narrower and more sectarian nationalism (an implicit criticism of Sinn Féin) and signals to unionists and Protestants that their traditions and identities are, and will be, respected (see, *inter alia*, Hume, 1986; O'Connor, 1993, p. 94).

Hume's readiness to invoke historical parallels and locate himself within these traditions is of interest because, by contrast, much of his rhetoric has emphasised the need to break free from a past which includes the 'archaic supremacism' of unionism and the fixities and shibboleths of territorial nationalism (Hume, 1988a, p. 3) and he has invoked the term 'New Republicanism' (Kearney, 1991, p. 41). A reading of Hume's statements leaves a strong impression that he and the SDLP believe themselves to have adjusted to current political realities which have escaped other parties and political actors.

Post-nationalism

This emphasis is to be found in considerations on post-nationalism; the second of the key concepts identified. Again, this is rather an imprecise concept; however, Delanty (1996) has identified some of the basic implications of the term. The focus is principally on the question of identity. Unlike nationalism, a post-national identity encompasses, or has the capacity to encompass, multiple identities, is not historically based and is premised on the acceptance of dissent and cultural difference. This last point is echoed in the work of Kearney whose sympathetic reading of the concept emphasises that post-nationalism does not necessarily supersede nationalism but can incorporate its more positive aspects; for example those that are cultural rather than territorial and democratic rather than sectarian and exclusive (1991, pp. 40–1). If we are now held to be living in a post-nationalist world, as Hume claims, this bolsters the visions outlined above. The nation-state is outdated which undermines both nationalist and unionist claims which are, according to Hume, based on territorial formulations of self-determination. The implication of post-nationalism is that both individual and communal identity and political structures are being (and should be) constructed and forged at both sub-national and supra-national levels. Therefore, the dichotomous Britain v. Ireland and unionist v. nationalist mindsets frozen in the nineteenth century and made manifest in the settlements of the 1920s are redundant. It could be countered that Kearney's formulation means that there is no simple contradiction between a national (cultural) identity and post-nationalism; however I would contend that there is a tension between Hume's nationalism and his invocation of post-nationalist language.

The European dimension

The political system in which these new identities can be harmoniously represented is that of the European Union and Hume has long advocated the concept of a 'Europe of the Regions' (Hume, 1988b; SDLP, 1994). This term has both a functional and normative strand to it, in that its more optimistic advocates believe that regions are gradually replacing the nation-state as the locus for economic activity within Europe and also provide the scope for a more pluralistic and diverse expression of cultural identity. The creation of a Council of European Regions in 1985 and a Committee of the Regions under the Maastricht Treaty, with the right to be consulted by the European Commission and the Council of Ministers, has provided an institutional expression of regionalism within the European Community/European Union (EC/EU). However, many authors remain sceptical about the pace of regional development and the concomitant decline in the power of the nation-state (Keating, 1995; Anderson and Goodman, 1995; Kennedy, 1994; Hooghe, 1995).

There are various reasons why Hume has set such store on the European dimension. On one reading, expressing the normative and functional elements sketched above, it is because he genuinely believes that 'ever closer union' has the capacity, if not to eradicate the old-fashioned antagonistic duality of identities, at least to downgrade them via the emergence of other, more benign, ones and that unionist and nationalist identities will become separated from their malign association with territorial integrity. If European integration has fostered the co-operation of France and Germany, those former adversaries, why cannot the disputes of one small island be resolved through this framework? In addition, there is the practical reason that co-operation between the two parts of Ireland in the European context would have an economic rationale.[2]

Other readings, however, can be constructed concerning Hume's use of the European dimension. As with his deployment of post-nationalism, it is an attempt to seize the moral high grounds of both realism and progress. With respect to the former, Hume often gives the impression that the SDLP deals in political realities; in other words it is not only that irredentist nationalists (*viz* Sinn Féin) and supremacist unionists who desire, for example, simple majority rule in NI hold positions of dubious morality but that they lack realism. The world has moved on and it is only the SDLP, of the northern parties at least, that has moved with it. Allied to this sense of realism is the implication that progress, the future, reinforces the SDLP analysis. European and global developments are moving in one direction and these have profound implications for Ireland which give rise to some of Hume's more glib soundbites: 'The world is a much smaller place today, not least because of developments in telecommunications and transport. Interdependence is today more important to people than independence. We cannot live apart' (Hume, 1994); and his desire to see 'an Ireland that is whole in a Europe that is whole, in a world that is whole' (Hume cited in Kennedy, 1994, p. 167).

A third reading of Hume's European emphasis is that the rationalist attack on nationalism and archaism which is part of the project masks a disingenuous restatement, rather than repudiation, of nationalist aims. There are two different critiques of Hume's European rhetoric; one being that his view of the process of integration and its promotion of regional identities is over-optimistic and naïve and the other that it is deliberately framed to promote *de facto* nationalism.

With respect to the second point, an emphasis on new relations between NI and the Republic of Ireland within the European Union, the advocacy of new structures to give practical expression to this and support in 1992 for a six-person Executive Commission to govern NI including representatives from the Republic and one from the European Commission are rooted in a nationalist, not post-nationalist, framework. This is because they reject the concept of an internal settlement in NI and the unionist right legitimately to oppose such trends. Therefore, despite the post-nationalist gloss, the conceptualisation of NI, the rights of unionists and the role of the Republic are located within a broadly nationalist tradition. Hume's most recent, and broadly sympathetic, biographer has noted this tension when he speaks of Hume's 'post-nationalist vision' and also remarks that 'countless commentators have been disarmed by his apparently flexible language and have mistaken him for an honest broker instead of the Nationalist politician he really is' (Drower, 1995, p. 14 and p. 17) and Jennifer Todd points out that Hume's view of self-determination shares some traditional nationalist assumptions (1991, p. 6).

Conclusion

If the three key political terms considered above have been seized upon by critics as an attempt by Hume to disguise a fundamentally unreformed nationalist agenda, similar accusations have been made of the use of less specifically political terminology. 'This island' takes on loaded nationalist connotations which are reinforced by the use of the term 'agreement' or elided into the phrase 'an agreed Ireland' (Longley, 1993). Take for example the following statements:

> They (unionists) have nothing to worry about if they are committed to reaching agreement. What I want to know from the unionists is 'Do you want to reach agreement with the people you share a piece of earth with or do you want to live in eternal disagreement?'
>
> (*Fortnight*, 322, November 1993, p. 18)

and

> The SDLP has always espoused and respected the principle of consent and remains committed to the creation of an agreed Ireland.
>
> (Hume, 1994a)

In trying to placate unionists' concerns and fears, Hume has stressed respect for their traditions, the concept of an Ireland which can accommodate these and the belief that unionists cannot be coerced because their numbers and geographical concentration are both a reality which has to be recognised and a fact that should instil in them self-confidence. Taking succour from these facts unionists have nothing to fear from agreement; to paraphrase an oft-repeated claim of Hume at the time of the Downing Street Declaration and the publication of the Joint Framework Document (see, for example, Hume, 1994b; SDLP, 1995, p. 13). There are two aspects to be highlighted from the first quotation. Firstly, there is an implicit claim to both reason and reasonableness in the formulation; those who favour peace and progress seek agreement and the notion of wanting to live in 'eternal disagreement' carries pejorative overtones. Secondly, the idea of sharing a piece of earth can be read not as a neutral statement about the need for tolerance or the evils of sectarianism but one that carries the implication of political structures framed within a broadly nationalist perspective.

Within the second quotation the concepts of 'consent' and 'agreed Ireland' are in tension, if not actually contradictory. An 'agreed Ireland' is a slippery concept, and probably deliberately so, but one that transcends an internal settlement within NI. At least one critic, Conor Cruise O'Brien, has maintained that united and agreed Ireland are synonymous terms (*Independent*, 1 April 1994) and another claims his political language 'has much in common with George Orwell's metaphor for Marxist jargon: "prefabricated phrases bolted together like the pieces of a child's Meccano set" ' (Longley, 1990, p. 13; and see Longley, 1994). This may be overstating the case since Hume may well conceive of, and settle for, an agreement which is 'more' than an internal one yet less than unification. However conceived it remains difficult to see how consent can be squared with an 'agreed Ireland'. It seems to me that the point is not to question Hume's sincerity in his respect for the unionist tradition(s) but that his use of the term and view of the people who compose it is limited and circumscribed.

The formulation can be read thus: the two traditions (nationalism and unionism) can and should be reconciled through new structures (the agreed Ireland) and expression of the unionist tradition is perfectly legitimate. What is illegitimate is for the expression of that tradition or identity to demand separate institutional and political structures. 'We cannot confuse the legitimacy of the two traditions with the *supposed* legitimacy of "two distinct entities" ' (SDLP paper cited in Aughey, 1993). Thus we have returned to the conception of consent which is in turn related to the question of what is the valid unit of self-determination. The persistence of seemingly incompatible unionist and nationalist conceptions of this can be blurred and fudged by terms such as 'equality of two traditions', 'parity of esteem' and the invocation of diversity, plurality and agreement as 'hurrah' words but cannot be removed.

It appears that, despite attempts at transcending the linguistic parameters of nationalist discourse, John Hume remains wedded to its fundamentals. This does not imply that Hume's formulations are consciously designed to deceive or are disingenuous but rather that his reassurances and concessions to unionism are ultimately likely to prove inadequate because they are informed by a conception of the Northern Ireland 'problem' and a reading of history which cannot be reconciled with unionism through the reworking of language.

The focus of this article has been on the language of Hume which is worthy of study in its own right. In conclusion, some brief thoughts on the development and influence of Hume's ideas will be presented. It is difficult to chart precisely the chronology of the ideas discussed above; however, according to Hainsworth, in the early 1970s the SDLP shared with other NI parties an ill-defined mistrust of the EC but by the time of the 1979 European election presented Europe as a means of 'peace and reconciliation' (1985, p. 127). What seems clear is that from the early 1980s Hume had moved to a position of pushing for both an enhanced 'Irish dimension' (the lack of which in Prior's Assembly led to the SDLP boycott) and had convinced the EC that the Irish 'question' was a legitimate concern, as evidenced by the Haagerup Report of 1983. Although the report was wary of British sensibilities it did endorse the basic position that NI was not solely an internal matter for the UK government and that the EC was a forum in which inter-state relations could be improved.

Despite the increased emphasis on regionalisation within the EC/EU outlined above, it appears that this particular aspect of the European dimension remains more a Humeian ideal than a reality and this process is hindered by the high degree of centralisation of the British and Irish states. This needs to be distinguished from advances in functional economic cross-border co-operation which EC Commissioners have advocated since 1982 (Anderson and Goodman, 1995) and which is acceptable to many unionists provided no political implications are drawn from it.

If one compares the 'conventional wisdom' of the two governments in the contemporary period with, for example, 20 years ago the ideas to which Hume subscribes seem to have been influential; a result of both his own assiduous lobbying and structural developments. Many commentators record the influence he has over the Irish government in relation to Northern policy (see, for example, Girvin, 1994; O'Brien, 1993; Cox, 1996; O'Leary 1987) and this has helped to 'soften the edges' of irredentism in Fianna Fáil and much British policy since the Anglo-Irish Agreement bears the imprint of Hume's thinking. However, a cautionary note should be posted. The more ambitious of Hume's ideas around 'post-nationalism' and regionalism have had relatively little impact on other politicians and policy-makers and developments promoted by Hume have been adopted largely because they coincide with the self-perceived interests of the respective governments in attempts both to manage the conflict and satisfy their electorates.

COMMENTARY BY JONATHAN TONGE

Analysis of the language and discourse of politicians and political parties is important for a number of reasons. It is through such analysis that we can accurately place the politicians in terms of policy. This type of scrutiny allows one to challenge the consistency in the thinking of politicians and better understand the motivations of political actors. Michael Cunningham's evaluation of the political language of John Hume has obvious importance. It dissects the thinking of arguably the most influential politician to emerge during the Northern Ireland conflict. Hume played a seminal role in the construction of the peace process and his political thinking dominated the 1998 Good Friday Agreement.

Leader of the SDLP from 1979 until 2001, Hume made substantial contributions to the articulation of constitutional nationalism and the moderation of militant republicanism. Given these inputs, Cunningham's analysis of Hume's ideological approach and political principles to conflict resolution is surely one of the most important contributions to *Irish Political Studies*. Certainly the article has lost little of its salience in the decade since publication and needs to be examined by all scholars of nationalism and conflict resolution.

Despite the plaudits often received by Hume, Cunningham does not deify his subject, a charge which *is* applicable to other works in the area. The biographies of Hume produced by Barry White (1985) and Paul Routledge (1998) are of course aimed at a rather different audience, of lay readers desirous of insights into Hume the man in addition to Hume the political thinker. In White's hagiography, the clues in the title are none-too-subtle: *John Hume: Statesman of the Troubles*. Cunningham cites Drower's biography of Hume, noting how the biographer claims that for all Hume's honeyed words, the onetime SDLP leader was always primarily an Irish nationalist. This appears a correct interpretation, but disappointingly, until recent times the researcher on Hume's philosophy was largely bereft of serious interpretive material. Astonishingly, McAllister's (1977) work on the SDLP represented the only major intellectual study of Hume's party. This deficit was finally rectified by Cunningham's article and a similarly critical assessment by McGovern (1997). These were followed by Gerry Murray's (1998) positive analysis of Hume's ideological approach, which was accompanied by a critical appraisal of the leader's often semi-detached relationship with his party.

Instead of lauding his subject, Cunningham offers a critical appraisal of the ambiguities underpinning Hume's nationalistic sentiments and aspirations. Hume's epiphanies were often derided, even by sympathisers, as woolly 'Humespeak', delivered via a 'single transferable speech', rather than lauded as the substantial political thought they represented. Cunningham examines three key aspects of Hume's political thought: self-determination; post-nationalism; and the European dimension. Each was crucial to Hume's ideological approach. At the core of 'Humespeak' was a vision: Hume argued for the right of the people on the island of Ireland to determine their own future; claimed that the concept of the nation state was dated; and insisted that the future of Ireland lay within a European context – a Europe of regions – in which competing nationalisms were irrelevant.

Cunningham notes that the Hume conception of Irish self-determination is within the republican Wolfe Tone tradition of a 32 county Ireland, in that the future of Ireland must be determined by the entire population of the island. In this respect, Hume offers a classical republican analysis of an indivisible island.

The landmass of Ireland is seen as the unit for the exercise of self-determination. Hume thus comes close to adopting a position based on geographical determinism. For Hume, the problem is less one of the unit of self-determination than the means of its exercise *within* that unit. Cunningham is effective in highlighting the republican underpinnings of Hume's position. Moreover, as Cunningham hints, Hume's argument is far from post-nationalist, whatever the protestations of the former SDLP leader. It allows the potential creation of a united independent Irish nation state, should that be the outcome of the exercise of self-determination.

Surprisingly, Cunningham is rather light on the other 'classic republican' assumption made by Hume in emphasising island-wide principles: that the people of the island are Irish. This assertion would come as news to many of the majority population in Northern Ireland, whose Britishness remains stridently asserted. Hume appears to accept that there are two *traditions* rather than two *nations* on the island of Ireland. Cunningham appears to suggest that the logical consequence of this thinking is that separate institutional structures in the north might not be supported by Hume. Whilst the assumption is reasonable given Hume's positioning, the institutional working-out of the Hume position was rather different. The two traditions were reconciled via formal power sharing in Northern Ireland and institutional attachments to the Irish Republic via Strands Two and Three of the Good Friday Agreement. Hume's two traditions were treated as two nations in the Agreement; affiliation to either of these nations was supposedly afforded equal legitimacy, or 'parity of esteem'.

The 1997 article illuminates the tensions between Hume's advocacy of a 32 county-based agreement and the post-national and European themes that the former SDLP leader persistently articulated. Hume was from the nationalist wing of the SDLP and steered his party in that direction, against the more socialist, internal-settlement leanings of other party founders, such as Gerry Fitt and Paddy Devlin, both of whom found themselves marginalised by the new political direction (Murray, 1998; Murray and Tonge, 2005). Under Hume a 'greener' type of member joined the party (Evans *et al*, 2000). Concurrently, however, Hume argued that the world had entered a post-national era which had crushed the relevance of ancient British versus Irish, or unionist versus nationalist, rivalries. Correctly, Cunningham casts a quizzical eye over how Hume's continuing advocacy of a unitary Irish state, albeit one at ease with its different traditions, can be construed as 'post-national'. Unionists rarely perceived Hume's nationalism as transcending traditional nationalist aspirations. Republicans offered an alternative perspective sceptical both of Hume's nationalism and his post-national musings. Bernadette McAliskey witheringly retorted to Hume's insistence that the world had moved into a post-nation state era that she had yet to experience her nation state, given the partition of her country and continuing British rule in the North.

The post-national ideas of Hume are very much linked to his faith in Europeanisation. Hume's articulation of this concept was perhaps vague and often conflated, as Cunningham implies, with broader ideas of globalisation and a shrinking world. For Hume, the European Union amounted to a form of supra-nationalism which made redundant the notion of independent nation states, displaced by growing interdependence. This had important, if short-lived, ramifications for SDLP policy. During the early 1990s, the party adopted the bizarre and unworkable policy of advocating an EU Commissioner to assist in the governance of Northern Ireland, an approach which at least united many unionists and nationalists in opposition, given the questions of democracy, legitimacy and practicality that were raised. The policy was quietly dropped, but Hume's zest for European ideals was undiminished. Hume's final election as leader was characterised by his advocacy of the post nation-state ideal, a set of principles scorned by the Sinn Féin President Gerry Adams throughout the 2001 campaign (Tonge, 2002).

Cunningham could usefully have highlighted a further tension in Hume's writings. Whilst Hume's ideological commitments to Europeanisation and post-nationalism were evident, much of his practical policy input was based upon bi-nationalism, a more limited transcending of narrow Irish nationalism. From 1975 onwards, Hume was central to the facilitation of Anglo-Irish inter-governmentalism. This approach was designed to place the Northern Ireland problem within a broader process of healing between Britain and Ireland. Meanwhile, the Irish government, after the 1985 Anglo-Irish Agreement, in which Hume's role was influential, adopted the role of custodian of northern nationalist interests. Hume's influence did assist in the removal of the supposed irredentism of the Irish government's constitutional claim to Northern Ireland. As such, Hume brokered a different form of Irish nationalism, but it still looked, smelt and felt like nationalism, set in a new bi-national arrangement, rather than supra-nationalism or Europeanism.

Hume was also active in generating American and European involvement in Northern Ireland and encouraged the US administration and EU Commission and Parliament to act as restraining forces upon militant Irish nationalism. Hume's encouragement of exogenous forces reflected his belief in the need to transcend a petty local squabble. A generous verdict might be that Hume saw his fostering of Anglo-Irish bi-nationalism as the means to create a peace process in which increasing external inputs would also help transcend the conflict. This was the Hume version of post-nationalism, which remains a slippery concept.

The structure of Cunningham's article is odd, with the conclusion overly long at nearly half the article. More importantly, however, there are substantive criticisms. At times, the article is overly suspicious of the former SDLP leader's attempts to dilute the 'principle' of 'Unionist consent' (a gerrymandering later elevated to the status of a principle by seemingly all except the most robust republicans). For all the supposed obfuscation of the principle, the SDLP's wavering of the need for Unionist consent as a prerequisite for a united Ireland was short-lived, amounting to a single motion passed at a solitary party conference, in 1976 (Murray and Tonge, 2005). That departure from type reflected temporary rage at the demise of the Sunningdale Agreement and the Northern Ireland Constitutional Convention. It was not a permanent erosion of the SDLP's unity by consent preferences, outlined in the party's defining *Towards a New Ireland* document (SDLP, 1972).

Furthermore, in emphasising the island-wide basis of Hume's approach to self-determination, Cunningham underestimates Hume's capacity to endorse co-determination as the means of 'self-determination'. Hume's references to the inability of the two traditions to agree the mode of self-determination led him away from the territorial all-island formula envisioned by Sinn Féin until the Good Friday Agreement. Hume argued the Agreement was an exercise in self-determination on the grounds he desired. Sinn Féin backed the deal, but Gerry Adams declared at his party's 1998 Ard Fheis that the Agreement was not an exercise in Irish self-determination. Notwithstanding the importance of the Good Friday Agreement being subject to referenda north and south, Adams' position is more consistent. Hume's position was based upon co-determination, a different beast from self-determination and a crucial departure from Toneite 32 County territorial determinism. Had the unthinkable happened in the Irish Republic's referendum and voters backed the retention of the constitutional claims to Northern Ireland in Articles 2 and 3 of the constitution, it would have made no difference to Northern Ireland's place in the United Kingdom. The vote in Northern Ireland effectively determined the fate of the Good Friday Agreement – co-determination on a separate north and south basis is a heavily modified version of self-determination and Hume appeared comfortable with this downgrading.

Cunningham's dissection also needs to take into account the context of Hume's articulations. Whilst Hume's ideological approach is sincerely held, the construction of pan-nationalism commonalities which formed the basis of the peace process required emphasis upon what nationalists throughout Ireland held in common. This allowed the SDLP to help foster the peace process and gave Sinn Féin the fig-leaf for political change by which the party could claim that all nationalist forces throughout Ireland were rowing in the same direction. Whilst Cunningham could hardly anticipate the precise contents of the Good Friday Agreement, the benign nature of Hume's nationalism and the principles of political settlement had been apparent in the Downing Street Declaration issued by the British and Irish governments in 1993.

Cunningham's article has considerable merit in highlighting the imprecision associated with Hume's formulations of post-nationalism, Europeanism and, most importantly, self-determination. The lack of clarity concerning Hume's approach to self-determination raised suspicions among unionists and some academics, including to some extent Cunningham, that the concept was being used as an ideological vehicle designed to, borrowing a phrase from the SDLP's Hugh Logue, trundle unionists into a united Ireland. Constructing his article during the mid-1990s, Cunningham could not be certain that Hume's approach to self-determination was perhaps more benign, part of the constructive ambiguity of the peace process. Although Hume's 32 county approach to self-determination was itself watered down by the British government and unionists, it is now clear that the former SDLP leader *did* accept that agreement on the exercise of a mechanism of self-determination was more important than that exercise resulting in a united Ireland. Therein lies the key to the ending of 30 years of conflict, which is why John Hume will remain identified as a major political figure and why Cunningham's article will continue to be read during the next 25 years – and beyond – of *Irish Political Studies*.

Notes

1 The following exegesis is based upon a sample of Hume's speeches as reported in newspapers, SDLP election literature and statements, and Hume's articles since the late 1980s.
2 There is a growing literature on the implications of 'Europeanisation' for the Northern Ireland question; see e.g. Anderson and Goodman, 1994, 1994a, 1995; Goodman, 1996; and Tannam, 1995.

References

Anderson, James and James Goodman (1994) 'European and Irish Integration: Contradictions of Regionalism and Nationalism', *Journal of European and Regional Studies*, 1 (1), pp. 49–62.

Anderson, James and James Goodman (1994a) 'Northern Ireland: Dependency, Class and Cross-Border Integration in the European Union', *Capital and Class*, 54, pp. 13–24.

Anderson, James and James Goodman (1995) 'Euro-Regionalism: National Conflict and Development', pp. 39–53 in Peter Shirlow (ed.) *Development Ireland*. London: Pluto Press.

Aughey, Arthur (1993) 'Irresistible Force?', *Fortnight*, 321, October.

Cox, W. Harvey (1996) 'From Hillsborough to Downing Street – And After', pp. 182–211 in Peter Catterall and Sean McDougall (eds.) *The Northern Ireland Question in British Politics*. Basingstoke: Macmillan.

Delanty, Gerard (1996) 'Habermas and Post-National Identity: Theoretical Perspectives on the Conflict in Northern Ireland', *Irish Political Studies*, 11, pp. 20–32.

Drower, George (1995) *John Hume: Peacemaker*. London: Victor Gollancz.

Evans, Jocelyn, Jonathan Tonge and Gerard Murray (2000) 'Constitutional Nationalism and Socialism in Northern Ireland: The Greening of the SDLP', pp. 117–32 in P. Cowley, D. Denver, L. Harrison and A. Russell (eds.) *British Elections and Parties Review 10*. London: Frank Cass.

Freeman, Michael (1996) 'Democracy and Dynamite: The People's Right to Self-Determination', *Political Studies*, 44 (4), pp. 746–61.

Gallagher, Michael (1990) 'Do Unionists Have a Right to Self-Determination?', *Irish Political Studies*, 5, pp. 11–30.

Gallagher, Michael (1995) 'How Many Nations Are There in Ireland?', *Ethnic and Racial Studies*, 18 (4), pp. 715–39.

Girvin, Brian (1994) 'Constitutional Nationalism and Northern Ireland', pp. 5–52 in Brian Barton and Patrick Roche (eds.) *The Northern Ireland Question: Perspectives and Policies*. Aldershot: Avebury.

Goodman, James (1996) 'The Northern Ireland Question and European Politics', pp. 212–28 in Peter Catterall and Sean McDougall (eds.) *The Northern Ireland Question in British Politics*. Basingstoke: Macmillan.

Griffin, Dean Victor (1993) cited in Andrew Pollak (ed.) *A Citizens' Inquiry: The Opsahl Report on Northern Ireland*. Dublin: Lilliput Press.

Hainsworth, Paul (1985) 'Northern Ireland in the European Community', pp. 109–32 in Michael Keating and Barry Jones (eds.) *Regions in the European Community*. Oxford: Clarendon Press.

Hooghe, Liesbet (1995) 'Subnational Mobilisation in the European Union', *West European Politics*, 18 (3), pp. 175–98.

Hume, John (1986) 'A New Ireland – The Acceptance of Diversity', *Studies*, 300, pp. 378–83.

Hume, John (1988) Letter to Gerry Adams, 17 March. Linenhall Library collection P3395.

Hume, John (1988a) Speech to SDLP 18th Annual Conference, Belfast, 25–27 November.

Hume, John (1988b) 'Europe of the Regions', pp. 45–57 in Richard Kearney (ed.) *Across the Frontiers: Ireland in the 1990s*. Dublin: Wolfhound Press.

Hume, John (1993) Joint Statement Issued With Gerry Adams, 23 April.

Hume, John (1994) 'Towards a New Century Together', *Belfast Telegraph*, 18 February.

Hume, John (1994a) 'We Want Equality, Not Dominance', *Belfast Telegraph*, 23 August.

Hume, John (1994b) 'Towards a New Ireland: Towards a New Century', Box 3, SDLP collection, Linenhall Library, 31 January.

Kearney, Richard (1991) 'Across the Frontiers: Ireland and Europe', pp. 36–48 in Maurna Crozier (ed.) *Cultural Traditions in Northern Ireland*. Belfast: Institute of Irish Studies, Queen's University.

Keating, Michael (1995) 'Europeanism and Regionalism', pp. 1–22 in Barry Jones and Michael Keating (eds.) *The European Union and the Regions*. Oxford: Clarendon Press.

Kennedy, Dennis (1994) 'The European Union and the Northern Ireland Question', pp. 166–88 in Brian Barton and Patrick Roche (eds.) *The Northern Ireland Question: Perspectives and Policies*. Aldershot: Avebury.

Longley, Edna (1990) *From Cathleen to Anorexia*. Dublin: Attic Press.

Longley, Edna (1993) Submission to Andrew Pollak (ed.) *A Citizens' Inquiry: The Opsahl Report on Northern Ireland*. Dublin: Lilliput Press.

Longley, Edna (1994) 'A Northern "Turn" ', *The Irish Review*, 15, pp. 1–13.

McAllister, Ian (1977) *The Northern Ireland Social Democratic and Labour Party*. Basingtoke: Macmillan.

McGarry, John and Brendan O'Leary (1995) *Explaining Northern Ireland*. Oxford: Blackwell.

McGovern, Mark (1997) 'Unity in Diversity? The SDLP's Approach to the Peace Process', pp. 54–71 in Chris Gilligan and Jonathan Tonge (eds.) *Peace or War? Understanding the Peace Process in Northern Ireland*. Aldershot: Avebury.

Murray, Gerard (1998) *John Hume and the SDLP: Impact and Survival in Northern Ireland*. Dublin: Irish Academic Press.

Murray, Gerard and Jonathan Tonge (2005) *Sinn Féin and the SDLP: From Alienation to Participation*. London: Hurst.

O'Brien, Conor Cruise (1993) 'A New Ireland?', *New York Review of Books*, pp. 38–42, 7 October.

O'Connor, Fionnuala (1993) *In Search of a State: Catholics in Northern Ireland*. Belfast: Blackstaff Press.

O'Leary, Brendan (1987) 'The Anglo-Irish Agreement: Folly or Statecraft?', *West European Politics*, 10 (1), pp. 5–32.

Routledge, Paul (1998) *John Hume: A Biography*. London: HarperCollins.

SDLP (1972) *Towards a New Ireland*. Belfast: SDLP.

SDLP (1988) 'SDLP Responses to Questions Raised in Discussion and in Previous Sinn Féin Papers', 11 July. Linenhall Library collection P3395.

SDLP (1994) 'Towards a New Century'. Handbill for 1994 European elections. Derry.

SDLP (1995) *Paths to a Political Settlement in Ireland: Policy Papers Submitted to the Forum for Peace and Reconciliation*. Belfast: Blackstaff Press.

Tannam, Etain (1995) 'The European Union and Northern Irish Politics', *Ethnic and Racial Studies*, 18 (4), pp. 797–817.

Todd, Jennifer (1991) 'The Conflict in Northern Ireland: Institutional and Constitutional Dimensions', pp. 3–7 in Myrtle Hill and Sarah Barber (eds.) *Aspects of Irish Studies*. Belfast: Institute of Irish Studies, Queen's University.

Tonge, Jonathan (2002) 'Northern Ireland: A Different Kind of Election', pp. 219–36 in Andrew Geddes and Jonathan Tonge (eds.) *Labour's Second Landslide: The British General Election 2001*. Manchester: Manchester University Press.

White, Barry (1985) *John Hume: Statesman of the Troubles*. Belfast: Blackstaff.

8   Modern Irish republicanism

The product of British state strategies

Anthony McIntyre

Originally published in *Irish Political Studies*, 10, 1995, pp. 97–121.

Setting up the board

Irish republicanism has been a constant factor in the overall political equation in the North of Ireland for the past 25 years. Its vibrancy and resilience have fascinated many and confounded most. For an organised body of thought and activity so central to the conflict, addressed daily in the newspapers, and almost hourly in the broadcasting media, it comes as no surprise that translation of this voluminous material into written work has been plentiful.

John Whyte, in his book, *Interpreting Northern Ireland*, has claimed that the North of Ireland relative to its size is the most researched place on earth (1990, p. vii). Much of that research constitutes a macro analysis of the totality of the conflict while others are more micro, and perhaps therefore more modest, in their approach. A considerable percentage of these works are directly addressed to the question of 'modern' Irish republicanism.

Yet to understand modern Irish republicanism it is necessary to think beyond the content of what has been published up to now. Much of that work is defective in that it concentrates either directly on the dominant personalities within republicanism, its supposed militaristic ethos, its 'hawks' and 'doves', its ineradicable terrorist culture, or views republicanism through its own interpretative grid. Each of these in its own way may contribute something to our understanding of the phenomenon. But in achieving this much they tend to leave a great deal more unexplained.

The modern republican movement has persistently been the product of British state strategies rather than a body which has existed for the sole purpose of completing the 'unfinished business' of uniting Ireland. It represents the crystallisation of nationalist opposition to structural exclusion *within* the North of Ireland. Danny Morrison has articulated the point fluently:

> The IRA [Irish Republican Army] doesn't claim to be representing the people in the twenty-six counties. Nor does Sinn Féin. The IRA claims to represent the IRA and the oppressed nationalists who support it. The IRA don't plant bombs in the name of the people of the twenty-six counties – the IRA plant bombs to bring about a political resolution to the problems of the North.
>
> (Jackson, 1988)

For this reason the republican movement and its activities, including the use of political violence, is not merely – or even mainly, despite the intentions of republicans – a dynamic towards a united Ireland, but is also a dynamic for reform within the North of Ireland. Because of that, modern republicanism, its earlier purist rhetoric notwithstanding, is situated on a structural fault line which can quite easily cause it to pull up, in spite of itself, considerably short of its stated goals.

Perhaps as importantly, by way of explanation for the longevity of the armed campaign, modern Irish republicanism functions as the politics of an 'underclass' of nationalists who feel economically marginalised and politically minimalised ('Susini', 1991, pp. 68–9). This results in participation in *political* activity (an end in itself) through 'unconventional' means.

A problem with much writing on the subject, therefore, immediately becomes apparent. It subscribes to a public discourse which holds that for most of the past 25 years the republican movement has been the expression of the dominance of the 'militarist' tendency over the 'political'. An autonomy has been ascribed to a 'militarism' operating under its own dynamic, impervious to 'political' reasoning. Where this is not evident in the literature, and efforts are made to strike a balance, there is a tendency nevertheless to impose an artificial dichotomy between 'political' and 'military' thinking, which it is inferred generally results from internal republican contradictions. This is perplexing for those trying to enhance their understanding of modern Irish republicanism. It is much more fruitful to analyse republicanism as a specifically 'political' phenomenon, not just pursuing political goals by military means, but performing political activity through a combination of 'conventional' and 'unconventional' means.

A necessarily superficial overview of some of the literature and a cursory observation on each work selected may suffice to demonstrate the above contentions. The more long-standing works on the subject are those of Bell (1979) and Coogan (1980). The former is heavily mechanistic and concentrates almost exclusively on the IRA as a quintessential military machine operating under the weight of an historical imperative. The latter is anecdotal, structureless and disappointingly threadbare in terms of explaining strategic considerations, preferring to presume the existence of an almost exclusivist militaristic mindset within republicanism. Bell, in a later work examining IRA targets and tactics, while more streamlined, fails to avail of the opportunity to be more probing in his analysis, contenting himself to identify an 'escalation imperative' as the underlying dynamic of republican political violence (1990).

Other works, largely journalistic but not sensationalist, do manage in part to trace the evolution of political thought within republicanism. Bishop and Mallie (1987), Kelley (1988), Keena (1990) and O'Brien (1993), while all constituting useful insights into changes within republican thinking, fail to locate these directly in a dialectic of republican/British state conflict. To varying degrees, there is a tendency within all four works to account for change as resulting from internal republican factors.

There are a number of autobiographical accounts which are less than adequate. McStiofain (1975) and O'Doherty (1993) leave the reader with a distinct impression of a military imperative guiding all activity. McGuire (1973) attempts to outline the development of a clear line of non-military thinking, but her work covered too short a timespan leaving her with insufficient subject matter to fully consider the impact on that thinking of British state strategies. The works of Adams while in no sense militaristic suffer from the deficiency of being somewhat propagandistic and are as such open to question in terms of what they omit rather than any factual inaccuracies contained within (1976, 1985, 1986, 1988a, 1988b, 1988c and 1990).

The era when republicanism was perhaps under the most intense spotlight ever, the hunger strikes of 1980–81, failed to produce the literature one might expect. The work of Metress (1983), Collins (1986) and Beresford (1987) are at best super-ficial treatments of the politics of republicanism during the hunger strikes. Clarke (1987) and O'Malley (1990) are much more substantive. However, the former treats Sinn Féin as if it emerged out of a vacuum and contends that by the second half of the mid-1980s the armed struggle was being used mainly for the purpose of maintaining internal discipline rather than for any political objective it was initially intended to achieve. O'Malley, while thorough in terms of identifying significant political movement within republicanism, steeps republican motiva-tion in some hazily defined culture of martyrdom, thus confusing ideological legitimising props for dynamics.

Of the more academic produce, the Research Institute for the Study of Conflict and Terrorism (1991), although concentrating on the IRA's 'fixation with violence', nevertheless identifies debate taking place in the republican movement, which it predicted would ultimately lead to a suspension of military operations due to the pressure applied from within the Catholic community. Again, this type of 'internalist' analysis ignores the relationship between Irish republicanism and the British state. Smith (1991) in his doctoral thesis, despite attaining a high standard of rigour, still only manages to construct a much more elaborate and academic version of Bell's 'escalation imperative', concluding that republicans, largely because of the weight of inherited militarism, could never discern at what point political violence had outlived its usefulness. White (1993), in his pioneering work, which combines a 'political process' analytical framework with a 'resource mobilisation' perspective, aimed at explaining the motivating factors in political protest, does not address his inquiry to the general political thought behind republican strategic evolution, choosing instead to confine himself to teasing out explanations from republicans as to why they, as individuals, participated in political violence.

Patterson (1989) arguably offers the best understanding of modern Irish republicanism with his utilisation of 'social republicanism' as an analytical and interpretative framework. But in using this organising principle he ascribes a continuity to republicanism which does not in fact exist, or at least is so fractured by periodisation that continuity as a concept is seriously compromised. Furthermore, in a vein similar to Clarke, he traces 'political' thinking within republicanism only back to 1977. Additionally, he exaggerates the extent to which republican thinking is the outcome of an engagement with traditional ideological currents rather than viewing this as an obvious response of a group trying to outmanoeuvre, or avoid being outmanoeuvred by, the British state. Patterson's approach is in a sense too seamless to identify incisively the specificity of republican activity.

Rather, therefore, than tracing the course of republican developments through a historically-given militarist/politicist grid, it is academically more productive to utilise the concept of 'political thought'. For many, republican 'political thinking' has been taken to mean the development of trends favouring a departure from the military campaign of the IRA and toward building Sinn Féin as an alternative to the political violence of the IRA. But this gives us at best a fractured and fragmented view of the republican 'whole'.

If politicism is interpreted as meaning a totally unarmed way of republicans achieving the goal of a British declaration of intent to withdraw from the north then there has been no politicist/militarist divide within republican ranks. On armed struggle being an essential means to achieve the goal, republicans have generally always been united. For example, in 1983, Morrison argued that if every nationalist in Ireland voted Sinn Féin the British would still not withdraw and that the only way, therefore, to force a disengagement was through armed struggle (Hernes, 1983). At the 1983 Sinn Féin Ard Fheis, Gerry Adams, in his inaugural address as party president, stated that 'there are those who tell us that the British Government will not be moved by armed struggle...the history of Ireland and British colonial involvement throughout the world tells us that they will not be moved by anything else' ('Susini', 1991, p. 33). Three years later Adams argued that armed struggle 'is a necessary form of resistance...armed struggle becomes unnecessary only when the British presence has been removed...if at any time Sinn Féin decide to disown the armed struggle they won't have me as a member' (*Andersonstown News*, 1986). The following year he argued that 'no one has outlined a scenario by which unarmed struggle would achieve Irish independence and peace' (Shanahan, 1987). At the strategically crucial 1986 Sinn Féin Ard Fheis, Martin McGuinness emphatically stated 'our position is clear and it will never, never, never change. The war against British rule must continue until freedom is achieved' (Browne and O'Toole, 1986). So, in giving up the armed struggle, it may be argued that republicans are not merely switching tactics but are in fact ceding the goal – the goal being a declaration of intent by the British state to withdraw regardless of whether the unionists consented or not.

There will of course be the suggestion that there exists a tradition which republican leaders later melted into where armed struggle was seen as a contingent strategy rather than an essential means to an end. This runs counter to a general theme of this paper that it is not 'traditions' that shape modern Irish political and strategic thought, but necessity arising from the confrontation with the British state. What the 'tradition' argument overlooks is firstly, the previous hostility by the present republican leadership to any such tradition and, secondly, the rationale given by republican leaders for armed struggle no longer being essential is premised on highly questionable assumptions.

Firstly, of the three traditions within republicanism identified by Adams, militarist, radical and constitutional (Adams, 1986, pp. 7–8), the latter approximates most closely to a position of holding armed struggle to be a contingent rather than essential strategy (Smith, 1991, p. 176). But this was the tradition most ridiculed by Adams (Patterson, 1989, p. 196).

Secondly, Adams, in justifying the departure from his earlier position of armed struggle being a necessary and morally correct position, stated 'once the British Government had said that they cannot see a defeat of the IRA . . . it seems to me just totally and absolutely clear that we need then to move on' (Tynan, 1994a). The difficulty with this position is that it seems never to have been stated by republicans in advance that such a statement from the British government would be sufficient to move the situation on.

Moreover, republicans as far back as 1971 were of the view that the British government had declared to the world that the IRA could not be defeated (*An Phoblacht*, 1971a). In December of the same year, the British Army General Officer Commanding (GOC) Harry Tuzo conceded the point when in reference to the IRA campaign he said, 'it's obviously an activity that could be carried on until they choose to desist finally from what they are doing' (Kelly, 1976, p. 49). The latter, coupled with the transparent despair of British Home Secretary Maudling, led republicans by the start of the new year to observe that the British were on the verge of admitting defeat due to a self-professed inability militarily to defeat the IRA (*An Phoblacht*, 1972). Arguably, the political fall-out from Maudling's 'acceptable level of violence' statement constrained British ministers' future public utterances on the matter. But the message was quite often, although not always, there implicitly. Prior, for example, conveyed as much when he said that economic as well as political measures were needed if violence were to be defeated (Prior, 1986, p. 203). Rees, while Secretary of State for Northern Ireland, told the British cabinet that more military measures were not going to solve the problem (Rees, 1985, p. 51).

The history of the modern republican movement – from the early 1970s – has basically been one of adapting to survive in the face of British state strategies. As space on any one particular front has been denied it, republicanism has surged up to reappear in a different theatre. Quite often, it would seem that republican engagement in certain activities, such as broadening out in the Republic of Ireland, or electoral activity in the north, is less the result of far-sighted and intelligent thinking, or the outcome of dipping into the experience and tradition of social republicanism, but rather the consequence of a body following the line of least pressure and appearing on that part of the stage least protected by the British state.

There has been a constant strategic thread linking all British state thinking since 1970 at least. Although there are more structural constraints governing the containment of republicanism than acknowledged by Rolston, his observation on British state strategy is far from invalid:

> There has always been a very consistent strategy of the British state, though not always at the forefront of the policies of each British Government; that is

the strategy of containing the 'Northern Ireland problem', militarily, ideologically and otherwise, not only within Northern Ireland but also within clearly geographically defined ghettos in Northern Ireland.

(1986, p. 262)

More specifically, it is not imprudent to go beyond Rolston and argue that the overriding policy of successive British governments has been to render ineffectual the military capacity of the IRA. This is not to say, however, that the British state has at all times striven to secure a military victory over the IRA, despite this objective being given much greater emphasis during the term of some governments, for example, Labour from 1976 to 1979, and the Conservatives in 1981. Rather, all its political initiatives were of much less concern to it in any normative sense and were more instrumentalist in character, in that they were aimed at eroding the ground where the IRA sank its roots. In other words rendering militarily ineffectual the IRA and consequently its political/military capacity to effect political change – foremost, that change which would have led to a British withdrawal without the consent of the unionists – while the dominant priority of the British state, was not necessarily to be secured through military means. For example, in the first months of Direct Rule Whitelaw tried to use republicans' 'manifest political weaknesses to undermine their military capacity' (Bew and Patterson, 1985, p. 49). In the 1990s, a military victory over the IRA was not considered necessary if 'political success in exploiting the weakness of the republican movement' could be attained (Ryan, 1994, p. 17).

A security mindset has constituted the hegemonic element within overall British state strategy, but that mindset has been nourished by both political and military inputs, the principal objective of which has been to bring to an end the conflict which makes it difficult for Britain to rule from afar. This is not to contend that 'ruling' means that Britain has any long-term self-interest for being in the north of Ireland. But while here, the British state behaves in accordance with a general imperative of states in the modern international arena to promote and protect its own self-interest over and above that of any other party. Contrary to what imperialistic type motives republicans attribute to the British state, it remains in Ireland in response to the unionists.

But it is not out of respect for the democratic wishes of unionism, but in response to what Kelly termed the unionist 'strategy of threat' (1989, p. 10), or likely potential to destabilise the British Isles in the event of a British declaration of intent to withdraw. As Rees put it in the early 1970s, 'we have not the faintest desire to stay in Ireland and the quicker we are out the better' (Fisk, 1975, p. 153); which decoded meant Britain would go if only the unionists allowed them. The British state need not be ideologically or politically pro-unionist – by virtue of its presence, which underwrites the constitutional guarantee and a consequent sectarian hegemony (Moxon-Browne, 1981, p. 50), it is structurally pro-union. It cannot therefore be neutral. Consequently, it will always be locked in permanent conflict with those most victimised by the union.

Given this constraint, British government policy has been to do that which maximises the likelihood of the least possible political involvement on the part of the British state (Bew and Patterson, 1985, p. 95). But in so doing, Britain has engendered the conditions which have invariably made it more difficult to achieve precisely that.

Because the strategies of the British state, including that of reproducing its own role as the constitutional guarantor, have effectively militated against the development of a non-violent political response, and shaped to a larger extent than generally appreciated the parameters within which a republican non-military organisation such as Sinn Féin could operate, politically violent anti-partitionism – as clearly distinct from inherent militarism – has come to be the dominant expression within modern Irish republicanism. Contrary to much of the conventional reading of the situation, this politically violent anti-partitionism cannot be explained away in terms of it being the residual product of a republican past being exploited by physical force opportunistic individuals. Equally so, the development of Sinn Féin, which labours under no organisational or functional imperative to perform political violence, cannot be reduced to republicanism merely drawing on the experience and tradition of the so-called 'revolutionary tendency' that existed in the movement of Irish republicanism since the 1920s. It too, like its military counterpart, can only properly be fully understood *vis-à-vis* the strategies of the British state.

But perhaps more crucially, it is through tracing the development of Sinn Féin to the point where its unarmed activities became the only active politics in republicanism that a central point of this paper may be demonstrated. British state strategy brought into being against itself the only form of political struggle which republicans insisted could work to end partition. It did not work and republicans consequently felt compelled to adopt the stance of constitutional nationalism, which they had persistently claimed could not work. The impetus behind such a shift lies in the dialectic of conflict between the British state and modern Irish republicanism. Ultimately, British state strategy was the major determinant in neutralising any effective anti-partitionist struggle against it.

As a means to trace developments within republicanism it is useful to examine the responses of republicanism to the three major policy initiatives in the course of this conflict which incorporated some form of 'Irish dimension'. These are the Sunningdale Agreement of 1973–1974; the Anglo-Irish Agreement of 1985; and the Downing Street Declaration of 1993.

Through a thorough examination and comparison of these areas – of which only a skeletal version is possible within the scope of the present paper – light may be thrown on the changing nature of republican thought, its nuances, ambiguities, tensions, contradictions, re-evaluations of political violence, its developing cognisance of its own marginalisation, its discourse shifting in emphasis and consequently repitching in inflexion in response to the ever-present pressure of the British state, culminating in republicanism's attempt to take the commanding heights on the discursive battlefield. A height from which it would be locked into a logic that could only lead to the abandoning of political violence without ever having achieved its main demands: no declaration of intent by the British state to withdraw; no change in the constitutional guarantee; and no indication that the British will become persuaders for Irish unity (Tynan, 1994b).

The Irish dimension: Opening moves

Prior to the power-sharing Executive of 1974 the 'provisional' republican movement had been in existence for three years. Conjured out of its bottle by the British state – in the act of preserving its own self-interest – attempting to limit its intervention in the North of Ireland to measures designed to restore the credibility of unionist rule internationally, the Provisional IRA became the only effective political expression of many northern nationalists in a context where more conventional political activity hardly seemed relevant (Guelke and Smyth, 1992, p. 104). That it grew in size and influence was directly related to the repressive measures – such as the Falls curfew and internment – utilised by the British state in its attempt to maintain unionist rule with a view to permitting itself an early exit and allow the unionists to carry on governing. That Direct Rule was not initiated in 1969, nor the constitutional guarantee removed to London at the same time, inevitably meant that the existing political conditions left no political space for nationalists to campaign in an exclusively peaceful manner.

But its emphasis on the use of political violence should not serve to obscure its political thinking in relation to unarmed activity. In a book on her involvement in the IRA, Maria McGuire draws attention to the view of a senior IRA leader, Daithí Ó Conaill, that it was essential for republicans to build an unarmed political base, the success of which would be determined by the size of any such movement and its basis for unity (McGuire, 1973, p. 73). In August 1971, republicans attempted to launch such a project by staging a convention for the purpose of building the movement in a non-military fashion (*An Phoblacht*, 1971b). Republicans were also heavily involved in the Irish Civil Rights Association (*Republican News*, 1972b). In addition, Sinn Féin was central to attempts to set up four regional parliaments under a Comhairle Eireann (*Republican News*, 1973a).

Contrary to the view that it was not until the 1980s that republicans arrived at the conclusion that the IRA could not drive the British Army into the sea, Tugwell correctly perceived that republicans appreciated from early in the campaign of political violence, that theirs would be a campaign of political leverage. That campaign would use the international, domestic and economic side effects of armed struggle on the British government and public to cause a necessary shift from the British state viewing the North of Ireland as an asset to a liability (Tugwell, 1981, p. 18).

In the period preceding Sunningdale a major sensitivity within republicanism related to constitutional nationalism and the perceived threat posed by it to the unity between the republican movement and the northern nationalists. Prior to the 1972 truce, Ó Conaill was preoccupied with talking to John Hume of the Social Democratic and Labour Party (SDLP), who was endeavouring to convince the former of the merits of an unarmed alliance between the SDLP and elements of the republican movement (McGuire, 1973, p. 125). SDLP concerns at the time were largely taken up with the problem posed by republicans. Paddy Devlin, in his autobiography, makes it clear that much of the party's time was spent trying to neutralise the republican challenge (1993). In its first substantial policy document,

Towards A United Ireland, the party advocated a British declaration of intent to withdraw and, as an interim measure, a provincial government based on a coalition of nationalists and unionists which would be subordinated not to Westminster but to a joint Anglo-Irish condominium (Bew and Patterson, 1985, p. 53).

But then, republicans were under no illusions about the SDLP, and were unambiguous in their view of the party as a 'partitionist nationalist' body – nationalists who may indeed aspire to a united Ireland but are prepared to wait until the unionists consent to such unity, a position later described by Adams as 'a partitionist fudge' (1988c, p. 51). This was an anathema to republicans at this juncture (MacLiam, 1973). British state reinforcement for the republican view of the SDLP lay in the Whitelaw strategy, confirmed in his memoirs, of building up the SDLP not because of the party's intrinsic merits but because it was in competition with the IRA (1989, p. 93).

The first incorporation of an Irish dimension in a British state policy proposal came in the British government's Green Paper of October 1972. That particular document effectively set the parameters of the forthcoming debate about Sunningdale. The underlying British state thinking came out in the manner of articulation chosen by Julian Critchley, a senior member of the Conservative Party: 'The Irish dimension exists. It is a fact of life which we must acknowledge and accept. Mr Lynch's attitude to the IRA in the south... is the key to the eventual military victory for which the security forces are working in the north' (Bew and Patterson, 1985, pp. 53–4). Garret FitzGerald, the Republic's foreign minister in the coalition government which helped negotiate Sunningdale, was in no doubt that this was a clear statement of British intent, claiming in his memoirs that the British state at Sunningdale was obsessed with security (1991, p. 237).

Seán McStiofain, Chief of Staff of the IRA until November 1972, believed that the Green Paper was an acknowledgement by the British state that it could no longer proceed with the pretence that the North of Ireland was the concern of Britain alone. In writing the editorial comment on the paper for the *Republican News*, he called for a boycott of the proposed North of Ireland plebiscite which would decide the constitutional status of the area on the grounds that it was designed 'to thwart the right of the majority in the whole of Ireland to determine the future of the country' (McStiofain, 1975, p. 330).

Ruairí Ó Bradaigh, president of Sinn Féin at the time, felt the resulting Sunningdale arrangement had to be destroyed before it destroyed the republican movement. He was concerned about the opportunities the arrangement afforded the SDLP to establish itself as the undisputed hegemon within northern nationalism. This was viewed in terms of the detrimental impact it would have on republican attempts to prosecute the anti-partitionist struggle (Bishop and Mallie, 1987, p. 209).

Although Ó Bradaigh felt the most effective way to resist the challenge of the SDLP – and consequently Sunningdale – was to fight the party in elections, his view did not prevail (Bishop and Mallie, 1987, p. 209), and the means to destroy the agreement soon became evident in an IRA vow to wreck anything that emerged from it through an upsurge in its armed campaign. Consequently, the organisation indulged in a bombing campaign in England (Kelley, 1988, pp. 205–10). The only time it eased up was during the Ulster Workers' Council (UWC) strike of 1974, and then only out of tactical considerations. Ó Conaill won the debate at leadership level within the republican movement that there was no point in the IRA using up scarce resources when the loyalists might obtain their objectives for them, namely, the destruction of British policies in the north of Ireland and the consequent reluctance of the British state to continue supporting the north as a viable political entity (Fisk, 1975, p. 208).

Aware that a gap between a 'partitionist nationalism' and an anti-partitionist nationalism was unbridgeable – precisely because the unity by consent formula made no middle ground possible, and Sunningdale had, in the opinion of Adams, 'succeeded for the first time in producing a fully fledged Catholic partitionist party, in the form of the SDLP' (Adams, 1986, p. 110) – republicans directed a concentrated propaganda offensive against the SDLP and the Catholic hierarchy in a bid to win the hearts and minds of northern nationalists by showing that the two forces were working in collaboration with the British state. They also focused on the hunger strikes in English prisons by the Price sisters and Michael Gaughan as a means to divert attention away from the power-sharing Executive and also to compromise constitutional nationalism in the eyes of northern nationalists (Davis, 1989, pp. 54–5). In addition, they lined up with the more radical groups such as People's Democracy and Bernadette McAliskey in a continuous propaganda barrage against Sunningdale (McAliskey, 1994). The lines of a clear class demarcation within the northern nationalist community were being drawn. Republicanism was in no mood for compromise.

Although the discourse of republicanism in this era did not primarily emphasise the security nature of the Sunningdale Agreement, its strategic thinking was very much premised on it. Assertive, unambiguous and unapologetically rejectionist, republicans forged ahead with their campaign. Significantly, however, republicans made the point that interim arrangements leading in the direction of a united Ireland would not be rejected (*Republican News*, 1973b). But they correctly analysed that the British were not making any move toward a united Ireland and were merely seeking to bolster the constitutional guarantee while at the same time incorporating constitutional nationalism into the framework of the state, in a bid to marginalise republicanism (*Republican News*, 1973c).

The Irish dimension: Stalemate

The next occasion on which an Irish dimension was introduced was with the Anglo-Irish Agreement of 1985. In the intervening years the British state had failed to render militarily ineffectual the IRA. Mason only managed to snatch defeat from the jaws of victory in his ham-fisted implementation of the Rees strategy. Of the IRA, Rees said, 'we set out to con them and we did' (Ryan, 1994, p. 58). The resulting ceasefire proved disastrous for the IRA. But they survived it with the help of Mason and the repressive measures he oversaw, which helped create the space in which there would develop an oppositional current within republicanism (Pollak, 1994), possessed of firm strategic ideas which would permit the continued prosecution of the war.

The emphasis was shifted to a 'long war' strategy. Furthermore, Rees' decision to legalise Sinn Féin for the purpose of creating what Reed terms (in a different era) a constitutional/legal Sinn Féin in contradistinction to an unconstitutional/ illegal IRA (Reed, 1984, p. 407), while at the same time refusing to create the necessary political space in which such a party could meaningfully function by removing the constitutional guarantee, only served to militate against the development of the unarmed political movement Rees sought to create.

At this post-ceasefire juncture republicans were very much of the opinion that the armed struggle would succeed in forcing a British withdrawal. Gerry Adams, who was a strong opponent of both the 1972 truce – which Seán McStiofain, the 'arch-militarist' of the media, favoured (Keena, 1990, p. 18; Bishop and Mallie, 1987, pp. 178–9) – and the 1975 one (Pollak, 1994), argued as late as 1979, 'that the British face military defeat is inevitable and obvious', and that the IRA's armed struggle 'would be sufficient to secure victory' (Adams, 1988a, p. 26). But this was a position that even Ó Conaill had seemingly begun to move away from as far back as 1973 (Kelley, 1988, p. 201). Moreover, prior to that again, republicans were professing openly that the IRA was not strong enough to defeat the British Army (*Republican News*, 1972a).

By 1980, Adams, while maintaining that the armed struggle would secure a declaration of intent to withdraw, was adding the qualification that it would be made that much quicker if political violence was complemented by 'an alternative political movement' which would minimise 'the influence of Dublin Government and SDLP types' (Adams, 1988a, p. 29).

The republicans' attempt to build an unarmed political movement was energised and expedited beyond their highest expectations by the British state's attempt to smash the IRA during the hunger strikes of 1981. Not only was the space created for a significant electoral machine to function, but the British strategy of rendering ineffectual the military capacity of the IRA was significantly knocked off course. British state strategy was merely reproducing the problem it was designed to eradicate.

Flushed with their new-found electoral success, international sympathy and a massive resource pool for the IRA, republicans confidently braced themselves for the long war. Euphoric at the prospect of overtaking the SDLP, and encouraged that they would do so by the paranoia of Garret FitzGerald, the twin approaches of 'armalite and ballot box' became the dominant strategic current within republican political thought (Morrison, 1986, p. 8).

But by 1984, the euphoria had dampened considerably. Republicans had come away from the experience of the National H-Block/Armagh Committee with the conviction that the way to crack constitutional nationalism was through a strong political party rather than a broad front (Clarke, 1987, p. 207). That constitutional nationalism had to be cracked was an imperative in republican considerations. In their post-hunger strike statement the republican prison leadership had this to say:

> We believe that the Dublin block of Fianna Fáil, Fine Gael and Labour are accessories to the legalised murder of ten true and committed Irishmen...
> [the SDLP] should now be recognised for what it is, an amalgamation of

middle class Redmondites, devoid of principle, direction and courage. This party is spineless and weak and is very capable of selling out to unionist intimidators for imperialist perks...nationalist pacifism in the Northern Ireland context dooms the nationalist population to subserviency, perpetuates partition, and thwarts the quest for a just and lasting peace in Ireland.

(Campbell *et al*, 1994, pp. 262–4)

But republicans were now once again searching for allies to compensate for the inability of Sinn Féin to become the hegemonic force in northern nationalist politics. In that sense republicans realised what FitzGerald did not – that they were not going to oust the SDLP from its position. Thus the new line adopted by Adams was that it might be a bad thing to overtake the SDLP as the leading force in northern nationalism as to do so would inevitably lead to a diminution in social radicalism (Bew and Patterson, 1985, p. 125).

But the British state seized on the paranoia of FitzGerald to craft yet another initiative aimed at rendering ineffectual the IRA. The Anglo-Irish Agreement of 1985 was, in the view of Thatcher, a question of security. What role Dublin would be permitted to have would at all times be shaped by its ability to enhance security from a British perspective (Thatcher, 1993, p. 403). FitzGerald, for his own part, said the Agreement was a device for making the 'status quo work' (Bew, 1989, p. 153).

The republican response to the Agreement was to present it in terms of a security initiative. In *A Pathway to Peace*, the only article of the Agreement referred to by Adams as 'extremely important' was Article 7, which in his view dealt with the intensified collaboration and harmonisation of the efforts to repress opposition to the British presence (1988b, p. 16). Its objective was the consolidation of British rule (Adams, 1988b, p. 19). It was also a levering mechanism by which the British state would force the unionists to come to terms with a new internal settlement (Adams, 1988b, p. 30). The British state's primary success lay in its tying in Dublin as a junior partner in Britain's own strategy while placing primary emphasis on security and simultaneously insulating itself from international criticism over the situation in the north of Ireland (Adams, 1986, p. 106).

For the republican leadership, the Agreement demonstrated the crucial role of the SDLP in British state strategic objectives to undermine national self-determination. Any vestige of nationalist or separatist sentiment within the SDLP leadership vanished with Seamus Mallon's acceptance of the Agreement (Adams, 1986, p. 112). Furthermore, in the view of Adams, the Dublin government had become the guarantor of the 'unionist veto', and partition had been copperfastened, while both the Dublin government and the SDLP had become part of the nationalist nightmare (O'Leary and McGarry, 1993, p. 220; Coughlan, 1986, p. 73). Ultimately, Adams claimed that there was nothing in the Agreement which would persuade the IRA to call a halt to its armed struggle (Kenny, 1986, p. 103).

Yet there was evidence of a republican hesitancy. The IRA, unlike its response to Sunningdale, claimed that none of its operations were directed against the Agreement (Clarke, 1987, p. 232). Morrison, somewhat disingenuously, claimed that no republican had claimed that the Agreement was a sell-out (Morrison, 1986, p. 15). A general republican theme beginning to emerge at the time was that any benefits the Agreement brought would be as a consequence of republican sacrifices (O'Malley, 1990, p. 237). This was an implicit acceptance by republicans that their activities could quite readily dynamise a reformist thrust. Morrison admitted as much three years after the signing of the Anglo-Irish Agreement when, in dismissing suggestions that the IRA should halt the armed struggle, he argued that the equation the SDLP 'work on with the British Government is "give us reforms and support drops for Sinn Féin and the IRA". So they need the IRA' (Jackson, 1988).

The hesitancy can most plausibly be explained by the increasing difficulties republicans were experiencing in both their armed and unarmed activity. Neither seemed to be bringing the earlier anticipated success. Moreover, republicans were becoming increasingly sensitive to the narrowing space in which they were being forced by the strategies of the British state to operate. As a consequence, republicans had to move to end their increasing isolation. This they attempted to do by urgently expediting the dropping of their abstentionist policy in the Republic of Ireland. But without actually appreciating it, republicans, rather than ending their isolation through abandoning abstentionism, were in fact confirming it. This monumental decision was an implicit acknowledgement by republicans that the people of the Irish republic were satisfied that they already had their nation state ('Susini', 1991, p. 18). They were also slowly conforming to the grinding logic of a process described by one commentator, Peter Mair, as follows:

> A new nationalism and a new nationalist consensus began to emerge in the late 1950s. Nationalist ideology proved as potent as ever, and Fianna Fáil remained the standard bearer par excellence, but the emphasis on territorial unity per se no longer played a crucial role... the national aim was to be the achievement of social and economic self-respect in the twenty-six county state, rather than the achievement of territorial self-respect in a new thirty-two county state.
>
> (Bew *et al*, 1989, p. 98)

Therefore, the ideology of anti-partitionism could only have a limited resonance. The consequences of this would unfold many years later. Moreover, the dropping of abstentionism was the outcome of a leadership change within the republican movement. The new leadership was northern based. Although the ascendancy of the northerners was widely interpreted as the arrival of politically astute people with a strategy that would ensure the whole of Ireland, rather than the north, would become the focus of attention and an all-Ireland anti-imperialist struggle, it was in fact the confirmation of everything the northerners generally sought to deny – that the north was indeed the issue. Consequently, the northern hegemonisation of the republican struggle was, contrary to the wishes of those promoting the new direction, an unconscious admission of the consigning of the struggle almost exclusively to the north. But this was something realised under the previous leadership. As far back as 1976, Peter Arnliss, writing in the *Republican News*, characterised the struggle as a 'ghetto people's war' (Patterson, 1989, p. 164).

With abstentionism no longer an obstacle, republicans could not continue seeking comfort in the consolation of 'if only'. Confronted with a realisation that they were little more than the political expression of a ghettoised northern nationalism, the search for new allies began with an urgency. In *A Pathway to Peace*, Adams outlined a strategy for constitutional nationalism, part of which would involve persuading the British government and the unionists that the future of the people of the north of Ireland could only lie in an all-Ireland context (Adams, 1988b, pp. 64–9). The London and Dublin governments were urged to meet and decide a date for withdrawal within a specified time period (Adams, 1988b, p. 69). However, Adams had no faith in the leaderships of constitutional nationalism, whom he labelled 'partitionist' and denigrated for their role in the Anglo-Irish Agreement (1988b, pp. 30 and 68).

The thinking behind the proposed strategy was therefore – similar to the old republican socialist logic of Peadar O'Donnell – to expose the leaderships of constitutional nationalism as being inconsistent on the national question by pressurising them to live up to their rhetoric (Adams, 1988b, p. 62). The structural, strategic and political myopia lay, however, in identifying who precisely they were to be exposed to. The 1986 Ard Fheis decision in spite of itself had effectively precluded the southern popular classes as an interested audience. Furthermore, the mechanisms for applying this pressure – the 68 Committees, the Irish National Congress, and the Forum for a Democratic Alternative – all failed to translate themselves into vehicles for what republicans termed 'broadening the base' (*An Phoblacht/Republican News*, 1988).

Increasingly, leading republicans spoke in terms of a stalemate having been reached: the IRA could not defeat the British nor could the British defeat the IRA. The major arms shipments in the latter half of the 1980s may have made republicans more emboldened in their dismissal of the Anglo-Irish Agreement, but the signs were there that republicans knew they could not continue indefinitely. Hence, IRA spokespeople, in interviews with the media, by 1988 began to allude to a big push over a period of 18 months to two years, by the end of which the IRA would know if it had the capacity to end the struggle (Mallie, 1988 and 1989). Significantly, when it became patently clear during the latter half of that timeframe that the struggle was not going to be ended on IRA terms, Peter Brooke began his 'feeling out' process with comments that Britain had no selfish strategic or economic reasons for remaining in Ireland and that the IRA could only be contained but not militarily defeated. And furthermore, that the British state would be 'flexible and imaginative' if the IRA renounced violence (Moloney, 1994, p. 9; Bew and Gillespie, 1993, p. 227). The most plausible interpretation of the Brooke gesture is that the British state was signalling to the IRA a way out of its armed campaign, rather than a way out of Ireland for itself.

It is in this context that attempts by republicans to argue that the union, and by implication the veto, is not safe, ring hollow. Republicans contend that the present situation is different from the eras of Sunningdale and the Anglo-Irish Agreement on the basis that in the post-Cold War world the strategic importance of Ireland is no longer of any great significance (*An Phoblacht/Republican News*, 1995). But the extent to which the strategic value of Ireland to Britain has been a factor in Britain continuing to remain in the North has declined in significance since the end of what Halliday has termed 'Cold War One' (1987). Weighed against the unionist 'strategy of threat' as a consideration in the minds of British state policy makers it arguably has little bearing (Bew and Patterson, 1985, pp. 141–3). Furthermore, there is evidence to suggest that the Republican leadership may not have seriously believed that the reason Britain remained in Ireland was strategic (Patterson, 1989, p. 182).

Aware of the pressures facing republicans, the British state had earlier adopted a two-pronged approach. On the one hand it intensified the military aspect of its strategic objective of rendering ineffectual the IRA with a particular emphasis on killing IRA volunteers caught on active service. On the other, it introduced a range of political and legal measures to isolate republican public discourse from the armed struggle. As the Adams leadership, unlike that of O'Bradaigh, had placed major emphasis on a public fusing of the armed and unarmed struggles (O'Brien, 1993, p. 116), this tactic was crucial in boxing Sinn Féin into a corner.

Ultimately, the British state was not concerned with Sinn Féin *per se* or the fact that Sinn Féin would campaign for a united Ireland, but that it would not find it possible to support the activities of the IRA in public. Britain would have been aware that if, ultimately, it could engineer a situation in which republicanism would exist without the IRA, there would, given the constitutional guarantee, no longer be a threat of any significance to the terms on which Britain had stated the union would remain – by the consent of a majority in the north of Ireland. Crucially, Britain perceives itself to have no quarrel with constitutional nationalism or its terms for uniting the country – by the latter's own attempts to persuade the unionists (Bew, 1989, p. 154). From the British state point of view republicans in an exclusively unarmed struggle could say what they want and even argue that their agenda remained unchanged, but the reality would be that the possibility of implementing that agenda would be greatly reduced (Bew *et al*, 1995, p. 231).

Failing the securement of the optimum situation in which republicanism would exist without the armed struggle, the British state could exploit to the full circumstances in which Sinn Féin could not publicly identify with the IRA. This would inevitably weaken the international legitimacy of the IRA.

The Irish dimension: Checkmate?

Confronted with a military campaign that required greater input for fewer results, and a political party incapable of attracting any support outside of its limited northern constituency, republicans were forced to turn to the leaderships of constitutional nationalism. Although the initial 'feeling out' process began with the SDLP/Sinn Féin talks of 1988, the real republican *volte face* only came in the 1990s.

Republicans had not wanted to abandon the armed struggle. That it was an essential means of achieving a British declaration of intent to withdraw had formed the central spine of republican discourse since the formation of the 'provisionals'. In the verbal sparring with Peter Brooke and others from late 1989, republicans had insisted that a ceasefire was an unacceptable precondition for talks. Less than two years prior to the 1994 'complete cessation' of armed struggle, representatives of the IRA leadership were asserting that there would never be a ceasefire until the British government gave a declaration of intent to withdraw from Ireland (Hazelkorn and Patterson, 1994, p. 70). But the new emphasis on peace in Sinn Féin public discourse – an attempt in itself to escape the 'marginalisation squeeze' of the British state by discursively seizing the moral high ground – was exposing republicans to ever greater pressure to call off the armed campaign. In a bid to field the flak Adams, by 1992, was claiming that the 'ballot box and armalite' strategy was outdated (Moloney, 1994, p. 15).

The turn to constitutional nationalism resulted in the Hume/Adams principles which, republicans claimed, could lead to an IRA cessation if the British government were to make a positive response. These principles included: the Irish people as a whole have the right to self-determination; an internal settlement is not a solution; unionists cannot have a veto over British policy but their consent and allegiances, expressed through an accommodation with the rest of the Irish people, are essential; and the British government must join the persuaders (Adams, 1994).

The response of the British state to this movement within nationalist politics was to join with the Dublin government in issuing the Downing Street Declaration. Despite its discursive shift with a refracted acknowledgement of Irish self-determination – constituting the Irish dimension – the declaration was not only a clear statement of intent by the British state to stay in Ireland, it also reconfirmed the constitutional guarantee. Indeed what has been termed 'the guarded acquiescence of the official Unionists' to the declaration (Patterson, 1994), raises grounds for suspicion that the British government viewed the document as an opportunity to claw back some of the ground it felt it may have conceded in the Anglo-Irish Agreement.

In spite of this, republicans did not reject it in the manner McStiofain had previously dismissed the British Green Paper of 1972, or as their predecessors had ruled out Sunningdale, both of which possessed all the structural obstacles to unification, from a republican perspective, that the Downing Street Declaration contained. Nor was it criticised in the same strident manner that was proffered in response to the Anglo-Irish Agreement. The discursive seizing of the high ground by republicans had left them marooned upon it when the tide of public expectancy generated by that very discourse threatened to drift out. Consequently, rather than state clearly and precisely what the Downing Street Declaration constituted, republicans felt compelled to procrastinate by means of a 'strategy of seeking "clarification"' (Brennock, 1994). More significantly, they did not encourage community groups or prominent personalities, such as Bernadette McAliskey, to identify the Declaration for what in fact it was, which would have allowed them the cushion for a softer landing in the event of any intended rejection.

After many months of 'clarification seeking' and internal and public debate, republicans gave the appearance of rejecting the Downing Street Declaration at their Letterkenny conference in the summer of 1994 (Sinn Féin, 1994). But given that the IRA ceasefire was announced shortly after that conference, it appears that republicans have in fact accepted the declaration under the very guise of having rejected it. Dublin and London have both made it clear that any future negotiations will have to take place within the partitionist parameters stipulated within the Declaration (Reynolds, 1994; *Irish News*, 1994).

In stark contrast to the Sunningdale Agreement, republicans have deferred to the interests they have always claimed stood in the way of Irish unity. By discursively relocating the forces of constitutional nationalism to a position they have never politically or strategically occupied since 1970 – being closer to the republican interpretation of partition than that of the British state – republicans have been able to claim that their own movement has not been as substantial as it would otherwise have been seen to be. However, of crucial significance here is that Reynolds made it clear to Sinn Féin that the unity by consent principle in the Downing Street Declaration was there to stay and that the party could never have been under any illusion about the issue – the government's position being clear on the matter. Nor did the Dublin government seek an alternative to 'unity by consent' and only then reluctantly accept the British position. It fully supported the consent principle (O'Reilly, 1994).

Arguably, Dublin felt it was pushing an open door. Certainly, Martin Mansergh interpreted the much lauded 1992 address to unionists by Mitchel McLaughlin as a significant shift by the republican leadership towards the unity by consent principle (Mansergh, 1995). In that address McLaughlin spoke of it being neither possible nor desirable to coerce unionists into a united Ireland, and of the need for republicans to convince Protestants of the rightness of their cause (McLaughlin, 1992). Since the Declaration, republican leaders have been trying conceptually to divide the indivisible. Adams has spoken of not permitting a veto to unionists while stating that their consent is necessary (Adams, 1994). McLaughlin reiterated the idea soon after, claiming that if there was to be a durable and democratic settlement, a rapprochement with the unionists was necessary as their agreement was essential. At the same time, he said their veto must go (McLaughlin, May 1994). The Sinn Féin vice president, Pat Doherty, continued in this vein in June 1994, arguing that the words consent and veto were significantly different (Carolan, 1994). But the unionist right to consent is precisely what republicans have always claimed constituted that veto.

Ultimately, what the British state will offer is an essentially internal settlement – with a few 'externalities' grafted on – differing little from the Sunningdale Agreement, and falling considerably short of the proposals contained in the SDLP policy document of 1972, *Towards a United Ireland*. And constitutional nationalism will not demur. It possesses neither the structural capacity nor the political will or inclination to confront Britain over the question of partition. Reynolds already made the position clear that he was not seeking self-determination 'in Ireland as a whole collected in a single entity. There will be no change in Northern Ireland without a change of opinions there' (Moloney, 1994, p. 40).

Republicans will have the burdensome task of selling the internal settlement as an interim arrangement which will weaken the institution of partition and hence act as a dynamic toward eventual unity. There is little room for seriously challenging the view of Meulemans (1994) that the realists within republican ranks accept that a united Ireland is not likely soon, if ever, but a close association between the two parts of the country may be possible. This is a scenario seemingly very much accepted by Mitchel McLaughlin when he said that any North–South institutions must have a dynamic to develop, and if so republicans would have no difficulty seeing them as part of a transitional process. In stressing that such a process would have to be open-ended he specifically refrained from stipulating that in order for it to be transitional the British state would have to pronounce clearly that it was leaving the country within a certain time (White, 1995). And in the absence of such a specific commitment by Britain, republicans are left with no option but to accept partition indefinitely. A reading of the comments of Martin McGuinness reveals as much:

> Our position has not changed. We would like to see a unitary state, we would like to see a thirty-two county republic but we recognise that we are only a small percentage of the total people of this island. The people of this island might decide on some other type of structure. I am not going to oppose it. I might oppose it politically but there is no way I would defend anybody's right to use armed force to go against the democratic wish of the people of this island.
>
> (Toolis, 1994)

That the people of Ireland have the right to decide on an option outside of a unitary state was made possible by the crucial concession from republicans, as articulated by Adams, that not only had the people of Ireland the right to national self-determination but they had also the right to choose how to exercise national self-determination (O'Brien, 1993, p. 275). Once this has been conceded, as Mansergh has argued, that right can legitimately be exercised when a people together agree to institutions that fall short of full independence or a change of sovereignty (1995).

Despite the major sea-change in republican political thought it has not resulted from what the former Sinn Féin president, Ruairí Ó Bradaigh, alleges to be the politicians in the movement cashing in the cheques that have been accumulated over the previous years of the struggle to get power and position for themselves (Moriarty, 1994). There has been no 'sell out'. Republicans have ultimately proved unable, despite their tremendous fortitude and resilience, to defeat the British state. That state by persistently exploiting the structural limitations republicans faced as a result of partition, and by conceding enough of an 'Irish dimension' to satisfy constitutional nationalism, has ensured that republicanism would never hegemonise the nationalist constituency. That republicans and constitutional nationalism can now occupy the same line-up in a post-armed struggle environment is of infinitely much less concern to the British state than it undoubtedly would have been in a situation where armed struggle was going full throttle. Republicans, rather than continue with an armed struggle for another 20 years which may have proved able 'to obtain compromise at the margins but not at the centre of the disputed object' (Smith, 1991, p. 375), have succumbed to the pressures generated by the massive array of forces and structural obstacles confronting them, and are prepared to settle for a compromise considerably short of their public 'Brits out' position (Brennock, 1994).

Northern Ireland, 'because of [its] complex, dense and overlapping history, will remain "British", but with an increasing "Irish dimension"' (Patterson, 1989, p. 210). Despite the volubility of republican discourse in continuing to oppose the constitutional guarantee, republicans have been locked into a political vice, the handle of which is in the firm grasp of the British state. And it is not about to relax its grip.

COMMENTARY BY THOMAS HENNESSEY

Anthony McIntyre's 1995 article in *Irish Political Studies* was a landmark essay in the analysis of modern Irish republicanism. The essay tried to restore some sophistication to the debate on republicanism by emphasising its political rather than military nature in a way Cronin (1980) had done over a decade earlier. Coming from a republican perspective McIntyre identified the British state as having had one consistent strategic objective – to render ineffectual the military capacity of the Irish Republican Army (IRA). But it is possible to identify one other British strategic objective – to balance any agreement that might achieve, or lay the foundations for, nullifying the IRA's armed struggle alongside a commitment to the consent of the people of Northern Ireland to any change in their constitutional position. McIntyre, ironically, identifies how the British state is not necessarily pro-unionist, although structurally pro-union, and probably would disengage if the unionists would allow this. It was the steadfast British adherence to the consent principle, combined with the inability to break the military stalemate, which forced the republican movement to seek allies within the wider nationalist family that led them into a peace process.

One of McIntyre's key arguments is that the republican movement is the product of British state strategies and, despite the rhetoric, does not exist solely for the 'unfinished business' of ending partition. It is the product of structural exclusion within Northern Ireland, driven not by a dynamic towards a united Ireland but by reform within Northern Ireland. But it is also possible to interpret modern republicanism as being driven by an ideology of anti-partitionism, seeking to finish 'unfinished business', as well as by structural exclusion. Each element needed the other to produce the modern republican movement. The one strategic objective of the republican movement was to force a British declaration of intent to withdraw from the north. British withdrawal would allow normal class politics to emerge because unionism was based not upon a sense of Britishness but on ascendancy. Sinn Féin argued in 1988 that 'Equality is synonymous with national rights. Partition is a direct contradiction to that' (*Irish Times*, 17 September 1988). This interpretation of unionism was not unique to republicanism.

McIntyre is correct to highlight how violence was not the only aspect of modern republicanism; however, the political element existed, in the early 1970s, in a primitive form compared to other expressions of nationalism. Retrospectively, Gerry Adams regarded the early years of the liberation struggle as a period in which there had been a popular base for republicanism. At this stage Sinn Féin really was a 'second cousin' to the Provisional Irish Republican Army (PIRA), and a 'very poor cousin at that' (*An Phoblacht/Republican News*, 1 March 1984). There had been an 'unconscious slipping into "spectator politics"', whereby people who had been previously involved in the struggle were pushed into the sidelines (*An Phoblacht/Republican News*, 17 November 1983).

Armed struggle remained part of the republican strategy because, as Adams explained in 1987:

> I would be prepared to consider an alternative, unarmed struggle, to attain Irish independence. If someone would outline such a course I would not only be prepared to listen, but I would be prepared to work in that direction. The difficulty is that no one has outlined a scenario by which unarmed struggle would achieve Irish independence and peace... There's no military solution, none whatsoever... And Dublin has failed to show any vestige of any political solution. They don't give a damn at all as far as I can see.
>
> (*Hot Press*, 17 December 1987)

The Sinn Féin–SDLP talks that followed in 1988 were an attempt, on the part of republicans, to build a nationalist coalition against the British government. Mitchel McLaughlin, a member of Sinn Féin's delegation, indicated that the time had come for all shades of nationalism to

> agree one simple proposition, namely, the Irish people's right to national self-determination... Irish self-determination is a principle to which every Irish nationalist can subscribe. The SDLP, Fianna Fáil and the other parties in the 26 counties are on record supporting the concept of independence in one way or another. This support must now become a practical campaign with a minimum objective of a negotiated British withdrawal. After that it will be up to Irish men and women to decide in an amicable fashion the structures within which the Irish people can live and prosper.
>
> (*Irish Times*, 18 May 1988)

Sinn Féin's position was that an irreversible declaration of intent would minimise any loyalist backlash and would go a 'long way towards bringing around to reality' most Loyalists and their representatives genuinely interested in peace and negotiation (*Irish Times*, 17 September 1988). In effect this meant the ending of the current British government policy and the removal of the unionist veto: 'We believe that consent can be obtained if the relevant parties, and particularly the two governments concerned, demonstrate the political will to achieve it. As a first step both governments must establish Irish reunification as a policy objective.' It was 'desirable' that unionists, or a significant proportion of them, gave their support to the means of achieving reunification and promoting reconciliation between all traditions. For Sinn Féin the key questions were, firstly, how to get the British government to recognise Irish national rights; and, secondly, to change its present policy to one of ending partition and the union, within the context of Irish reunification and, having done so, how to secure the co-operation of a majority in the north to the means of implementing those rights (*Irish Times*, 13 September 1988).

McIntyre was absolutely right in highlighting that Sinn Féin were trying conceptually to 'divide the indivisible' when Adams spoke of not permitting a veto to unionists while stating their consent was necessary. Mitchel McLaughlin, in 1991, wrote that

> It should never be disputed that Unionist agreement is not only desirable but vital if we are to have lasting peace and stability in Ireland. The Unionist community must be encouraged to recognise that their future lies in a newly negotiated Ireland, in which their power and influence will have a legitimate determining effect. Such a national agreement is unattainable within the context of Partition which denies the Irish people their right to self-determination… Britain created the Unionist veto and Britain created the 'consent' misnomer. Because Britain has the power to remove the veto, it holds the key to resolution of this problem.
>
> (*Fingerpost Monthly*, May 1991, Volume 8, No.1)

In 1992, Sinn Féin published *Towards a Lasting Peace in Ireland*. It called on the British government to 'join the persuaders' for a united Ireland, to use its influence to convince unionists that their future did not lie within the Union. It also called on the Irish government to persuade the British that partition had failed, to persuade unionists of the benefits of reunification, and to persuade the international community that it should support a 'peace process' in Ireland (Adams, 1995, p. 209). In republican thinking the consent of unionists was achievable *after* the British government declared an interest in seeing a united Ireland. Unionists would then have to negotiate their new position in an agreed Ireland.

But the problem for the republican leadership was that the Conservative government of the day, like all British governments before it since 1949, were immovable on this fundamental principle. During the secret exchanges between republicans and the British the latter were explicit in rejecting the idea that they should seek to 'persuade' unionists that their best interests lay in a united Ireland ('Messages between the IRA & the Government', 19 March 1993). Hume–Adams was the last attempt by republicans to create, at least, an Irish nationalist consensus on persuasion before the Downing Street Declaration closed the door on it. In that sense the Downing Street Declaration was a major strategic defeat for the concepts contained in Hume–Adams. But, by now the republican leadership must have known that options were limited given the logic of the peace process – expectations had been created and the prospect of a never-ending military stalemate was unattractive.

But the fall-back position appears to have been to allow the Irish government to bat for the republican movement in negotiations with the British over a North–South body. This was making common cause with both Dublin and the SDLP who both sought an Irish dimension that would constitute an embryonic all-Ireland government. This was probably the most remarkable shift in republican thinking. In 1984, Adams had called Anglo-Irish co-operation, such as in Sunningdale, as 'basically sell-outs' (*An Phoblacht/Republican News*, 1 March 1984). By 1995, after the first IRA ceasefire, this had changed. The North–South institution, promulgated by London and Dublin, in the Framework Document, encouraged a widely-held nationalist expectation that closer economic co-operation between the two parts of the island would induce unionists to shift their loyalties away from Britain and towards the Republic. As a result of this gradual process, the political foundations would be laid for unification. The North–South body outlined in the Framework Document possessed the crucial element of the Sunningdale Agreement's Council of Ireland: executive power – authority for decisions and their execution, on an all-Ireland basis, rested with that body. Contrast this with the North–South Ministerial Council (NSMC) that emanated from the Belfast Agreement of 1998: the NSMC had no executive power. Authority in this institution emanated from the Dáil and the Northern Ireland Assembly respectively via those ministers attending the NSMC in their designated executive capacity.

Thus the Council of Ireland had the ability to evolve into an embryonic all-Ireland government. There need not be a *de jure* formal transfer of British sovereignty to Dublin in the near to middle future; but, over time, the *de facto* creation of an all-Ireland administration would eventually occur. Thus there need not be any formal consent to a united Ireland by the population of Northern Ireland. Consent would be formally accepted but actually by-passed. At some, unspecified, point in time, unionists would awaken one day in an all-Ireland state without the lowering of the Union Flag; that would soon be a formality to tie up loose ends, though. This would have removed the necessity for the formal consent of the people of Northern Ireland to a united Ireland. The unionist veto would have been negated. The origins of this strategy, of course, were not to be found in the republican movement but in the Department of Foreign Affairs in Dublin, leading back to Sunningdale. But an embryonic all-Ireland government could not occur with the NSMC. The Adams strategy finally collapsed when Bertie Ahern saved the Belfast Agreement by acceding to Tony Blair's demand that the NSMC should take the form outlined by David Trimble – the republican strategy was sensible up to this point at which it collapsed. Republicans faced accepting the Belfast Agreement or returning to war. The latter was not really an option. It was at this point that the republican movement lost the war. The road to partitionism – and being tied into the consent principle – was complete. It was not a British government that delivered the final blow but an Irish one.

References

Adams, Gerry (1976) *A Broad Analysis of the Present Situation*. Belfast: Republican Press Centre.

Adams, Gerry (1985) 'Breaking the Silence', pp. 2–11 in Martin Collins (ed.) *Ireland After Britain*. London: Pluto Press in association with Labour in Ireland.

Adams, Gerry (1986) *The Politics of Irish Freedom*. Dingle: Brandon.

Adams, Gerry (1988a) *Signposts to Independence and Socialism*. Dublin: Sinn Féin.

Adams, Gerry (1988b) *A Pathway to Peace*. Dublin: Mercier.

Adams, Gerry (1988c) 'A Republican in the Civil Rights Campaign', pp. 39–53 in Michael Farrell (ed.) *Twenty Years On*. Dingle: Brandon.

Adams, Gerry (1990) *Cage 11*. Dingle: Brandon.

Adams, Gerry (1994) 'An Unacceptable and Intolerable Stand-Off', *An Phoblacht/ Republican News*, 13 January.

Adams, Gerry (1995) *Free Ireland: Towards a Lasting Peace*. Dingle: Brandon Press.

An Phoblacht (1971a) 'No Surrender', July.

An Phoblacht (1971b) 'Dáil Uladh', September.

An Phoblacht (1972) 'Year of Decision', January.

An Phoblacht/Republican News (1988) 'Broadening the Base', 30 June.

An Phoblacht/Republican News (1995) 'Editorial: Facing the Challenge', 23 February.

Andersontown News (1986) Interview with Gerry Adams, 22 November.

Bell, J. Bowyer (1979) *The Secret Army: The IRA 1916–1979*. Dublin: Poolbeg Press.

Bell, J. Bowyer (1990) *IRA Tactics and Targets*. Dublin: Poolbeg Press.

Beresford, David (1987) *Ten Men Dead*. London: Grafton.

Bew, Paul (1989) 'The Ambiguous Dynamics of the Anglo-Irish Agreement', pp. 149–57 in Alan O'Day and Yonah Alexander (eds.) *Ireland's Terrorist Trauma: Interdisciplinary Perspectives*. New York: St Martin's Press.

Bew, Paul, Peter Gibbon and Henry Patterson (1995) *Northern Ireland 1921–1994: Political Forces and Social Classes*. London: Serif.

Bew, Paul and Gordon Gillespie (1993) *Northern Ireland: A Chronology of the Troubles 1968–1993*. Dublin: Gill and Macmillan.

Bew, Paul, Ellen Hazelkorn and Henry Patterson (1989) *The Dynamics of Irish Politics*. London: Lawrence and Wishart.

Bew, Paul and Henry Patterson (1985) *The British State and the Ulster Crisis: From Wilson to Thatcher*. London: Verso.

Bishop, Patrick and Eamonn Mallie (1987) *The Provisional IRA*. London: William Heinemann.

Brennock, Mark (1994) 'Sinn Féin Brought in from the Margins to the Centre of Political Activity', *Irish Times*, 27 August.

Browne, Vincent and Fintan O'Toole (1986) 'The Ballot and the Bullet', *Magill*, 13 December.

Campbell, J. Brian, Lawrence McKeown and Felim O'Hagan (eds.) (1994) *Nor Meekly Serve My Time: The H-Block Struggle 1976–1981*. Belfast: Beyond the Pale Publications.

Carolan, Mary (1994) 'SF Report is Strong for Peace', *Irish News*, 25 June.

Clarke, Liam (1987) *Broadening the Battlefield: The H-Blocks and the Rise of Sinn Féin*. Dublin: Gill and Macmillan.

Collins, Tom (1986) *The Irish Hunger Strike*. Dublin: White Island.

Coogan, Tim Pat (1980) *The IRA*. Glasgow: Fontana.

Coughlan, Anthony (1986) *Fooled Again? The Anglo-Irish Agreement and After.* Cork: Mercier.

Cronin, Sean (1980) *Irish Nationalism: A History of its Roots and Ideology.* Dublin: Academy Press.

Davis, Richard (1989) 'Irish Republicanism v Roman Catholicism: The Perennial Debate in the Ulster Troubles', pp. 34–74 in Alan O'Day and Yonah Alexander (eds.) *Ireland's Terrorist Trauma: Interdisciplinary Perspectives.* New York: St Martin's Press.

Devlin, Paddy (1993) *Straight Left: An Autobiography.* Belfast: Blackstaff.

Fisk, Robert (1975) *The Point of No Return: The Strike Which Broke the British in Ulster.* London: André Deutsch.

FitzGerald, Garret (1991) *All in a Life: An Autobiography.* Dublin: Gill and Macmillan.

Guelke, Adrian and Jim Smyth (1992) 'The Ballot Bomb: Terrorism and the Electoral Process in Northern Ireland', pp. 103–24 in Leonard Weinberg (ed.) *Political Parties and Terrorist Groups.* London: Frank Cass.

Halliday, Fred (1987) *The Making of the Second Cold War.* London: Verso.

Hazelkorn, Ellen and Henry Patterson (1994) 'The New Politics of the Irish Republic', *New Left Review*, 207, pp. 49–71.

Hernes, Lisbeth (1983) 'Interview with Danny Morrison', unpublished manuscript lodged with the Linenhall Library, Belfast.

Irish News (1994) 'Referendum Will Guarantee Honest Outcome Says Major', 17 September.

Jackson, Joe (1988) 'Oh Danny Boy: Interview with Danny Morrison', *Hot Press*, 25 August.

Keena, Colm (1990) *Gerry Adams – A Biography.* Dublin: Mercier.

Kelley, Kevin (1988) *The Longest War: Northern Ireland and the IRA.* London: Zed.

Kelly, James (1976) *The Genesis of Revolution.* Dublin: Kelly and Kane.

Kelly, James (1989) *The Courage of the Brave: The Anglo-Irish Agreement – A Politico-Military Analysis.* Kells: Kells Publishing.

Kenny, Anthony (1986) *The Road to Hillsborough: The Shaping of the Anglo-Irish Agreement.* Oxford: Pergamon.

MacLiam, Cathal (1973) 'Let Us . . . Keep Faith', *Republican News*, 24 March.

Mallie, Eamonn (1988) 'The Provos' Resurgance: There's More to Come', *Fortnight*, 265.

Mallie, Eamonn (1989) 'Twenty Years On: Where do the Provos Go From Here?', *Sunday Press*, 5 February.

Mansergh, Martin (1995) 'Agreement Makes the Nation', *Sunday Business Post*, 29 January.

McAliskey, Bernadette (1994) Interview with the author, September.

McGuire, Maria (1973) *To Take Arms: A Year in the Provisional IRA.* London: Macmillan.

McLaughlin, Mitchel (1992) 'Protestantism, Unionism and Loyalism', *Fingerpost Monthly*, Spring/Summer.

McLaughlin, Mitchel (1994) 'Unionist "Consent" in an Agreed Ireland', *Fingerpost Monthly*, 8 (1).

McStiofain, Seán (1975) *Memoirs of a Revolutionary.* Edinburgh: Gordon Cremonisi.

Metress, Seamus (1983) *The Hunger Strike and the Final Struggle.* Detroit, MI: Connolly Books.

Meulemans, Bill (1994) 'Republicans Enter Uncharted Lands', *Irish News*, 15 November.

Moloney, Ed (1994) *Peace Chronology.* Unpublished manuscript.

Moriarty, Gerry (1994) 'British Disengagement from North "Only Way to End Armed Struggle" ', *Irish Times*, 29 August.

Morrison, Danny (1986) *The Hillsborough Agreement*. Belfast: Republican Publications.

Moxon-Browne, Edward (1981) 'The Water and the Fish: Public Opinion and the IRA in Northern Ireland', pp. 41–72 in Paul Wilkinson (ed.) *British Perspectives on Terrorism*. London: George Allen and Unwin.

O'Brien, Brendan (1993) *The Long War: The IRA and Sinn Féin – 1985 to Today*. Dublin: O'Brien Press.

O'Doherty, Shane (1993) *The Volunteer*. London: Fount Paperbacks.

O'Leary, Brendan and John McGarry (1993) *The Politics of Antagonism: Understanding Northern Ireland*. London: Athlone Press.

O'Malley, Padraig (1990) *Biting at the Grave: The Irish Hunger Strikes and the Politics of Despair*. Belfast: Blackstaff.

O'Reilly, Emily (1994) 'Where the Power Lies', *Irish Press*, 22 January.

Patterson, Henry (1989) *The Politics of Illusion: Republicanism and Socialism in Modern Ireland*. London: Hutchinson Radius.

Patterson, Henry (1994) 'Ireland: Looking for a Way Out?', *New Agenda*, 2, pp. 1–2.

Pollak, Andy (1994) 'Veterans Face Record of Gains, Setbacks and Lost Opportunities', *Irish Times*, 29 August.

Prior, Jim (1986) *A Balance of Power*. London: Hamish Hamilton.

Reed, David (1984) *Ireland: The Key to the British Revolution*. London: Larkin Publications.

Rees, Merlyn (1985) *Northern Ireland: A Personal Perspective*. London: Methuen.

Republican News (1972a) 'Agony in the Six Counties', 7 October.

Republican News (1972b) 'Sinn Féin Back New Civil Rights Body', 22 December.

Republican News (1973a) 'Comhairle Eireann', 2 February.

Republican News (1973b) 'What Next?', 10 March.

Republican News (1973c) 'Don't Vote. Use Your Head', 19 May.

Research Institute for the Study of Conflict and Terrorism (1991) *Northern Ireland: Reappraising Republican Political Violence: A Special Report*. London: Research Institute for the Study of Conflict and Terrorism.

Reynolds, Albert (1994) 'Now it's Time for Liberty, Equality and Fraternity', *Irish News*, 15 September.

Rolston, Bill (1986) 'The British State and the Ulster Crisis: From Wilson to Thatcher by Paul Bew and Henry Patterson', *Journal of Law and Society*, 13 (2), pp. 257–62.

Ryan, Mark (1994) *War and Peace in Ireland: Britain and the IRA in the New World Order*. London: Pluto.

Shanahan, Kate (1987) 'Under Fire', *Hot Press*, 17 December.

Sinn Féin (1994) *The Downing Street Declaration – Sinn Féin's Analysis*. Sinn Féin National Internal Delegate Conference.

Smith, M.L.R (1991) *The Role of the Military Instrument in Republican Strategic Thinking: An Evolutionary Analysis*. Unpublished PhD thesis. London: King's College, University of London.

'Susini' (1991) 'Armed Struggle; A Strategic Imperative', unpublished manuscript lodged in the Linenhall Library, Belfast.

Thatcher, Margaret (1993) *The Downing Street Years*. London: HarperCollins.

Toolis, Kevin (1994) 'Peace and the Provo', *Guardian Weekend*, 19 November.

Tugwell, Maurice (1981) 'Politics and Propaganda of the Provisional IRA', pp. 13–40 in Paul Wilkinson (ed.) *British Perspectives on Terrorism*. London: George Allen and Unwin.

Tynan, Maol Muire (1994a) 'IRA "Has No Mandate" ', *Irish Times*, 20 January.

Tynan, Maol Muire (1994b) 'IRA Has "Vested Interest" in Advancing Peace, Says Adams', *Irish Times*, 2 September.

White, Barry (1995) 'Arms Issue May Prove to be an Obstacle', *Belfast Telegraph*, 18 January.

White, Robert W. (1993) *Provisional Irish Republicans: An Oral and Interpretative History*. Westport, CT: Greenwood Press.

Whitelaw, William (1989) *The Whitelaw Memoirs*. London: Aurum.

Whyte, John H. (1990) *Interpreting Northern Ireland*. New York: Oxford University Press.

9 The politics of language and literature in pre-independence Ireland

Tom Garvin

Originally published in *Irish Political Studies*, 2, 1987, pp. 49–63.

Pre-independence Ireland witnessed an extraordinary linking of linguistic revivalism and hostility to English popular culture, a linking that was eventually to lead to the formation of a semi-official ideology for the independent Irish state. The Gaelic League, the 'onlie begetter' of so many nationalist organisations, was the central vehicle by which this ideology was formulated and promulgated. It should be remembered that most of the 1916 leaders and most of the leading figures in the Free State, whether pro-Treaty or anti-Treaty, had been members of the League in their youth and had imbibed versions of its ideology of cultural revitalisation. Although formally non-political and even anti-political, the League had profoundly political purposes, and offers a prime example of how culture can be bent to purposes that are very non-cultural. It could be argued that in the long run the true loser was general Irish culture and intellectual life, whether expressed in the English or the Irish languages. The politicisation of culture effected by the League in the early years of the century was to create an official cultural ideology which was arguably hostile to much of the real culture of the community; 'Gaelic Unrealism' might be a just term for it. This official ideology was to dominate much of Irish cultural life for a generation after independence.

The Irish language had been dying in Ireland for a considerable time. The mediaeval social order which had been associated with it was finally defeated in the seventeenth century; it had not even survived that century as the first language of Irish Catholicism. The considerable cultural achievements of the Gaelic tradition were forgotten. The Famine of the 1840s, of course, further weakened the language and by the end of the century it was in full retreat even in its last western redoubts. Unlike Scottish Gaelic, it did not even have the advantage of being the normal language of worship, as Catholicism's support of the English language, even in Irish-speaking areas, was consistent.

The League came out of a tradition of antiquarian research into Gaelic civilisation, fundamentally similar to other nationalist movements in Europe dedicated to the rediscovery and, perhaps, revival of national pasts. Anglo-Irish liberal interest in Celtic remains and nationalist political purpose joined hands. Gaelic was apparently particularly popular among the Irish emigrants in London and New York and many of the ideas of the League appear to have been derived from *émigré* political feeling.

The League was inaugurated in 1893 and was formally dedicated to the preservation and revival of the language and the celebration of, and, if possible, the resuscitation of traditional dress, dances and customs, in so far as these could be reconciled with the canons of late-Victorian respectability. Its mixture of scholarly research and social recreation appealed enormously to a wide variety of people, in particular perhaps the newly-educated young of the villages and towns. Twenty years after its foundation, it had become a mass movement, with 100,000 members and 1,000 branches (Redmond-Howard, 1913, pp. 217–18). Much of this mass membership was young.

Originally, however, the League was a coterie rather than a mass movement and its character changed very significantly when it grew beyond its original membership. It had grown out of an impulse towards unionist/nationalist encounter in Trinity College, Dublin and in its first years it was dominated by a mainly Dublin-based group of middle-class scholars and dilettantes (O Cobhthaigh, 1917, pp. 37–40). Douglas Hyde, the son of an Anglican clergyman from Sligo, was its first president and served from 1893 to 1915. He claimed consistently that he had originally insisted on the League's taking a non-political stance for pragmatic reasons, wishing to avoid the divisions endemic in Irish politics, but had always anticipated that in the long run it would evolve into a great political movement once its cultural purposes had been fulfilled. He also observed that even those members of the League who wished to use it for political purposes accepted the non-political pose for pragmatic reasons (Hyde Papers).

Again according to Hyde, the reasons for the League's avoidance of politics were many. In the first place, it preserved the League from attack by the British government and from the attentions of the police; actually the police took little interest in it and appear to have underrated its long-term political potential. Secondly, as most of the League's branches around the country were run by 'officers and secretaries who were largely either National Teachers or Customs and Excise Officers' and as these men were forbidden by their terms of employment to engage in normal political activity, an openly political stance would have crippled the League at local level. These teachers and civil servants were 'full of national feeling of the best type but could find no outlet for it'. Essentially, the League gave an outlet for repressed political passion and 'let loose a lot of energy for the good of Ireland which would otherwise have been lost' (Hyde Papers; Cleary, 1919, p. 401; *United Irishman*, 9 December 1899).

Another reason was, of course, the attempt to keep unionists and nationalists, Protestants and Catholics and the various classes of society, together in harmony in the League in as far as it was possible. Ironically, in the light of subsequent events, the Irish language had quite an appeal to certain Protestants who saw in it a way of claiming an Irish identity without having to pay the heavy price of giving up their religion and conforming to the Catholic faith of most Irish people. After all, an Irish-speaking Protestant could logically claim to be more 'Irish' than a monoglot English-speaking Catholic; he might also irritate him. Conversely, many Catholics distrusted linguistic revivalism because it appeared to be some kind of Protestant Trojan Horse.

The League had a strange political evolution between 1893 and 1915, being eventually turned not just to political purposes but to insurrection. It was colonised by people with different purposes from those of the founders. It was, as already suggested, a perfect vehicle for those whose occupation forbade or discouraged political action of a conventional kind. Given the political vacuum that existed in the aftermath of the fall of Parnell, its appeal as a substitute for politics was all the greater; culture became a surrogate for politics.

One study of 32 early Leaguers and 'Irish-Irelanders' found that three were Protestants, seven were civil servants, two were teachers, four were journalists, three were priests, a further three were in business and four were 'gentlefolk writers'. Six were unclassifiable. Interestingly, at least 17 had been emigrants and of these at least 12 had become involved in the League first while living outside Ireland. At least half were of 'peasant origin'. They appeared to be generally 'energetic and moderately successful men whose careers provided inadequate scope for their talents and ambitions' (Waters, 1977).

Many of the League's leaders saw early on that it was going to need the support of certain powerful groups in Irish society if it were to prosper and become a mass movement. Eoin MacNeill, possibly the original inventor of the League, was a young law clerk in Dublin at the beginning of the 1890s. A Catholic from the glens of Antrim, he was, unlike many nationalists, trusted by the Catholic clergy. As early as 1891, MacNeill urged in the pages of the *Irish Ecclesiastical Record* that the Catholic priesthood take up the cause of the language on the grounds that it would help preserve an Irish identity and would defend Irish Catholicism against the inroads of English culture (*Irish Ecclesiastical Record*, Third Series, XII, 1891, pp. 1099–1108). It should be remembered that MacNeill was striking, rather cleverly, while the iron was hot; in 1891 the Church was at odds with advanced popular nationalism because of Parnell and presumably would be receptive to any proposal by which the authenticity of its claims to be the leader of the Catholic nation could be bolstered. Not for the last time, the Irish language was to be used for purposes external to itself.

MacNeill's appeal to the clergy had some success. In 1898, a priest writing in the *Irish Ecclesiastical Record* drew a specific parallel with the priest-led Flemish linguistic revival movement of the period, noting that the linguistic revival in Belgium had been supported by the priests because it offered a barrier against what he termed 'the inroad of corrupting French literature' from Paris. Irish, he argued, was well suited to performing a similar function in Ireland against the presumably equally corrupt literature in English, as traditional pious Christian phrases were embedded in its everyday idioms (*Irish Ecclesiastical Record*, Fourth Series, III, 1898, pp. 551–2). Hyde himself used this kind of argument to sell the language to the clergy; like MacNeill, he realised very early on that they would have to be seduced politically if the Gaelic League's cultural project were to be truly successful (*Irish Catholic*, 5 January 1902). The Catholic Church as an institution never accepted the language or the League wholeheartedly. The Church's historical commitment to English was well entrenched, and elements in the ideology of the Gaelic revival movement looked suspiciously pagan.

However, many of the lower clergy did become neo-Gaelic ideologues, and the Christian Brothers accepted the language as a vehicle for building an ethos of self-respect and patriotism. Clericalist lay Catholics, as represented by the *Leader* or the *Catholic Bulletin*, used the language as a means of denigrating English culture. It was typically suggested that Irish was somehow a Catholic language and that English was therefore a Protestant, or, even worse, a pagan language (*Leader*, 28 October 1905, 23 November 1907, 21 November 1908, 12 December 1908 and 9 January 1909).

The League appealed to those who wished for cultural reform, but more, perhaps, to those who wanted to raise Irish political consciousness. In particular, the League attracted many whose objectives were political and to whom its cultural activities were of little interest. Many of these were clerics, but more were laymen; the Irish Republican Brotherhood (IRB) became involved in the League quite early on. In many areas, the Catholic clergy adopted it as a way of regulating the social life of the young, particularly the better educated and more adventurous of the younger generation. Despite occasional collisions between local priests and Leaguers such as the famous one in Portarlington in 1906, by and large the lower clergy and the League cooperated fairly well (Gaelic League, 1906; Waters, 1977).

In a penetrating and prophetic article published in 1904, the *Belfast Newsletter* saw the League's political potential (28 May 1904). It noted the artificial character of the organisation. Its appeal to adults was limited, and it attracted children and adolescents rather more, often because of adult encouragement. The adult classes having lost momentum, the League had turned to the children and was attempting to use compulsion on them and on their teachers. In particular, the League had used political pressure, through the clergy and the Commissioners of National Education, to force teachers to learn Irish. Furthermore, the branches of the League did not confine their discussions to cultural matters, but were essentially centres of political indoctrination, where loyalty to the tongue and religion of the forefathers were combined ideologically with a hatred of England and its culture.

The League grew rapidly in the first years of the new century, partly because of the impact of the Boer War on public opinion, dividing nationalists into pro- and anti-imperial camps. As the League became larger, it became more Catholic, less Dublin-oriented and more clericalist; it evolved into an organisation with significant rural connections, particularly in the south and the west of Ireland. MacNeill and Hyde had invited this evolution, but sometimes appeared less than totally happy with its consequences. Hyde remarked delphically later on that the League had been very charming until it became powerful (Hyde Papers). It was argued later that the clerical–nationalist campaign waged by the *Leader* had the effect of driving out the Protestants and bringing in the clergy (Cleary, 1919, pp. 402–3). Certainly the *Leader* disliked the claims of some Protestants to the political leadership of advanced nationalisms (27 July 1901).

Protestants clearly came to distrust the League, whether out of prejudice or justifiable fear. While individual Protestants remained loyal to it, it never became a mass movement among the non-Catholic population. Furthermore some Protestant Leaguers encountered hostility from some lay and clerical Catholic Leaguers.

By March 1904, the *Church of Ireland Gazette* had denounced it and in 1905 a Church of Ireland bishop seriously suggested a separate Gaelic League for Protestants. The famous Dublin branch *Craobh na gCúig gCúigí* ('Five Provinces Branch') became known sarcastically as the 'Branch of the Five Protestants' (*Leader*, 12 March 1904 and 28 October 1905).

It should be recalled that the League appealed to many, perhaps most, for essentially non-political, non-religious and even non-cultural reasons. Like most successful mass organisations, the League appealed to many for reasons of recreation and socialising. In particular, of course, it offered a legitimate occasion for the young of both sexes to meet; in the 'flat dullness of an Irish village or country town, the League class was an unexpected source of light and gaiety' (Cleary, 1919, p. 404). Most of the middle class fought shy of it and those who aspired to rise further under the existing social and political regime avoided it for prudential reasons. It did, however, appeal to clerks, a minority of the doctors, solicitors and teachers in country towns. 'The lady members will be the more eager and serious-minded women of the town, with perhaps a few who like dancing or eager-minded men' (Cleary, 1919, p. 404). These seem to have been in many cases those who were kept out of the charmed circle of Masonic and Hibernian clubs and who did not have powerful friends or relatives at court.

The League interacted oddly with the often labyrinthine snobberies of small-town life in Ireland. Moran, with the optimism of a cultural pioneer, had claimed in 1899 that it would be able to transcend the local snobberies that made community action so difficult to organise (*Claidheamh Soluis*, 8 April 1899). However, by 1907, he was complaining that the League could scarcely provide 40 different branches for the 40 different grades of society which inhabited the average Irish town (*Leader*, 7 December 1907). A general problem the League had to deal with was that Irish was seen still as the language of lower prestige, of poverty and of backwardness and the League found itself having to fight ingrained attitudes of all kinds.

Resentment, self-respect and language

The Gaelic League offered a psychological escape from the rather extreme restrictions of Irish society as experienced by young men and women at the turn of the century. It appealed particularly to certain kinds of young men whose personal ideology and value-system were conservative and who had imbibed, in the austere and heavily disciplined schools of the Christian Brothers and the Holy Ghost Fathers, a strong work ethic of a kind perhaps not traditional in Ireland. They valued themselves higher than did the social system, which commonly discriminated against them. People in that position found normal political action closed to them because constitutional politics had been crippled by the fall of Parnell. Politics was seen as a dirty game and those who engaged in it would inevitably, regardless of good intentions, be soiled. The abstract, romantic and anti-political radicalism of the League offered an admirable substitute for politics.

Hyde was well aware of the psychological comfort which the cult gave young men and women of this kind. Hyde, Moran and the other leaders appear to have been quite clear in their minds that the true value of teaching the Irish language in schools was actually psychological rather than pedagogical; it built character as much as it did intellect. Hyde argued that Irish people from rural or small-town backgrounds, of post-Gaelic stock and lower-class cultural backgrounds, were engaged in a hopeless and humiliating attempt to become accepted in the English-speaking world; they were socially 'impossible', to use that word in a Nancy Mitford sense, and could never become 'possible'. No matter how hard they tried, no matter how many examination triumphs they had, they would never become accepted. Instead, they should keep their pride and build up a non-English counter-culture which would allocate status independently of the prevailing Anglo-Saxon one. This doctrine had appeal in Ireland, and even more among the Irish emigrants in London, particularly among those in lower white-collar positions in the civil service (House of Commons, 1899, Appendix, pp. 482–4).

The *Leader* in 1902 argued in typical fashion that the psychological boost that the League gave to its members had the effect of dispelling the sense of the paralysis, of absence of political will, so well described by James Joyce as being the dominant feature of Irish social culture in Edwardian times. The League was held to offer a psychological escape-route from the enervating sense of self-contempt, inferiority and mediocrity which colonialism generated:

> The Irish revival, the arriving at the conviction of its necessity by process of thought, the effort to follow where that conviction leads, the immediate effect on the self-respect of an Irishman once he is possessed of the Irish-Ireland conviction – all this at once tends to operate on our energies, to give us real ideals and drag us out of the ruck of general mediocrity.
>
> (*Leader*, 24 May 1902)

Status resentment lay behind much of the enthusiasm which the League attracted. One's style of speaking English could be used to 'place' one very accurately by class, region and even religion; Irish, on the other hand, reflected regional dialects only, and echoed no elaborated and oppressive class system. Ironically, conflicts between the various dialects at times became as obsessive as was concern with accent in English. Resentment was aggravated by both deliberate and unconscious slighting of these thin-skinned people by a remote and insensitive establishment. Possibly an even more intense resentment was aimed at those Catholics who had made their peace with the regime and who had achieved some preferment. The 'Cawstle Cawtholics' aspired to ascent within the system by imitating English manners, accepting English ideological assumptions, sending their child to Catholic imitations of English grammar or public schools or even to Protestant schools in England or Ireland. They were also willing to acquire higher education for their children, often in the face of Episcopal disapproval. The *Leader* and other papers railed against the deracination which they imagined such education involved (*Leader*, 1 September 1900 and 2 January 1904).

Many of these resented people were actually descended immediately from well-known nationalist families, often with a violent past behind them. Even the students of the new University College in Dublin appeared excessively snobbish and anglicised to the *Leader*. In 1912, four years before many of the students and some of their lecturers took part in an insurrection, it described UCD students as 'poor white-livered lads' who had no understanding of Irish history, whose upbringing had been 'mean' and who were inclined 'to think it "smart" to despise (the) Irish (language)' (*Leader*, 1 June 1912). Not only the Anglo-Irish establishment but also the rather insecure Catholic upper middle class were targets for the resentment of the newly educated Catholic upwardly mobile lower middle class and its working-class allies.

Status resentment, then, could be cured only at the high price of assimilation into the establishment, a cure available only to a few. The alternative status system offered by the League was cheaper – fluency in Irish, proficiency in rural dances, adherence to a strict Catholic morality and an informed (even obsessive) knowledge of the history and antiquities of Ireland, together added up to a considerable challenge to the system, which valued non-Catholic religious affiliations and English upper-class manners far more than things Irish, commonly seen as quaint, provincial and backward. W.P. Ryan saw the League as a symptom of what might nowadays be described as psychic political modernisation acting on the minds by the young laymen and priests (Ryan, 1912, p. 33).

The American consul in Queenstown, County Cork, writing in the immediate aftermath of the 1916 Rising, was struck by the effect the Gaelic League had on young Catholic students. The League had tried to build up national character by inculcating an awareness of past cultural achievement. 'In fact, the movement was a character cult fully as much as a political manifestation.' Most Catholic students were politicised by Sinn Féin and 'it appears to really inspire and improve them' (Despatches from Consuls, 841.00/5–85, 30 September 1916, National Archives, Washington, DC).

What I have termed status resentment had a permanent impact on the ideology of the young men who were to become the founding fathers of independent Ireland. The emergent elite was obsessed by a sense of moral superiority and anger at the contempt in which it sensed it was held by the establishment. A curious inverted snobbery encouraged the embracing of a partly artificial counter-culture, constructed as a compensation for the discomfort generated by the existing status system. The neo-Gaelic counter-culture also acted as a convenient source of ideological stances, in particular an alliance between separatism and certain sections of the Catholic clergy.

The internal politics of the Gaelic League

The League was essentially a political party which denied that proposition. Its expansion after 1899 was spectacular, its membership expanding enormously and its revenues increasing also; its annual income increased from about £1,000 to about £7,000 between 1900 and 1904 (Redmond-Howard, 1913, pp. 217–18; *United Irishman*, 5 March 1904). Before 1899 it scarcely had a formal constitution as it was dominated by a small Dublin group who knew each other well. It staged its first Oireachtas, or general meeting at which various cultural activities such as dancing and singing competitions were held, only in 1897 (Tierney, 1980, p. 44). The 1899 constitution provided for a regular representative structure, with an executive committee (Coiste Gnótha) elected annually by a delegate conference (Ard-Fheis) from the branches. The Ard-Fheis delegates were elected by the branches (craobhachta) in proportion to the certified memberships of the branches. There were periodic constitutional shake-ups every few years as the organisation grew larger and more impersonal. The basic structure remained intact and appears to have been an important prototype for later nationalist political parties (Tierney, 1980, p. 53; *Claidheamh Soluis*, 7 February 1900 and 24 May 1902). Two types of member of the Coiste Gnótha were stipulated by the 1899 and later constitutions – residential and country. The former were required to reside in the Dublin area, whereas the latter were to represent the provinces. Originally, half the members were residential; this proportion tended to decrease, under pressure from the new country branches. Because of the expense of travel, residential members of the Coiste Gnótha (by definition those who lived in the Dublin area) tended to dominate its business. The early Ard-Fheiseanna had about 150 delegates but later ones had swollen memberships of up to 400. The Coiste Gnótha originally had 20 members, but grew rapidly to 45 in the mid-1900s in part at the insistence of the new, more rural membership. Rural voters came to elect people to the governing bodies of the League who were unsympathetic to the founding fathers and who did not always share their view of the League's purpose.

As the League grew in popularity, it came to be looked upon with unease by many party politicians, who sensed that it somehow represented a threat to their quasi-monopoly of nationalist public opinion. It also became the target of entryist tactics on the part of the IRB, there were personality clashes, while regional dialectical differences sometimes aggravated differences over policy and ideology. At times, the League's internal politics were spectacularly bad-tempered; the tradition of the cabal soon dominated its politics.

A basic opposition, combining regional feeling and political ideology, existed in the League between those who wished to construct a standard version of the language which would be acceptable to speakers of the three main dialects (Ulster, Connacht, and Munster) and those who claimed that the southern, Munster dialect, because it could claim a respectable literary tradition, should have primacy. The supporters of the Munster dialect, sometimes referred to as 'Provincialists', tended to despise the Connacht dialect in particular, as being the language only of poor and unlettered peasants and fishermen. Hyde and Pearse, who spoke Connacht Irish, naturally defended dialectical pluralism, as did MacNeill. The Munster branches, together with some Leinster branches (there was no developed Leinster dialect), supported the southern dialect. In particular, the very active Keating branch in Dublin tended to represent the southern cause against the dialectical pluralism of Central Branch and the League's Dublin-based establishment. The Keating branch, founded in 1901, consisted mainly of expatriate Munstermen living in the capital, in particular J.J. O'Kelly (known as 'Sceilg') and Father Patrick Dineen, S.J., compiler of a famous and entertaining dictionary. Cathal Brugha, a Dubliner of part-English descent and an extreme separatist, was also a member (Tierney, 1980, p. 176). In the early 1900s, 'Sceilg' published a little magazine, *Banba*, in opposition to the League establishment as personified by Pearse, Hyde and MacNeill, but also vitriolic in its criticism of many Cork Leaguers. The Munster opposition was particularly active in opposing the appointment of Pearse to the editorship of the League paper, *An Claidheamh Soluis* ('the Sword of Light'), in 1902 (Hyde Papers).

According to Hyde, it was Munster 'Provincialism' that instigated factional politics in the League, culminating in competitive elections to the Coiste Gnótha every year. Admittedly, the growth in size of the League probably encouraged the development of stable factions. Connacht imitated Munster, and both provinces ran 'tickets' against each other and against the Dublin establishment. Ironically many of their candidates were themselves Dublin-dwellers. The increase in size of the Coiste Gnótha to 45 members in 1904–5 turned what was originally an executive into a large, less decisive and more discursive body; 'thus if there ever was anything like a full meeting of the Executive it was more like a little parliament than a Cabinet meeting' (Hyde Papers).

Munster had a strong Gaelic tradition and one that had long been self-consciously political; the province had a tradition of Jacobite and agrarian political sentiment which survived particularly in Irish-language verse. In Munster the League had plenty of raw material to work on, and the province soon got a reputation for efficient and energetic organisation. Munster performers did exceptionally well at national competitions, the west Cork branches being particularly conspicuous. An ex-civil servant returned from London, Fionan MacColuim, had a reputation as the most effective organiser the League had and concentrated those energies on Munster (Hyde Papers). The result of the League's expansion and of Munster's self-assertiveness was the gradual weakening of Dublin's dominance and the dominance of Central Branch. The city's strength at the Ard-Fheis and the power of the resident members of the Coiste Gnótha waned. At the 1902 Ard-Fheis, Dublin still had 56 out of a grand total of 187 delegates, or 30 per cent, whereas Munster had only 29 delegates, 16 per cent of the total. The following year, Dublin had 43 delegates out of 257, or a mere 17 per cent, whereas Munster had climbed to 20 per cent and Connacht had also expanded. By 1912, of 202 delegates from the four provinces, Munster was to boast a massive 84, or 42 per cent (*Leader*, 10 May 1902; *Claidheamh Soluis*, 9 May 1903, 18 June 1904, 18 August 1906 and 19 June 1912).

This pattern was not just confined to the level of branches or Ard-Fheiseanna. Forces based in non-Dublin areas and in Munster in particular penetrated the Coiste Gnótha decisively. In 1904, six of the 15 non-resident members were from Munster and seven were in 1907. However, 'on the ground' Munster's superior organisational tradition showed itself. By the end of 1906, the League had established district committees (coisti ceanntair), mainly at Munster insistence, to fund and administer the travelling teacher systems locally and generally supervise the local areas' revival efforts. Of 49 such committees in Ireland, nine were in Leinster, ten in Ulster, 12 in Connacht and 18, or 37 per cent, were in Munster. By early 1908, this Munster dominance had become even greater than two years previously;

the figures were 64 in Ireland, out of which 17 were in Leinster, 12 in Ulster, seven in Connacht and 28, or a massive 44 per cent, in Munster. In that year 46 of 111 League teachers, or 41 per cent, were active in Munster (*Claidheamh Soluis*, 18 June 1904, 11 December 1906, 24 August 1907 and 15 February 1908).

One consequence of this expansion was to increase the numbers of rural clergy serving as delegates and committee members. In the League as in other Irish political and social organisations, clergy were particularly important activists in areas which were remote and poor and lacked educated laymen: the clergy 'stood in' for a middle class in these areas. Regional tensions became greater as Munster and even Connacht became more assertive. The League also became vulnerable to penetration as it became less of a caucus and more generally a branch organisation. Arthur Griffith's group, named Sinn Féin ('Ourselves') in 1905 but in existence since the late 1890s, was an early interested watcher of the League. Griffith tried to evolve a policy that was intermediate between the constitutionalism of the Irish party and the separatism of the IRB. Sinn Féin was Dublin-centred and was noticeably weak in Cork (*Sinn Féin*, 28 August 1909). Griffith believed in industrialisation to an extent that made him hostile to labour, as is often pointed out, but also to the ruralism of many priests. He was rather hostile to the neo-Gaelic clericalism of D.P. Moran's *Leader*. Sinn Féin, perhaps the purely 'burgeois moderniser' of the nationalist groups, rather impressed observers with its energy and detachment from the emotionalism of separatist politics (Brooks, 1907, p. 14).

Although Griffith was not particularly sympathetic to the League's ideology, his lieutenants were quick to exploit its political potential. They were 'nearly always among the more active members' of the League (O Cobhthaigh, 1917, p. 54) and they tended to push out the more lethargic committee members in the 1900–1906 period. However, Sinn Féin remained a narrow cabal and was apparently unable to compete with IRB entryism from about 1907 on. While the Catholic hierarchy probably never seriously considered capturing the League, despite dark rumours to that effect, the League did become very clericalised. It could be argued that the League was penetrating the Church as much as the reverse; it had a strong ideological appeal to many of the younger clergy. They listened sympathetically to the League's exhortations to teach Irish in the schools and imbue the young with a knowledge of Irish history and a pride in the remnants of its traditional culture.

The League's original posture of aloofness from parliamentarianism eventually crystallised into a settled distrust of it. This was eventually to make it more vulnerable to the anti-political politics of many of the radicals. Hyde remembered that because Patrick Ford of the *Gaelic-American* approved of the League and controlled much of the parliamentarians' money-bags, he had little trouble from the parliamentarians or agrarians: 'The trouble was to keep out politics of the Wolfe Tone or Fenian type', whose adherents moved in on the League after 1909 and took it over in 1914–15, expelling Hyde in the process.

The hostility to the parliamentarians, descended from the old rancours surrounding the fall of Parnell, antedated the IRB coup, however, and helped to make it possible (*Freeman's Journal*, 31 August 1910). Even the Sinn Féiners of

Griffith's little party were in two minds about the League. A similar ideological ambivalence toward linguistic revival existed in the minds of the physical-force separatists, who colonised the League for political reasons. Hyde believed many of them cared little for the Irish language, but the young men who they inducted both into the League and the IRB were inculcated with a combination of linguistic and militaristic ideologies. Eventually even socialists belatedly saw the League's political potential and the Dublin regional council became penetrated by Larkinites. Hyde complained that the leftist influence on the Coiste Gnótha drove away the rich and influential; he himself was compelled to wear old clothes so as not to raise the ire of the new democracy.

Several contemporary observers saw the League was being taken over by revolutionaries (*Irish Independent*, 28 September 1911; *Cork Constitution*, 25 September 1911). Of course there were revolutionaries and revolutionaries in it, to use an Irish phrase; the IRB were to be more successful than either the Sinn Féiners or the socialists. By 1910 the take-over of the League by the Brotherhood was well underway. Classic Irish committee politics was used: Ard-Fheis delegates in rural areas were persuaded to give their proxy votes to Dublin-based activists, who voted for their own people. The IRB also had its own 'ticket' and advised its activists to vote for them (*Irish Independent*, 3 September 1911; Ó Ceallaigh, 1963, pp. 50–1; Hyde Papers). By 1912, Seán T. O Kelly had engineered for himself the third-highest delegate vote for residential member and Thomas Ashe the seventh-highest, out of 15 seats.

The growing politicisation of the League reflected itself in various ways. Pearse, although not a member of the conspiracy, became increasingly 'political' and strident in his writings. The atmosphere of acrimony in the League's affairs deepened. In some ways the League became more energetic, efficient and aggressive. The Coiste Gnótha was made smaller and more an executive than a deliberative body. A reorganisation of the branch organisation was put in train (*Claidheamh Soluis*, 16 August 1913, 23 August 1913 and 20 September 1913). Essentially, caucuses of the IRB based mainly in Dublin took advantage of the ruralised and decentralised character of the Gaelic League. Another tactic was to blame the establishment for the slowness of the linguistic revival campaign. The depressing linguistic statistics in the 1911 census, which documented the unrelenting expansion of the English language, were laid squarely at the establishment's door. Hyde described the older and less outgoing members of the leadership being driven from office and even out of the League by a simple campaign of personal abuse (Hyde Papers).

In effect, the extremists confiscated the language, much as they had confiscated Gaelic games. By doing so they identified the language and the games with a particular political ideology and thereby ensured that anyone who did not share that ideology or who was not willing to pay at least lip-service to it would boycott them. Protestants naturally excluded themselves but so did most of the Catholic middle class.

The IRB appear to have convinced themselves in 1914 that there would be an early German victory in the War, and that out of that victory would come a dismemberment of the British Empire and, of course, an independent Ireland, presumably allied with the Reich. By 1915 the subversion of the League was complete and it became another front, like the Irish Volunteers, for the IRB and the insurrectionist wing of the League led by Pearse. Eventually the insurrectionist cabal was to deceive the IRB leaders themselves and stage the 1916 Rising. Pearse had prophesied the subordination of the League to the purposes of the Irish revolution in the *Calidheamh Soluis* as early as November 1913.

The politics of violence was everywhere in Europe, and orange and green both were arming in anticipation. It may be, however, that a subconscious sense of the Quixotic hopelessness of the League's programme of linguistic revival prompted a retreat from cultural failure to the paradoxically easier task of staging a revolution; British power in Ireland was less impervious than was the wall of quiet but implacable resistance to Gaelicisation which the common people of Ireland erected against the League's teachers. Although political agitation had established Irish as a taught subject in many schools and had eventually forced the National University of Ireland to require it for matriculation, the revival remained essentially artificial and confined to certain middle sections of society. The Census recorded the tide of English rising implacably even in the *Gaelteachtaí* despite the Canute-like efforts of the *muinteóirí taistil*. From 1905 on, the League paper asked periodically if their efforts were indeed to be in vain. Pearse railed against defeatism and labelled it 'treachery... in the face of the enemy' (*Claidheamh Soluis*, 4 October 1905, 18 January 1908 and 15 February 1908). By then, Pearse himself was desperately fighting pessimism and resorting to the imagery of warfare, although so far the war was visualised as a cultural one.

From 1906 on, contributions to the central language fund began to fall off, and the League became more dependent on Irish-American funding. The *Claidheamh* suggested the decrease was due to increased local retention of money but a certain diminution of energy and interest is to be suspected. In 1908, a Mayo teacher contributed a depressing and convincing account of the very limited impact the teaching of Irish had on the long-term linguistic habits of pupils. The League at times appears to have become uneasy and to lose its sense of purpose; disagreements such as that about dialects festered (*Banba*, June 1906; *Claidheamh Soluis*, 23 May 1908 and 30 May 1908). By 1910, sales of the League's publications were falling off and financial bankruptcy was seriously contemplated in public (*Claidheamh Soluis*, 26 August 1911). Some feared failure, others used it as a stick with which to beat the leadership.

Increasing bad-tempered desperation and authoritarianism was the reaction of some Leaguers. *Irish Freedom*, the IRB paper, called for Ireland to hold fast to her 'soul' in 1911; it was felt that eventually people would have to be forced to save their cultural and political souls. The desperation of failure bred a truculence and the paper called for 'language bigots' to speak Irish and 'Shove it down the throats of all and sundry' (October 1911).

Desmond FitzGerald, an IRB activist in Kerry in the years before the Great War, saw the language even then as a dying one. It was becoming impoverished in vocabulary and syntax; older men spoke a richer version of it than did the younger: 'We were subconsciously aware that the continued decay of the Irish language was bringing ominously near a further great break with the past' (FitzGerald, 1968, pp. 13–15 and 32–4). A common theme later on was to blame politics and politicians for the decline of the revival movement and the continued retreat of the *Gaelteachtaí*; in fact the Irish government has, since independence, been berated for permitting the language decline to continue. Siobhán Lankford, a north Cork activist, recalled that in Mallow the League's classes went on amid great fervour throughout the Anglo-Irish war until the news came down from Dublin in 1922 that a compromise Treaty had been accepted:

> Almost overnight the enthusiasm evaporated and the classes faded away. At first we couldn't believe the classes were not going to continue...one of the most intellectual of the students...said 'Well, the enthusiasm was great because we expected to have a Republic and its dignity would demand the native language, but now we'll still be part of the British Empire and have a divided country – not worth the effort of learning a language – English will be good enough for us'.
>
> (Lankford, 1980, pp. 124–5)

An alternative explanation would be that the essentially politically motivated interest in the language could not be a long-term substitute for a general and genuine public interest in language change, an interest that is historically very unusual in circumstances analogous to Ireland's. The end of the political revolution in 1922–23 exposed the hollowness of the cultural movement which the revolutionaries had hijacked. The IRB separatists were men of secret societies, authoritarian and obsessed by political goals to the near-exclusion of cultural, economic or social considerations (O'Casey, 1946, pp. 346–50). Essentially, the Irish language was valued not for itself but as a symbol of national distinctiveness. Beyond that, it was fit only for children and for others who needed protection against English civilisation.

Behind the idealism of Pearse, the ruralism of clergy and the single-mindedness of IRB leaders, there sometimes lurked another emotion: status resentment and personal ambition cloaked in nationalism. In 1910, a letter to the League's paper complained about the unfairness of the public service examinations, which did not accept Irish as a subject, while accepting foreign modern languages such as French and German. Significantly, the Irish ethnic identity was seen by this writer actually to exclude not just the upper classes or Protestants, but apparently anyone who had had a Jesuit education in Ireland (*Claidheamh Soluis*, 10 September 1910).

The Gaelic League had originally been offered to the Catholics as a means of vaccinating the public against English popular culture, held to be erosive of traditional morality. A major theme of Irish-Ireland and Catholic thought was, of course, the menacing growth of a large market in Ireland for English popular culture generally. This was a by-product of mass literacy, ironically itself a result of the upgrading of national school education under clerical auspices. As already suggested the Gaelic League itself was in part a reaction to this growth of an anglicised popular culture and its consequent real or imagined demoralising and deracinating effects on the minds of the young and easily influenced. Countrymen noticed how much further this process had gone in the big towns and in Dublin; to a countryman, a Dubliner of the period seemed at least as English as he was Irish.

An obsession with public morality and with the powers of the popular press to corrupt the population was common among the young patriots as it was among the priests. Dublin was the symbol of not only the arrogant achievements of eighteenth-century Anglo-Ireland but also of the receptivity of the native Irish, in their debased urban form, to Anglo-American vulgarity and corruption. Naturally, the idea of cultural protectionism became popular; it is striking how much more popular cultural protectiveness was than was economic protectionism – after all, the latter divided, whereas the former united.

The League's evident inadequacy as a vehicle of linguistic revival and as a bulwark against secular vulgarity caused some clericalists to abandon it in favour of direct censorship of English publications. From 1910 on, regular burnings of English newspapers occurred. The *Leader* was joined by a more extremist paper, the *Catholic Bulletin*, edited by 'Scelig' (J.J. O'Kelly), an old Keating branch hand. The old Munster critique of the League was reiterated in this paper, which recommended the publishing of suitable books in *English* to act as substitutes for the English 'penny dreadfuls'. Censorship was also to be resorted to (*Catholic Bulletin*, March 1911, April 1911 and March 1913). The Gaelic League had been found wanting, but not before it had been used as a stalking-horse for separatist and clericalist forces who were soon to be given a chance to try out their views on culture on an entire nation-state.

COMMENTARY BY MAURA ADSHEAD

Politics and culture are never far apart, and this is especially so in new nations. On the face of it, Tom Garvin's 1987 article provides an historical narrative of the evolution of the Gaelic League and the influence of the League upon post-independent politics – though in doing so, it is also clearly as much about the influence of post-independence politics on the development of the League and Irish culture. Probing further, it is this 'chicken and egg' conundrum that points to the heart of the article's interest for scholars of Irish politics. Exploration of the relationship between the construction of political identity and the creation of political culture is as pertinent an issue now as it ever was, raising important questions about the fundamental assumptions that underpin the Irish polity and the dynamics of politicking within it.

In relation to the construction of national identity and political culture, Garvin notes that the political leaders of the Free State were all previous members of the League, so that the League served to some extent as the 'ideological spawning ground' for the politics of nationalism and independence prior to the foundation of the state. In consequence, the politics of Irish independence became irretrievably combined with the politicisation of Irish culture: cultural expression became a means of political expression, where formal political involvement was prohibited and such expression reflected the creation of a counter-culture that acted as 'a compensation for the discomfort generated by the existing status system'. Despite providing comfort to nascent nationalist sentiment and a locus for the proxy-political mobilisation, the successful creation of 'an official cultural ideology' was a bitter-sweet victory.

Whilst initially appealing to Protestants as a means to express their Irishness without giving up their religion, the League soon became a breeding ground for 'a hatred of England and its culture' and from there, it was but a short step for the membership to begin to equate Protestantism with Englishness, so that the Protestant claim to the language and membership of the League was gradually loosened by popular denial. So began the foundations for *holistic* as opposed to *liberal* nationalism in Ireland – an unusual juxtaposition that is not normally found in democratic states. Whereas liberal nationalism is concerned with estab-lishing national values and rights (usually in the context of values of tolerance and pluralism), holistic nationalism is usually based on an ethnic conception of the nation that stresses the conversion, or the expulsion (or possibly worse) of the 'other' in defence of a traditional conception of community.

In contemporary Ireland, this narrowly based prescriptive description of Irish identity is being challenged by inwards migration and increasing cultural diversity. As a result, in addition to the 'usual' economic, political and technical issues associated with the politics of immigration, the changing demographic also constitutes a challenge to the state on another level, in terms of current and long-standing constructions of identity and conceptions of the body politic, 'which render the "we" of contemporary Ireland obsolete as an "authentic" (mono) cultural voice' (Lentin, 2002, p. 236).

A further peculiarity relating to the development of Irish political culture is a popular fascination with violence (arguably sustained largely as a consequence of our lack of exposure to it) and epitomised, for example, in Pearse's renowned rationalisation of the Easter Rising as an expression of 'blood sacrifice' (Lee, 1989, pp. 25–6). In a later work, Garvin notes that violence played an important part in the formation of Irish democracy between 1913 and 1923 with serious consequences for Irish political culture, suggesting that even in contemporary Ireland elected politicians must 'pay homage' to the 'romantic rhetoric of mili-tarist nationalism' (2004, p. 6). It is perhaps an ironic quirk of history that Pearse's earlier recourse to the imagery of warfare, documented in Garvin's 1987 article, occurs in the context of his stewardship of the League and his defiant fight against pessimism about the chances for success of Gaelic revival. As it was, the struggle for independence proved much more successful than the struggle to Gaelicise Ireland.

That this should be so, reflects the greater significance of the League in providing political opportunity structures to would-be leaders of Irish independence than as a vehicle for the preservation of Gaelic culture – attracting in turns the (ambivalent) attentions of Sinn Féin and other 'physical-force separatists', as well as the Irish Republican Brotherhood and (belatedly) Larkinite socialists. To this list, we might also add the 'footsoldiers' of the Catholic Church, represented by a growing cadre of young priests, for whom the League offered a means to both promote and preserve the enshrining of an essentially *Catholic* Irish identity against the 'inroads of English culture'. The Church's somewhat cynical support for the League as a means to promote *Irish Catholic patriotism* points to that organisation's political acumen in recognising the League as an instrument of influence for the masses, not just the political elite. It might also contribute to explaining the limited success of contemporary attempts at linguistic revival: as a stand-alone political project that is not tied to other strategic interests or state goals, it seems that language revival *per se* is not perceived as a priority or promoted with any great enthusiasm by Irish politicians and key state interests. As Garvin notes, 'Essentially the Irish language was valued not for itself but as a symbol of national distinctiveness'. Once this distinction could be made politically, there was no further need for its cultural expression.

It is already apparent that the inferences to be made from the evidence presented in this case are legion. Further consideration should also be given, however, to what might be more explicitly uncovered were an alternative methodology or framework for analysis to be deployed. The article clearly documents, for example, the emergent cleavage structure of Irish politics during this period – a conspicuous comparator that is taken up elsewhere by Garvin (1974 and 1977) and also by others in later work (Sinnott, 1984, 1995, 2001 and 2002). Details of divisions between the provinces and Dublin point to a nascent centre/periphery cleavage. The part played by the Catholic Church in the 'nationalist project' provides clear evidence of a church/state cleavage, where Protestantism loses out to the establishment of Catholicism as the religion of the state. Moreover, the patterning of Gaeltacht areas and the association of 'Irish and poverty, Irish and social inferiority' (Lee, 1989, p. 133) sets the context for a significant urban/rural cleavage. Finally, references to the class cleavage (by any other name) are multiple throughout the text.

Whilst Garvin acknowledges the strongly stratified nature of society and makes a good deal of the importance of 'status resentment' as a significant determinant of post-nationalist Irish identity, he eschews explicit references to class. Still, however, it is hard to view Hyde's 'distaste for the lefties', epitomised by his feeling 'compelled to wear old clothes so as not raise the ire of the new democracy' as anything but an implicit reference to the significance of social class in explaining the League's development. We see that what began essentially as a pursuit of the middle classes in Ireland and the Irish Diaspora outside it had, by 1899, ceased to be an elite organisation and turned into a well-organised institutional structure that was popular with the masses and may even be regarded as a prototype for later nationalist parties. The failure – by the protagonists recorded and the political scientists recording – to explicitly recognise the class dimensions to this narrative point to another peculiarity of Irish politics, that is, the steadfast refusal to acknowledge class in popular political discourse. Instead, the idea was promulgated that because British rule and the Protestant Establishment had been overthrown, Ireland was somehow a classless society (McLaughlin, 1993, p. 209). The fact that this is not true (see O'Leary, 1990) is less important than the fact that so many believed it to be true and as a consequence, in Ireland *social* class did not translate into class *politics* (Mair, 1992, p. 389). This attitude is borne out by 'the striking electoral debility of class-based, left-wing parties' in Ireland and the fact 'there is no other single country in western Europe that even approaches the weak position of the Irish left' (Mair, 1992, pp. 384–5).

As it stands, Garvin's study provides an elegant example of how the Gaelic League succeeded in promulgating an over-arching Irish identity that was able to subsume any latent class identity, and helped establish the foundations to contemporary political culture – one which deliberately emphasised the importance of Catholicism and Irishness (as opposed to Anglo-Irish or British traditions) in the name of Irish 'nation building'. More generally, however, it points to the significance of recognising what is *politics*. The idea, for example, that a movement designed to address the (re)construction of national identity could be anything but fundamentally political is difficult to swallow: its political potential was clearly recognised by the League's founders; by the major political movements for independence; by the lower-middle-class professionals who, barred from overt political activity, took to the League as a means of politicking by another means; and even, eventually, by the masses who 'found normal political action closed to them because constitutional politics had been crippled by the fall of Parnell'. A new institutionalist analysis (Powell and DiMaggio, 1991) of this material would surely bring forth a much clearer enunciation of the establishment of socio-cultural norms and values and their subsequent promulgation throughout society. Thus, to suggest that 'culture was bent to politics' or that the League at times 'appealed as a substitute for politics' is – by insisting on a highly suspect notional separation of the two – to fail to recognise their implicit intertwining in the first place (Lukes, 1974 and 2005). In fact, when the story of the Gaelic League is viewed in the context of contemporary political concerns regarding the cultivation of popular opinion by media savvy politicians, the role of political 'spin doctors' and the manipulation of issues for political gain, one is tempted to ask: were it not ever thus?

References

Brooks, Sydney (1907) *The New Ireland*. Dublin: Maunsel.

Cleary, Arthur E. (1919) 'The Gaelic League, 1893–1919', *Studies*, VIII, pp. 398–408.

FitzGerald, Desmond (1968) *Memoirs*. London: Routledge and Kegan Paul.

Gaelic League (Portarlington Branch) (1906) *Autobiography of the Ruairi O More Branch*. National Library of Ireland pamphlet collection.

Garvin, Tom (1974) 'Political Cleavages, Party Politics and Urbanisation in Ireland: The Case of the Periphery-Dominated Centre', *European Journal of Political Research*, 2 (4), pp. 307–27.

Garvin, Tom (1977) 'National Elites, Irish Voters and Irish Political Development: A Comparative Perspective', *Economic and Social Review*, 8, pp. 161–86.

Garvin, Tom (2004) '*Cogadh na gCarad*: The Creation of the Irish Political Elite', pp. 6–18 in Tom Garvin, Maurice Manning and Richard Sinnott (eds.) *Dissecting Irish Politics*. Dublin: UCD Press.

House of Commons (1899) *Final Report of the Commissioners on Intermediate Education*. Cd. 9511.

Hyde Papers (various dates) Collection of uncatalogued papers held at the Delargy Centre for Irish Folklore and the National Folklore Collection, University College Dublin.

Lankford, Siobhán (1980) *The Hope and the Sadness: Personal Recollections of Troubled Times in Ireland*. Cork: Tower.

Lee, J.J. (1989) *Ireland 1912–1985*. Cambridge: Cambridge University Press.

Lentin, Ronit (2002) 'Anti-Racist Responses to the Racialisation of Irishness: Disavowed Multiculturalism and its Discontents', pp. 226–36 in Ronit Lentin and Robbie McVeigh (eds.) *Racism and Anti-Racism in Ireland*. Dublin: Beyond the Pale Publications.

Lukes, Steven (1974) *Power: A Radical View*. London: Macmillan

Lukes, Steven (2005) *Power: A Radical View*. Second Edition. London: Palgrave Macmillan

Mair, Peter (1992) 'Explaining the Absence of Class Politics in Ireland', pp. 383–410 in John H. Goldthorpe and Christopher T. Whelan (eds.) *The Development of Industrial Society in Ireland*. Oxford: Oxford University Press.

McLaughlin, Eugene (1993) 'Ireland: Catholic Corporatism', pp. 205–37 in Allan Cochrane and John Clarke (eds.) *Comparing Welfare States: Britain in International Context*. London: Sage.

O'Casey, Sean (1946) *Drums Under the Window*. New York: Macmillan.

Ó Ceallaigh, Seán T. (1963) *Seán T*. Dublin: Foilseacháin Náisiunta.

O Cobhthaigh, Diarmid (1917) *Douglas Hyde*. Dublin: Maunsel.

O'Leary, Brendan (1990) 'Setting the Record Straight: A Comment on Cahill's Country Report on Ireland', *Governance*, 3 (1), pp. 98–104.

Powell, Walter W. and Paul J. DiMaggio (1991) (eds.) *The New Institutionalism in Organizational Analysis*. Chicago, IL: Chicago University Press.

Redmond-Howard, Louis G. (1913) *The New Birth of Ireland*. London: Collins.

Ryan, William Patrick (1912) *The Pope's Green Island*. London: Nisbet.

Sinnott, Richard (1984) 'Interpretations of the Irish Party System', *European Journal of Political Research*, 12 (3), pp. 289–307.

Sinnott, Richard (1995) *Irish Voters Decide: Voting Behaviour in Elections and Referendums Since 1918*. Manchester: Manchester University Press.

Sinnott, Richard (2001) 'Attitudes and Behaviour of the Irish Electorate in the Referendum on the Treaty of Nice. Flash Eurobarometer Survey for the European Commission'. Dublin: Institute for the Study of Social Change, University College Dublin.

Sinnott, Richard (2002) 'Cleavages, Parties and Referendums: Relationships Between Representative and Direct Democracy in the Republic of Ireland', *European Journal of Political Research*, 41 (6), pp. 811–26.

Tierney, Michael (1980) *Eoin MacNeill: Scholar and Man of Action, 1867–1945*. Oxford: Clarendon Press.

Waters, Martin James (1977) 'Peasants and Emigrants: Considerations of the Gaelic League as a Social Movement', pp. 160–77 in Daniel J. Casey and Robert E. Rhodes (eds.) *Views of the Irish Peasantry, 1800–1916*. Hamden, CT: Archon.

Part Two

Electoral politics and political institutions

10 Does Ireland need a new electoral system?[1]

Michael Gallagher

Originally published in *Irish Political Studies*, 2, 1987, pp. 27–48.

Every general election to take place in independent Ireland has been held under the system known as the Single Transferable Vote (STV) in multi-member constituencies; for descriptions of how the system works, see Hand (1979) and Chubb (1982, pp. 350–3). The reasons why STV, not then used elsewhere in Europe, was bestowed on Ireland are worth looking into briefly, because they are still relevant to the way Irish people and politicians evaluate their electoral system.

STV came to Ireland because it was the system favoured by Britain's electoral reformers. The Proportional Representation (PR) Society was founded late in the nineteenth century to press for the introduction of STV at British elections. In 1911 it put forward STV as a way of easing the Home Rule crisis; STV in Ireland, the PR Society suggested, would be particularly appropriate because it would guarantee minority representation. The society's president came to Dublin and elaborated the case in a lecture, which was sufficiently persuasive to bring about the formation of a PR Society of Ireland, whose members included Arthur Griffith (O'Leary, 1979, pp. 5–6). This was a key event as far as the future of electoral law in Ireland was concerned. It meant that there was henceforth a strong lobby in favour of PR as opposed to the British single-member plurality (SMP) system, but it also meant that PR came almost to be equated with the Single Transferable Vote, and that where other forms of PR, involving lists, were concerned, there was a profound ignorance. From the start, STV seems to have been known in Ireland simply as 'PR', which, as we shall see, leads to considerable confusion in some quarters as to what proportional representation actually entails.

STV was used in 1919 to elect Sligo Corporation, which brought it widespread and favourable publicity (O'Leary, 1979, pp. 7–8), and was prescribed in the 1920 Government of Ireland Act for the parliaments of the future northern and southern Ireland. The constitution of the Irish Free State laid down in Article 26 that the Dáil be elected 'upon principles of Proportional Representation'. This may conceivably have reflected an intention to allow the legislators to decide which particular PR system was to be used, but is far more likely to have reflected a belief that 'Proportional Representation' denoted STV. O'Leary (1979, pp. 15–16) observes that when this part of the draft constitution was debated in the Dáil, Article 26 was assumed to be prescribing STV, and when the first electoral laws were debated in 1923 there were no signs of awareness that PR could mean anything but STV.

The electoral system, then, constitutes at best only a partial exception to the Irish Free State's pattern of simply continuing or adopting British norms and procedures in the area of providing government. It is true that the use of any PR system marked a radical break from British practice, but it is also true that the introduction of STV (which has been described by Gudgin and Taylor (1979, p. 164) as 'the Anglo-Saxon' form of PR) was due to that system's popularity with an active British pressure group, who hoped that if it performed satisfactorily in Ireland its chances of being adopted in Britain would be improved. The willingness to be guided by British advice, and the lack of interest in, let alone knowledge of practices in continental Europe, have to some extent set the tone for most subsequent discussion of Irish electoral reform.

In this paper we shall consider recent calls for a change to Ireland's electoral system, examining the factors which seem to have brought the issue back to the political agenda, such as proportionality, government stability and deputies' behaviour patterns. Finally, some alternative systems will be briefly considered.

The record of STV: Proportionality and government stability

Electoral systems tend to be judged mainly by two criteria: proportionality (or 'fairness') and governmental stability. These are often seen as being inherently in conflict: full proportionality (which denotes that every party receives exactly the same share of the seats as it wins of the votes) is associated in some minds with a fragmented legislature, containing many small parties, from which no stable government can emerge. In contrast, less proportional systems tend to give major parties, especially the largest, a 'bonus' of seats at the expense of smaller groups and thus facilitate stable single-party government. This way of looking at the utility of electoral systems has characterised especially the British (and hence the Irish) debate on the subject; Britain's SMP system is defended on the ground that, even if it does penalise small parties, it usually produces single-party government, which would be highly unlikely under any form of PR. In much of continental Europe, though, proportionality (or 'one person, one vote, one value') tends to be seen as more fundamental, and as necessary a feature of a democracy as universal suffrage, although some countries with PR systems employ thresholds which deny representation to parties whose support falls below a certain level (Israel, West Germany) or make life difficult for them (Sweden).

Whether it is generally true that PR encourages multi-partism and hence unstable government, does not concern us here (the issues are aired in several essays in Grofman and Lijphart, 1986). What is relevant is that STV in Ireland cannot convincingly be faulted on either criterion.

Proportionality

When it comes to proportionality, Irish elections display a high degree of correspondence between parties' shares of the votes and seats (this is discussed in Gallagher, 1986, pp. 255–60; and Sturm, 1986, pp. 58–60). There are several ways in which the concept of proportionality can be measured, but whichever method is chosen the conclusion is much the same: Ireland holds an upper mid-table position in the league table of 24 liberal democracies (see Lijphart, 1985, pp. 10–12 for the table and for discussion of measuring proportionality). For example, as measured by the widely-used Loosemore–Hanby index, the 1981 Irish election (the one Lijphart uses) produced the eighth most proportional result out of 24 held in different countries at around the same time. The disproportionality produced was 4.4 per cent; the range was from 1.1 per cent in Austria (the most proportional) to 21.4 per cent in France (the least proportional). No system, then, produces much more proportional results than STV in Ireland, but several produce much less proportional results.

Moreover, STV has delivered this impressive degree of proportionality in the face of a severe obstacle, namely an exceptionally small district magnitude (the number of deputies elected from each constituency). The larger the district magnitude, the more proportional the electoral system. The reason is not hard to see. In a small constituency there are few seats to share out, and thus little likelihood that each contending party will receive the number which corresponds to its proportion of the votes. For example, if in a three-seat constituency party A wins 50 per cent of the votes, while B wins 30 per cent and C wins 20 per cent, then there is no 'fair' allocation of the seats. If A is given two seats and B one, then C is grossly under-represented, but if each party is given one seat, then A is harshly treated, having won two and a half times as many votes as C, but receiving no more seats. Thus there is a view that PR systems need a district magnitude of at least five seats if they are to 'work properly'.

In Ireland, though, district magnitude at recent elections has averaged only 4, and fell to as low as 3.4 at the elections of 1969 and 1973. Even the figure of 4 is lower than that for any other country using a PR system (see Mackie and Rose, 1982, pp. 410–11). With such a small district magnitude, no electoral system could be expected to have delivered more proportionality than STV has in Ireland. The strange suggestion that STV is a type of majority system rather than a PR system, as seems to be implied by Katz (1984, especially pp. 135–7 and 141), has no basis either conceptually or empirically.

Government stability

Between 1922 and 1977, STV's record with regard to government stability was equally beyond reproach (this is discussed in Gallagher, 1986, pp. 260–4). Since the first general election in 1922, there have been another 22 in 65 years, so each Dáil has lasted on average about three years. Over the period 1945–77 (for which figures are presented by King, 1981, p. 299), Ireland held nine general elections, slightly below average for most liberal democracies (the range was from six in India to 14 in Australia and Denmark). The case for the abolition of PR on the issue of government stability was a weak one, even though it was the main plank in the arguments of the anti-PR side in the referendums of 1959 and 1968 (see O'Leary, 1979, pp. 46–58 and 68–9; Chubb, 1982, pp. 162–3), sometimes laced with Ferdinand Hermens-inspired rhetoric about the inevitable collapse of democracy in any country foolish enough to use a PR system of election.

The party system too does not correspond to the chaotic fragmentation which defenders of SMP voting sometimes suggest must result from the introduction of PR. Even at the February 1987 election, which produced the most fractionalised Dáil since 1961, the 'effective number of parties' in the Dáil was only 2.9.[2] This figure is relatively low by comparative standards. Lijphart (1984, p. 160) presents a table showing the average number of effective parties in parliament for each of 22 countries over the period 1945 to 1980. The range is from 1.9 in the USA to 5.0 in Finland and Switzerland, and only seven have a lower average than 2.9. Of course, it might be argued that the non-fractionalised nature of the Dáil is caused more by Irish voting patterns than by the electoral system; it comes about because the great majority of voters usually back one of the two major parties. This is no doubt correct, but the essential point remains: the electoral system has not caused a fragmented party system, and has not prevented the Irish people enjoying, or at least experiencing, stable government over the last 65 years.

However, critics would point to the absence of a majority government after three of the most recent four elections, and the holding of three general elections in a 17-month period in 1981–82, to argue that STV has failed to guarantee stable government over the last six years. This is obviously true, but the question arises of whether an electoral system is obliged to deliver majority government regardless of the way people vote or the willingness of parties to co-operate with each other. It is hard to see why STV should be reprimanded for not giving Fianna Fáil an overall majority in February 1987, when it won 44.1 per cent of the votes, yet praised for doing the same in November 1982, when it won 45.2 per cent. The notion that any party or alliance of parties has an automatic right to form a majority government, regardless of how many votes it wins, is certainly incompatible with the philosophy behind every kind of PR system, and indeed seems hard to reconcile with the reasons for holding democratic elections in the first place.

Critics also observe that Ireland has had frequent experience of coalition governments, which opponents of PR allege are inherently inferior to 'strong, decisive' single-party governments. Fianna Fáil has consistently argued (see Mair, 1979, pp. 453–6; Gallagher, 1985a, pp. 34–5) that coalitions are by their very nature weak, indecisive and internally divided. This point cannot be dismissed out of hand, for there have been obvious signs that, in recent Irish coalitions, Fine Gael and Labour have been pulling in different directions on certain issues, the result being characterised by some economic commentators as 'drift' and, additionally, being unsatisfactory in the eyes of both parties' members and supporters. But it is not a strong argument. For one thing, Fianna Fáil governments since 1946 have displayed something less than 'rock-like unity' and single-mindedness of purpose. Moreover, although this is not the place to embark on a wide-ranging discussion of the relative merits of single-party or coalition governments, a cursory glance at European experience is enough to discredit any facile assertion of the innate superiority of the former. The comparative economic growth records over the past 30 years of West Germany and Switzerland (governed by coalitions) and Britain, for example, show that 'one-party government good, multi-party government bad' is a difficult view to defend.

The record of STV: Deputies' behaviour patterns

Much recent discontent with STV springs not from alleged shortcomings in the areas of government stability or proportionality, but from discontent at the behaviour patterns which, it is said, it imposes upon deputies. The argument is a familiar one, and is summed up, and sometimes endorsed, by various academic writers (see, for example, Parker, 1983, p. 21; Farrell, 1985, p. 260; Carty, 1981, p. 134; Chubb, 1982, pp. 156 and 227–8; Katz, 1984, p. 144). It can be summed up as 'STV causes brokerage – causes a weak Dáil'. It runs to the effect that candidates of the same party cannot compete against each other on policy grounds, and therefore they must find another way of distinguishing themselves from their 'running mates'. They are thus compelled to engage in brokerage, to try to establish a better 'record of service to their constituents' than the other candidates of their party. Consequently, deputies have to spend an excessive amount of their time dealing with the problems of individual constituents, to the detriment of their 'proper' parliamentary duties.

There is a difficulty in trying to tackle the proposition that 'STV causes brokerage – causes a weak Dáil', namely that although this seems to be widely accepted, there is no fully developed case to sustain it. Analysing a case which has not been made is not easy. It may be that its widespread acceptance has led to an assumption that its validity can be taken for granted. Because of this, it has never been cast in a testable form, a task which this section of the paper is forced to attempt.

The argument seems to involve four assumptions. The first is that an electoral system involving intra-party competition is a sufficient precondition of brokerage; where one exists, deputies must 'inevitably spend a lot of time on brokerage work'.[3] The second is that STV is a necessary precondition of deputies engaging heavily in brokerage; if a new electoral system not involving intra-party competition were introduced in Ireland, TDs' casework burdens would greatly decrease. The third is that if TDs' brokerage workloads decreased, the Dáil would become significantly stronger. The fourth is a normative argument, that constituency work is somehow not what deputies should be doing; they should instead be 'legislating' or 'helping to run the country'. We shall argue that none of these assumptions is valid.

Does STV cause brokerage?

The first assumption, that intra-party competition compels deputies to resort to brokerage in order to bolster their positions against internal party rivals, is certainly not sustainable as a cross-national proposition. This is borne out by recent studies of voter–deputy relations in a number of countries, some of which have preferential party list electoral systems, under which candidates of any one party are in competition with each other to just the same extent as under STV. In Denmark, one country with such a system, there is little casework contact between deputies and voters, and Thomas (1985, p. 218) speaks of 'the relative insignificance of the case-work function of MPs in Scandinavia'. In Switzerland (whose electoral system is even closer to Ireland's, since it allows voters to vote across party lines as well as to express preferences for candidates within each party), it has been estimated that the average deputy deals with fewer than 40 requests for help from constituents a year (Hughes, 1985, p. 232). Although some of STV's Irish critics have pointed to Tasmania's combination of STV and brokerage politics, O'Connell's careful analysis casts doubt on the causal connection. He concludes (O'Connell, 1983, p. 61) that brokerage 'is more *associated* with PR-STV *under certain conditions* than *caused* by it'.

In Switzerland, the explanation for the absence of brokerage demands appears to be that citizens have alternative forms of redress, via someone else in the all-encompassing network of one's political party or professional group. This, it might be argued, reduces the usefulness of comparisons between Ireland and Switzerland, as it does not prove that a preferential electoral system will not cause heavy constituency workloads in countries, such as Ireland, where social integration is lower. But the explanation in Denmark is much more relevant. It is, firstly, that local government is relatively strong, so that 'the appropriate level for the resolution of the problems or grievances of the individual citizen in relation to the provision of a wide range of services will be the local and not the national level'; and, secondly, that citizens are relatively well 'informed about which office to approach in the administrative structure, and less inhibited about making a direct approach' (Thomas, 1985, pp. 219–20).

STV may cause deputies to be responsive to the voters' wishes, but it does not cause the voters' wishes to concern deputies' 'availability' rather than their legislative ability, ministerial potential or ideological soundness. The causes of this must be found in other aspects of Irish politics and society. The fact is that there is no logical basis to the claim that candidates of one party cannot, under STV, compete on any basis other than brokerage. There are obvious differences of emphasis within both Fianna Fáil and Fine Gael which rival candidates could, and indeed sometimes do, highlight. Nor is there anything to prevent candidates of the same party trying fervently to establish reputations not as active constituency workers but as active parliamentarians. Why, then, do they choose to compete primarily on the terrain of constituency work? Is this forced upon them?

Defenders of the 'STV causes brokerage' hypothesis seem to be undecided on this. Some argue that it is indeed forced upon TDs: they have to compete on the basis of casework ability rather than parliamentary ability because only the former impresses voters. But to give such an answer is tacitly to acknowledge that the demand that TDs engage in brokerage work is present in the population for other reasons, and is not created by STV. STV does not cause brokerage demands to arise; it merely gives TDs a powerful incentive to respond to them.

Other supporters of the hypothesis would argue that voters do not really need as much casework assistance as they get from TDs. They would say that STV's role really is causal, in that voters are to some extent responding to TDs' behaviour patterns; they would not have so many demands if deputies did not seem so eager to deal with them. Doubt could be cast on this, implying as it does that Irish voters, induced by their TDs into believing wrongly that they need assistance in dealing with the bureaucracy, are suffering from false consciousness on a massive scale. But if it were true, then the remedy would surely lie in TDs' own hands; if they stopped looking for constituency work, most of it would go away. If TDs decided to stress their legislative rather than their brokerage abilities, then presumably, according to this argument, the electorate would shift its perceptions accordingly.

Would brokerage exist without STV?

The second assumption underlying the 'STV causes brokerage – causes a weak Dáil' argument is that intra-party competition is a necessary cause of brokerage, so that if the former could be eliminated, by means of a change in the electoral system, the brokerage workload would lighten significantly. The suggestion that deputies would not face brokerage demands if the electoral system did not involve intra-party competition is simple to refute empirically. There is much evidence to suggest that brokerage is a very widespread – though, as we have just seen, not a universal – phenomenon. For example, Mezey (1979, p. 159) observes that 'members of every type of legislature say that they are subjected to an incessant flow of such [particularised] demands, and they indicate that coping with them requires a substantial portion of their time and resources'.

There are two further points which show that intra-party competition is not a necessary cause of brokerage in Ireland. The first is that brokerage was practised by Irish politicians in the last century, long before STV arrived (see, for example, Buckland, 1972, p. xx); the same point is made about Tasmania (O'Connell, 1983, p. 54). The second is that if TDs do so much constituency work purely to stave off electoral threats from party running mates, then we should expect to find that Labour and Workers' Party deputies, who usually stand alone, do a bare minimum of constituency work. There is no evidence for this, and impressionistic observations of rural Labour TDs at work run strongly counter to it. One newspaper report (*Sunday Independent*, 8 March 1987, p. 32) stated that Frank McLoughlin, Labour TD for Meath from November 1982 to February 1987, dealt with the cases of 29,000 different people during his time in the Dáil.

Of course, even if constituency work is, almost everywhere, part of a deputy's duties, it might still be argued that in Ireland it forms an exceptionally and unhealthily high part. Trying to find out whether this is so is not easy, because of a lack of information in most countries as to just how much time deputies do spend on casework.

For Ireland, there have been eight different attempts to elicit the truth on this subject. The first came in 1961, when the High Court heard various deputies' descriptions of their activities. One deputy, for example, said he personally 'interviewed' about 110 constituents a week (see Chubb, 1983, p. 121). The next information comes from December 1964, when Tuairim sent questionnaires to deputies. The results here also were not very precise, but Whyte (1966, p. 7) was able to conclude that 22 of the 42 deputies answering the relevant question in full spent more than half their political working time (which averaged 44 hours a week) dealing with constituency work. The only attempt to measure the phenomenon from the consumers' side came in 1971, when a survey found that four out of five respondents had never contacted a politician for any reason (reported in Komito, 1984, p. 180), but the survey was confined to Dublin and the number of respondents was only 499. By 1972, when the Review Body on public service body pay reported, the average TD's self-reported working week had risen to 72 hours a week when the Dáil was in session and 58 hours a week when it was in recess. Once again, no precise breakdown of activities was given, but it seems that deputies reported that in an average week when the Dáil was in session, they spent 25 hours 'attending Dáil' and 47 hours 'on all other activities as TD' (Review Body, 1972, pp. 210–11).

In 1974, an unpublished survey by D.P. Murray, mentioned in passing by Barrington (1980, p. 177), concluded that 'about 140,000 representations' were received by deputies and senators in that year, an average of about 700 each a year or 14 a week. The Public Service Review Body conducted another survey in 1978. This time TDs said that they worked a 70-hour week when the Dáil was in recess, and 78 hours when it was sitting; they spent 40 hours a week on constituency work when the Dáil was in recess, and 32 hours when it was sitting (Review Body, 1979, p. 235). The report noted that the increase in working hours compared with 1972 'is largely attributable to constituency work' (Review Body, 1979, p. 241). In 1980, a Dublin TD reported receiving 244 communications in one particular month, of which it seems about half contained requests for assistance (Chubb, 1982, p. 227). Finally, we come to the fullest exploration of the question, by Roche, who interviewed 115 TDs in 1981. He found that they reported receiving, on average, 140 representations every week; holding three to four clinics a week; and working a 75-hour week, of which about half was devoted to constituency work. Sixteen deputies claimed to deal with 201 to 300 representations each week, and 12 reported over 300 cases a week (Roche, 1982, pp. 99–100).

What can be made of all these figures? The first point is that often they are difficult to reconcile with each other, and they should all be regarded with a degree of scepticism. The deputies giving evidence in the 1961 constitutional case were especially selected to give evidence in support of the claim that rural deputies had a high burden of constituency work and, even if they did not exaggerate, cannot be regarded as any kind of random sample. In examining responses to the 1964 questionnaire, Whyte (1966, p. 6) notes that they were 'in some cases implausible'; one deputy, for example, claimed to work a 100-hour week. Roche (1982, p. 100), too, notes the danger of exaggeration, and points out that many of the 'representations' received by deputies are extremely minor, amounting only to requests for information or for application forms. The inquiries of the review bodies are particularly susceptible to what was tactfully termed 'some degree of unconscious overstatement' (Review Body, 1972, p. 125; 1979, p. 235). These bodies were, after all, trying to decide how much deputies should be paid; in this context, expecting, on the basis of respondents' own reports, to find a deputy who is not overburdened with constituency work is as optimistic an endeavour as expecting to find a rich farmer or a lazy academic.

The second point is that despite the vagueness which has not really been dispelled despite all these studies, two clear impressions remain: constituency work looms large in a deputy's working week, and its volume has been growing steadily. Cross-national comparisons are difficult to make given the absence of reliable figures, but the volume of cases, coupled with the low number of people represented by each deputy, do seem exceptional. Roche's figure of 140 cases per week per TD suggests a total of 23,240 per week for the entire Dáil, or about 1,200,000 a year, approximately half of the electorate. Even allowing for exaggeration, and for individual cases cropping up repeatedly, this seems an extraordinary level of voter–deputy contact. Some comparative evidence (Gallagher, 1985b, p. 390) suggests that the level is indeed exceptionally high.

It does seem, then, that Irish voters make unusually heavy casework demands on their deputies. But what has the electoral system got to do with this; why would they make fewer demands if a new electoral system, not involving intra-party competition, were introduced? Admittedly, a few demands could be eliminated if a single-member constituency system were introduced. Individuals, or groups based in one part of the present multi-member constituency, who at present take a problem to more than one deputy would henceforth be able to approach only one. Moreover, some cases are no doubt at present 'called up' by deputies' frenetic efforts to advertise their availability through provincial newspaper advertisements and other methods, and would not arise under a different electoral system. But Roche's conclusion (1982, p. 103) that 'public representatives in providing constituency service are primarily responding to a demand that exists and are not creating it' seems realistic, especially as there is no argument or evidence to the contrary. Most of a deputy's cases would be likely to remain regardless of a change in the electoral system.

It is interesting to observe that very few TDs blamed the electoral system for their volume of constituency work during a debate, in January and February 1983, on reform of the Dáil. Of the 43 TDs to speak in the debate, only eight (Seamus Brennan, Maurice Manning, Des O'Malley, Ted Nealon, Rory O'Hanlon, Michael Keating, Liam Skelly and George Birmingham) said that STV was among the causes of the Dáil's weakness because of its impact on their casework loads. Of course, since the debate was not explicitly about the electoral system, it cannot be assumed that no other deputy holds this view, but it does not appear to have been in the forefront of their minds. Some of the other deputies did blame the volume of casework, at least in part, for the weakness of the Dáil, but attributed this volume to inefficiency, unhelpfulness or bureaucracy in the civil service or to a lack of decentralisation, rather than to STV.

Overall, then, there is neither empirical evidence nor a logical argument to support the claim that STV is a cause of deputies' casework loads, or that changing the electoral system would lead to any significant diminution in the volume of casework. This is not really surprising. A recent cross-national examination of voter–deputy relations concluded that 'electoral systems are *not* fundamental in determining parliamentarian/constituency relationships', and that 'electoral systems are, perhaps, rather more passive elements...than either supporters or opponents of electoral reform tend to believe' (Bogdanor, 1985b, p. 299).

Is brokerage the cause of the Dáil's weakness?

The third assumption is that the Dáil is a relatively weak parliament, and that if TDs were faced with fewer brokerage demands it would be stronger. It seems to be generally accepted that most parliaments are significantly stronger than the Dáil, although those implying this have failed to produce either criteria by which the strength of a legislature can be measured or a demonstration that the Dáil is very different from most parliaments. In the absence of such argument, it can be pointed out that parliaments everywhere have much less power than classical constitutional theory ascribes to them, and that the 'decline of parliaments' is one of the clichés of the twentieth century. In any case, if TDs had more time as a result of a reduction in their constituency work, how would they use it to increase the power of the Dáil?

There are, in theory, three ways in which TDs could put the extra time to good effect. First, they could spend more time on debates in the Dáil chamber; second, they could be more active in formulating legislation; third, they could establish and participate in an active committee system.

The first suggestion, then, is that if TDs had less constituency work, the Dáil would be able to sit for longer, and so more TDs would have a chance to speak. However, when deputies debated Dáil reform in 1983, several of them made it clear that the problem is not one of finding time to speak but of filling up the existing time. Bernard Durkan said that 'the first thing I tried to learn when I was elected here was how to speak for half an hour on a subject that could be dealt with in ten minutes' (*Dáil Debates*, 339: 1136–7, 3 February 1983). John Kelly recalled without much fondness the days when the Dáil sat late, and deputies would 'get up at 8.45 and womble through until 10.30' (*Dáil Debates*, 339: 658, 27 January 1983). Bertie Ahern admitted that during his time as government chief whip he had been guilty of persuading deputies to come into the Dáil chamber and 'keep talking for 45 minutes', without being especially concerned what they said while on their feet. 'During the years', he recalled, 'there have been people in this House who were excellent at saying nothing for one hour and 45 minutes' (*Dáil Debates*, 339: 443, 26 January 1983). If so many Dáil sitting hours consist of 'having people waffle on', in his words, then it is doubtful whether there would be much point in burdening deputies with even more speaking time to be padded out.

Some deputies mentioned the second possibility, namely that they should have a central role in policy-making. Liam Skelly felt that TDs should be 'dealing with the most vital task facing the country, finding a solution of our economic ills'

(*Dáil Debates*, 339: 1014, 3 February 1983). Quite a few deputies seemed to share the sense of surprise expressed by Liam Fitzgerald when he said, 'It was always my belief that in being elected to this House one was being elected to be a legislator in some form or other. I have wondered since coming in here if that is the case' (*Dáil Debates*, 339: 1132–3, 3 February 1983). However, such views represent a rather naive view of the political process. In no parliamentary system does policy emerge from the debates of deputies, and laws are not fashioned in the debating chamber. The vision of deputies debating a topic back and forth, reaching a collective decision as to the solution to a problem such as unemployment, encapsulating their decision in law, and instructing the government to implement the law, is a quixotic one. Among other things, it ignores the role of political parties in any modern society. Almost all deputies are elected, first and foremost, not because of their wisdom or even their record of constituency service, but because they are among the nominees of a political party, and can be relied upon to support the proposals emanating from the government when that party is in office. They are not elected to exercise their judgement when voting on each issue, whatever the constitution in any particular country might imply. It is not lack of time caused by the pressure of constituency work, nor the archaic procedures of the Dáil, which prevent TDs from being law-makers; it is the reality of modern political life.

In acknowledgement of this, most of those who are concerned at TDs' behaviour patterns have suggested a third role they could usefully fill, namely that of participating in a strong committee system. This is undoubtedly the only realistic way in which any free time accruing to deputies as a result of a decline in constituency work could be used to strengthen the role of parliament. The attractions of such a committee system are obvious. Deputies could look systematically into the consequences of government decisions and their implementation by the civil service, forcing greater accountability and subjecting decision-makers to a degree of public scrutiny. It is hard to dispute that this is, of itself, desirable, but it is necessary to be cautious about the possible benefits of such a system.

It is not true, as is sometimes suggested, that parliaments in virtually every country in the world apart from Ireland have a committee system which produces a high degree of scrutiny of the executive. Comparisons with the U.S. Congress or the European Parliament are pointless, because neither body sustains a government, and so party discipline is relatively unimportant. In most parliaments which do sustain governments, committees play a less significant role than is sometimes suggested. A cross-national study of the power of committees has concluded that, in all the countries covered apart from the United States, 'administrative oversight is undertaken with varying degrees of ineffectiveness' (Shaw, 1979, p. 375). In Japan, 'most committee work in the Diet is an exercise in futility', and committees are judged, by Diet members and officials, 'to be impotent in the face of the power of the bureaucracy, of vested interests, and of the political parties' (Baerwald, 1979, pp. 345 and 355). In Italy, committees have found it 'almost impossible...to undertake an active and coherent supervision of the Administration' (D'Onofrio, 1979, p. 98).

There are some parliaments where committees are stronger, such as West Germany and Austria, but it is doubtful whether these are models to be copied. The committees in key areas are highly penetrated by interest groups: deputies who are teachers sit on the education committee, civil servants on the committee to deal with civil servants' pay, farmers on the agriculture committee, and so on (Johnson, 1979, pp. 132–3 and 136; Mezey, 1979, pp. 214–18; Steiner, 1972, p. 307). Reviewing the Irish evidence, O'Halpin (1986, p. 8) raises the possibility that committees may be more susceptible than the Dáil as a whole to the arguments of interest groups. This, or a related, danger was adverted to in the Dáil by John Bruton, who argued that committees should not, therefore, as some had recommended, be charged with overseeing the work of a particular department (*Dáil Debates*, 339: 1266–7, 8 February 1983). However, if they are given a brief which does not relate directly to a specific department, there is the possibility that any recommendations they make will be ignored. Past practice in Ireland has been that committee reports do little but gather dust; they are rarely debated by the Dáil and, said Bruton (*Dáil Debates*, 339: 1263–4, 8 February 1983), suffer the ignominious fate of being used only by academics.

All of this is not by any means to dismiss completely the idea of an effective parliamentary committee system; it can be of some value. For example, Giddings (1985, p. 380), while acknowledging that 'the committees have not changed the basic patterns and relationships of British parliamentary government', argues that 'increased accountability of government has been the main outcome' of the recent expansion of the Westminster committee system. It is, rather, to suggest that there are limits to what can realistically be anticipated from such a reform. There is always the danger that, in a parliament where loyalty to the party is expected, committees will become simply miniature versions of the Dáil, paralysed by disagreements between government and opposition, a fate which seemed to befall the Joint Committee on Marriage Breakdown in the 1982–87 Dáil. Moreover, in a small parliament like the Dáil, where about a third of government deputies are cabinet or junior ministers, every ambitious backbencher can entertain hopes of fairly rapid advancement provided he or she displays fidelity to the party line, and so there will be a temptation for able government backbenchers to be as supportive of their ministers in the forum of a committee as in the Dáil chamber. Therefore, even if brokerage duties were removed entirely from TDs' backs, and if in consequence a Dáil career attracted the philosopher-kings who some seem to feel would make better deputies than the present incumbents, it still does not follow that the Dáil would be significantly stronger *vis-à-vis* government, let alone in any sense a better institution.

It has been argued, then, that the belief that TDs should spend less time on casework and more on parliamentary work is very loosely grounded. It has not been shown that any tangible benefits to anyone would ensue if deputies spent more time on parliamentary work than they do at present. If TDs did find themselves with much more time on their hands as a result of a reduction in their constituency work, it is perfectly possible that the consequence would simply be that the recent downward trend in the number continuing with their extra-parliamentary occupation would be reversed. This is not to deny that there might well be advantages in tilting the balance of deputies' activities somewhat away from constituency work and towards parliamentary work. It is to suggest that this part of the case against STV has not been addressed, let alone established, by the opponents of STV, and that the benefits which would supposedly outweigh the costs of changing the electoral system have not been established.

Should deputies' casework loads be lower?

The fourth and final assumption underlying the view that the electoral system should be changed to reduce deputies' casework load is that TDs should be concentrating on parliamentary duties rather than constituency work. Some cite the constitution to back up the argument, observing that it makes no mention of deputies having a brokerage role, but this is no more realistic than arguing that political parties should not play an important role in politics since the constitution does not mention them either. It sometimes seems to be taken for granted, both by deputies and by commentators, that the common weal would be better served if TDs spent less time on constituency work, but it can also be argued that TDs are performing a necessary service by the constituency work they do.

The balance of evidence seems to suggest that deputies' efforts do achieve something for their constituents. Komito (1984), whose careful examination marks a clear advance on earlier studies (Bax, 1976; Sacks, 1976), concludes that

> Bureaucrats responded to politicians when they would not to voters... Brokerage sometimes forced a case to be reviewed, a decision to be speeded up, or a service to be provided... Brokerage often resulted in the provision of a legitimate service which might not otherwise have been obtained.
> (pp. 183 and 184)

A TD's intervention can help, not by winning benefits that constituents are not entitled to, but by ensuring that they know what they are entitled to and how to obtain it, and by speeding up the provision of their entitlements. Roche (1982) makes a similar point. He shows that deputies report that most of the cases presented to them concern delays in the Department of Social Welfare, and concludes that public representatives, unlike most voters, 'possess the limited expertise, the authority and the access needed to bring a case to a successful conclusion' (Roche, 1982, p. 107).

As against this, two analyses of Dáil questions have taken a rather different view. Kerrigan (1983) concluded that about 60 per cent of questions are 'for electoral use', i.e. they are asked purely to enhance the image of the deputy. This seems a sweeping judgement, based as it is on the assumption that every question relating to an individual case has a purely electoral motivation and could not possibly arise out of maladministration or the sheer difficulty of getting an answer in any other way. However, Kerrigan backs up his label by ascertaining, in an analysis of 745 of these individual-related questions, that 27 per cent of them were 'faulty', in that they contained inaccurate or insufficient details. In these cases at least, questions were not highlighting injustices; instead, 'any and all entreaties are shovelled together and thrown into the Dáil'.

A rather similar conclusion was reached by another study, this time of Dáil questions to the Minister for Social Welfare later in 1983 (Relate, 1983). This makes rather high-handed assertions as to what sort of questions TDs 'should' and 'should not' ask, and it seems that all questions relating to individual cases come into the latter category as far as the anonymous author is concerned. The author argues that only one of the 351 questions looked at brought about an improvement for the person concerned, apart from a 'few cases' where a question may speed up a payment. Many of the rest, it is said, were based on inaccurate information, and 'it is obvious...that the TDs made no attempt to find out the most basic details about the case'. However, the author does admit that 'most of the problems of misunderstanding need never have arisen if the Department of Social Welfare explained clearly why a person didn't get a benefit or got a reduced rate'. A relevant point here is that if TDs simply 'shovel cases into' the Dáil without even a cursory examination, they can hardly complain that such cases occupy much of their time.

When deputies debated Dáil reform early in 1983, although many TDs expressed the wish that they had less constituency work, only two (John Kelly and Maurice Manning, both academics) cast overt doubt on its usefulness as far as constituents are concerned. In contrast, many TDs stressed that they felt it was useful. Alan Shatter (*Dáil Debates*, 339: 550, 27 January 1983) said: 'Much constituency work is due to the inefficiency of the Government, the civil service and Government Departments in their administrative affairs which renders it impossible for an individual to get simple answers to simple queries without going to their local TD'. Bernard Durkan, too, defended the holding of clinics and engagement in constituency work: 'I believe there are many people who would not get their rights unless someone took up the cudgels on their behalf' (*Dáil Debates*, 339: 1138, 3 February 1983). A similar viewpoint was expressed by other deputies, including Frank Fahey, Myra Barry, Nora Owen, Michael Keating and John Boland (*Dáil Debates*, 339: 462, 575, 634, 948 and 1055–6, 26 January – 3 February 1983), although the last two also argued that some at least of their letter-writing activity was merely a 'charade', consisting as it did of pretending to be able to get preferential treatment for constituents (*Dáil Debates*, 339: 944–6 and 1066, 2 and 3 February 1983). Gene Fitzgerald added the point that by engaging in constituency work, deputies not only assist constituents but also keep in touch with the people and become aware of areas of government activity where problems are arising (*Dáil Debates*, 339: 924, 2 February 1983).

As with the volume of deputies' casework, then, it is hard to draw firm and reliable conclusions, but it seems reasonable to suggest that some at least of what deputies do is valuable from the viewpoint of their constituents, even if some is not. The claim that TDs' representations are themselves the main cause of the delays they complain about, in that they simply clog up the works, and that without them all government departments would function to the complete satisfaction of their clients, is ingenious but seems rather too trusting of the administrative agencies.

Other electoral systems

If STV were abolished, what could replace it? There are five main options: the single-member plurality system, lists with preferential voting, lists without preferential voting, a hybrid system, or the Alternative Vote.

Single-member plurality system

The single-member plurality system ('the British system') seems to have little support in Ireland. It has twice been rejected by the electorate; it produces an obvious and high amount of disproportionality; and it is under severe criticism in some of the countries where it is used, such as the United Kingdom, Canada and New Zealand. In the Dáil debates of 1983, only one TD (Rory O'Hanlon) suggested that SMP voting should even be 'looked at'. It is hard to see it being offered to the electorate again.

List systems with preferential voting

A list system with preferential voting (i.e. voters can cast a preference for one or more of their party's candidates, as in, for example, Italy, Finland and Denmark) also seems a non-starter. It would not, of itself, bring about any significant changes in proportionality or government stability, and in particular the aspect of intra-party competition would still be present.

Perhaps it should not be dismissed quite so hastily, as there is an argument which sees it as likely to have different consequences from STV. In particular, Katz (1984, p. 142) states that 'there remains a substantial difference between intraparty choice under STV and the choice allowed in most other systems'. The main difference is that under list systems with preferential voting, deputies would need to concern themselves only with the support of those who will, or might, vote for their party, whereas under STV even the fifth or sixth preference of a supporter of another party could be important, so that deputies need to be concerned about their reputation in every voter's eyes.

It is hard, though, to see how this could make any difference to deputies' incentive to respond to their constituents' demands. In theory, deputies could safely refuse to help those they felt certain would never vote for their party, since there would no longer be any prospect of receiving a lower preference vote. But they would surely be more likely to assume, as they do at present, that everyone approaching them was a potential supporter, and so they would still feel it worthwhile to assist every constituent who sought help. Besides, there would be a serious problem of representation if deputies applied political tests to constituents before deciding whether or not to help them. So the type of change in deputies' behaviour seemingly predicted by Katz is unlikely to happen and could well be seen as undesirable if it did.

Another objection to a list system with intra-party preferential voting (which is recommended by Katz, 1984, p. 145) is that it would greatly increase Fianna Fáil's bonus of seats by leaving Fine Gael, the PDs and Labour with wasted votes which they could no longer transfer to each other. This could be overcome only by the technique of *apparentement*: the unused votes of parties which declare that they are contesting the election in alliance are pooled, and seats are awarded to the alliance if the number of votes in the pool is large enough (Lakeman, 1974, p. 98). One problem with *apparentement* is that the question of alliances is decided by party leaders, whereas under STV party voters can express their own attitude to other parties.

List systems without preferential voting

A rigid list system, in which voters can simply express a preference for a party list, with the party itself deciding which candidates receive the seats it wins (as in Israel, France in 1986 and, effectively, in Norway, Sweden, Belgium and the Netherlands), might be more popular with politicians, albeit not with the voters. It would provide PR, but would avoid the element of electoral competition between candidates of the same party which some critics of STV find objectionable. Although, as we saw earlier, such a system seemed unknown to those discussing electoral laws in the 1920s, the idea of party lists may be better understood now. In the debates on Dáil reform in 1983, three deputies (Des O'Malley, Ted Nealon and George Birmingham) suggested that a list system should be considered (along with the Alternative Vote), and it can be assumed that they were thinking of a non-preferential version. Such a system would reduce voter participation in the choice of deputies, but would it, as a corollary, have a positive effect on the behaviour of deputies? We shall consider this further below when discussing the Alternative Vote.

A hybrid system

The fourth type of electoral system which might be considered as an alternative to STV is a hybrid system, under which there would in effect be two different routes to the Dáil. The West German Bundestag is elected in this way: half the deputies are elected under the plurality system, and the other half from non-preferential lists. List seats are allocated to parties in such numbers as to ensure that their total seats (not their list seats) are proportionate to their share of the list votes. A hybrid system in Ireland might see, say, two-thirds of deputies elected under STV in constituencies of the present magnitude, with the other one-third being elected from lists at the provincial or even national level. The latter group of deputies would not be tied to any particular constituency and would, thus, be free to concentrate on parliamentary or ministerial duties. Such a system might be thought complicated, but the same is often said of STV itself, and, besides, the hybrid system does not cause confusion in West Germany. Another objection is that this system might be more proportional than the existing one, with a resulting increase in the difficulty of obtaining stable governments, but this could, if necessary, be overcome by using a relatively high threshold (say 10 per cent of the provincial/national votes) which a party would need to reach in order to qualify for a share of the list seats.

A hybrid scheme was included in the Fine Gael manifesto (p. 24) for the February 1987 election, although it is too vague to be evaluated in detail. The scheme proposed is essentially the same as the West German system. The only difference is that the constituency seats would be filled by the Alternative Vote rather than by plurality, a modification which seems pointless since a party's total number of seats is not affected by the outcomes in the single-member constituencies. This proposal was clearly the brainchild of Garret FitzGerald (he adumbrated it in his last Dáil speech as Taoiseach – see *Dáil Debates*, 370: 3846, 19 December 1986), and it remains to be seen whether the post-FitzGerald Fine Gael retains interest in it.

The Alternative Vote

The fifth and final option, the Alternative Vote (STV in single-member constituencies, which is used at by-elections) has emerged as the most likely candidate to replace STV if any change is made in the future. In the 1983 Dáil debates, two deputies (Maurice Manning and Michael Keating) came out in favour of it, and four others (the three who also said a list system should be considered, plus Rory O'Hanlon) mentioned it as one of two possibilities. Most importantly, the introduction of the Alternative Vote (AV) has been Fianna Fáil policy since the party's 1984 Ard-Fheis endorsed a motion to this effect, reportedly (*Irish Press*, 1 April 1984) by 'a large majority'. Both the party's then spokesman, Bobby Molloy, and the *Irish Press* reporter, said that this system would have considerable support among TDs of both Fianna Fáil and Fine Gael, as it would free them from many constituency duties and would make life harder for minor parties and independents and thus produce 'more clear cut results' at general elections. In July 1986, the Progressive Democrats' director of policy, Stephen O'Byrnes, expressed his support for AV (*Irish Press*, 15 July 1986 and 21 July 1986).

The first point to be made about AV is that it is not a PR system, because it is based on single-member constituencies. Any single-member constituency system is, by definition, a 'winner takes all' system within each constituency, regardless of whether the winner is determined by a plurality or a majority formula. The tendency in Ireland to describe AV as 'PR in single-member constituencies' is presumably based on the belief that since AV differs from the British system, and since the British system is not PR, AV must be a form of PR. Article 12.2.3 of Bunreacht na hÉireann, which requires that the President be elected 'on the system of proportional representation', embodies this misconception. 'PR in single-member constituencies' is a contradiction in terms, as there is no way of dividing up a single seat proportionately.

Table 10.1 Results of Australian general elections 1975–84 under Alternative Vote

		1975	1977	1980	1983	1984
Labor	% vote	42.8	39.6	45.1	49.5	47.5
	% seats	28.3	30.7	40.8	60.0	55.4
Liberals	% vote	41.8	38.1	37.4	34.4	34.4
	% seats	53.5	54.0	43.2	26.4	30.4
National/Country	% vote	11.3	10.0	8.9	9.2	10.6
	% seats	18.1	15.3	16.0	13.6	14.2
Others	% vote	4.1	12.3	8.6	6.9	7.4
	% seats	0	0	0	0	0

Source: Mackie and Rose, 1982, pp. 16–19; Hughes, 1983, p. 336.

How would AV work out in practice? It is used only in Australia, where, as would be expected from a non-PR system, it produces a sizeable bonus in seats for the largest party. Table 10.1 shows that Labour and small parties generally suffer at the expense of the Liberal–National coalition, although the swing of the pendulum favoured Labour in 1983 and 1984. Above all, it shows that whatever merits AV may have, being a form of PR is not one of them. The electoral system used in France (except in 1986) is similar: it is a single-member two-ballot system, in which, if no candidate wins a majority on the first round of voting, a second round is held and the candidate with a plurality of votes is declared the winner. This too produces highly disproportional results. For example, in 1981 the Socialists won 56.3 per cent of the seats with only 37.8 per cent of the votes (Mackie and Rose, 1982, pp. 137 and 139).

What sort of results AV would produce in Ireland, given the present fluidity in the Irish party system, is a matter for speculation, but it is clear that considerable disproportionality is possible and that very few, if any, independents or Workers' Party candidates would be elected. Labour, too, would find its Dáil representation practically eliminated without a transfer agreement with another party. All of these prospects, of course, might enhance the appeal of AV in the eyes of the major parties.

The Alternative Vote, like any other single-member system, would also produce regionally-biased parliamentary groups. Fianna Fáil would be likely to take nearly all of the seats in the west of Ireland, where it wins over 50 per cent of the votes, and very few in many areas of the east and south. Consequently, the Fianna Fáil parliamentary party would be dominated by western deputies, whereas hardly any Fine Gael TDs would be from the west. The parties would inevitably be less responsive to the areas from which they had few deputies, and this would no doubt be reflected in the policies of governments, as it has been in recent years in Britain, where the Conservatives hold relatively few seats in northern England and Scotland. Regional divisions would thus be accentuated. In addition, fewer voters would be represented in the Dáil by the candidate who received their first preference. In the November 1982 election, 71.4 per cent of voters saw their first choice elected, but in the Australian elections of 1980 and 1983 the figures were only 53.5 per cent and 55.2 per cent respectively (Gallagher, 1986, p. 266; Wright, 1986, p. 131). Compared with nearly half of Australian voters, relatively few Irish voters (16.4 per cent at the February 1987 election) are not represented by a deputy of the party to whom they gave their first preference.

The question remains as to what changes AV or a non-preferential list system would make to TDs' behaviour. It may well be that it would bring about much less change than is sometimes assumed. For one thing, it is hard to see how the volume of demands coming in to TDs would be significantly reduced. AV might reduce it slightly, by cutting out cases from people or groups who currently 'do the rounds' of several TDs' clinics, but the majority of cases would remain. The argument appears to be, in fact, not that it would reduce the volume of requests for a TD's assistance, but that it would insulate deputies against the need to respond to these requests. This, if it happened, might make life easier for TDs, but offers little to anyone else. In any case, it might not happen, for in small constituencies – under AV, each TD would represent only 20,000 people – other sanctions might be employed against a deputy who professed himself too busy to deal with what he regarded as unnecessary requests for help. Irish proponents of AV may not be aware that Australian MPs 'complain of the pressure of electoral work and the constant requests for help from their constituents' (Rydon, 1985, p. 99).

A second factor to be borne in mind is that if competition between candidates of the same party was removed from the election itself, it would simply be transferred to the nomination stage. Local party members would decide on the candidate(s) and, if a list system was used, their position on the list. At present, deputies and aspiring deputies build up a base in their local party organisation, and ensure that the members of their network channel constituents' problems to them rather than to another deputy (see Carty, 1981, pp. 130–4). Under a new electoral system, a deputy who neglected this activity would be vulnerable to being unseated at the nomination stage by a challenger who had built up a stronger base within the local party.

Amendments to STV

Finally, it is worth mentioning two alterations which might profitably be made to the existing system. One would be the abolition of by-elections, which are an absurd anomaly under a PR system. They demonstrate again Ireland's excessive dependence on British practice in this whole area, since no other country in the world to use a PR system employs by-elections to fill casual vacancies arising between general elections, for the obvious reason that they make it impossible for a local minority to retain a seat won at a general election, even if its support has increased in the meantime. An improvement would be to adopt either the procedure used for European Parliament elections, when the parties appoint 'reserves' at the time of the general election, or the practice in Malta and Tasmania (the other places where STV is employed), where the vacating deputy's papers are recounted and the seat is awarded to the candidate elected from them. A second desirable amendment would be to randomise the order of names on the ballot paper, in view of the well-attested advantage (see Robson and Walsh, 1974) of candidates whose names begin with letters early in the alphabet; of the 166 deputies elected in February 1987, 45 had surnames beginning with the letters A, B or C, and there were 89 in the A–H range. Consideration could also be given to introducing the Gregory method for the distribution of surpluses, because the present random sampling technique introduces an unnecessary arbitrary element into the counting of votes and can lead to the 'wrong' candidate being elected (Coakley and O'Neill, 1984; Gallagher and Unwin, 1986).

Conclusion

It has been argued that the case against STV in Ireland is not a strong one. Its record in delivering proportionality – not that this seems to be a prime criterion for most of those advocating change – is impeccable, and this has not been purchased at the expense of government stability, for the incidence of general elections in Ireland is lower than in, for example, Britain. Most of the criticism directed against STV in Ireland in recent years has concerned its alleged tendency to weaken the Dáil by compelling deputies to engage extensively in constituency work for sheer electoral survival. It has been argued here that this line of criticism is rather muddled. STV is neither a sufficient nor a necessary cause of the brokerage work performed by TDs. Moreover, the view that deputies should not devote so much time to brokerage, because this prevents them making some potentially weighty but unspecified contribution to solving the nation's problems, can be questioned. If TDs are really serious about wanting to reduce the brokerage demands made by voters, they would be better employed tackling the problem at source. Establishing the office of Ombudsman represented one step in this direction, but it is curious that they have shown so little interest in ideas like establishing citizens' advice bureaux and accessible administrative tribunals, or the decentralisation of decision-making.

All of this is not to argue that STV is a perfect electoral system, or that the subject of electoral reform is not worthwhile. Examination of the alternative possibilities, though, suggests that none is likely to rectify the alleged defects of STV, and most would increase disproportionality, penalising all but the largest parties, without making governments more stable. As yet, the case in favour of any of the alternatives remains to be clearly stated.

COMMENTARY BY DAVID M. FARRELL

It is instructive to re-read Gallagher's 1987 article alongside his most recent statement on this question (2005). In the intervening period, there have been a series of electoral reforms in the established democracies – 14 in total, according to Katz (2005) – as well as the rather colossal wave of electoral system design for the new democracies of East and Central Europe, Latin America, and parts of Africa, thus providing one of the main reasons why the study of electoral systems has become one of the most dynamic parts of the political science discipline (for a good review of the 'maturation' of the field of electoral systems research, see Shugart, 2005). Whereas electoral reform was an extremely unlikely prospect in 1987, two decades later we know that not only is it more likely, we also know a lot more about what it might entail, how it might occur, and how successful it might be. We also know that, with the exception of some prominent sub-national cases of electoral system design (including for state/territory parliaments across Australia, local government elections in New Zealand and Scotland, and still ongoing efforts to reform elections in the Canadian province of British Columbia) and at national level the briefest exception in Estonia for just one election, the Single Transferable Vote (STV) has not proven a popular option among electoral reform policy-makers. Despite all this, despite the fact that we now know that electoral reform can occur and how it might occur, despite the fact that the trend is away from (rather than to) STV, Gallagher's views on whether Ireland needs a new electoral system remain unchanged (Gallagher, 2005).

We know that the absence of electoral reform in Ireland is not for want of trying on the part of some prominent politicians. The entrenchment of STV in the Irish constitution has clearly 'helped' in this regard – as witnessed by the failed attempts to switch to the single-member plurality system in referendums held in the 1950s and 1960s. But this has not stopped attempts to review the existing system with a view to its possible replacement, most recently the request in 2000 by the then Minister for the Environment, Noel Dempsey, for the All-Party Oireachtas Committee to consider the question 'as a matter of urgency'. The Committee's report was unequivocal in recommending against any reform of the existing electoral system (Gallagher, 2005, p. 528).

Gallagher's 1987 paper reviews the main points generally made in favour of reforming the existing electoral system. In the first instance, and most specifically associated with the reform proposals in the 1950s and 1960s, there is the question of government stability, something that Gallagher (rightly) quickly dismisses as simply not much of a problem in the Irish case, in part because the version of STV used in Ireland has relatively low proportionality trends due to the small district magnitude. (The term 'district magnitude', or 'M', refers simply to constituency size: the general rule of thumb is that an average M of less than 5 produces less than perfect proportionality. Given that constituency size in Ireland falls within the band of 3–5 seats, there is little danger of highly proportional electoral results.) The bigger question – which at the time of Gallagher's paper ironically had not yet featured that prominently in political debates over the system, but which has certainly now become the main bone of contention (FitzGerald, 2003) – was whether STV was the cause of constituency 'turf war' politics in Ireland. This takes up the lion's share of Gallagher's paper, and is its principal contribution.

Pre-Gallagher a casual observer could have been forgiven for concluding that a major factor (if not *the* major factor) behind Irish politicians' love of constituency casework was the electoral system. After all, it makes some sense, for here we have an electoral system that pitches politician against politician (often from the same party) in election battles focused on the constituency. Here we have a system in which literally every vote counts, so that unlike virtually all other electoral systems, politicians are fighting for every and any vote preference they can get ('If you won't give me your number 1, or number 2, can I have your number 3?'). Here we have an electoral system in which, despite all the centralising of campaign strategies that has occurred (Farrell, 2004), the national election campaigns of the parties are more accurately described as 41 separate constituency contests.

In short, and to put things more technically, the focus of criticism has switched from the two most prominent features of electoral system design ('district magnitude' and 'electoral formula') to the third feature which for so long – but no longer (Shugart, 2005) – remained neglected in electoral system research generally: namely 'ballot structure'. The point at issue is that STV's ballot structure design, in which voters can rank order all the candidates on the ballot paper regardless of party affiliation, promotes a candidate-orientation that in Ireland manifests itself in the form of brokerage politics.

In his 1987 paper, Gallagher clinically disabuses the casual observer of any view that STV is to blame for the way Irish politics has come to be. His argument follows four steps, carefully and painstakingly dismantling a series of (often implicit) assumptions or hypotheses that drive the argument that STV leads to brokerage politics. The first question – which is the core one – is whether STV causes brokerage. Gallagher's analysis is that it is less a case of the electoral system *causing* the style of politics, and more one of it *facilitating* that style, which is consistent with comparative analysis that demonstrates a statistical relationship between electoral system design and the constituency orientation of politicians (Farrell and Scully, 2007). This leads naturally to the second question, whether brokerage would exist without STV, to which the answer is that it most likely would, especially given that the Irish electorate evidently expect this of their politicians (Marsh *et al*, 2007). The third question is whether brokerage is the cause of the Dáil's weakness. It is impossible to disagree with Gallagher's observation that:

> even if brokerage duties were removed entirely from TDs' backs, and if in consequence a Dáil career attracted the philosopher-kings who some seem to feel would make better deputies than the present incumbents, it still does not follow that the Dáil would be significantly stronger *vis-à-vis* government, let alone in any sense a better institution.

Finally, there is the issue of whether TDs' casework loads should be lower, freeing up their time to focus on parliamentary work. Gallagher provides evidence of how constituency casework does actually achieve results, thus begging the question of whether good linkage between politicians and their constituents is not necessarily 'bad'.

In one respect, and for obvious reasons, the paper is somewhat out of date and this is over the question of what electoral system might replace STV were there to be electoral reform. Gallagher reviews the obvious alternatives which, at the time he was writing, pointed to the Alternative Vote (the system used for electing the Irish President) as the most obvious candidate. At that stage, the 'German system' was not seen as a likely contender, in large part because it was then largely unique to (West) Germany. Twenty years later, the mixed-member system (as this family has come to be known) has become one of the most fashionable of electoral systems (Shugart and Wattenberg, 2001) and the electoral system of choice for those promoting reform in Ireland (Laver, 1998).

Quite apart from the question of *change of* electoral system, there is the separate issue – dealt with in rather cursory fashion towards the end of Gallagher's 1987 paper – about *changes to* the electoral system. The onset of computer technology, the (slightly) greater use of STV in other jurisdictions, and the availability of more information on how STV operates elsewhere, makes it possible to give more thought to alterations to the existing system (Farrell and McAllister, 2006), few if any of which would necessitate constitutional reform in order to be implemented. Gallagher refers to three: replacement of by-elections with the 'count back' procedure, randomisation (or 'rotation') of candidates' names on the ballot paper, and the adoption of more appropriate methods for transferring surplus ballot papers than the current random transfer procedure (such as the Weighted Inclusive Gregory method recently adopted in Western Australia). We now know that the (so far failed) experiment to introduce computerised voting and counting to Irish elections would have facilitated such needed 'tweaks' to the STV system, and so assuming that computerised voting is eventually adopted, we can expect to see change in the future.

Gallagher's 1987 paper stands the test of time (which is more than can be said for the rather flimsy binding in the early volumes of *Irish Political Studies*!), and its arguments remain highly pertinent two decades later. It is still the first (and last) thing someone should read to gain a true understanding of the issues associated with Ireland's electoral system, the questions raised about why (and how) it might be reformed, and the reasons why it shouldn't be reformed.

Notes

1 I should like to thank Michael Laver, Peter Mair and Richard Sinnott for comments on an earlier draft.
2 The concept of the 'effective number of parties' was devised by Laakso and Taagepera (1979). It is essentially a measure of fragmentation: the higher the figure, the more fragmented the parliament. Its usefulness is elaborated in Lijphart (1984, pp. 120–3).
3 The assumption made by critics of STV in Ireland does seem to relate to intra-party competition generally rather than to STV specifically, although it could be argued, as indicated in the discussion on list systems with preferential voting in the last section of the paper, that there is a significant difference between the two.

References

Baerwald, Hans H. (1979) 'Committees in the Japanese Diet', pp. 327–60 in John D. Lees and Malcolm Shaw (eds.) *Committees in Legislatures: A Comparative Analysis*. Oxford: Martin Robertson.

Barrington, Thomas J. (1980) *The Irish Administrative System*. Dublin: Institute of Public Administration.

Bax, Mart (1976) *Harpstrings and Confessions: Machine-Style Politics in the Irish Republic*. Assen: Van Gorcum.

Bogdanor, Vernon (ed.) (1985a) *Representatives of the People?* London: Gower.

Bogdanor, Vernon (1985b) 'Conclusion', pp. 293–301 in Vernon Bogdanor (ed.) *Representatives of the People?* London: Gower.

Buckland, Patrick (1972) *Irish Unionism – Volume One: The Anglo-Irish and the New Ireland, 1885–1922*. Dublin: Gill and Macmillan.

Carty, R. Kenneth (1981) *Party and Parish Pump: Electoral Politics in Ireland*. Waterloo, Ontario: Wilfred Laurier University Press.

Chubb, Basil (1982) *The Government and Politics of Ireland*. Second Edition. London: Longman.

Chubb, Basil (1983) *A Source Book of Irish Government*. Dublin: Institute of Public Administration.

Coakley, John and Gerald O'Neill (1984) 'Chance in Preferential Voting Systems: An Unacceptable Element in Irish Electoral Law?', *Economic and Social Review*, 16 (1), pp. 1–18.

D'Onofrio, Francesco (1979) 'Committees in the Italian Parliament', pp. 61–101 in John D. Lees and Malcolm Shaw (eds.) *Committees in Legislatures: A Comparative Analysis*. Oxford: Martin Robertson.

Farrell, Brian (1985) 'Ireland: From Friends and Neighbours to Clients and Partisans', pp. 237–64 in Vernon Bogdanor (ed.) *Representatives of the People?* London: Gower.

Farrell, David (2004) 'Before Campaigns were "Modern": Irish Electioneering in Times Past', pp. 178–97 in Tom Garvin, Maurice Manning and Richard Sinnott (eds.) *Dissecting Irish Politics: Essays in Honour of Brian Farrell*. Dublin: UCD Press.

Farrell, David and Ian McAllister (2006) *The Australian Electoral System: Origins, Variations and Consequences*. Sydney: University of New South Wales Press.

Farrell, David and Roger Scully (2007) *Representing Europe's Citizens? Electoral Institutions and the Failure of Parliamentary Representation*. Oxford: Oxford University Press.

FitzGerald, Garret (2003) *Reflections on the Irish State*. Dublin: Irish Academic Press.

Gallagher, Michael (1985a) *Political Parties in the Republic of Ireland*. Manchester: Manchester University Press.

Gallagher, Michael (1985b) 'Social Backgrounds and Local Orientations of Members of the Irish Dáil', *Legislative Studies Quarterly*, 10 (3), pp. 373–94.

Gallagher, Michael (1986) 'The Political Consequences of the Electoral System in the Republic of Ireland', *Electoral Studies*, 5 (3), pp. 253–75.

Gallagher, Michael (2005) 'Ireland: The Discreet Charm of PR-STV', pp. 511–33 in Michael Gallagher and Paul Mitchell (eds.) *The Politics of Electoral Systems*. Oxford: Oxford University Press.

Gallagher, Michael and Antony Richard Unwin (1986) 'Electoral Distortion under STV Random Sampling Procedures', *British Journal of Political Science*, 16 (2), pp. 243–53.

Giddings, Philip (1985) 'What Has Been Achieved?', pp. 367–81 in Gavin Drewry (ed.) *The New Select Committees: A Study of the 1979 Reforms*. Oxford: Clarendon.

Grofman, Bernard and Arend Lijphart (eds.) (1986) *Electoral Laws and Their Political Consequences*. New York: Agathon Press.

Gudgin, Graham and Peter J. Taylor (1979) *Seats, Votes and the Spatial Organisation of Elections*. London: Pion.

Hand, Geoffrey (1979) 'Ireland', pp. 121–39 in Geoffrey Hand, Jacques Georgel and Christopher Sasse (eds.) *European Electoral Systems Handbook*. London: Butterworths.

Hughes, Christopher (1985) 'The Relationship of the Citizen to "His" Member of Parliament in the Swiss System of Government', pp. 224–36 in Vernon Bogdanor (ed.) *Representatives of the People?* London: Gower.

Hughes, Colin A. (1983) 'Appendix C', pp. 335–7 in Howard R. Penniman (ed.) *Australia at the Polls, 1980 and 1983*. Washington, DC: American Enterprise Institute.

Johnson, Nevil (1979) 'Committees in the West German Bundestag', pp. 102–47 in John D. Lees and Malcolm Shaw (eds.) *Committees in Legislatures: A Comparative Analysis*. Oxford: Martin Robertson.

Katz, Richard S. (1984) 'The Single Transferable Vote and Proportional Representation', pp. 135–45 in Arend Lijphart and Bernard Grofman (eds.) *Choosing an Electoral System: Issues and Alternatives*. New York: Praeger.

Katz, Richard (2005) 'Why are There so Many (or so Few) Electoral Reforms?', pp. 57–78 in Michael Gallagher and Paul Mitchell (eds.) *The Politics of Electoral Systems*. Oxford: Oxford University Press.

Kerrigan, Gene (1983) 'Question Marks', *Magill*, 6 (11), August, pp. 27–30.

King, Anthony (1981) 'What Do Elections Decide?', pp. 293–324 in David Butler, Howard R. Penniman and Austin Ranney (eds.) *Democracy at the Polls*. Washington, DC: American Enterprise Institute.

Komito, Lee (1984) 'Irish Clientelism: A Reappraisal', *Economic and Social Review*, 15 (3), pp. 173–94.

Laakso, Markku and Rein Taagepera (1979) 'Effective Number of Parties: A Measure with Application to West Europe', *Comparative Political Studies*, 12 (1), pp. 3–27.

Lakeman, Enid (1974) *How Democracies Vote*. Fourth Edition. London: Faber and Faber.

Laver, Michael (1998) *A New Electoral System for Ireland?* Dublin: The Policy Institute, Trinity College Dublin.

Lijphart, Arend (1984) *Democracies*. New Haven, CT: Yale University Press.

Lijphart, Arend (1985) 'The Field of Electoral Systems Research: A Critical Survey', *Electoral Studies*, 4 (1), pp. 3–14.

Mackie, Thomas T. and Richard Rose (1982) *The International Almanac of Electoral History*. Second Edition. London: Macmillan.

Mair, Peter (1979) 'The Autonomy of the Political: The Development of the Irish Party System', *Comparative Politics*, 11 (4), pp. 445–65.

Marsh, Michael, Richard Sinnott, John Garry and Fiachra Kennedy (2007) *The Irish Voter: Parties, Issues and Candidates*. Manchester: Manchester University Press.

Mezey, Michael L. (1979) *Comparative Legislatures*. Durham, NC: Duke University Press.

O'Connell, Declan (1983) 'Proportional Representation and Intra-Party Competition in Tasmania and the Republic of Ireland', *Journal of Commonwealth and Comparative Politics*, 21 (1), pp. 45–70.

O'Halpin, Eunan (1986) 'Oireachtas Committees: Experience and Prospects', *Seirbhís Phoibli*, 7 (2), pp. 3–9.

O'Leary, Cornelius (1979) *Irish Elections 1918–1977*. Dublin: Gill and Macmillan.

Parker, Anthony J. (1983) 'Localism and Bailiwicks: The Galway West Constituency in the 1977 General Election', *Proceedings of the Royal Irish Academy*, 83 (C2), pp. 17–36.

Relate (1983) 'Dáil Questions on Social Welfare', *Relate*, 11 (3), December, pp. 2–5.

Review Body on Higher Remuneration in the Public Sector (1972) *Report to the Minister for Finance*. Dublin: Stationery Office.

Review Body on Higher Remuneration in the Public Sector (1979) *Report to the Minister for the Public Service*. Dublin: Stationery Office.

Robson, Christopher and Brendan Walsh (1974) 'The Importance of Positional Voting Bias in the Irish General Election of 1973', *Political Studies*, 22 (2), pp. 191–203.

Roche, Richard (1982) 'The High Cost of Complaining Irish Style', *Journal of Irish Business and Administrative Research*, 4 (2), pp. 98–108.

Rydon, Joan (1985) 'MPs and Their Constituents in Australia', pp. 86–102 in Vernon Bogdanor (ed.) *Representatives of the People?* London: Gower.

Sacks, Paul M. (1976) *The Donegal Mafia: An Irish Political Machine.* New Haven, CT: Yale University Press.

Shaw, Malcolm (1979) 'Conclusion', pp. 361–434 in John D. Lees and Malcolm Shaw (eds.) *Committees in Legislatures: A Comparative Analysis.* Oxford: Martin Robertson.

Shugart, Matthew (2005) 'Comparative Electoral Systems Research: The Maturation of a Field and New Challenges Ahead', pp. 25–57 in Michael Gallagher and Paul Mitchell (eds.) *The Politics of Electoral Systems.* Oxford: Oxford University Press.

Shugart, Matthew and Martin Wattenberg (eds.) (2001) *Mixed-Member Electoral Systems: The Best of Both Worlds?* Oxford: Oxford University Press.

Steiner, Kurt (1972) *Politics in Austria.* Boston, MA: Little, Brown.

Sturm, Roland (1986) 'Elections and the Electoral System', pp. 55–70 in Brian Girvin and Roland Sturm (eds.) *Politics and Society in Contemporary Ireland.* Aldershot: Gower.

Thomas, Alistair H. (1985) 'Members of Parliament and Access to Politics in Scandinavia', pp. 199–223 in Vernon Bogdanor (ed.) *Representatives of the People?* London: Gower.

Whyte, John H. (1966) *Dáil Deputies: Their Work, Its Difficulties, Possible Remedies.* Dublin: Tuairim Pamphlet.

Wright, Jack F.H. (1986) 'Australian Experience with Majority-Preferential and Quota-Preferential Systems', pp. 124–38 in Bernard Grofman and Arend Lijphart (eds.) *Electoral Laws and Their Political Consequences.* New York: Agathon Press.

11 Religion, national identity and political change in modern Ireland[1]

John Coakley

Originally published in *Irish Political Studies*, 17 (1), 2002, pp. 4–28.

Conventional historical definitions of important time periods frequently clash with formal calendar definitions. In the judgement of many historians, for example, the twentieth century began not in 1900 but in 1918; the nineteenth century, similarly, can be seen as having begun not in 1800 but in 1815; and there are those who argue that it really only began in 1848. When does 'modern Ireland' begin? In conventional discourse, it may well have begun as recently as the 1990s, or, at the earliest, by a date at which the twentieth century was well advanced. For historians, the concept of modernity is more elastic and it may, indeed, be stretched out to cover four or five centuries. Modern history began, in this view, with the Renaissance; and modern Ireland began in 1603, if we are to cite the title of the great work of one of the country's most distinguished historians, the late J.C. Beckett (1981).

The social scientist's understanding of modernity tends to be rather narrower. Although the word lacks an agreed meaning and obviously rests on boundaries that are relative, in the minds of many social scientists it implies an economy that has advanced well into the capitalist phase, a society in which spatial and occupational mobility are matched by high levels of educational attainment and literacy, and a polity in which the rights of the individual and basic democratic values have taken at least tentative root (for an early, classic statement, see Lerner, 1958; the term and the concept were subsequently the subject of vigorous debate, though this has been largely sidelined by 'new' issues such as globalisation).

The object of this article is to provide a general interpretative overview of the interplay between religion and electoral politics in an Ireland that had emerged by the end of the nineteenth century as a society to which the adjective 'modern' could legitimately, if not necessarily uncontentiously, be applied. More specifically, the paper looks at the interplay over a long time span (from the mid-nineteenth to the late twentieth century) between four types of division: the religious boundary, the ethnic frontier, the electoral divide and the political border. While the relationships between these dimensions are complex and multi-directional, only one subset of these is explored: the impact that religion has had on geopolitical arrangements, both directly and as mediated through patterns of ethnic identity and electoral behaviour.

The broad picture that emerges from this analysis begins with a bipolar religious denominational axis that permits us to distinguish between predominantly Protestant zones and overwhelmingly Catholic ones on the island of Ireland, but that also requires us to recognise a high degree of interdenominational spatial mingling between these; and the character of this polarisation has been changing as the Catholic share of the population has increased. Although the religious division once coincided starkly with a relatively clearly defined line of ethnic division, this pattern has altered considerably in recent decades, undermining the formerly clear-cut character of religion as an ethnic determinant. The dynamics of the relationship between religion and ethnic identity have taken very different forms in the two parts of Ireland, and their articulation in electoral politics has followed contrasting paths in the north and the south. From a comparative perspective, electoral politics in the north was exceptionally stable from 1885 to 1969, but was utterly disrupted by unpatterned electoral rebellion in the 1970s. The south's period of electoral instability spanned the period from 1918 to the 1920s, and was followed by remarkable stability since then. These developments had an impact on the character of the two Irish states, but also themselves reflected some of the political consequences of partition. We may now examine these four dimensions in turn.

Religious divisions

The significance of religion for political life in Ireland is so widely acknowledged that it is not necessary here to rehearse its origins or to summarise its social and political influence.[2] Instead, four points about the pattern of religious affiliation in Ireland are worth making; each of them has had particular social and political consequences.

First, the religious boundary is exceptionally clear-cut at the individual level. The child is typically marked with the symbols of religious affiliation at an early stage, perhaps within days of birth. While it may be possible to shake off outward signs of religious commitment and inner belief later in life (or even to manage never to acquire them in the first place), a baptismal record can never be deleted. At least at the level of formal allocation of individuals to a small number of denominational categories, religious affiliation is relatively easily measurable.

This remark needs to be modified by drawing attention to certain features of religion that qualify its categorical nature. It is true that some are born into an entirely secular family life, but absence of religion is itself a belief system and the religious boundary applies here too, at least in an exclusionary sense. It is also true that some technically distinct religions may be theologically adjacent or identical (for example, Catholicism and Orthodoxy, especially when their area of overlap in the Uniate churches is considered). It is also the case that some conflicting belief systems – or ones that vary in the emphasis that they place on central articles of faith or practices – may find a home within a single organisational structure, as in the case of Pietism within the Lutheran churches of Northern Europe in the eighteenth century, or Methodism within the Church of Ireland in the nineteenth century. It is also clear that formal adherence to a particular belief system may not be incompatible with rejection of its principles (the phenomenon of the formally atheistic Communist Party secretary who was a practising Catholic was not unknown in Poland, nor is the vicar who is a closet atheist absent from the Anglican tradition). Finally, it is of course true that a single religious denomination may contain an enormous diversity of views, from the sceptical to the committed, and that this may be so great that divisions *within* a particular denomination may be greater than those *between* denominations (the transition from charismatic or radical Catholicism to fundamentalist Protestantism is an example).

But, having said all of that, the reality is that religious labelling is, by comparison with other forms of measurement, exceptionally easy. In the west, religious belief is exclusive, though different religions may appeal to the same foundation myth (they may disagree on its nature and interpretation). Thus Catholics and Protestants alike trace the foundation of their churches back to Jesus Christ, and in Ireland the role of St Patrick is acknowledged by the main Christian churches; indeed, in the past, members of the Roman Catholic, Anglican and Presbyterian churches have alike claimed him exclusively as one of their own; but this does little to diminish the perceived significance of theological differences in the post-Reformation period. The history of census taking in the western world is eloquent testimony to this feature of religious affiliation: individuals can relatively easily be placed in denominational boxes by the observer, even if one of these is a residual agnostic or atheistic one.

The second politically significant feature of religion is its relationship to territory. In the modern world, the clarity with which a human being may be tagged with a denominational label becomes overshadowed as we move from the individual level to that of territorial communities: spatial religious boundaries tend to be zonal rather than linear, and this has been a pronounced feature in the Irish case. By contrast to linguistically divided societies such as Belgium, denominationally divided ones as the Netherlands, Germany, Switzerland or Latvia, though their populations may once have been more clearly spatially segregated, are now denominational patchworks, and this was true also of Bosnia–Hercegovina until the early 1990s. It may be possible to identify territories that belong predominantly to particular religions, but these tend to be separated by mixed zones where there are small majorities, or none.

This may be illustrated clearly in the case of the Catholic–Protestant geographical boundary in Ireland: there is no single means of defining this, and no line can be drawn on a map – or, at least, none that makes administrative sense – that will entirely separate these two major denominations (not to mention attempting to map divisions within Protestantism). This may be seen from Table 11.1, which seeks to define a boundary between Catholic Ireland and Protestant Ireland by using the results of the 1911 census, the main measurement instrument in the hands of those who planned the partition of Ireland. The formula is deceptively simple: units with a Catholic majority are placed on one side of the border, while

Table 11.1 Five versions of the Catholic–Protestant border in Ireland, 1911

Unit	No. of units	Units with a Protestant majority				Nature of northern area
		No.	Area (000 acres)	Population	Percent Protestant	
Province	4	1	5,332	1,581,696	56.3	Coherent
County	39	5	2,152	1,005,250	70.8	Coherent
County district	309	43	1,834	903,867	74.9	Fragmented
District electoral divisions	3,673	424	2,147	959,436	78.2	Highly fragmented
Six-county unit	[1]	[1]	3,352	1,250,531	65.6	Coherent

Source: calculated from *Census of Ireland, 1911.*

Note: 'County' refers to administrative counties, of which there were 39: 33 counties (including one divided into two Ridings) and six county boroughs. 'Nature of northern area' refers to its geographical characteristics where 'fragmented' refers to the existence of Protestant enclaves outside the core territory and Catholic enclaves within it. All but one of the predominantly Protestant county districts lay within the present borders of Northern Ireland (the exception was Cootehill No. 2 rural district, Co. Monaghan). Almost all of the district electoral divisions with Protestant majorities lay within the same area, but there were 18 in Donegal, nine in Monaghan, and six in Cavan, with a further six outside the province of Ulster: two in Wicklow and one each in Dublin, Kildare, Offaly and Sligo. The population figures include military personnel stationed in Ireland.

those with a Protestant majority are placed on the other side. But the problem with this formula is also clear: what kind of unit are we to use? Table 11.1 illustrates the outcome by selecting only four of the large number of possible units: the shape of the border, and the territorial integrity of the two resulting areas, varies greatly depending on whether one selects the province, the county, the county district or the district electoral division as the unit for aggregating individuals. The Table also includes, for comparison, the six-county unit that ultimately became Northern Ireland, the inclusion within this of predominantly Catholic counties with large Protestant minorities clearly reflecting unionist political influence rather than any attempt at delineation of a 'fair' demarcation line. The four 'objective' sets of units considered here produce four very different types of territories, varying, in the case of the 'Protestant' segments, in surface area (from 1.8 to 5.3 million acres), in population (from less than a million to more than a million and a half) and in the size of the minorities they produce (ranging from 21.8 per cent to 43.7 per cent). But these examples could be expanded by considering other units (such as parliamentary constituencies, baronies, parishes, dispensary districts or other administrative units), each of which would produce a very different map of the border.

This illustration of the tendency of religious frontiers to be imprecisely defined leads us into the third point, which focuses specifically on the issue of religion in Ireland. This is to the effect that the religious frontier in Ireland is not only imprecise; it is also changing. After possibly centuries and certainly many decades of relative stability, the demographic relationship between the two major communities has begun to shift, with the higher rate of natural population increase on the part of Catholics gradually translating itself into a steadily increasing overall share of the population. This has had a dramatic impact at local level, with the striking growth of the Catholic population west of the Bann and in Belfast as obvious examples.

One obstacle to the examination of long-term population trends has been instability in the boundaries of the units used for aggregating census data. This has been especially acute since the reform of local government in Northern Ireland in 1973. However, we may try to reconstitute Northern Ireland's old counties by grouping districts and wards, and we may make various allowances for the high non-response rate to the question on religious affiliation in recent censuses. This will lead us to the conclusion that of Northern Ireland's six traditional counties, only two, Antrim and Down, now have Protestant majorities. The long-established Catholic majorities in two others have been consolidated: that of Fermanagh increased from 56 per cent in 1926 to 59 per cent in 1991, while that of Tyrone increased from 55 per cent to 63 per cent over the same period. But between 1926 and 1991 the Catholic share of the population of Armagh increased from 45 per cent to 55 per cent, while that of Londonderry (grouping the city with the county) increased from 48 per cent to 59 per cent.

Indeed, it makes sense to look at the evolution of denominational relations in terms of four zones in the island of Ireland. Defined crudely in terms of counties, these are as follows:

- a predominantly Protestant zone (Antrim and Down), with a sizeable Catholic minority;
- a mixed zone (the other four counties of Northern Ireland), with an increasing Catholic majority;
- a predominantly Catholic zone (the other three counties of Ulster), with a sizeable Protestant minority; and
- an overwhelmingly Catholic zone (the rest of Ireland), with a very small Protestant minority.

Using units as large as counties produces a rather crude result, but the overall pattern emerges very clearly, and is illustrated in Table 11.2: following a drop-off in the Catholic proportion of the population as the nineteenth century proceeded (a consequence in large measure, presumably, of emigration), the Catholic share in all zones increased dramatically in the twentieth century. The political consequences of this are considered later.

The fourth point has to do with the social concomitants of religion in Ireland. The reality is that the religious cleavage was in major respects associated with what might be called a 'denominational division of labour', an association whose impact persists to the present. This linkage is well known, and is at its most stark in terms of occupational status when one contrasts Catholics with members of the Church of Ireland, and in terms of educational attainment and literacy when one contrasts Catholics with Presbyterians. These relationships emerge clearly from

Table 11.2 Percentage of Catholics by denominational zone, 1834–1991

Year	East Ulster	Mid-Ulster	South Ulster	Rest of Ireland	Total
1834	31.4	50.5	74.9	92.8	80.9
1861	29.7	51.6	76.3	91.1	77.7
1911	24.3	50.5	81.8	93.8	75.0
1991 (a)	29.3	54.8	87.6	91.8	75.1
1991 (b)	33.7	59.2	90.0	96.0	80.2

Sources: calculated from *Commissioners of Public Instruction, 1835*; *Census of Ireland, 1861, 1911, 1991*; *Census of Northern Ireland*, 1991.

Note: East Ulster is defined as Antrim, Down and Belfast; Mid-Ulster as the remaining counties of Northern Ireland and South Ulster as Cavan, Donegal and Monaghan. The 1834 figures were derived by grouping data for Established Church parishes (when these overlapped with county boundaries they were included in the county in which the majority of their population lay). The two rows for 1991 express the numbers of Catholics as percentages respectively of (a) the total population and (b) the total population minus those not indicating their religious affiliation and those defining themselves as having no religion.

Table 11.3 Selected male occupational groups by religion, 1861

Occupational group	Catholic	Church of Ireland	Presbyterian	Number
Titled nobility	12.5	87.5	0.0	80
Gentlemen	30.1	63.0	4.0	1,802
Landed proprietors	40.9	50.6	6.2	5,789
Learned professions	41.7	44.7	9.6	11,695
Farmers	76.4	10.4	11.8	413,309
Farm labourers, servants	88.0	5.7	5.9	374,425
Total occupied males	78.3	11.6	8.8	1,844,793

Source: calculated from *Census of Ireland*, 1861.

Note: all figures except those in the last column are percentages. Percentages do not total to 100 due to omission of smaller religious groups.

the census of 1861, the first at which a question on religious affiliation was asked. As Table 11.3 shows, if we extract the four leading social groups from the rest of the population we can see that the more prestigious the group, the lower the proportion of Catholics. Although the numbers in the higher social groups were quite small, their influence was very great indeed. Table 11.4 similarly shows the relationship between religion and literacy in 1861. The lower level of educational attainment of Catholics as measured by this yardstick is obvious.

While the relationship between religions and social position was at its starkest in 1861, it was still pronounced in the early twentieth century, as census reports and local studies show.[3] Although it has survived in more attenuated form to the present in both parts of Ireland, it is, of course, in Northern Ireland that it has been most actively documented. The 1971 census showed that Catholics were disproportionately likely to be unemployed, and to be located lower on the social scale

Table 11.4 Religion and literacy, 1861

Denomination	Percent able to: Read and write	Read only	Neither read nor write
Catholic	35.1	19.1	45.8
Church of Ireland	63.8	20.2	16.0
Presbyterian	60.1	28.1	11.1
All	41.3	20.0	37.8

Source: *Census of Ireland*, 1861.

in terms of occupational status than Protestants (Rowthorn and Wayne, 1988, p. 107). Indeed, there was evidence of further, finer distinctions (to the advantage of Protestants) within particular occupational groups, and even a degree of 'vertical' stratification, with a tendency towards religious segregation by industry (Aunger, 1975). By 1991 there were still marked differences in these respects, and the Catholic unemployment rate was double the Protestant rate (Gallagher *et al*, 1995); and although the relative inequalities diminished during the 1990s, differences remained (Equality Commission for Northern Ireland, 2000).

Ethnic frontiers

Of course, the significance of religion for Irish politics is based mainly on its relationship to ethnic identity, the dimension to which we now turn. The question of cause and effect – whether religion simply promoted a particular pattern of ethnic identity or whether, alternatively, religious affiliation at the level of the family was a choice conditioned by ethnic identity – is being side-stepped here. Instead, we may consider four points about the character of ethnic identity and its relationship to religion.

First, at the level of the individual, ethnic affiliation is exceptionally complex. It lacks the discrete or categorical character of religion; one may identify simultaneously as an Ulster person, as Irish, as British and as European, though it is likely that one will identify very strongly with one of these levels. Difficult though it may be, one may even opt altogether out of ethnic identification, as did the Belorussian-speaking population of eastern Poland in the inter-war period, many of whom described themselves simply as *tuteszy* (meaning 'people from around here', or locals). But there are systems of government (such as consociationalism) that require unambiguous group identification. The British government adopted a cumbersome form of wording to avoid confronting this issue in the Constitution Act of 1973 (which required any government to be 'likely to be widely accepted throughout the community),[4] but it was addressed more explicitly in the Good Friday Agreement, which requires all Members of the Legislative Assembly (MLAs) to identify as unionist or nationalist – but which, unusually in a consociational system, also allows them to opt out by accepting the designation 'other'.

Evidence as to the gains emanating from attempts of this kind to build ethnic identity so explicitly into public policy is mixed. There have been cases such as Moravia in the dying years of the Habsburg monarchy, or inter-war Estonia, where the registration of ethnic minorities as such has been hailed by the minorities themselves as an important step towards their recognition. On the other hand, ethnic labelling may also be used as a basis for discrimination against minorities (as Jewish and other minorities have discovered) or even against majorities (as in the case of South Africa under apartheid). It may also reduce a multi-dimensional pattern of identification to a single dimension, and sow seeds of conflict. As two Hungarian authors warned about the process of ethnic categorisation by states in attempting to measure population size over 60 years ago,

> The censuses forced declarations and decided attitudes out of persons who might otherwise have served as connecting links between divergent groups of human beings – in particular between different nationalities to which they were bound by family ties. Had European science and politics not classified, defined and analysed so much during the nineteenth century – a process by which the rich and valuable syntheses of life were so often torn asunder – the persons referred to, together with the transitional groups of human beings, might well have been employed for the purpose of eliminating antagonism.
>
> (Teleki and Rónai, 1937, p. 28)

Second, the aggregation of complex patterns of individual ethnicity at the level of the territorial collectivity is likely to result, other things being equal, in rather less precise ethnic frontiers. If the spatial edges of denominationally defined communities are fuzzy, in other words, and if religious identity is not perfectly translated into ethnic identity, then the spatial edges of ethnic communities are likely to be still fuzzier.

However, ethnic identity depends not just on religion but on geopolitics. Lines on a map that may initially have been drawn casually, or arbitrarily, can come eventually to have very considerable social significance. The boundary between Northern Ireland and the south, like the border separating Finland from Karelia, or Romania from Moldova, is likely to have had a considerable impact, in the long term, on people's sense of ethnic identity. Ironically, however, in the Irish case this impact is likely to have been more pronounced *within* the two main communities than *between* them. In other words, rather than simply reinforcing the gulf between the two main traditional communities on the island, it is likely to have helped to differentiate northern Catholic from southern Catholic, and northern Protestant from southern Protestant, as part of a wider process of political differentiation. The town of Lifford, for example, is likely now to be closer in a social psychological sense to Letterkenny than to physically adjacent Strabane, and Clones to Monaghan rather than to nearby Newtown Butler. The third and related point has to do with the changing character of ethnic identification. The evidence of a strong convergence between religious and ethnic affiliation at the beginning of the twentieth century is overwhelming. As Frank Wright (1996, p. 515) put it, 'the only difference between the north of Ireland and most other national conflicts was that the settler-native division ran between peoples of different religions rather than of different language groups'. When the location of the border was being debated in the 1920s – especially in the course of the work of the Boundary Commission – the view was widely taken that there was a complete coincidence between religious and political preferences in this respect. But there is evidence that patterns of ethnic identity have been significantly ruptured by partition. Although empirical evidence for these points is limited and many observers would contest them, there is some intuitive support for the following tentative generalisations:

- in the south, nationalism may have lost its Catholic communal basis and increasingly acquired a territorial one, with the development of a new form of state patriotism; but the imagined community of mainstream southern nationalism arguably now has 26 counties rather than 32 (see Power, 1996);
- also in the south, what was a *British* Protestant *ethnic* minority has not alone shrunk in size but has also become an *Irish* Protestant *religious* minority – simultaneously moving closer to the southern majority while distancing itself from its northern co-religionists (Coakley, 1998);
- in the north, while Irish Catholics left on the 'wrong' side of the border in general clung to an older form of Irish identity, significant 'British' identification has appeared, and there are signs of the emergence of a form of 'northern Irish' identity, as may be seen from Table 11.5 (see also Elliott, 2000, pp. 476–82; O'Connor, 1993); and
- also in the north, as may be seen from Table 11.5, although Protestants have normally defined themselves as 'British', there are traces of an 'Ulster' identity, and here, too, there are ambiguous signs of a potentially more inclusive 'Northern Irish' identity that implies a sharing of communal affiliation with northern Catholics (two perceptive and careful assessments of a range of subjective evidence point to the complex and ambiguous nature of Northern Ireland Protestants' 'British' identity; see Loughlin, 1995, and McBride, 1996).

Fourth, because ethnicity is more closely linked to religion than to language, it faces particular challenges in a secular age. In the contemporary world, the public policy importance of language has in general been increasing, while that of religion has been diminishing. Although burgeoning ethnic sentiment may be associated with assertive religious behaviour, in reality the doubting agnostic and the convinced atheist may be just as committed 'Protestants' or 'Catholics' in the ethnic sense as their devout neighbours. But to the extent that ethnicity depends on possibilities of collective communal celebration, religion in either a secular or an ecumenical age constitutes an increasingly threadbare cultural framework. Ethnic identification, in other words, must in these circumstances be able to assert a degree of autonomy with respect to religious denominational affiliation.

Table 11.5 Religion and national identity, Northern Ireland, 1968–2000

Label	British	Irish	Ulster	Northern Irish	Other
Protestant					
1968	39	20	32	–	9
1978	67	8	20	–	5
1986	65	3	14	11	6
1989	68	3	10	16	3
1994	71	3	11	15	0
2000	72	3	7	15	3
Catholic					
1968	15	76	5	–	4
1978	20	69	6	–	5
1986	9	61	1	20	9
1989	10	60	2	25	4
1994	10	62	0	28	0
2000	9	59	1	28	2

Sources: Rose, 1971: 485; Moxon-Browne, 1983; Whyte, 1990: 69; Trew, 1996; Devine, 2001.

Note: The question asked in 1968 was 'which of these terms best describes the way you usually think of yourself?'; by 2000 this was substantially the same: 'which of these best describes the way you think of yourself?'. The 'Northern Irish' option was first introduced in 1986. Other responses included 'sometimes British, sometimes Irish' (Protestants, 1968, 6%, 1986, 4%; Catholics, 1968, 3%, 1986, 6%) and 'Anglo-Irish' (Protestants, 1968, 2%; Catholics, 1968, 1%).

Electoral cleavages

We may turn now to the electoral expression of the divisions discussed in the last two sections. Again, the main lines of the relationship between voting behaviour and such background factors as religion and ethnicity are so well known as not to require summary here. There is nevertheless a case for examining the long-term impact of these social factors on patterns of electoral behaviour, and the comparative literature may help to highlight significant features of developments in Ireland. The obvious starting point is the well-known model of Lipset and Rokkan, developed in the 1960s but exerting a continuing influence over research into party systems, whether this is conscious or unconscious (Lipset and Rokkan, 1967; for recent interpretations, see Mair, 1997). This sought to explain the party systems of the 1960s in terms of long-term trends and inherited voting habits, and pointed to social cleavage structures inherited from the nineteenth century or earlier as the main source of explanation.

Efforts to apply this model to politics in the Republic of Ireland have highlighted its limited capacity to explain the nature of the Irish party system (Garvin, 1974; Whyte, 1974; Coakley, 1986; Mair, 1987; Sinnott, 1995), and the most sustained analyses of party politics in Northern Ireland over a long time frame have substantially ignored it (McAllister, 1983; Mitchell, 1999). This arises in part from the allegedly deviant cleavage structure in Ireland, but there is another sense in which Ireland contrasts with the countries on whose political histories the model was based: all of them had a long-established geopolitical identity, typically – but not always – predating the nineteenth century. The two Irish states, by contrast, came into existence only in the 1920s, very late in the framework of the Rokkan model. Nevertheless, the Rokkan model is an important heuristic instrument in considering the long-term path of development of Irish parties. Indeed, if we move forward with the model from the nineteenth century to the present, rather than seeking to project contemporary party politics backwards, we may obtain a revealing perspective on the present.

Two features of the Rokkan model are of particular relevance. The first is the notion of organic evolution of the party system. From a simple, typically bipolar structure in the nineteenth century emerged a more complex multi-party system in the twentieth century, whose broad shape was 'frozen' around the period at which mass suffrage was introduced – typically, in the 1920s. The second feature is the suggestion that this fossilised party system adapted itself to changing political issues as the twentieth century progressed, sticking to the mould in which it had been set on its establishment. This mould was a function of the cleavage structure in the country in the early twentieth century, the major cleavages being social class, the urban–rural division, religion and ethnicity. The classical European party system was kick-started by the early mobilisation of liberalism, with conservative counter-mobilisation following (in southern Europe the pattern was rather different, with liberalism being linked to anticlericalism, and conservative interests mobilising behind a Catholic or, later, Christian Democratic party). The advent of a powerful socialist party at the end of the nineteenth century was a further defining factor, and the core party system was completed with the secession of the Communists around 1920. Other political forces (such as agrarian, ethnic or religious parties) may also have appeared at this time.

The middle decades of the nineteenth century saw a superficially similar development in Ireland, with a growing polarisation between a conservative party (emerging from the older Tory tradition) and a liberal party (with its origins in the Whig tradition). There the similarity with the European pattern and the Rokkan model ends. The defining features of Irish conservatism and liberalism quickly became bound up with religious and ethnic identity: the conservative tradition was to transmute into the unionist one, while Irish liberalism – eccentrically, by European standards, strongly linked to a Catholic support base – was unable to resist the challenge of other competitors for the Catholic vote. The outcome is illustrated in Figure 11.1. We may identify four critical junctures in the subsequent development of party politics in Ireland, each of them raising serious questions about the applicability of the model in this country.

The 1885 election

This was the election most closely associated with the development of modern party politics in Ireland. The introduction in the Representation of the People Act of 1884 of substantial male suffrage contributed to three political shifts. The

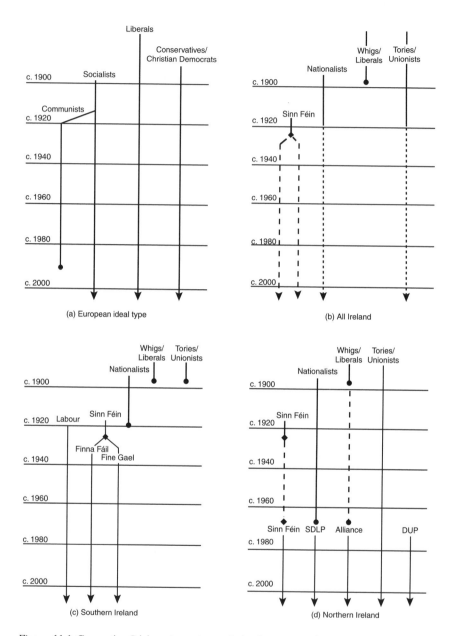

Figure 11.1 Competing Irish party systems: skeletal representations.

Note: in (b), heavy dashes refer to Southern Ireland and light dashes to Northern Ireland.

first was the conclusive defeat of liberalism by nationalism in the south and the establishment there of a zone of virtual one-party control. The second was the inauguration of a pattern of bipolar nationalist–unionist electoral competition in the north that was to last until the end of the 1960s. The third was the introduction of the modern political party on both nationalist and unionist sides – an organisation with thousands of members, hundreds of branches, a permanent secretariat, a large, representative decision-making national convention, and a disciplined parliamentary group (see Walker (1981) on this process in general; O'Brien (1957) and Lyons (1951) for this process in the case of the Nationalist Party; Buckland (1972 and 1973) in the case of the Unionist Party; and Walker (1989, pp. 176–225) on the 1885 election itself).

The 1918 election

Though of great significance *for* the north (in that it underlined the north–south gap, making partition more difficult to resist), this was of less significance *in* the north, except insofar as it showed that nationalists could expect to be challenged from time to time by a new radical party, Sinn Féin. Apart from this new intra-nationalist cleavage, the old inter-bloc division between nationalism and unionism remained. In the south, however, the 1918 election was of enormous importance, confirming the complete replacement of the Nationalist Party by the new radical nationalist force, Sinn Féin, in a result without parallel in the history of other mass party systems (Coakley, 1994).

The 1922 election in the South

The twin themes of this election were, first, the major split in Sinn Féin that was eventually to produce the two main parties that dominate southern politics today, Fianna Fáil and Fine Gael, and, second, the electoral intrusion of new political forces, of which the Labour Party was most significant in the long term (Gallagher, 1979). Although the elections of 1885 and 1918 show a level of electoral instability in the south that we would not expect in terms of the Rokkan model, elections from the 1920s onwards conformed closely to the pattern of electoral stability that the model predicted.

The 1973 election in the North

If the pattern of party politics in the south was shaken to its core by the elections of 1918 and 1922, the pattern in the north was characterised by a degree of stability without parallel elsewhere in Europe. Essentially, the same two parties fought elections on substantially the same issue, with the same outcome, from 1885 to 1965. The outbreak of civil unrest, however, posed a fundamental threat to the established parties, which found themselves seriously challenged in the 1969 Stormont and 1970 Westminster elections. The suspension of Stormont in 1972 was the blow that finally toppled the electoral dominance of the Ulster Unionist

Party (as Rokkan would have reminded us, the existence of a parliamentary structure to which a government is answerable has a crucial effect in stabilising a party system). Although the process of electoral re-alignment was long drawn out (extending from the Stormont election of 1969 to the local elections of 1977), it was at the Assembly election of 1973 that the new party system began to crystallise, with the consolidation of the electoral power of the Social Democratic and Labour Party (SDLP), which had replaced the Nationalist Party; the further splintering of unionism (though ultimately only one major challenger to the Ulster Unionist Party, the Democratic Unionist Party, was to survive); and the establishment of a permanent presence for a single biconfessional party, the Alliance Party.[5] The only major subsequent change in this pattern was the addition of a fifth party, Sinn Féin, in the early 1980s. Notwithstanding this high degree of electoral fragmentation, though, the two major blocs remained strikingly unidenominational (Mitchell, 1995).

Although electoral behaviour in Ireland has been characterised as 'politics without social bases', there is one sense in which party politics has had an over-whelmingly powerful social base: this is religion. This emerges vividly from a consideration of the emergence of the party system in the nineteenth century, in which, as Figure 11.2 shows, we can see a steady assimilation of the electoral map of the country to the religious denominational map. Elections from 1832 to the 1880s essentially reproduced the pattern of electoral control by middle-level elites that was already obvious in the early seventeenth century. In 1885 this was translated into substantial popular control, as the election results began to reflect denominational divisions almost perfectly (the results at constituency level in 1885 are illustrated in Figure 11.3, which plots the Conservative-Unionist vote in 1885 against the percentage of Protestants in each constituency according to the 1891 census, and shows an almost perfect correlation between the two).[6]

It is true that ecological and survey data dealing with social characteristics are of limited value in explaining inter-party variation within the south after 1922 and within blocs in the north after 1973. The reality is that, by contrast to the rest of Europe, where class and religion were the dominant fault lines of the party system, with weaker challenges from ethnicity and the urban–rural division, in Ireland ethnicity has been central, the challenge of class has been weak, that of religion (in the pure sense) even weaker and that of rural interests only ephemeral. But the powerful effect of religion, as a surrogate for ethnicity, may be seen in Table 11.6, which summarises the results of all elections to the Northern Ireland House of Commons from 1929 (the first election after the abolition of propor-tional representation and the reintroduction of single-member constituencies) to 1965 (the last election before these boundaries were changed, and new political forces began to have their first impact). Outside Belfast, the determining effect of the religious composition of a constituency was complete; and within Belfast the challenge from other forces (in particular, those of the left) was uneven, and tended itself to derive from a communal support base.

The dominance of ethnicity in the north has, if anything, increased over the last three decades, as the middle ground has struggled to survive. Ethnic mobilisation

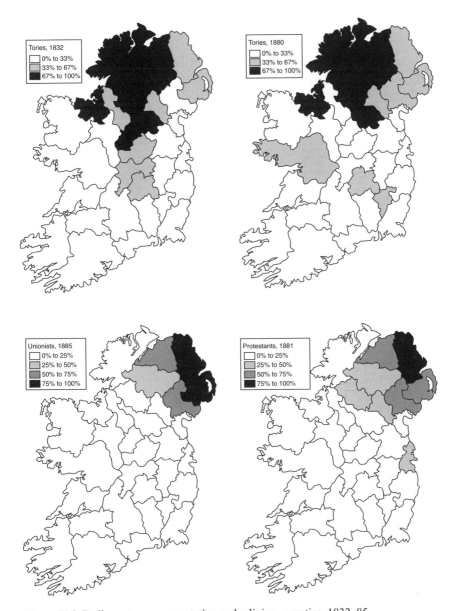

Figure 11.2 Parliamentary representation and religion, counties, 1832–85.

Note: the data refer to county constituencies only, i.e. they exclude parliamentary boroughs.

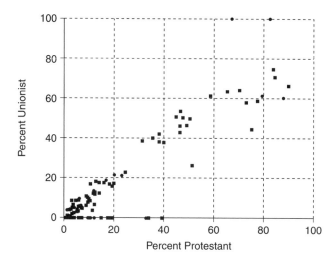

Figure 11.3 Conservative/Unionist vote, 1885, by percentage Protestant, 1891.

Note: the data points refer to parliamentary constituencies. Those where Unionists registered 0 were uncontested; those registered as 100 were contested only by Unionists.

Table 11.6 Results of Northern Irish elections by zone, 1929–65

Zone	Total number of seats by party			Total
	Unionist	Nationalist	Other	
Rural constituencies				
Unionists (23)	207	0	0	207
Nationalist (9)	0	74	7	81
Total (32)	207	74	7	288
Belfast				
Unionist (13)	90	0	27	117
Nationalist (2)	0	7	11	18
Mixed (1)	4	0	5	9
Total (16)	94	7	43	144
General total (48)	301	81	50	432

Source: calculated from Elliott, 1973

Note: excludes the for-member Queen's University constituency. In Belfast, the Central and Falls constituencies have been classified as nationalist and the Docks as mixed. 'Other' includes, in rural Northern Ireland, two Anti-Partitionist, an Independent Nationalist, an Independent Unionist, a Republican, one Northern Ireland Labour Party (NILP) and one Fianna Fáil (Éamon de Valera, elected for South Down in 1933); in Belfast Unionist constituencies, 13 NILP, mainly in the post-war years, 11 Independent Unionists, mainly in the inter-war years, and three independent Labour MPs; in Belfast nationalist constituencies four Independent Labour, four Republican Labour, two Socialist Republican and one National Democratic Party, all in the post-war years; and in the 'mixed' constituency two NILP and in the post-war years, two Irish Labour and one Republican Labour.

was especially noticeable on the nationalist side, which accounted for an average of 26 per cent of the total vote in the 1970s and 31 per cent in the 1980s (Mitchell, 1999), rising to 38 per cent in the 1990s.

Political consequences

In a democracy, of course, citizens expect their votes to have an effect, and it is time to turn to the political level and to examine the effect on this of the background factors that have been considered. In the south, religious denominational divisions declined steadily in political significance. More recently, it is true, religion acquired a new political salience, but the line of conflict now separates fundamentalist Catholics from those of a secular background (themselves mainly Catholic by origin) on such areas of public morality as abortion and divorce. The small Protestant minority was traditionally to be found on the liberal side on issues of this kind; but it is likely that it now mirrors the division between the religiously committed and the secular that has been so prominent a feature of the rest of southern Irish society in recent years.

In Northern Ireland, of course, the position is rather different. It is clear that, whatever its public policy significance in the past, religion now has little direct effect on the political process in Northern Ireland. There are sectors where this assessment needs to be modified: all of the churches take an active interest in education, and their voices are also frequently heard in the area of health services and certain aspects of social policy, including the issue of sabbatarianism. Although the interests and perspectives of the various churches may have been in conflict to some degree in certain of these areas in the past, there is little sign that the political system (either under Direct Rule from London or under recent devolved administrations) has found them excessively problematic.

Religion plays a much more central role through a more indirect channel, though this issue is now largely confined to Northern Ireland. Given its close link to ethnic identity, it is reasonable to define the major actors in Northern Irish politics in terms of religious blocs, or portions of such blocs – but blocs whose defining characteristic is ethnic rather than theological. The blocs clearly carry great weight within the political system, as Northern Ireland's recent history has shown. Thus the early dents in the armour of the old Stormont system were a consequence of predominantly Catholic street protests in the early days of the civil rights movement. The fall of Stormont in 1972 was a consequence in large part of an armed rebellion by a section of the Catholic population. In the fall of the power-sharing institutions in 1974, a general strike by Protestant workers played a central role. The negotiations that led to the Anglo-Irish Agreement of 1985 were prompted in part by the enhanced political status of the republican movement following the 1981 hunger strikes. Finally, of course, the talks that led to the Good Friday Agreement were designed to copper-fasten a peace process that had seen paramilitaries within both communities embark on a sustained ceasefire.

Given the undoubted political clout of these blocs and the capacity of armed violence, bombing, intimidation and civil protest to bring about political change, what space remains for the kind of electoral politics that has been discussed above? Again, the importance of this issue is now largely confined to Northern Ireland; in the south, the victory of conventional politics was clear already by the 1930s. In any society, elections act as a barometer of public opinion, conferring legitimacy on those groups which can claim a 'democratic mandate', however that is to be defined. In Northern Ireland they have a particular importance in providing personnel for local district councils and in returning representatives to the parliaments in London and Brussels.

The significance of domestic Northern Irish elections has been more restricted. Since the last elections to the old Northern Ireland House of Commons in 1969, only five elections to domestic assemblies have taken place. Three of these (in 1975, 1982 and 1996) have been to bodies that were essentially chambers for discussion. The real power of the ballot box thus received its most promising outing in the two remaining cases (1973 and 1998), when the assemblies were parliamentary type bodies. In these two cases, elected members broadly reflected, of course, divisions within society at large. This means that while all parties have a capacity to advance the interests of their supporters, they have an even greater capacity to obstruct proposals from other parties. This arises in large measure from a very necessary weighted voting mechanism; but the net effect of this conjunction of profound ethnic divisions with consociational structures of government is to confer vetoes on the major groups rather than facilitating progress. What is remarkable in this context is not the set of political crises that have beset the new government structures of Northern Ireland since 1998, but rather the extent of very real political progress that has been made since then.

Conclusion

What of the long-term trend, then, in the interplay between the factors considered here: how may one generalise about the political consequences of religious and ethnic dynamics as reflected in electoral behaviour? The bitter inter-ethnic conflict that was fought out in the form of religious wars in the seventeenth century remained substantially submerged until the late nineteenth century; then it was resuscitated in the form of electoral politics in the 1880s. But this new form of politics in turn fell victim to reliance on older, more violent methods, as unionist and nationalist mobilisation took on military shape just before the outbreak of the First World War. The early twentieth century appears to have been the high point of the marriage between religious groups and ethnic blocs. Partition, as is well known, failed to produce 'a Protestant state for a Protestant people' in Northern Ireland. It may have come closer to success in the South in carving out 'a Catholic state for a Catholic people': the Protestant minority declined dramatically, but the most recent stages in this decline overlapped, coincidentally, with what has been described as an increasing 'protestantisation' of the Catholic population (Inglis, 1998, p. 204).

This process, which might also be described as essentially one of secularisation, appears to have had its counterpart in steady patterns of ethnic redefinition. In the

Republic, although hard empirical evidence to this effect is difficult to come by, there are signs that an older form of ethnic nationalism has been yielding – probably rather unevenly – to a newer form of 'civic' nationalism, its reach defined in terms of geography rather than putative descent (and there are compelling theoretical reasons for expecting this outcome). Civic nationalism is normally seen as more inclusive than ethnic nationalism, and this feature has undoubtedly been present in the Irish case: accommodation of the Protestant tradition is now apparently more complete than ever in the past, and an 'ethnic fusion' of the two traditions in the Republic seems to have taken place. But there is an important respect in which it may be more exclusive: precisely because of its characteristic territorial definition, it could be argued that, for many, it now no longer extends to the Catholic population of Northern Ireland (see Garvin, 1998, pp. 152–4). Perhaps because of a perception that this change has been taking place – but clearly not only because of this – Northern Catholics, as we have seen, tend to be less unanimous in describing themselves as 'Irish', and appear no longer to be as attached to the notion of Irish unity as they once were.

At the level of the island, this development is of considerable importance. It is clear that national identification and political preferences can no longer be crudely inferred from religious affiliation. The growing demographic weight on the island of that portion of the population which is of Catholic background can thus no longer be seen as implying the political consequences it might once have had. A 'Catholic' demographic majority in Northern Ireland will not immediately translate itself into an electoral majority, because of the very different age structures of the Catholic and Protestant populations. Although a Catholic electoral majority may lead to a political majority for the two main nationalist parties combined, it will not, unless, there is a sharp shift in the political priorities consistently endorsed by Catholics in opinion polls, lead to a majority in favour of a united Ireland.[7] Similarly, southern acceptance of the constitutional *status quo*, strikingly demonstrated in the 1998 referendum that followed the Good Friday Agreement, suggests that the pursuit of political stability has taken a decisive lead over traditional irredentism in the mind of the southern electorate.

In the narrower context of Northern Ireland, the outcome of the interplay between religion, ethnicity, electoral behaviour and structures of government has, as we have seen, led after many years of civil strife to an uneasy but so far stable accommodation. The complex 1998 settlement can, of course, lead to paralysis at the level of domestic decision-making structures, leaving space for intervention by external actors, or even rendering such intervention necessary. It may, indeed, be precisely this external context that will constitute the most effective guarantor of future political stability. One might even indulge in a rather blunt paraphrase of Stein Rokkan's sceptical assessment of the political impact of electoral politics in western Europe: votes in Northern Ireland count, paramilitary and other forms of mobilisation in Ireland matter, resources from Europe assist, but governments in London and Dublin decide. The stark character of bi-national conflict that emerges in traditional historical writings may always have been an oversimplification of political reality; but of the geopolitical complexity to which the interplay of religion, ethnicity and politics has brought the conflict by the beginning of the twenty-first century there can be little doubt.

COMMENTARY BY EOIN O'MALLEY

When one looks for an example to explain and illustrate cleavage divisions – an institutionalised social division between groups in a country or geographical area – Northern Ireland provides a classic case. Furthermore it presents an example of a cleavage division that is reinforced by a number of different social strata.

Here we see two groups, Catholics/nationalists and Protestants/unionists, who are not only separated by religion, but also by national identity, politically, physically and, to a lesser extent, economically. The cleavage divisions in Northern Ireland are deeply institutionalised. Catholics/nationalists and Protestants/unionists in Northern Ireland read different newspapers (the *Irish News* versus the *Ulster Newsletter*), go to different schools (Catholic versus State schools), live in different areas (segregation is high) and tend to work in different professions (Catholics tend to be better represented in the professions whereas Protestants have dominated business). These religious/ethnic identities tend to get projected onto party choice. We know therefore that if someone is Protestant that he will most likely vote for a unionist party. Moreover, we know that if someone is a church-going, middle-class Catholic she will probably vote SDLP.

Which cleavage division is *prior* is not clear. Are Protestants loyal to Britain because they are Protestant or is their *Britishness* separate from religious dogma? Equally do Catholics feel loyalty to the Irish state because of religion or are they Catholic because they are Irish? Or are religious and national identities separate but reinforcing? When one looks at the conflict in Northern Ireland to what extent can we say that it is a religious as opposed to ethnic conflict? Is religion or ethnic identity important in separating people in Ireland north and south? And is it of any relevance to explaining political choice in the Republic?

These are not questions which John Coakley answers in the preceding article; it is, in his own description, a speculative piece. It is questionable whether we can ever have definitive answers to these questions. However these are some of the many questions Coakley raises in an article that considers the importance of religion in Irish politics. And he offers some clues to the answers of these and other questions. Using census data on the geographical distribution of religion in Ireland and social differences of Irish people divided by religion we are exposed to its impact on a number of areas – broadly, to the containment of ethnic conflict and specifically, to the ongoing political or 'peace' process in Northern Ireland; and to the impacts on party systems and voting behaviour north and south.

While the religious boundary seems quite clear-cut, the geographic boundary separating Protestants and Catholics is far from it. The choice of the unit for the partition of Ireland was important in terms of stabilising the Northern Irish state, but as Coakley points out, the divisions were imprecise and have been subject to change. Northern Ireland, and in particular Belfast, has become more Catholic. This leads us to consider the difficulties in using separation as a peace strategy.

Indeed Coakley points out that these identities are often more complex than is usually made out. He argues that the position of the border has had an impact on the identities of people who may have found themselves (arbitrarily) on either side of the border. Irish Catholics north of the border have developed much different identities to those in the south.

The Northern Ireland party system, remarkably stable, even stagnant, for so long has obvious roots in the religious cleavage. The roots of the southern party system are less easily explicable in these terms. It is long argued that southern Irish politics are without social bases. So where class, religion or linguistic background explain votes in other countries, in the Republic of Ireland there are no clear cleavages that can explain Irish political attitudes and voting behaviour. Most studies can only point to weak effects of class on party support, but we still have the situation that a plurality of people in all classes tends to support Fianna Fáil. Some parties, it is true, are more purely one class than others, so the Progressive Democrats and Sinn Féin derive support primarily from the middle classes and working classes respectively. But these effects are not strong.

Religion has been an even less important cleavage. The cleavage division was 'solved' by the secession of Ireland from the UK. Catholics dominated the new state. Coakley points out that southern Protestants have been more liberal and that in the last twenty years the dominance of Catholic thinking in public policy has been challenged by liberal secularists (usually of a Catholic background). But religion cannot explain voting for the parties or the shape of the party system. Or can it?

While there has been a good deal written about the seemingly tribal loyalties of the parties in Irish politics, particularly Fianna Fáil and Fine Gael, much of this assumes that these divisions came about as a result of the Treaty divisions and the Civil War. There has been little or no research on the sources of these divisions. While some historians look at the importance of personal loyalties (FitzPatrick, 1998), it seems too easy to assume that the Treaty issue did not reflect some existing, underlying cleavage.

One possibility is that the tribal party politics to some extent reflected the tribal loyalties of people in Ireland. Irish history is all too often, inaccurately, characterised as Gaelic Ireland revolts against English invasion and rule, eventually overthrowing it to reinstate a Gaelic state. This pastiche has suited Irish and British politicians but ignores many of the subtleties of history. The tribes of Ireland are not two-fold – there were at least four significant groups in Ireland. Ireland was invaded by Anglo-Normans or Old English who dominated certain parts of the country for many centuries. The Reformation had a major impact in England, but the Old English in Ireland remained loyal to the Catholic faith and wished to remain loyal to the English Crown. However, the Crown was aggressive in its opposition to the Catholic Church and attempted to replant the country with Protestants. Penal law drove the Old English and Gaelic Irish together. The Old English differed from the native Irish in that their religion was much more continental. They tended to attend Jesuit churches and schools. They were loyal to the Crown of England and looked to it for protection. The native Irish Catholicism was much more of the mystical kind compared to the more European Catholicism of the Old English (Foster, 1988, pp. 9 and 47). There is a debate as to the extent of this 'two nations' of Irish Catholics, and there was certainly a degree of assimilation and intermarriage (Duffy *et al*, 2001, p. 38). But Foster (1988, p. 51) argues that the Old English were

> firmly entrenched in urban and trade interests...As a social group, they were closely knit, both through their adherence to Catholicism and through their interlinked marriage arrangements. They were utterly sure of themselves socially.

The other identifiable tribal groups in Ireland are the New English or Anglo-Irish and the Ulster-Scots Presbyterians or Dissenters. The latter group remained primarily in Ulster and its presence formed the basis for the division of Ireland. The Anglo-Irish became the socially and politically dominant group. In the various uprisings against English rule, many on the grounds of religion, the three groups united against the Anglo-Irish. Religion and geographical separation prevented Ulster-Scots from assimilating with the other Irish rebels against English rule, but the divisions between the Old English and the Gaelic Irish broke down. At the same time, however, we can identify a number of different traditions in Irish nationalism, which came to a head at the time of the Treaty. The Treaty split revealed 'sharply divergent conceptions of the meaning of the Irish nation' (Prager, 1986, p. 30). There is the constitutional nationalism of the Irish Enlightenment, which basically admires the institutions of the English state but wishes to see them used for the benefit of Irish people, and the Irish Ireland or Gaelic Romantic nationalism of the Fenians, which viewed British institutions and traditions with suspicion (Prager, 1986). Garvin's *1922: The Birth of Irish Democracy* distinguishes between anti- and pro-Treatyites. The former saw the republic as 'a moral and transcendental entity analogous to the Church of Christ...[whereas the latter] saw the republic as a bargaining device in achieving rational-legal self-government' (Garvin, 1996, p. 143). Where the roots of these traditions lie is debatable. It is unclear if there were social bases for these divisions, but it would be unusual if there were not. One possible explanation, and it should be emphasised that this is just a possibility, is that the ethnic divisions between Gaelic Ireland and Old English persisted and are reflected in these ideological divisions. This would mean that there may be an ethnic basis for the Civil War divisions and hence the Irish party system.

It is a big jump from saying that these distinct traditions existed and arguing that there is an ethnic basis for them. Another leap is required to make the claim that these traditions form the basis for the Irish party system. Further research is required to make the connection between ethnic divisions and the party system, and any such research will have significant obstacles. One obvious problem is that people will not be aware of the ethnic divisions. Though it is not a requirement of ethnicity that the groups are self-aware of the divisions, it will make it difficult for survey research to be used to explain the differences between Fianna Fáil and Fine Gael. If this does form the basis of the division between the parties, we would expect that this 'cleavage' would show up in attitudinal differences. The areas that might be useful to study include attitudes towards Britain; attitudes to the Irish language; attitudes to Northern Ireland; and attitudes to law and constitutionalism.

But we do not see Fine Gael and Fianna Fáil voters differing radically in their attitudes to Northern Ireland. Evans and Sinnott (1999, p. 440) show that these voters are equally likely to support an Irish nationalist solution, although Fine Gael voters are slightly more accommodating of unionist positions. In the new Irish state nationalism became the only acceptable position – only the hues differed. What Coakley points out is that pre-partition loyalties were often eroded. Many southern Protestants became attached to the Irish state and became *Irish* Protestants where they or their ancestors may have previously thought of themselves as British Protestants.

Taking up Coakley's challenge I have looked briefly at one aspect of the impact of religion and national identity on politics in modern Ireland and in particular on electoral politics. The questions Coakley raises are important intellectual puzzles that reflect the real stuff of Irish politics. Coakley's insights will provide the basis for their solutions.

Notes

1 This article is a revised version of the Frank Wright Memorial Lecture, Queen's University Belfast, 10 February 2000.
2 See, for example, Whyte (1980), for the definitive study in the case of the Republic; in Northern Ireland, studies that examine the impact of religion typically focus on the ethnic dimension, but several, such as Brewer and Higgins (1998), address religious features of the conflict more explicitly.
3 For a detailed study of a large sample of the Belfast population in 1911, see Hepburn and Collins (1981); for an overview of trends in Belfast from 1861 to 1911 see Hepburn (1983).
4 The 1973 British Government White Paper that preceded the Act was a little more forthcoming: 'the Executive itself can no longer be solely based upon any single party, if that party draws its support and its elected representation virtually entirely from only one section of a divided community'.
5 This outcome had been anticipated in the results of the local elections of May 1973.
6 The correlation coefficient for the 72 contested constituencies was 0.96.
7 In a large survey in 2000, for instance, 52 per cent of Catholics opted for a united Ireland as a long-term policy for Northern Ireland, while 25 per cent opted for continued union with the UK, with 23 per cent preferring alternative political arrangements (these results are consistent with those of earlier surveys). In 2000, 55 per cent of SDLP supporters and 86 per cent of Sinn Féin supporters in the sample selected a united Ireland as a long-term goal; calculated from Northern Ireland Life and Times Survey (2000), data downloaded from <http://www.ark.ac.uk/nilt/>.

References

Aunger, Edmund A. (1975) 'Religion and Social Class in Northern Ireland', *Economic and Social Review*, 7 (1), pp. 1–18.
Beckett, J.C. (1981) *The Making of Modern Ireland 1603–1923*. New Edition. London: Faber.
Brewer, John D. and Gareth I. Higgins (1998) *Anti-Catholicism in Northern Ireland, 1600–1998: The Mote and the Beam*. Basingstoke: Macmillan.
Buckland, Patrick (1972) *Irish Unionism – Volume One: The Anglo-Irish and the New Ireland, 1885–1922*. Dublin: Gill and Macmillan.

Buckland, Patrick (1973) *Irish Unionism – Volume Two: Ulster Unionism and the Origins of Northern Ireland, 1886–1922*. Dublin: Gill and Macmillan.

Coakley, John (1986) 'The Evolution of Irish Party Politics', pp. 29–54 in Brian Girvin and Roland Sturm (eds.) *Politics and Society in Contemporary Ireland*. London: Gower.

Coakley, John (1994) 'The Election That Made the First Dáil', pp. 31–46 in Brian Farrell (ed.) *The Creation of the Dáil*. Dublin: Blackwater Press.

Coakley, John (1998) 'Religion, Ethnic Identity and the Protestant Minority in the Republic', pp. 86–106 in William Crotty and David E. Schmitt (eds.) *Ireland and the Politics of Change*. London: Longman.

Commissioners of Public Instruction (1835) *First Report of the Commissioners of Public Instruction in Ireland*. London: HMSO.

Devine, Paula (2001) 'Northern Ireland Life and Times Survey: Results', available at <http://www.ark.ac.uk/nilt/>.

Duffy, Patrick J., David Edwards and Elizabeth FitzPatrick (2001) 'Introduction: Recovering Gaelic Ireland c.1250–c.1650', pp. 21–73 in Patrick J. Duffy, David Edwards and Elizabeth FitzPatrick (eds.) *Gaelic Ireland c.1250–c.1650: Land, Lordship and Settlement*. Dublin: Four Courts Press.

Elliott, Marianne (2000) *The Catholics of Ulster: A History*. London: Penguin.

Elliott, Sydney (1973) *Northern Ireland Parliamentary Election Results 1921–1972*. Chichester: Political Reference Publications.

Equality Commission for Northern Ireland (2000) *Profile of the Monitored Workforce in Northern Ireland: Summary of the 1999 Monitoring Returns*. Belfast: Equality Commission for Northern Ireland.

Evans, Geoffrey and Richard Sinnott (1999) 'Political Cleavages and Party Alignments in Ireland, North and South', pp. 419–56 in Anthony F. Heath, Richard Breen and Christopher T. Whelan (eds.) *Ireland North and South: Perspectives from Social Science*. Oxford: Oxford University Press for The British Academy.

FitzPatrick, David (1998) *The Two Irelands, 1912–1939*. Oxford: Oxford University Press.

Foster, R.F. (1988) *Modern Ireland 1600–1972*. London: Penguin.

Gallagher, Anthony M., Robert D. Osborne and Robert J. Cormack (1995) *Fair Shares? Employment, Unemployment and Economic Status: Religion and the 1991 Population Census*. Belfast: Fair Employment Commission for Northern Ireland.

Gallagher, Michael (1979) 'The Pact General Election of 1922', *Irish Historical Studies*, 21 (84), pp. 404–21.

Garvin, Tom (1974) 'Political Cleavages, Party Politics and Urbanisation in Ireland: The Case of the Periphery-Dominated Centre', *European Journal of Political Research*, 2 (4), pp. 307–27.

Garvin, Tom (1996) *1922: The Birth of Irish Democracy*. Dublin: Gill and Macmillan.

Garvin, Tom (1998) 'Patriots and Republicans: An Irish Evolution', pp. 144–55 in William Crotty and David E. Schmitt (eds.) *Ireland and the Politics of Change*. London: Longman.

Hepburn, Anthony C. (1983) 'Work, Class and Religion in Belfast, 1871–1911', *Irish Economic and Social History*, 10, pp. 33–50.

Hepburn, Anthony C. and Brenda Collins (1981) 'Industrial Society: The Structure of Belfast, 1901', pp. 210–28 in Peter Roebuck (ed.) *Plantation to Partition: Essays in Ulster History in Honour of J.L. McCracken*. Belfast: Blackstaff Press.

Inglis, Tom (1998) *Moral Monopoly: The Catholic Church in Modern Irish Society*. Second Edition. Dublin: UCD Press.

Lerner, Daniel (1958) *The Passing of Traditional Society: Modernizing the Middle East*. New York: The Free Press.

Lipset, Seymour M. and Stein Rokkan (1967) 'Cleavage Structures, Party Systems, and Voter Alignments: An Introduction', pp. 1–64 in Seymour M. Lipset and Stein Rokkan (eds.) *Party Systems and Voter Alignments*. New York: Free Press.

Loughlin, James (1995) *Ulster Unionism and British National Identity Since 1885*. London: Frances Pinter.

Lyons, F.S.L. (1951) *The Irish Parliamentary Party 1890–1910*. London: Faber and Faber.

Mair, Peter (1987) *The Changing Irish Party System*. London: Frances Pinter.

Mair, Peter (1997) *Party System Change: Approaches and Interpretations*. Oxford: Clarendon.

McAllister, Ian (1983) 'Territorial Differentiation and Party Development in Northern Ireland', pp. 37–63 in Tom Gallagher and James O'Connell (eds.) *Contemporary Irish Studies*. Manchester: Manchester University Press.

McBride, Ian (1996) 'Ulster and the British Problem', pp. 1–18 in Richard English and Graham Walker (eds.) *Unionism in Modern Ireland: New Perspectives on Politics and Culture*. London: Macmillan.

Mitchell, Paul (1995) 'Party Competition in an Ethnic Dual Structure', *Ethnic and Racial Studies*, 18 (4), pp. 773–93.

Mitchell, Paul (1999) 'The Party System and Party Competition', pp. 91–119 in Paul Mitchell and Rick Wilford (eds.) *Politics in Northern Ireland*. Boulder, CO: Westview Press.

Moxon-Brown, Edward (1983) *Nation, Class and Creed in Northern Ireland*. Aldershot: Gower.

O'Brien, Conor Cruise (1957) *Parnell and His Party, 1880–90*. Oxford: Clarendon Press.

O'Connor, Fionnuala (1993) *In Search of a State: Catholics in Northern Ireland*. Belfast: Blackstaff Press.

Power, Paul F. (1996) 'Revisionist Nationalism's Consolidation, Republicanism's Marginalisation, and the Peace Process', *Eire-Ireland*, 31 (1), pp. 89–122.

Prager, Jeffrey (1986) *Building Democracy in Ireland: Political Order and Cultural Integration in a Newly Independent Nation*. New York: Cambridge University Press.

Rose, Richard (1971) *Governing Without Consensus: An Irish Perspective*. London: Faber.

Rowthorn, Bob and Naomi Wayne (1988) *Northern Ireland: The Political Economy of Conflict*. Cambridge: Polity Press.

Sinnott, Richard (1995) *Irish Voters Decide: Voting Behaviour in Elections and Referendums Since 1918*. Manchester: Manchester University Press.

Teleki, Count Paul and Andrew Rónai (1937) *The Different Types of Ethnic Mixture of Population*. Budapest: Athenaeum.

Trew, Karen (1996) 'National Identity', pp. 140–52 in Richard Breen, Paula Devine and Lizanne Dowds (eds.) *Social Attitudes in Northern Ireland: The Fifth Report 1995–96*. Belfast: Appletree Press.

Walker, Brian M. (1981) 'Party Organisation in Ulster, 1865–92: Registration Agents and their Activities', pp. 191–209 in Peter Roebuck (ed.) *Plantation to Partition: Essays in Ulster History in Honour of J.L. McCracken*. Belfast: Blackstaff Press.

Walker, Brian M. (1989) *Ulster Politics: the Formative Years, 1868–86*. Belfast: Ulster Historical Foundation and Institute of Irish Studies.

Whyte, John H. (1974) 'Ireland: Politics Without Social Bases', pp. 619–52 in Richard Rose (ed.) *Electoral Behavior: A Comparative Handbook*. New York: Free Press.

Whyte, John H. (1980) *Church and State in Modern Ireland, 1923–1979*. Dublin: Gill and Macmillan.

Whyte, John H. (1990) *Interpreting Northern Ireland*. Oxford: Clarendon Press.

Wright, Frank (1996) *Two Lands on One Soil: Ulster Politics Before Home Rule*. Dublin: Gill and Macmillan.

12 Transformation with a small 't'

Candidates for the Dáil, 1948–82[1]

Michael Marsh

Originally published in *Irish Political Studies*, 4, 1989, pp. 59–82.

In any liberal democratic political system it seems reasonable to expect a link between social change and political recruitment, even if the nature of that linkage is problematic. One review of legislative recruitment in a number of countries suggested that variations in the social profile of deputies could be 'explained' by variations in the societies they represented (Quandt, 1970). It should presumably follow that a change in the society will be reflected in a change in those recruited to fulfil particular political roles, yet few would see this reflection as being a simple and undistorted one. Political parties normally play a far from nominal role in recruitment. The nature of particular parties and party systems provides an 'opportunity structure' which constrains recruitment. Schlesinger has pointedly remarked that 'in the game of politics, the political as well as the social system determines the players' (1966, p. 12). This paper examines the balance between these two elements in determining the composition of one group of players in the Irish political system. It looks at candidates for legislative office, not just at those actually selected. First, it begins by describing occupational profiles and trends in the group of candidates as a whole to see what degree of change has taken place. Second, it looks at the direct link between the changes that have been observed and trends in social structure. Third, it assesses the extent to which changes between or within parties best account for those observed trends and considers the consequences of the changes on each party's profile.

The changing social background of Dáil candidates

Candidates have received little academic attention, certainly by contrast with deputies, despite a widespread recognition that it is the selection of candidates which is often the most decisive stage in the process of recruitment (Czudnowski, 1975, p. 219; Gallagher and Marsh, 1988). This is particularly true of Irish elections, where the proportional representation (PR) system offers each party a better chance of success than is the case in majoritarian systems. There are fewer safe seats for parties than in, for instance, Britain and – in contrast to much of Western Europe – there are very few safe seats for individuals. Voters select individuals, not parties, and there is no equivalent to the list ordering which virtually guarantees seats to favoured candidates in most other PR systems.

Hence, particularly amongst the candidates of the major parties, there are very few 'hopeless' candidacies. Yet, in contrast to the attention paid to TDs (McCracken, 1958; Whyte, 1966; Farrell, 1971 and 1975; Chubb, 1982; Gallagher, 1984 and 1985; Farrell, 1984), candidates have received little attention. A few studies have concentrated on explaining the role of electors in turning candidates into TDs (Robson and Walsh, 1974; Marsh, 1981a and 1987; Darcy, 1988). The direct role played by voters in recruitment is, however, conditional upon the earlier role played by the parties which select the candidates (Gallagher, 1988). It is the parties and the party system that structure the opportunities for participation by aspiring politicians, and for choice by voters.

The context

Candidates as a whole may differ from TDs in a number of ways. Three seem particularly important for a consideration of political participation and recruitment. First, there are a lot more candidates than TDs. This means that the number of cases for analysis is larger, and the basis for generalisations about profiles and trends is more reliable. Second, candidates comprise a more unstable group. Turnover amongst candidates is more rapid than it is amongst TDs.[2] Newly-elected TDs tend to reflect environmental change more rapidly and clearly than TDs as a whole and this will be even more true of candidates. Third, TD profiles are in part determined by the pattern of party successes. Only by looking at candidates as a whole can we see if some social groups provide no candidates at all, or just none for successful parties.

Candidate selection is for the most part a decentralised process, carried out by a relatively large number of activists from constituency party organisations. The central organisation has traditionally intervened to offer guidance on the number of candidates to be selected, but not the personnel. In more recent times, particularly since 1977, party leaderships have played a stronger role, but the procedure remains one essentially under local control (Gallagher, 1988). This has consequences for the way in which parties can respond to social change, as we shall see later. Not all candidates represent parties. Many stand as independents, or are one of a small handful of candidates of a very small party. In almost every Dáil there are a few of these. Their candidacies owe much more to individual than to party factors; they are, for the most part, essentially self-starting candidates, and may be untypical in consequence.

The data

The data examined here comprise social and political background information on all candidates who stood for election to the Dáil at the general elections of 1948, 1954, 1961, 1969, 1977, 1981 and February 1982. This includes every other election from 1948 to 1977, and then the next two successive ones. It does not cover the two most recent elections, of November 1982 and of 1987. Every election has its exceptional circumstances. The success of Clann na Poblachta in

1948, Labour's attempt to provide a nationwide slate of candidates in 1969 and the hunger-striker candidates of 1981 are all good examples of such uniqueness. The particular features of any one election go some way towards justifying the sort of study intended here, which goes beyond the single election to look at the wider picture. However, in making generalisations about trends, care must be taken not to place too much emphasis on the results of any one election.

The series of elections covered here dates from a quarter of a century after the foundation of the state. This allows time for the founding 'revolutionary elite' (Cohan, 1972 and 1973) to have worked its way through the system. Initially recruitment depended substantially on candidates' roles in the struggle for independence, but turnover in the early years was rapid. Peillon calculates that less than half of the complement of the first Dáil survived the next two Dala, and by 1933 only 25 per cent survived. Thereafter, political careers became rather more stable (Peillon, 1982). The character of the Dáil in 1948 was most unlike that of 1922 in terms of its occupational profile, but quite similar to that of 1932. McCracken's study (1958) shows that professional people had declined and had been replaced by farmers and those in industry and commerce. McCracken also showed that the average age of the Dáil increased until 1948, and thereafter declined. This can be interpreted as further evidence that the system had settled down, and that the revolutionary era was closing.[3] Only one deputy in the current, 25th, Dáil was born before independence (Gallagher, 1987).

Most earlier studies of TDs have adopted a simple categorisation of occupations, which serves to distinguish groups of similar size. This categorisation has been followed here, for reasons of comparability, and because anything much more complex would make demands which could not be met by available data sources.[4] The basic categorisation is four-fold, separating out farmers, those in commerce (mostly small businessmen), those in the professions and employees (mostly clerical and manual workers).[5] In addition, the professionals are further subdivided into higher and lower professional groups, and the employees into non-manual and manual workers. Higher professionals are largely lawyers, solicitors, doctors, accountants and university teachers. Lower professionals are mostly teachers. A difficulty with occupation, noted in almost all such studies, is that many politicians often report more than one occupation. The solution adopted here follows that in Whyte (1966), which is to accept the fact of multiple occupations, unless an occupation is known to be superseded by a later one. An alternative solution, to select only the major occupation (e.g. Gallagher, 1984 and 1985; Farrell, 1971), proved beyond the limits of the data, and, in addition, seems unjustifiably arbitrary. In consequence, the percentages in the Tables normally sum to more than 100.

Changes in the occupational profile of candidates

Figure 12.1 shows the changing occupational profile over various elections since 1948, taking the four main groups described above. There are some clear trends. Most striking is the decline in the number of farmer candidates from 34 per cent in 1948 to 17 per cent in 1982 in almost linear fashion.

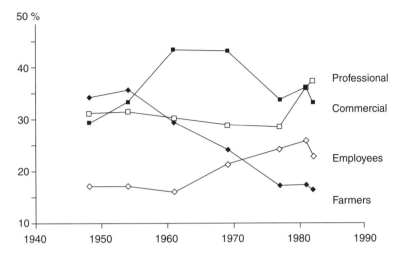

Figure 12.1 Social profile of candidates.

There is no sign that this figure has been subject to the fluctuations that have been observed in other countries (Czudnowski, 1975, p. 203). Over the period as a whole, this fall in the number of farmers is compensated for by increases of almost equal size in the other groupings. However, closer inspection indicates that the pattern is a more complex one. Initially, the decline in farmers was balanced by an increase in commercial candidates, but that group too has latterly shown some decline from its peak, achieved in the 1960s. Professionals and employees have shown a more recent increase. In the case of professionals, this dates from the late 1970s and follows a period of gentle decline; for the employees group the upsurge dates from 1969. This is not to say there has been no change within the various categories. Amongst commercials, there has been some decline in the small-scale retailer category – grocers and publicans in particular – and an increase in vaguely-defined businessmen, company directors and, more specifically, auctioneers, with the last-named the fastest-growing component of this category.

Further variations are apparent when the professional and employee groups are examined more closely in Figure 12.2, which shows the changes in higher and lower professionals and non-manual and manual workers. The stability in the professional group conceals a considerable transformation. The importance of candidates from the higher professions has declined, whilst that of those from the lower professions has increased. Only since 1969 has the increase more than cancelled out the decline. This is in part because the decline in higher professionals has been halted but also because the increase in the lower professions was very sharp, particularly between 1977 and 1981. From only ten per cent of all candidates in 1948, lower professionals comprised 20 per cent in 1982. Whilst in 1948 almost 70 per cent of professionals were 'higher', by 1982 it was the 'lower'

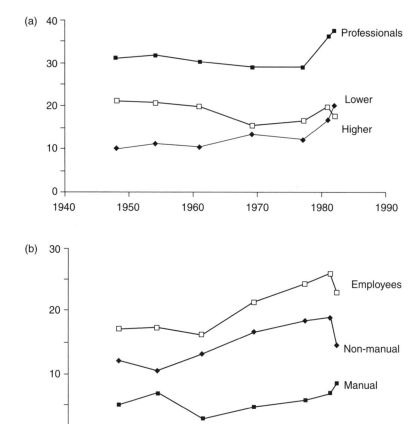

Figure 12.2 Detailed social profile of candidates. (a) Professionals; (b) Employees.

group that was dominant, comprising over 50 per cent of the group, although this dominance was not obvious until 1982. Some transformation of the employee group is also apparent. Both manual and non-manual workers have fluctuated around a slight upward trend but the fluctuations have not been synchronised. Non-manual occupations have shown the more steady increase, despite a fall back in 1982. Manual occupations entered a trough in 1961 from which they did not emerge until 1981, but the overall trend has been an upward one from 5.6 per cent in 1948 to 8.2 per cent in 1982. Generally, then, farmers and higher professionals have declined over the period, whilst commercials have declined over the second part of it. The rising groups have been lower professionals, particularly teachers, and to a lesser extent other non-manual (largely clerical) and manual workers.

The trends are even more marked amongst new candidates. It might be expected that candidates standing for the first time would be drawn more from the growing and less from the declining groups. There are generally fewer farmers and commercial candidates standing for the first time, and more professionals and those from the residual category. The only remarkable difference apart from this is in the professional category. New professional candidates declined sharply to a low of only 22 per cent in 1961, before rising steadily to almost 40 per cent in 1981. This fluctuation is in contrast to the stability apparent in Figures 12.1 and 12.2.

Social change and changes in candidate profiles

It has been argued that change in the profile of candidates will follow social change, although not everyone agrees on what sort of change will occur. Quandt has suggested that the comparative cross-sectional evidence is that manual workers, and those from the liberal professions, increase with modernisation; farmers, merchants and bureaucrats decline (1970, pp. 193–4). Matthews has made similar suggestions, indicating that in more advanced countries the profiles of legislators and citizens are closer than they are in developing ones (1984). Cross-sectional comparative studies of this nature can be very misleading to the extent that they adopt an excessively deterministic view of development. Even so, in the absence of much detailed comparative time series study, their findings are worth consideration. The available information on the changing profiles of Irish TDs has led Farrell to suggest that changes over the last few decades have mirrored social change, judged by the decline in those in the retail trade and the increase in professionals (1984, pp. 328 and 338). An increase in skilled workers in Labour's ranks in 1969 has also been linked to the increase in that group in the population (Busteed and Mason, 1970). However, some have cautioned against expecting social changes to be reflected in political elites. Cohan (1972 and 1973) argues, from an examination of cabinets, that the elite has really adapted only marginally to social change. Gallagher (1981) suggests that this is because parties are decentralised and not formally linked to social groups; they are 'direct' parties, not 'indirect' ones in Duverger's classic formulation. He argues too, on the basis of changes in the composition of the Dáil, that the rise in professionals is marginal, as is that in non-manuals, and though farmers have declined this is not necessarily due to social change (Gallagher, 1981, p. 280).

Table 12.1 shows the pattern of occupational social change over the 1951–79 period. It is based only on the male workforce; in consequence it probably underestimates the growth in lower non–manual workers relative to manual workers, but it serves to illustrate the broad picture. It is adapted from a table presented by Rottman and O'Connell (1982). The match between the professional category in their data and the data used here is not exact, as their social structural data put salaried non–manual workers into the professional category, while in Table 12.1 here they are placed with non–manual employees. The decline in farmers is the most obvious feature, down to 21 per cent in 1979 from 38 per cent in 1951. This is very similar to the extent of the decline in farmer candidates. Commercials (employers and self–employed) have stayed relatively stable, increasing only in the 1970s and then by a small amount. The farmer decline is compensated for by

Table 12.1 Changes in occupational social structure 1951–79 (males only)

	1951 %	1961 %	1971 %	1979 %
Farmers	38	36	27	21
Employers and self-employed	8	8	9	10
Professionals	4	6	9	11
Employees: non-manual	15	16	20	23
Employees: manual	35	33	35	35

Source: adapted from Rottman and O'Connell, 1982, p. 70.

the increase in professionals, from four per cent to 11 per cent, and other categories, from 50 per cent to 58 per cent. Most of this increase is in the non-manual category, from 15 per cent to 23 per cent. Manual workers have stayed quite stable, although this conceals a sharp increase in skilled workers at the expense of unskilled ones.

These data illustrate the point that change in the profile of candidates is in accord with the direction of social change. That is not to say that the candidate profile mirrors social structure but that changes in social structure leave an impression on it.

Political parties and changes in candidate profiles

The key to change is held by political parties. Change can occur within parties, as a party attracts a different sort of candidate, or through a change in the balance of parties, perhaps with new parties representing rising social groups whilst those representing old ones go into decline. Such processes have been charted most clearly by Pedersen, who has shown how the rise of socialist parties and decline of conservative ones in Denmark broadened political recruitment (Pedersen, 1976). We have seen that some changes have taken place in the profile of Irish candidates. To what extent has that followed change within rather than between parties? Irish parties are generally considered to be socially heterogeneous. This applies particularly to their bases of electoral support. Whyte's (1974) description of Irish politics as being 'without social bases' is much cited, usually in order to qualify the description (e.g. Laver, 1986). Studies of electoral support since Whyte's have generally concluded that there are significant differences in the support profiles of Irish parties even if the dominant pattern of inter-party conflict has not served to emphasise these. At elite level, McCracken's assertion that there is 'no pronounced difference in the occupational composition of the two major parties' (McCracken, 1958, p. 116) has been less disputed. Carty has used this as rather doubtful evidence for his belief that the Irish party system cannot be explained through Lipset and Rokkan's social cleavage approach (Carty, 1983). In a different vein, Gallagher notes differences in the parties' support at mass level but suggests that these are not reflected in their parliamentary profiles, with only the Labour Party showing much variation (Gallagher, 1987). In the light of this it must be expected that any change in the overall profile of candidates will owe more to similar changes and adaptations within the different parties than to alterations in the system of parties.

This expectation is strengthened by the fact that the party system since 1948, at least to 1982, has shown increasing stability. The three oldest parties, Labour, Fianna Fáil and Fine Gael, persisted, with Fine Gael in particular growing in strength from its low point of 1948. These three parties have provided the stable core to the party, system. The biggest change has been amongst the 'minor' parties. In 1948 there were two other significant parties, Clann na Poblachta, a radical protest party, and Clann na Talmhan, a farmers' party, plus a lot of independents. These declined quite rapidly after 1948. Taking all these as 'others', their vote dropped from 27 per cent in 1948 to 3 per cent in 1969. There was some revival in the 1970s, with the new Workers' Party taking votes from Labour and in February 1982 'others' won over 6 per cent of the vote. Compared with the 1940s and early 1950s, however, this figure is still low. Figure 12.3 shows the proportions contributed by each of these four groupings to the candidate lists in the elections covered here.[6] Changes have been most pronounced in the 'others' category. The proportion of Fine Gael candidates increased in the 1950s whilst Fianna Fáil and Labour levels remained fairly steady with the exception of 1969 in the case of Labour. The proportion of 'other' candidates traces a v-shaped curve, declining until 1969 and then rising again, reaching in 1982 its highest level since 1948. Independents account for a consistently large proportion of these candidates. Although over 60 per cent of 'other' candidates were fielded by Clann na Poblachta in 1948, independents and minor parties fielded equal numbers in 1954 and 1961 and since then two-thirds or more have been independents.

Bearing these figures for candidates in mind we shall move on to look at the contribution of changes in the party system to changes in the profile of candidates presented to the electorate. We shall be searching for evidence that increases or

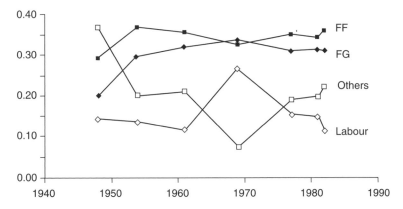

Figure 12.3 Share of candidates, by party.

decreases in the proportions of candidates from the different social groups are in any way a consequence of changes in the weight of candidates from each party (or group of parties in the case of 'others'). Following that, we will then examine the contribution to the candidate profile made by changes in the types of candidate offered by different parties.

Changes between parties

Figure 12.4 shows the changes in the total proportions of candidates from each occupational category by party. The area charts show first, in their general profile, the change in the proportion of candidates from the occupational group and second, in the layers, the distribution of those candidates in the four political groups. Hence we can see the contribution of parties to the trends already identified. For a change in party system to account for an overall increase or decrease in the number of candidates from a particular group we should need first to see a change in the size of any one of the layers, comparable to a change in the height of the overall chart, and, second, to be able to show a similar change in the proportions of candidates fielded by that party.

The decline of the weight of farmer candidates is in significant part a consequence of the reduction in the relative number of farmer candidates from 'other' parties. Fianna Fáil and Fine Gael both field fewer such candidates now, but the clearest drop is on the periphery of the party system. There has not been much of a drop in total candidates from 'other' parties, at least after 1954, which suggests that it is a change in the partisanship of farmer candidates which explains the decline. The demise of Clann na Talmhan, explicitly a farmers' party, accounts for some of this pattern but the party fielded very few candidates after 1948 and the relative number of farmer candidates from 'other' parties fell steadily until 1969, after which it remained small but constant. Farmers now tend to seek political careers only through established parties.

Commercial candidates increased until the 1970s, after which their proportions fell. Some growth in the relative number of Labour commercials in 1969 served to prolong the peak of these candidates through the 1960s but the pattern owes most to the increases in Fianna Fáil and Fine Gael, and, more recently, a declining proportion of such candidates from Fine Gael. Only the short-lived surge in Labour commercials can be accounted for by an increase in the relative numbers of Labour candidates; again, the obvious conclusion is that there has been a change in the parties' own candidate profiles, with Fianna Fáil in particular putting forward more such candidates.

The number of professional candidates remained quite stable until 1977, but since that time it has grown quite sharply. The stability transcended increases and decreases in different parties as these tended to cancel one another out. Labour fielded more as 'others' fielded less, while fluctuations in Fine Gael mirrored those in Fianna Fáil. The recent surge is attributable to their growing weight within the major two parties, in particular Fine Gael. Again, these results suggest that change within parties, not change in the party system, is responsible for

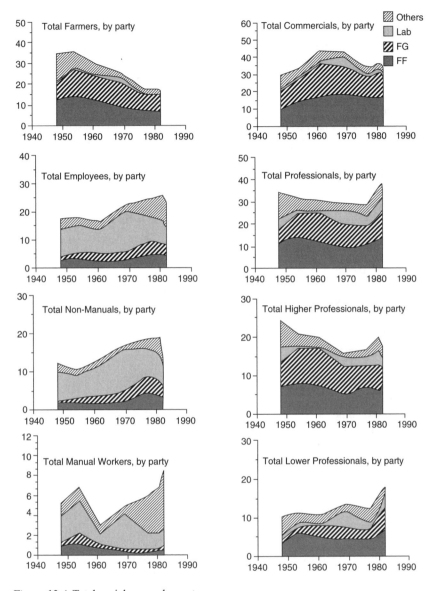

Figure 12.4 Total social group, by party.

change in the candidate profile, since there has been no increase in these two parties' share of the candidates list. It seems possible that the increasing proportion of professional candidates reflects the drive in that party under Garret FitzGerald to raise the quality of candidates (see O'Byrnes, 1986), although it is not obvious why it should be the lower professionals who comprise most of Fine Gael's growing professional component. What is clear is that the Fine Gael profile has changed; there has been no recent increase in the relative number of Fine Gael candidates.

The changes in the weight of employee candidates describe a curve which is the reverse of that for commercial candidates: in this case an initial decline, followed by a long period of growth. Slight increases in employee candidates in Fine Gael, Fianna Fáil and, more recently, 'other' parties all contribute to the greater incidence of such candidates. The big upturn in 1969 was due largely to the increase in Labour's candidate share, but since then has been sustained by the other party groupings. Originally, the bulk of such candidates were in the Labour Party, many of them being trade union officials, but this is no longer the case. Labour now provides a third, rather than the half it did formerly. Figure 12.4 also suggests that the other parties have changed their profiles, giving more places to such employee candidates. Non-manual workers constitute the bulk of employee candidates so it is not surprising that this trend is equally true of non-manual workers. It is, however, not true of manual workers. Their increase since 1969 is due entirely to 'other' parties. As 'other' candidates became more prevalent in that period, it provides the best example of system change accounting for profile change. Certainly there must have been some alteration within the 'others' category since 1948. While the growth of a new party (the Workers' Party) accounts in part for the profile change, most such candidates in more recent years have been independents of various kinds. These are now different in character to their 1948 counterparts.

The general conclusion must be that there is little evidence that long-term change in the candidate profile was due to change in the party system. This was suggested initially by the general stability of candidate shares between the four political groupings, and is confirmed in these charts. No social category is represented at all exclusively by any one party, although the share of employee candidates within the 'others' category in 1982 is striking. However, the variations in the contribution of different parties to the potential representation of different social groups are noticeable. Professionals appear to be spread most widely, with all groups contributing significantly to their representation. The great majority of farmers (particularly since the 1960s) and commercial candidates come from the two major parties, with Labour and 'others' providing only a thin layer of icing on top of that cake. In contrast, employee candidates come almost entirely from Labour and from parties on the fringe of the political system. This is even more true of manual workers, where the contribution of Fine Gael and Fianna Fáil is barely visible on the chart.

Changes within parties

Figure 12.5 shows the changes in the profiles of the four groups with respect to the broad categories of occupations already described. The eight charts show the party shares of each of the social groups and subgroups examined before. In contrast to Figure 12.4, these pictures do not show whether the overall proportions

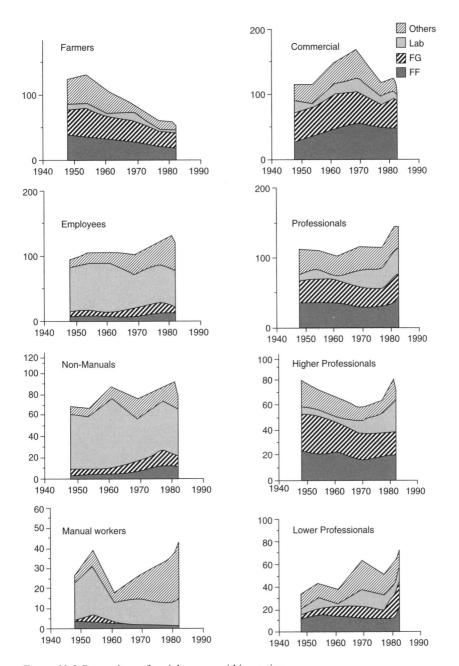

Figure 12.5 Proportions of social groups within parties.

in each category have increased or decreased but only reflect the category's share in each party's overall list of candidates. In other words, the layers in both Figure 12.4 and Figure 12.5 represent the same groups of candidates, but in Figure 12.4 they are shown relative to the total number from a single occupational group and in Figure 12.5 they are shown as a proportion of a particular party's candidates. Thus, for example, Fianna Fáil farmer candidates are shown in Figure 12 4 as a proportion of all farmer candidates and in Figure 12.5 as a proportion of all Fianna Fáil candidates. In examining these charts we expect to see significant changes in the proportions of candidates from the different social groups inside the different parties. We suggested that, if there was no change in its structure, the party system could only respond to social change by the parties changing their own social balance. We will also look for evidence of similarities in social profiles across parties to see whether if, in responding to social change, the parties have become more alike.

The universal picture as far as farmers are concerned is one of decline; the overall fall in the weight of farmer candidates is repeated everywhere. It is most striking in the 'others' grouping. Clearly, the collapse of Clann na Talmhan was partly responsible for the sharp drop in the early part of the period, with the effect staved off initially as Clann na Poblachta disappeared even faster. Farmers were not a significant element outside the two major parties after 1969. Whereas in 1948, Labour stood out for its lack of recruitment from this sector, in 1982 the division was between the major and the minor parties.

The reduction in the numbers of farmers was compensated for initially by the growth in candidates from commerce, particularly in small-scale retailing. All four political groups show an upward trend for commercial candidates until the 1960s, and a downward one since that time. The Fianna Fáil pattern is the clearest: a linear increase until 1969, with a decrease at each election since apart from 1977. As was the case with farmers, there is again some suggestion that 'others' now resemble Labour in their commercial profile whilst in the early part of the period they were closer to the other two parties. However, unlike the case of farmers, whose incidence in each party converged as their overall proportion declined, parties are no closer in the proportions each has of commercial candidates than they were in 1948. It is a feature which still serves to distinguish the parties.

The reverse is true of professional candidates. Labour was again the odd one out in 1948 but from 1969 all four 'parties' have been grouped closely. Only Labour has changed its profile very much, being less than ten per cent professional in 1948 and increasing to over 30 per cent by 1982. The decisive increase was evident in 1969, when, along with its most socialist message, it put forward its most middle-class profile. Brian Farrell was moved to point out the irony 'that an increasing ideological emphasis on class and privilege in Irish society should occur as the public representatives as a group become a less accurate cross-section of that society' (1971, p. 323)[7] but this is not untypical of European social democratic parties. Most of them have become more middle class in the post-war years, particularly since the 1960s, without this necessarily having any connection with their ideological outlook (Marsh, 1980).

The pattern in the professional category conceals a very different development amongst higher and lower professionals. The overall trend in higher professionals is downwards. However, when the patterns in the different parties are examined it is clear that this category provides the most remarkable example of convergence between parties. The party with most higher professionals declined more sharply in its proportion than any other; the party with the fewest increased in proportion most sharply. Earlier studies of TDs have remarked on the similarity in profiles between Fine Gael and Fianna Fáil. However, a clear difference was evident in 1948 and this persisted until 1969. It was eroded because of the reduction in the number of higher professionals amongst Fine Gael candidates. Labour's higher professionals increased considerably after the early 1960s to the extent that in 1981 it had a higher proportion of such candidates in its ranks than did any other party. This had the effect of halting the overall decline in higher professionals, although lower professionals now far outweigh them.

Lower professionals are universal and increasing. They are the success story of Irish political recruitment. In 1948 only Fianna Fáil and 'others' (Clann na Poblachta) put forward many such candidates but by 1982 they formed a significant proportion of all political slates. The increase within Fine Gael is the most remarkable; the party changed from having the smallest proportion in 1948 to the largest in 1982. If we speculate that many of the higher professionals would have been self-employed,[8] Fianna Fáil/Fine Gael differences would be quite clear in respect of an employed/self-employed classification in 1948; whilst the two parties resembled one another quite closely with respect to the self-employed (farmers, commercials and higher professionals), differences were much more evident for lower professionals and, although numbers are small, for 'employees'.

The charts showing the comparative incidence of employee candidates, both manual and non-manual, are the most uneven of all those displayed. They also manifest some of the most rapid changes. Only Labour drew a significant proportion of its candidates from this grouping in 1948, and in comparison with the proportion in that party, those in the other parties were minimal. As Labour's profile broadened, employees became more conspicuous in the other parties, but really only in the 'others' grouping do they appear as more than a thin band on the chart. Farmers constitute small minorities outside the two main parties; employees are tiny minorities inside them. They are prominent in Labour and amongst 'other' parties but their character in these two groups differs. Labour employees are much more likely to be non-manual. In fact, Labour dominates the non-manuals chart with a share within the party twice as large as in any other party. The 'others' grouping dominates the manual chart in similar fashion with the majority of manual candidates located outside the established parties.

The charts provide ample evidence of expected changes in social profiles within parties as bands changed in width. We also looked for evidence of convergence between parties. Only professionals proved to be anything like a similar sized grouping in all parties, with some signs of convergence between parties in both the higher and lower professional groups. In the remaining social categories, Labour and 'others' differed increasingly from Fianna Fáil and Fine Gael in their profiles. The expected similarity between Fianna Fáil and Fine Gael is generally evident, but, when the professional category is analysed in detail, is more pronounced in 1982 than in 1948.

The conclusions from Figures 12.4 and 12.5 can be reinforced by examining more formally the changes which might be expected in the candidate profile according to whether party system change or within-party change is decisive. We can do this by holding either of these two factors constant and calculating the number of candidates that would be expected in a particular category if the other factor alone were responsible for change.[9] This projection can then be compared with the actual proportion of professional candidates. The calculations for the four main occupational groups are displayed graphically in Figure 12.6. For each occupational group three series are displayed: P1, a projection keeping the within-party profiles constant; P2, which holds the proportion of candidates nominated by each party constant; and the actual data series. If the P1 series is closest to the actual one, it suggests that changes in the overall candidate profile are a consequence largely of alterations in the party system. However, if the P2 series is more accurate, then we can say that it is a shift within one or more parties which is more decisive. The general conclusion from Figure 12.6 must be that the actual series is normally closer to P2 than to P1, supporting the earlier conclusion that it is change within parties, rather than change in the party system, that is most important. This is best illustrated in the graphs for farmers and commercial candidates. Only the projection which allows for within-party change (P2) predicts the sort of decline in farmer candidates which has occurred. Similarly, only the P2 projection produces the rise and fall pattern which describes the recent history of commercial candidates. The picture is less clear for employee candidates, partly because trends in that group are less dramatic, but P2 again provides the more accurate projection. For professionals, neither projected series is very inaccurate until the elections of the 1980s. Only then are the assumptions of the within-party model of change obviously more accurate. In general, then, we must conclude that observed trends owe much more to changes within parties than to changes in the numbers of candidates put up by each party.

Party profiles

We have seen that the trends in the overall candidate profile can be attributed essentially to changes in the profiles within the separate parties. How similar are the patterns of overall development in the different parties, and to what extent has the change which has taken place left the parties more or less similar to each other than they were in 1948? The assertion made earlier about the similarity of the Fine Gael and Fianna Fáil profiles is demonstrated in Figure 12.7, which summarises the pattern of changes within each party and grouping (each band refers to the percentage of a party's candidates in a particular occupational category).

Although there are slight differences, the clear impression from the area charts must be that the Fine Gael and Fianna Fáil slices are cut from the same cake. Each has a significant but declining layer of farmers and substantial blocks of

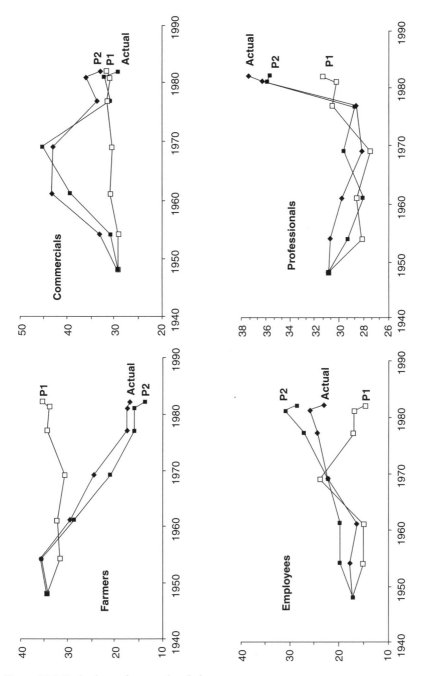

Figure 12.6 Projections of occupational change.

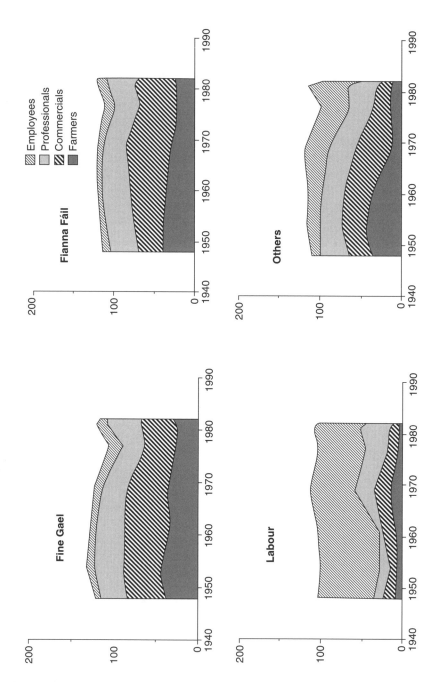

Figure 12.7 Party profiles by social group.

professionals and commercials, and is topped by a thin crust of employees. The right-hand, current (1982) sides of the wedges match more closely than the left-hand sides; the parties resemble one another more now than in 1948. Labour's pattern is very different. The employee crust is very deep; underneath it, only professionals now constitute a clearly visible layer. Its profile is now probably a little closer to those of Fine Gael and Fianna Fáil because of the decline in the proportion of Labour's employees and the drop in farmers elsewhere, but still differences outweigh similarities. Finally, the picture of the 'others' profile shows a major transformation. In 1948, 'other' candidates were not very different from those in Fianna Fáil and Fine Gael, but by 1982 they looked much more like those in the Labour Party. This change dates from 1969, although signs of the transformation were there much earlier as employees gradually replaced farmers as independent and minor party candidates.

Conclusion

This paper has examined the changing occupational profiles of candidates in Dáil elections over the period 1948 to 1982. The major changes are a big decline in farmers, an unsustained increase in commercial candidates, a small recent increase in professionals and a steady, but slight growth in employee candidates. Overall, there is first a net shift from farmers to employees and commercials, and then from commercials to employees and professionals. We have examined three sources of this change: changes in the social structure, then changes in the system of parties and lastly, changes within the parties themselves.

On a casual inspection, social change appears to underlie the direction of changes observed in the candidate profile. Those groups which have grown tend to provide more candidates, and those which have declined provide fewer. However, the relationship between social and political change is clearly not a direct one. Change in candidate profiles has generally been slower than occupational social change. Farmers have been slower to decline and professionals and employees slower to increase. Commercials have declined politically despite evidence of increases socially. Furthermore, and contrary to some expectations, these changes have not produced a more socially representative profile of candidates, but only made it no less unrepresentative than it was in 1948.

Social changes are mediated through parties and the party system. There is little sign that change in the candidate profile has followed the growth or decline of parties. This is suggested by the general stability of candidate numbers and is reinforced by the charts showing the contribution of different parties to the proportions of candidates in each social group. The analysis of changes within parties is more positive, showing that parties have altered their candidate profiles, often in line with social change. This analysis also shows some convergence between the largest two parties, but a growing diversity in many ways between the big two and the rest in their social profiles. 'Others' show the most upheaval, not surprisingly perhaps as the parties and independents which make up the category are themselves unstable. Change within the 'others' category is arguably party system change as much as change within parties, although the weight of independents in this category qualifies this argument.

A summary analysis estimating trends in the candidate profile first under the assumption of no change in party size and second under the assumption of no change in party profile demonstrates that much more accurate projections follow when variations in the within-party profiles are allowed. Whilst some of the changes in candidates in the short term may be due to a rise or fall in the proportions nominated by different parties, the long-term trends are for the most part a consequence of shifts within those parties.

There are four obvious transformations. First, there has been a shift from farmer to commercial candidates. This is most evident in Fianna Fáil, whose profile over the period shows a reversal of the relative proportions of these two groups in the party. Second, there has been a shift from (non-manual) employee candidates to professional ones in the Labour Party. This has no direct basis in social change, and is a purely political shift, though one with ample precedent

Table 12.2 Appendix: Number of candidates by party, occupation and election year

Year	Party	Farmer	Commercial	Higher Prof.	Lower Prof.	Non-manual	Manual	Other	No data	Total
1948	FF	44	32	26	13	7	3	1	9	119
	FG	27	32	21	3	1	1	0	11	82
	Labour	4	8	3	2	27	9	0	6	57
	Other	45	31	24	17	7	5	1	31	149
1954	FF	40	40	22	17	5	3	0	3	112
	FG	35	36	25	4	3	3	1	8	89
	Labour	3	2	2	4	17	9	1	4	41
	Other	22	15	8	6	4	4	0	9	61
1961	FF	32	45	21	13	4	2	1	9	107
	FG	31	51	24	8	6	1	2	0	96
	Labour	2	5	1	1	21	3	0	3	35
	Other	14	15	7	6	5	2	0	36	57
1969	FF	33	68	19	16	8	1	1	0	122
	FG	43	60	26	12	10	1	2	0	125
	Labour	12	21	10	15	40	13	1	0	99
	Other	3	12	3	7	5	3	1	0	27
1977	FF	25	62	25	16	16	1	6	0	132
	FG	29	42	21	9	17	1	4	1	116
	Labour	2	7	9	7	26	6	1	1	57
	Other	9	15	7	13	10	14	5	1	71
1981	FF	28	71	27	22	16	2	4	0	139
	FG	31	53	24	25	15	0	5	1	126
	Labour	1	8	14	7	27	7	2	0	60
	Other	10	13	14	13	18	19	2	2	79
1982	FF	29	58	24	29	14	3	2	0	131
	FG	27	45	20	27	8	1	2	1	113
	Labour	1	4	9	5	18	5	2	0	41
	Other	4	14	11	12	13	22	13	0	81

elsewhere. Third, 'others' showed a shift from farmers to (manual) employees. This reflects a change in the nature of minor Irish parties, from Clann na Talmhan to the Workers' Party and several minor socialist lists. Finally, within Fine Gael, there has been a clear shift from higher to lower professionals, broadening that party's candidate profile and bringing it even closer to Fianna Fáil's.

Overall then, the evidence here supports Schlesinger's assertion that social and political factors play a part in shaping recruitment. Irish parties appear to have responded to social change by accommodating some growing groups and allowing declining ones to move slowly to one side. This has been accomplished without any dramatic shift in the party system. In this respect, parties have responded in the recruitment context to social change as they have responded in the broader political context: by within-party adaptation rather than by party system change. For those impressed by the flexibility of Irish parties, this is another point to those parties' credit. A more critical interpretation must emphasise the limits to that adaptation. The social profile remains hugely distorted, though no more than it was in 1948; and those serving most to reduce that distortion are increasingly to be found only on the periphery of the party system, amongst minor parties and independents.

COMMENTARY BY ADRIAN KAVANAGH

In writing this commentary, I searched through the periodicals shelves of the NUI Maynooth library to find the particular edition of *Irish Political Studies* that this article by Marsh appeared in. It was out, but this search brought to my attention the fascinating array of topics and diversity of approaches that marked the electoral studies research papers in the earlier editions of *Irish Political Studies*, as well as similar papers in other Irish journals such as *Economic and Social Review* and *Irish Geography*, in decidedly marked contrast to present academic trends where the focus is firmly on survey-based statistical modelling. The rather place-based focus of the 1980s electoral literature proves particularly appealing to an electoral geographer, including the work on clientelism by Komito (1992), the 'friends and neighbours effect' by Parker (1982) and the persistence of localism in Irish politics by Marsh (1981b) and O'Carroll (1987), in addition to Michael Marsh's 1989 article, which analyses the changing socio-economic backgrounds of Irish election candidates over the 1948–82 period. By contrast, however, electoral studies papers in recent conferences have tended to particularly focus on the findings of statistical analyses based on large-scale questionnaire surveys.

I expected to see such a trend also replicated in the more recent issues of *Irish Political Studies*. While the electoral output is slightly less prominent than it was in the journal in the 1980s (probably due to fewer general elections!), a review shows that the variety that characterised the electoral studies papers in the earliest issues of *Irish Political Studies* still remains. As well as reports of recent elections (including Kennedy (2002) and Kavanagh (2004a)), recent *Irish Political Studies* articles have included studies of: activism levels and internal politics within political parties (Gallagher *et al*, 2002; Rafter, 2003; Kennedy *et al*, 2005), party policy positions (Benoit and Laver, 2003), the decline in Fine Gael support between 1982 and 2002 (O'Malley and Kerby, 2004), the Constituency Commission (Kavanagh, 2003), and political bias in the Irish media (Brandenberg, 2005). The themes and strong localised flavour of the 1980s articles have largely not been revisited however, probably due to reluctance on behalf of contributors not to retread old ground. This also applies to the article under consideration here, one of a number of seminal articles by the same author appearing in the early editions of the journal (see also Marsh, 1987 and 1991).

The paper begins by positing that changes in the nature of political recruitment will, to some degree, reflect general changes in society, allowing for various opportunity structures associated with different parties that may act to limit recruitment from certain sectors of society. A key point is made at the onset, namely that studies of election candidates have been rather few in number, particularly when contrasted with the greater focus on those who have proven successful in elections, Dáil deputies. This is quite apt, given that the subsequent revisitings of this research have largely tended to just focus on the backgrounds of the elected candidates, with the notable exception of Galligan (1999). The process of candidate selection, writing from a 1980s context, is portrayed as largely driven by constituency activists, with the only intervention on the part of party headquarters concerning advice on the numbers of candidates to be selected. Recent studies of the candidate selection process (Galligan, 1999 and 2003; Galligan and Kavanagh, 2007), however, point to growing levels of influence by party headquarters for the 1997, 2002 and 2007 general elections. Marsh also draws attention to differences that exist between the general group of election candidates and the sub-group that proves to be successful, namely the deputies – the candidate group is larger, more volatile and less dependent on patterns of party support in subsequent electoral contests. Furthermore, as will be discussed later, the socio-economic background of deputies can differ significantly from that of election candidates.

Based on his analysis of various candidate datasets, covering the period between 1948 and 1982, Marsh finds a significant decline in the number of farmer candidates, as well as those drawn from the higher professions, with a general increase in the number of candidates drawn from the lower professional (particularly teachers) and employee groups. While these changes are found to mirror general social trends to a degree, the relationship is not an especially robust one and makes for a growing variance between the social profiles of election candidates and Irish society at large. Studying the social profiles of the three main parties, Fianna Fáil, Fine Gael and Labour, as well as the 'others' category, Marsh portrays these as largely 'socially heterogeneous' – as he argues, 'no social category is represented at all exclusively by any one party' – but he does draw out significant distinctions between Fianna Fáil and Fine Gael, on the one hand, and the Labour and others group in terms of their socio-economic profiles. By 1982, farmer candidates are predominantly associated with the two main parties, as opposed to the late 1940s when the 'others' group accounted for a significant proportion of these. The decline of farmer candidates amongst the 'others' group is linked to the changing nature of the smaller parties over this period and, in turn, acts as the most significant component in the overall decline in farmer candidate numbers during the study period. The commercial and professional sectors were also found to account for a more significant proportion of Fianna Fáil and Fine Gael candidates, while candidates for Labour and the other parties were found to be more likely to be drawn from the manual and non-manual employee groups.

These are but a few insights from what amounts to a highly comprehensive analysis of the changing socio-economic backgrounds of election candidates. Perhaps one dimension that may have further added to this study – and this is to betray my bias as a geographer – would have been to draw out the regional dimension of these changing patterns. For instance, such an approach could have studied whether the decline in farmer candidacies was largely a nationwide trend or more a factor of ongoing population shifts between rural and urban Ireland over this period, reducing the number of seats in the more rural constituencies and, subsequently, the number of candidates contesting these. Similarly, one could also detect whether certain regions – especially the less volatile regions – largely resisted these overall trends at the same time as changes were being exacerbated in other parts of the state.

While this paper has not been revisited in detail in more recent issues of *Irish Political Studies*, it has proven to be widely cited in publications relating to specific general election contests, most notably the *How Ireland Voted* series. Such treatments are generally set within a wider context of the under-representation of other sectors of society in political life, often with a particular focus on female participation in electoral politics (O'Sullivan, 1999). The specific candidate-focused analysis of this paper has, however, only been replicated once within this series – in the Galligan (1999) 'Candidate Selection' chapter in *How Ireland Voted 1997* – and the general trend has been to discuss the social backgrounds of Dáil deputies as opposed to a much wider study of the larger candidate base. Thus, Galligan (1999) offers the most useful point of comparison to detect whether Marsh's concept of 'transformation with a small t' can be viewed as having continued relevance for more recent contests. Comparison with the 1997 statistics and – in some instances – extending this analysis through to the 2007 context draws out some interesting trends. One related aspect to note is the change in the actual numbers of candidates being selected by the larger parties over the 1980s, 1990s and 2000s. In the case of Fianna Fáil, 131 candidates were selected to contest the February 1982 contest, the last election studied by Marsh, but this figure falls to 112 for the 1997 contest and further drops to 106 for the 2007 election – despite a slight increase in the number of constituencies being contested over the same time period (from 41 to 43). Similarly, the number of Fine Gael candidates fell from 112 in 1982 to 90 in 1997, although the number has increased slightly to 91 for the 2007 contest. By contrast, the number of candidates for Labour (41 in 1982, 44 in 1997 and 49 in 2007) and especially the 'Other' category (from 81 in 1982 to 236 in 1997) have increased over this time period.

Table 12.3, which uses figures drawn from Galligan (1999) to update the Marsh analysis, shows the impact that changing recruitment levels amongst the different political parties has had in relation to the social backgrounds of candidates. The number of farmer and commerce-based candidates selected by the two main parties declined over the 1982–1997 period, although these trends were offset somewhat by an increase in the numbers within these categories for the 'Others' category, due in part to the influence of rural-based independent candidates drawn from the Fianna Fáil and Fine Gael gene pool in the case of the farmer category, and Progressive Democrat candidates in the case of the commerce category. The number of professional candidates is shown to have increased between 1982 and 1997 (and these categories now account for a significantly larger share of the total candidate base), with this representing a continuation of the trend noted in Marsh's 1989 article for lower professionals and a significant reversal of the observed decline in the number of higher professional candidates in that article. The advent of the Progressive Democrats had a significant impact on the increase in the number of professional candidates in the 1997 contest

Table 12.3 Number of candidates by party, occupation and election year, excluding 'Other' and 'Don't Know' categories

	Fianna Fáil	Fine Gael	Labour	Others	Total
Farmers					
1948	44	27	4	45	120 *(30.7%)*
1982	29	27	1	4	61 *(15.2%)*
1997	13	12	1	15	41 *(10.4%)*
Commerce					
1948	32	32	8	31	102 *(26.1%)*
1982	58	45	4	14	121 *(30.1%)*
1997	29	21	1	36	87 *(22.1%)*
Higher Professionals					
1948	26	21	3	24	74 *(18.9%)*
1982	24	20	9	11	64 *(15.9%)*
1997	22	14	11	31	78 *(19.8%)*
Lower Professionals					
1948	13	3	2	17	35 *(9.0%)*
1982	29	27	5	12	73 *(18.2%)*
1997	21	26	13	27	87 *(22.1%)*
Salaried Employees					
1948	7	1	27	7	42 *(10.7%)*
1982	14	8	18	13	53 *(13.2%)*
1997	23	11	11	31	76 *(19.3%)*
Manual Employees					
1948	3	1	9	5	18 *(4.6%)*
1982	3	1	5	22	30 *(7.5%)*
1997	0	0	5	20	25 *(6.3%)*

Sources: Marsh, 1989: 79; Galligan, 1999: 72.

(11 of the 30 Progressive Democrat candidates were drawn from either the higher or lower professions), as indeed has the increasing influence of other smaller political parties, such as the Green Party, over this period. Again marking a continuation of the trend observed in Marsh's 1989 article, the number of salaried employee candidates continued to grow up until the 1997 contest, with this increase also reflected in the numbers selected by all the different political parties, with the notable exception of Labour. Finally the number of manual employee candidates declined between 1982 and 1997, with neither of the main political parties selecting any candidate from this category in the latter contest. The growing political strength of Sinn Féin and other smaller left-wing parties, such as the Socialist Party and Socialist Workers' Party, has probably acted to redress that trend during elections held in the 2000s, although it is telling that these parties are to some extent attempting to increase the number of candidates drawn from the professional and commerce categories as an attempt to widen their electoral appeal outside their traditional urban working-class bases.

The overall trend acts to illustrate the impact that the increased number of small party and independent candidates has had on the social profile of general election candidates. In some cases, the impact of these new parties has been to confirm the overall candidate social profile, for instance, although new Green Party candidates do offer radically different viewpoints, they do not differ significantly from the main parties in terms of their social backgrounds. However, the increasing numbers of left-wing small party or independent candidates have proven key in maintaining manual employee candidate levels at, or above, those of 1982 for the most recent general election contests (2002 and 2007) – the growing importance of these parties not being fully evident at the time of the 1997 contest, as reflected in the Galligan (1999) figures. Despite this, manual workers remain significantly under-represented in terms of candidate selection – particularly in relation to the two main parties – and prove to be even less represented when the focus is on successful candidates, or Dáil deputies. The manual grouping accounted for only one per cent of all deputies after the 1997 contest, increasing slightly to two per cent for 2002, as opposed to the farmer (13 per cent in both contests) and professional (47 per cent in both contests) categories, which proved to be of even greater significance in terms of Dáil representation, relative to these groupings' contribution to candidate selection (O'Sullivan, 1999, p. 188; Gallagher, 2003, p. 115).

Marsh's 1989 article has provided a useful benchmark against which more recent candidate selection trends may be measured. It remains to be assessed how relevant this topic is, apart from satisfying academic curiosity. I would argue, based on insights arising from my doctoral studies into the determinants of low voter turnout in socially deprived areas, that it is still an important topic – and perhaps even more important given the trend of declining electoral participation in general election contests. A strong theme that emerged from the qualitative analysis I carried out (Kavanagh, 2002) was the link that existed between turnout propensity and electoral choice, namely the suggestion that certain types of election candidates might prove to be more successful in drawing people from certain socio-economic backgrounds out to the polls. One South West Inner City resident saw this as a key factor underpinning the low turnouts in his home area:

> By and large you never had a Tony Gregory (type candidate). And I reckon if you had two Tony Gregory's in this side of the city that we would be an awful lot better off. They can say what they like, but on the north-side of the city I think they're about five years ahead of us both in their political aware-ness, their community awareness and the way they have got in to trying to work the system. And I think that's down to people like Gregory...that's what I think is very, very badly needed here – to get somebody who is of the area and from the area.

Others argued that there was a linkage between candidate selection and socio-economic biases in turnout and political representation levels, suggesting that social biases in turnout and candidate selection may result in significant differences in terms of the levels of interest awarded to specific issues or concerns. As one politician noted:

> The result of low voter turnout is that you get a Dáil where the interests of wealthy people are represented and not those of the poorer in society. As well as that the issues that are causing most excitement in the Dáil are farmers' issues as the politicians all know that the farmers vote en masse. I can do a number of months work on a Social Welfare Bill and I will not get a similar electoral return from working on this.

Such claims are further evident in the light of the impact that locally-based, mainly working-class, candidates had on local election turnouts in the 2004 local elections, where political mobilisation by such candidates – including Sinn Féin, Socialist Party, Socialist Workers Party and other 'bin charges' candidates – proved to be one of the key factors accounting for significantly higher turnout levels in a number of working-class areas in Dublin in those contests (Kavanagh, 2004a and 2004b). In a similar vein, similar associations can be developed relat-ing to demographic and gender biases in candidate selection. Thus, Marsh's 1989 article is not only important in terms of the extent of scholarship evident, but also in creating a context against which the ongoing political under-representation of different social groups in Irish society may be measured.

Notes

1 An earlier version of this paper was presented at the workshop on Patterns of Elite Transformation in Western Democracies, ECPR Joint Sessions, Bologna, 1988, and I am grateful to members of that group for their comments. Desmond King carried out some of the data collection, which was assisted by a grant from the TCD Faculty Benefaction Fund.
2 In the dataset described below, 42 per cent of all candidates were standing for the first time but only 26 per cent of successful candidates were elected for the first time.
3 It took longer at cabinet level. Cohan argues that 'the personnel in Fianna Fáil governments remained virtually unchanged until 1949' (1973).

4 Information was obtained from local and national newspapers, notices of polls, the political parties and directories: Thom's Directory, Nealon's Guides, the Magill election books, and Knight and Baxter Moore, 1973 (see Marsh, 1987, p. 74).

5 The term 'employees' is not an exact one, as many professionals are also employees. There was also a small number of unclassifiable candidates. These have not been shown in the Tables. See the Appendix for details.

6 The Labour proportion includes candidates from the National Labour Party in 1948. This graph is based on total candidate figures, not just on those for whom occupational data are available. There is some difference between these figures and those on which later graphs are based, as for 1948 and 1961 there is a significant (over 20–25 per cent) missing data problem for 'others', and hence 'others' are under-represented in the data for those years. For details of missing data see the Appendix.

7 The prominence of university teachers on Labour's lists was also noted: 'It might even be suggested that the Labour Party is...becoming symbolically representative not merely of the new university graduate group in society but of the university teacher' (Farrell, 1971, p. 323). The party's handbook for canvassers made a similar point, if less knowingly: 'Among our candidates are farmers, industrial workers, solicitors, university lecturers, businessmen, professors, housewives, shopkeepers and teachers', cited in Horgan (1986, pp. 172–3), who notes particularly the need for three categories of university lecturers, professors and teachers!

8 Peillon notes that census information suggests that most higher professionals have not been self-employed, despite the fact that the higher/lower distinction was initially based on this expectation (1982). However, it is probable that the distinction is normally valid for politicians and that those from the higher professions (doctors, solicitors and barristers in particular) are more likely to be self-employed than the professional group as a whole.

9 This technique has become quite popular in electoral analysis (see for instance Heath *et al*, 1985).

References

Benoit, Kenneth and Michael Laver (2003) 'Estimating Irish Party Positions Using Computer Wordscoring: The 2002 Election – A Research Note', *Irish Political Studies*, 18 (1), pp. 97–107.

Brandenberg, Heinz (2005) 'Political Bias in the Irish Media: A Quantitative Study of Campaign Coverage during the 2002 General Election', *Irish Political Studies*, 20 (3), pp. 297–322.

Busteed, Mervyn A. and Hugh Mason (1970) 'Irish Labour in the 1969 Election', *Political Studies*, 18 (3), pp. 373–9.

Carty, R. Kenneth (1983) *Party and Parish Pump: Electoral Politics in Ireland*. Dingle: Brandon Press.

Chubb, Basil (1982) *The Government and Politics of Ireland*. Second Edition. London: Longman.

Cohan, Alvin S. (1972) *The Irish Political Elite*. Dublin: Gill and Macmillan.

Cohan, Alvin S. (1973) 'Career Patterns in the Irish Political Elite', *British Journal of Political Science*, 3 (3), pp. 213–28.

Czudnowski, Moshe M. (1975) 'Political Recruitment', pp. 155–242 in Fred I. Greenstein and Nelson W. Polsby (eds.) *Handbook of Political Science – Volume 2: Micropolitical Theory*. Reading, MA: Addison-Wesley.

Darcy, Robert (1988) 'Election of Women to Dáil Éireann: A Formal Analysis', *Irish Political Studies*, 3, pp. 63–76.

Farrell, Brian (1971) 'Dáil Deputies: "The 1969 Generation"', *Economic and Social Review*, 2 (3), pp. 309–27.

Farrell, Brian (1975) 'Irish Government Re-observed', *Economic and Social Review*, 6 (3), pp. 405–14.

Farrell, David M. (1984) 'Age, Education and Occupational Backgrounds of TDs and "Routes" to the Dáil: The Effects of Localism in the 1980s', *Administration*, 32 (3), pp. 323–41.

Gallagher, Michael (1981) 'Societal Change and Party Adaptation in the Republic of Ireland, 1960–1981', *European Journal of Political Research*, 9 (3), pp. 269–85.

Gallagher, Michael (1984) '166 Who Rule: The Dáil Deputies of November 1982', *Economic and Social Review*, 15 (4), pp. 241–64.

Gallagher, Michael (1985) 'Social Backgrounds and Local Orientations of Members of the Irish Dáil', *Legislative Studies Quarterly*, 10 (3), pp. 373–94.

Gallagher, Michael (1987) 'The Outcome', pp. 63–98 in Michael Laver, Peter Mair and Richard Sinnott (eds.) *How Ireland Voted*. Dublin: PSAI/Poolbeg Press.

Gallagher, Michael (1988) 'Ireland: The Increasing Role of the Centre', pp. 119–44 in Michael Gallagher and Michael Marsh (eds.) *Candidate Selection in Comparative Perspective: The Secret Garden of Politics*. London: Sage.

Gallagher, M. (2003) 'Stability and Turmoil: Analysis of the Results', pp. 88–118 in Michael Gallagher, Michael Marsh and Paul Mitchell (eds.) *How Ireland Voted 2002*. Basingstoke: Palgrave Macmillan.

Gallagher, Michael and Michael Marsh (eds.) (1988) *Candidate Selection in Comparative Perspective: The Secret Garden of Politics*. London: Sage.

Gallagher, Michael, Vanessa Liston, Michael Marsh and Liam Weeks (2002) 'Explaining Activism Among Fine Gael Members: A Test of the General Incentives Model', *Irish Political Studies*, 17 (1), pp. 97–113.

Galligan, Y. (1999) 'Candidate Selection', pp. 57–81 in Michael Marsh and Paul Mitchell (eds.) *How Ireland Voted 1997*. Boulder, CO: Westview Press.

Galligan, Yvonne (2003) 'Candidate Selection: More Democratic or More Centrally Controlled?', pp. 37–56 in Michael Gallagher, Michael Marsh and Paul Mitchell (eds.) *How Ireland Voted 2002*. Basingstoke: Palgrave Macmillan.

Galligan, Yvonne and Adrian Kavanagh (2007) 'Candidate Selection for the 2007 Election: The Politics of Place and Gender'. Unpublished paper presented at 'Place, Environment and Politics in the Republic of Ireland' conference, NUI Maynooth, 23 March.

Heath, A.F., Roger Jowell and John Curtice (1985) *How Britain Votes*. Oxford: Pergamon Press.

Horgan, John (1986) *Labour: The Price of Power*. Dublin: Gill and Macmillan.

Kavanagh, Adrian (2002) *Social Deprivation, Political Alienation and Community Empowerment*. Unpublished PhD Thesis. Maynooth: National University of Ireland Maynooth.

Kavanagh, Adrian (2003) 'The Constituency Commission', *Irish Political Studies*, 18 (2), pp. 89–99.

Kavanagh, Adrian (2004a) 'The 2004 Local Elections in the Republic of Ireland', *Irish Political Studies*, 19 (2), pp. 64–84.

Kavanagh, Adrian (2004b) 'Turnout or Turned Off? Electoral Participation in Dublin in the Early 21st Century', *Journal of Irish Urban Studies*, 3 (2), pp. 1–24.

Kennedy, Fiachra (2002) 'The 2002 General Election in Ireland', *Irish Political Studies*, 17 (2), pp. 95–106.

Kennedy, Fiachra, Pat Lyons and Peter Fitzgerald (2005) 'The Members of Labour: Backgrounds, Political Views and Attitudes towards Coalition Governments and the Party System', *Irish Political Studies*, 20 (2), pp. 171–86.

Knight, James and Nicolas Baxter-Moore (1973) *Republic of Ireland: The General Elections of 1969 and 1973*. London: The Arthur McDougal Fund.

Komito, Lee (1992) 'Brokerage or Friendship? Politics and Networks in Ireland', *Economic and Social Review*, 23 (2), pp. 129–45.

Laver, Michael (1986) 'Ireland: Politics with Some Social Basis; An Interpretation Based on Survey Data', *Economic and Social Review*, 17 (3), pp. 193–213.

Marsh, Michael (1980) 'European Social Democratic Party Leaders and the Working Class', pp. 47–74 in K. Lawson (ed.) *Political Parties and Linkage: A Comparative Perspective*. New Haven, CT: Yale University Press.

Marsh, Michael (1981a) 'Electoral Preferences in Irish Recruitment: The 1977 Election', *European Journal of Political Research*, 9 (1), pp. 61–74.

Marsh, Michael (1981b) 'Localism, Candidate Selection and Electoral Preferences in Ireland: The General Election of 1977', *Economic and Social Review*, 12 (4), pp. 267–86.

Marsh, Michael (1987) 'Electoral Evaluations of Candidates in Irish General Elections, 1948–1982', *Irish Political Studies*, 2, pp. 65–76.

Marsh, Michael (1991) 'Accident or Design? Non-Voting in Ireland', *Irish Political Studies*, 6, pp. 1–14.

Matthews, Donald R. (1984) 'Legislative Recruitment and Legislative Careers', *Legislative Studies Quarterly*, 9 (4), pp. 547–85.

McCracken, J.L. (1958) *Representative Government in Ireland: A Study of Dáil Éireann 1919–1948*. London: Oxford University Press.

O'Byrnes, Stephen (1986) *Hiding Behind a Face: Fine Gael under FitzGerald*. Dublin: Gill and Macmillan.

O'Carroll, J.P. (1987) 'Strokes, Cute Hoors and Sneaking Regarders: The Influence of Local Culture on Irish Political Style', *Irish Political Studies*, 2, pp. 77–92.

O'Malley, Eoin and Matthew Kerby (2004) 'Chronicle of a Death Foretold? Understanding the Decline of Fine Gael', *Irish Political Studies*, 19 (1), pp. 39–58.

O'Sullivan, Mary-Clare (1999) 'The Social and Political Characteristics of the Twenty-Eighth Dáil', pp. 181–94 in Michael Marsh and Paul Mitchell (eds.) *How Ireland Voted 1997*. Boulder, CO: Westview Press.

Parker, Anthony J. (1982) 'The "Friends and Neighbours" Effect in the Galway West Constituency', *Political Geography Quarterly*, 1 (3), pp. 243–62.

Pedersen, Mogens N. (1976) *Political Development and Elite Transformation in Denmark*. London: Sage.

Peillon, Michel (1982) *Contemporary Irish Society: An Introduction*. Dublin: Gill and Macmillan.

Quandt, William B. (1970) *The Comparative Study of Political Elites*. London: Sage.

Rafter, Kevin (2003) 'Leadership Changes in Fine Gael and the Labour Party, 2002', *Irish Political Studies*, 18 (1), pp. 108–19.

Robson, Christopher and Brendan Walsh (1974) 'The Importance of Positional Voting Bias in the Irish General Election of 1973', *Political Studies*, 22 (2), pp. 191–203.

Rottman, David B. and Philip J. O'Connell (1982) 'The Changing Social Structure of Ireland', pp. 63–8 in Frank Litton (ed.) *Unequal Achievement: The Irish Experience 1957–1982*. Dublin: Institute of Public Administration.

Schlesinger, Joseph A. (1966) *Ambition and Politics*. Chicago: Rand-McNally.

Whyte, John H. (1966) *Dáil Deputies: Their Work, Its Difficulties, Possible Remedies*. Dublin: Tuairim Pamphlet.

Whyte, John H. (1974) 'Ireland: Politics Without Social Bases', pp. 619–52 in Richard Rose (ed.) *Electoral Behavior: A Comparative Handbook*. New York: Free Press.

13 Party choice and social structure in Ireland

Michael Laver

Originally published in *Irish Political Studies*, 1, 1986, pp. 45–55.

The social bases of voting choice in Ireland will remain without a definitive interpretation until the advent of a full-scale academic election study. Until then, political scientists will continue to be thrown back upon two basic types of data. The first is a collection of aggregate statistics, based mainly on census returns and constituency-level voting figures. Such data have recently been used to good effect by Gallagher (1976), Garvin (1981) and Parker (1984). The second is a series of commercial public opinion polls dating back to the early 1970s. These are based on quota samples of about 1,000, and were collected mainly for Irish national newspapers. Such data informed Whyte's well-known 'politics without social bases' interpretation of the Irish party system (Whyte, 1974), as well as that of Carty (1981). However, both Gallagher (1985) and Sinnott (1987) have used survey data to criticise the 'politics without social bases' thesis, basing their arguments on the different propensities with which different occupational groups vote for the different Irish parties.

This paper presents a reanalysis and reinterpretation of both survey and aggregate data. The first part follows a method used by Laver (1984) to analyse local voting in Liverpool. A principal components analysis is used to reduce a large set of aggregate variables to a manageable set of inputs to a series of regressions on constituency voting patterns. This enables us to scan quite a wide range of data while retaining a small enough number of basic indicators to allow sensible causal modelling. The second part of the paper offers a possible solution to the problem posed by the relatively small size of the samples used by the commercial opinion polls. This involves joining the results of the cross-tabulations of 67 polls taken over 11 years into a single time series. A mathematical smoothing operation is then used to remove most of the more erratic fluctuations in the data. This enables more confident interpretations of voting patterns *within subsections of the electorate.*

Whether the analyses that follow support or undermine the 'politics without social bases' argument is a matter of interpretation. There can be no doubt that the social patterning of party preference is not as stark in Ireland as it is in some European systems. There can be no doubt that class conflict in Ireland has only a very pale reflection in the party system. Nevertheless, both the aggregate and the survey analyses that follow do show the quite definite effects on party choice of certain aspects of the social structure. Things, in short, are quite a lot more predictable than they would be if party politics in Ireland had no social basis whatsoever.

A reinterpretation of aggregate data

A fundamental problem facing aggregate analyses of voting behaviour in Ireland is the very small number of available data points. Multi-member constituencies are quite large and the population is quite small. The various data sources can be matched to voting figures, therefore, only at the level of the county and the county borough. Even so, voting figures for constituencies combining two counties must be apportioned between counties. (For the analysis reported here, such votes were apportioned on the basis of voting patterns in the previous county council elections, giving 26 data points; see Laver (1986a) for the full figures.) In short, we must live with the small number of data points, while finding a method that allows us to look at a wide range of potentially interesting variables.

The method used is to generate indices from a wide range of variables, using principal components analyses. Sixty-six input variables were used. These related to the age structure of the county concerned, to its occupational structure, social and economic wellbeing, agricultural structure and housing structure, together with a range of general cultural variables, dealing with religion, population turnover and so on. This analysis is reported in Laver (1986a), and the principal components that emerged are summarised in Table 13.1, which also shows the simple correlations between the aggregate socio-economic factors and voting patterns in the Irish counties in the November 1982 general election. These results strongly reproduce the findings of Gallagher and Parker in relation to the Fine Gael vote, which proves once more to be very difficult to interpret in terms of aggregate data. In contrast, the Fianna Fáil vote seems quite clearly structured at county level, particularly by Factors 2, 4, 5 and 7. The same factors also structure the Labour vote, albeit to a lesser extent.

Table 13.1 Simple correlations between socio-economic factors and vote share: November 1982

Factor	Interpretations (positive versus negative loadings)	Fianna Fáil	Fine Gael	Labour
1	Young families vs. over 40s	−.15	−.39	+.39
2	Agriculture vs. other occupations	+.76	*	−.38
3	Manual occupations vs. professions	+.13	−.45	+.18
4	Low soc. econ. well-being vs. high	+.65	+.42	−.55
5	Poor housing amenities vs. rest	+.75	*	−.50
6	Rentals vs. mortgages	*	*	*
7	Cattle farming vs. tillage/horticulture	+.77	+.34	−.57
8	Prosperous versus marginal farming	−.14	*	+.15
9	Protestants vs. Catholics/Irish speakers	−.25	+.20	*
10	No religion/High turnover vs. rest	−.30	−.24	+.44

The *independent* effects of the various socio-economic variables, however, can only be assessed properly in terms of multiple regression analyses, the results of which are reported in Table 13.2. While the effects of all of the socio-economic factors were explored, only those of Factors 2, 4, 5 and 7 are reported here. The others add nothing to the explanatory power of the model. The Table shows quite clearly that, while the relevant factors are inter-related, the factor describing the pattern of agricultural land use maintains the strongest link with Fianna Fáil voting once the effect of the other factors is held constant. The simple relationships between the other factors and Fianna Fáil voting shown in Table 13.1 thus seem to be an artefact of their covariation with the agricultural structure factor. Thus the relationship that appears to exist between the proportion of the workforce engaged in agriculture and the proportion of voters supporting Fianna Fáil seems, on closer inspection, to be spurious.

Having uncovered one potential set of spurious effects, we must be careful not to replace them with another. Most of the factors extracted have strong regional, and especially east–west, overtones. An attempt was therefore made to check the possibility that the socio-economic factors were simply acting as surrogates for an east–west regional dimension that was 'really' structuring voting patterns. An independent definition of the 'west' was used (taken from Scully (1971)), since to take a definition from previous voting analyses would have been self-defeating. This east–west dichotomy was run as a dummy variable in a multiple regression (Model G) that also included the agricultural structure factor. The results suggest

Table 13.2 Multiple regressions on Fianna Fáil and Labour voting, November 2002

Model	Variables (factors)	Fianna Fáil		Labour	
		Beta coef.	R squared	Beta coef.	R squared
A	2 Agricultural occupations	.36	.50	.38	.39
	4 Low socio-economic well-being	.41		−.30	
B	2 Agricultural occupations	.39	.60	−.38	.27
	5 Poor housing amenities	.40		−.84	
C	2 Agricultural occupations	.26	.63	.33	.35
	7 Cattle farming	.61*		.37	
D	4 Low socio-economic well-being	.40	.46	−.26	.30
	5 Poor housing amenities	.32		−.38	
E	4 Low socio-economic well-being	.19	.60	−.39	.36
	7 Cattle farming	.62*		−.35	
F	5 Poor housing amenities	.14	.59	−.31	.37
	7 Cattle farming	.66*		.34	
G	7 Cattle farming	.60*	.60	–	–
	East/ west dummy 0/1	.19		–	–

Note: all *R*-squared values significant at .001 level for Fianna Fáil and .05 for Labour. Betas marked with an asterisk are significant at a .001 level or better.

that Fianna Fáil voting is higher in the west *because* the level of livestock farming is higher. It does not seem to be the case, therefore, that the explanatory power of the agricultural structure derives solely from the fact that it varies between east and west, while the 'westness' of a county determines the level of Fianna Fáil voting. If anything, this analysis is consistent with the reverse interpretation. This is that the link between 'the west' and Fianna Fáil voting is a product of regional variations in the agricultural structure.

The very low levels of the relationship between Fine Gael voting and the various socio-economic factors do not allow for more detailed analysis. None of the multiple regressions used to predict the Fine Gael vote yield coefficients that are significant, either in statistical or in any other terms. Furthermore, when each of the original input variables is correlated with the Fine Gael vote, nothing of significance emerges either. Such a robust non-relationship must be regarded as a significant finding in its own right, though care must once more be taken when generalising aggregate results to individual behaviour.

The non-relationship of Fine Gael voting and the aggregate level socio-economic factors does not mean that there is no social basis for the Fine Gael vote. Rather it means that we have yet to find a social basis for it that is patterned at the level of the constituency. This is in contrast with the Fianna Fáil vote, which does vary on this scale. Since, as we shall see from the analysis of survey data that follows, Fine Gael voting clearly *is* related to socio-economic factors, it must be the case that these vary more within constituencies than between them.

The predictability of Labour voting lies between that of Fianna Fáil and that of Fine Gael, as Table 13.2 also shows. If we take the agricultural structure as the best predictor of Labour voting, however, the analysis of mispredictions is most revealing and can be found in Table 13.3. This shows that the Labour vote is underpredicted in precisely the constituencies in which the party won seats. Given that Dublin constituencies are excluded, Labour voting seems to be concentrated quite disproportionately on certain candidates, who generate wild outliers. Votes for these candidates can be seen to fit in not at all with the general variation of the Labour vote across the country, but to pop up in statistically unexpected places such as Kerry and Tipperary! This shows a strong 'incumbency' or 'candidate' effect, or at least a strong unexplained local effect, quite unlike anything that can be found for Fianna Fáil.

Table 13.3 Mispredictions of Labour vote by tillage/livestock factor

Overpredictions (% Labour vote)		Underpredictions (% Labour vote)	
Waterford	9.9	Kerry	18.2
Laois	7.5	Tipperary North	12.0
Donegal	7.3	Tipperary South	9.2
Offaly	5.5	Meath	6.5
Wexford	5.5	Wicklow	5.5

We can draw some general conclusions from the aggregate analysis:

(i) Fianna Fáil voting appears to be more consistently predictable from aggregate data than previous analyses suggest, once variables relating to the agricultural structure are introduced. These also indicate that the link between Fianna Fáil voting and 'the west' may well not be to do with 'the west' itself, or with employment in agriculture, but rather with patterns of landholding and usage.

(ii) Fine Gael voting does not appear to be related to anything patterned at county level.

(iii) Overall patterns of Labour voting show some linkage with aggregate socio-economic factors. However, Dáil seats appear to be won on the basis of local surges of support that are not at all easy to predict in aggregate terms.

In general, many of the factors that might affect voting behaviour, social class for example, vary more within counties than between them. Obviously, only factors that pattern the social and economic structure at county level can have even a chance to influence county level voting behaviour. For an insight into the effect of other socio-economic variables we need to use survey data, to which we now turn.

A reinterpretation of survey data

John Whyte's 'politics without social bases' thesis was based on a Gallup Poll conducted in 1969. Regular commercial polling in Ireland, however, began in earnest only in November 1974, after which we do have a series of polls conducted at least quarterly and often monthly. These were based on quota samples of about 1,000 voters each, and were conducted by two reputable commercial market research organisations, Irish Marketing Surveys (IMS) and the Market Research Bureau of Ireland (MRBI). The main problem is that the small sample sizes realise even smaller numbers within particular sub-samples, resulting in a considerable month-by-month variation in survey estimates of party support within any given social group. The erratic nature of the figures provided by the survey data on party support within social groups is illustrated in Figure 13.1. The dotted line shows the 'raw' time series of figures for the Fianna Fáil share of the vote within the ABC1 (non-manual) social grouping in the 67 different polls analysed between November 1974 and May 1985. There seems a strong probability that sampling error is superimposing a lot of 'noise' on the underlying 'signal' in the data. Operating precisely on this analogy, it is possible to use mathematical smoothing techniques to remove the effect of the noise. The solid line in Figure 13.1 shows the effect of applying the smoothing routines available in the MLAB modelling package to the same opinion poll data, and shows the very considerable dangers of basing any firm conclusions on the findings of single polls. Individual poll results lie on the broken, not on the solid, line. Thus the difference between 1979 and 1982 depends very much upon *which* of the raw polls the analyst happens to select.

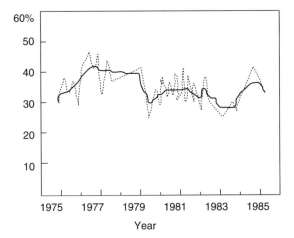

Figure 13.1 Raw and smoothed Fianna Fáil share of ABC1 electorate.

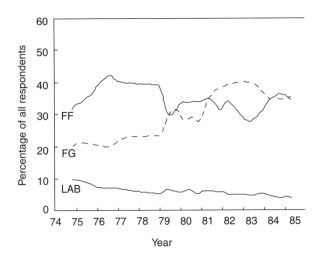

Figure 13.2 Party shares of ABC1 electorate.

Figure 13.2 shows the shares of the middle-class electorate attracted by each of the main parties over the period at issue. One obvious trend is the decline in the level of the middle-class Labour vote, from about ten per cent at the outset to about five per cent in 1985. In contrast we see a considerable, though rather more erratic, increase in the level of middle-class Fine Gael voting. Even after the reverses of 1984 and 1985 the Fine Gael share of the non-manual electorate is still markedly higher than it was in the late 1970s. The Fianna Fáil share of the non-manual vote simply seems to have fluctuated, though it did go up and down in inverse relationship to that of Fine Gael. We should beware of a version of the ecological fallacy when dealing with a series of poll results based on unconnected samples. The fact that the Fine Gael vote share goes up when that of Labour goes down does not necessarily mean that voters switched from one party to another. An equally plausible interpretation is that voters moved into and out of the 'undecided' group in particular ways. Nevertheless, the patterns shown in Figure 13.2 are certainly consistent with an interpretation based on a competition between Fianna Fáil and Fine Gael for the non-manual vote and, underlying this, a steady leakage of middle-class Labour support, mostly to Fine Gael. We also see that the suggestion that Fine Gael was becoming, in the early 1980s, the party of the middle class clearly has some basis in the polling data. Fine Gael overtook and led Fianna Fáil in this group for most of the period.

The situation in the farming electorate (Figure 13.3) is broadly similar, though Labour has effectively no support in this sector. Fine Gael shows a more modest (about ten per cent) and a more erratic increase over the 12 years from 1974 to 1985, while the level of Fianna Fáil support has fluctuated around a broadly static position. Starting far behind Fianna Fáil, and with no Labour support to eat into, Fine Gael has been less successful at overtaking Fianna Fáil among the farmers. In both the farming and non-manual electorates, however, there is no doubt that the two big parties are much more evenly-matched in 1985 than they were in 1975.

In the skilled (C2) and semi- and unskilled (DE) manual electorates, the position is rather different (see Figures 13.4 and 13.5). In the first place, there is much more significant Labour support at the beginning of the period. In the second place, Fianna Fáil starts much further ahead of the other two parties. The recent decline in Fine Gael is more marked in the manual electorate, and is accompanied by a more sustained revival of Fianna Fáil. Indeed, while the Fine Gael advance

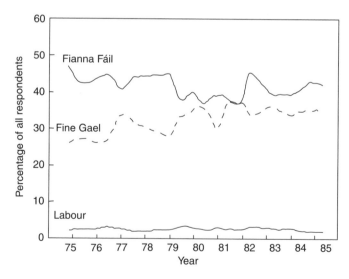

Figure 13.3 Party shares of farming electorate.

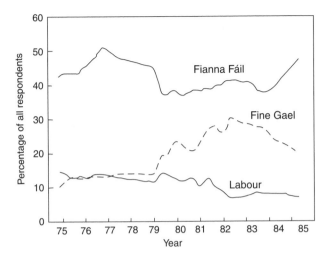

Figure 13.4 Party share of C2 electorate.

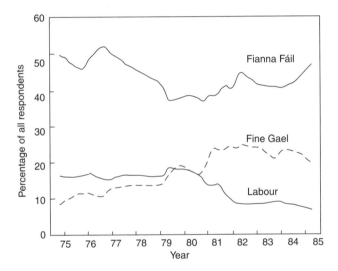

Figure 13.5 Party share of DE electorate.

within the skilled working class was as marked as that within the middle class, these gains have proved more volatile. In contrast Fine Gael gains within the unskilled working class have been both less spectacular and less volatile. Labour has more to lose in this sector of the electorate; it would appear to have lost it to both of the big parties, which have each increased their vote share during periods of Labour decline. Recent Fine Gael losses have been accompanied by Fianna

Fáil gains, however, so that the net result over the whole period is that the Fine Gael vote share has increased at the expense of that of Labour.

Overall, however, the different social bases of party support in Ireland can be seen from a simple inspection of Figures 13.2–13.5. More detailed analysis of patterns within both the non-manual and the farming electorates provides further evidence of social patterning (see Laver, 1986b). Moving from occupational category A (professional) to E (unskilled manual), therefore, the Fine Gael vote share decreases consistently, and the Fianna Fáil and Labour vote shares increase, at any one point in time. Looking at changes over time, the main story is the Fine Gael advance from the low baseline of the early 1970s. And the main social basis of that advance seems to have been in the middle class.

Conclusion

The aggregate and the survey data highlight quite different aspects of the social patterning of voting choice in Ireland. On the one hand, the Fine Gael vote share has been found by others, and is found again here, to defy aggregate analysis. Yet on the other, a very clear social patterning of the Fine Gael vote appears in the survey data. In contrast, Fianna Fáil appears as a catch-all party in the survey data, but with quite a clear social patterning in its vote at constituency level. What is clear from all of this is that the social environment appears to be patterning the Fianna Fáil vote. This creates constituency-level variations captured in variables, such as the agricultural structure factor, that are not simple aggregations of individuals, but rather related to matters such as the pattern of land use. The Fine Gael vote appears to be patterned, in contrast, within rather than between constituencies, with the party appealing to social groups that do not tend to generate environmental effects on the scale of a constituency. This would make variations in its vote difficult to explain in aggregate terms despite the fact that the party offered a quite distinctive social appeal. What is clear above all else, however, is that it takes a combined analysis of both types of data to illustrate the social patterning of Irish voting behaviour. To take only one source of inspiration, whether it be survey or aggregate data, is to ensure that the social patterning of support for one or other of the main parties will be very difficult to interpret.

COMMENTARY BY JOHN GARRY

'Why do people vote the way they do?' is a fundamental political science question. Library shelves groan under the weight of books tackling the topic and the debates the question gives rise to are perhaps the most heated in the discipline. One key approach to the question focuses on the potent underlying political divisions in society, most notably divisions arising from national and industrial revolutions (Lipset and Rokkan, 1967). Distinct attitudes to the nation state (between, for example, strong and weak nationalists) may strongly shape voting, as might the particular socio-economic class one belongs to. Ireland has long been considered an interesting case comparatively, due to the apparent unimportance of class in driving voting and the high salience of 'the national question' in shaping party support, certainly in the early years of the state. Hence, Ireland has often been contrasted with Britain in terms of the role played by social class at election time. Pulzer famously stated that 'class is the basis of British party politics: all else is embellishment and detail' (1967, p. 98). Another ubiquitous summary of the Irish case by Whyte portrays Ireland as having 'politics without social bases' (1974). Neither author is shy of over-statements and, in the Irish case, the challenge Whyte's punchline posed was to identify whether any class basis to Irish voting behaviour was observable and, if so, how much and in what direction. In his 1986 article, Laver takes up this challenge.

Laver's analysis is brave, innovative and scene-setting. It is brave in that it draws on two very distinct sets of data in order to address a question. This strategy almost inevitably leads to two different results and the analyst is then faced with the challenge of making sense of apparently contradictory findings. Many analysts thus typically err on the side of safety and simplicity and use a single data source which leads to a single set of results. These results may be right or wrong, interesting or uninteresting, but at least are not contradictory. Thus, Laver's approach is indeed a bold one. In using both aggregate level and individual level data, he leaves himself open to the possibility of arriving at two answers and, unsurprisingly, two answers is what he gets. Sometimes getting two different answers is very upsetting as it demonstrates a breaking of the fundamental law of scientific inquiry – replicability. If a scientist repeats an experiment and cannot reproduce the original results then the findings cannot be taken seriously. Laver does not break this law as he elaborates sound theoretical reasons that explain why the aggregate level findings are different from the individual level findings.

Aggregate level analysis tells us how the context of the voter (their county in this case) is related to the election results (at the county level). We know quite a lot about each county in terms of the proportion of people in the county who have certain characteristics. Some counties have more old people than other counties, more farmers, more Protestants, more religious people, and so on. Laver demonstrates that it is impossible to explain Fine Gael voting from the aggregate data. However, it is possible from the individual level survey data. The survey data suggest 'a clear patterning' of the Fine Gael vote, with the party support in this period having a middle-class bias. In relation to Fianna Fáil, Laver finds that the party's vote is strongly predictable from the aggregate data. It is related to type of agricultural land use, with the party doing much better electorally in counties that have more cattle farming than tillage farming. However, from the survey data the party appears to be, overall, a cross-class party. The reason for these different findings depending on which data source is used is that some social factors are very strongly geographically based. Some counties have a lot more tillage farming than cattle farming and for other counties the reverse is true. This leads to the generation of a county-based variable which has a large degree of variation and thus predictive potential. Social class, on the other hand, is much less patterned by county, there are middle-class and working-class people in each county. Thus, the class-based variation is likely to occur much more within than between counties and will thus be more effectively captured by individual level survey data. The original contention by Whyte that Ireland has 'politics without social bases' has long acted as an advertisement for hunters of a social structure to voting in Ireland. Laver neatly demonstrates that such a hunter needs two bullets for each party and may strike it lucky with either aggregate or individual level evidence.

Laver's analysis is also innovative. He uses a vast array of information in a very neat and concise way. In the aggregate level analysis he is faced with the challenge of a dependent variable (vote choice by county) which has a miserly 26 data points. This low N places great constraints on the number of predictor (explanatory) variables that can sensibly be employed. This is a great shame as Laver has a vast array of predictor variables – 66 in total – relating to, for instance, the age, agricultural and religious structure of each county. One option would be simply to pluck the three or four variables from these 66 that seem most plausible or useful in terms of vote prediction. This strategy, however, would throw in the bin all the nuance and richness of the other variables. Thus, Laver 'summarises' the 66 variables into a much smaller number of indices (10 in all). Using a principal components analysis he distils the large number of variables into a small number on the basis of the observed inter-relationships between all the variables. Thus, the variables relating to age are 'bunched' together, as are the variables relating to housing, and so on. Because ten variables is still a lot with which to interrogate a dependent variable with an N of 26, Laver sneaks up the question by first conducting a series of bivariate correlations in order to identify which of the 10 variables has no predictive power. At this stage, four variables are left in play. Because these four are likely to be related to each other, a multivariate analysis is necessary in order to isolate the unique influence of each on the dependent variable. However, four variables is still regarded by Laver as too many to use in the multiple regression and so he plays the four variables off each other in a series of head to heads. It is from this process that the relationship between Fianna Fáil vote and cattle farming emerges. Overall, this particular research design is one based on a determination to use all available evidence but to do so in a way that is very sensitive to the constraints relating to the inference of causal relationships in analyses with a low N. It is probably still a useful model for analysts using aggregate level data who often cannot resist the temptation to conduct what Laver would likely refer to as 'kitchen sink' regressions in which all available predictor variables are lobbed into the analysis simultaneously in a much less careful way than that in Laver's analysis.

The research design is innovative in Laver's use of a wealth of survey data to tell a story in a simple and straightforward style. The opinion poll evidence is based on samples of 1,000 respondents which means a single poll may not have enough data to examine the behaviour of sub-samples (how do the different social classes vote?) with a great degree of certainty. The problem is lessened when a range of polls are added together. Laver wishes to get the best of both worlds.

He wants to merge polls together to increase the certainty of his estimates but he also wants to tell an over-time story in terms of trends in the class-vote relationship. Thus, he relies on an analysis in which the relationship between class and vote is calculated using evidence from five polls at a time. The first five polls are analysed, then polls two through six are analysed, then polls three through seven, and so on until the end of the series of polls. This smoothed time series makes the key trends in the data easy to observe. One might quibble, however, with the way Laver presents the over-time trends graphically. Figures 13.2–13.5 take a particular social class and show the proportion of that class voting for each of the three main parties. Perhaps taking each party one at a time and showing the proportion of each class voting for it would have been more helpful. The question then becomes: does party x do better among class y or class z? For instance, to see whether Labour tends to do better in the higher or lower classes one has to look at the height of the Labour line in all the graphs simultaneously. The same applies to the other two parties. Presenting the data one party at a time also helpfully controls for over-time trends in party support.

Finally, Laver's paper is scene-setting in that it sets up the stage for an analysis of class voting in Ireland based on a fully-fledged election study with high-quality individual-level data gathered at election time. Variations of Laver's opening sentence have appeared in a number of his publications and he deserves more credit than anyone in actually getting an election study in Ireland established. In an academic election study a great deal of attention can be paid to the careful and theoretically grounded measurement of class. Specifically, many analysts believe that the social class grades (A/B/C1/C2/D/E/F) used in opinion polls are less than ideal as they do not capture important distinctions between classes based on whether or not one is self-employed, the level of autonomy and security one enjoys in the workplace, and whether one is in a position of power in the workplace in terms of supervising others. The 'Goldthorpe' class scale is based on such distinctions and was included in the first Irish National Election Study conducted directly after the 2002 general election. As Laver predicted, this more nuanced measure of class does yield insights into the class basis of voting in Ireland, over and above that yielded by the social grades approach. The results are particularly interesting for Fianna Fáil and Labour (Marsh *et al*, forthcoming). The social grades approach suggests a cross-class Fianna Fáil party while the more nuanced Goldthorpe measure suggests a somewhat working-class bias with the party doing best among skilled manual workers and worst among the higher salaried middle class. In relation to Labour the social grades measures do not suggest a class basis to the party's support in 2002, it is just as likely to be middle class as working class. However, using the Goldthorpe measure does yield a class basis, in a middle-class direction. The party performs best among the higher salaried middle class and the routine non-manual class and does worst among manual workers (particularly skilled manual workers). Fine Gael emerges as a cross-class party.

The Irish National Election Study is not the only dataset being used to grapple with the question of the social bases of Irish voting. The Irish Social and Political

Attitudes Survey (ISPAS) conducted in 2001–2002 has also been used to good effect by Kennedy and Sinnott (2006). Using level of educational qualification as a proxy for social class they find Fianna Fáil supporters tend to come from the lower-educated groups. Also, because they analyse party preferences rather than party choice they avoid low N problems associated with the analysis of the social basis of small parties. They find, for example that Progressive Democrat supporters and Green Party supporters tend to be relatively highly educated. Overall, the future looks bright for the study of the social structural basis of Irish voting, particularly given that Ireland is now included in a series of cross-national survey projects, such as the Comparative Study of Electoral Systems (CSES), the European Election Study (EES), and the European Social Survey (ESS). These data sources will allow analysts not only to tease out the class basis of Irish party support but to sensibly situate their findings in an international context. So we can see that Whyte's challenge, profitably taken up by Michael Laver, will continue to be contested. New work should hope to emulate the theoretically-driven, innovative empirical research that Laver's article displays.

References

Carty, R. Kenneth (1981) *Party and Parish Pump: Electoral Politics in Ireland*. Waterloo, Ontario: Wilfred Laurier University Press.

Gallagher, Michael (1976) *Electoral Support for Irish Political Parties 1927–73*. London: Sage.

Gallagher, Michael (1985) *Political Parties in the Republic of Ireland*. Dublin: Gill and Macmillan.

Garvin, Tom (1981) *The Evolution of Irish Nationalist Politics*. Dublin: Gill and Macmillan.

Kennedy, Fiachra and Richard Sinnott (2006) 'Irish Social and Political Cleavages', pp. 78–93 in John Garry, Niamh Hardiman and Diane Payne (eds.) *Irish Social and Political Attitudes*. Liverpool: Liverpool University Press.

Laver, Michael (1984) 'Are the Liverpool Liberals Really Different? A Path Analytical Interpretation of Local Voting in Liverpool 1973–82', *British Journal of Political Science*, 14 (2), pp. 243–9.

Laver, Michael (1986a) 'Ireland: Politics with Some Social Basis; An Interpretation Based on Aggregate Data', *Economic and Social Review*, 17 (2), pp. 107–31.

Laver, Michael (1986b) 'Ireland: Politics with Some Social Basis; An Interpretation Based on Survey Data', *Economic and Social Review*, 17 (3), pp. 193–213.

Lipset, Seymour M. and Stein Rokkan (1967) 'Cleavage Structures, Party Systems, and Voter Alignments: An Introduction', pp. 1–64 in Seymour M. Lipset and Stein Rokkan (eds.) *Party Systems and Voter Alignments*. New York: Free Press.

Marsh, Michael, Richard Sinnott, John Garry and Fiachra Kennedy (forthcoming) *The Irish Voter: Parties, Issues and Candidates*. Manchester: Manchester University Press.

Parker, Anthony J. (1984) 'An Ecological Analysis of Voting Patterns in Galway West, 1977', *Irish Geography*, 17 (1), pp. 42–64.

Pulzer, Peter G.J. (1967) *Political Representation and Elections in Britain*. London: Allen and Unwin.

Scully, John J. (1971) *Agriculture in the West of Ireland: A Study of Low Farm Income Problems*. Dublin: Stationery Office.

Sinnott, Richard (1987) 'The Voters, the Issues and the Party System', pp. 57–103 in Howard R. Penniman and Brian Farrell (eds.) *Ireland at the Polls 1981, 1982 and 1987: A Study of Four General Elections*. Durham, NC: Duke University Press.

Whyte, John H. (1974) 'Ireland: Politics Without Social Bases', pp. 619–52 in Richard Rose (ed.) *Electoral Behavior: A Comparative Handbook*. New York: Free Press.

14 The Northern Ireland political process

A viable approach to conflict resolution?

Kirsten E. Schulze

Originally published in *Irish Political Studies*, 12, 1997, pp. 92–110.

Conflict in multi-communal, multi-ethnic and multi-national states has been considerably greater than conflict in culturally homogeneous states. Empirical evidence shows that two-thirds of all internal conflicts have not been solved through negotiation, but have ended in the surrender or elimination of one of the main parties involved. Further, a closer inspection of those conflicts which were solved by some form of compromise reveals that the 'compromise' settlement was often 'imposed' through the use of force by the majority community. Thus the history of conflict resolution does not provide a rosy backdrop for ending the Troubles in Northern Ireland. Neither does the semantic evolution of the negotiations from being a 'peace' process, to being a 'talks' process, to having become a 'political' process.

This article seeks to explore the possibility of achieving a settlement which will provide lasting stability as a result of the current negotiations in Northern Ireland. It will look at the decisions by loyalists and republicans to call a ceasefire in 1994, the perceptions of the parties to the 'talks' with regard to what is on the negotiation table, and the overall obstacles in the political process. The main focus is on the applicability and limits of so-called conflict resolution 'theories' in explaining first, the shift from conflict to negotiation and, secondly, the possibility of concluding a stable and lasting negotiated settlement.

Conflict resolution 'theories'

Since most states do not conform to the ideal of the one nation state and since many conflicts are rooted in competing national, religious, and ethnic claims, there has been an increase in conflict resolution studies and theories. Within this field there are a number of prevailing views. One of the most common ones is that multi-communal states are inherently predestined for instability and that stability can only be achieved by undemocratic means, i.e. the subjugation of one community by another as argued by Rabushka and Shepsle (1972). The example of South Africa's Apartheid system is a case in point. The problem with this approach, however, is that in many cases even undemocratic means such as the use of force cannot create stability, but rather will provoke counter-violence.

Most studies of conflict and conflict regulation or resolution have been of an empirical nature. More often than not they have had specific regional foci such as the Middle East (Ben Dor and Dewitt, 1987), Africa (Zartman, 1989) or Latin America. Or, they have approached conflicts from within a Cold War (Kriesberg, 1992) or post-Cold War (Vasquez *et al*, 1995; Sandole, 1992) global framework. Even the purely theoretical studies of conflict resolution which have focused on peace processes, mediation, negotiation and the ending of civil wars have often had their roots in a specific case study. Rabie's thought-provoking book on conflict resolution and ethnicity (1994) is one such example, being inspired primarily by the Arab-Israeli dialogue.

Hanf (1989), Ohlson (1989), Touval and Zartman (1985), and O'Leary and McGarry (1993b) have approached selected case studies through some form of general analytical framework. O'Leary and McGarry's book is particularly noteworthy in this context as it outlines an extensive taxonomy looking at methods of conflict regulation ranging from those for eliminating differences to those for managing differences.

The studies of individual conflict situations in Europe, the Middle East, Africa and Latin America tend to confirm that far from resolution, conflict has become a relatively permanent and in its own way even stable situation. To add to this bleak picture, those few conflicts that were resolved either ended in partition, recognising that mutual coexistence is not possible, or in a 'compromise' or 'settlement' which was more often than not achieved through the overwhelming use of force.

Generally, theories and approaches towards conflict resolution fall into one of two broader categories: those that focus on the circumstances which facilitate a shift from violence to negotiation and those that focus on the type of settlement that would resolve or regulate the conflict. Underlying many of the studies of how parties to a conflict enter into negotiations is the concept of a stalemate (Pillar, 1983; Zartman, 1989; Kriesberg and Thorson, 1991). The likelihood of an agreement to coexist is greatest when all communities realise that none of them is strong enough to gain a clear victory, yet none of them so weak as to be vanquished. What has been reached is what Zartman refers to as the 'ripe moment' composed of a structural element, a party element, and a potential alternative outcome – that is, a mutually hurting stalemate, the presence of valid spokespersons, and a formula for a way out (1995, p. 18; 1989, pp. 134–69).

The second category encompasses proposals such as integration/assimilation, consociation, depoliticisation, and syncretistic nationalism. The integrationist school of thought on conflict resolution is situated within the realms of modernisation theory. The argument here is that social integration advanced through a process of modernisation will eliminate parochial particularisms within communities and permit an inclusive process of nation-building to emerge. While this approach has often been promoted by western liberal intellectuals, its success remains empirically unsubstantiated.

Consociation, depoliticisation, and syncretistic nationalism are all based on the assumption that it is unrealistic to believe that existing communities will disappear and thus these three theories are essentially differing approaches to the creation of unity by giving space to diversity. The consociation theory advances an institutionalisation of existing communities, thereby organising coexistence. The right 'democratic' institutional framework is able to regulate the coexistence of different communities, maintaining stability and democratic ideals at the same time (Lijphart, 1977). A number of models have developed within this theoretical framework which are case-specific: the Lebanon model (Hanf, 1993; Kewenig, 1965; Hudson, 1985), the Switzerland model of *Konkordanzdemokratie* (Steiner, 1970), and the Belgium model (Lijphart, 1981) among others.

Another approach of institutionalisation is depoliticisation. As the name implies, it aims at depoliticising communal identities by institutionalising and encouraging cultural diversity in order to prevent symbolic cultural deprivation. This theory arose within the Austrian context in the early twentieth century and has its foundation in the work of Bauer (1924) and Renner (1902 and 1918). Such a policy, for instance, has been adopted by Canada, India and Indonesia.

The creation of a syncretistic nationalism is another approach to removing the symbolic ethnic element from the inter-communal discourse. The aim is creating an all-inclusive nationalism, a universal umbrella, and thereby giving all communities a stake in the state. The Soviet and Yugoslav approaches fall into this category. A more recent example with less negative connotations is the formulation of a syncretistic civil religion symbolised by the 'rainbow people' in South Africa in the current peace process.

Within this second category of conflict resolution 'theories' a sub-category focusing on cross-communal institutions and inter-community relations on a micro-level has emerged. In essence, this aims at what Horowitz (1993) refers to as reducing the level of overt ethnic conflict behaviour by heightening incentives for inter-ethnic co-operation. This sub-category has attempted to apply methods of conflict resolution used in personal and organisational disputes to intra- and inter-state conflict. Approaches which fall into this category include community mediation, citizen diplomacy, and co-operative education (Burton and Dukes, 1990; Smith, 1996; Schwerin, 1995) and have at their core the notion of achieving civil justice (Smith, 1996), community empowerment (Schwerin, 1995), or what in the case of Northern Ireland is called parity of esteem. They are generally termed 'Alternative Dispute Resolutions' (ADR) and evolve around community activities to deal with social tension and seek cooperative relationships on a society level (Schwerin, 1995). The attraction of this approach is clear: in the absence of progress on often mutually exclusive and deadlocked macro-political issues such as the constitutional position of Northern Ireland, comparatively significant progress can be achieved on a micro (community) level. On the other hand, however, by not touching upon the conflict at a macro level, ethno-nationalist conflicts cannot ultimately be resolved by such an approach.

This overview of some of the approaches and theories on conflict resolution reveals a number of stated and unstated assumptions which conflict resolution 'theories' have in common and which are important when considering the Northern Irish case. First, coexistence is the desirable outcome for communities in conflict with each other. Secondly, democratic approaches are more desirable than non-democratic approaches. Thirdly, compromise is seen as positive. And finally nationalism is generally seen as negative. These assumptions, which in themselves should be questioned, are situated in an even more problematic 'western liberal' context which promotes democracy on the one hand while at the same time stressing the right to self-determination.

The ceasefires of 1994: a shift towards accommodation?

The concept of the 'ripe moment' or the 'right timing' is at the core of those conflict resolution theories which focus on the initiation of negotiations or the shift from conflict to resolution. According to Zartman the 'ripe moment' results from the existence of a stalemate, the presence of spokespersons for all sides, and the availability of a formula for a way out. Thus, the question is whether a stalemate was the underlying motivation for the ceasefires of 1994, and whether the Frameworks Document is indeed a formula for a way out. In short, has the 'ripe moment' for conflict resolution been reached in Northern Ireland?

The republican ceasefire

The republican shift from conflict to negotiation can be attributed to a number of specific events as well as generally changing perceptions. First, the Irish Republican Army (IRA) received a substantial amount of arms in a shipment from Libya in 1986 (Mallie and McKittrick, 1996, pp. 40–50). Up to that point it had been the view that the IRA was close to achieving its military aims and all that was really needed was that extra shipment of arms to carry out a large-scale campaign. By 1988 the IRA was no closer to victory. The second event was the Enniskillen Remembrance Day bomb in 1987 and the public revulsion south of the border which politically isolated the republican movement. The physical and material ability to carry on the war almost indefinitely was not in doubt. But the moral capacity to do so was. There was no realistic prospect of a military or political breakthrough accompanied by the gradual realisation by some of the republican leadership that political aims could not be advanced through violence (Mansergh, 1995). Paramilitary violence was capable of prolonging a stalemate and frustrating political initiatives, but it was not capable of achieving a united Ireland.

> There was a military stalemate and a political stalemate. Neither side had the capacity to defeat the other. There was a growing realisation that there was a possibility to sustain the struggle as pressure indefinitely but it did not add up to resolution of the conflict on a nationalist agenda.
>
> (Gibney, 1996)

The unacceptability of violence for some constitutional nationalists split and consequently weakened the nationalist community as a whole, dividing republicans and nationalists, north and south, and affecting public opinion particularly in the

United States. What was needed to move the situation forward was unity. Elements within the leadership which had already been advocating a more proactive political role for Sinn Féin to escape from the environment of political and military stalemate of the 1980s (Hartley, 1996) gained support in their efforts to engage with the Social Democratic and Labour Party (SDLP). Born out of this were 17 months of direct Sinn Féin–SDLP contacts (Smith, 1995, p. 198) and a continuing private dialogue between John Hume and Gerry Adams to 'hammer out a nationalist realignment' (Gibney, 1996). While Hume was trying to wean the IRA away from violence two additional significant changes occurred in the international environment which aided the republican attempt to bring in other nationalists and to find a catalyst to break the logjam without signalling surrender (Gibney, 1996). In 1992 Albert Reynolds succeeded Charles Haughey as Taoiseach in the Republic of Ireland and Bill Clinton took on the U.S. Presidency. Both Clinton and Reynolds became part of the dialogue on how to move the situation forward. In essence, what started to emerge is the often referred to pan-nationalist front. This nationalist alliance, in republican circles, was interpreted as 'a nationalist consensus that a united Ireland was feasible' (Gibney, 1996).

The ceasefire of 1994 was called within this context. The IRA had to make a political judgement and deal with political circumstances. It had to trust the Sinn Féin leadership. The ceasefire was established with the aim of negotiations following within a reasonable time-frame. Through negotiation Sinn Féin wanted 'to bring reality as close to their political vision as possible' (Hartley, 1996). It effectively was to redefine the situation for republicanism in the sense that the conflict had defined republicanism in terms of what was being fought against while the peace process defined it in terms of what was being fought for. How much of this redefinition is left after the return to violence is debatable.

Interesting is the IRA analysis of the British government's motivation for the negotiations. The IRA called the ceasefire in order to create the circumstances that would allow 'the British to leave Ireland' (Gibney, 1996) – the assumption being that the British wanted out. While the IRA had admittedly reached a stalemate situation in its war with Britain, it was quite clear that this situation was to be moved forward through British withdrawal (defeat), the formula for the resolution of the conflict being a united Ireland.

The loyalist ceasefire

The loyalist position in the Northern Ireland conflict started to change with the 1985 Anglo-Irish Agreement which emphasised the necessity to find a political way forward as well as giving the loyalist working class a political voice. The transition from being a paramilitary actor to becoming a political one, however, was made difficult by the dynamics within unionism as a whole (Bruce, 1992 and 1994). Attempts to shift from conflict to negotiation are evident in the 1991 unilateral ceasefire which was aimed at providing the four main parties with a chance to come up with an agreement during the Brooke talks. It was an opportunity to create an environment of as little provocation as possible. 'Loyalists had not demanded participation in return, being content to exert political influence on a situation without direct involvement' (McMichael, 1996). Unionist politicians, however, were as unsatisfactory a representation as ever from a loyalist perspective. The ceasefire broke down, the talks collapsed and the conflict in Northern Ireland plunged into a renewed cycle of violence with loyalist violence surpassing republican violence. This 1991 attempt had made it clear that the Ulster Democratic Party (UDP) and Progressive Unionist Party (PUP) should be involved in future talks and that loyalist paramilitaries and parties had to work together for a united loyalist voice.

Unlike the republican situation, the loyalist military position was not perceived as a stalemate:

> The people felt that they militarily had achieved what they wanted to achieve. They had prevented the IRA from bombing us into a united Ireland. There was no point of further military action which would have been detrimental to the cause. So we started planning a ceasefire long before that of the IRA.
> (Hutchinson, 1996)

In 1993, after the breakdown of the Mayhew talks, the loyalist parties started playing a more active role in bringing about a shift to negotiation. The UDP set up a group within the Combined Loyalist Military Command (CLMC) to analyse the political situation and make recommendations. Parallel to this development, loyalists were also in contact with the Irish Government through a number of mediators (Finlay, 1996). The secret contacts initiated by Dublin, however, were not embraced by all in the CLMC. Approaches had been made to both the Ulster Volunteer Force (UVF) and Ulster Defence Association (UDA), which the latter rejected (McMichael, 1996). Relations with the British government were fraught with even more suspicion. It prompted the loyalists to keep their distance, while the British government for the sake of 'evenhandedness' did not contact the loyalists until it was able *officially* to talk to the republicans (Ancram, 1996).

In 1994 the CLMC started discussing a ceasefire because the Downing Street Declaration had provided the opportunity for talks and forced the IRA to lay its position on the table. There were intense discussions surrounding loyalist strategy as a result of the emerging nationalist position and great efforts were made to move the entire situation in a meaningful direction.

Some comparative remarks should be made about the loyalist and republican shifts from conflict to negotiations. The republican shift within broader republican strategy must be seen as a purely tactical shift with the underlying motivation being a military stalemate (see the 'TUAS document', *Sunday Tribune*, 23 April 1995). The ultimate goal of a united Ireland had not changed. Rather, it had become clear that the IRA would not be able to defeat Britain in conventional terms. Negotiation opened up a political avenue which was seen as a way of moving out of the stalemate. Thus, it can be said that the situation of the IRA–British conflict was clearly a stalemate, possibly signifying the 'ripe moment'. While there were no problems with the spokespersons, the formula (Downing Street Declaration and Framework Document) for the way out was 'dubious'. Yet, one could say that Zartman's 'ripe moment' had been achieved with some minor reservations. This then raises the question why the IRA decided to return to violence despite the stalemate, and if the problem was not really in achieving the 'ripe moment' then it must be sought in the resolution proposals or the interim process.

The motivation for the loyalist ceasefire was not a stalemate situation. This is due to the tripolar structure of the conflict itself. The IRA sees the British state as its enemy, reducing loyalism to no more than a 'nuisance factor' in this war of liberation. The loyalists see republicanism as their enemy, perceiving themselves to be on the same side as the British Army (Miller, 1978; Boulton, 1973; Bruce, 1992). Thus, structurally a stalemate situation is needed between the IRA and the British in order to attempt to resolve the conflict. A stalemate between republicans and loyalists is not necessary and, indeed, it did not and does not exist. The motivation for the loyalist shift to negotiation comes from a different source: the desire to move forward politically not only on the constitutional issue but also to promote and represent broader urban loyalist working-class interests. The latter aspect is linked to a growing class consciousness – the realisation that working-class Protestants may have felt better off than Catholics but were not in fact.

Interesting within the process of shifting from conflict to negotiation are the dynamics between loyalists and republicans, which shed light on the respective accounts of the two ceasefires:

> In 1994 everybody knew that the IRA was going to call a ceasefire. We knew what the score was. The IRA knew what was going on in the loyalist community...As far as they were concerned they were going to be the only show in town. They had to be in control. They tried to make sure that they called a ceasefire when the loyalists did not call a ceasefire. And if a loyalist ceasefire was called, that there was no political leadership (thus the assassination of Ray Smallwoods) in loyalism.
>
> (McMichael, 1996)

Like the debate in republicanism which is often portrayed through the inadequate paradigm of 'hawks' and 'doves' and which instead should be seen as a combination of conventional and unconventional means within an essentially political activity (McIntyre, 1995), there was an ongoing debate in loyalism between those who saw the ceasefire as the way forward and those who did not (McMichael, 1996). The IRA decision to return to violence changed the situation for the loyalists significantly as the loyalist ceasefire had been made conditional on the republican one (*CLMC Ceasefire Statement*, 13 October 1994). It has made the loyalist ceasefire more difficult to uphold and has resulted in internal tensions as evident in the challenge by Billy Wright in September 1996 and the withdrawal of loyalist prisoner support in October 1996.

Conflicting interpretations of the peace process

The republican and loyalist cessations of violence initiated the pre-talks but post-violence phase of the political process. It is a phase which most conflict resolution 'theories' do not focus on in detail and not with regards to moving towards substantial negotiations. Yet it could be argued that it is the most important phase characterised by initial euphoria, then uncertainty, impatience, and distrust. Above all, as a period sandwiched between two more active phases, it is governed by perceptions and misperceptions which, beyond doubt, influence future actions. The collapse of the IRA ceasefire in February 1996 is a case in point – as are Drumcree, and the loyalist prisoners' withdrawal of support for the peace process. The key issues are really quite simple: What is on the negotiating table and where is the process going?

Both loyalists and republicans had expected that after six to eight weeks following the ceasefires real and substantive negotiations would begin. There was little sympathy from either for the extensive political games the unionists, the SDLP and the Northern Ireland Office had become used to playing over the past years. From the republican perspective the decontamination period, the demands for prior decommissioning, and the call for elections were all seen as a way of avoiding all-party talks, sending the message that they had 'lost' and that remaining part of the talks meant 'letting the British government make Sinn Féin into another SDLP'. Moreover, the talks were increasingly perceived as an internal solution (Dodie McGuinness, Sinn Féin Ard Fheis, 1996), as surrender (Sinn Féin *Submission to the International Body on Decommissioning*, 1995), and to many as abandoning republican aims.

The breakdown of the ceasefire after 17 months' lack of movement was partly a reaction to the republican interpretation of the process and partly due to internal dynamics within the IRA which had been put under strain through this very absence of progress. The centrality of republican aims within Irish republican ethno-nationalism meant that not only the IRA but also the nationalist community had descended into an 'identity crisis'. The IRA's end of the ceasefire statement made this clear when stating that 'we take this opportunity to reiterate our total commitment to our republican objectives' (*Statement*, 9 February 1996). A couple of weeks later, at the Ard Fheis, Sinn Féin Vice President Pat Doherty stressed this theme further:

> We are republicans. It is our republican analysis that guides everything we do. We want to see a united, independent Ireland because a united, independent Ireland will best serve our people. It is as republicans that we built our strategy for peace, for a new Ireland. We met and worked with other components of the peace process as republicans. And as republicans we will rebuild it.
>
> (Ard Fheis, March 1996)

Loyalist assessment of the republican position at that time was bleak:

> Since Canary Wharf they've realised that they've done Sinn Féin more damage than good. Going back to the peace process will not achieve what they

want and going back to violence is not what their support base wants... They will have to call another ceasefire... Once in the negotiations they won't have a chance to achieve even a quarter of what they want. The Frameworks Document is the maximum of what can be achieved for nationalists.

(David Adams, 1996)

It is thus not surprising that Pat Doherty referred to 'rebuilding the peace process', and rebuilding it in such a way that republican aims could be achieved, possibly based on another tactical cessation of violence. Sinn Féin having been barred from the negotiations because of the IRA return to violence, and despite receiving 15 per cent of the vote in the May 1996 elections, has made it clear that it will not settle for anything less than full inclusiveness:

The resolution of the conflict demands an inclusive negotiated settlement. That is not possible unless and until the British government faces up to its responsibility. The blame for the failure of the Irish peace initiative lies squarely with John Major and his government.

(*An Phoblacht/Republican News*, 10 October 1996)

Thus, from a republican perspective it is essential that the Union must be on the negotiating table and the process should be going in the direction of a united Ireland. The question, however, from a conflict resolution perspective is whether republicans with their ethno-nationalist framework for republicanism, their perception of compromise equalling surrender, and their objection to anything that is even slightly perceived as an internal settlement, can be part of and agree to any negotiated settlement short of a united Ireland.

Loyalist perception is influenced by the mainstream parties traditionally trying to keep those parties associated with paramilitary violence out of any negotiations. The mainstream's insistence on prior decommissioning can be interpreted as such a move, the logic being as follows: The arms were the reason why parties such as UDP and PUP had to be dealt with. Once decommissioning had taken place, there was no longer any reason for these parties being there when all they did was split the unionist vote. They really should leave political representation to the established parties.

Loyalist perceptions towards the peace process echoed some of the republican statements. Gary McMichael's comment that 'the indoctrination has been that compromise is surrender and that reconciliation is also surrender' (*Faces*, November 1995) and the loyalist gunman quoted as saying that 'peace at any price should rather be called defeat' (*Sunday Life*, 3 March 1996) reflect this. With these perceptions it comes as no surprise that for the loyalists the constitutional framework of Northern Ireland is not on the negotiating table. What they would like to achieve is 'some form of agreed solution which will take the gun out of politics and make the people feel that their nationality – British or Irish – is protected' (Hutchinson, 1996). Similar ideas are discussed in the UDP's *Common Sense* (1987) proposals.

The mainstream unionists concur that unification is not on the agenda. As an Ulster Unionist councillor stressed 'it's the furthest off it has ever been during the Troubles' (Nelson, 1996). What is on the agenda is greater Irish influence in Northern Ireland:

> We need more cooperation between the security forces and intelligence in order to defeat terrorism. We would like to see a commitment equal to that of preventing minced beef from getting through.
>
> (Nelson, 1996)

Accommodation within Northern Ireland is also up for discussion. Several attempts have been made to reach an agreement with the SDLP. The Ulster Unionist vision of this agreement is 'a form of power-sharing, preferably with a devolved administration but a unitary legislature' (Nelson, 1996). A structure would be created that the majority of the community of Northern Ireland could give allegiance to, a structure that would address the democratic deficit, and one that would make the constitutional status of remaining part of the Union clear with the abolition of Articles Two and Three of the Irish Republic's constitution.

The SDLP's aim is similarly conceptual, but less specific with regard to structure. Moreover, the nationalist position remains that a united Ireland is desirable and thus any agreement will be perceived as a step towards unification. The differences between the nationalist and unionist visions of power-sharing become clear when looking at what the nationalists believe must be on the negotiating table. They want to discuss the relations between all communities on the island of Ireland:

> We would like to see a situation on the island where everyone respects each other's traditions. We want an environment of reconciliation – to get rid of the blinkers of history and look at reality as it exists today ... In this new agreed Ireland economics will take the lead and the borders will gradually disappear.
>
> (Farrell, 1996)

A side note on the interpretations of the peace process should be on the initiators of the process and their expectations. The British and Irish governments have stated repeatedly that the aim is all party negotiations, that the settlement has not been predetermined, and that the object of the talks is to create a lasting peace. Only a solution acceptable to both parts of the population through negotiations can create a stable agreement. Essentially, 'the people of Northern Ireland will decide the future of Northern Ireland and we will accept their views' (Ancram, 1996). Interesting are the British and Irish views on the problems of interpretation and mistrust. Finlay's (1996) perceptive statement that 'if Sinn Féin want to see it (the settlement) as a transition and loyalists as permanent – we want to see it as durable', touches upon the depths of mistrust resulting from these conflicting interpretations. 'We need to remove this mistrust and establish a degree of confidence ... What we are doing at the moment is redressing this situation of mistrust' (Ancram, 1996).

Closer analysis of the views and perceptions reveals that the expectation of what will be negotiated and the vision of the solution are tied directly to the respective parties' national identity. Returning to the assumptions underlying conflict resolution, nationalism and ethnic nationalist interpretations are clearly the largest obstacle to compromise. For unionists/loyalists the current constitutional arrangement matches their identity, making the Union non-negotiable. Nationalists/republicans, on the other hand, who are unable to identify will continue to push for a re-negotiation of state identity – until a match has been achieved.

The limits of conflict resolution 'theories'

When applied to the current Northern Ireland political process and to the Northern Ireland conflict in general, conflict resolution 'theories' are limited by their underlying assumptions and also by their overall applicability to the specific dynamics of the conflict. Theories such as the 'ripe moment' for a shift from conflict to negotiation are able to generally look at motivations which might move actors towards reconciliation. They are, however, limited in the sense that they assume that a stalemate is an intolerable situation. The return to the armed struggle by the IRA shows that a stalemate might trigger a consideration of a non-violent political option, but that the choice between a stalemate situation accompanied by unsuccessful political action will be interpreted as a defeat while a stalemate accompanied by military action will not necessarily be perceived as such. Thus a stalemate is not at all intolerable if the alternative is perceived to be surrender. That does not, however, mean that tactical intervals of non-violence do not make sense. Further, considering the history of repeated negotiation attempts in Northern Ireland, it can be seen that there probably is no such thing as one 'ripe moment', but that there are a number of 'moments' which make resolution more likely than others. And finally, it is more useful to consider the 'ripe moment' as a process rather than a specific point in time – such as the ceasefires of 1994.

While the 'ripe moment' deals with the shift, theories on possible settlement are dealing with the end product. This leaves the highly important interim phase inadequately studied. Indeed, it is this phase in which most peace processes start to falter. The current Northern Ireland peace initiative, like the current Arab-Israeli one, has faced its main obstacles on the way to substantive negotiations, losing actors along the way due to perceptions that they were being 'sold out' or forced to surrender. So the problem has been one of keeping the process going for long enough to actually have a discussion about a settlement.

Theories focusing on the solution or settlement are also limited. Obviously, there will be preferred options and options that are completely unsuitable. Ethnic cleansing, as one extreme, clashes with the values of the state as Northern Ireland is part of a liberal democracy. In that sense the paradigm of conflict resolution will be restricted by the democratic framework. The paradigm is further limited by competing ethnic nationalisms which make the integrationist/assimilationist approach another futile exercise. O'Leary and McGarry (1993a, table 8.2, pp. 292–3) give an excellent overview of the acceptability of one option over the other for nationalists and unionists in Northern Ireland, and the British and Irish electorates, as well as going through the drawbacks of each of these options. Like most other conflict resolution theorists, O'Leary and McGarry argue that a form of power-sharing is the most likely to succeed. Consociationalism falls into this category. The problem with consociationalism, however, is that it can only work if all communities are committed to it. As a delicate system it can easily be brought down as the Lebanon example shows. Moreover, it does not solve the question of allegiance. Assuming this power-sharing would take place under a British constitutional arrangement, it would, no doubt, run up against republican opposition. Joint British–Irish authority would, conversely, provoke a violent unionist reaction.

Depoliticisation and syncretistic nationalism run up against the obstacle of ethnic nationalism. Reducing nationalism to cultural rights as the depoliticisation approach does, may appease some nationalists but will not satisfy republicans. It will also not find much support in unionist circles as unionism and nationalism would be equally reduced to a mere cultural particularism as well as implying a contestable equality between the two traditions (English, 1995 and 1996). Syncretistic nationalism is more likely to succeed in the sense that space is given to ethnic national identity and at the same time, on a different level, to a universal inclusive nationalism. Such attempts have been made through civic unionism focusing on the idea of the Union (Aughey, 1995) and the concept of Britishness (McBride, 1996) as opposed to Englishness as a 'mechanism' of equality. But it too has run up against the obstacle of the exclusive appeal of ethnic unionism and ethnic nationalism.

Beyond the problems that each settlement proposal entails, there are much more fundamental problems in the assumptions underlying conflict resolution theories. The key assumption is that compromise and coexistence are desirable. This is almost diametrically opposed to the aims of most of the parties to the conflict, for whom compromise means giving up their vision of the state or giving up their political project. Any compromise would weaken the Union and thus be unacceptable to unionists while at the same time it falls short of a united Ireland making it unacceptable for republicans and some nationalists. So for the parties to the conflict compromise is far from desirable. And since the unwillingness to compromise is directly linked to the zero-sum perceptions in this conflict, it can be said that compromise really is possible only when the symbolic and ideological prerequisites for compromise exist. It only becomes a viable option if every side feels that its existence is no longer threatened. This, so far, has not been the case in Northern Ireland.

With an unwillingness to compromise and even an unwillingness to sit down at the same table and negotiate, conflict resolution 'theories' focusing on settlements have become purely academic. The main obstacle is not the lack of willingness to shift to a non-violent political strategy, nor is it the absence of alternative solutions. Rather it is the unwillingness to compromise based directly on each party's ethnic identity and political project, and its perception of what could be gained from negotiations. Thus, conflict resolution theories are limited by intransigence on the ground.

An interim assessment of the peace process

In many ways, from a comparative perspective it seems that the conflict in Northern Ireland can be much more easily resolved than other conflicts in the sense that it is quite clear who needs to talk to whom and what the key issues are. Yet, at the same time, resolution seems more difficult as there has been little success in getting the parties to the conflict to engage in a constructive debate, never mind agree to a settlement.

With the primary obstacle being the absence of a readiness to negotiate and compromise, the question of the possibility of imposing a solution is often raised. A revised version of the Anglo-Irish Agreement or an elaboration of the Frameworks Document would be an option in this scenario. However, while the threat of an imposed solution might provide the unionists with an incentive to negotiate a settlement, an actual imposition would not achieve a stable and lasting peace. From an institutional perspective, the only feasible cross-border institutions would be those which would not require unionist participation. More generally, though, it is highly likely that unionist/loyalist opposition and violence would increase in response to an imposed solution, probably accompanied by a drive for an independent Ulster. At the same time there is no indication that republicans would be less disaffected or would abandon the armed struggle as their willingness to settle for less than a 32 county democratic socialist republic is debatable. In short, an imposed solution would not work unless, like in the Lebanese comparison, it would be backed by substantive military force. Instead, an imposed solution would lead to an increase in violence.

In essence, this means that the current political talks are the only way forward with mutual distrust and perceptions being at the heart of the problem. With regard to removing these obstacles, the joint British–Irish government initiative has been less than successful. For instance, a transfer of republican prisoners from English prisons to Irish prisons would have contributed substantially to creating some republican confidence in the British government. Equally, for loyalists, a review of prison sentences would have been a way to counter the overall perception that there has been no real movement. And finally, the perpetual fear of the unionists of being 'sold out' by the British through shady back door agreements with the Irish has also not been alleviated.

More important, however, is the joint-governmental perception of violence as the main problem. While it cannot be overemphasised that nine out of ten political parties have agreed to 'resolve' this conflict through democratic means and are pursuing their aims within the joint-governmental framework, the fact that a dynamic of interacting violence and democracy has existed for the past 27 years and continues to exist must also be taken into account. Violence is a symptom and not the cause of the conflict. The current peace talks thus appear to have the wrong emphasis by focusing on the issue of decommissioning. This is not to say that a reinstatement of the IRA ceasefire is unnecessary. From a comparative perspective, however, there are few cases – if any – in which a complete absence of violence has preceded or even accompanied negotiations. While violence remains one of the most crucial issues, the emphasis should be on striving towards a settlement – no matter how improbable – which will eliminate the reasons for resorting to the use of force for political ends.

Conclusion

Resolution of the Northern Ireland conflict is unlikely as long as both unionist/loyalist and nationalist/republican political positions and interpretations of the peace process are inextricably intertwined with national identity. The liberal ideals of compromise, accommodation, national reconciliation, and coexistence which are at the core of most conflict resolution 'theories' cannot but be rejected as they will be perceived as producing a loser and a winner, especially taking into consideration the demography of Northern Ireland. Thus, the limits of conflict resolution 'theories' are in their implementation and the often rather large gap between the ideal and the situation on the ground.

While permanent *resolution* is unlikely (without resorting to ethnic cleansing and expulsion), *regulation* of the conflict is possible. Drawing upon the approaches available, the one most likely to succeed – if one may indulge in such a purely academic exercise – is that of a syncretistic nationalism, meaning the creation of an inclusive, overarching nationalism which can accommodate ethnic, cultural and religious differences, combined with power-sharing on the micro (community/institutional level). It is the option most likely to succeed as the foundations already exist. The required universal nationalism is present in the civic concept of unionism in which Welsh, Scottish, English and Irish nationalism can exist within the ideal of the union. Irish nationalism and Britishness would not be conflicting but coexisting and even complementary identities. But as long as unionism is expressed in ethnic terms such inclusiveness is not possible.

Another option for a syncretistic nationalism, given the historical connotations of unionism, lies within a broader European Union as civic Europeanness rather than Britishness. With both, however, it should be pointed out that some segments of the population will probably opt out and decide to define themselves separately. And moreover, a syncretistic nationalism like a syncretistic religion will never evoke the kind of emotional response that an ethnic nationalism does. Despite this, the approach of syncretistic nationalism if combined with micro level 'Alternative Dispute Resolution', is probably the one conflict resolution 'theory' in which the gap between the ideal and reality may be marginally smaller.

COMMENTARY BY PAUL ARTHUR

When the Good Friday Agreement was signed in 1998 Tony Blair felt the 'hand of history' on his shoulder; and not much later he detected a 'seismic shift' in Irish republican thinking. Yet in a speech on 18 October 2002 he recalled 'four and a half years of hassle, frustration and messy compromise' (Blair, 2002, no pagination). This contrast in tone serves as a timely warning that political rhetoric does not always measure up to political reality and that pessimism is the common denominator of political discourse.

It is well to bear this in mind when reviewing Kirsten Schulze's invigorating and innovating analysis of conflict resolution theory and the Northern Ireland problem. The timing of her article recalls E.H. Carr's dictum that it is just as important to note the date as it is the author and the title of publication. The bulk of her research was carried out in 1996 – long before it was inevitable that an Agreement would be signed, but within a timeframe that suggested that fundamental political change could be on its way. It was a year that had seen the ending of the Irish Republican Army (IRA) cessation of violence with the Canary Wharf bombing on 9 February. But it was to be the year, too, when 'The Northern Ireland Forum/Entry to Negotiations Election 1996' was held (to borrow from the title of Sydney Elliott's 1997 article).

Elliott's clumsy title was indicative of confusing times. Republicans had insisted on being part of inclusive all-party talks whereas the British Government demurred, offering instead an elective process as an essential confidence building measure short of clear evidence of decommissioning by the paramilitary groups. Clumsiness was built into the method of the electoral mechanism. Besides the election of 90 delegates from the 18 constituencies, there was to be a regional list in which 20 delegates from the ten parties with the highest aggregates from Northern Ireland as a whole could also be appointed with a maximum of two from each party. This unique 'top-up' system was a mechanism to allow the system to be totally inclusive. Hence a Labour grouping that achieved less than one per cent of the poll had two delegates allocated to the Forum. More importantly the Progressive Unionist Party (PUP), the Ulster Democratic Party (UDP) and the Northern Ireland Women's Coalition (NIWC) joined Sinn Féin (SF) as part of an inclusive process.

It is instructive to look at the state of those parties more than ten years later. The NIWC and UDP are extinct and the PUP is moribund. Their contribution to the process that led to the 1998 Agreement cannot be underestimated but the political geometry has moved on. The Agreement was fashioned by the two governments, the international community (notably the United States and European Union) and a 'strong centre' – borrowing on the South African example of the African National Congress (ANC) and National Party – comprised of the Ulster Unionist Party (UUP) and Social Democratic and Labour Party (SDLP). Schulze's understated pessimism was understandable in 1997 but her insight was impressive.

She produced a good survey of the theoretical literature with its emphasis on the 'ripe moment' which was 'composed of a structural element, a party element, and a potential alternative outcome – that is, a mutually hurting stalemate, the presence of valid spokespersons, and a formula for a way out'. Here she was following the pioneering work of William Zartman who had developed the notion of the ripe moment and the mutually hurting stalemate (Zartman, 1989, 1995). But her contribution was to suggest that

> there probably is no such thing as one 'ripe moment' but that there are a
> number of 'moments' which make resolution more likely than others... it is

more useful to consider the 'ripe moment' as a process rather than a specific point in time – such as the ceasefires of 1994.

That is an important observation for two reasons. It is a valuable refinement of Zartman's theory; and it has a particular resonance in terms of the Northern Ireland conflict.

To illustrate: in what he referred to his single transferable speech, John Hume had been peddling the notion of the 'healing process' for many years. What had appeared to be a cliché was in reality a shift in the lexicon of political discourse in Northern Ireland. 'Process' had succeeded 'zero-sum'. In that respect Dr Schulze assumed too much when she asserted that from a comparative perspective the Northern Ireland conflict could be more easily resolved than others because 'it is quite clear who needs to talk to whom and what the key issues are'. If we can assume that there are three components in the life cycle of a conflict – analysis, negotiation and implementation – one must ask why did analysis take so long? Why did Richard Rose's dictum that the 'problem is that there is no solution' (1976, p. 139) remain the norm for so long? The answer is that there was no agreement as to who the parties to the conflict were – or, at least, as to how they were to be treated. It veered from the two communities, to both governments and the communities as represented by the constitutional parties to, finally, all of those who had veto powers.

This is reflected in the rich vein of interviews the author conducted in researching her article. It includes interviews with the 'pariahs' as represented by the paramilitary parties. It is implicit in the peculiar arrangements for the 1996 Forum elections and in its emphasis on negotiation and inclusion. It is acknowledged in the distinction between a *political* process – part of her title – and the *peace* process which is embedded in her narrative. And all of this is serviced by distinguished third parties who brought an experienced dispassionate approach to the problem. What the author captures brilliantly is the transitional phase between negotiation and a durable settlement: 'While the "ripe moment" deals with the shift, theories on possible settlement are dealing with the end product. This leaves the highly important interim phase inadequately studied.'

That is something she does with panache. She identifies the motivations of the main players at a crucial stage in the negotiations. Of course she cannot anticipate its outcome but she would have every reason for quiet theoretical satisfaction as she surveys the scene a decade later. The 1998 Agreement may have been a case of *coitus interruptus* – that would be one interpretation of the Prime Minister's remarks on 18 October 2002. It revealed a serious, but obvious, flaw in the process. The Agreement was not an enduring settlement but merely a significant staging post towards such. In his comparative work on peace agreements Robert Rothstein has commented that often they are weak and tentative but that they can alter the basic nature of a long and profoundly bitter conflict:

> It is also very important for the leaders on both sides recognize that the game has changed, that the behaviour necessary to get to a provisional agreement is not always the behaviour appropriate for the post-agreement period; needs

and priorities change, interests must be redefined or revisioned, and a joint learning process must be institutionalized and accelerated.

(1996, p. 7)

By shifting the emphasis from the big bang of the 'ripe moment' to a series of events/accidents/personnel changes that compose a process, Schulze has encapsulated the messiness of the past eight years as well as allowing for the further refinement of theory. Consider, for example, the recent work of Dean Pruitt in his Working Paper 'Whither Ripeness Theory?' (2005). Pruitt, who seems unaware of Schulze's work, complements it in his critique of ripeness theory through the addition of such as 'shock' and 'readiness' 'theories'. In her article Schulze was careful to apostrophise theory because, as she says, most studies of conflict regulation/resolution have been of an empirical nature and it is as well to be sceptical of what passes for theory. Nearly two decades ago Rogowski noted, sagely, the proclivity of 'grand' theories being proposed in which 'rewards go, not to the good experimentalist or the good critic, but first to those who erect new theoretical edifices and second to those who adapt and extend them most rapidly and inventively' (1978, p. 306).

With that health warning in mind we can proceed to look at the current status of the peace process in the light of developments and obstacles since 1998. Schulze has drawn our attention to the IRA's physical and material ability to continue the long war but she doubted its moral capacity. That has been borne out by subsequent events. Indeed it has enhanced the peace wing's ability to isolate 'spoilers' in republicanism generally. What is remarkable about this generation of republican leaders is that it has managed to induce fundamental political change without incurring the perennial split, and has done so through virtually the same leadership that led them through 30 years of armed struggle.

Their capacity to deliver total decommissioning by July 2005 and an acceptance of the reformed policing system early in 2007 reinforces the notion that we should eschew the idea of one ripe moment. More importantly it suggests that that leadership followed Rothstein's injunction for redefinition or revisionism. Adams and McGuinness have brought the same discipline that sustained the armed struggle to the political process. Presciently Schulze noted that the 1994 ceasefire redefined Sinn Féin and the IRA 'in the sense that conflict had defined republicanism in terms of what was being fought against while the peace process defined it in terms of what was being fought for'.

That is not to say that this carefully honed strategy always ran smoothly, nor indeed to deny that serendipity had a role to play. A check list reminds us that IRA involvement with the Revolutionary Armed Forces of Colombia (FARC) at the turn of the millennium, the robbery of nearly £25 million in Belfast in December 2004 and the murder of Robert McCartney in January 2005, all severely tested the political skills of the Adams/McGuinness leadership. But the FARC involvement may have been turned to advantage in the most unlikely circumstances. On 11 September 2001 President Bush's 'point man' happened to be in Belfast to read the riot act to the Sinn Féin leadership over the Colombian adventure. Now he was able to present them with the ultimate choice – either they were part of the

War on Terror or they were totally committed to peace. Current evidence suggests that the Sinn Féin leaders turned this, and the other, events to their mutual advantage. It is conceivable that they speeded up the move towards decommissioning and the acceptance of policing. What one analyst may describe as shock theory another may simply suggest serendipity and opportunity.

Our final comment refers to Pruitt's refinement of ripeness through readiness: 'Readiness is the extent to which an individual disputant is interested in negotiation'. It focuses on 'motivation to end a conflict – rather than on hurting stalemate – and by making third-party pressure one source of this motivation' (Pruitt, 2005, pp. 6 and 8). It is an apt concept on which to conclude this paper. The present tense lies in the new Northern Ireland Assembly and the putative creation of a new 'strong centre' composing Sinn Féin and the DUP. Most commentators are agreed that republicans have delivered and that the pressure is now on the DUP leader, the Rev Ian Paisley. Tim Hames, no friend of Irish republicanism, noted (2007) the 'vast ideological transformation' of Sinn Féin: 'The sheer scale of this change is astonishing. It should be recognised as such and welcomed with an appropriate spirit. It is historic.' And an editorial on the same day commented that it 'took Mr Trimble to lay the foundations for a political settlement but it will require Mr Paisley to erect the house' (*Times*, 2007).

Kirsten Schulze would appreciate the metaphor. Her pioneering work captures precisely the contours and the time-scales entailed in delivering a peace process. Hers was a timely and perceptive piece that brought both clarity and realism to a messy situation.

References

Adams, David (1996) Interview with the author: Ulster Democratic Party (Lisburn), 18 April.

Ancram, Michael (1996) Interview with the author: Northern Ireland Office (Stormont), 17 September.

Aughey, Arthur (1995) 'The Idea of the Union', pp. 8–19 in John Wilson Foster (ed.) *The Idea of the Union: Statements and Critiques in Support of the Union of Great Britain and Northern Ireland*. Vancouver: Belcouver Press.

Bauer, Otto (1924) *Die Nationalitätenfrage und die Sozialdemokratie*. Vienna: Verlag der Wiener Volksbuchhandlung.

Ben Dor, Gabriel and David B. Dewitt (eds.) (1987) *Conflict Management in the Middle East*. Lexington, MA: Lexington Books.

Blair, Tony (2002) 'Prime Minister's Speech on Northern Ireland', 18 October. <http.www.pm.gov.uk/output/Page1732.asp>.

Boulton, David (1973) *The UVF 1966–1973: An Anatomy of Loyalist Rebellion*. Dublin: Gill and Macmillan.

Bruce, Steve (1992) *The Red Hand: Protestant Paramilitaries in Northern Ireland*. Oxford: Oxford University Press.

Bruce, Steve (1994) *The Edge of the Union: The Ulster Loyalist Political Vision*. Oxford: Oxford University Press.

Burton, John and Frank Dukes (1990) *Conflict: Practices in Management, Settlement and Resolution*. London: Macmillan.

Elliott, Sydney (1997) 'The Northern Ireland Forum/Entry to Negotiations Election 1996', *Irish Political Studies*, 12, pp. 111–22.

English, Richard (1995) 'Unionism and Nationalism', pp. 135–8 in John Wilson Foster (ed.) *The Idea of the Union: Statements and Critiques in Support of the Union of Great Britain and Northern Ireland*. Vancouver: Belcouver Press.

English, Richard (1996) 'The Same People with Different Relatives? Modern Scholarship, Unionists and the Irish Nation', pp. 220–35 in Richard English and Graham Walker (eds.) *Unionism in Modern Ireland: New Perspectives on Politics and Culture*. Basingstoke: Macmillan.

Farrell, Marietta (1996) Interview with the author: Social Democratic and Labour Party (Belfast), 17 April.

Finlay, Fergus (1996) Interview with the author: Irish Labour Party (Dublin), 22 May.

Gibney, Jim (1996) Interview with the author: Sinn Féin (Belfast), 17 May.

Hames, Tim (2007) 'Don't Swap Your Guns for Begging Bowls', *The Times*, 29 January.

Hanf, Theodor (1989) 'The Prospects of Accommodation in Communal Conflicts: A Comparative Study', pp. 313–32 in Peter A. Döring (ed.) *Bildung in sozio-ökonomischer Sicht*. Cologne and Vienna: Böhlau.

Hanf, Theodor (1993) *Coexistence in Wartime Lebanon: Decline of a State and Rise of a Nation*. London: I.B. Tauris.

Hartley, Tom (1996) Interview with the author: Sinn Féin (Belfast), 17 May.

Horowitz, Donald (1993) 'Conflict and the Incentives to Political Accommodation', pp. 173–88 in Dermot Keogh and Michael H. Haltzel (eds.) *Northern Ireland and the Politics of Reconciliation*. Washington, DC: Woodrow Wilson Center Press/Cambridge University Press.

Hudson, Michael (1985) *The Precarious Republic: Modernization in Lebanon*. Boulder, CO: Westview.

Hutchinson, Billy (1996) Interview with the author: Progressive Unionist Party (Belfast), 11 July.

Kewenig, Wilhelm (1965) *Die Koexistenz der Religionsgemeinschaften im Libanon*. Berlin: de Gruyter.

Kriesberg, Louis (1992) *International Conflict Resolution: The US–USSR and the Middle East Cases*. New Haven, CT: Yale University Press.

Kriesberg, Louis and Stuart J. Thorson (eds.) (1991) *Timing the De-escalation of International Conflicts*. Syracuse, NY: Syracuse University Press.

Lijphart, Arend (1977) *Democracy in Plural Societies: A Comparative Exploration*. New Haven, CT: Yale University Press.

Lijphart, Arend (1981) *Conflict and Coexistence in Belgium: Dynamics of a Culturally Divided Society*. Berkeley, CA: University of California Press.

Mallie, Eamonn and David McKittrick (1996) *The Fight for Peace: The Secret Story Behind the Irish Peace Process*. London: Heinemann.

Mansergh, Martin (1995) 'The Background to the Peace Process', *Irish Studies in International Affairs*, 6, pp. 145–58.

McBride, Ian (1996) 'Ulster and the British Problem', pp. 1–18 in Richard English and Graham Walker (eds.) *Unionism in Modern Ireland: New Perspectives on Politics and Culture*. Dublin: Gill and Macmillan.

McIntyre, Anthony (1995) 'Modern Irish Republicanism: The Product of British State Strategies', *Irish Political Studies*, 10, pp. 97–122.

McMichael, Gary (1996) Interview with the author: Ulster Democratic Party (Lisburn), 17 July.

Miller, David W. (1978) *Queen's Rebels: Ulster Loyalism in Historical Perspective*. Dublin: Gill and Macmillan.

Nelson, Drew (1996) Interview with the author: Ulster Unionist Party (Belfast), 19 April.

Ohlson, Leif (1989) *Case Studies of Regional Conflicts and Conflict Resolution*. Göteborg: Padrigu Papers.

O'Leary, Brendan and John McGarry (1993a) *The Politics of Antagonism: Understanding Northern Ireland*. London: Athlone Press.

O'Leary, Brendan and John McGarry (eds.) (1993b) *The Politics of Ethnic Conflict Regulation*. London: Routledge.

Pillar, Paul R. (1983) *Negotiating Peace: War Termination as a Bargaining Process*. Princeton, NJ: Princeton University Press.

Pruitt, Dean (2005) 'Whither Ripeness Theory?', Institute for Conflict Analysis and Resolution Working Paper No. 25. Fairfax, VA: George Mason University.

Rabie, Mohammed (1994) *Conflict Resolution and Ethnicity*. Westport, CT: Praeger.

Rabushka, Alvin and Kenneth A. Shepsle (1972) *Politics in Plural Societies: A Theory of Democratic Instability*. Columbus, OH: Merill.

Renner, Karl (1902) *Der Kampf der österreichischen Nationen um den Staat*. Leipzig and Vienna: F. Deuticke.

Renner, Karl (1918) *Das Selbstbestimmungsrecht der Nationen, in besonderer Anwendung auf Österreich*. Leipzig and Vienna: F. Deuticke.

Rogowski, Ronald (1978) 'Rationalist Theories of Politics: A Midterm Report', *World Politics*, 30 (2), pp. 296–323.

Rose, Richard (1976) *Northern Ireland: A Time for Change*. London: Macmillan.

Rothstein, Robert (1996) 'After The Peace: The Political Economy of Reconciliation'. Inaugural Rebecca Meyerhoff Memorial Lecture, Harry S. Truman Institute, Jerusalem University.

Sandole, Dennis J.D. (1992) *Conflict Resolution in the Post-Cold War Era: Dealing with Ethnic Violence in the New Europe*. Fairfax, VA: Institute for Conflict Analysis and Resolution.

Schwerin, Edward W. (1995) *Mediation, Citizen Empowerment, and Transformational Politics*. London: Praeger.

Smith, M.L.R. (1995) *Fighting for Ireland? The Military Strategy of the Irish Republican Movement*. London: Routledge.

Smith, Roger (ed.) (1996) *Achieving Civil Justice: Appropriate Dispute Resolution for the 1990s*. London: Legal Action Group.

Steiner, Jürg (1970) *Amicable Agreement Versus Majority Rule: Conflict Resolution In Switzerland*. Chapel Hill, NC: University of North Carolina Press.

The Times (2007) 'Editorial: Not So Alone', 29 January.

Touval, Saadia and I. William Zartman (eds.) (1985) *International Mediation in Theory and Practice*. Boulder, CO and London: Westview Press/Foreign Policy Institute.

Vasquez, John A., James Turner Johnson, Sanford Jaffe and Linda Stamato (eds.) (1995) *Beyond Confrontation: Learning Conflict Resolution in the Post-Cold War Era*. Ann Arbor, MI: University of Michigan Press.

Zartman, I. William (1989) *Ripe for Resolution: Conflict and Intervention in Africa*. Oxford: Oxford University Press.

Zartman, I. William (ed.) (1995) *Elusive Peace: Negotiating an End to Civil Wars*. Washington, DC: Brookings Institution.

15 Who voted for peace?

Public support for the 1998 Northern Ireland Agreement[1]

Bernadette C. Hayes and Ian McAllister

Originally published in *Irish Political Studies*, 16, 2001, pp. 73–93.

Over the past 30 years of communal conflict, Northern Ireland has seen many attempts to reach a lasting political settlement.[2] The April 1998 Northern Ireland ('Good Friday') Agreement appears to represent the most promising of these. Previous attempts at a settlement had excluded the main paramilitary organisations, but when militant republicanism began to reassess the effectiveness of its military campaign, the preconditions emerged to include them in negotiations. Although the Agreement was formally ratified by 71 per cent of voters in the referendum held on 22 May 1998, only a narrow majority of Protestants voted to support it. Moreover, in the period since the vote, there have been major doubts about the commitment of the Irish Republican Army (IRA) and Sinn Féin to constitutional politics and to the decommissioning of paramilitary weapons, casting a further shadow over the long-term viability of the political institutions created by the Agreement.

Whatever the caveats and future uncertainties surrounding the Good Friday Agreement, it remains an historic turning point in Northern Ireland politics, with, for the first time in the province's history, the formation of an Executive composed of unionists and the representatives of physical force republicanism. Such a scenario would have seemed wildly improbable even five years ago. In this article we use the 1998 Northern Ireland Referendum and Election Study Survey[3] to analyse the referendum campaign and the patterns of voting. The survey data are used to test four explanations of why a narrow majority of Protestants voted to support the Agreement, and to examine the beliefs of Catholic nationalists and republicans about the Agreement.

The origins of the peace process and the Agreement

The peace process has its immediate roots in the 1985 Anglo-Irish Agreement, which, for the first time, formally acknowledged that the Irish Republic had a legitimate role to play in Northern Ireland affairs (Arthur, 1999). Public reaction to the Anglo-Irish Agreement differed significantly between the two communities in Northern Ireland. Arguing that the Agreement was nothing more than a device to further Irish unity, unionists mounted street protests against its introduction

(Aughey, 1989). All 15 Unionist MPs immediately resigned their parliamentary seats at Westminster in protest, resulting in a series of by-elections in which, under the slogan 'Ulster says no', both moderate Ulster Unionist Party (UUP) and more extreme Democratic Unionist Party (DUP) representatives united to attempt to defeat the Agreement.

Less dramatic discontent also emerged within some sections of the nationalist community. For the first time, the Agreement highlighted the distinction between republicans and their more moderate nationalist colleagues in their approach to Irish unity (O'Leary and McGarry, 1993, pp. 222–3). Sinn Féin was deeply suspicious of the initiative, claiming that it had surrendered the Irish Republic's legitimate constitutional claim to the reunification of Ireland and instead delivered *de jure* recognition to Northern Ireland as part of the United Kingdom. In contrast, the leader of the Social Democratic and Labour Party (SDLP), John Hume, saw it as the first step in the process of persuading unionists as to the legitimacy of their case and the inevitability of Irish unity (Hume, 1996).

But more so than any other factor, it was the response of the paramilitary organisations that signalled a fundamental change in party politics. In January 1987 a group aligned with the Ulster Defence Association (UDA) issued a strategy document called *Common Sense*, which advocated the return of devolved government to Northern Ireland, based on a model of shared responsibility in government (McMichael, 1999, p. 24). A similar move towards a more overtly political strategy came from Sinn Féin (McIntyre, 1995). Although Sinn Féin had made impressive electoral gains since the introduction of its 'Armalite and ballot box' strategy at the beginning of the decade, it still attracted the support of only one in ten Northern Ireland voters. Sinn Féin realised that it had to build strategic alliances with other groups, and in 1988 Gerry Adams secretly met John Hume, an initiative that sowed the seeds of Sinn Féin's transition to a constitutional party (Murray, 1998, pp. 161–86).

These continuing talks led to the so-called Hume–Adams initiative which in turn formed the basis for the Downing Street Declaration, formally signed by the British and Irish governments on 15 December 1993. In the Declaration, the two governments outlined the principles that they hoped would lead to a political settlement.[4] The Declaration eventually paved the way for the establishment of the Northern Ireland Forum and the start of all-party negotiations, which commenced in June 1996, presided over by a former U.S. Senate majority leader, George Mitchell. However, it was not until the election of the Blair Labour government in May 1997 that progress was made. In order to further the talks, the new government deliberately blurred the decommissioning issue, reasoning that the most divisive issues could be dealt with last. The talks finally concluded with the ratification of the Good Friday Agreement on 10 April 1998.

The Good Friday Agreement is based on 'parity of esteem' – the principle of providing full expression for differing identities. In practice, this means that there is recognition for the political rights of both communities, and the freedom to express those rights in political institutions.[5] Each of the three strands represents a trade-off between unionist and nationalist aspirations. In return for nationalist demands for the creation of cross-border bodies, nationalists and republicans endorsed the return to devolved government and the creation of an elected Assembly. To make the creation of cross-border bodies more acceptable to unionists, the north–south dimension was complemented by an east–west dimension via the establishment of a British–Irish Council. For nationalists, in return, the elected Assembly would be based on the principle of proportionality with a power-sharing Executive composed of all groups within the Assembly, chosen by the d'Hondt procedure.

Reactions to the Agreement

These compromises were not equally acceptable to all unionists and nationalists alike. No sooner had the Agreement been signed than significant divisions began to emerge within the mainstream unionist groups. In addition to those unionists (mainly Democratic and UK Unionists) who had adopted an anti-Agreement stance almost from the very beginning of the negotiations, significant opposition to the Agreement also came from many mainstream unionists.[6] The major dispute was less over constitutional matters, which had already been debated intensely during the negotiations, but rather over the issues of weapons decommissioning by the paramilitaries, reform of the Royal Ulster Constabulary (RUC), and the accelerated release of paramilitary prisoners.

For many unionists, the concession to Sinn Féin and the two loyalist fringe parties with paramilitary links to introduce a phased early prisoner release programme was unacceptable (von Tangen Page, 2000). The scheme would see all prisoners released within two years and many released within the first six months. Although early release was confined to prisoners affiliated with organisations that had established and maintained an unequivocal ceasefire, this failed to ameliorate unionist concerns. Many unionists reacted with horror at the thought of the release of convicted murderers who might, in some cases, be released after having served less than three years.[7] There was also some nationalist concern, albeit to a lesser degree, when it was realised that sectarian murderers would also be eligible for early release.[8]

A related issue was the continuing ambiguity over the decommissioning of paramilitary weapons. Despite British assurances to the unionists that the decommissioning of IRA weapons was a necessary precondition to the inclusion of Sinn Féin in government, much confusion surrounded the issue. Pro-Agreement and anti-Agreement unionists both argued that the immediate surrender of all paramilitary weapons was a necessary prerequisite for Sinn Féin's inclusion in government, typified in the slogan: 'no guns, no government'. Republicans adopted a different interpretation; decommissioning remained a necessary but long-term aspiration, whose eventual success should be seen as a consequence of, rather than a precondition for, access to political office.[9] Support for this position was also echoed, albeit to a lesser extent, by John Hume as well as by senior SDLP figures on the Hume wing of the party (see De Breadun, 2001, pp. 195–6).

There were also widespread unionist concerns over the proposed Independent Commission on Policing, a key concession to nationalists. Among even moderate unionists, it was viewed as a mechanism to undermine the RUC, and many feared that it would pave the way for the force's eventual disbandment. Nationalists, in contrast, viewed the reform of the RUC as a crucial step in making the police more widely acceptable.[10] They envisioned that not only would the recommendations of the commission suggest the establishment of a new police service that would attract support and consent from all sections of the community, but one which would, for the first time, be representative of both communities. The Commission was established in June 1998 under the chairmanship of Chris Patten, a former Conservative minister. The subsequent report, published in September 1999, contained a total of 175 recommendations, the most contentious of which was to change the name of the RUC to the Northern Ireland Police Service.[11]

There were also some anti-Agreement nationalist dissenters. While the vast majority of nationalists saw the Agreement as an important advance in meeting their aspirations and demands, many republicans saw the establishment of cross-border bodies and the power-sharing Executive as inadequate. They pointed out that not only did the Agreement fail to deliver a united Ireland, but through its principle of majority consent for any future change in the constitutional position of Northern Ireland it again reaffirmed partition and the unionist veto.[12] Furthermore, they argued that although the Agreement promised a review of policing, it contained no firm commitment to either disband or reform the RUC. Eventually, however, most republicans added their voices to the pro-Agreement camp, no doubt encouraged by the promised prisoner release programme.

The campaign and the vote

In late March 1998, Senator George Mitchell announced that 9 April was the deadline for the parties to reach an agreement; as he put it, 'the time for discussion is over. It is now time for decision' (*Times*, 26 March 1998). The negotiations that followed continued almost constantly and involved the British Prime Minister, Tony Blair, as well as the Irish Taoiseach, Bertie Ahern. President Clinton called the main party leaders on the telephone several times, urging them to compromise. After dramatic all-night negotiations on the eve of Mitchell's deadline, agreement was finally reached at 6am. The referendum to ratify the agreement was set for 22 May with an Assembly election following a month later, if the referendum proposal was passed.

The Agreement received differing receptions within the two Northern Ireland communities. The Ulster Unionist Party executive, meeting on 11 April, supported it by a vote of 55 to 23, despite the opposition of several mainstream unionists, notably Jeffrey Donaldson and William Ross.[13] At a subsequent meeting of the Ulster Unionist Council on 18 April, delegates voted 540 to 210 in favour of the Agreement and endorsed the leadership of David Trimble (*Sunday Times*, 19 April 1998). However, the Council also passed a resolution supporting Trimble's efforts 'to resolve those areas where concerns still exist among our people', a clear indication of disquiet about the Agreement's provisions for reform of the police, the release of prisoners and the decommissioning of terrorist weapons. For their part, the Democratic Unionists, led by Ian Paisley, pledged to oppose the Agreement, as did Robert McCartney's United Kingdom Unionists.[14] In general, the loyalist parties with paramilitary links supported the Agreement.

There were fewer divisions among nationalists, with both the SDLP and Sinn Féin welcoming the Agreement. Gerry Adams called the Agreement 'a high point where republicans are now a pivotal and growing force in Irish politics' (*Times*, 13 April 1998). The IRA viewed the Agreement as a significant step, but said that it fell short of 'presenting a solid basis for a lasting settlement' and stated that there would be no decommissioning of weapons (*Times*, 1 May 1998). At a special Sinn Féin conference held in Dublin on 10 May, 331 of the 350 delegates present voted in favour of the Agreement, and to permit members to take their seats in the proposed Assembly. The high point of the meeting was the triumphal appearance of 30 republican prisoners, who had been given parole by the Irish government in order to attend the conference.

The initial popularity of the Agreement and the positive media attention that it attracted ensured that early public reactions were very favourable. The first poll to test public opinion, conducted in mid-April, showed that almost three out of every four voters said that they intended to vote yes, with just 14 per cent saying no and even fewer, 13 per cent, saying that they were undecided (Figure 15.1). As unionist leaders articulated more concerns about how the Agreement would work, Protestant fears about the Agreement grew; as a result, support dropped markedly,

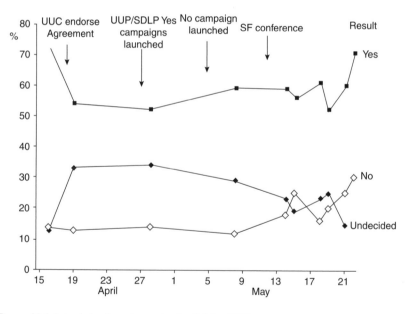

Figure 15.1 Intended referendum vote, April–May 1998.

Note: estimates include non-voters. Details of publication of surveys, survey companies and sponsors (with fieldwork dates in parentheses) are as follows: 16 April, MRBI/ICM/Harris, *Guardian* and *Irish Times* (11–14 April); 19 April, Ulster Marketing Surveys, *Sunday Independent* (16 April); 28 April, Lansdowne Market Research, *RTÉ* (28 April); 8 and 14 May (NIO, private poll); 15 May, MRBI, *Irish Times* (12–13 May); 18 May, MRC, *Daily Telegraph* (9–15 May); 19 May, Market Research Group, *Belfast Telegraph* and *UTV* (8–10 May); 21 May, MRBI, *Irish Times* (19 May).

to between 50 and 60 per cent. It remained at this level throughout the campaign, even dropping to 52 per cent according to one survey just five days before polling day. The proportion of undecided voters stood at around three out of every ten voters during late April and early May; it was not until just before polling day that they dropped below 20 per cent.

Although supporters of the Agreement outnumbered opponents by about three to one, the lack of decisive support among Protestants was a source of concern for the British government. The government had planned to mount a major television advertising campaign to encourage participation (and a strong yes vote), but accusations that they were seeking to manipulate the outcome forced them to abandon the plan. At the start of the campaign, Figure 15.2 shows that the largest group of Protestants were undecided about their vote, numbering more than four out of every ten Protestants. Both the yes and no groups increased during the campaign, as undecided voters made up their minds; however, by the end of the campaign, the final polls showed that the yes and no groups were almost equal in size. By contrast, Catholic support for the Agreement never dropped below 76 per cent, and averaged 87 per cent; Catholic 'no' voters never numbered more than four per cent of all Catholic voters.

The result of the referendum was a yes vote of 71.1 per cent, and a no vote of 29.9 per cent, based on a turnout of 81.1 per cent (Table 15.1). The turnout was the second highest in Northern Ireland in the postwar years, confirming the importance placed on the issue by the electorate. In the Irish Republic the result was even more decisive: on a turnout of 56.3 per cent (similar to the turnout in other

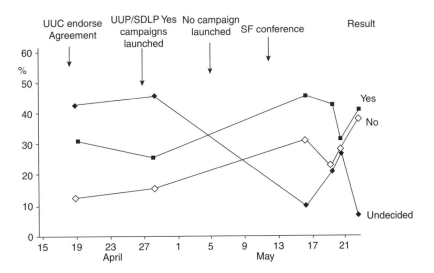

Figure 15.2 Intended referendum vote among Protestants, April–May 1998.

Note: estimates exclude non-voters. In the 15 and 21 May surveys, 'loyalist' is used instead of Protestant. See Figure 15.1 for details of surveys, not all surveys in Figure 15.1 include religion or political preference breakdowns.

Table 15.1 The results of the referendums, 22 May 1998

	Northern Ireland		Republic of Ireland	
	N	Percent	N	Percent
Yes	676,966	71.1	1,442,583	94.4
No	274,879	28.9	85,748	5.6
Total valid votes	951,845	100.0	1,528,331	100.0
Spoilt votes (turnout)	1,738	(81.1)	17,064	(56.3)

Source: Northern Ireland Office.

Note: in Northern Ireland, the question was: 'Do you support the agreement reached in the multi-party talks on Northern Ireland and set out in Command Paper 3883?' In the Irish Republic: 'Do you approve of the proposal to amend the Constitution contained in the undermentioned Bill the Nineteenth Amendment of the Constitution Bill, 1998?'

referendums, though significantly lower than in general elections), 94.4 per cent voted yes and just 5.6 per cent no. There were, however, ten times more spoiled votes in the Irish Republic than in Northern Ireland, indicating some republican dissatisfaction with the Agreement's explicit recognition of the constitutional position of Northern Ireland. Nevertheless, the result in the Irish Republic was never in doubt, since all of the major parties campaigned for a yes vote.

Patterns of voting

Although the referendum result produced a decisive yes vote, it also indicated the deep divisions that existed among unionists. The Northern Ireland Referendum and Election Study shows that 57 per cent of Protestants voted yes, while 43 per cent voted no (Table 15.2), a finding confirmed by an exit poll which showed that 55 per cent of Protestants who voted supported the Agreement, and 45 per cent opposed it (*Sunday Times*, 24 May 1998). The survey provides little evidence of differential turnout between the two communities; one of the governments' concerns had been that a low turnout in one or other community might undermine the result. This did not occur, and if non-voters had cast their ballots, based on their intending vote the result of the referendum would have been virtually unchanged, with the yes vote increasing slightly to 76 per cent.

Although the results produced a clear Protestant majority in favour of the Agreement, closer inspection of the patterns of voting suggests considerable fragility in the Protestant vote. The final part of Table 15.2 shows that one-quarter of Protestants said that they had considered changing their vote during the course of the campaign, compared to just 7 per cent of Catholics. Of the Protestants who fell into this category, most (16 per cent) had considered moving from a yes to a no vote. If all of these wavering voters (irrespective of the direction of the change) had actually changed their final vote, then the outcome would have been 67 per cent yes and 33 per cent no. But more importantly, Protestant opinion would have been equally divided on the Agreement, with exactly half voting in favour and

Table 15.2 Religion and the referendum vote

	Protestant	*Catholic*	*Other/indep.*	*Total*
Voted	85	84	80	84
(N)	(472)	(335)	(106)	(913)
Vote choice (voters only)				
Yes	57	99	76	75
No	43	1	24	25
(N)	(371)	(277)	(82)	(730)
Vote choice (non-voters only)				
Yes	49	82	57	63
No	26	4	14	16
Don't know	25	14	29	21
(N)	(71)	(59)	(24)	(154)
Considered changing vote				
Yes	26	7	34	20
(Yes voters considered No)	(16)	(7)	(24)	(14)
(No voters considered Yes)	(10)	(0)	(10)	(6)
No	71	91	62	78
Don't know	3	2	4	2
(N)	(361)	(269)	(81)	(711)

Note: 'Talking to people, we found that some people did not manage to vote. How about you? Did you manage to vote in the referendum? How did you vote?' (Non-votes only) 'If you had voted would you have voted yes to the Agreement or no to the Agreement? Was there any time during the referendum campaign when you considered voting in a different way?'

half voting against.[15] Among Catholics, the yes vote would have declined just marginally, from 99 per cent to 92 per cent. Indecision among Protestants therefore came close to altering the referendum outcome.[16]

Explaining the vote

Identifying Protestant voters according to their views of the Agreement presents few problems, since their vote in the referendum produced a sizeable minority against.[17] By contrast, identifying divisions within Catholic opinion using referendum vote is more problematic; the results presented in Table 15.2 indicate that only one per cent voted against the Agreement, and just seven per cent considered changing from a yes to a no vote. There is also little leverage to be gained from examining Catholic non-voters, since the vast majority said that they would have voted yes had they actually cast a ballot.

The main division in Catholic opinion was less in attitudes to the Agreement *per se*, than in its implications for constitutional change. Catholics have traditionally been divided between those wanting Irish unity, who constitute about two-thirds of all Catholics, and the remaining one-third who want Northern Ireland to remain part of the United Kingdom (Breen, 1996). However, among those wanting Irish unity, only a minority wish to see it come about quickly; most see it as a long-term aspiration. Accordingly, we divide Catholic voters into those who want Irish unity to occur in the short- to medium-term (who we term republicans, and constitute 35 per cent of all Catholic voters) and those who oppose it or who see it as a long-term goal (who we term nationalists, and are 65 per cent of the Catholic total).[18] We assume that nationalists viewed the Agreement as an important political milestone in its own right, while republicans perceived it as a mere stepping stone to their ultimate goal of Irish unity.[19]

There are several potential explanations for why voters decided to support the Agreement, the most obvious of which is that voters simply identified with its basic principles. The Good Friday Agreement set out three basic dimensions as a basis for a settlement. The first, devolution, was supported by almost all Catholic voters and most Protestant yes voters, but two of the three institutions failed to attract majority support among Protestant no voters (Table 15.3). Second, the decommissioning of paramilitary weapons has been a major source of dispute, and three of the four groups in Table 15.3 supported its phasing with the creation of new institutions and prisoner releases, the exception being republicans. Finally, the Agreement also dealt with territorial issues: the proposal for self-determination by Northern Ireland's people attracted majority support from all four groups, although Catholics (and notably republicans) were less supportive of any change in the Irish Republic's constitutional claim to the province.

Related to views of the Agreement's principles is the extent to which the electorate understood the basic mechanics of how the new system of government would

Table 15.3 Support for aspects of the Belfast (Good Friday) Agreement

	(Percent support)			
	Protestants		*Catholics*	
	Yes	*No*	*Nationalist*	*Republican*
Devolution				
Establish NI Assembly	97	65	97	91
Power-sharing in the new executive	83	48	94	94
Create North–South bodies	71	24	92	93
Decommissioning				
Paramilitaries decommission before enter government	86	88	60	38
Prisoners only released after decommissioning	83	87	62	44
Territorial				
NI remain part of the UK	98	98	86	61
Removal of Republic's claim to NI	81	85	56	37
'A new beginning'				
All parties make Assembly a success	98	69	98	91
Agreement brings economic prosperity	67	29	78	63
Agreement broke political deadlock	61	21	77	51
Agreement leads to lasting peace	34	7	61	39
(N)	(257)	(173)	(180)	(95)

work. The Agreement itself (a copy of which was delivered to every household in Northern Ireland prior to the referendum) had 11 sections and no less than 136 clauses, excluding annexes. The complexities of the Agreement may have defeated many voters and influenced the outcome of the vote. The survey included six statements about the new system of government and respondents were asked to state whether each was true or false.[20] The mean number of correct answers was 3.1 out of a possible total of six, but there were differences between the four groups: Catholic republicans were most politically knowledgeable about the Agreement (3.7 correct answers), followed by Catholic nationalists (3.3), Protestant yes voters (3.0) and finally Protestant no voters (2.9).

A second explanation for voting in the Good Friday Agreement is that it represented a 'new beginning'. Three decades of civil conflict have seen many cathartic events – such as the Omagh bombing in August 1998 – which temporarily galvanise public opinion against violence.[21] The circumstances surrounding the Good Friday Agreement appeared to fit this perception of 'a new beginning'. The frantic all-night talks before the deadline and the religious symbolism of Easter all fostered the belief that the Agreement might indeed represent a fundamental break with the past and deliver peace. The last part of Table 15.3 suggests that this explanation has some validity for Protestants. A majority of Protestant yes voters believed that the Agreement represented a new beginning in three of the four statements, the exception being that only one in three believed that it would deliver a lasting peace. By contrast, Catholics supported all four of the statements about the Agreement, and republicans three of the four.

A third explanation for voting in the referendum is exposure to political violence. Since the start of the current Troubles in 1968, more people have died in the communal violence than in any similar period in Ireland with the possible exception of the 1922–23 Irish Civil War (O'Leary and McGarry, 1993, pp. 8ff). Since 1968, about one-quarter of the population have lived all of their lives surrounded by violence, and have known nothing else, with major consequences for their political beliefs and behaviour (Hayes and McAllister, 1999). We would expect individuals with more exposure to political violence to be more likely to support its use for political goals and, therefore, to oppose the Agreement.

There are three forms of political violence that the population has been exposed to. First, direct experience of violence – being the victim of a violent event and experiencing intimidation – is widespread, and Table 15.4 shows that Protestant no voters and Catholic republicans were more likely to have experienced such exposure. Second, indirect experience, through having a family member, close relative or friend killed or injured, is also widespread, but again occurs more frequently among Protestants who voted no and Catholic republicans. Finally, collective exposure to violence, through being caught up in a violent act, either an explosion or a riot, is also higher among Protestant no voters. There is, then, *prima facie* evidence to support the hypothesis that greater exposure to political violence increases the probability of opposing the Agreement.

A final possible explanation for the referendum vote is popular support for empowering leaders to negotiate an overarching settlement on behalf of the society

Table 15.4 Exposure to political violence

	Percentages			
	Protestants		Catholics	
	Yes	No	Nationalist	Republican
Direct experience				
Victim of violent incident	9	20	14	19
Intimidated	15	17	22	28
Indirect experience				
Family/relative killed/injured	16	24	17	31
Know someone killed/injured	54	64	56	62
Collective exposure				
Caught up in explosion	25	28	25	29
Caught up in riot	14	33	22	37
(N)	(257)	(173)	(179)	(95)

Source: Northern Ireland Referendum and Election Study, 1998.

Note: 'A lot of people have suffered during the Troubles in one way or another. We would like to ask you some questions about you and your family's experiences. During the Troubles were you ever ...?' Estimates are for voters only. Ns for individual items vary slightly due to missing data.

Table 15.5 Trust in major political leaders (percent trust)

	Protestants		Catholics	
	Yes	No	Nationalist	Republican
David Trimble	89	51	73	48
John Hume	62	28	95	95
Ian Paisley	27	70	3	0
Gerry Adams	4	0.3	41	73
(N)	(249)	(157)	(178)	(91)

Source: Northern Ireland Referendum and Election Study, 1998.

Note: 'Here is a list of the main political leaders in Northern Ireland. Which of these, if any, would you generally trust to act in the best interests of all the people of Northern Ireland?' Estimates are for voters only. Ns for individual items vary slightly due to missing data.

as a whole. One key element which was missing from previous settlements has been the ability of political elites to deliver the consent of their respective communities for a political accommodation (Wilford, 1999). We would expect, therefore, that the greater the popular trust in the major political leaders by their supporters, the greater the influence such leaders would have on the outcome of the referendum.

Each of the four major political leaders were trusted by at least seven out of ten of their supporters. The two main advocates of the Agreement, David Trimble, the Ulster Unionist leader, and John Hume, leader of the SDLP, were trusted by 89 and 95 per cent of Protestant yes and Catholic nationalist voters respectively.

Ian Paisley, the Democratic Unionist leader who campaigned against the Agreement, was trusted by 70 per cent of Protestant no voters, while Gerry Adams gained the trust of 73 per cent of Catholic republicans. Most notable is the cross-community support for Trimble; while he gained the trust of only 51 per cent of Protestant no voters, only slightly more than was given to him by republicans, 73 per cent of nationalists trusted him, almost twice as many as who were prepared to trust Gerry Adams.

Evaluating the explanations

We have, then, four major explanations of voting in the referendum – support for the Agreement's principles, the perception of a 'new beginning', exposure to political violence, and trust in political leaders. To what extent do these explanations collectively explain the indecision shown by Protestant voters during the referendum campaign, and ultimately the decisions that were taken by voters on referendum day itself? Table 15.6 addresses the first of these two questions by predicting whether or not the respondents considered changing their vote from each of the four explanations.[22] In addition, controls for age, gender and education are included in the models. The results suggest that indecision was significantly

Table 15.6 Explaining indecision in the Referendum vote

	Protestants		Catholics	
	Est.	*(SE)*	*Est.*	*(SE)*
Supports Agreement				
Devolution	.06	(.08)	−.29	(.23)
Decommissioning	.01	(.06)	−.25	(.14)
Territorial	.11	(.08)	.02	(.14)
Knowledge of Agreement	.08	(.09)	.03	(.17)
'A new beginning'	−.03	(.20)	−.23	(.54)
Exposure to violence	.71	(.48)	1.48	(.83)
Trust in leaders				
Trimble/Hume	.88**	(.29)	1.09	(1.17)
Paisley/Adams	−.10	(.28)	−.15	(.53)
Controls				
Age	.03**	(.01)	−.05**	(.02)
Gender	.48*	(.25)	−.01	(.53)
Education	.10	(.18)	−.09	(.40)
Constant	−1.74		2.00	
Pseudo R-squared	.09		.09	
(N)	(440)		(268)	

Source: Northern Ireland Referendum and Election Study, 1998.

Note: ** $p < .01$; * $p < .05$. Logistic regression estimates showing parameter estimates and standard errors predicting whether or not considered changing vote in the referendum (coded one for yes, zero for no). Trimble and Paisley refer to the Protestant equation, Hume and Adams to the Catholic equation. See footnote 22 for details of independent variables and coding.

Table 15.7 Explaining the Referendum vote

	Protestants		Catholics	
	Est.	*(SE)*	*Est.*	*(SE)*
Supports Agreement				
Devolution	.55**	(.11)	−.23	(.14)
Decommissioning	.22**	(.09)	.12	(.08)
Territorial	−.22**	(.10)	.40**	(.09)
Knowledge of Agreement	.07	(.11)	.03	(.17)
'A new beginning'	1.37**	(.26)	.49	(.34)
Exposure to violence	−1.75**	(.61)	−.64	(.57)
Trust in leaders				
Trimble/Hume	1.27**	(.32)	.94	(.60)
Paisley/Adams	−.32	(.32)	−1.11**	(.32)
Considered changing vote	.29	(.32)	1.84**	(.75)
Controls				
Age	.02*	(.01)	−.02	(.02)
Gender	−.05	(.31)	−.10	(.32)
Education	−.24	(.23)	−.48*	(.24)
Constant	−6.54		−1.03	
Pseudo R-squared	.46		.21	
(N)	(440)		(268)	

Source: Northern Ireland Referendum and Election Study, 1998.

Note: ** $p < .01$; * $p < .05$. Logistic regression estimates showing parameter estimates and standard errors predicting a yes or no vote in the referendum (coded one for yes, zero for no) among Protestants and nationalism (coded one) or republicanism (coded zero) among Catholics. Trimble and Paisley refer to the Protestant equation, Hume and Adams to the Catholic equation. See footnote 22 for details of independent variables and coding.

related to only one of the four explanations, and then only among Protestants. Protestants who considered changing their vote were more likely to express trust in David Trimble (who we show below was a major factor in influencing overall Protestant support for the Agreement). The only other significant factor is age, and in both communities younger respondents were more likely to be undecided than their older counterparts, net of other things.

There are much more extensive effects, particularly among Protestants, when we examine the referendum vote itself. For Protestants, the major influences in promoting a yes vote were the perception that the Agreement represented a 'new beginning', support for the new devolution arrangements, and trust in David Trimble. Although the other two institutional arrangements – decommissioning of paramilitary weapons and territorial factors – emerge as statistically significant, Protestants who voted yes were particularly motivated by the return of devolved government to the province. Trusting David Trimble was also a major element shaping the Protestant yes vote, while views of Paisley had little impact. Exposure to political violence is important, even after a wide range of controls; as predicted, those who reported such exposure were more likely to oppose the Agreement.

Knowledge of the Agreement as well as indecision during the referendum campaign did not influence the voting decision, net of other things.

Among Catholics, predicting nationalist from republican sentiments produces a weaker model. Nevertheless, it is notable that it was support for the territorial principles of the Agreement which were particularly important for nationalists, followed by a lack of trust in Gerry Adams. Indeed, it would appear that while feelings about John Hume did not discriminate between the two groups, views about Adams provided an important divide. Finally, unlike Protestants, those who considered changing their vote were more likely to be nationalists than republicans; clearly the latter possessed a firmer view about the potential benefits of the Agreement to further their political goals.

Discussion

Of the many attempts that have been made in the past 30 years to reach a permanent political settlement in Northern Ireland, the Agreement has by far the greatest chance of success. Unlike previous failed attempts to solve the Northern Ireland problem, the Good Friday Agreement is based on the assumption that all of the parties to the conflict, constitutional as well as extra-constitutional, should be included and this principle extends to the political institutions proposed in the Agreement. Not least, the Agreement embodies the strategic reassessments that have taken place within the various paramilitary organisations, away from violent conflict and towards constitutional politics. But while the Agreement has great potential to deliver permanent peace, fundamental disagreements remain between the parties to the settlement and were exemplified in the referendum vote.

The results presented here have shown that although a majority of unionists – 57 per cent – supported the Agreement, there was considerable indecision and unease right up to the referendum vote itself. Indeed, if those who reported considering changing their vote had done so, unionist opinion would have been equally divided and the Agreement would most probably have collapsed. Unionists were motivated in their support for the Agreement by the belief that it represented a 'new beginning' and by support for the political institutions it proposed, particularly devolution. By contrast, for Catholic nationalists the territorial provisions in the Agreement were most important. For both communities, the influence of the main party leaders in shaping the vote underlines the important role political leaders possess in arguing the case for such fundamental change among their supporters.

The desire for a 'new beginning' among Protestants explains the difficulties in implementing the Agreement. In the absence of widespread agreement on fundamental political principles, such a desire represents an insecure basis for a permanent settlement. While unionists wanted a 'new beginning', there was little support for reviewing the role of the police or for releasing paramilitary prisoners. Equally, republicans were unenthusiastic about the removal of the Irish Republic's constitutional claim over Northern Ireland. More practically, the Agreement blurred issues such as how and under what political circumstances the decommissioning of paramilitary weapons would take place, as well as in what circumstances Sinn Féin would be permitted to join the Executive. Unionists believed that decommissioning would be well underway prior to the establishment of the Executive, while republicans believed there was no requirement to commence the process prior to the establishment of the Executive.[23]

It was the decommissioning issue that led to the collapse of the first attempt to establish the Executive on 15 July 1999,[24] and the beginning of a new series of talks in September, again under the auspices of Senator George Mitchell. Mitchell completed his review on 19 November, arguing that 'devolution should take effect, then the Executive should meet, and then paramilitary groups should appoint their authorised representative, all on the same day and in that order' (*Times*, 19 November 1999). At a meeting of the Ulster Unionist Council on 27 November, the delegates voted 58 per cent to 42 per cent to participate in the Executive with Sinn Féin, subject to progress on decommissioning having been made by February 2000. In the absence of satisfactory progress, it was agreed that the Unionists would withdraw from the Executive, thereby collapsing the Executive and its institutions.

The Executive was finally established on 29 November 1999, with ten ministers taking their seats, the most controversial being the Sinn Féin appointment of Martin McGuinness as Minister for Education.[25] However, because of the lack of progress on decommissioning, David Trimble and his party threatened to resign their Executive positions on 12 February 2000. In response, despite strenuous objections from nationalists, the British government, to save David Trimble from his own threat of resignation, suspended the Assembly and Direct Rule was restored to Northern Ireland. It was not until 30 May, after the IRA had released a formal statement saying that they would 'initiate a process that will completely and verifiably put IRA arms beyond use' as well as allowing the inspection of arms dumps 'by agreed third parties' (*Times*, 11 May 2000), that the Executive was formally restored, and with the support of the Ulster Unionist Council, the Ulster Unionist Party re-entered a power-sharing Executive with Sinn Féin.[26]

The future of the Executive

Although the Executive has survived in office since November 1999, many caveats and uncertainties remain, and its long-term viability will be decided by four factors. First, election results since 1999 suggest increasing unionist fragmentation, with the anti-Agreement faction on the ascendancy. The election of the Democratic Unionist candidate William McCrea over the Ulster Unionist candidate David Burnside in the South Antrim by-election in September 2000, shocked pro-Agreement unionists. Traditionally considered one of the safest Ulster Unionist seats in Northern Ireland, McCrea won by 822 votes, despite the hard-line stance adopted by Burnside on prisoner release, police reform and decommissioning. Although Burnside managed to recover the South Antrim seat at the subsequent Westminster election, held in June 2001, overall the general election was the worst ever for the Ulster Unionist Party. The UUP lost two seats to Sinn Féin and three to their arch rivals in the DUP (Cochrane, 2001; Totten, 2001).

A second concern is continued tension over decommissioning and police reform. In January 2001 David Trimble banned Sinn Féin from taking their ministerial positions on the North–South ministerial council because of lack of progress on decommissioning, although the ban was subsequently deemed unlawful by the High Court. The reform of the police continues to anger both unionists and nationalists, and despite the launch of a recruitment campaign in February 2001, to date neither the SDLP nor Sinn Féin have encouraged Catholics to join the restructured police force. Controversy also surrounds the newly established police authority, an independent, representative body set up to monitor policing in Northern Ireland; once again, both the SDLP and Sinn Féin have refused to either endorse or join it.

Third, although the paramilitary ceasefires remain, in principle at least, intact, there has been an upsurge in paramilitary activity, particularly among loyalists. In Belfast an internal loyalist feud between the Ulster Volunteer Force and Ulster Freedom Fighters erupted in August 2000, resulting in eight deaths and since the start of 2001, sectarian attacks on Catholic homes by loyalists has become a regular occurrence. On the republican side, despite the Provisional IRA commitment to open their arms dumps for inspection, no inspection has taken place by the independent commission charged with this task since October 2000, although the IRA renewed contact with the commission in March 2001. And, although it announced a ceasefire after the Omagh bombing in August 1998, the Real IRA has continued its sporadic bombing campaign in both Northern Ireland and Britain.

The most important factor affecting the future of the Executive is declining support among Protestants. The Northern Ireland Life and Times Survey, conducted in late 2000, found that 42 per cent of Protestants would definitely vote no if the referendum were held again, while just under a quarter were either undecided or said that they would not vote.[27] Of those who voted yes, a minority said that they would now either vote no (14 per cent) or abstain (four per cent). Two key factors in explaining this switch in electoral support among Protestants previously supportive of the Agreement are declining levels of support for devolution and the lack of progress on the decommissioning of IRA weapons (Hayes and Dowds, 2001). Given the importance of devolution in explaining original Protestant support for the Agreement, unless this issue in combination with decommissioning is addressed, the fragile edifice of the Good Friday Agreement may finally collapse.

COMMENTARY BY STEFAN WOLFF

Ever since the 1998 Agreement was achieved in the early hours of Good Friday 1998, voices of gloom and doom have accompanied its rocky implementation and the frequent and lasting suspension of its institutions. Assembly elections in 1998, 2003 and 2007, and general elections in 2001 and 2005 that saw a steady increase of votes and seats for parties widely regarded as representing the extremists rather than the moderates of their respective communities, have not contributed to a more positive view of the future of Northern Ireland either. Yet, in spite of it all, the process that began almost 20 years ago with a series of initially secret meetings between the president of Sinn Féin, Gerry Adams, and the then leader of the Social Democratic and Labour Party (SDLP), John Hume, has proven remarkably stable and successful.

Published in 2001, three years after the Agreement was endorsed in Northern Ireland and in the Republic of Ireland, Bernadette Hayes and Ian McAllister's article seeks to explain the differential support from the two communities for the Agreement. The article is tightly argued and well-supported by empirical evidence.

There are four different hypotheses that the authors establish and then evaluate: (1) voting behaviour was conditioned by support of the underlying principles of the Agreement; (2) a yes-vote was dependent on whether voters saw the Agreement as a new beginning; (3) the decision to support or oppose the Agreement in the referendum was dependent on the degree to which voters had been exposed to political violence (the higher exposure to violence among unionists, the more likely an opposing vote); and (4) trust in political leaders is a strong incentive to vote one way or the other. As can be expected in a society as deeply divided as Northern Ireland, the results of Hayes and McAllister's analysis highlight the divisions both between the two communities and within them. Unionist support for the Agreement is said to be based on perceptions of it representing a 'new beginning' and support for devolution, as well as having been shaped significantly by Protestant yes-voters' trust in the Ulster Unionist Party (UUP) leader David Trimble. Catholic nationalists (as opposed to Catholic republicans) are said to have supported the Agreement primarily because of its territorial provisions (the North–South dimension). The main distinction between the two segments of Catholics, who both overwhelmingly supported the Agreement, appears to be the lack of trust that nationalists had in Gerry Adams, the Sinn Féin president. (The distinction between nationalists and republicans is based on an alleged difference in terms of how soon they want their aspiration of a united Ireland to be realised – republicans are said to desire this in the short to medium term (35 per cent), while nationalists are assumed to oppose this goal or only want to see it realised in the long term (65 per cent). Not even in 1998, however, were these assumptions reflected in the votes polled by the SDLP and Sinn Féin.)

I have no reason to doubt the factual accuracy of the tests conducted by the authors, but I wonder whether the hypotheses proposed capture the complex dynamics of both the political process *and* the peace process in Northern Ireland since 1998. One key explanation for the difficulties that the political process in Northern Ireland has experienced since 1998, in my view, has to do with perceptions of credible commitment to the Agreement. The notion of credible commitment has emerged as a powerful explanation among scholars of conflict resolution since the late 1990s and is associated with, among others, the work of Fearon (1998), Walter (2002) and Lake and Rothchild (1996). Relying on rational choice accounts of human behaviour, it argues that perceptions of a lack of credible commitment can be mutually reinforcing among the parties to a peace agreement and lead to both sides defecting from it despite the fact that it would be in their best interest to honour it.

Some elements of a credible commitment explanation are implicit in Hayes and McAllister's hypothesis about trust in political leaders. The attitudes that voters in both communities had towards David Trimble and John Hume, and towards Ian Paisley and Gerry Adams, reflect, at least partially, that perceptions of how credibly committed the 'other' community is to the Agreement did play a role in how people cast their vote. An important further test, however, is missing: What impact did different interpretations of the Agreement have on the vote? In other words, were some Protestants swayed towards a no-vote because nationalists and republicans so overwhelmingly supported the Agreement, in spite of (or perhaps because of), their long-standing aspiration to a united Ireland? This assumption, of course, cannot be separated from trust in leaders. Protestant no-voters displayed high levels of trust in Paisley (who argued against the Agreement as a sell-out); while yes-voters overwhelmingly supported Trimble (who argued that the Agreement secured Northern Ireland's status as part of the United Kingdom).

Yet, the issue of different interpretations of the 'true meaning' of the Agreement reaches deeper than that. Protestant support for devolution, singled out as a major factor in a Protestant yes-vote by Hayes and McAllister, has lower levels of support than the territorial dimensions of the Agreement – that Northern Ireland remains part of the UK and that the Republic's claim to the region is provisionally removed from its constitution. Likewise, support by Protestants for the assumption that the Agreement makes provisions requiring decommissioning to precede the establishment of a power-sharing Executive and prisoner release seems at least at a similar level than support for devolution, and certainly higher than the assumption that the Agreement represents a 'new beginning'. The one aspect of devolution and 'a new beginning' that does enjoy very high levels of Protestant (yes-voter) support is the establishment of the Northern Ireland Assembly. Taken together, support or opposition by Protestants seems to centre on an interpretation of the Agreement delivering peace (via decommissioning), the region's continued status as part of the UK (via its territorial provisions), and control of the political process in Northern Ireland (via a unionist majority in the Assembly). The authors' own discussion of the 'Future of the Executive' strongly points in the direction of the peace dimension having become, by 2001, perhaps the most crucial issue for Protestants' support of, or opposition to, the Agreement.

There can be little doubt that this is crucially correlated with trust in political leadership. On the one hand, David Trimble himself fed into this Protestant interpretation of the Agreement, initially by emphasising that the Agreement secured, rather than undermined, the Union, and subsequently with his ill-devised mantra of 'no guns, no government'. Not only did this deprive the UUP leader of any sense of initiative (as it was now up to the IRA to decide whether there would be power-sharing or not), it also fatally undermined his leadership and electoral support for his party as those who had trusted Trimble to deliver on the

Agreement saw their hopes increasingly disappointed as the political process stalled and eventually came to a halt over the suspension of the institutions by the British government. The continued support of the Agreement by both Sinn Féin and the SDLP, at the same time, is likely to have reinforced Protestant misgivings about what exactly they had signed up to in the Agreement, and, more importantly, that Catholics might not at all be committed to the Protestant interpretation of the Agreement.

Credible commitment, of course, works both ways. The more Protestants resisted the implementation of the Agreement's institutions, especially power-sharing and the North–South bodies, both enjoying well over 90 per cent nationalist and republican support, the more reluctant did the IRA become about engaging in decommissioning, which in turn only seemed to confirm Protestant anxieties about the permanence of peace. Increasingly, both communities viewed each other as *not* credibly committed to what each one of them valued highly – peace vs. power-sharing and North–South bodies. While any existing sense of a 'new beginning' began to evaporate, opponents of the Agreement in the UUP and Democratic Unionist Party (DUP) saw their hand strengthened, first in the Assembly, and then at the polls.

The authors more or less predicted such an outcome in 2001 – that 'declining levels of Protestant support for devolution and the lack of progress on decommissioning of IRA weapons' may prove crucial in the demise of the 1998 Agreement. With the benefit of six more years of observing the political and peace processes in Northern Ireland, this conclusion now requires some modification. The 1998 Agreement has not (yet) collapsed, but has seen some important changes to its institutions, above all a strengthening of the collective responsibility of the Executive and of the accountability of each of its members, as well as the extension of the d'Hondt principle to the selection of the First and Deputy First Minister (NIO, 2006). While the former clearly addresses concerns that many in Northern Ireland had about devolved government in the region, the latter is necessitated by a political reality on the ground that has seen the DUP and Sinn Féin become the strongest political parties in their respective communities. At the same time, what few ever believed to be possible eventually happened: the IRA decommissioned its weapons, and Sinn Féin endorsed new structures of policing for Northern Ireland. Thus, while the two main concerns among Protestant supporters of the Agreement seem to have been addressed, the upshot of these parallel, yet closely connected, developments remains an electoral result that is not exactly the most promising for the restoration of all institutions created by the 1998 Agreement and their subsequent stability.

The hypotheses developed and tested by Hayes and McAllister in their 2001 contribution to *Irish Political Studies*, in my view, cannot fully explain this outcome. My contention, thus, is that expectations of credible commitment can potentially offer a convincing account in that the electoral trend over the past several years that saw the support for the DUP and Sinn Féin rise at the expense of the UUP and SDLP provides the background against which voters in both communities made their decision at the polls in March 2007. (It is also important to note that the UUP and SDLP have lost their long-term leaders since 1998, and now lack the kind of credible leadership that, despite all their faults, David Trimble and John Hume could provide.) Precisely because Protestants distrust the commitment of Sinn Féin (and the IRA) to peace, and because Catholics are wary of the DUP's commitment to devolution in all its aspects (that is, Assembly *plus* power-sharing *plus* North–South institutions), they voted for those parties who they saw as most likely to represent their interests in an uncompromising way. The expectation of an overwhelmingly Protestant DUP vote among Catholics, and of a similar Catholic Sinn Féin vote among Protestants, again resulted in a self-fulfilling prophecy that strengthened those two parties who will find it most difficult to make a success of the political process in Northern Ireland. Unless the leaderships of the DUP and Sinn Féin find it in themselves to trust each other enough to share power, the 1998 Agreement may indeed be doomed. This, as regrettable as it would be, however, would only be a verdict on the political process in Northern Ireland, as no vote since 1998 can be regarded as a vote against peace. In my view, the people of Northern Ireland have long decided for peace, what they cannot agree on is its political framework.

Notes

1 The 1998 Northern Ireland Referendum and Election Survey was conducted by John Curtice, Lizanne Dowds, Geoffrey Evans and Bernadette C. Hayes and funded by the Economic and Social Research Council. Our thanks to Sidney Elliott (Queen's University Belfast) and Maura Murphy (Market Research Bureau of Ireland) for providing the commercial poll data used in Figures 15.1 and 15.2. An earlier version of the paper was presented at the meeting of the American Political Science Association, Atlanta, 2–5 September 1999. Our thanks to two anonymous reviewers and to the editors of *IPS* for constructive comments; the usual disclaimer applies.

2 The best recent accounts of the conflict are to be found in Mitchell and Wilford (1999) and Ruane and Todd (1996, 1999). Several autobiographies provide useful backgrounds, notably Hume (1996) and Mitchell (1999). The terms 'unionist' and 'Protestant' are used interchangeably in the paper. The term 'nationalist' refers to Catholics who generally support constitutional political groups, mainly the Social Democratic and Labour Party; 'republican' refers to Catholics who generally support extra-constitutional political groups such as Sinn Féin and the IRA.

3 The Northern Ireland Referendum and Election Survey was funded by the Economic and Social Research Council and was a nationally representative post-election survey of all adults aged 18 years or older conducted immediately after the Northern Ireland Assembly elections in June 1998. Using face-to-face interviews, the survey is based on a randomly selected sample of 948 respondents and has an overall response rate of 71 per cent.

4 The Downing Street Declaration set out the principles under which a peace process based on an inclusive dialogue between the various political parties in Northern Ireland could proceed. The Framework documents dealt with proposals for the internal governance of Northern Ireland (Strand One), relationships between Northern Ireland and the Republic of Ireland and those between Ireland and Britain (Strands Two and Three). See Wilford (1999) for a comprehensive overview of the terms and proposals contained in the Framework documents.

5 See Ruane and Todd (1999), Cox *et al* (2000) and Wilford (2001) for comprehensive overviews of the terms and conditions of the Agreement.

6 Aughey (2000) provides a comprehensive account of unionist reaction to the Agreement.

7 As the 1998 Assembly election manifesto of the DUP, in typifying the view of many unionists, bluntly stated: 'All decent people recoil with moral contempt at the prospect of the mass release of those who have murdered and maimed the innocent, whilst the RUC is to be demoralised and disarmed'.

8 The first opinion poll on the early release of prisoners confirmed the greater disquiet among Protestants. Conducted by MRC (Ireland) between 9 and 15 May (*Belfast Telegraph*, 18 May 1998), the results showed that an overwhelming majority of Protestants – 84 per cent – said that terrorist prisoners should not be released in two years, compared to 45 per cent among Catholics.

9 Opinion poll data conducted immediately after the ratification of the Good Friday Agreement lends further support to this finding. A poll conducted by the Harris Research Centre on 1–2 June (*Irish Times*, 5 June 1998) found that 61 per cent of Protestants believed that decommissioning should begin immediately, before the introduction of any other reforms including the establishment of the Executive, compared to just 31 per cent among Catholics.

10 A poll conducted by MRC (Ireland) between 9 and 15 May (*Belfast Telegraph*, 18 May 1998) found that an overwhelming majority of Catholics – 79 per cent – said that the RUC needed to be reformed, compared to just 36 per cent among Protestants.

11 These proposed changes produced a 400,000 signature petition in opposition, delivered to Downing Street in January 2000 by the Police Federation of Northern Ireland. Despite both unionist and, to a lesser extent, nationalist opposition, much of the Patten report was finally implemented in November 2000 with the passage of the Police (Northern Ireland) Act (see Walker, 2001).

12 Some senior members of the IRA resigned over republican support for the Agreement, forming what in time would become the 'Real IRA'. Nine senior Sinn Féin members also resigned, including Bernadette Sands McKevitt, a sister of the IRA hunger-striker, Bobby Sands, to form the 32-County Sovereignty Movement (De Breadun, 2001, pp. 73–5; see also McIntyre, 2001).

13 As Ross put it, 'There is going to be one awful struggle in the party and the community when people absorb what is in that document. This is bad enough to destroy Ulster as far as I am concerned' (*Times*, 12 April 1998).

14 This view was epitomised by the chairperson of the DUP, Nigel Dodds: 'the Northern Ireland recognised in this document is a different one from the Northern Ireland that I knew prior to this agreement. This is a Northern Ireland in transition to a united Ireland' (cited in Aughey, 2000, p. 69).

15 The actual figures are 50.1 per cent (survey n = 186) voting yes, 49.9 per cent (n = 185) voting no.

16 Indecision among Protestants is also demonstrated by the timing of the respondents' voting decision. Among Protestants 44 per cent said that they made up their minds either during the last week of the campaign (32 per cent) or on polling day itself (12 per cent). This compares with just 16 per cent of Catholics who made a similar timing in their voting decision. Among Protestants who said that they considered changing their vote, no less than 74 per cent said that they only decided on their vote during the last week of the campaign, compared to 48 per cent of Catholics.

17 In these analyses, the 'other/independent' category was allocated to either Protestant or Catholic based on parents' religion. This has few practical consequences for the analyses, and helps to preserve the sample size.

18 The question was: 'Please tick the box which comes closest to your view about the future of Northern Ireland: Northern Ireland should never leave the UK ... Northern Ireland should unify with the Irish Republic straight away'. Respondents had 11 boxes between these two extremes; nationalists are coded as those who ticked one of the first six boxes, republicans as those who ticked one of the last five boxes.

19 This division of Catholic opinion also corresponds with party preferences, with almost half of republicans identifying with Sinn Féin, compared to two-thirds of nationalists who identified with the SDLP. In addition, 36 per cent of republicans said that they had some sympathy for republican violence, compared to 22 per cent of nationalists.

20 The statements were: 'Northern Ireland has the right to become part of a united Ireland if a majority of people in Northern Ireland vote to do so' (true); 'Prisoners will not be released if the paramilitary organisations to which they belong have not decommissioned weapons' (false); 'Parties which win a significant number of seats in the Assembly are guaranteed a place in the Northern Ireland Executive so long as they keep to the conditions of the Agreement' (true); 'No key decision can be made by the Assembly unless 40 per cent of both unionist and nationalist representatives agree' (true); 'Parties with links to paramilitary organisations that have not decommissioned their weapons are not allowed a place on the Northern Ireland Executive' (false); and 'The commission on policing could recommend the creation of a new police force to replace the RUC' (true).

21 The Omagh bombing was also an important catalyst in changing opinion within the republican movement as, for the first time, Sinn Féin issued an outright condemnation of the Real IRA, whose members carried out the Omagh bombing. As Gerry Adams put it: 'Sinn Féin believe the violence we have seen must be for all of us now a thing of the past, over, done with and gone'. This statement opened the door to face-to-face talks for the first time between Adams and Trimble. Within a week of the bombing, the Real IRA announced an indefinite ceasefire (see De Breadun, 2001, pp. 169–75).

22 Multiple item scales were created from the groups of variables presented in the preceding Tables. The reliabilities for the four scales (Cronbach's alpha) generated from Table 15.3 are 0.73, 0.76, 0.69 and 0.80 respectively. In the case of exposure to political violence, an additive scale was created from the six items in Table 15.4. Age is coded in single years; gender is coded 1 = male, 0 = female; and education is coded 1 = primary, 2 = secondary, 3 = tertiary.

23 The Agreement does not endorse either interpretation, and simply affirms that the parties will 'continue to work constructively and in good faith with the Independent Commission, and to use any influence they may have, to achieve the decommissioning of all paramilitary arms within two years following endorsement in referendums North and South of the agreement and in the context of the implementation of the overall settlement'.

24 Because of their concern over decommissioning, the Ulster Unionist Party boycotted the inauguration of the Executive. The lack of UUP participation meant that the Executive had to be dissolved after just three minutes because of the absence of cross-community support. In response, Seamus Mallon, the Deputy First Minister, resigned his position before the Assembly was formally adjourned at 1.30 pm.

25 In the ten-member Executive both the UUP and SDLP were allocated three ministerial appointments and the Democratic Unionists and Sinn Féin two each.

26 On 27 May the Ulster Unionist Council voted 459 to 403 in favour of a return to the power-sharing Executive. Trimble's margin of victory – just 56 votes – was his narrowest win yet (*Times*, 27 May 2000).

27 The survey was a random sample of the population in Northern Ireland aged 18 years or over (n = 1,800) and was conducted between October and December 2000. The data and documentation are available at <http://www.ark.ac.uk/nilt/>.

References

Arthur, Paul (1999) 'Anglo-Irish Relations and Constitutional Policy', pp. 242–64 in Paul Mitchell and Rick Wilford (eds.) *Politics in Northern Ireland*. Boulder, CO: Westview Press.

Aughey, Arthur (1989) *Under Siege: Ulster Unionism and the Anglo-Irish Agreement*. Belfast: Blackstaff Press.

Aughey, Arthur (2000) 'The 1998 Agreement: Unionist Responses', pp. 62–76 in Michael Cox, Adrian Guelke and Fiona Stephen (eds.) *A Farewell to Arms?: From 'Long War' to Long Peace in Northern Ireland*. Manchester: Manchester University Press.

Breen, Richard (1996) 'Who Wants a United Ireland? Constitutional Preferences Among Catholics and Protestants', pp. 33–48 in Richard Breen, Paula Devine and Lizanne Dowds (eds.) *Social Attitudes in Northern Ireland: The Fifth Report 1995–96*. Belfast: Appletree Press.

Cochrane, Feargal (2001) 'The 2001 Westminster General Election in Northern Ireland', *Irish Political Studies*, 16, pp. 179–90.

Cox, Michael, Adrian Guelke and Fiona Stephen (eds.) (2000) *A Farewell to Arms?: From 'Long War' to Long Peace in Northern Ireland*. Manchester: Manchester University Press.

De Breadun, Deaglan (2001) *The Far Side of Revenge: Making Peace in Northern Ireland*. Cork: Collins Press.

Fearon, James D. (1998) 'Commitment Problems and the Spread of Ethnic Conflict', pp. 107–26 in David A. Lake and Donald Rothchild (eds.) *The International Spread of Ethnic Conflict: Fear, Diffusion, and Escalation*. Princeton, NJ: Princeton University Press.

Hayes, Bernadette C. and Ian McAllister (1999) 'Generations, Prejudice and Politics in Northern Ireland', pp. 457–91 in Anthony F. Heath, Richard Breen and Christopher T. Whelan (eds.) *Ireland North and South: Perspectives from the Social Sciences*. Oxford: Oxford University Press.

Hayes, Bernadette C. and Lizanne Dowds (2001) 'Underpinning Opinions: Declining Levels of Support Among Protestants for the Good Friday Agreement', paper presented at a round-table discussion by Democratic Dialogue, 10 April, Europa Hotel, Belfast.

Hume, John (1996) *Personal Views: Politics, Peace and Reconciliation in Ireland*. Dublin: Town House.

Lake, David A. and Donald Rothchild (1996) 'Containing Fear: The Origins and Management of Ethnic Conflict', *International Security*, 21 (2), pp. 41–75.

McIntyre, Anthony (1995) 'Modern Irish Republicanism: The Product of British State Strategies', *Irish Political Studies*, 10, pp. 97–121.

McIntyre, Anthony (2001) 'Modern Irish Republicanism and the Belfast Agreement: Chickens Coming Home to Roost, or Turkeys Celebrating Christmas?', pp. 202–22 in Rick Wilford (ed.) *Aspects of the Belfast Agreement*. Oxford: Oxford University Press.

McMichael, Gary (1999) *An Ulster Voice: In Search of Common Ground in Northern Ireland*. Boulder, CO: Roberts Rinehart.

Mitchell, George J. (1999) *Making Peace*. London: William Heinemann.

Mitchell, Paul and Rick Wilford (eds.) (1999) *Politics in Northern Ireland*. Boulder, CO: Westview Press.

Murray, Gerard (1998) *John Hume and the SDLP: Impact and Survival in Northern Ireland*. Dublin: Irish Academic Press.

NIO (2006) *The Agreement at St. Andrews*. Belfast: Northern Ireland Office. <http://www.nio.gov.uk/st_andrews_agreement.pdf>.

O'Leary, Brendan and John McGarry (1993) *The Politics of Antagonism: Understanding Northern Ireland*. London: Athlone Press.

Ruane, Joseph and Jennifer Todd (1996) *The Dynamics of Conflict in Northern Ireland*. Cambridge: Cambridge University Press.

Ruane, Joseph and Jennifer Todd (1999) 'The Belfast Agreement: Context, Content, Consequences', pp. 1–29 in Joseph Ruane and Jennifer Todd (eds.) *After the Good Friday Agreement: Analysing Political Change in Northern Ireland*. Dublin: University College Dublin Press.

Totten, Kelly (2001) ' "Two Elections, One Day. Simple But Important". The Northern Ireland District Council Elections 2001', *Irish Political Studies*, 16, pp. 225–32.

Von Tangen Page, Michael (2000) 'A Most Difficult and Unpalatable Part – The Release of Politically Motivated Violent Offenders', pp. 93–103 in Michael Cox, Adrian Guelke and Fiona Stephen (eds.) *A Farewell to Arms?: From 'Long War' to Long Peace in Northern Ireland*. Manchester: Manchester University Press.

Walker, Clive (2001) 'The Patten Report and Post-Sovereignty Policing in Northern Ireland', pp. 142–65 in Rick Wilford (ed.) *Aspects of the Belfast Agreement*. Oxford: Oxford University Press.

Walter, Barbara F. (2002) *Committing to Peace: The Successful Settlement of Civil Wars*. Princeton, NJ: Princeton University Press.

Wilford, Rick (1999) 'Regional Assemblies and Parliament', pp. 117–41 in Paul Mitchell and Rick Wilford (eds.) *Politics in Northern Ireland*. Boulder, CO: Westview Press.

Wilford, Rick (ed.) (2001) *Aspects of the Belfast Agreement*. Oxford: Oxford University Press.

16 Devolution and the diffusion of power

The internal and transnational dimensions of the Belfast Agreement[1]

William A. Hazleton

Originally published in *Irish Political Studies*, 15, 2000, pp. 25–38.

From the early 1970s to the present, devolution has occupied a central role in efforts to accommodate unionists and nationalists in Northern Ireland. Other constitutional arrangements were discussed and debated, but none managed to pre-empt or exclude a devolved framework for governing Northern Ireland. The 1998 Belfast Agreement marks the latest, and in many ways the most ambitious, attempt to reconstruct and reform the northern state-within-a state created under the now repealed 1920 Government of Ireland Act (Hadfield, 1998). In this rendition, devolution is part of a multi-strand approach, integrating devolved and transnational elements, with power-sharing arrangements, cross-border initiatives, legal safeguards, and new inter-governmental arrangements intended to secure cross-community acceptance.

We tend to think of devolution as strictly an internal matter in that decentralisation of administrative responsibility and/or legislative authority within a state does not affect its political independence or territorial integrity in terms of international law. Powers are transferred to regions recognised as distinctive parts of a country. However, unlike federal systems where power is divided and authority co-ordinated and shared between the central and regional governments, devolved institutions remain subordinate.

In states combating the centrifugal forces of ethnic nationalism, devolution, in combination with consociational principles and human rights guarantees, is seen as a flexible alternative to secession. Because the external aspects of national self-determination stress separation and independence, self-determination is not regarded as an absolute right of peoples or minority groups within existing states. Short of major human rights violations, such as genocide, expulsion, or wholesale repression, or a regime's persistent refusal to address minority rights and demands for local self-government, diplomats and scholars have tended to argue for ethno-national autonomy within less-than-independent political entities (Hannum, 1994, pp. 14–49; Levine, 1996; Lapidoth, 1996, pp. 29–58; Sisk, 1996, pp. 47–75). The emphasis, then, becomes 'internal' self-determination; that is, democratic self-government, meaningful participation, human rights safeguards, communal autonomy, and equal protection for minority communities. The idea, as expressed by Hurst Hannum (1998, p. 15), is 'self-determination should be concerned primarily with people, not territory'.

Until very recently, devolution remained an anathema for Irish republicans who struggled to end partition, for it represented, even in the short-run, an internal settlement that left Northern Ireland subservient to Westminster. While nationalists, and particularly republicans, adhere to a territorial interpretation of self-determination, the basic premise for devolution in Northern Ireland and the rest of the United Kingdom is the recognition of separate political wills. The territorial boundaries of the state are preserved, at least for the present, but as Vernon Bogdanor (1999a, p. 185) points out, devolved institutions create new centres of political power that promise 'to be anything but subordinate' in representing their peoples' interests. In Northern Ireland, unlike Scotland and Wales, the political autonomy of its inhabitants is expressly recognised in the 'principle of consent', whereby the majority has the right to determine whether the region remains part of the United Kingdom.[2]

To explore devolution's centrality to the Agreement, this article is divided into four parts. The first describes the debate over devolution prior to 1997. The second explores changing conditions and shifts in negotiating positions that facilitated a political compromise on devolved power-sharing and cross-border arrangements in the Belfast Agreement. The third explains the Northern Ireland Assembly's pivotal role in establishing the North/South Ministerial Council. The fourth assesses the Agreement's prospects, particularly in light of the continuing impasse over decommissioning (MacGinty, 1999).

The central argument for devolution, under the terms of the Agreement, is that it allows Northern Ireland to be shared on several dimensions; more importantly, it transfers primary responsibility for internal conflict management to the people of Northern Ireland and their elected representatives. The difficulty, as evidenced by the Agreement's painfully slow implementation, is that democratic accountability requires political flexibility, particularly within a multi-layered arrangement that diffuses governmental power within and across state jurisdictions. With political outcomes still seen in many quarters as communal victories or defeats, not all of Northern Ireland's parties have discovered that 'as in law or business, statecraft illustrates the maxim that the real negotiation begins only *after* the agreement is signed' (Crocker and Hampson, 1996, p. 57).

Devolution with an Irish dimension

'Sunningdale for slow learners' was the Social Democratic and Labour Party's (SDLP) negotiator Séamus Mallon's oft-repeated characterisation of the talks leading to the Belfast Agreement. For the blueprints from which the Agreement was constructed were not new, but rather well worn, with origins that could be traced back to the ill-fated Sunningdale Conference of 1973, if not the Government of Ireland Act of 1920 (Bogdanor, 1999b, pp. 60–9; Kendle, 1989, pp. 224–33). At Sunningdale, it was agreed to establish a power-sharing Northern

Ireland Executive, along with developing a new political framework that included an Irish dimension in the form of a Council of Ireland. This spawned a unionist backlash, and within five months the Executive collapsed under the weight of a fourteen-day general strike (Anderson, 1994). Subsequent attempts at power-sharing also failed, but rather than placing a dunce cap squarely on unionists, Gordon Gillespie (1998) claims that *all* parties had been slow to learn from the Sunningdale experiment. It was doomed from the outset, he asserts, not so much because of faulty architectural design, but because it lacked clear support from majorities in both communities. For Gillespie, Sunningdale's lesson was that any agreement required 'sufficient consensus', and this was finally understood in negotiating the Belfast Agreement and submitting it to a popular referendum (1998, pp. 112–13).

From 1972 onward, British governments sought to accommodate the aspirations of both communities through various partnership arrangements (Dixon, 1997, pp. 25–6). Along the way were limited efforts to put Northern Ireland on a more equal footing with Scotland and Wales at Westminster, but the region's complete integration into the United Kingdom, which appealed to elements of the Ulster Unionist Party (UUP) (Hume, 1996, pp. 74–105), never received serious consideration. Parliament's commitment to devolution for Northern Ireland reflects a view, long shared by most Britons, that the region is a 'place apart', and one that requires 'exceptional' measures (Ward, 1993, pp. 47–8).

Enthusiasm for integration began to wane among unionists as they grudgingly acknowledged the permanence of Anglo-Irish co-operation in shaping Northern Ireland's future. But as their attention shifted toward devolution, unionists split over the form it should take (Cochrane, 1997, pp. 103–8). Some sought refuge in proposals for administrative devolution, with few powers to share, while others, including David Trimble (1988, p. 92), held out the modest prospect of limited legislative devolution, with some type of regional council, in return for 'significant concessions' on cross-border ties. Debates over how much and what powers to share, and in Ian Paisley's case whether power should be shared at all, continued; however, the 1991–1992 Brooke/Mayhew Talks found the principal unionist parties supporting a devolved assembly.

Meanwhile, nationalists and republicans were sharply divided over the desirability of devolution. Both denounced Northern Ireland as a 'failed political entity', but the SDLP, unlike Sinn Féin, was open to discussing internal alternatives short of British withdrawal and unification. The SDLP attracted moderate elements of the Catholic minority, who aspired to a united Ireland but also sought accommodation with their unionist counterparts. As a result, they would only consider a devolved, power-sharing executive in the context of a consultative role for the Irish government. The latter was recognised in the 1985 Anglo-Irish Agreement,[3] after which the SDLP's leader, John Hume, appeared to back away from a devolved assembly, preferring some type of Anglo-Irish co-sovereignty, or joint-authority for the North instead (*Irish Times*, 7 August 1992).

This caused a split in nationalist opinion on whether to hold out for co-sovereignty and made the SDLP's negotiating position difficult to decipher during the

Brooke/Mayhew Talks. Fearing future bargaining opportunities would be squandered, the devolutionist wing, which included pragmatists like Eddie McGrady, Joe Hendron, and Seán Farren, advocated linking the re-establishment of a Northern Ireland assembly to tangible expressions of North–South co-operation (Bloomfield, 1998, pp. 20–6). Opinion in the party began to turn away from co-sovereignty, but most had doubts that unionists would share 'real' power. Having benefited from reforms and economic programmes under Direct Rule, the Catholic middle class, in particular, harboured suspicions that devolution 'might unhelpfully repoliticise questions', with no substantial guarantees of fair-play and equal treatment (McKittrick, 1994, pp. 18–19).

The 1993 Downing Street Declaration, and subsequent publication of the Joint Frameworks Documents, placed devolved power-sharing arrangements squarely on Northern Ireland's political agenda. UUP strategists realised that an Irish dimension formalising cross-border links would have to be conceded if devolution was to take place. But what would be the basis for such a compromise? The key elements, according to Paul Bew (*Irish Times*, 8 June 1998), were contained in statements made by Ulster Unionist MP John Taylor and Ireland's Taoiseach, John Bruton. In 1995 both men endorsed 'practical' cross-border co-operation that would be underpinned by changes in Articles 2 and 3 of the Irish constitution that contained the Republic's territorial claim to the North. The problem at that stage, Bew notes, was that 'neither Taylor nor Bruton could deliver enough people within unionism or nationalism for such an accommodation'. Three years later, Bruton's successor, Bertie Ahern, and David Trimble, both of whom had originally shied away from the idea, would advance 'practical' North–South links as the only way to achieve a cross-party consensus.

Negotiating Strands One and Two

The institutions created by the Belfast Agreement were largely the product of negotiations between the SDLP, UUP, and the British and Irish governments. Numerous compromises and trade-offs resulted in this process. For devolution to return to Northern Ireland, the most significant by far involved the future relationship between 'internal' democratic institutions (Strand One) and the transnational North/South Ministerial Council (Strand Two). In the Agreement, unionists achieved important concessions on the status of North–South bodies and the SDLP secured meaningful powers for nationalists in a new Northern Ireland Assembly.[4] These arrangements were buttressed by communal autonomy regarding education and the Irish language, enhanced legal safeguards, and a commitment to equality of opportunity in economic, social, and cultural affairs (O'Leary, 1999, pp. 76–8). Accommodation was found in devolution with an Irish dimension through an agreed set of rules and procedures, allowing both communities to 'live together, not only sharing power, but sharing cultural space with one another' – no small feat in the lingering shadow of Sunningdale (Cochrane, 1998, p. 14).

Tony Blair's New Labour government, which assumed power in 1997, saw devolution within the larger context of rejuvenating, modernising and democratising the United Kingdom. Devolution, be it in Scotland, Wales, or Northern Ireland, was intended to strengthen the union, and Labour recognised the need for 'flexibility' in developing different arrangements for each region (Tonge, 1998). Labour's vision of greater democratic accountability and new and more inclusive forms of governance found resonance in the Strand One submissions and proposals made by Alliance, the Northern Ireland Women's Coalition (NIWC), and two loyalist parties with paramilitary ties, the Progressive Unionist Party (PUP) and the Unionist Democratic Party (UDP).[5] At the risk of over-generalisation, it is fair to say the smaller participants favoured a form of devolution for Northern Ireland that would be more inclusive in terms of participation, more expansive in terms of authority, and more extensive in terms of executive and legislative powers. Each endorsed power-sharing and proportional representation, with the NIWC also calling for gender balance in the Assembly (Farry and Neeson, 1999, pp. 1229–34; Fearon and McWilliams, 1999, pp. 1260–2). Their appeals for inclusiveness and diversity reflected shared concerns that the voices they represented risked being marginalised or excluded from the new body.[6]

While not a participant in the multi-party talks by choice, Paisley's Democratic Unionist Party (DUP) advocated an assembly with the greatest amount of devolved power over the widest range of functions, including security, and having the means to determine spending priorities. The catch was the elected body would be 'truly democratic', i.e. uphold the principle of majority rule, and not be tied to 'any form of cross-border or all-Ireland structures'.[7] By excluding itself, the DUP avoided the prospect of having to compromise its well-entrenched positions, preferring instead to mobilise unionist opposition in an attempt to undermine Trimble's negotiating position.

Refusing to concede republicanism's commitment to abolishing partition, Sinn Féin also opted for self-exclusion on devolution, but did so from 'inside' the multi-party talks. Having consistently argued that no 'internal' settlement could work, republicans called for 'fundamental' political and constitutional change, based upon freedom, justice, democracy, and equality (*Irish Times*, 5 February 1998). When pressed for specifics, Sinn Féin offered an ambitious proposal for a three-tiered federal arrangement, starting with 'community councils' that would 'ensure maximum involvement of communities with maximum control over their own affairs'. At the next level were several regional bodies and, at the apex, a national parliament for a unitary Irish state.[8] Sinn Féin's submission drew no response, nor could it; for unification, like integration, was not up for discussion at the all-party talks. Republicanism's opposition to 'partitionist' solutions prevented Sinn Féin from engaging, in any practical way, in negotiations concerning the executive and the new assembly. In the end, Sinn Féin's silence on a devolved parliament communicated, at best, their reluctant acquiescence. Nevertheless, the prospects of returning to Stormont brought accusations from disillusioned republicans that Sinn Féin's leadership had become captive to its own peace strategy by ensuring the continuation of British rule (McIntyre, 1998, pp. 13–15).

With Sinn Féin preferring to concentrate on their 'equality agenda', the SDLP and Irish government assumed responsibility for representing nationalist interests in negotiations on the institutional arrangements in Strands One and Two. The SDLP tabled proposals for a power-sharing executive to administer Northern Ireland; weighted majorities to ensure a 'sufficient consensus' of cross-community support for important decisions; and the inclusion of guarantees for human, political and cultural rights (*Irish News*, 18 February 1998). However, devolution presented a political risk for the SDLP, and the UUP still evidenced a lack of enthusiasm for sharing power in any substantial way. As negotiations progressed, Northern Ireland correspondent, David McKittrick (*The Independent*, 23 March 1998), reported growing distrust and apprehension among nationalists that granting powers to an unproven assembly might jeopardise the political, social, and economic advances which they had made in the last 25 years. It was not surprising, then, that both the SDLP and the Ulster Unionists accorded a higher priority to the Strand Two deliberations on creating North–South bodies.

For a party that once ruled Stormont, the UUP proposed a devolved institution with, in McKittrick's words, 'powers so modest that it could be described as minimalist'. Rather than Scotland, the SDLP's preferred model, Ulster Unionists desired an administrative and executive assembly modelled along Welsh lines.[9] They saw no need for an executive committee acting as a cabinet, believing instead that the executive should be the body as a whole, with administrative functions being handled by committees whose membership and chairs would be determined by proportional representation. Their submission also stressed that the assembly 'must have political efficacy and be "boycott proof" with no incentive for nationalists to make it fail' (*Irish Times*, 24 February 1998). Given the proposal's tenor and substance, other parties openly questioned whether the UUP leadership viewed the devolution of legislative powers, essential if Northern Ireland was to have self-government, as attainable or necessarily advantageous. In the larger context of simultaneously discussing North–South co-operation, a cautious UUP appeared wedded to a policy of weak institutions across the board.

Ultimately, the nature and functions of devolved government for Northern Ireland would be heavily influenced by the high-stakes game of institutionalising cross-border co-operation in Strand Two. Ensuring the Agreement had a tangible Irish dimension or, in Sinn Féin's view, an 'all-Ireland context'[10] was of enormous symbolic and political significance to nationalists and republicans alike. A proposed North/South Ministerial Council provided an instrument for translating their aspirations for closer connections with the Irish Republic into reality. The problem was that the purposes and functions of the Council were also presented largely in aspirational language, which caused considerable confusion and concern among unionists. For nationalists, phrases like 'fail-safe mechanisms', 'harmonising functions', and 'injecting a new dynamic' resonated with progress and hope of one day achieving a united Ireland. In unionist ears they raised the spectre that any new North–South arrangements 'would develop a life of their own' and weaken, if not destroy, the union (*Irish Times*, 23 March 1998).

While successive Irish governments had strongly endorsed closer co-operation with the North, there was good reason for Ahern to be cautious and pragmatic, because the future actions of the North/South Ministerial Council would potentially affect his side of the island as well as Northern Ireland. To protect the autonomy and independence of the Irish Dáil, the North/South Council and its implementation bodies would have to be based on legislation passed by the Dáil and its counterpart in the North, making it in effect accountable to both parliaments. For this to transpire, the Northern Ireland body had to have a decision-making executive and broader legislative authority than either the SDLP or UUP envisioned.

By early March, Trimble had agreed in principle to formal North–South structures. This marked the beginning of what would be regarded as a major concession by the UUP negotiators, who remained fearful of a rank-and-file backlash to formalising cross-border ties. But what areas of co-operation would be mutually practical and how and to whom would North–South bodies be accountable? Negotiations concentrated on defining membership, role, remit, functions, decision-taking and implementation powers in precise and neutral terms.[11] In the end, however, the keystone for constructing the bridge between North and South was the new assembly. It, along with the Dáil, would designate the functions of the new bodies; they would each appoint the members, who would remain accountable to their respective legislatures; and once a body was established, neither party could change it without the other's consent. The other important link was that neither the assembly nor the North/South Ministerial Council should be free-standing. This meant that both had to come into effect at roughly the same time, and that if the assembly, for example, should collapse, the Ministerial Council would also cease operation.[12]

Practical considerations, in the end, essentially determined how these all-Ireland bodies would be established and operate. The most effective way of guaranteeing the degree of northern participation in cross-border institutions that nationalists demanded, while still ensuring the accountability that unionists and, for different reasons, the Irish government required, was through a devolved assembly with executive and legislative powers. Ulster Unionist negotiators recognised this linkage and modified their position on Strand One accordingly. For unionists and nationalists, devolution and democratic accountability provided the basis for agreeing to North–South bodies; by sharing power in a cabinet-type government at home, they could also share responsibility for deciding the North's role in future cross-border initiatives. In reaching this conclusion, the link forged between devolved government and the North/South Council was neither an expedient trade-off nor a watered-down compromise, but rather a realistic recognition on the part of the parties of the mutual interdependence between the institutions in Strands One and Two.

Moving beyond a narrow political deal

The Belfast Agreement did not mark the conclusion of the peace process, for it is not a political settlement; nor was it the intention of the British and Irish governments to impose a settlement on the people of Northern Ireland. Rather, it is the end product of intensive political bargaining, which explains why certain issues were deliberately fudged while others appear mired in a complex procedural and legal maze. Still, there is much that can be said for the Agreement, both in terms of what it offers and what it promises. The first is that despite its complexity, the Agreement's multi-strand, consociational approach creates a framework for internal conflict management through devolved self-government. Second, communal interests receive recognition and protection through an ambitious set of measures that include executive power-sharing, proportionality across the public sector, parity of esteem, and minority veto rights (O'Leary, 1999, pp. 67–79). The third, and perhaps most innovative, is that people are free to transcend communal divisions through the Civic Forum in Strand One and territorial divisions through the North/South Ministerial Council in Strand Two, and the British-Irish Council in Strand Three (Bogdanor, 1999c).

The Agreement, then, not only provides individual and communal safeguards, but also the means whereby their different interests can be managed and their competing aspirations co-exist, with the possibility of transforming Northern Ireland, including its constitutional status, through peaceful change. In this context, devolution detaches the region from a single community and a single state; Northern Ireland is to be shared. This is not how devolution is traditionally portrayed in legal texts, where careful attention is paid to enumerating powers and defining territorial and administrative boundaries. To the contrary, devolution for Northern Ireland is based partly on constitutional precedents, partly on theories of conflict management, partly on trial and error over the past 30 years, and partly on sheer political expediency. The product that eventually emerged, though far from perfect, seeks to bridge the communal divide by giving people a range of choices that are truly multi-dimensional. The prospects of this capture the imagination. In the words of Irish journalist Fintan O'Toole:

> The search for peace has turned a place that nobody quite wanted into a place that nobody claims. Northern Ireland has become a new kind of political space. Its people are in an extraordinary position – free to be anything they can agree to become. They have escaped from nations.
>
> (*New Yorker*, 27 April 1998, p. 56)

If the deadlock over the continuation of the multi-party Executive and decommissioning can be breached, the Assembly will become the principal arena of the peace process. Under the Agreement, devolution is the crucial linchpin for conflict management as well as for any future political settlement. The Assembly's deliberations are not confined to strictly Northern Ireland matters, but include issues relating to the North/South Council and, when and where appropriate, the British-Irish Council and the British-Irish Inter-governmental Conference.[13] Devolution, in this case, draws its legitimacy from the principle of 'popular sovereignty', which extends to the Assembly's active participation in the confederal arrangements of Strands Two and Three (Meehan, 1999, pp. 20–2). It gives voice to Northern Ireland's political will or wills as expressed by the majority or, in specified cases, concurrent majorities from each community. In this way, self-determination is continually exercised through devolved self-government, reflecting great faith in democracy and, more accurately, in the people of Northern Ireland and their political representatives.

But can it work? Unfortunately, the record of political initiatives in Northern Ireland over the past 30 years, and for 'identity' conflicts generally, is not promising.[14] Even the best-designed legal or procedural arrangements, reinforced with a fundamental faith in democratic principles, cannot always guarantee successful outcomes. Regardless of the Agreement's strengths or failings, the answer to whether or not it will work ultimately rests with Northern Ireland's political parties. More specifically, it will depend upon their intentions, their objectives, and their aspirations. Encouragement can be found in the 71 per cent who voted in favour of the Agreement, and in subsequent polls indicating that most parts of the Agreement, including executive power-sharing and the North/South Ministerial Council, continue to enjoy cross-community support (*Belfast Telegraph*, 21 February 2000). Ironically, though not surprisingly, confidence-building measures, particularly the early release of prisoners, police reform, and decommissioning, have fuelled a prolonged, emotionally charged, and highly divisive debate. In February 2000, the standoff between unionists and republicans over decommissioning resulted in the Northern Ireland Secretary of State's decision to suspend the Assembly (*Sunday Times*, 6 February 2000; *Irish Times*, 14 February 2000). Only when a new series of IRA confidence-building measures followed, and the Ulster Unionist Council narrowly endorsed continued participation in the Executive, was the Assembly reinstated at the end of May (*Irish Times*, 29 May 2000).

The lack of trust evident in the debate over decommissioning has highlighted a potentially more serious problem, the degree of commitment in all quarters to implementing the entire Agreement. Anti-Agreement unionists continue to speak of alternatives, which are, one assumes, devices of their own making that should amend or replace the Agreement (*Irish Times*, 11 October 1999). As John Lloyd has noted, republicans have pledged their commitment to 'the peace process', but the Assembly is portrayed as a 'transitional phase' in achieving Irish unity (*New Statesman*, 24 August 1998, p. 9). Meanwhile, pressure for IRA decommissioning is met by insistent demands for the removal of all causes of conflict (*Irish Times*, 16 February 2000). For both anti-Agreement unionists and hard-line republicans, the issue is not trust; it is one of incompatible objectives or, more precisely, who will ultimately determine Northern Ireland's future. If the Agreement is but 'a narrow political deal', in Gerry Adams' words (*Irish Times*, 4 October 1999), it leaves Northern Ireland's entrenched political positions in place, offering little prospect for accommodation, let alone a transformative process to erode communal antagonism.

Conclusion

In the context of the Agreement, devolution is designed to create a broader, more flexible political space. The Assembly is intended to serve as the anchor for arrangements that diffuse political power within and across international borders, and thus relax, if not blur, Northern Ireland's identity with any one state. Devolution provides limited self-government, and with it, greater self-determination for the recipients. But the expanded range of choice and opportunity that the Agreement makes available will have little attraction for those whose single-minded goal is the attainment of an exclusive form of territorial sovereignty. This kind of self-determination, regardless of how illusionary, can only be exercised in Northern Ireland at someone else's expense.

Even under more favourable conditions, the road ahead for Northern Ireland is bound to be difficult. Self-government in divided societies requires concessions and compromise. Besides deeply symbolic issues such as decommissioning, marching, and retaining the name and the badge of the Royal Ulster Constabulary, urgent concerns over hospitals, schools, roads, and economic development require the attention of politicians who have little or no experience in these matters. For the peace process to move forward, uncomfortable choices will have to be made, which is particularly difficult for a society that is used to the zero-sum politics of fear and recrimination.

Devolved self-government for Northern Ireland represents more than a set of institutional relationships. To operate, it requires that nationalists and unionists manage their differences through political accommodation and compromise. Decommissioning, minority safeguards, and changes in the criminal justice system are not intended as compensation or punishment, to be imposed on or rewarded to only one side, but instead intended to make all sides more secure in engaging each other. In the end, it is not the Agreement *per se*, but the subsequent 'state of mind' of the participants that will largely determine whether its provisions allow for peaceful co-existence. Devolved self-government and transnational institutions have created a new political space, a unique arrangement that could make Northern Ireland the envy of other regions in Europe. However, with this comes the responsibility for managing their own political differences, leaving the people of Northern Ireland and their political leaders to determine whether or not they move forward under the Belfast Agreement.

COMMENTARY BY NIALL Ó DOCHARTAIGH

The Belfast or Good Friday Agreement (GFA) of 1998 was the culmination of almost a decade of tortuous negotiations, beginning in earnest in 1990 with the re-opening of secret contact between the British government and the Irish Republican Army (IRA) through a long-established and closely-guarded channel of communication that had lain dormant since the 1981 hunger strikes (Taylor, 1997; Mallie and McKittrick, 1996; Rowan, 1995 and 2003; Hennessey, 2000; Cox *et al*, 2000).

By the time William Hazleton was writing his article it seemed to many as though the long process had finally come to a conclusion with the signing of the Agreement. All that remained was to tie up the loose ends and to resolve some of the more difficult outstanding issues. As Hazleton notes, the issue of decommissioning loomed largest of all. This issue had almost scuppered the process but a series of fudges and compromises pushed the issue of decommissioning forward, making it a problem to be resolved after the signing of the Agreement (O'Kane, 2007).

While there was caution and pessimism about the capacity of the parties to resolve this and other difficult issues, a caution that Hazleton shared, only a few would have predicted that it would take almost a further decade before the devolved institutions would get up and running on a reasonably firm basis in 2007. The 'peace process' was to continue for almost as long as the conflict it was intended to resolve.

Nor were there many who expected that the institutions would ultimately come into operation under the leadership of the Democratic Unionist Party (DUP) and Sinn Féin. Neither party had been actively involved in the design of the institutions. As Hazleton points out, the Ulster Unionist Party (UUP) and the Social Democratic and Labour Party (SDLP) had been to the fore in the detailed negotiations on institutional design. The DUP had not only rejected the Agreement, it had refused to take part in the negotiations that led to the Agreement and rejected the very principle of a peace process that the party as recently as 2005 regarded as a 'surrender to the IRA' (*Irish Times*, 2 August 2005). Some commentators see the new-found dominance of the two 'extremist' parties as the inevitable product of the sectarian logic of the consociational structures of government established under the Agreement. They argue that these structures deepened and institutionalised communal divisions by embedding them in the structures of government. As Eamonn McCann, one of the most prominent left-wing critics of the Agreement, puts it:

> The Agreement was always certain to consolidate sectarianism in that it established a system based on striking a balance between the wishes and interests of 'the two communities'. This ensured that the battle within each community concerned which party could be counted on to vindicate and advance its interests vis-à-vis the interests of the other side.
>
> (*Belfast Telegraph*, 5 January 2006)

But as the DUP and Sinn Féin gathered strength these 'extreme' parties were transformed. A once-rejectionist DUP moved slowly but decisively to accept the principle of power-sharing, even when it involved republicans who ultimately remained committed to ending the existence of Northern Ireland as a political entity. Sinn Féin enjoyed a dramatic surge in support even as it moved away from what many republican purists saw as core values. Both the DUP and Sinn Féin had built support by moderating their positions. In the 2007 Assembly elections the DUP and Sinn Féin successfully warded off challenges from opponents on their respective flanks who felt that the parties had compromised excessively, that they had sold out their core principles. The poor showing of these challengers demonstrated that the parties had the capacity to bring their supporters with them, and to attract new supporters, despite the major shifts in their positions.

As Hazleton notes, there are obvious continuities between the Good Friday Agreement and earlier attempts to resolve the conflict by establishing devolved power-sharing arrangements with an all-Ireland dimension, most notably through the Sunningdale Agreement of 1973. But the Good Friday Agreement was different, principally because it sought to incorporate and include Provisional republicans rather than to marginalise and isolate them. Loyalist paramilitaries were also included in the process but they did not have the kind of electoral support that Sinn Féin enjoyed and that made the inclusion of Provisional republicans such a significant political issue. Unlike the Sunningdale Agreement, the Good Friday Agreement involved prisoner releases, a major reform of policing, and a gradual removal of the British army presence on the ground. There are many who might argue, of course, that all of these issues would have been resolved much earlier had Sunningdale been allowed to get up and running. These measures addressed minority alienation from state security forces to an extent not attempted since the late 1960s and were a crucial element in ending the Provisional IRA campaign.

William Hazleton's article is concerned primarily with how government structures can help to provide a framework for peaceful political competition in deeply divided societies. It connects with a much broader literature on government structures in deeply-divided societies that has been dominated by debates over the merits of the kind of exceptional consociational structures for government established for Northern Ireland under the Agreement (McGarry and O'Leary, 2006a and 2006b). While Hazleton is good on the negotiations and the origins of the compromise that emerged, it is necessary to go elsewhere for detailed analysis and description of the devolved structures that emerged from the negotiations. The work of Brendan O'Leary and John McGarry has been at the heart of both academic and policy debates on government structures for Northern Ireland for well over a decade and their work is deeply embedded in wider debates on consociationalism (O'Leary, 2002; McGarry and O'Leary, 2004a and 2004b). It is essential for anyone wishing to further explore the debates Hazleton touches on.

McGarry and O'Leary's work on consociationalism and on British government policy in Northern Ireland has been critiqued by Paul Dixon in an academic interchange that was notable for its intensity and that illustrates some of the more contentious issues in the debates on consociationalism in Northern Ireland (Dixon, 1996a and 1996b; McGarry and O'Leary, 1996). A number of other recent works also deal in more detail with many of the issues that Hazleton touches on in his article (Elliott, 2002; Neuheiser and Wolff, 2002; Smith, 2002; Tonge, 2000 and 2005).

Hazleton's article reminds us that the current consensus in support of power-sharing devolution is a relatively recent development. The minimalist devolved Executive that the Ulster Unionist Party initially proposed in the negotiations reflected the powerful and long-established integrationist tendency within the party, a tendency that saw devolution as a threat to unionism to the extent that it distanced Northern Ireland from the rest of the United Kingdom. It also reflected the preference of the party for avoiding what its long-time leader James Molyneaux used to call 'high-wire acts' (House of Lords *Hansard*, 22 October 2003, col. 1624). In effect, the party feared that any negotiated settlement involving compromise with nationalists would weaken the connection with Great Britain. The fact that devolved governments were established in Scotland and Wales in 1999 and that the British government was clearly determined to bring an end to Direct Rule from London, made this minimalist position untenable. Despite this, there remains a lingering integrationist tendency within the UUP, a tendency that took hope and comfort from the difficulties in implementing the Good Friday Agreement. Senior UUP MP David Burnside gave voice to this sentiment in 2004 at a time of crisis in the process:

> It will be no major disadvantage to the unionist people if the Belfast Agreement is never seen again, and we work at Westminster to make direct rule more acceptable and seek more powers for local government throughout the province.
>
> (*Belfast Telegraph*, 5 January 2004)

Sinn Féin too found that its initial proposals for new government structures covering all of Ireland were not a realistic basis for negotiation. From this distance in time, after several years during which Sinn Féin has been focused above all on taking power in a devolved government in Belfast, it can be difficult to remember that Provisional republicans set their face against a devolved power-sharing government in Stormont for so many years, and actively argued against devolution in the negotiations.

As Hazleton notes, one of the most innovative features of the new devolved government structures for Northern Ireland is the way in which they are intertwined with new all-Ireland structures, stretching the devolved institutions beyond the boundaries of the United Kingdom. In the international context the intertwining of internal and cross-border structures was an innovative and radical step. Central to the consociational bargain, as defined by Lijphart (1977, p. 2), is 'an overarching sense of loyalty' to the state by the different segments that share power. A place in government is guaranteed to minorities within state boundaries that those minorities accept. The Good Friday Agreement, by contrast, acknowledged that external connections were an internal issue, that relationships with the rest of Ireland could not be separated out from the position of the minority community within Northern Ireland. Institutions that stretched beyond the boundaries of the state were recognised as a crucial element in securing the position of the minority within Northern Ireland, and securing minority acceptance of the state.

One of the great question marks over the Agreement is how these new all-Ireland institutions will work. Many nationalists see them as a way to knit together the two political jurisdictions in Ireland by gradually expanding co-operation in a range of areas. Even if unionists remain strongly resistant to such links, nationalist ministers in the Northern Ireland Executive will have considerable power to push forward co-operation and integration in their areas of ministerial responsibility, meeting regularly with Irish government ministers who might be expected to be sympathetic to such efforts. Some nationalists who stress the significance of the all-Ireland elements of the Agreement envision a future point at which co-operation and north–south institutions have become so embedded and so naturalised that the island is effectively unified. Unionists, by contrast, stress that they support cross-border co-operation only to the extent that it is of direct practical benefit to Northern Ireland, and can be expected to resist any creeping integration of the two parts of the island.

But few analyses of the all-Ireland institutions consider the very real possibility that they may reinforce the border. Politicians and civil servants south of the border may well seek to protect the interests of their part of the island at every point at which the all-Ireland context comes into play. Simultaneously, unionists and nationalists in the north may find themselves regularly united by the desire to ensure that the interests of the north as a territorial entity, of their electorate and constituencies, are defended in any situation in which Ireland as a whole is involved. There is a distinct possibility that the new all-Ireland structures could become a forum for the embedding of divided territorial identities on the island as increased contact oriented around the border serves to reinforce that border.

Hazleton concludes by arguing that the future of the institutions and the Agreement lies in the hands of the parties, that no system, no matter how carefully designed, can work well if elected representatives do not co-operate. There are hopeful signs. In some ways, the long drawn-out character of the peace process has made the settlement more secure. The violence that aroused intense emotions and mutual distrust has receded in time. Politicians and the electorate have become used to the shape of the new institutions, even if they have not been functioning for much for the period. The extended period of peace has allowed northern nationalists to become more comfortable with a demilitarised northern state which no longer presents such a naked repressive face. Unionist politicians have become more regular visitors to Dublin and the extended period of peace has allowed unionists to look at the rest of Ireland in a different way, no longer viewed through the prism of the IRA campaign. When Ian Paisley met Taoiseach Bertie Ahern in Dublin in spring 2007, his remarks on 'this great city of Dublin' and his comments on how his father 'fought to see, as a member of Carson's army, Ireland remain within the Union' (*Irish Times*, 5 April 2007) provided a reminder that separation from the rest of Ireland was not the original core of unionism in Ireland. The long peace opens up the prospect that northern nationalists can begin to identify with, and become more comfortable within, the northern state, but also that northern unionists can begin to reassess the Irish context, and become more comfortable with the building of stronger links between the two jurisdictions.

Notes

1 The author wishes to acknowledge the helpful comments made by Cathal McCall, Gordon Gillespie, Allan Leonard, Arthur Aughey, Sydney Elliott, Colin Irwin, and Carmel Roulston.
2 Under Constitutional Issues, para. 1(1) states: the British and Irish governments 'recognise the legitimacy of whatever choice is freely exercised by a majority of the people of Northern Ireland with regard to its status, whether they prefer to continue to

support the Union with Great Britain or a sovereign united Ireland' (*The Agreement between the Government of the United Kingdom of Great Britain and Northern Ireland and the Government of Ireland*, Belfast, 10 April 1998; herein cited as *The Agreement*).

3 While most citizens of the Republic of Ireland shared the view that Northern Ireland had 'failed', they were more interested in stabilising the situation than in changing the *status quo*. This is reflected in the Irish government's qualified support for devolution in Northern Ireland, contained in Article 4 of the Anglo-Irish Agreement.

4 For comparison, see John Hume, 'Opening Statement', Multi-Party Talks, SDLP Press Release, 7 October 1997; SDLP Submission to Strand One (Agenda Item Three) of the Multi-Party Talks, October 1997; and SDLP Submission on 'Principles and Requirements', presented to Strand One of the All-Party Negotiations, 13 October 1997.

5 Alliance Party, 'A New System of Government for Northern Ireland', paper submitted to Strand One of the Multi-Party Talks, 27 October 1997; Northern Ireland Women's Coalition Submission to Strand One of the Multi-Party Talks, 27 October 1997. For the positions of the PUP and the UDP, see Northern Ireland Forum, Committee A, *Report*, Annex C, 24 April 1998.

6 In response to efforts by NIWC and Alliance, a consultative Civic Forum was included in Strand One to allow other voices, particularly those of the private and voluntary sectors, to be heard. See *The Agreement*, Strand One, para. 34.

7 Democratic Unionist Party Submission, Northern Ireland Forum, Committee A, *Report*, Annex C, 24 April 1998.

8 Sinn Féin, 'Nature, Form and Extent of New Arrangements', submitted to Strands One and Two, 27 October 1997, pp. 43–6.

9 More than a year later, many UUP activists, including former party leader Lord Molyneaux, continue to favour an alternative devolved arrangement based on the new Welsh Assembly (*Belfast Telegraph*, 2 October 1999).

10 See Gerry Adams, 'Hope of a New Beginning', Opening remarks to Strand Two, 7 October 1997.

11 Mark Durkan, the SDLP negotiator, recalls that he and his UUP counterpart, Jeffrey Donaldson, took to writing related words and phrases on a large clipboard and systematically excluding those that were neither neutral nor mutually acceptable.

12 The order to suspend the Northern Ireland Assembly and Executive, which Secretary of State Peter Mandelson signed on 11 February 2000, did, in effect, suspend the Ministerial Council, if only temporarily (*Irish Times*, 12 February 2000).

13 In the British–Irish Inter-governmental Conference, executive members of the Northern Ireland Administration will be consulted prior to decisions (*The Agreement*, Strand Three, para. 7).

14 An estimated 15 to 20 per cent of identity conflicts have ended through negotiation, and of those roughly two-thirds eventually collapse into renewed fighting (Licklider, 1995).

References

Anderson, Don (1994) *14 May Days: The Inside Story of the Loyalist Strike of 1974*. Dublin: Gill and Macmillan.

Bloomfield, David (1998) *Political Dialogue in Northern Ireland: The Brooke Initiative, 1989–92*. New York: St Martin's Press.

Bogdanor, Vernon (1999a) 'Devolution: Decentralisation or Disintegration?', *Political Quarterly*, 70 (2), pp. 185–94.

Bogdanor, Vernon (1999b) *Devolution in the United Kingdom*. Oxford: Oxford University Press.

Bogdanor, Vernon (1999c) 'The British–Irish Council and Devolution', *Government and Opposition*, 34 (3), pp. 287–98.

Cochrane, Feargal (1997) *Unionist Politics and the Politics of Unionism since the Anglo-Irish Agreement*. Cork: University of Cork Press.

Cochrane, Feargal (1998) 'Learning to Agree', *Fortnight*, 370, pp. 14–15.

Cox, Michael, Adrian Guelke and Fiona Stephen (eds) (2000) *A Farewell to Arms?: From 'Long War' to Long Peace in Northern Ireland*. Manchester: Manchester University Press.

Crocker, Chester A. and Fen Osler Hampson (1996) 'Making Peace Settlements Work', *Foreign Policy*, 104, pp. 54–71.

Dixon, Paul (1996a) 'The Politics of Antagonism: Explaining McGarry and O'Leary', *Irish Political Studies*, 11, pp. 130–41.

Dixon, Paul (1996b) 'Explaining Antagonism: The Politics of McGarry and O'Leary', *Irish Political Studies*, 11, pp. 155–9.

Dixon, Paul (1997) 'Consociationalism and the Northern Ireland Peace Process: The Glass Half Full or Half Empty?', *Nationalism & Ethnic Politics*, 3 (3), pp. 20–36.

Elliott, Marianne (ed.) (2002) *The Long Road to Peace in Northern Ireland*. Liverpool: Liverpool University Press.

Farry, Stephen and Sean Neeson (1999) 'Beyond the Band-Aid Approach: An Alliance Party Perspective Upon the Belfast Agreement', *Fordham International Law Journal*, 22 (4), pp. 1221–49.

Fearon, Kate and Monica McWilliams (1999) 'The Good Friday Agreement: A Triumph of Substance Over Style', *Fordham International Law Journal*, 22 (4), pp. 1250–72.

Gillespie, Gordon (1998) 'The Sunningdale Agreement: Lost Opportunity or an Agreement Too Far?', *Irish Political Studies*, 13, pp. 100–14.

Hadfield, Brigid (1998) 'The Belfast Agreement: Sovereignty and the State of the Union', *Public Law* (Winter), pp. 599–614.

Hannum, Hurst (1994) *Autonomy, Sovereignty and Self-Determination*. Philadelphia, PA: University of Pennsylvania Press.

Hannum, Hurst (1998) 'The Specter of Succession: Responding to Claims for Ethnic Self-Determination', *Foreign Affairs*, 77 (2), pp. 13–18.

Hennessey, Thomas (2000) *The Northern Ireland Peace Process: Ending the Troubles?* Dublin: Gill and Macmillan.

Hume, David (1996) *The Ulster Unionist Party, 1972–92*. Lurgan: Ulster Society.

Kendle, John (1989) *Ireland and the Federal Solution: The Debate over the United Kingdom Constitution, 1870–1921*. Kingston, Ontario: McGill–Queen's University Press.

Lapidoth, Ruth (1996) *Autonomy: Flexible Solutions to Ethnic Conflicts*. Washington, DC: United States Institute of Peace Press.

Levine, Alicia (1996) 'Political Accommodation and the Prevention of Secessionist Violence', pp. 311–40 in Michael E. Brown (ed.), *The International Dimension of Internal Conflict*. Cambridge, MA: MIT Press.

Licklider, Roy (1995) 'The Consequences of Negotiated Settlements in Civil Wars, 1945–1993', *American Political Science Review*, 89 (3), pp. 681–90.

Lijphart, Arend (1977) *Democracy in Plural Societies: A Comparative Exploration*. London: Yale University Press.

MacGinty, Roger (1999) ' "Biting the Bullet": Decommissioning in the Transition from War to Peace in Northern Ireland', *Irish Studies in International Affairs*, 10, pp. 237–47.

Mallie, Eamonn and David McKittrick (1996) *The Fight for Peace: The Secret Story Behind the Irish Peace Process*. London: Heinemann.

McGarry, John and Brendan O'Leary (1996) 'Proving Our Points on Northern Ireland (and Giving Reading Lessons to Dr Dixon)', *Irish Political Studies*, 11, pp. 142–54.

McGarry, John and Brendan O'Leary (eds.) (2004a) *The Northern Ireland Conflict: Consociational Engagements*. Oxford: Oxford University Press.

McGarry, John and Brendan O'Leary (2004b) 'Stabilising Northern Ireland's Agreement', *The Political Quarterly*, 73 (3), pp. 213–25.

McGarry, John and Brendan O'Leary (2006a) 'Consociational Theory, Northern Ireland's Conflict, and its Agreement. Part 1: What Consociationalists Can Learn from Northern Ireland', *Government and Opposition*, 41 (1), pp. 43–63.

McGarry, John and Brendan O'Leary (2006b) 'Consociational Theory, Northern Ireland's Conflict, and its Agreement. Part 2: What Critics of Consociation Can Learn from Northern Ireland', *Government and Opposition*, 41 (2), pp. 249–77.

McIntyre, Anthony (1998) 'Is Sinn Féin a Victim of its Own Design?', *Parliamentary Brief*, 5 (6), pp 13–15.

McKittrick, David (1994) *Endgame: The Search for Peace in Northern Ireland*. Belfast: Blackstaff Press.

Meehan, Elizabeth (1999) 'The Belfast Agreement – Its Distinctiveness and Points of Cross-Fertilization in the UK's Devolution Programme', *Parliamentary Affairs*, 52 (1), pp. 19–31.

Neuheiser, Jorg and Stefan Wolff (eds.) (2002) *Peace at Last: The Impact of the Good Friday Agreement on Northern Ireland*. New York: Berghahn.

O'Kane, Eamonn (2007) 'Decommissioning and the Peace Process: Where Did It Come From and Why Did It Stay So Long?', *Irish Political Studies*, 22 (1), pp. 81–101.

O'Leary, Brendan (1999) 'The Nature of the British–Irish Agreement', *New Left Review*, 233, pp. 66–96.

O'Leary, Brendan (2002) 'The Belfast Agreement and the British–Irish Agreement: Consociational, Confederal Institutions, a Federacy and a Peace Process', pp. 293–356 in Andrew Reynolds (ed.) *The Architecture of Democracy: Constitutional Design, Conflict Management and Democracy*. Oxford: Oxford University Press.

Rowan, Brian (1995) *Behind the Lines: The Story of the IRA and Loyalist Ceasefires*. Belfast: Blackstaff.

Rowan, Brian (2003) *The Armed Peace: Life and Death After the Ceasefires*. Edinburgh: Mainstream.

Sisk, Timothy D. (1996) *Power Sharing and International Mediation in Ethnic Conflicts*. Washington, DC: United States Institute of Peace Press.

Smith, Jeremy (2002) *Making the Peace in Ireland*. Harlow: Longman.

Taylor, Peter (1997) *Provos: The IRA and Sinn Féin*. London: Bloomsbury.

Tonge, Jonathan (1998) 'Labour & Northern Ireland: The Long Road Back to Devolution', Working Papers in Contemporary History & Politics No. 17. Salford: European Studies Research Institute, University of Salford.

Tonge, Jonathan (2000) 'From Sunningdale to the Good Friday Agreement: Creating Devolved Government in Northern Ireland', *Contemporary British History*, 14 (3), pp. 39–60.

Tonge, Jonathan (2005) *The New Northern Irish Politics*. Basingstoke: Palgrave Macmillan.

Trimble, David (1988) 'Initiatives for Consensus: A Unionist Perspective', pp. 73–94 in Charles Townshend (ed.) *Consensus in Ireland: Approaches and Recessions*. Oxford: Clarendon Press.

Ward, Alan J. (1993) 'A Constitutional Background to the Northern Ireland Crisis', pp. 33–51 in Dermot Keogh and Michael H. Haltzel (eds.) *Northern Ireland and the Politics of Reconciliation*. Washington, DC: Woodrow Wilson Center Press.

17 The North

Party images and party approaches in the Republic[1]

Richard Sinnott

Originally published in *Irish Political Studies*, 1, 1986, pp. 15–31.

The inter-party conflict that rumbled beneath the surface of the New Ireland Forum, erupted in its immediate aftermath, and culminated in the rejection of the Hillsborough Agreement by Fianna Fáil raises important questions about the nature, depth and significance of the differences between Irish political parties on the Northern Ireland issue. The interpretation of these that prevailed until recently has been that nationalist/constitutional issues no longer divide the parties. In the revised edition of his standard text on Irish politics, Chubb points to the year 1948 as the date by which the 'issues which had split Sinn Féin were either resolved or increasingly irrelevant'. He goes on to argue that from the 1950s, 'all parties were to a great extent drained of ideology; they overlapped considerably in the policies they proposed; and they competed for the votes of a public increasingly concerned with welfare and consumer politics and less and less with national issues' (Chubb, 1982, pp. 98 and 104). In the light of recent events, an alternative interpretation is that differences on the Northern Ireland issue have increased since the changes in the leadership of the two main parties in the late 1970s. Having restated the view that 'in later years differences between the parties became progressively harder to identify', Gallagher adds 'after 1977, though, when Garret FitzGerald became leader [of Fine Gael], and especially after Charles Haughey became Fianna Fáil leader, there were signs that the former bipartisan approach had ended and that the two parties had drifted apart on the issue' (Gallagher, 1985, pp. 60–1).

Both interpretations rely mainly on the evidence of public documentation of various sorts: party or government statements, election manifestos, speeches and media interviews by party leaders and party spokesmen on Northern Ireland. The problem is that such policy statements, being public, are constrained by the particular circumstances in which they are issued. Whether a party bears the responsibility of government or enjoys the freedom of opposition is one obvious conditioning factor. Tactical electoral considerations constitute another set of constraints on how much is said and with what degree of emphasis.[2] Of particular importance since 1980 is the fashioning of party pronouncements on Northern Ireland in terms of the very severe exigencies of inter-governmental and diplomatic negotiation in what has become known as the 'Anglo-Irish process'.

Finally, there is the strong and quite limiting assumption that bipartisanship on the issue is a good thing. All of this implies that one must distinguish between official party positions and underlying party approaches. The distinction is in fact frequently implicit in discussions of inter-party differences. For example, O'Malley, having extensively analysed current policy positions, implies that there is something beyond these:

> The events of 1980 and 1981 revealed the deep-rooted differences between the two major parties, differences exacerbated by the acrimonious relationship between the party leaders themselves. The Anglo-Irish process has...brought out the differences between Fianna Fáil's and Fine Gael's *conceptions* of the Northern problem.

> (1983, p. 55, emphasis added)

The argument is not that one type of inter-party difference is more real or more important than the other. The fact is, however, that relatively little systematic attention has been paid to differences in party approach, as opposed to formal party policy. This paper is intended as a contribution to redressing that imbalance.

Methodology

Party approach differs from stated policy position in three ways. First, it is more general. It denotes the ways in which a party thinks about and understands an issue, the aspirations it holds in relation to the issue and the broad outline policies it espouses. Secondly, party position is articulated by the party leader or by an appointed spokesperson. It is an attribute of the party as a single collective actor. Party approach, on the other hand, is the aggregate of the approaches of the individuals who make up the party. It obviously follows that, except in the unlikely event of total unanimity, there is no one single party approach. There are rather dominant approaches or, in the absence of some degree of agreement, there may be conflicting but co-existing approaches. Party approach may also vary according to the level of the party being considered – whether it is the party in the electorate, the party in the constituencies or the party in parliament.

The analysis presented here focuses on the parliamentary parties. Gathering data on party approaches at this level requires extensive in-depth elite interviewing. A series of such interviews was conducted in 1974–1975 and this paper is based on data from that source.[3] There has been considerable turnover in the composition of the Dáil since then and this, together with the developments that have occurred in Anglo-Irish relations, means that the data do not necessarily represent current party approaches. The data are important, however, for our understanding of the development of current party approaches and positions. At a minimum, they constitute a benchmark in relation to which subsequent changes can be measured.

Table 17.1 Nationalist references in party images, by party

Difference mentioned	All parties %	Fianna Fáil %	Fine Gael %	Labour %
Nationalist outlook, republicanism	32	43	24	11
Irish language	8	16	0	0
Policy on Northern Ireland	16	14	20	11
Civil war differences	18	14	20	33
Total number of respondents	70	37	25	9

Note: because of multiple responses the percentages in this table are not cumulative. The base used in calculating the percentages in this and the following tables is the number of responses.

Party image

When asked, 'What do you see as the main differences between the parties?', politicians from all parties had recourse to the 'national question'. They did so, however, to quite a different extent and with considerable differences of emphasis. Thus nationalism in some form figured prominently in the discussion of party differences with half the Fianna Fáil parliamentary elite, but with less than one-third of that of Fine Gael and Labour. More significant than these quantitative differences, however, were the differences in emphasis and evaluation.

Fianna Fáil

Fianna Fáil deputies referred most frequently to the very broadest aspects of the phenomenon, in terms of 'national outlook' or 'republicanism'. Such references constituted 27 per cent of Fianna Fáil first-mentioned differences, and 43 per cent of total mentions, whereas they occurred only once as a first-mentioned difference in Fine Gael discussions and in only 24 per cent of all mentions. A Fianna Fáil TD distinguished between a national outlook and its opposite, a 'West British outlook', as follows:

> The reason why I joined Fianna Fáil was because I saw in it a party which had a tradition...I saw in it the party which by tradition and by aim was the one which would cater best for my aspirations as an Irishman having what I regard as a national outlook and I think that Fianna Fáil has that, more so than any of the other parties.

He went on to apply the distinction to Fine Gael:

> I think that there are certain elements, and influential elements, in Fine Gael who haven't yet realised that in Ireland there are people who are as good and possibly better at and as well equipped to administer their own affairs as there are in England. I think that...there are in Fine Gael, as I see it, people who still retain the West British outlook.

A party colleague who used the same term was more specific about its implications:

> Take ourselves first of all. We are committed and have always been committed
> to a united Ireland and the present Constitution and we have more and more
> of a national outlook than Fine Gael have, in my opinion. It appears that it
> wouldn't worry them very much changing Articles Two and Three of the
> Constitution. This is . . . to us sacred if you like, and to our supporters . . . It is
> a big difference between the two parties. They seem to look at it in such a
> frivolous way; our nationalism seems to be much more deep-rooted.

The term 'republican' is used with the same broad meaning as the term
'national outlook', but tends to add a connotation of equality. When asked what
he would see as the essence of the problem in Northern Ireland, a Fianna Fáil
deputy responded as follows:

> I see the essence of the problem as interfering from outside. I am a republican
> in the sense that Irishmen have the right to rule over their own land the same
> as any other nation has the right to rule over their own land and that every
> individual citizen has equal rights and equal obligations to himself, his
> family, and his state. And that the state has obligations to the citizens.

The same respondent later went on to deny emphatically that the term republican
carried any connotation of endorsement of the use of violence for political ends:

> We are the only republican party in this country, true republican party. I am
> not talking about the gun-man party, republicanism comes back to two
> people in this country – Tone and de Valera. Now you have the parades to
> Bodenstown by the Provisionals and the Officials every year, and Tone must
> turn in his grave when he hears some of the speeches above his head, because
> Tone always preached love for fellow man, he preached freedom, he preached
> rights and obligations, he abhorred assassination and he particularly abhorred
> religious assassination.

As well as emphasising a distinction based on national outlook and republicanism
more than the other parties, Fianna Fáil was the only party to mention policy
towards the Irish language as a differentiating factor.

Fine Gael

In contrast to this Fine Gael deputies were, as we have seen, less likely to refer to
nationalist differences in any form. They were, however, more likely than Fianna
Fáil to refer either to specific policy differences arising out of the Civil War. The
contrast between the party images is further emphasised by the fact that half of
the Fine Gael references to national outlook were dismissive, whereas all Fianna
Fáil references to it were positive. The dismissive Fine Gael references tended to
recognise the Fianna Fáil claim to distinction on this score but to place a very

different evaluation on it. One Fine Gael politician defined the difference between the two parties as follows:

> I honestly think that Fianna Fáil is the party of shamming and humbug, affecting if you like a special kind of Irishness, which is not only skin deep but in fact is a film on a glass – leave it for a minute and it is blown away and disappeared. They set up to be more nationally minded, they attach great importance to the word 'republican' and all that arid stuff. In fact it means absolutely nothing, they have done no more than anybody else.

The contrast between defining differences in issue-specific terms and defining them in terms of 'national outlook' can be seen by comparing the following Fine Gael extract with the quotations from Fianna Fáil TDs given above:

> Well I think...the major difference between the parties...is in relation to Northern Ireland, in the recent change by the Fianna Fáil party on their Northern stand,[4] that the British should go and, they haven't said so explicitly, but implicit in that is that the Northern majority shouldn't impede the will of the majority of the island. I think that it is a significant change and...we are poles apart on that. We believe that the British should stay until there is a solution on the North and that [withdrawal] should post-date a solution rather than ante-date it. Secondly, we are firmly of the belief that until the majority in the North want a United Ireland, it can't happen.

Labour

Labour deputies were less likely to see differences in nationalist terms at all. Only two of the nine Labour deputies saw nationalism as a prominent distinguishing element in the system, and one of these was a reference to 'the republicanism of the past' as the only distinguishing feature of Fianna Fáil. Three other Labour respondents referred to the Civil War but isolated references to the Civil War as an explanation of party differences tend to imply historical rather than genuine ideological or policy differences. This does not, of course, mean that differences arising from the Civil War are themselves seen as insignificant. Indeed, one Labour deputy emphasised their strength and persistence and saw in them a very real obstacle to the development of the kind of left–right differences he would prefer. Having referred to his belief that it was 'the accident of their attitude to the Treaty that divided Fianna Fáil and Fine Gael', he went on,

> if in the long term Fine Gael and Fianna Fáil were to coalesce I think it would remove a lot of the miseries and hates and 'seventy-sevens' and Ballyseedys[5] and obscenities out of Irish life. We can blame that on the Civil War, which is the most awful thing which happened to us.

The evidence so far thus suggests that, by the mid-1970s, nationalism continued to play a role, at the very least in differentiating the images of the parties. The more important test, however, is whether nationalist differences manifest themselves in the parties' analyses of the problem.

Party analyses of the problem

The causes of the Northern Ireland problem cited by TDs are listed in Table 17.2. Discrimination against the Catholic or minority community in Northern Ireland was both the most frequently cited cause and the one most agreed upon. The response to perceived inequality can, however, take two forms. It may either take the form of a demand for redress, or it may take the form of emphasising the ethnic or national distinctiveness of the group that is seen to be discriminated against. When the discussions are analysed in these terms we find that the parties diverge considerably. Many more Fianna Fáil than Fine Gael respondents saw identity as the central issue. Fine Gael respondents pointed much more to equality as the central issue. On the matter of the relative emphasis on identity and equality, Labour fell roughly half-way between the two main parties. In summary, because the perception of inequality is compatible with either a nationalist or a non-nationalist interpretation, the fact that the parties tended to agree that inequality was a cause is of only limited significance.

Table 17.2 Causes employed in explanations of the Northern Ireland problem, by party

Cause	Use	All parties %	Fianna Fáil %	Fine Gael %	Labour %
Discrimination/ inequality	Yes, central	43	41	46	46
	Yes, not central	11	13	11	0
	No	46	46	42	55
Inherited mutual fear	Yes, central	34	27	42	36
	Yes, not central	5	3	8	9
	No	61	70	50	55
Britain	Yes, central	28	46	8	18
	Yes, not central	7	11	0	9
	No	65	43	92	73
Unionist intransigence	Yes, central	19	30	12	0
	Yes, not central	11	8	8	27
	No	70	62	81	73
Religion	Yes, central	19	14	19	36
	Yes, not central	10	5	15	9
	No	72	81	65	55
Partition	Yes, central	20	30	12	9
	Yes, not central	7	8	4	9
	No	73	62	85	82
The IRA	Yes, central	14	5	19	27
	Yes, not central	3	0	8	0
	No	84	95	73	73
(N)		(74)	(37)	(26)	(11)

Two causes that obviously belong to a more nationalist analysis of the problem are 'Britain' and 'partition'. Table 17.2 shows that Britain or British actions were cited much more by Fianna Fáil than by Fine Gael and Labour. Britain was, in fact, the cause most frequently cited by Fianna Fáil politicians and for 46 per cent of them it was a central element in their argument. Partition also divided Fianna Fáil from Fine Gael and Labour. One Fianna Fáil TD argued, for example, that

> the essence of the problem is that our country is divided by British law and this is an unnatural division in itself and an undemocratic division, but the division is there and the essence of the problem is that the British support that decision that they made in the 1920s up to the present time.

In contrast to the foregoing nationalist interpretation, references to religion and inherited mutual fear tend to imply analyses of the problem in terms of conflicting groups or communities rather than in terms of conflicting national aspirations. Having referred to the problem of mistrust between the communities, for example, a Labour politician went on to identify its origins in a religiously segregated educational system as

> the whole basis and the essence of the problem. I think it [action towards a solution] must begin in a very slow way through education, through the people who run the educational system, be it the Church people or whatever, agreeing on certain basics: to get children together as a start, to get children to accept one another as people and to try to get away from this idea that their religion is the thing that divides them.

Community tensions rather than nationalist aspirations were also highlighted by a Fine Gael TD:

> Of course, I think that the core of the problem is ignorance, ignorance on the part of... unionists as to the contentions of the minority or as to what might follow if they have any sort of a workable arrangement with the Republic and ignorance, I suppose, on the side of the nationalists, with a certain amount of engendered hatred for the other side... Then, of course, ignorance begets fear and fear begets violence, there you have it.

Inherited mutual fear was, after discrimination, the cause most frequently cited by Fine Gael politicians. The remaining causes frequently cited by Fine Gael were unionist intransigence and the Irish Republican Army (IRA). The IRA was specifically singled out as a cause much more often in Fine Gael and Labour responses than in those of Fianna Fáil.[6]

Rather than pointing to republican paramilitary extremism, Fianna Fáil deputies were more likely to point to what they saw as extremism of another sort, unionist intransigence. Thus the intransigence of the bulk of the loyalist community

Table 17.3 Equality and identity as issues in discussions of the Northern Ireland problem, by party

Central issues	All parties %	Fianna Fáil %	Fine Gael %	Labour %
Equality	27	14	46	27
Identity	38	50	23	27
Both equality and identity	20	30	8	18
Other	14	5	23	27
Total number of respondents	(74)	(37)	(26)	(11)

is contrasted by one Fianna Fáil TD with what he sees as his own side's willingness to compromise:

> Well, the essence is that we have two communities. The loyalist community are intransigent, they haven't changed, they haven't co-operated. Some of them are changing, they see that we here genuinely mean [it] when we say that we don't want any solution other than a peaceful solution to the Northern problems. We are prepared to accommodate the loyalist population. We are prepared to work with them and assist them and give reasonable undertakings even to the extent of federalism.

Overall, Fianna Fáil TDs tended to see things within a nationalist framework, emphasising Britain, partition and unionist intransigence as causes. Fine Gael and Labour, in contrast, were more inclined to point to causes such as mutual fear, religion, and the IRA, which do not imply a nationalist interpretation.

Desired solutions to the problem

The interviews were not designed to explore all of the complexities of possible solutions to the problem in Northern Ireland. While some respondents did choose to elaborate in detail on appropriate institutional arrangements, the discussions, taken as a whole, allow for an analysis of the general shape of a solution rather than of its particulars. Thus the solutions preferred by respondents were coded on a continuum pitched at a fairly general level. One end of the continuum was defined as co-operation or reconciliation within the existing state of Northern Ireland, the other end as reunification of Northern Ireland and the Republic in a new all-Ireland state. There were three intermediate positions on the scale. As Table 17.4 shows, near-majorities of Fine Gael and Labour on the one hand, and of Fianna Fáil on the other, were at opposite ends of this continuum.

The orientation of 46 per cent of both Fine Gael and Labour politicians was exclusively towards the solution of co-operation/reconciliation within Northern Ireland, whereas 46 per cent of Fianna Fáil politicians took the direct opposite approach of exclusive emphasis on Irish unity as the solution. The latter approach

Table 17.4 Proposed solutions to the Northern Ireland problem, by party

Type of solution	All parties %	Fianna Fáil %	Fine Gael %	Labour %
Co-operation/reconciliation within Northern Ireland	26	5	46	46
Co-operation/reconciliation within Northern Ireland, some emphasis on Irish dimension	31	22	42	36
Both co-operation/reconciliation and a united Ireland	5	11	0	0
A united Ireland, some emphasis on co-operation/reconciliation within Northern Ireland	10	16	4	0
A united Ireland	28	46	8	16
(Total number of respondents)	(74)	(37)	(26)	(11)

is articulated with considerable emphasis by a Fianna Fáil TD:

> The problem to me is very plain. I should say I am prejudiced in so far as I am a complete believer in the reunification of the country … There will always be, always be, eternally and perpetually, a sense of nationalism in the people that will at some stage or other, down through the years, say that they must assert themselves and not allow their country to be governed partly by somebody else.

Even taking into account the intermediate positions on the continuum, the situation remains fairly polarised. This is because Fine Gael and Labour were cohesive in supporting either an exclusively or a mainly internal settlement. Fianna Fáil was less cohesive. While almost half of Fianna Fáil was exclusively reunificationist, there was a substantial minority which was aligned with the bulk of Fine Gael and Labour in emphasising the need for an internal settlement in Northern Ireland.

While the foregoing discussion emphasises differences between the parties, one should note that as a consequence of the very large majorities on one side of the issue within Fine Gael and Labour, combined with the existence of a significant dissenting Fianna Fáil minority, the majority position among interviewees as a whole was in favour of an internal settlement. Given that this was the majority position, it is perhaps worth illustrating with an example from each party. A Labour deputy was quite clear on where the emphasis must lie:

> I am a firm advocate of power-sharing. I am not a pusher as regards the Council of Ireland … Power-sharing was supremely necessary and a very basic ingredient, but there were a few frills that were unnecessary … and then, of course, the post-Sunningdale nonsense started, even including Garret

FitzGerald, who spoke about a united Ireland as though it were around the corner, ten years hence kind of thing...I think that power-sharing is an answer.

A Fine Gael deputy laid equal emphasis on power-sharing as a sufficient condition for a solution but held out the long-term prospect of a united Ireland:

> I suppose the major problem that I see is the lack of stable and acceptable political institutions in Northern Ireland. I feel that if a power-sharing administration could be devised, even without an all-Ireland dimension...I think the raison d'être of the IRA would very largely disappear...Unity has, I think, receded into the background because of the recognition of the realistic fact that the majority in the North don't want unity. That has to be recognised and accepted and, in recognising and accepting it, I think paradoxically you bring the day of unity nearer.

Any Fianna Fáil deputy coming down on this same side of the spectrum of solutions to the Northern Ireland problem was, as we have seen, part of a dissenting minority within his party elite and, accordingly, was likely to be less than comfortable about his view. The discomfort is evident in the somewhat convoluted formula ('the ultimate interim solution') adopted by the Fianna Fáil deputy who said:

> so the way I see it is that it is not a problem that we solve at all, it is possibly a problem that Britain can solve – or might be able to solve – but the ultimate interim solution does seem to me to be a sort of working system for the Northern Ireland area, for them as a community.

Party policies on Northern Ireland

Responses to the question, 'What, if anything, can we do to contribute to a solution?', are summarised in Table 17.5, and show considerable conflict between Fianna Fáil on the one hand and Labour and Fine Gael on the other. The conflict is between the policy of seeking a British withdrawal and the policy of putting less emphasis on the demand for a united Ireland. The British withdrawal proposal was mentioned by a majority of Fianna Fáil TDs and given a central role by nearly all who mentioned it. In most of these cases British withdrawal was seen as an element in a wider strategy, the objective of which was to deal with unionist opposition to a united Ireland. As one Fianna Fáil deputy put it, the outcome would be a 'change of attitude' on the part of the unionists:

> I don't feel myself that if you had the long line of British mistakes removed that things would fall into place immediately...I am saying that if they committed themselves to leaving that you would see a change of attitude in the unionist camp, that would...eventually see that you would have a federation probably, that would eventually come back down to just one

Table 17.5 Policy proposals relating to Northern Ireland, by party

Cause	Use	All parties %	Fianna Fáil %	Fine Gael %	Labour %
Overtures to	Central	28	24	31	36
Unionists	Not central	12	19	8	0
	Not mentioned	60	57	62	64
Practical	Central	32	35	42	0
co-operation with	Not central	4	3	4	9
NI/travel to NI	Not mentioned	64	62	54	91
British withdrawal	Central	24	43	4	9
from NI	Not central	10	16	0	9
	Not mentioned	66	41	96	82
Deemphasise demand	Central	22	0	46	36
for a united Ireland	Not central	8	3	12	18
	Not mentioned	70	97	42	46
Improve economy/	Central	19	27	8	18
social welfare etc.	Not central	5	5	0	18
to make Irish unity	Not mentioned	76	68	92	64
attractive					
Action against	Central	18	3	35	27
the IRA	Not central	0	0	0	0
	Not mentioned	82	97	65	73
Pluralist legislation	Central	12	3	15	36
in the Republic of	Not central	7	11	0	9
Ireland	Not mentioned	81	87	85	55
(N)		(74)	(37)	(26)	(11)

government – not necessarily in Dublin, if it is an emotive thing for them to have it in Dublin, have it somewhere else.

The precise implications of seeking to change the attitude of the unionists by means of British withdrawal were, however, seen in somewhat different ways by different politicians within Fianna Fáil.

One deputy used the analogy of the melting pot in which different traditions could work out a relationship with each other, were it not for the outside backing received by one tradition:

In this island you have different traditions which in the normal society, in the normal political environment, would have had to sort themselves out and work out a relationship with each other. That has never been allowed to happen in an open, healthy, democratic way on this island because one or other of the traditions has always been supported on the outside, backed up or supported. Until such time that it is made clean to all traditions, whoever they are, that no one is going to be supported or encumbered or inhibited from the outside, that they are all in that little melting pot and just work it out between you and find a *via media* . . . But once you start saying that the border is inviolable, there is no solution. There is no way you can work out a solution in that context, because he is thereby saying, in the case of one particular tradition saying, 'we are backing you'. Why should they make any concessions to any common *via media*?

A party colleague expressed confidence that the Northern majority would do very well for themselves in the working out of such a relationship. He rejected any proposals for unilateral constitutional change on the part of the Republic of Ireland but went on:

> I am agreeable to change our course when the time comes to sit down and say, 'right what is between us, let's sort it out in a business-like fashion'. Then I would be prepared to do something about it. I have no doubt in the world that if the majority, the unionists, in Northern Ireland knew that in five or ten years time that all right they are going to be on their own that they would sit down in five minutes and, by Jasus, work out a scheme there that, I'd tell you something, the shrewd hardy businessmen that they are, they wouldn't let themselves short at all, they would do terribly well, they know that too.

There is, however, a more hardline interpretation of this argument than that implied in the foregoing references to little melting pots and shrewd and hardy unionist businessmen. It was expressed by the Fianna Fáil deputy who, referring to the goal of 'the whole island being under one government', said 'that will never come about until the British begin to pull the rug out from under the obstinate Loyalist majority up there'. A party colleague expressed this essentially coercive view of the rationale for British withdrawal as follows:

> The essence of the problem is the stranglehold that the majority in the North of Ireland have had on affairs in the North of Ireland from the time partition was inaugurated. I do feel that part and parcel of being able to upset that and being able to bring the majority to heel, despite the threats of UDI [Unilateral Declaration of Independence], is a straightforward positive declaration by the Brits in the long term not alone of their willingness to get out but of the straightforward view that they want to get out.

In contrast to the articulation of the policy of British withdrawal by a majority in Fianna Fáil, the policy was mentioned by only a small minority of Fine Gael and Labour, whose TDs instead stressed the policy of de-emphasising the demand for Irish unity. This is not the opposite of British withdrawal in the sense that a policy positively advocating the permanent maintenance of the British presence would be. In fact many of the politicians who advocated the de-emphasis approach shared the same objective as the advocates of British withdrawal, a united Ireland. The essential difference between the two approaches had to do with the means used in achieving the objective, in particular the means of dealing with unionist opposition. The contrast is underlined by a Fine Gael TD:

> This idea of claiming rights and the Irish dimension...as far as I am
> concerned, it means nothing. The Irish dimension will always be there in the
> fact that it is a part of Ireland whether they like it or anyone else likes it, it is
> part of Ireland and that is the Irish dimension for me...When you start
> demanding rights and we must have an Irish dimension and this, it does make
> people up there fearful.

Contrasting approaches were also apparent on the issue of action specifically
directed against the IRA. A substantial minority of Fine Gael and Labour
deputies, as Table 17.5 shows, gave such a policy a central place in their
discussion. Only one Fianna Fáil deputy took a similar view. It is noteworthy that
in all the cases in which this policy was articulated, it was accorded a central role
as, for example, by this Fine Gael TD:

> All we can do is ensure, as we are ensuring, that this is not a hidey-hole for
> people who run across the border after they have committed a murder if things
> get too hot for them down there and to ensure that if they commit a murder
> here they can be tried in the North and if they commit a murder in the North
> they can be tried here and that is what the Criminal Justice Bill is all about.[7]

The Labour Party's main distinctiveness arose from the articulation of a policy
of pluralism. The approach takes the view that Northern Ireland unionists cannot
be expected to be open to the prospect of a united Ireland as long as aspects of
the Republic of Ireland's legislation reflect the views of the Roman Catholic
Church. Accordingly, the policy advocates greater pluralism in constitutional,
legislative and administrative matters in relation to issues such as family planning
and divorce and in relation to education. One Labour deputy covered most of the
relevant issues in a forceful argument in favour of a pluralist state:

> I think we should be making it quite clear that this is a pluralist and not a
> unitary state. I cannot understand the ambivalence of people like Fr. Denis
> Faul[8] who is so excellent on British brutality in Long Kesh and then goes off
> and makes speeches about the necessity to maintain denominational education
> and about the horrors of contraception. We could recommend our willingness
> to work as equal partners by introducing such things as divorce and
> contraception in the South. I am not suggesting that all Protestants are sex
> maniacs or anything like that but I think that these are symbolic gestures.

Policies of this sort were mentioned by 45 per cent of Labour deputies and most
of these accorded them a central role. The policy was mentioned by only a few
Fianna Fáil and Fine Gael TDs. The Labour Party was also distinctive (see Table 17.5),
giving virtually no support to a policy that was relatively popular among the two

larger parties, the policy of practical co-operation and travel between Northern Ireland and the Republic.

Conclusion

Given the nature of the issue and of the evidence employed, the limits of this analysis should be underlined. First, the purpose has been descriptive rather than evaluative. The objective has been to document the parties' approaches and to uncover basic concepts and assumptions of party political thought on this issue. The assessment of the strengths and weaknesses of the various approaches is part of political debate in the widest sense and is, no doubt, best left to that process. Second, and most obviously, the evidence relates to the mid-1970s, is conditioned by the circumstances prevailing at that time and is not intended as a portrayal of the contemporary situation. Third, the analysis presents an incomplete account of inter-party differences on the Northern Ireland problem. The account is incomplete because it concentrates on party members' approaches, leaving aside officially-stated policy, and because the sample was limited to the parliamentary elite.

Bearing all these qualifications in mind, we can conclude that, in the mid-1970s, the parties differed substantially on the Northern Ireland issue. There were considerable contrasts in the role that the national question played in the self-images of the parties. The analyses and interpretations of the nature of the problem put forward by the parties diverged significantly. The solutions envisaged fell at different points on a continuum ranging from a purely internal solution to a purely unificationist solution. Finally, consistent with these differences, the parties advocated different policies. The alignment underlying all these differences was Fianna Fáil versus Fine Gael, with Labour tending to be close to Fine Gael but also showing some distinctiveness in virtue of its advocacy of pluralism. One interesting discrepancy in this alignment was the tendency for a minority within Fianna Fáil to be towards the Fine Gael end of the continuum that ranged from a purely internal settlement to one putting exclusive emphasis on reunification.

In so far as our interpretation of the Irish party system is concerned, these findings suggest some qualification to the thesis that no significant differences exist between Irish political parties.[9] Despite its normal lack of electoral salience and despite strong pressures towards bipartisanship, the Northern Ireland issue continued to produce considerable differences in approach through to the mid-1970s at least. Nor should this situation be surprising. The comparative theory of party systems points to a strong tendency for party alignments and, by implication, party differences to be perpetuated over extended periods of time (Sinnott, 1984).

When it comes to the question of the wider implications of the findings, two views are possible. One is that, with the recent developments in Anglo-Irish relations, in particular with the Hillsborough Agreement, all is changed utterly. The problem is now on a different plane; the terms of reference have been radically altered. Thus the thinking of the 1970s has become outmoded and irrelevant. An alternative view, and one that does not necessarily imply criticism of the Hillsborough Agreement, is that, in terms of the underlying issues that must be dealt with, little has changed. Hillsborough is, as it were, Sunningdale upside-down. Whereas the latter implemented power-sharing and treated the Irish dimension as a potentiality, the former implements the Irish dimension and treats the internal aspect as a matter for subsequent negotiation. This reflects the dual problem arising out of the double minority situation that obtains on the island (Whyte, 1978, p. 276). The point to bear in mind in so far as the Republic of Ireland is concerned is that the political parties do not approach these problems *de novo* but with an inheritance derived from stands taken in the past. The evidence presented here suggests that this inheritance was still identifiable in party approaches in the mid-1970s. It remains to be seen whether the mid-1980s will transform it.

COMMENTARY BY CHRISTOPHER FARRINGTON

Sinnott's article is an important part of the literature on Ireland, north and south, because it looks at connections between the politics of the two parts of the island. He focuses on political parties and uses an approach which seeks to ascertain 'party approach' rather than party policy. He widens the scope of analysis by moving away from party leaders' speeches and carefully thought out policy documents to examining how 'a party thinks about and understands an issue'. Sinnott shows that, in 1974, there were significant differences between the main political parties in the Republic of Ireland on key issues related to Northern Ireland and the British–Irish relationship. His empirically grounded analysis of the differences between the political parties in the Republic of Ireland on Northern Ireland is not only useful in and of itself but also because it provides an important baseline from which future analysis can judge movement.

Sinnott presents a primarily descriptive analysis of the approaches of the parties and, as such, prompts several more analytical questions. What role does Northern Ireland play in politics in the Republic of Ireland? What is the significance of these different approaches for the search for a settlement in Northern Ireland? Has there been a change in party approaches in the Republic of Ireland on Northern Ireland? Obviously Sinnott was not able to address all of these questions and some of the debate has developed since the article was published. However, it is through these three inter-related questions that the article has made a contribution to the literature.

It is well known that the study of nationalism has dominated the study of Irish politics. Politics in Ireland was seen as odd in a comparative context, as the Irish party system reflected the divisions over the 1921 Anglo-Irish Treaty (Mair and Weeks, 2005, pp. 135–8). Thus, Irish democracy and Irish nationalism were entwined at an early stage in Irish political development, an entanglement which party leaders still find it necessary to acknowledge. The leaders of all the main political parties have to pay annual homage to their 'founding fathers': the Fine Gael leader at Béal na mBláth for Collins; the Fianna Fáil leader at Bodenstown (in careful cognisance of Sinn Féin's annual commemoration) for Tone; and the Labour Party leader at Arbour Hill for Connolly. Sinnott demonstrated that the

Northern Ireland issue is an important part of these differences between the parties on attitudes to nationalism in Ireland.

However, the broader question is how these differences relate to competition between the parties for votes. There is a paradox in Irish politics regarding Northern Ireland: the issue is clearly most important in Irish politics, given its connections with Ireland's struggle for independence and given the levels of violence experienced there since the 1960s, but it does not feature as an electoral issue in most elections. This has been the subject of some debate. One side of this debate argues that Irish public opinion is as disinterested in Northern Ireland as British public opinion and that there are no strong opinions on a future for Northern Ireland (Cochrane, 1994; Cox, 1985). The other side of this debate disputes the relative significance of public opinion; here it is argued that Irish public opinion has more of an interest in Northern Ireland than British public opinion because the Northern Ireland question is tied up in ideas of nationhood that have been central to Irish public and political discourse (Dixon, 1995; Trumbore, 1998).

This debate never really reached a consensus. However, what it does indicate is that a disconnection developed between scholarship on Northern Ireland and scholarship in the Republic over the course of the Troubles. The Irish government and Irish political parties have almost been written out of the analysis of Northern Ireland. For example, most general histories of Northern Ireland include extensive discussions on the role of the British government (Dixon, 2001) and there are some key texts on British government policy on Northern Ireland (Cunningham, 2001; Bloomfield, 1996) and work on the policy of British political parties on Northern Ireland (Cunningham, 1995; Bew and Dixon, 1994; Dixon, 1994) but very little on the policy or approach of Irish political parties and particularly how these have developed over time. This has recently begun to change (Ivory, 1999; Hayward, 2004; O'Donnell, 2007a and 2007b) but there is a corollary risk that the role of Northern Ireland is written out of the analysis of Irish politics because it does not have saliency for voters. For example, it was the fourth edition of the standard textbook on politics in the Republic of Ireland before a chapter was included on Northern Ireland and the North–South and British–Irish dimensions (Coakley and Gallagher, 2005). Sinnott's analysis does suggest a potential explanation. He suggests that party approaches on Northern Ireland may be less important for short-term electoral strategies and issues and more important for longer-term processes of party identification. As Sinnott himself argues elsewhere:

> it is clear that economic issues predominate over traditional nationalist issues or over the problem of Northern Ireland in the appeals of the parties. The explanation of this lack of relative lack of emphasis on nationalism or the Northern Ireland issue lies in the distinction between the dimension or domain of identification and the dimension or space of competition.
>
> (1995, p. 73)

The divisions within the Republic of Ireland on Northern Ireland have been overshadowed by the inter-governmental relationship that has developed between Ireland and the United Kingdom since the Anglo-Irish Agreement of 1985.

Academic attention has understandably focused on why that relationship changed and how it impacted upon politics in Northern Ireland (Arthur, 2000). However, this did not mean that divisions within the Republic had disappeared or had stopped becoming politically salient. The divisions between political parties in the Republic over the Northern Ireland question are important because of how these affect the search for a settlement. It is a question not adequately discussed, let alone answered, as to whether the political composition in government in Dublin was as important as that in London. Given Sinnott's findings that the parties differed in their approach to Northern Ireland, is it a coincidence that Fine Gael, rather than Fianna Fáil, Taoisigh signed the Sunningdale communiqué and the Anglo-Irish Agreement?

It seems to be the case that the Fine Gael–Labour coalition was able to sign the two agreements precisely because their approach to Northern Ireland de-emphasised Irish unity, promoted reconciliation between unionists and nationalists, and emphasised an inter-governmental approach and Irish dimension. All of these characteristics were identified by Sinnott. It was in the context of the first of these initiatives, the Sunningdale experiment, that Sinnott conducted his interviews in 1974–75. The Sunningdale communiqué was signed in December 1973 but the experiment collapsed after the Ulster Workers' Council strike of May 1974. The communiqué was the first serious attempt to resolve the Northern Ireland conflict that involved the Irish government and the period from 1973 to 1985, from Sunningdale to the Anglo-Irish Agreement via the New Ireland Forum of 1983, represented the high point of Fine Gael influence on Irish government policy and Irish political discourse on Northern Ireland. This policy and discourse was constructed under the stewardship of Garret FitzGerald and other notables in the party, such as Paddy Harte. The Sunningdale communiqué was the first time where a revisionist nationalism was seen to inform Irish government policy on Northern Ireland. Differences exist between how this revisionist nationalism and a more traditional nationalism see the causes of the conflict and how this then impacts views about potential solutions (Farrington, 2007). Although Sinnott does not place these two differing approaches into different categories, these have represented the broad division in Irish politics on this issue.

Fianna Fáil has been associated with a more traditional interpretation of Northern Ireland so the involvement of Fianna Fáil at a later stage of development of the search for a settlement is almost as interesting as Fine Gael's involvement in the first few initiatives. Therefore, how significant a change is it that Fianna Fáil was in power for Good Friday 1998? We should not forget that Fianna Fáil opposed the Anglo-Irish Agreement in the Dáil, Charles Haughey came out against the New Ireland Forum report and, while Jack Lynch held to a bipartisan line in the Dáil in 1973–74, had he attempted to make this official Fianna Fáil policy, he would have faced stiff opposition from many of his parliamentary party and his grass roots. We may overplay the differences and underplay the significant continuity provided by the civil service but this evidence does give credence to the argument that the more republican approach of Fianna Fáil was not conducive to making significant political breakthroughs in Northern Ireland prior to the movement of the republican movement towards constitutional politics.

If we endorse this argument, we need to acknowledge that the development of the peace process during a Fianna Fáil-led government is significant. What did a Fianna Fáil-led government bring to the process that a Fine Gael–Labour coalition could not? The answer may well be republicanism and by bringing republicanism to the process, they may well have helped bring about a peace process (O'Donnell, 2003; 2007a; 2007b).

Thirty years is a significant length of political time and Ireland – north and south – has changed absolutely in that time. The question is whether those attitudes on nationalism, partition and Northern Ireland have also changed in that time frame? An examination of the various positions cannot be undertaken here but we have to acknowledge that a consensus appears to have developed on Northern Ireland underpinned by the principles of the Good Friday Agreement. It might reasonably be pointed out that there are divergent views on what the Good Friday Agreement means for the prospects of Irish unity (Coakley, 2001) but we can identify the principle of consent, cross-border co-operation and political safeguards for each community as key parts of the consensus.

However, once we identify that a consensus exists, we have to account for its emergence, given the divergent views that Sinnott identified. There are a number of alternative explanations. In the first, Hayward (2004) argues that many of the labels of republican discourse in the south have remained the same but the meanings have changed. This would indicate that there has been an ideological shift in southern Irish politics. A second interpretation is that the consensus that has developed has been a pan-nationalist political alliance between the Irish government, Sinn Féin and the SDLP (O'Donnell, 2007a). This second interpretation does not necessarily rule out ideological change but does emphasise a common nationalist agenda, particularly built on the republican conception of Irish self-determination.

Much has changed from the period of Sinnott's interviews to today. Most importantly, when Sinnott was conducting his interviews, the Troubles were at their most violent. The period had also witnessed a significant shift in the types of claims that were being made. The initial impetus for the Troubles was the civil rights campaign which stressed issues such as housing and discrimination. By the time of the Sunningdale experiment it is clear that the issues have changed to competing national identity claims. This makes the form of nationalism espoused by the main political parties in the Republic crucial. Northern Ireland nationalists and republicans have ideological connections with ideological developments in the Republic and we need to understand those connections in much greater detail. Sinnott's article provides a staging post but much more work is needed on what is a relatively neglected aspect of politics on the island of Ireland.

Notes

1 The research on which this article is based was carried out with the aid of a grant from the Committee for Social Science Research in Ireland.
2 The November 1982 election was notable for an attempt to raise Northern Ireland as an issue. Analysis of election manifestos, however, indicates that the issue is generally not officially emphasised in electoral competition (Mair, 1982).

3 The stratified sample of 75 politicians included all current and former ministers and parliamentary secretaries, all current opposition frontbench spokesmen and 15 prominent backbenchers identified by the political correspondents. A further 18 randomly selected backbenchers were included to make up the target number. The response rate for frontbenchers (government and opposition) was an impressive 83 per cent; for backbenchers it was 94 per cent. The maximum number of cases in the present analysis is 74 because one of the former ministers interviewed was an independent deputy. The interviews, which were of the open-ended conversational kind, were tape-recorded, and then transcribed verbatim. Previous studies in this area have also relied on elite interviews (Cohan, 1977; O'Malley, 1983). The number of interviews in each case (14 and four respectively) is too small, however, to warrant generalisations about party approach as we have used the term.

4 On 29 October 1975, Fianna Fáil issued a policy statement on Northern Ireland that was widely regarded as signalling a considerable change in its publicly stated policy position. This view was based on that part of the statement that said 'Fianna Fáil calls on the British Government to encourage the uniting of Ireland by agreement, in independence and in a harmonious relationship between the two islands, and to this end to declare Britain's commitment to implement an ordered withdrawal from her involvement in the Six Counties of Northern Ireland' (reported by the *Irish Times*, 30 October 1975).

5 Seventy-seven is given as the number of 'executed republicans' for the period of the Civil War of 1922–23 in Macardle (1937, Appendix 2, pp. 984–5). 'Ballyseedy' refers to a reprisal carried out by government forces at Ballyseedy, Co. Kerry in March 1923, in which nine men were roped to a log and a mine was exploded. The incident is discussed by Calton Younger (1970, pp. 501–10).

6 Since the issue was not explicitly raised with each respondent one cannot draw inferences from these data about overall party attitudes to paramilitary violence.

7 The reference would appear to be to the Bill subsequently passed as the Criminal Law (Jurisdiction) Act 1976.

8 Fr Denis Faul, parish priest of Dungannon, and a prominent critic of British Government security and prison policy.

9 For further documentation of the 'no differences' thesis and for a systematic spatial analysis of Irish party differences based on evidence from discussions of both the Northern Ireland problem and economic problems, see Sinnott (1986).

References

Arthur, Paul (2000) *Special Relationships: Britain, Ireland and the Northern Ireland Problem*. Belfast: Blackstaff.

Bew, Paul and Paul Dixon (1994) 'Labour Party Policy and Northern Ireland', pp. 151–65 in Brian Barton and Patrick J. Roche (eds.) *The Northern Ireland Question: Perspectives and Policies*. Aldershot: Avebury.

Bloomfield, David (1996) *Peacemaking Strategies in Northern Ireland: Building Complementarity in Conflict Management Theory*. Basingstoke: Macmillan.

Chubb, Basil (1982) *The Government and Politics of Ireland*. Second Edition. London: Longman.

Coakley, John (2001) 'The Belfast Agreement and the Republic of Ireland', pp. 233–44 in Rick Wilford (ed.) *Aspects of the Belfast Agreement*. Oxford: Oxford University Press.

Coakley, John and Michael Gallagher (eds.) (2005) *Politics in the Republic of Ireland*. Fourth Edition. London: Routledge.

Cochrane, Feargal (1994) 'Any Takers? The Isolation of Northern Ireland', *Political Studies*, 42 (3), pp. 378–95.

Cohan, Alvin S. (1977) 'The Question of a United Ireland: Perspectives of the Irish Political Elite', *International Affairs*, 53 (2), pp. 232–54.

Cox, W. Harvey (1985) 'Who Wants a United Ireland?', *Government and Opposition*, 20 (1), pp. 29–47.

Cunningham, Michael (1995) 'Conservative Dissidents and the Irish Question: The Pro-Integrationist Lobby 1973–1994', *Irish Political Studies*, 10, pp. 26–42.

Cunningham, Michael (2001) *British Government Policy in Northern Ireland 1969–2000*. Manchester: Manchester University Press.

Dixon, Paul (1994) ' "The Usual English Double Talk": The British Political Parties and the Ulster Unionists 1974–94', *Irish Political Studies*, 9, pp. 25–40.

Dixon, Paul (1995) 'Internationalization and Unionist Isolation: A Response to Feargal Cochrane', *Political Studies*, 43 (3), pp. 497–505.

Dixon, Paul (2001) *Northern Ireland: The Politics of War and Peace*. Basingstoke: Palgrave.

Farrington, Christopher (2007) 'Reconciliation or Irredentism: The Irish Government and the Sunningdale Communiqué 1973', *Contemporary European History*, 16 (1), pp. 89–107.

Gallagher, Michael (1985) *Political Parties in the Republic of Ireland*. Manchester: Manchester University Press.

Hayward, Katy (2004) 'The Politics of Nuance: Irish Official Discourse on Northern Ireland', *Irish Political Studies*, 19 (1), pp. 18–38.

Ivory, Gareth (1999) 'Revisions in Nationalist Discourse Among Irish Political Parties', *Irish Political Studies*, 14, pp. 84–103.

Macardle, Dorothy (1937) *The Irish Republic: A Documented Chronicle of the Anglo-Irish Conflict and the Partitioning of Ireland, With a Detailed Account of the Period 1916–1923*. London: Gollancz.

Mair, Peter (1982) 'Issue Dimensions and Party Strategies in the Irish Republic, 1948–81: The Evidence of Manifestos', EUI Working Paper 41. Florence: European University Institute.

Mair, Peter and Liam Weeks (2005) 'The Party System', pp. 135–59 in John Coakley and Michael Gallagher (eds.) *Politics in the Republic of Ireland*. Fourth Edition. London: Routledge.

O'Donnell, Catherine (2003) 'Fianna Fáil and Sinn Féin: The 1988 Talks Reappraised', *Irish Political Studies*, 18 (2), pp. 60–81.

O'Donnell, Catherine (2007a) 'Pan-Nationalism: Explaining the Irish Government's Role in the Northern Ireland Peace Process, 1992–98', *Contemporary British History*, 21 (2), pp. 223–45.

O'Donnell, Catherine (2007b) *Fianna Fáil, Irish Republicanism and the Northern Ireland Troubles, 1968–2005*. Dublin: Irish Academic Press.

O'Malley, Padraig (1983) *The Uncivil Wars: Ireland Today*. Belfast: Blackstaff Press.

Sinnott, Richard (1984) 'Interpretations of the Irish Party System', *European Journal of Political Research*, 12 (3), pp. 289–307.

Sinnott, Richard (1986) 'Party Differences and Spatial Representation: The Irish Case', *British Journal of Political Science*, 16 (2), pp. 217–41.

Sinnott, Richard (1995) *Irish Voters Decide: Voting Behaviour in Elections and Referendums Since 1918*. Manchester: Manchester University Press.

Trumbore, Peter F. (1998) 'Two-Level Games in the Anglo-Irish Peace Process', *International Studies Quarterly*, 42 (3), pp. 545–65.

Whyte, John (1978) 'Interpretations of the Northern Ireland Problem: An Appraisal', *Economic and Social Review*, 9 (4), pp. 257–82.

Younger, Calton (1970) *Ireland's Civil War*. London: Fontana.

18 The DUP as a politico-religious organisation

Clifford Smyth

Originally published in *Irish Political Studies*, 1, 1986, pp. 33–43.

Although the Democratic Unionist Party (DUP) has been in existence for nearly 14 years, the interaction between the party and the Free Presbyterian Church of Ulster is not widely understood. There are a number of reasons for this. In the first place, Dr Ian Paisley's very high profile style of political leadership has encouraged a particular image of the DUP and prompted outsiders to formulate assumptions about the type of party which Ian Paisley would lead. Equally important, however, has been the veil of secrecy that has been drawn across certain areas of the party's internal operations, a veil of secrecy that has served to conceal the strength of the relationship between the Free Presbyterian Church of Ulster and its political alter-ego, the DUP. This relationship does not merely consist in the fact that Ian Paisley is both party Leader and Moderator of the Free Presbyterian Church or in the curious situation where four out of the DUP's 21 members in the present Northern Ireland Assembly are Free Presbyterian ministers. The relationship is much more intimate and has influenced major aspects of the party's infrastructure, including the selection of candidates, its electioneering techniques, financial development and ideology.

Candidate selection

On four occasions in the early 1970s the Presbytery, the governing body of the Free Presbyterian Church, took vital decisions of a highly political nature which had a direct bearing on whether the DUP would be in a position to select certain Free Presbyterian ministers as candidates for the party. Such Presbytery meetings were highly secret and neither the paid-up grass-roots membership of the DUP, nor activists holding positions of responsibility within the party, appreciated what was going on or the way in which the decisions that were taken at these secret Presbytery meetings influenced the development of the party.[1]

On the eve of the first elections to the former Northern Ireland Assembly in June 1973, a bitter wrangle broke out at one such meeting. The dispute arose because a leading Free Presbyterian minister, Rev. Alan Cairns, was adamant that the Presbytery should endorse the decision that only Dr Paisley and Rev. William Beattie would be permitted to go forward as DUP candidates at the election. Ian Paisley and William Beattie had been before the Presbytery on previous occasions because both ministers had gone on to win seats in the Stormont Parliament. Both had stood for Westminster, Beattie in North Belfast where he was unsuccessful, and Ian Paisley in North Antrim which he won under the banner of Protestant Unionism. It would therefore have been difficult for Presbytery to reverse their previous decision, but the demise of Protestant Unionism and the emergence of the DUP had created a new situation.[2]

The DUP was in effect a coalition of the Protestant Unionist Party with a much more inchoate grouping of disillusioned and radical members of the Ulster Unionist Party. The dissident Unionist Party members looked to Desmond Boal, the MP for Shankill in Belfast, for leadership but Boal was a highly individualistic personality. While he welcomed the support of those who endorsed his views, he never went out of his way to organise a distinctive grouping of the dissidents. Those Ulster Unionist Party members who joined the DUP did so as individuals, influenced to a greater or lesser degree by Boal's strident and powerful criticisms of the Glengall Street party, rather than as followers whose leader had called them to embrace this new political alignment, known initially as the United Loyalist Party. The emergence of the DUP encouraged a number of Free Presbyterian ministers to follow their Moderator's example and throw their weight behind the new party. Alan Lucas, an associate of Boal's from West Belfast, was elected organising secretary to the new party and has graphically described how Free Presbyterian ministers played a key role in setting up the new party's organisation. It is therefore hardly surprising, given that Ian Paisley and William Beattie had already established themselves as politicians, that in the run-up to the elections to the Northern Ireland Assembly other Free Presbyterian ministers would entertain political ambitions. Alan Cairns' resolution that only Dr Paisley and Rev. William Beattie should be given Presbytery's blessing would have had the effect of debarring three other Free Presbyterian ministers who, it was generally supposed, were interested in standing for the Assembly. The ministers were Rev. James McClelland, Rev. Ivan Foster and Rev. William McCrea.

There is a strong undercurrent of pietistic disengagement to be found among a number of the Protestant sects in Ulster.[3] For generations many Reformed Presbyterians had taken no part in the political life of the Province, and they were not alone: others amongst the Christian Brethren, the Baptists and even Presbyterians influenced by Faith Mission teaching eschewed politics and regarded the exercise of voting as an expression of worldliness. This disinterest in political affairs is also reflected amongst a minority of Free Presbyterians who would argue that the Christian's task is to preach 'the simple gospel' rather than to engage in the cut and thrust of political activism. Alan Cairns' resolution articulated that sentiment among some of those at Presbytery, and in the end only William Beattie and Ian Paisley were given permission to go forward to selection at their respective DUP Constituency Associations and thereafter as candidates of the DUP.

In the event the DUP fielded 17 candidates in that election, one of whom turned out to be Dr Paisley's wife, Eileen. Had the Presbytery taken another view and approved of all five Free Presbyterian ministers standing, then over a quarter of the DUP's candidates would have been publicly associated with the Free

Presbyterian Church. The impression thereby created in the minds of the mass of Unionist electors in Northern Ireland would inevitably have undermined the original intention of Desmond Boal and Ian Paisley, which was to form a party which was secular in character, which would appeal to the media, and would be sufficiently distanced from Protestant Unionism.

Certain Free Presbyterians would put a more benign interpretation on these events, arguing that, as each Free Presbyterian minister undertakes at his ordination to give himself full-time to the ministry and work of a pastor, it was not unreasonable of the courts of the Free Presbyterian Church to insist that ministers apply to the Presbytery before taking up responsibilities that would inevitably come into conflict with their role as pastors. One leading member of the Church even suggested that, in the mid-1970s, at a time when there had been a lowering of the political temperature in the Province, some of the more pietistic members of Presbytery contemplated the proposition that Dr Paisley be asked to resign from political office and devote himself exclusively to his gospel ministry![4]

Electioneering techniques

It is one thing to launch a political movement and proceed to put up candidates; it is quite another matter to go out and actually win seats, but this is precisely what Ian Paisley was able to do. The second example of the convergence of religious and political attitudes within the DUP relates to Ian Paisley's electioneering technique. This shared many of the aspects of a religious crusade. Indeed, Ian Paisley has never been averse to using the term 'crusade' to typify the kind of political campaigns in which he has become engaged. As he sees it, his party has been called into existence to defend the Protestant position in Ulster and to safeguard the Union. Though there is an inherent tension between Paisley's Protestantism and his concept of unionism, the religious emphasis suggests that crusading accurately describes the DUP's political activity, and helps outsiders understand something of the party's evident militancy.

The crusaders have an inner motivation, and a good example of this is to be found in the constituency of North Antrim at election time. There campaigning is accompanied by a series of prayer meetings held either in private homes or in the Ballymena Free Presbyterian Church. At such meetings God's blessing is called down upon the electoral campaign. Not all stalwart DUP supporters will attend such religious meetings, but those who do fervently and sincerely believe that their prayer 'availeth much'.

This form of commitment inevitably encourages a far higher level of political involvement on the part of such DUP supporters. They regard campaigning with Rev. Ian Paisley as 'doing God's work'. This is because they accept that Paisley has been raised up by God at this critical hour in Ulster's history (McCrea, 1980). The religiously motivated activists have never been discouraged from holding such views by the DUP leader himself, and their willingness 'to go the second mile' – to work extremely hard for the DUP leader – gives the DUP a considerable advantage over rival political parties because of the work load that each DUP activist is willing to bear in order to gain a political triumph.

Every election victory is interpreted in such circumstances as a special sign of God's blessing upon a party which seeks to magnify His name and uphold the cause of Protestant Ulster. Electoral reverses suffered by DUP candidates have never prompted the opposite reaction amongst the more spiritually-minded party activists: that the rejection of the candidate should be adjudged as the disapproval of the Almighty. This is a curious facet of the DUP activists' thinking; electoral victories signify God's blessing upon them, but political reverses are interpreted differently, as a challenge to redouble their efforts.

One respondent offered another way in which religious commitment advanced the interests of the DUP, pointing out that Ian Paisley is able to promote his political mission seven days a week. The respondent, who attends Paisley's Martyrs' Memorial Church on occasion, referred to the DUP leader's habit of making a strong political point in the course of the weekly church announcement, particularly at moments of crisis in the Province. In the days of Protestant Unionism, before the Martyrs' Memorial was opened, Ian Paisley's sermons to packed congregations in the Ulster Hall were overtly political in tone, but when the Free Presbyterian Church made the transition to the new church building on the Ravenhill Road, Paisley tempered his approach, restricting any political thrust in his message of the day to the church notices. However, the DUP leader had long recognised the value of building some pithy political comment into the advertisements for his church services published in the local papers.

Though a number of Free Presbyterian ministers emulated the DUP leader's crusading zeal, Paisley's approach has never been universal within the Free Presbyterian Church, and this is only to be expected when a minority within the denomination remains pietistic in its theology. Where religious dynamism and political activism do converge within the DUP, the party gains supporters who are extremely highly motivated and this inner strength helps to explain why the party has developed as a formidable electoral machine.

On polling day an even more practical aspect of the convergence of religious and political interests within the DUP becomes apparent. The DUP is able to call upon the assistance of a large number of auxiliary workers on election day, together with a significant pool of minibuses and larger vehicles belonging to various congregations of the Free Presbyterian Church throughout Ulster. It is not unusual for these auxiliary workers, who are mainly but not exclusively adherents of the Free Presbyterian Church, to outnumber the paid-up members of the local DUP branch in the constituency, and their support is of critical importance to the DUP election machine. Ian Paisley's determination to defend the Protestant cause succeeds in mobilising not only active party members in the DUP but a considerable number of Free Presbyterians who never attend a DUP branch meeting but who rally to the party on the one day in an election year when it really counts.

Financial development

If winning seats is of primary importance to political parties like the DUP, then finding the cash to fund this frenetic political activity must be second on the list of priorities. Surprisingly, though, it is precisely in the area of financial organisation that the interaction between the DUP and the Free Presbyterian Church has proved to be a serious disadvantage.

By the time the DUP came into existence in 1971, Rev. Ian Paisley had already gained a reputation as something of a financial wizard. His ability to encourage the giving of vast sums of money to support the extension of the Free Presbyterian Church had already entered into Northern Ireland folk memory, and even local comedians and entertainers referred to the famous 'plastic buckets' which were used to collect the offering at Dr Paisley's 'Protestant rallies' or gospel campaigns.

This image of the Free Presbyterian Church as a financially sound and expanding evangelical movement rebounded on the DUP. It was wrongly assumed from the very outset that the party would in some sense be a recipient of the Free Presbyterian Church's financial largesse. In fact this has never been the case and the party has had to survive financially without being able to call directly on the Free Presbyterian Church for aid to cover administrative and political commitments. An added difficulty occurred in respect of those DUP activists who were also Free Presbyterians, who believed that as they already made generous contributions to the 'Free Church' they were under less of an obligation to give generously to the party.

From the point of view of the party leader, the party's financial predicament placed him in an embarrassing dilemma. He could not acknowledge the actual state of the party's finances without damaging his own image, or his ability to continue to attract considerable financial support. As a result the financial problems which press in upon the DUP are not public property and it is only the DUP activists and branches, upon which considerable financial demands are made, which are made aware of the party's debts and encouraged to raise sums of money to cover the party's expenses.

The second difficulty arises at this point because the Free Church's self-image is that of God-fearing and holy-living citizens, and this has led to the imposition of doctrinal restraints on the way in which the DUP's membership is encouraged to raise financial support. The party has turned to the usual sources in order to build up its funds, finance its headquarters secretariat and publicise its aims and objectives (Calvert, 1981). At branch level, every member pays an annual subscription, and each of the branches contributes to the central fund of the Imperial Constituency Association.[5] The party has also had the support of wealthy benefactors whose generosity and loyal support have more than once eased it out of financial difficulties.

Individual commitments to the party, no matter how generous, proved insufficient to meet the DUP's requirements, however. Additional funds had to be secured and Calvert (1981) has recorded, in *A Decade of the DUP*, two instances when special fund-raising efforts separately raised sums of £12,000. Wallace Thompson, formerly the party's Finance Officer, has described in an interview another occasion when he accompanied Dr Paisley on a province-wide tour to raise extra funds to meet a financial emergency which the party faced. Interestingly, Thompson alluded to the fact that not all the donations came from members of the party. The circumstances in which these methods were employed suggest that the party showed little foresight in coping with the financial demands made upon it.

Running a political party is expensive (see Rose, 1976, p. 213, for a discussion of party finance). The financial support of party members and the assistance of a few benefactors would hardly suffice to keep the party solvent and it is at this point that the tension between running a political party and maintaining a 'Protestant witness' emerges once again. Evangelical Christians have a clearly-defined position, rejecting fund-raising measures that involve raffles, ballots and methods which can be construed under the general head of games of chance or gambling. Dr Paisley has publicly decried other church organisations or institutions which rely on 'pea soup suppers and dandelion teas' to augment their bank accounts and meet day-to-day running expenses. By late 1972, however, it became apparent that large public meetings were no longer appropriate and, as a consequence, plastic buckets could no longer be used to collect financial contributions from those in attendance. The DUP found itself in growing financial difficulties and the question then arose as to how to meet the shortfall in income.

One school of thought articulated at Executive level by Sandy Spence, chairman of the Bannside Democratic Unionist Association and Mayor of Ballymena, held closely to the line taken by Dr Paisley in his capacity as leader of the Free Presbyterian Church. This was that all financial support should come as a response of loyal and faithful supporters to the needs of the situation. Spence did not go so far as to suggest that other means would be a form of 'compromise', but he inferred that it would be inappropriate for the DUP, considering the stand that it had taken, to adopt a 'worldly' method of raising funds. The problem was that, although Sandy Spence was not a Free Presbyterian, he was an Elim Pentecostal lay preacher. Yet such was the nature of the DUP's crusade that he felt strongly that the party could not demean itself by adopting fund-raising methods in any way different from those used by the small independent evangelical churches, specifically freewill offerings.

Many of the party activists from Ballymena, coincidentally a town renowned for the parsimony of its citizens, a veritable Aberdeen planted in North Antrim, saw that such a stance was impracticable. Not only would fund-raising on a larger scale bring them into contact with an electorate much wider than the numbers represented by their own party followers, but they admitted to a distinction between the circumstances which governed the activities of a church and its members and the activities of a political party. The Mid-Antrim branch went on to organise 'cake sales' which were a considerable financial success, and also 'sacred music evenings'. The latter were held in Orange Halls scattered across North Antrim, and were chaired by leading personalities in the party. The programme consisted of gospel groups, drawn from evangelical churches, and usually invited by personal contact, who 'entertained' the audience with selections of sacred music, solo pieces and the like. The party speaker then addressed the meeting in terms in keeping with the mood of the evening, after which supper was served. Initially, these evenings of sacred music drew large crowds and brought in much-needed revenue, and they also carried in their wake the added advantage that quite a number of members of the audience were not followers of the party. Thus they saw the DUP on favourable terms, recognised that its influence was growing in the province and acquainted themselves with the local party activists in that area.

Apparently, 'sacred music evenings' held the answer to the DUP's financial problems, and they had the seeming advantage that they did not offend against the consciences of those of the party workers who would have preferred to rely on the giving of individuals than to hawk their party wares in the market place in the same way as the 'worldly' political parties. Two problems arose, though, both in their own way external to the DUP's immediate needs. Firstly, some Christians recognised that there were items on the programmes that were presented in a style which differed little from that of rock and roll and dance bands, in appearance, in musical beat and in the mannerisms of the vocalists and musicians. Admittedly the words had a Christian content but, objectively, it was hard to restrain the opinion that these young people had found the best of both worlds, rock music and trendy clothes inter-faced with godliness and spirituality. There were murmurs of discontent among the faithful. Secondly, the evenings of sacred music proved such a valuable asset that far too many concerts were organised and inevitably the audiences began to fall away.

Wallace Thompson has stated that there was another problem which could arise over these sacred music evenings. Apparently the gospel music artists had to be acceptable to the Free Presbyterian Church; if the artists were members of a church in the World Council of Churches they would be regarded as 'apostate' and barred from performing. The DUP was expected to comply with the Free Presbyterian Church's religious standards and taboos on such matters.

Richard Rose (1976, p. 213) has commented that 'like churches, parties are dependent upon many contributors supplementing cash gifts with an investment of time in voluntary work'. This research indicates that Rose's general statement is not only applicable to the DUP but is open to an even more specific application. That is, not only is the financing of the DUP comparable with the financing of other voluntary organisations like churches, but even more significantly, the religious motivations and techniques which the strict Protestant sects apply to fund-raising have been adopted by the DUP. The consequences of this have been that the DUP, having denied itself the possibility of raising funds through the well-established channels open to political parties, has resorted to whipping up semi-religious fervour at a number of set-piece meetings throughout the party's history, during which party members have pledged themselves to subscribe generously to party funds. It is difficult to estimate whether this self-denying ordinance has cut the DUP off from financial resources which it might otherwise have tapped. The likelihood is that financial support for the party engendered by a feeling of commitment has more than made up for any loss the party might have suffered as a result of separating itself from 'worldly' methods of financing.

Ideology

Finally, it is necessary to make reference to the relationship between Ian Paisley's theology and the ideology of the DUP. Ian Paisley has a remarkable facility for communicating his beliefs to his followers, and those beliefs strike a chord which enables the leader to claim with some justification that he is the voice of Protestant Ulster. Paisley has brought about a synthesis between American religious fundamentalism which is vibrant, brash, and full of energy and dynamism, and Ulster's loyalist or Orange tradition.[6] The Ulster loyalist tradition embraces those of the Gaelic-speaking Irish who were converted to the Reformed Faith, Puritan settlers from England, Huguenots and the Scots Presbyterians who had settled in increasing numbers in the north-east of Ireland as the seventeenth century progressed. Today the Ulster loyalist tradition is as fragmented as it was during plantation times, and in addition the process of secularisation has helped to create a form of loyalism which is severely nominal in its Protestantism. Ian Paisley, by contrast, proclaims beliefs that have their roots in the seventeenth-century covenanting spirit of Ayrshire's lowland Scots.

The Covenanters 'were the pioneers of full civil and religious freedom. They stood for the rule of the people against the domination of arbitrary princes. They resisted the totalitarian claim of their day that the king was supreme in all causes, religious as well as civil' (Barr, 1946, p. 230). The democratic experience of these Scots Presbyterians reached its apogee in the political treatise written by Samuel Rutherford in 1644, entitled *Lex, Rex* (1980).[7] Rutherford refuted the Stuart monarch's divine right doctrines. As a consequence, these democratic ideals expounded by Rutherford and contended for by other Covenanters on the battlefield at Drumclog and Aird's Moss forged a particular form of assertive and conditional political allegiance which is patently evident in Ulster right down to the present day.

In a discussion about his political ideology, Ian Paisley has stated that some of the Covenanters had a very clear perception of the Bible's teaching on the relationship between the governing authority and the governed. It is Paisley's opinion that the Reformers (Luther and Calvin) had not entirely freed themselves from some of the Church of Rome's teaching, particularly in the area of the relationship of the subject to the prince. Paisley therefore claimed that a more democratic approach emerged a century after the Reformation within Scots Presbyterianism, and in particular within the Covenanting movement. Following the signing of the Anglo-Irish Agreement on 15 November 1985, there was a massive rejection of the new relationship between Britain and the Irish Republic by the unionists of Ulster. The slogan 'Ulster Says No' hurled defiance not only at the Agreement, but also in the face of those who claimed that Ulster must accept the sovereign will of Parliament if so directed. The determination of the unionists was symbolised in a renewal of the coalition between Ian Paisley's DUP and the Unionist Party, but it also reflected the extent to which Paisley's political beliefs dominated the political scene in Ulster. Those who wish to understand the political theories at the root of this Ulster resolve had best acquaint themselves with the principles and militant activities of the Covenanters.[8]

Though the historic roots of Paisley's political ideas may be in Scotland, his revivalist preaching style, his fund-raising ability, his Arminian theology, and even to some extent his energy, have all been influenced by a more recent twentieth-century transatlantic religious phenomenon. Dr Paisley's affinity with American fundamentalist Protestantism first became apparent in the early days of his Christian ministry, and by the time he helped to launch and then lead the DUP his identification with fundamentalism was complete.[9] Inevitably the religious beliefs which have motivated the DUP leader shaped his thinking and gave a particular style to his larger-than-life revivalist ministry. This provided the foundations and intellectual presuppositions upon which the DUP leader constructed his political ideology. It is an ideology which expresses Paisley's determination to defend the Protestant and unionist cause in Northern Ireland in a manner which draws heavily on Ulster's Orange tradition and the folk symbols of loyalism, but the verve with which Paisley communicates his beliefs and policies to his supporters and the watching world has been profoundly influenced by the DUP leader's fundamentalist experience. Although the religious convictions of the movement appear somewhat anachronistic, Paisley's facility for synthesising the Orange and Protestant tradition of Ulster with the parallel values of American fundamentalist religion suggests that the Ulster Protestant Party has a strong affinity with contemporary trends in the United States of America associated with fundamentalist pressure groups like the Moral Majority (Viguerie, 1980).

Conclusion

This paper indicates that the influence which the Free Presbyterian core exerts over the Democratic Unionist Party pervades many aspects of the party's structure including the leadership exercised by Dr Paisley himself. There is also a uniformity of politicised fundamentalist attitudes shared by the party's membership, and a willingness to endorse the promotion of individual Free Presbyterian adherents to positions of authority within the DUP's structure.

This Free Presbyterian influence within Democratic Unionism is not exercised self-consciously because, provided the members remain devoted in their loyalty to Dr Paisley and accept wholeheartedly his paternalistic articulation of Ulster Protestant and unionist sentiment, there will be no friction between a DUP member who subscribes to another Protestant denomination and his local party colleagues who may also be Free Presbyterians. There are indications that Free Presbyterians within the DUP are blind to the anomalous role enjoyed by adherents of their Church within a party which makes much of its claim to be democratic. This suggests that in some sense the Free Presbyterian influence within the DUP has submerged itself within a somewhat broader inner-party consensus which may be characterised as politicised fundamentalism. This explains why Pentecostalists, Baptists and members of the major Presbyterian denomination in the Province are made to feel at home within the party, provided they share the kind of adulation of Ian Paisley as DUP leader and 'man of God' to which the Free Presbyterians within the party subscribe.

As the Free Presbyterian core within the DUP is blind to the significance of its role within the party, this core is not to be confused with either a 'tendency' or a 'party within a party'. This fully accords with a view of the DUP which suggests that integration between the Free Presbyterian core and other DUP activists who subscribe to other sects or denominations is for all practical purposes complete. It also helps to explain, however, why outside commentators tend to describe the DUP as being cohesive and highly disciplined.

In conclusion, the DUP has often been characterised in the past as Ian Paisley's one man band.[10] This description is but the seed to a more complete understanding. Paisley's twin commitments to Protestantism and loyalism are replicated throughout the DUP, and this helps to explain both the party's extraordinary cohesion and its ruthless electioneering zeal.

COMMENTARY BY CLAIRE MITCHELL

In 1986 Clifford Smyth helped kick-start the fledgling *Irish Political Studies* journal with an account of the mysterious relationship between the Democratic Unionist Party (DUP) and the Free Presbyterian Church (FPC). Indeed, 1986 saw a flurry of publications about the DUP with Steve Bruce's *God Save Ulster! The Religion and Politics of Paisleyism*, and Ed Moloney and Andy Pollak's *Paisley*, also appearing. Smyth's own biography of Paisley, *Ian Paisley: Voice of Protestant Ulster*, was published the following year. Each of these books expressed a fascination with the larger than life figure of Paisley. None, however, were overly complimentary. Of the three books, Bruce's is the most 'objective' in tone. Moloney and Pollak quickly pin their colours to the mast, branding Paisley a 'malign colossus' on the back cover of their book. Similarly, Smyth's account is not particularly fulsome. The difference with Smyth's account – in this article and in his 1987 book – is that whereas Bruce, Moloney and Pollak were 'outsider' researchers, Smyth was in many senses an 'insider'. As a former deputy leader of the DUP who had won a variety of seats for the party in the early 1970s, Smyth would have had access to a wide range of inside information based on personal experience and contacts.

This insider angle, however, also provides one of the biggest puzzles of the article. Smyth was purged from the DUP in late 1976. Although he still identifies himself as an evangelical, Smyth has also described a number of negative experiences with Protestant churches in Northern Ireland as a result of his transvestism – this was not at the hands of the FPC, which he also left in 1976, but another Protestant denomination (Smyth, 2005a and 2005b). So it is clear that Smyth has experienced at first hand the authoritarian side of Protestant religion as well as of Democratic Unionist politics. Highlighting this authoritarianism has been a constant thread in Smyth's work. Writing recently, Smyth compares the DUP to Fianna Fáil, arguing that both 'exhibit a form of "democratic centralism" similar to that in Stalin's Soviet Union. Both parties are unforgiving towards those who speak out of turn, or buck tight internal discipline. Including…jettisoning party candidates who have lost favour' (2006, no pagination). Of course this begs the question of how the author's own biography intertwines with his telling of the story of the DUP. What was his motivation in writing this article, and indeed in his commentary on the DUP ever since?

The fact that Smyth is not explicit about his methodology in this article also prompts us to ask how we should read his conclusions. Whilst he indicates that interviews have informed his study, we are not given any detail about the sample or the process. Indeed, in his PhD thesis (1984), he acknowledges that most of his data after 1976 comes from DUP 'defectors'. This obviously impacts the type and tone of information presented, and the article ought to be read with this in mind.

Indeed, in this article Smyth's tone verges on that of exposé. He says he wants to explain the significance of a relationship he felt was 'not widely understood'. He indicates that a 'veil of secrecy' has been drawn deliberately by the DUP across its internal operations to 'conceal' its 'intimate' relationship with the FPC. Smyth does not indicate in this article why the DUP would wish to obscure the details of this relationship. However, again in his PhD thesis (1984, pp. 54–7), he has argued that the electoral fortunes of the DUP may have been damaged by too close an association. This resonates strongly with the modern DUP who seem even more acutely aware of the potential unpopularity of its religious connection.

Overall, Smyth provides a fascinating insight into the workings of the DUP, outlining four areas where the religion of the Free Presbyterian Church overlaps with the DUP. Firstly, it has had a say over candidate selection. Secondly, the crusading zeal of Church members in election time is highlighted. Thirdly, the Church has had an impact on the development of DUP finances and fourthly, an ideological overlap is identified. In at least the first three of these dimensions Smyth describes a dual effect of the FPC, which on one hand enhances the DUP's campaigning and finances, but on the other, can constrain the DUP's wider political repertoire. For example, the FPC tried in the early 1970s to limit the number of DUP candidates drawn from within its ranks. This was because of a long-standing evangelical tradition of pietistic disengagement from politics (Brewer, 1998; Jordan, 2001). This pietistic tradition has been continually underestimated in Northern Irish public life, particularly amongst commentators who assume that strong Protestant religious beliefs are inseparable from strong unionist politics. As later work has shown, this is not the case and strong evangelical beliefs can in fact mitigate against political involvement (Brewer, 1998; Jordan, 2001; Ganiel, 2004; Mitchell, 2005). In this sense it is interesting that the party link creates tension for the FPC. Although Smyth says the pietists are a minority within the FPC, he also indicates that they have been influential enough to place limitations on the political role of the Church, particularly with regard to limiting candidates and 'worldly' fundraising techniques.

One of the most interesting things about the article is the emphasis on the early pragmatism of the DUP and indeed of Paisley himself. Particularly in the post-Good Friday Agreement and St Andrews Agreement era, with Paisley's un/willingness to compromise keeping commentators on tenterhooks, it is interesting to remember that Paisley has often been on the pragmatic side of his party. Smyth tells us that Paisley's initial intention was to 'form a party which was secular in character, which would appeal to the media, and would be sufficiently distanced from Protestant Unionism'. This is an important reminder that Paisley's politics may in fact be more pragmatic than his ultra-Protestant posturing may indicate.

The DUP's recent move towards compromise is of course an important political shift, but it also builds upon this longer tradition of pragmatism. Moreover, Smyth reminds us that the DUP of the 1970s was itself very divided over the religious connection. Thus it is important to remember that the, rather erroneously dubbed, 'secular wing' of the DUP is not a recent development. Despite the tightly controlled, united front presented for public inspection, the DUP has always housed internal tensions.

Twenty years after Smyth's article, *Irish Political Studies* is still following the religion and politics debate, with recent research articles engaging in particular with this more flexible side of the DUP. Ganiel's (2006) 'Ulster Says Maybe' article, for example, argues that the DUP have proven very capable of reorienting their politics to a post-Agreement situation, including the necessary compromise of dealing with Sinn Féin. Similarly, again in *Irish Political Studies*, Southern (2005) has highlighted the DUP's more moderate side, showing how they have edged away from policies such as Sabbatarianism (the infamous 'chaining up the swings on Sundays') and are in fact rather ideologically malleable when circumstances require. Elsewhere, Mitchell and Todd (2007) have shown how DUP voters, not just the party elite, have adapted their identities and ambitions to the changed political context, reducing their opposition to the Republic of Ireland. In many ways Smyth's 1986 article planted the seeds of this debate, and although this side of the DUP has largely been ignored since, it is significant that it has been picked up once again in the 2000s.

Having drawn attention to their past and present flexibility, it is important to balance this by pointing out that the DUP remains an incredibly religious organisation. A network of small conservative evangelical churches continue to populate the main leadership positions. Of the 30 DUP MLAs elected in 2003/ defected into the DUP after 2003, 17 are members of the FPC, six are members of other small Protestant denominations (Elim, Baptist, Free Methodist), six are Presbyterians and one is an Anglican (Mitchell, 2005, p. 51). Other MLAs – Mervyn Storey and George Dawson – are involved in the Caleb Foundation, a conservative evangelical pressure group. David Simpson and Willie McCrea are both gospel singers. Many more are involved in lay roles in churches and other religious organisations. Prayers of thanks and hymns from the podium are still the standard DUP approach to election victories. In the light of this, it would be grossly inaccurate to pronounce the DUP to be a secular, flexible animal. The ideological overlaps Smyth identified between religion and politics are still very real, even if they may now manifest themselves in slightly different forms. As the idea of power-sharing and an 'Irish dimension' become increasingly normalised, the political battles of the future for the DUP may well come to focus on conservative sexual morality and lifestyle choices (Mitchell and Tilley, 2004). Indeed, this would be a very promising avenue for future research into the DUP.

Finally, it is interesting to note how terminology has changed since the 1980s. Smyth never mentions the word 'evangelical', a term that now dominates academic discourse, as well as the internal religious discourse of conservative Protestants throughout the modern world. Instead, where religion is named at all, Smyth says that Paisley has borrowed from American 'fundamentalism'. Today 'fundamentalism' has rather different connotations (Bruce, 2001), and is a term conservative Protestants rarely use to describe themselves. It is also of interest that Smyth describes the DUP as part of the 'loyalist' tradition, whereas today the DUP's literature claims that it is a unionist political party. Perhaps in both these instances, the softening terminology indicates an awareness of the changing context of Northern Irish politics and a craving for respectability in a world where fundamentalism is associated with terrorism, where loyalists are thought to be tattooed thugs and where anti-Romanist discourse jars uncomfortably with a secular, multicultural Britain.

In all, revisiting Smyth's article provides evidence of both continuity and change within the DUP. Today the language is different, the reality of post-Agreement politics has almost been accepted, the message is a little softer and some new issues are on the agenda. But re-reading Smyth's article reminds us that the DUP has always had internal tensions, has always agonised over the role of the FPC – and vice versa – and has always had a pragmatic streak when necessary. Such insights are important to keep in mind when analysing the role of the DUP through contemporary crises and changes.

Notes

1 The minutes of these Presbytery meetings have never been made public and Dr Paisley often stated that Presbytery members were not even to tell their wives what went on. Passed off in good humour, Paisley's remark carried a barb nonetheless.
2 See Harbinson (1973) for a brief account of the origins of Protestant Unionism.
3 See Schaeffer (1982, pp. 18f) for a brief introduction to the political implications of pietism.
4 This anonymous informant was well placed within the Free Presbyterian Church.
5 For some insight into the party's organisation see, for example, Ulster Democratic Unionist Party (1978).
6 See Douglas (1974, p. 397) for the attributes of religious fundamentalism.
7 Rutherford took a keen interest in the welfare of the Presbyterians of Ulster (Bonner, 1894).
8 See Paisley (1985, pp. 33f) for a succinct statement of his position.
9 See the Free Presbyterian Church magazine *The Revivalist* (1957).
10 *Irish Times*, 18 June 1980.

References

Barr, James (1946) *The Scottish Covenanters*. Glasgow: John Smith and Son.
Bonner, Horatio (ed.) (1894) *Letters of Samuel Rutherford*. Edinburgh: Oliphant, Anderson and Ferrier.
Brewer, John (1998) *Anti-Catholicism in Northern Ireland 1600–1998: The Mote and the Beam*. London: Macmillan.
Bruce, Steve (1986) *God Save Ulster: The Religion and Politics of Paisleyism*. Oxford: Oxford University Press.
Bruce, Steve (2001) *Fundamentalism*. Oxford: Polity Press.
Calvert, David (1981) *A Decade of the DUP*. Belfast: Crown Publications.

Douglas, J.D. (ed.) (1974) *The New International Dictionary of the Christian Church.* Exeter: Paternoster Press.

Ganiel, Gladys (2004) 'Evangelical Political Identity in Transition: Mapping the Intersections of Religion, Politics, and Change in Post-Belfast Agreement Northern Ireland', ISSC Working Paper 2004/1. Dublin: Institute for the Study of Social Change.

Ganiel, Gladys (2006) 'Ulster Says Maybe: The Restructuring of Evangelical Politics in Northern Ireland', *Irish Political Studies*, 21 (2), pp. 137–55.

Harbinson, John (1973) *The Ulster Unionist Party 1882–1973: Its Development and Organisation.* Belfast: Blackstaff Press.

Jordan, Glenn (2001) *Not of this World? Evangelical Protestants in Northern Ireland.* Belfast: Blackstaff Press.

McCrea, William (1980) *In His Pathway: The Story of the Rev. William McCrea.* London: Lutterworth Press.

Mitchell, Claire (2005) *Religion, Identity and Politics in Northern Ireland: Boundaries of Belonging and Belief.* Aldershot: Ashgate.

Mitchell, Claire and James Tilley (2004) 'The Moral Minority: Evangelical Protestants in Northern Ireland and Their Political Behaviour', *Political Studies*, 52 (4), pp. 585–602.

Mitchell, Claire and Jennifer Todd (forthcoming, 2007) 'Between the Devil and the Deep Blue Sea: Nationality, Power and Symbolic Trade-Offs Among Evangelical Protestants in Contemporary Northern Ireland', *Nations and Nationalism*, 13 (4).

Moloney, Ed and Andy Pollak (1986) *Paisley.* Dublin: Poolbeg Press.

Paisley, Ian R.K. (1985) *The Crown Rights of Jesus Christ.* Belfast: Martyrs' Memorial Publications.

Rose, Richard (1976) *The Problem of Party Government.* Harmondsworth: Pelican.

Rutherford, Samuel (1980) *Lex, Rex, or the Law and the Prince.* Harrisonburg, VA: Sprinkle Publications.

Schaeffer, Francis (1982) *A Christian Manifesto.* Basingstoke: Pickering Publications.

Smyth, Clifford (1984) *The Ulster Democratic Unionist Party: A Case Study in Religious and Political Convergence.* Unpublished PhD thesis. Belfast: Queen's University Belfast.

Smyth, Clifford (1987) *Ian Paisley: Voice of Protestant Ulster.* Edinburgh: Scottish Academic Press.

Smyth, Clifford (2005a) 'Dealing with My Sexual Brokenness', *Belfast Telegraph*, 20 July.

Smyth, Clifford (2005b) Interview with William Crawley on Sunday Sequence, Radio Ulster, 24 July.

Smyth, Clifford (2006) 'Fury of the Faithful as Dr. No Says "Yes"', *Parliamentary Brief*, November, <http://www.thepolitician.org/articles.php?articleID=364>.

Southern, Neil (2005) 'Ian Paisley and Evangelical Democratic Unionists: An Analysis of the Role of Evangelical Protestantism Within the Democratic Unionist Party', *Irish Political Studies*, 20 (2), pp. 128–45.

Ulster Democratic Unionist Party (1978) *Ulster Democratic Unionist Party Year Book 1975–1976.* Belfast: Ulster Democratic Unionist Party.

Viguerie, Richard A. (1980) *The New Right: We're Ready to Lead.* Falls Church, VA: The Viguerie Company.

Index